# THE ROUTLEDGE COMPANION TO MEDIA AND RACE

*The Routledge Companion to Media and Race* serves as a comprehensive guide for scholars, students, and media professionals who seek to understand the key debates about the impact of media messages on racial attitudes and understanding. Broad in scope and richly presented from a diversity of perspectives, the book is divided into three sections: first, it summarizes the theoretical approaches that scholars have adopted to analyze the complexities of media messages about race and ethnicity, from the notion of "representation" to more recent concepts like Critical Race Theory. Second, the book reviews studies related to a variety of media, including film, television, print media, social media, music, and video games. Finally, contributors present a broad summary of media issues related to specific races and ethnicities and describe the relationship of the study of race to the study of gender and sexuality.

**Christopher P. Campbell** is a professor in the School of Mass Communication and Journalism at the University of Southern Mississippi. He is the author of *Race, Myth and the News* (Sage Publications, 1995) and co-author of *Race and News: Critical Perspectives* (Routledge, 2011).

# THE ROUTLEDGE COMPANION TO MEDIA AND RACE

*Edited by Christopher P. Campbell*

NEW YORK AND LONDON

First published 2017
by Routledge
711 Third Avenue, New York, NY 10017

and by Routledge
2 Park Square, Milton Park, Abingdon, Oxon OX14 4RN

*Routledge is an imprint of the Taylor & Francis Group, an informa business*

© 2017 Taylor & Francis

The right of Christopher P. Campbell to be identified as the author of the editorial material, and of the authors for their individual chapters, has been asserted in accordance with sections 77 and 78 of the Copyright, Designs and Patents Act 1988.

All rights reserved. No part of this book may be reprinted or reproduced or utilised in any form or by any electronic, mechanical, or other means, now known or hereafter invented, including photocopying and recording, or in any information storage or retrieval system, without permission in writing from the publishers.

*Trademark notice*: Product or corporate names may be trademarks or registered trademarks, and are used only for identification and explanation without intent to infringe.

*Library of Congress Cataloging in Publication Data*
Names: Campbell, Christopher, 1955- editor of compilation.
Title: The Routledge companion to media and race / edited by
   Christopher Campbell.
Description: London ; New York : Routledge, Taylor & Francis Group,
   2017.
Identifiers: LCCN 2016027112| ISBN 9781138020726 (hardback) |
   ISBN 9781315778228 (ebk)
Subjects: LCSH: Minorities in mass media. | Race relations in mass
   media. | Racism in mass media. | Mass media and race relations.
Classification: LCC P94.5.M55 R68 2017 | DDC 302.2308—dc23
LC record available at https://lccn.loc.gov/2016027112

ISBN: 978-1-138-02072-6 (hbk)
ISBN: 978-1-315-77822-8 (ebk)

Typeset in Bembo Std
by Swales & Willis Ltd, Exeter, Devon, UK

# CONTENTS

Notes on Contributors   viii

Introduction   1

## PART I
### Studying Race and Media: Theories and Approaches   9

1. Representation: Stuart Hall and the "Politics of Signification"   11
   CHRISTOPHER P. CAMPBELL

2. Framing: The Undying White Racial Frame   19
   FRANK J. ORTEGA AND JOE R. FEAGIN

3. Cultivation Theory: Gerbner, Fear, Crime, and Cops   31
   VALERIE J. CALLANAN AND JARED S. ROSENBERGER

4. Historical Media Analysis: Oppression and Resistance   43
   VANESSA MURPHREE

5. Priming: Memory, Media, and Minorities   55
   FRANCESCA R. DILLMAN CARPENTIER

6. Critical Race Theory: Everything Old is New Again   65
   KIM M. LEDUFF

## PART II
### Race, the Medium, the Message   75

7. Primetime Television: Portrayals and Effects   77
   DANA MASTRO, ANDREA FIGUEROA-CABALLERO, AND
   ALEXANDER SINK

8   Film: Race and the Cinematic "Machine"                                87
    GERALD SIM

9   Popular Music: Translating Race and Genre from
    Ethnic to Epic                                                        96
    PAUL LINDEN

10  The Internet: Oppression in Digital Spaces                            107
    KISHONNA L. GRAY

11  Social Media: From Digital Divide to Empowerment                      117
    GINA MASULLO CHEN

12  Journalism and African Americans: Diversity and Perspective           126
    CHERYL D. JENKINS

13  Journalism and Latinos: Stereotypes, Underrepresentation,
    and Ignorance                                                         138
    RAUL REIS

14  Advertising: A Window to Race and Culture                             148
    ANTHONY J. CORTESE

15  Ethnic Media: Moving Beyond Boundaries                                160
    SHERRY S. YU

16  Sports Media in the United States: Trivializing Race                  173
    DANIEL SIPOCZ

17  Sports Media in Europe: An International Context                      185
    JACCO VAN STERKENBURG

## PART III
Race, Ethnicity, and Intersectionality                                    197

18  African Americans: From Minstrelsy to Reality TV                      199
    ROCKELL A. BROWN

19  Latin@s: Underrepresented Majorities in the Digital Age               210
    CELESTE GONZÁLEZ DE BUSTAMANTE AND JESSICA RETIS

20  Native Americans: The Denial of Humanity                              222
    DEBRA MERSKIN

21  Asian Americans: Model Minoritizing Digital Labor in
    a Post-Racial Age                                                     231
    VINCENT N. PHAM AND KENT A. ONO

22  Arabs, Muslims, and Arab Americans: Constructing an Evil Other        241
    EVELYN ALSULTANY

| | |
|---|---|
| 23 **Mixed Race: From Pathology to Celebration**<br>JI-HYUN AHN | 250 |
| 24 **Europe: Representation of Ethnic Minorities and Their Effects**<br>CHRISTIAN SCHEMER AND PHILIPP MÜLLER | 259 |
| 25 **East Asia: Looking In and Looking Out**<br>YASUE KUWAHARA | 269 |
| 26 **India: Insecurities of a Nation on the Rise**<br>SIDHARTH MURALIDHARAN | 276 |
| 27 **Gender and Black Feminist Theory: Examining Difference**<br>MIA MOODY-RAMIREZ | 289 |
| 28 **Race and Sexuality: Whitewashing Representation**<br>ROBERT D. BYRD, JR. | 304 |

*Index*     312

# CONTRIBUTORS

**Ji-Hyun Ahn** is an Assistant Professor of Global Media Studies in the School of Interdisciplinary Arts and Sciences at the University of Washington Tacoma. Her research interests include media globalization, Asian media/cultural studies, multiculturalism, and mixed-race/blood issues in East Asia. Her recent works have appeared in journals such as *Media, Culture & Society* and *Cultural Studies*.

**Evelyn Alsultany** is an Associate Professor in the Department of American Culture at the University of Michigan and Director of Arab and Muslim American Studies. She is the author of *Arabs and Muslims in the Media: Race and Representation after 9/11* (2012). She is co-editor of *Arab and Arab American Feminisms: Gender, Violence, and Belonging* (2011) and *Between the Middle East and the Americas: The Cultural Politics of Diaspora* (2013).

**Rockell A. Brown** is an Associate Professor in the School of Communication at Texas Southern University. She is the co-author of *Race and News: Critical Perspectives* (2012) and book chapters about Tyler Perry's films and the black family.

**Robert D. Byrd, Jr.** is an Assistant Professor in the Department of Journalism at the University of Memphis. His research examines LGBTQ media and media representations via a queer lens.

**Valerie J. Callanan** is a Professor of Sociology at Kent State University. Her research focuses on crime-related media, fear of crime, and suicide, and has been published in *Deviant Behavior, Policing & Society, Sociological Perspectives, Feminist Criminology*, and *Journal of Criminal Justice*. She is the author of *Feeding the Fear of Crime* (2005).

**Christopher P. Campbell** is a Professor in the School of Mass Communication and Journalism at the University of Southern Mississippi. He is the author of *Race, Myth and the News* (1995) and co-author of *Race and News: Critical Perspectives* (2012).

**Francesca R. Dillman Carpentier** is the James H. Shumaker Term Professor at the School of Media and Journalism at the University of North Carolina in Chapel Hill. Her research focuses on the unintended effects of media messages, merging literature on implicit memory, automatic information processing, and impression formation with communication literature that highlights the complexities of news and entertainment.

**Gina Masullo Chen** is an Assistant Professor in the School of Journalism at the University of Texas at Austin. Her research focuses on the online conversation around the news and how it influences social, civic, and political engagement. She is Co-Editor of *Scandal in a Digital Age* (2016) and authoring *Online Incivility and Public Debate: Nasty Talk* (forthcoming).

CONTRIBUTORS

**Anthony J. Cortese** is a Professor of Sociology at Southern Methodist University. He is the author of *Ethnic Ethics: The Restructuring of Moral Theory* (1990), *Provocateur: Images of Women and Minorities in Advertising*, 4th ed. (2016), *Walls and Bridges: Social Justice and Public Policy* (2004), and *Opposing Hate Speech* (2006).

**Joe R. Feagin**, the Ella C. McFadden Distinguished Professor at Texas A&M University, does research on racism, sexism, and class issues. He has published dozens of scholarly books and hundreds of scholarly articles in these research areas. Among his books are *Systemic Racism* (2006), *Two-Faced Racism* (2007, with Leslie Picca), *The White Racial Frame* (2nd ed., 2013), *Racist America* (3rd ed., 2014), *White Party, White Government* (2012), *Latinos Facing Racism* (2014, with Jose Cobas), *The Myth of the Model Minority* (2nd ed., 2015, with Rosalind Chou), and *Liberation Sociology* (3rd ed., 2015, with Hernan Vera and Kimberly Ducey).

**Andrea Figueroa-Caballero** is a doctoral student in the Department of Communication at the University of California, Santa Barbara. Her research is focused on the cultural effects of media within the context of race/ethnicity and sexual minorities.

**Celeste González de Bustamante** is an Associate Professor in the School of Journalism at the University of Arizona, where she is a Distinguished 1885 Scholar and an affiliated faculty member of the U.A. Center for Latin American Studies. She is the author of "*Muy buenas noches*": *Mexico, Television and the Cold War* (2012) and the co-editor of *Arizona Firestorm: Global Immigration Realities, National Media, and Provincial Politics* (2012).

**Kishonna L. Gray** is a Martin Luther King, Jr. Visiting Scholar in Women and Gender Studies and Comparative Media Studies/Writing at the Massachusetts Institute of Technology. She is also the founder of the Critical Gaming Lab at Eastern Kentucky University, which has transformed into the Equity in Gaming Initiative. Her work broadly intersects identity and digital media although she has a particular focus on gaming. Her most recent book is *Race, Gender, and Deviance in Xbox Live* (2014).

**Cheryl D. Jenkins** is an Associate Professor and Graduate Coordinator in the School of Mass Communication and Journalism and Associate Director of the Center for Black Studies at the University of Southern Mississippi. She is co-author of *Race and Media: Critical Perspectives* (2012).

**Yasue Kuwahara** is Professor of Communication and Director of Popular Culture Studies at Northern Kentucky University. Her research interest includes U.S. influence on postwar Japanese society and East Asian popular culture. She is the editor of *The Korean Wave: Korean Popular Culture in Global Context* (2014).

**Kim M. LeDuff** is Professor of Communication and Dean and Associate Vice Provost of University College at the University of West Florida. She is the author of *Tales of Two Cities: How Race and Crime Intersect on Local TV News* (2010) and co-author of *Race and News: Critical Perspectives* (2012).

**Paul Linden** is an Assistant Professor in the College of Communication at Butler University. He holds a Ph.D. in literature, a master's degree in mass communication, and twenty years of experience in the music business.

CONTRIBUTORS

**Dana Mastro** is a Professor in the Department of Communication at the University of California, Santa Barbara. Her research examines the influence of exposure to racial/ethnic images in the media on perceptions of self and other, as well as on intergroup relations in society.

**Debra Merskin** is a Professor in the School of Journalism and Communication at the University of Oregon. Her publications appear in journals such as *The Howard Journal of Communication*, *American Behavioral Scientist*, *Sex Roles*, and *Mass Communication and Society*. She is the author of *Media, Minorities, and Meaning: A Critical Introduction* and *Sexing the Media: How and Why We Do It* (2014).

**Mia Moody-Ramirez** is an Associate Professor and Graduate Program Director in the Department of Journalism, Public Relations and New Media at Baylor University. She has conducted research in the areas of minorities and women in the media, and her topics include reality television, rap music, and political campaigns.

**Philipp Müller** is a research associate in the Department of Communication at Johannes Gutenberg University in Mainz, Germany. His research deals with the production, uses, and effects of journalistic media content, with a special focus on social identity and on media change and innovation.

**Sidharth Muralidharan** is an Assistant Professor of Advertising in the Temerlin Advertising Institute at Southern Methodist University. His primary research interests are on cross-cultural studies and on advertising's impact on mitigating social and environmental issues in India and abroad.

**Vanessa Murphree** is an Associate Professor in the School of Mass Communication and Journalism at the University of Southern Mississippi. She is the author of *The Selling of Civil Rights: The Student Nonviolent Coordinating Committee and the Use of Public Relations* (2006), and she has written about the birth control movement, crisis communication, media relations, and historical perspectives of public relations.

**Kent A. Ono** is a Professor in and Chair of the Department of Communication at the University of Utah. He has authored/co-authored: *Contemporary Media Culture and the Remnants of a Colonial Past* (2009), *Asian Americans and the Media* (2009, with Vincent Pham), and *Shifting Borders: Rhetoric, Immigration, and California's Proposition 187* (2002, with John Sloop). He is working on a book with Vincent Pham titled *Asian American New Media*.

**Frank J. Ortega** is a Ph.D. candidate and graduate research assistant in the Department of Sociology at Texas A&M University. His research focuses on issues concerning race, class, and gender. His major interests center on Latina/o representations in the media and popular culture in addition to topics regarding education, labor, and health.

**Vincent N. Pham** is an Assistant Professor of Communication in the Department of Civic Communication and Media at Willamette University. He is the co-author of *Asian Americans and the Media* (2009, with Kent Ono). He is currently co-editing the forthcoming *Companion to Asian American Media* collection with Lori K. Lopez and is working on a book with Kent Ono titled *Asian American New Media*.

CONTRIBUTORS

**Raul Reis** is the Dean of the School of Communication at Emerson College in Boston. His academic articles have appeared in the *Journal of Broadcasting & Electronic Media*, *Journalism & Mass Communication Educator*, *Journal of Mass Media Ethics*, *Science Communication*, *World Communication Journal*, *Environmental Communication*, and the *Journal of Intercultural Communication*, among others. He has co-authored the books *Mass Communication: Producers and Consumers* (2010) and *Writing and Reporting for Digital Media* (2015).

**Jessica Retis** is an Associate Professor of Journalism and Communications at California State University Northridge. Her research focuses on Latin-American diasporas and the media, diversity and the media, the political economy of the media, and Hispanic media in the US and Europe. She is currently editing *The Handbook of Diaspora, Media and Culture*.

**Jared S. Rosenberger** is an Assistant Professor and Sociology Program Director in the Department of Political Science and Sociology at Murray State University. His research interests include media constructions of the criminal justice system, fear of crime, and the penal system. His publications examine the relationship between gender and fear of crime, media and penal attitudes, and race and attitudes toward the police.

**Christian Schemer** is a Professor of Communication in the Department of Communication at Johannes Gutenberg University in Mainz, Germany.

**Gerald Sim** is Associate Professor of Film Studies at Florida Atlantic University's School of Communication and Multimedia Studies. He is the author of *The Subject of Film and Race: Retheorizing Politics, Ideology, and Cinema* (2014).

**Alexander Sink** is a graduate student in the Department of Communication at the University of California, Santa Barbara. His research interests are on the role of media in issues of stereotyping, prejudice, and discrimination.

**Daniel Sipocz** is an Assistant Professor in the Department of Communication at Berry College. His research focuses on the representation of women and minorities in sports media as well as popular culture.

**Jacco van Sterkenburg** is an Assistant Professor in the Department of Media and Communication and the Erasmus Research Centre for Media Communication and Culture at Erasmus University in Rotterdam, the Netherlands. He is also a visiting research fellow at the Mulier Institute, a Dutch social science research center in the field of sport. He has published work in *Media Culture and Society*, *Journal of Sport and Social Issues*, *International Review for the Sociology of Sport*, *Soccer and Society*, and *Journal of Multicultural Discourses*.

**Sherry S. Yu** is an Assistant Professor in the Department of Journalism at Temple University and a member of the School of Media and Communication's doctoral program faculty. Her research explores cultural diversity and media in relation to cultural literacy, civic engagement, and intercultural dialogue in a multicultural society, with a specific focus on ethnic media, multiculturalism, and transnational migration.

# INTRODUCTION
## *Christopher P. Campbell*

Nearly every day, mass media audiences are confronted with issues related to race and ethnicity. In the United States, Barack Obama's election and re-election were routinely framed by news organizations as evidence of a "post-racial" America, a notion that casts racism and discrimination as vestiges of America's past and dominates racial representations in both journalism and entertainment media. Local TV newscasts and much entertainment media in the US are dominated by images of African-American and Hispanic men as violent, pathological criminals. Journalism and entertainment media in the US and abroad routinely cast immigrants as deviant, as dangerous. These representations take on even more significance given the general invisibility in the media of people who are part of the minority populations in the countries in which they live. *The Routledge Companion to Media and Race* is designed as a guide to understanding the key debates about the impact of media messages on racial attitudes and understanding. Its 28 chapters examine approaches to the study of race and media, the role that various media play in generating meanings about race, the representation of specific races and ethnicities, and the relationship of those meanings to studies of gender and sexuality. The work in this book offers scant evidence that media systems in the US and around the world are providing audiences with the kind of accurate, meaningful, and complex representations of people who live outside of the dominant cultures. Instead, mainstream media outlets continue to routinely ignore or stereotype "others."

The book is divided into three sections. Part I, Studying Race and Media: Theories and Approaches, looks at several of the most significant approaches that media scholars have used to examine the complexity of media messages. This section begins with my discussion of the work of British Cultural Studies scholar Stuart Hall and others who have examined race and media through the lens of *representation*. It provides a description of the roots of cultural-critical media analysis and cites multiple studies that describe the complex ways powerful meanings about race and ethnicity are generated through media texts, including those generated through social media. Hall described the complex ways that mediated messages function as the "politics of signification," an observation that is especially applicable to the hegemonic power of the myths about race and ethnicity that are reified in journalism and in entertainment media.

In the second chapter, Frank J. Ortega and Joe R. Feagin look at *framing theory* and how the persistence of the white/dominant racial "frame" is important to social science approaches that analyze media and society. The authors use framing analysis to highlight African-American and Latina/o stereotypes in the media and describe how prevailing media images often operate out of an anti-other subframe, resulting in the mischaracterization of people of color. The chapter concludes with a discussion concerning the challenges presented by racialized media framing, the great need for accurate racial depictions, and the necessity of a broader critical focus on the mostly white owners and controllers of mainstream media content in regard to racial matters.

Next, Valerie J. Callanan and Jared S. Rosenberger look at *cultivation theory*. They examine the seminal work of George Gerbner and his associates beginning in the 1970s, who looked at the impact of long-term television viewing on the attitudes of audience members, including the notion of the "mean world" syndrome, in which heavy television viewers perceive the world as a very scary place. The chapter summarizes research on media cultivation of perceptions about race and crime in three areas: fear of crime, punitive attitudes, and attitudes toward law enforcement. Those perceptions have heavily influenced significant, misguided public policy decisions in the US and elsewhere. As the authors observe, "When we portray crime in simple moral and racialized terms—dark evil doer versus the white heroic crime fighter—it invokes simple responses to a complex issue."

In Chapter 4, Vanessa Murphree examines scholarship that has addressed race as it has played out through media history. In describing *historical media analysis*, she explains that scholars have generally examined two aspects of that history: the story of racism in the mainstream, white media and the story of empowerment in alternative, minority-focused media. Through an examination of the scholarship surrounding the history of media and race, she describes the many perspectives that help to explain how the white majority has oppressed minority groups and how these same groups have employed the media to advance their causes and positions in society.

Next, Francesca R. Dillman Carpentier opens with a review of literature explaining *media priming* effects based on associative network models. Following this review, she highlights key studies about how media depictions of race and ethnicity "prime" stereotypes and bias social judgments. She discusses these studies in terms of how they have contributed to our general understanding of the relationship between media exposure and race-related beliefs and attitudes, as well as how they exemplify the typical methodologies used to address this area of research. Her chapter closes with a discussion of recent work that suggests ways to combat media effects that are detrimental to social progress toward understanding and acceptance of diversity, including media literacy solutions that work within existing associative networks to more effectively link concepts of race with positive, if not more representative, attributes.

In Chapter 6, Kim M. LeDuff explores how *Critical Race Theory* (CRT), a relatively recent legal theory, can be used by mass media scholars to better understand how contemporary media narratives have led to polarization based on race and class in America. LeDuff explains that the roots of CRT extend back to the 1970s when a group of legal scholars and activists realized that the waves of change following the Civil Rights era of the 1960s were not having the long-term impact on society that the movement had expected. She describes examples of news stories and narratives from contemporary media to illustrate the application of CRT in media criticism.

Part II, Race, the Medium, the Message, examines scholarship related to all types of media, from TV shows to social media to sports coverage. The authors identify disturbing patterns—primarily invisibility and stereotypes—of people of color across all forms of media, patterns rooted in the oldest forms of popular culture and persisting into the current landscape of social media and video games. In Chapter 7, Dana Mastro, Andrea Figueroa-Caballero, and Alexander Sink document *primetime television* portrayals of racial and ethnic minority groups across the decades and address the implications of exposure to this content on audience members. Their examinations reveal that representations vary over time and across racial/ethnic groups, in terms of both quality and quantity, and that content-analytic evidence also indicates that racial/ethnic groups are largely underrepresented and constrained to a narrow scope of character-types on television. Finally, they discuss evidence from experimental and survey-based studies that examine the negative effects of exposure to this content.

Next, Gerald Sim examines how racial ideology exists and functions in *film*. He considers the medium's material base, textual operations, modes of address, and genres, and he discusses cinema as a social and economic institution. Within each of those paradigms, he highlights key ideas from critical race film studies and illustrates them with examples from both canonical and contemporary film culture. The chapter reflects on the ways that cinema in all its forms is implicated in Eurocentrism and white privilege and on those in which counter-ideological strategies have been practiced and theorized.

In Chapter 9, Paul Linden examines *popular music* and the growth of rock 'n' roll, reggae, rap and *salsa*; he argues that their growth demonstrates the semantic instability of "race" and "musical genre" as interpretive categories. He explains that translation is employed as a methodological concept allowing for semantic analysis of musical forms as they pass through geographical, social, and economic contexts, and he argues that the careers of Elvis Presley and Bob Marley exemplify the movement of popular music forms into the American mainstream. His analysis looks at the systematic, hidden expenses of mainstream success, including the alienation of core fan bases as well as artists' loss of both creative control and authorship.

Chapters 10 and 11 look at "new" media. First, Kishonna L. Gray provides a contemporary context for the *Internet* as it relates to race and ethnicity. By examining the racialized dynamics in access (i.e., the "digital divide"), Internet usage (i.e., "Black Twitter"), and control (i.e., the lack of diversity and inclusion in the Internet industries), she examines just how unequal the Internet still is along racial lines. Her most significant contribution is providing an overview of whiteness as a hegemonic identity operating within Internet culture. She argues that if we are to truly dissect and transform how race is communicated within Internet culture, we need to focus our attention on the industry, on access, on Internet use, on experiences within virtual settings, on representations, and even on the politics of technological production. Next, Gina Masullo Chen focuses on the intersection of *social media* and race. She explores how social media have helped provide a public voice for people of color that has been lacking for decades in traditional forms of media, such as television, newspapers, and movies. In addition, she explores how the hashtag has provided a means for people of color to gather together virtually around specific topics and even shift the discourse around news events. Finally, she examines the role of social media in encouraging people of color to register to vote and cast their ballots.

The next two chapters look at race and journalism. First, Cheryl D. Jenkins focuses on *journalism and African Americans*, explaining that the often simplistic and episodic news coverage of complex issues like race and racism by the American mainstream media has helped to strengthen the decades-old argument by industry critics that a more diverse news media, with viewpoints that reflect the actual makeup of the communities being covered, would serve a true democracy better. She demonstrates that research in the area of newsroom diversity shows a troubling trend in mainstream media, which has consistently been less inclusive of voices outside of dominant power structures in society. In Chapter 13, Raul Reis describes similar issues by examining *journalism and Latinos*. He writes that communication researchers who have studied the representation of Latinos in both news and entertainment U.S. media have been arguing for decades that this portrayal is skewed and inaccurate. He explains that an academic discussion about Latinos and journalism could hardly fail to acknowledge how scholars have dealt with three main issues: stereotyping and its effects on popular perception; underrepresentation and its pitfalls; and ignorance about the group and the potentially negative consequences of that ignorance.

In Chapter 14, Anthony J. Cortese looks at the *advertising* history and explains that images of ethnic minorities in advertising shape cultural attitudes about race and are very powerful agents of socialization. He writes that advertising is a barometer of the willingness of whites to share mainstream culture with people of color and argues that studying these images fosters critical media literacy and allows audiences to challenge racist ideologies. He examines how ethnic images and race relations have been historically presented in advertising and how such portrayals correlate with patterns of intergroup relations and tensions.

Next, Sherry S. Yu explains that the mediascape in multicultural societies is transforming. She writes that, aside from increasing transnational migration, forces of globalization (both cultural and economic) and digitalization make media transcend their formal national boundaries, and that *ethnic media* are no exception. She explains that while ethnic media were once confined to the domain of ethnic or diasporic communities, these media go beyond not only geographic, but also ethnic boundaries. She argues that what is lagging behind this shift is the social perception and academic approach toward ethnic media, which consider ethnic media as media *by* and *for* immigrant, ethno-racial, and linguistic minorities only. Her discussion traces the evolution of ethnic media by examining various aspects—terminologies, historical trajectories, and trends in production and consumption—and suggests that new critical approaches to understanding ethnic media are needed.

The final two chapters in Part II look at sports media. In Daniel Sipocz's examination of *sports media in the United States*, he focuses on the power of sports and sports media to construct racial stereotypes. He discusses how sports and sports media, as institutions in daily life, contribute to the sociological understanding of the world around us. Through contemporary examples of racial stereotypes in sports coverage and through previous scholarship, he outlines why there is a need to study sports media and the sports media's role in reinforcing stereotypes. Finally, Jacco van Sterkenburg examines *sports media in Europe*. He explains that its massive popularity and the diversity of the players it features make "mediasport" an important producer of discourse surrounding racial and ethnic diversity. He also looks at European sports media audiences and how diverse audiences receive and negotiate racialized ideologies (re)produced by sports media.

In Part III, Race, Ethnicity, and Intersectionality, *The Routledge Companion to Media and Race* provides a broad summary of the scholarship about media issues related to specific races and ethnicities both in the US and around the world. It also looks at the relationship of the study of race and media to the study of gender and sexuality. The authors in this section make it clear that media in the US and elsewhere feed hegemonic notions about race and ethnicity, and that those notions often intersect with patriarchal and heteronormative ideologies.

In Chapter 18, Rockell A. Brown examines media representation of *African Americans*, primarily by exploring reality television. She shows how the reality television genre depicts African Americans in stereotypical ways similar to how they have been portrayed historically in popular culture. She describes the most common of those stereotypes that began in the era of minstrel shows as well as the contemporary, assimilationist representations that persist on primetime television. Next, Celeste González de Bustamante and Jessica Retis look at *Latin@s* (Latino and Latina Americans). They explain that despite the extraordinary growth of the Latin@ population in the US, news and entertainment media continue to ignore this segment of the population. They provide an overview of scholarship that has examined representations of Latin@s and describe common examples of mainstream media representations (and misrepresentations). They also discuss how Latin@s choose to portray and depict themselves and discuss the possibilities and challenges in so doing in a twenty-first-century digital landscape.

In Chapter 20, Debra Merskin looks at *Native Americans*. She explains that in books, magazines, newspapers, movies, and television programs, representations of American Indians have been stereotypical, with problematic representations that date back more than 200 years. These limited and limiting portrayals present, to both Indians and non-Indians, one-dimensional visions of Indian-ness that, for both men and women, emphasize violence, sexuality, and savagery. She contextualizes media representations by discussing contemporary conditions of being Native in America, describing the history of representations of American Indians in several mass media forms (cinema, newspapers, and television) and presenting perspectives and debates in existing scholarship about Native Americans.

Next, Vincent N. Pham and Kent A. Ono address media representations of *Asian Americans*. After providing an overview of those representations across media formats, they point out that Asians and Asian Americans have played a pivotal role in producing the contemporary Internet. They explain that while key figures – such as Steve Chen and Jawed Karim, co-founders of YouTube – appear centrally in discussions of the digital universe, little research has been done on media discourse about Asian Americans' pivotal role in building the Internet. They explore discourse about Asians and Asian Americans as new media pioneers and Internet entrepreneurs and argue that aspects of the predominant "model minority" myth discourse about Asians and Asian Americans are simultaneously complicated and reinforced in media narratives.

Evelyn Alsultany in Chapter 22 provides an overview of how *Arabs, Muslims, and Arab Americans* have been portrayed in the U.S. media. She begins with a discussion of how Arab and Muslim identities have been conflated and racialized in U.S. government and media discourses. She then explores two time periods of representations: 1898 to 2000 and September 11, 2001 to the present. She demonstrates how images have changed from romantic sheikhs to rich oil sheikhs to terrorists; from sultry belly dancers and harem girls to oppressed, veiled women; from one-dimensional terrorist characters to the introduction of sympathetic characters alongside representations of more complex terrorist characters.

Next, Ji-Hyun Ahn explains that media scholars have argued that the media/cultural representations of *mixed-race* people have shifted "from pathologization to celebration" and "from tragic to heroic." She addresses the causes of this shift and its significance for the larger social transformation by critically examining the politics of mixed-race representation in the American media landscape. She covers miscegenation and passing narratives in early Hollywood to the recent increase of multiracial representation in various forms of popular media. While she primarily focuses on scholarly discussion in the United States, she also examines transnational scholarship by introducing research on mixed-race representation in East Asia that takes a different historical trajectory from the West.

The next three chapters of Part III examine media representations of race and ethnicity outside of the United States. In planning this book, I had hoped to include discussions about ethnic media representations from around the globe, but, alas, I found that in some parts of the world—for instance, China, the Middle East, Latin America, and Africa—scholars appear to be reluctant to enter the debate about those representations.

If nothing else, I found that close investigation of media and ethnicity in developing countries remains an area ripe for examination, though such examinations likely will be coupled with a certain amount of political risk.

In Chapter 24, Christian Schemer and Philipp Müller examine the media in *Europe*. They find that despite differences in the way ethnic minorities are represented in the media of different European countries, general patterns apply to nearly all countries within the European Union. They write that ethnic minority groups are generally underrepresented, but that, like in the US, they are *overrepresented* in negative roles, often as delinquents or criminals. They argue that this negativity is especially pronounced for social groups that are culturally distant or considered somehow less beneficial to the receiving country, and that the political discourse on immigration is also often negative or not positive enough to reduce the negative image of ethnic minorities to the general population. They fear that the lack of positivity sometimes legitimizes the overt expression of prejudice and discrimination among the European public. Next, Yasue Kuwahara examines the internal and external aspects of racial and ethnic issues in mass media in *East Asia*. Internally, she writes, mass media have shaped and reflected the changing relationships among East Asian countries since the end of WWII—from animosity stemming from the colonial memory to economic alliance. Externally, she finds, while the perception of racial "others" has begun to change as the exposure to non-Asians increases, the representation of race in mass media still shows the strong influence of Western hegemony.

In Chapter 26, Sidharth Muralidharan surveys the racial climate in *India* and the role played by mass media (especially advertising) in this context. The first part of the chapter provides a brief historical background on the Indian perception of "whiteness" and how brands of fairness creams have capitalized on the skewed notions of beauty among men and women to sell their wares. The second part of the chapter delves into gender disparity caused by the caste system and how advertising campaigns and innovative media can help spread the message of preventing violence against women. He ends by describing the extraordinary physical and media racial abuse faced by African immigrants and the Indians of the Northeast, and provides suggestions on curbing racial and gender bias based on academic literature and his personal experience.

This section's final two chapters look at the notion of intersectionality—how ideas about race and ethnicity in media studies intersect with those about gender and sexuality. In Chapter 27, Mia Moody-Ramirez describes the relationship of *gender and Black Feminist Theory* to the study of race and media. She offers an overview of feminist theory, defines terms relevant to the study of race, gender, and Black Feminist Theory, and summarizes the contributions of Black Feminist Theorists such as Alice Walker, Patricia Hill Collins, bell hooks, Angela Davis, and Kimberlé Williams Crenshaw. In the final chapter, Robert D. Byrd, Jr. focuses on the intersection of race and *sexuality* and the media representations at that intersection. He explores the cultural phenomena that occur not only in media portrayals of LGBTQ people of color, but also the broader LGBTQ rights movement in society. He explains that most literature on the subject asserts media have followed a greater move toward an assimilationist movement that focuses on heteronormative and homonormative adherence to the status quo, and, ultimately, subordinates race, gender, class, and sexuality. He examines white, gay male privilege and the role of race and gender in asserting privilege. He also explores the role of co-opted black civil rights rhetoric in the modern gay rights movement, which has led to the symbolic annihilation of LGBTQ people of color—not only in the movement, but also in media representations of LGBTQ people and issues.

INTRODUCTION

In reflecting on the work that is contained in this book, I cannot find much evidence to be hopeful that the mass media in the US and elsewhere are providing audiences with representations that could diminish racism and ethnic resentment. Indeed, the authors have provided us with a gloomy view of the role that the media play in propagating misguided and hurtful portrayals of "others." Journalism, advertising, and the entertainment industry all have long histories of symbolically annihilating and stereotyping people and communities that exist outside of the dominant culture, and this book provides testimony that these problems persist in the twenty-first century. Other than cases in which new forms of media appear to be giving a voice to people who have often been voiceless—for instance, social media's success in advancing the Black Lives Matter movement—there is little evidence that we can expect dramatic changes in the mainstream media anytime soon. In an era in which American-style capitalism is dominating the international political economy, media companies that generate enormous revenues will surely cling to patterns that put profit motives above the higher purpose of providing audiences with the kind of accurate, complex, and meaningful portrayals that could have an impact on dominant cultures' racial and ethnic attitudes and on improved public policy decisions.

But I do not believe that all is lost. Minimally, as media empires realize that there is profit to be made from providing more diverse content for increasingly diverse audiences, things should change. New technologies have dramatically increased the number of media outlets to which audiences have access and represent another area of hope. Many media professionals are aware of the critiques described in this book, and there are many instances in which they do the right thing. The first step in identifying solutions is to clarify the magnitude of the problems. The value of this book, then, is in summarizing and describing the important issues about race and ethnicity that media organizations need to address. The work that follows makes it clear that media content can have profound cultural impacts and consequences. It also makes it clear that the potential for media systems in the US and around the world to provide audiences with improved representations of all of the world's peoples is enormous.

# Part I
# STUDYING RACE AND MEDIA
## THEORIES AND APPROACHES

# 1

# REPRESENTATION

## Stuart Hall and the "Politics of Signification"

*Christopher P. Campbell*

Stuart Hall, the Jamaican-born British Studies cultural critic whose work heavily influenced a generation of scholars' examinations of race and the mass media, died only a few months before the infamous 2014 fatal shooting of Michael Brown by a Ferguson, Missouri, police officer. Brown, an unarmed 18-year-old African-American man, was shot by a white police officer. After the shooting, some news organizations included in their immediate coverage of the event a photo of Brown taken from his Facebook page. In the photo, Brown stands in a tank top, unsmiling and flashing a peace sign (misidentified by some of those organizations as a gang sign). Later, other photos from Brown's Facebook page surfaced that presented a less incendiary figure. Within a few days of Brown's death, a hashtag—#IfTheyGunnedMeDown (as in, "If they gunned me down, which photo of me would the news media use")—"trended" on social media applications like Twitter and Tumblr. Young African Americans posted two photos of themselves, one in which they appeared less than angelic juxtaposed against a photo that reflected them in a positive light, for instance in a graduation gown or military uniform.

These postings reflected an insight into the notion of media *representation* that likely escapes many Americans who view with regularity news coverage of black men who have been arrested for (or victimized by) violent crime. That is, the young African Americans who posted the photos intuitively recognized the problems inherent in the dominant media representation of black people as pathological criminals, a representation that goes largely unchallenged in the journalism industry and affects both racial attitudes and public policy decisions.

Stuart Hall would have been quick to recognize the meaning of the social media postings that followed Brown's death. His work challenged the "preferred reading" of media texts, and he described the cultural power of those meanings as the "politics of signification" (1980: 138). Hall used the term *representation* to describe the complex ways in which the mass media not only *present* images, but how they are actually engaged in *re-presenting* images that have multiple meanings, especially when it comes to meanings about race and ethnicity. For Hall, the analysis of media representations is key to unlocking the power of the dominant meanings ascribed to those representations, meanings that serve the interests of the wealthiest and most powerful members of a society. His believed his notion of representation was transformational and

> a way of constantly wanting new kinds of knowledges to be produced in the world, new kinds of subjectivities to be explored and new dimensions of meaning which have not been foreclosed by the systems of power which are in operation.
> *(Quoted in Jhally 1997)*

The purpose of this chapter is to describe the work of Hall and others who have examined race and media through the lens of representation and how powerful meanings about race and ethnicity are generated through media texts.

## "Reading" the Media

As Fiske (1992) explains, "The definition of culture as a constant site of struggle between those with and those without power underpins the most interesting current work in cultural studies" (292). He cites Hall's seminal essay, "Encoding/Decoding," as a "turning point" in cultural studies, as it

> introduces the idea that television programs do not have a single meaning but are relatively open texts, capable of being read in different ways by different people. Hall also suggests that there is a necessary correlation between people's social situations and the meanings that they may generate from a television program.
> *(292)*

Hall described "decoding" media texts through three levels of analysis. The first level is the denotative or "preferred" reading—that which was intended by the producer—and is followed by connotative ("negotiated" and/or "oppositional") readings of the same message. Hall explains:

> The domains of "preferred readings" have the whole social order imbedded in them as a set of meanings, practices and beliefs; the everyday knowledge of social structures, of "how things work for all practical purposes in this culture," the rank order of power and interest and the structure of legitimations, limits and sanctions.
> *(1980: 134)*

What Hall would describe as a "negotiated" reading of media texts allows for analysis beyond the meaning intended by their producers. According to Hall, such a reading requires a recognition of the "dominant ideology" that is at work and how that ideology is "shot through with contradictions" (137). Hall writes, "Negotiated codes operate through what we might call particular or situated logics: and these logics are sustained by their differential and unequal relation to the discourses and logics of power" (137). For Hall, the denotative, commonsense meanings of the stories are insignificant without the connotative, interpretive readings.

Similarly, Fiske and Hartley (1978) say these deeper levels of analysis allow us to identify the potential of a message to create larger cultural meanings; they also describe three levels of codes to be found in television messages. Like Hall's "preferred reading," the first order is the denotative message and "the sign is self contained" (41). Like Hall's "negotiated reading," the second order calls for the connotative reading of the message, including its potential for cultural myth-making. In this analysis, Fiske and Hartley include the impact of television production techniques to connote meanings: "Camera angle, lighting and background music [and] frequency of cutting are examples" (45).

Hall describes "oppositional" readings of media messages in which a viewer "detotalizes the message in the preferred code in order to retotalize the message within some alternative framework of reference." He adds, "One of the most significant political moments . . . is the point when events which are normally signified and decoded in a negotiated way begin to be given an oppositional reading. Here the 'politics of signification'—the struggle in discourse—is joined" (138). Fiske and Hartley describe this highest level of analysis of media messages as that which recognizes the "mythology" or "ideology" that hides in the coding of media messages: "This, the third order of signification, reflects the broad principles by which a culture organizes and interprets the reality with which it has to cope" (46).

Other cultural studies scholars have advanced similar notions in interpreting media texts. Louis Althusser (1971), for instance, described the concepts of *hailing* and *interpellation* to explain the way in which media messages "hail" audiences into specific understandings that serve the interests of the message producers. As Fiske (1992) notes, "These terms derive from the idea that any language, whether it be verbal, visual, tactile or whatever, is part of social relations and that in communicating with someone we are reproducing social relationships" (1992: 289). Likewise, Antonio Gramsci (1971) used the concept of *hegemony*—the subtle, unseen political, social, and economic ideology that reflects the interests of the wealthy and powerful—to describe the way in which media representations function.

Like Althusser and Gramsci, Roland Barthes was concerned with the subtle way in which hegemony functioned, almost without notice. In introducing his seminal work *Mythologies* (1957/72), Barthes described his efforts to examine French popular culture through the prism of cultural myths:

> The starting point of these reflections was usually a feeling of impatience at the sight of the "naturalness" with which newspapers, art and common sense constantly dress up a reality which, even though it is the one we live in, is undoubtedly determined by history. . . . I hate seeing Nature and History confused at every turn, and I wanted to track down, in the decorative display of *what-goes-without-saying*, the ideological abuse which, in my view, is hidden there.
>
> *(11)*

Barthes was concerned with the way artifacts of popular culture—advertising, photojournalism, studio wrestling, and others—reflect a kind of groupthink that doesn't allow for more complicated interpretations of events. Similarly, the work of cultural anthropologist Clifford Geertz, especially his essay "Common Sense as a Cultural System," is often cited in critical examinations of the media. Geertz (1983) argued,

> As a frame for thought, and a species of it, common sense is as totalizing as any other: no religion is more dogmatic, no science more ambitious, no philosophy more general. Its tonalities are different, and so are the arguments to which it appeals, but like them—and like art and like ideology—it pretends to reach past illusion to truth, to, as we say, things as they are.
>
> *(84)*

Cultural studies scholars have frequently addressed the notion of representation in news coverage, which routinely reflects mythical *common sense* about the events of the day. Fiske and Hartley (1978) identified "myth chains" as one of the ways in which journalistic storytelling embeds ideological understandings, and they pointed out that "news reporting and fiction use similar signs because they naturally refer to the same myths in our culture" (65). Himmelstein (1984) identified the "myth of the puritan ethic" (205) in news coverage that routinely extolled the values of hard work and middle-class life while implicitly questioning the values of the underclass. Richard Campbell (1991a, 1991b), in describing the myth-making capacity of journalism, suggested that the notion of "balance" was itself a "code word for . . . middle American values." He continues,

> These values are encoded into mainstream journalism—how it selects the news, where it places its beat reporters, who and how it promotes, how it critically reports and thereby naively supports government positions.
>
> *(1991a: 75)*

## Race, Representation, and the News

Among the most significant analyses of contemporary racism and the media is embodied in the work of sociologist Herman Gray (1986, 1991, 1995), who has examined both primetime television programs as well as journalism. Hall identified in 1986 the "twin representations" of African Americans in fictional and nonfictional television (304). He contrasted the upper-middle-class life portrayed on the mega-hit sitcom *The Cosby Show* with the underclass black life portrayed in a 1985 PBS documentary titled *The Vanishing Family: Crisis in Black America*. Race as it is portrayed on fictional television, according to Gray, is consistent with the American Dream, and "appeals to the utopian desire in blacks and whites for racial oneness and equality while displacing the persistent reality of racism and racial inequality or the kinds of social struggles and cooperation required to eliminate them" (302).

Gray argues that the underclass black life on nonfictional TV, on the other hand, fails to

> identify complex social forces like racism, social organization, economic dislocation, unemployment, the changing economy, or the welfare state as the causes of the crisis in (the urban underclass) community.
>
> *(300)*

Gray concludes:

> The assumptions and framework that structure these representations often displace representations that would enable viewers to see that many individuals trapped in the under class have the very same qualities (of hard work and sacrifices as seen on Cosby) but lack the options and opportunities to realize them.
>
> *(303)*

My own work on race and news attempts to expand on Gray's examination of the "twin representations" of African Americans (as well as representations of Hispanic and "other" Americans); in describing my approach in *Race, Myth and the News* I wrote, "The danger of the commonsense claim to truth is in its exclusion of those who live outside the familiar world it represents" (1995: 18). My first study (Campbell 1995) found the racial mythology embedded in broadcasts across the United States represented "a hegemonic consensus about race and class that sustains myths about life outside of white, 'mainstream' America" (132).

I've identified three myths that appear to be persistent in representations of race in American journalism (Campbell 1995, 2012). In identifying a "myth of marginality," I argued that people of color are ignored and therefore less significant and *marginalized* in news coverage (1995). I first cited the general "invisibility" of people of color in the news, noting the underrepresentation of minority news sources and the lack of coverage of minority communities in the newscasts I reviewed, including newscasts from cities with large minority populations. Additionally, I cited other studies (including Entman 1990, 1992 and Gist 1990) that provided evidence of the underrepresentation and stereotypical portrayal of minorities in all forms of daily news coverage. I also analyzed coverage from two cities that I argued provided evidence of lingering "traditional" or "old-fashioned" racism—the kind of racism that most Americans believe to be a thing of the past. The first analysis, in which a TV station in Hattiesburg, Mississippi followed a brief story on the local celebration of the Martin Luther King, Jr. Holiday with a more detailed story about a local tribute to Robert E. Lee, questioned the curious juxtaposition of the stories as well as the symbolic nature of that juxtaposition. I also examined a story from Minneapolis about a fishing rights controversy that pitted white sportsmen against a regional Indian tribe; the coverage was dominated by the opinions of the sportsmen (led by Minnesota sports legend Bud Grant) and failed to include the perception of the tribe. I argued that the two stories represented "a persistence of racial insensitivity that—when compounded by the news media's general under-representation of minority life—can contribute to a dangerous ignorance about people of color and a continuance of discrimination and injustice" (57).

Second, I identified a "myth of difference," arguing that in local TV newscasts people of color are routinely represented, in a number of ways, *differently* than white people. I argued that many stories on local television news continued to reinforce historical stereotypes about people of color, including "positive" stereotypes of successful African-American athletes and entertainers as well as the negative stereotypes of people of color (especially African-American and Hispanic men) as violent criminals. I cited other studies (most importantly Gray 1991) that also found such stereotypes to be the dominant representation of African-American men in mainstream media. I closely analyzed several stories that reflected a pattern of subtle racial biases in the newsroom and argued that "however well intended they might be, journalists (and audience members) are likely unaware of the biases and stereotypical thinking that are deeply rooted" in the cognitive and cultural processes in a society that is dominated by white, middle-class perceptions (82).

Finally, I identified a "myth of assimilation." In my analysis of local television news coverage of Martin Luther King, Jr. Day, I described a cherished newsroom myth that represents people of color, especially African Americans, as having overcome racism and fully assimilated into the American mainstream, where equality has been achieved. This is now referred to as "post-racialism." I found that stories about the King holiday were dominated by a theme of racial harmony, despite the evidence of lingering racial hostility in many of the cities that adopted that theme. As I wrote:

That King Day was covered the way it was is not surprising. The social and professional processes that dictate how news is covered are based on an implicit common sense, a common sense that may have more to do with stereotyped notions about the world than with a true understanding of it. Most Americans would like to believe that their country is a tolerant and fair one, that discrimination does not exist, that equal opportunity is there for all. But what we would like to believe and what actually exists are clearly at odds.

*(111)*

I expressed specific concern about news organizations creating a mythical world in which racial harmony is the norm when seen in the broader context of newscasts that routinely include images of people of color as suspects in stories related to violent crime. In reflecting on the work of Gray (1986, 1991) and Jhally and Lewis (1992), I expressed this concern: "If our society is the just and fair one that was portrayed on King Day, the constant barrage of menacing images of minorities that more commonly appear on local TV news will undoubtedly fuel racist attitudes" (111). When I worked with colleagues to revisit representations of race on local television news in 2012 (Campbell, LeDuff and Brown), we found few changes to the mythic notions I had identified in 1995; indeed, we found the mythic representations of race in journalism in the age of the Barack Obama presidency to be even more problematic.

## Race, Representation, and Contemporary Media

Other scholars have examined aspects of representation of race and ethnicity in media across media types and across borders. Evelyn Alsultany, in *Arabs and Muslims in the Media: Race and Representation after 9/11*, examines primetime dramas and sitcoms, journalism, advertising, and public relations in identifying both stereotypical and more complicated media representations of Arabs and Muslims that served hegemonic understandings in post-9/11 America and into the Obama era. Her work describes the traditional representations of Arabs and Muslims in which audiences are "primed by the media to equate Arabs and Muslims first with dissoluteness and patriarchy/misogyny and then with terrorism" (9). But she also identifies media portrayals that surfaced after 9/11 that she describes as "simplified complex representations" (8) that reflect the notion of a co-opted "multiculturalism" that is a shallow attempt to counter the terrorist stereotype:

> This feature of post-9/11 representations is consistent with Mahmood Mamdani's (2004) claim that the public debate since the terrorist attacks have involved a discourse about "good" and "bad" Muslims in which Muslims are assumed to be bad until they perform and prove their allegiance to the US.
>
> *(14–15)*

Similar to Herman Gray's pleas for more complicated representations of African Americans in the media, Alsultany believes,

> If more and more Americans were to see more and more complex portrayals of Arabs, Muslims, Arab Americans, and Muslim Americans on television on film, who knows what the effect would be. Racism is endlessly flexible, resentment of the Other can be easily stoked; stereotyped assumptions are difficult to

overcome. Perhaps the emergence of honest, and varied, and *human* portrayals of Arabs and Muslims would make little difference in a country, and a world, on its viewers. Television shows . . . have the potential for more complexity than we often give them credit for. Perhaps, en masse, they could compel an audience to reject the logics that legitimize the denial of human rights.

*(Alsultany 2012: 177)*

Rolf Halse (2012) reached similar conclusions in his examination of the representations of a Muslim-American family on the hit primetime show on the Fox network in the US, *24*. Scholars who view race and the media through the lens of representation have established a significant body of work that helps explain the subtleties of contemporary racism and its impact on cultures around the world. Contemporary examples include examinations of Aboriginal identity in contemporary Australia (Fforde et al. 2013); the predictability of stereotypes of American Indians on primetime television (Fitzgerald 2010); portrayals of migrant women in Korean films (Kim 2009); the "new racism" in popular culture's representation of African-American women (Littlefield 2008); and news coverage of the Maori Party in New Zealand (Sullivan 2005).

Stuart Hall's influence on the important body of work that uses the concept of representation as a means of examining the relationship between race and the media will certainly continue well into the twenty-first century; that relationship becomes more complicated daily as the world's populations shift geographically, socially, and politically. As events in Ferguson, Missouri unfolded after Michael Brown's death in 2014, American news organizations' coverage of protests, especially those that erupted nationally after a grand jury failed to indict the white policeman who shot him, continued to rely on problematic journalistic processes that fail to reflect the complexities of contemporary racism. Like the observations of the many cultural critics who have studied those complexities, the young people who contributed to the #IfTheyGunnedMeDown social media campaign that followed Michael Brown's death recognized the political power of media representations and embarked on a kind of post-modern media criticism that is consistent with the observations of cultural studies scholars. This critique of racism in the media has also spread to other aspects of American popular culture (for instance, by stand-up comedians like Chris Rock or in satiric TV shows like *The Daily Show*), which is a positive indication that that critique is not limited to academic critique. Indeed, as Hall might have observed, "'The politics of signification'—the struggle in discourse—is joined" (1980: 138).

## References

Alsultany, E. (2012) *Arabs and Muslims in the Media: Race and Representation after 9/11*. New York: New York University Press.
Althuser, L. (1971) *Lenin and Philosophy and Other Essays* (Ben Brewster, trans.). London: Monthly Review Press.
Barthes, R. (1972) *Mythologies* (Jonathan Cape Ltd., trans.). New York: Hill & Wang. (Original work published 1957.)
Campbell, C. (1995) *Race, Myth and the News*. Thousand Oaks, CA: Sage Publications.
Campbell, C., LeDuff, K., and Brown, R. (2012) "Yes We Did?: *Race, Myth and the News* Revisited," in C. Campbell, K. LeDuff, C. Jenkins, and R. Brown (eds.), *Race and News: Critical Perspectives*. New York: Routledge, 3–21.
Campbell, R. (1991a) *60 Minutes and the News: A Mythology for Middle America*. Urbana, IL: University of Illinois Press.

——. (1991b) "Word vs. Image: Elitism, Popularity and TV News," *Television Quarterly* 26(1): 73–81.
Entman, R. M. (1990) "Modern Racism and the Images of Blacks in Local Television News," *Critical Studies in Mass Communication* 7(4): 332–345.
——. (1992) "Blacks in the News: Television, Modern Racism and Cultural Change," *Journalism Quarterly* 69(2): 341–361.
Fforde, C., Bamblett, L. Lovett, R. Gorringe, S., and Fogarty, B. (2013) "Discourse, Deficit and Identity: Aboriginality, the Race Paradigm and the Language of Representation in Contemporary Australia," *Media International Australia* 149: 162–173.
Fiske, J. and Hartley, J. (1978) *Reading Television*. London: Methuen.
Fiske, J. (1992) "British Cultural Studies and Television," in R.C. Allen (ed.), *Channels of Discourse, Reassembled*. Chapel Hill, NC: University of North Carolina Press, 287–326.
Fitzgerald, M. R. (2010) "'Evolutionary Stages of Minorities in the Mass Media': An Application of Clark's Model to American Indian Television Representations," *Howard Journal of Communications* 21(4): 367–384.
Geertz, C. (1983) *Local Knowledge: Further Essays in Interpretive Anthropology*. New York: Basic Books.
Giste, M. E. (1990) "Minorities in Media Imagery," *Newspaper Research Journal* 11(3): 52–63.
Gramsci, I. (1971) *Selections from the Prison Notebooks* (Quentin Hoare and Geoffrey Nowell-Smith, eds. and trans.). New York: International Publishers.
Gray, H. (1986) "Television and the New Black Man: Black Male Images in Prime-time Situation Comedy," *Media, Culture and Society* 8: 223–242.
——. (1991) "Television, Black Americans, and the American Dream," in R. K. Avery and D. Eason (eds.), *Critical Perspectives on Media and Society*. New York: Guilford, 294–305.
——. (1995) *Watching Race: Television and the Struggle for Blackness*. Minneapolis, MN: University of Minnesota Press.
Hall, S. (1980) "Encoding/Decoding," in S. Hall, D. Hobson, A. Lowe, and P. Wills (eds.), *Culture, Media, Language*. London: Hutchinson, 128–138.
Himmelstein, H. (1984) *TV, Myth and the American Mind*. New York: Praeger.
Jhally, S. (Producer). (1997) *Stuart Hall: Representation and the Media* (video). Northampton, MA: Media Education Foundation.
Jhally, S. and Lewis, J. (1992) *Enlightened Racism: The Cosby Show, Audiences, and the Myth of the American Dream*. Boulder, CO: Westview.
Kim, S. (2009) "Politics of Representation in the Era of Globalization: Discourse about Marriage Migrant Women in Two South Korean Films," *Asian Journal of Communication* 19(2): 210–226.
Littlefield, M. B. (2008) "The Media as a System of Racialization: Exploring Images of African American Women and the New Racism," *American Behavioral Scientist* 51(5): 675–685.
Mamdani, M. (2004) *Good Muslim, Bad Muslim: America, the Cold War, and the Roots of Terror*. New York: Pantheon Books.
Sullivan, A. (2008) "The Maori Party and the Media: Representations in Mainstream Print Leading to the 2005 Election," *Pacific Journalism Review* 14(1): 131–149.

# Further Reading/Viewing

Alsultany, E. (2012) *Arabs and Muslims in the Media: Race and Representation after 9/11*. New York: New York University Press. (Evelyn Alsultany's prescient examination of the representations of Arabs and Muslims in American media.)
Campbell, C., LeDuff, K., Jenkins, C., and Brown, R. (2012) *Race and News: Critical Perspectives*. New York: Routledge. (Contains six essays that examine race and the journalistic routine and six contemporary case studies.)
Gray, H. (1995) *Watching Race: Television and the Struggle for Blackness*. Minneapolis, MN: University of Minnesota Press. (Sociologist Herman Gray examines representations of race in primetime television shows from *In Living Color* to *A Different World*.)
Jhally, S. (Producer). (1997) *Stuart Hall: Representation and the Media* and *Race, The Floating Signifier* (videos). Northampton, MA: Media Education Foundation. (These two videos feature Stuart Hall in lectures that address race and representation in the media; other scholars are featured in the Media Education Foundation's remarkable series of cultural studies videos.)

# 2
# FRAMING

## The Undying White Racial Frame

*Frank J. Ortega and Joe R. Feagin*

This chapter explores contemporary racial framing as exhibited in today's mass media, particularly racial representations, images, and discourses. We first introduce framing theory as a conceptual social science approach to analyzing media and society. We build on this by adding the white racial frame as a theoretical perspective to assess racism in the media, especially racial depictions and the role of media owners in the reproduction of racial oppression. Framing theory and the white racial frame are then applied to better understand how contemporary portrayals in the mainstream media continue to reproduce damaging racial stereotypes and mischaracterizations of racial minorities.

More specifically, we analyze popular African American and Latina/o images to better understand the ways in which media outlets depict people of color. The first examples demonstrate the replication of racial frames in discourse surrounding black athletes and images of President Barack Obama. Following this, we inquire into the transmission of racial ideologies to youth, using the film *Despicable Me 2* and its Latina/o imagery. We chose these widely circulated examples to illustrate how contemporary media framing regularly influences individual and group interactions. The chapter concludes with a discussion concerning challenges presented by racialized media framing, the great need for accurate racial depictions, and the necessity of a broader critical focus on the mostly white owners and controllers of mainstream media content in regard to racial matters.

### Framing Theory

Frames, small and large, organize social reality and construct meanings while connecting individual interpretations to broader structural and ideological processes, including those of major media institutions (Carragee and Roefs 2004). Frames are essential communication components that structure everyday life; they help organize our lived realities as well as develop and reinforce our attitudes and behaviors on many subjects (Goffman 1974; Bateson 1955). Media framing in particular is a central part of U.S. culture and to a substantial degree influences our thoughts and actions. Research on framing has been used in media studies including analyses of news coverage and is significantly used in the fields of communication, anthropology, psychology, sociolinguistics, and social movement studies (Vliegenthart 2012; Van Gorp 2007). Sociologists such as Gitlin (2003), Tuchman (1978), and Goffman (1974) have contributed to framing theory and research especially through their constructivist and symbolic interactionist approaches (Vliegenthart and van Zoonen 2011; McCullagh 2002).

We recognize that frames and framing definitions vary across these academic disciplines. For our purposes, however, Gitlin (2003) best captures how we and many others view frames; he argues that framing involves "principles of selection, emphasis, and presentation composed of little tacit theories about what exists, what happens, and what matters" (2003: 6). In addition, his useful definition implies that frames have important variations (see also Van Gorp 2007). Thus, frames not only diverge but converge across different issues and events, and impact how the receiver thinks about an issue in a prescribed way. Moreover, we share the view that frames exist largely outside the individual and are clearly organizing forces in institutions like the mainstream media (Van Gorp 2007).

Studying media frames carefully reveals numerous latent assumptions about society that are embedded deeply within dominant cultural perspectives. Socially constructed frames often become repackaged and circulated through important mediums such as newspapers, magazines, billboards, music, social media, television, film, and radio. These frames influence media audiences to recall, evaluate, condense, and interpret an issue in particular ways (Van Gorp 2007). Frames can be obvious, but many are subtle and unnoticed, yet remain fundamental to the ways people construct social reality. They are located in communicators' minds, the texts, the receivers' minds, and the larger culture (Entman 1993).

Framing theory offers an analytical pathway to investigate how people process information and use relevant data to interpret society. Media frames accentuate pieces of information, through omission and inclusion, thereby making them more *salient* and meaningful to audiences (Entman 1993). Furthermore, identifying media frames is useful and important in understanding significant social biases. Thus, an empirical news study often involves an analysis of keywords, language of arguments, stock phrases, headlines, images, metaphors, and editorial and other journalistic actors (de Vreese 2012; Matthes 2009; Gamson and Modigliani 1989).

Generally speaking, media information that audiences receive is selective in nature and presented through frames that represent the interests of those choosing them (McCullagh 2002). Those with the power to construct and circulate frames, e.g., the decision-makers in the news industry, mostly emphasize specific facts to sway audiences to particular points of view (Carragee and Roefs 2004; Ryan et al. 2001). Thus, news stories are always affected by journalists' and editors' perceptions and biases, which in turn can shape audience perceptions and biases (Powell 2011). Media producers, consciously and unconsciously, highlight issues that reflect certain social interests (not others) and that are mostly in line with established ways of thinking (Entman 1993; Gamson 1989). The result is that subtle changes in media messages can dramatically alter how audiences interpret important societal events.

In addition to these commonplace features of framing, we should note the importance of how the media set particular agendas and primes. Media agenda-setting structures the amount of attention and importance that most people in media audiences adhere to, such as those societal events and issues accented in the media (McCombs and Shaw 1972). The related process of priming involves media decision-makers subtly calling attention in audience members' minds to certain limited aspects of a societal event or issue, and thereby ignoring often important aspects (Iyengar et al. 1982). On a regular basis, framing, agenda-setting, and priming are tools used to benefit those who create, control, and maintain the society's dominant economic, political, and other social frames.

However, we must remember that audiences, in part or as wholes, are not necessarily passive vessels ready to be filled with biased frames and subframes. Some, or most, people constantly challenge certain recurring frames. Moreover, the mainstream media is only one avenue through which people come to understand the world, since they often draw on frames generated by their own or their families' experiential knowledge (Gamson 1992). In addition, some audiences, especially those who have been victims of societal oppression, frequently make use of *counter-frames* to contrast and resist negative framing in the mass media (Feagin 2013).

Clearly, the process of framing is an integral part of human societies. Frames and the processes of framing have tremendous power over people's responses to regular media communications (Entman 1993). Framing theory offers valuable sociological insights into communication frames in accordance with how the mass media reflects, shapes, and influences social reality. Adding to this theoretical structure, we now discuss a broad societal frame termed the "white racial frame," which we use as a valuable tool in examining racialized worldviews as produced and circulated via the U.S. mass media.

## The White Racial Frame

Racial oppression remains foundational to U.S. society. It takes the form of the political, economic, and other social subjugation of Americans of color. This reality is seen in the historical white construction and maintenance of the society's racial hierarchy, which so adversely affects Americans of color. Whites are positioned atop the hierarchy and thereby benefit from major material and non-material advantages. The dominant ideology of white racial superiority and others' racial inferiority is a central part of the *white racial frame* (Feagin 2013). The white racial frame includes a centuries-old pro-white subframe and anti-black and anti-Other subframes. All these subframes are composed of racialized stereotypes, images, emotions, language accents, and inclinations to discriminate. Assessing this commonplace white framing of society involves evaluating both the anti-Other subframes and the pro-white (e.g., "white savior") subframe. The white racial frame is part of the racial oppression that is foundational and systemic in U.S. society, and evaluating it is necessary to fully explaining the continuing societal dominance of whites, of white power and privilege. The anti-Other and pro-white subframes are important theoretical concepts to consider when analyzing the racialization of people of color in the mass media and other major institutions.

Why do the anti-black frame and anti-Other subframes exist? The early white racist frame originated during first contacts with indigenous and African populations and was adopted to justify and legitimize (especially in white minds) whites' extraordinarily oppressive actions toward these groups. Anti-Other subframes became widely used in the seventeenth century and have remained part of the popular white imagination ever since (Feagin 2013). The anti-Other subframes were created to rationalize white mistreatment of people of color, whereas the establishment of a pro-white subframe verified and justified white superiority in the minds of whites—and often in the minds of those oppressed (Feagin 2013). For centuries these pro-white and anti-Other subframes have operated through all major institutions, thereby actively sustaining the mistreatment and racialization of Americans of color. These highly racist frames continue to negatively affect the lives of people of color.

The effects of historical white oppressions, such as anti-American Indian genocide and African-American enslavement, have had a profound impact on the formation of the U.S. racial hierarchy and, consequently, on the life chances of people of color (Bonilla-Silva 2010). In addition, the many manifestations of *systemic racism* beyond the white racial frame (for example, concrete racial discrimination) continue to subjugate and marginalize people of color while simultaneously providing whites with huge psychological, social, and economic gains (Feagin 2006). Today, some systemic racial oppression operates at a more covert level, yet in all its blatant and hidden forms it continues to have devastating economic, political, and social effects on the lives and communities of all Americans of color. The mainstream mass media remain highly complicit in people's understanding of societal racial matters. Racist media images, largely controlled by white media company owners and their top executives, require deep probing to uncover and disrupt their racist and other biased group misrepresentations (Hall 1981). Better theoretical concepts, such as the white racial frame, can help social science researchers to investigate more thoroughly how the mainstream media construct and maintain the still prevalent visual and non-visual racial characterizations of people of color.

## The White Racial Frame and the Media

In Europe and the United States, whites used this white racial frame in viewing social worlds and to make sense of racial matters within their everyday interactions and lives. The mass media make use of "anti-Other" and "pro-white" subframes, in programs that demonize people of color and reaffirm the virtues of whites (Feagin 2013; Hall 1981). Who benefits from this arrangement? Who owns the most influential mass media? Media ownership, particularly of television and radio companies, is largely in the hands of elite white men. For instance, television broadcast company ownership among people of color has remained extremely low: Latinos/as (3.0 percent) (see Dávila 2012), African Americans (0.6 percent) and Asian Americans (1.4 percent). This compares to 77.2 percent for white ownership (FCC 2014). Clearly, Americans of color have little control over U.S. television content. This lack of media ownership and control among Americans of color results from several factors: historical white control (emerging during Jim Crow segregation), mergers and conglomerate ownerships, elite-biased deregulation, and the Federal Communications Commission's reluctance to follow certain court rulings (Carolyn 2013).

In addition, elite white executives, mostly men, oversee the five major U.S. television networks: NBC, ABC, CBS, FOX, and the CW. As primary decision-makers, these elite white men, and their mostly white senior managers, are primarily responsible for the racist and gendered framing of racial minorities. Intentionally or subconsciously, the white media owners and their executives perpetuate an old anti-Other framing with inaccurate and/or racist portrayals of people of color that serve the social interests of whites. As a result, blacks, Latinos/as, and other Americans of color are frequently misrepresented in negative terms and are also underrepresented in positive settings. All whites benefit from this arrangement as it regularly reinforces the primary rationalization for the dominant racial hierarchy in the US along with the inherent white privileges it produces.

Most importantly, the racial characterizations only work if influential people and their major social institutions such as the mainstream media regularly perpetuate the white racial frame with its implicitly negative mental images and explicit racist messages about Americans of color (Entman and Rojecki 2000). The result of perpetuating such systems is that much of the public remains left out of media production and lacks significant control over its processes, and the voices, views, and interests of people of color are often ignored altogether. In our view we need a critical national dialogue concerning elite white hegemony in the production and reproduction of racist framing via the mass media. We would also benefit from better funding models for alternative media, particularly public media, as one possibility for creating a counter-discourse to these frames and narratives.

FRAMING

## The Anti-Other Subframe: African Americans

The anti-Other subframes of the dominant white racial frame have persisted over long periods of time and have regularly surfaced in the mass media, where they are manifested in countless racist constructions and depictions of people of color. Most anti-Other subframes are similar across groups of color but have been developed and articulated by whites in numerous forms depending on the historical setting and the past or present political and economic status of the particular group. Nonetheless, negative framing of people of color remains central to this country's systemic racism, including white people's desire to preserve the racial status quo. The effect is that these subframes shape the lived outcomes of people of color and have taken many variations such as those accenting "foreign-ness," "criminality," and omnipresent "inferiority" (for example, biological, intellectual, and cultural inferiority). The following two sections present examples from newsprint, film, and Internet sources illustrating the reality of white racial framing in regard to African Americans and Latinos/as in particular.

The sports arena is one segment of society where race and racism continue to be pronounced and relatively obvious. For example, consider these depictions and treatments of black athletes out of the anti-black subframe: (1) blacks as "thugs"—e.g., negative media portrayals of black football star Richard Sherman's post-game speech about his abilities (Plaschke 2014); (2) blacks as "deceitful and manipulative" —e.g., white basketball GM Danny Ferry's incendiary comments describing an African player as a liar and cheater (Joseph 2014); (3) blacks as (slave-like) commodities to be controlled—e.g., the comments of white basketball owner Donald Sterling (Cacciola and Witz 2014); and (4) the racial name-calling experienced by black athletes from white sports fans and media commentators (Chen 2012; Katzowitz 2014). These are just a few examples of how black athletes are racially framed as "thugs," "gangsters," and "deviants" in mainstream institutions including in the mainstream media.

Traditional white racist framing of African Americans includes emotionally loaded stereotypes such as the Mammy, Uncle Tom, Coon, Buck, and Jezebel. These are often shaped, nuanced, and repackaged in mainstream media to justify white dominance. The white racial frame used by most mainstream media commentators on U.S. athletics often designates black players as naturally gifted or "[bred] to play" (Hughey 2014). The biological references and breeding metaphors maintain the logic of racism inherent in the system of chattel slavery. However, this commonplace white framing reduces the black athletes to a source of white entertainment, as physically worthy but not intellectually worthy of human dignity, and usually fails to acknowledge a given athlete's strong dedication and thousands of hours of hard work. Furthermore, racist imagery targeting blacks is widely available on the Internet, including in the negative framing of black athletes and of President Barack Obama. The substantial time and effort whites dedicate to racially frame and admonish blacks is a testament to how ingrained the white racial frame has become in the minds of whites and other Americans.

Indeed, one would be hard-pressed to study race in the United States without making an honest examination of the often racialized politics within professional sports (Carrington 2013). The subordinated position of blackness in the realm of these sports remains transfixed in a process of commodification, no matter what their incomes might be. The modern black athlete has been described as a "million dollar slave" (Rhoden 2006), largely because the institution of slavery has many parallels to the ways in which powerful whites have exploited black players. In most professional sports institutions, for example, whites are the primary owners and beneficiaries of black labor. For this reason, whites have framed and rationalized their exploitation of blacks by pointing to their pay but simultaneously devaluing their (human) worth. Note that white men are usually the organizational decision-makers who enact sports team policies that are reinforced by officials, fans, and the wider public and amount to the constant policing of black players and their professional and personal lives. For instance, these athletes are often viewed, periodically and publicly, by white owners and sports fans as animalistic, thereby providing more white validation of white power and control of blacks in the sports arena. This, in turn, forcefully preserves white profiteering through the exploitation of black labor. The historical and contemporary economic injustice of black Americans continues to be carried out through the white racial frame.

Moreover, professional sports often provide a moral, socioeconomic, and political battleground where whites pass explicitly and implicitly racist judgments and make racist commentaries in the now extensive realm of social media. One of the views asserted in the Internet version of this white racial framing is an elaborated animalizing imagery (Saminaden et al. 2010). In many different areas besides sports, whites have often portrayed blacks as "monkeys" and "apes" (Nederveen 1995). This old racist logic often implies that blacks, similar to large animals, must be contained and controlled by superior whites, which effectively solidifies the racial hierarchy. These portrayals suggest that people of African descent are subhuman, irrational, and instinctive, traits linked to biological frames and animal characteristics (e.g., aggression, speed, and strength).

Recently whites have used this monkey imagery (for example, photos) and mocking symbols such as bananas to systemically denigrate black Americans, specifically the country's first black president Barack Obama and his family. Carefully crafted images of the Obamas as monkeys, apes, and chimpanzees, together with elaborate photo-shopped backdrops and hate speech captions, appear in the millions on the Internet. Such white racist framing again accentuates, often rather emotionally, the old racist view that blacks are genetically and categorically unequal to whites. This recurring strategy of biological and social distancing allows whites to again justify their dominant hierarchical position in society.

During their years in the White House, Obama and his family endured a constant barrage of racist aggression. Anti-black sentiment against Obama often took the form of racist ape or monkey images reproduced online. The Internet provides people with an easily accessible outlet to express themselves anonymously and un-anonymously. This is the case in an Internet search of the phrases "Obama and monkey" or "Obama and ape," which retrieves hundreds of thousands of racist images. The likely white-generated images usually contain altered or photo-shopped pictures of the Obamas as monkeys and apes. These images fall into various categories, including the Obamas portrayed with monkey ears or mouths or with faces superimposed on monkey or ape bodies. They also include pictures of monkeys or apes represented as the Obamas (e.g., cartoon character Curious George dressed as President Obama) or unaltered pictures of the Obamas with significant changes to the background or the inclusion of props and messages to animalize and mock them.

One infamous image of President Barack Obama as an animal was propagated nationwide through Sean Delonas' political cartoon in a 2009 issue of the right-wing *New York Post* (Paterniti 2009). The cartoon depicts a murder: two police officers (one with a smoking gun) standing over a dead chimpanzee. One officer says, "They'll have to find someone else to write the next stimulus bill," a reference to Obama's economic legislation and to a chimpanzee who had recently been shot dead after attacking a woman. Clearly, the cartoonist is portraying Obama in the imagery of a chimpanzee and invokes the "black criminal" framing while simultaneously playing on the fear of black men as "physically threatening" and "rapists." Shortly after publication of the cartoon, Delonas defended his work and "called the controversy 'absolutely friggin' ridiculous. Do you really think I'm saying Obama should be shot? I didn't see that in the cartoon,' Delonas told CNN. 'It's about the economic stimulus bill'" (CNN 2009). Operating out of the white racial frame, Delonas failed to acknowledge his white privilege and ignored the national black community's objection to his racist cartoon. Delonas and the *New York Post* editors suffered no substantial repercussions for their actions; this form of racism continues to appeal to the fear of a white majority that continues to feel it needs to protect white women from threats like Obama. In other words, there is a gendered/sexual politics that is attached to this imagery that facilitates acceptance of this form of racism.

Animalistic anti-black framing is integral to maintaining white supremacy in America and this precise framing mechanism continues to scare white America into complicity with white power structures. This is evident in the many ways black athletes are constantly animalized and racialized. And even the country's highest office does not protect a person of color from viciously animalizing white attacks. The sanctity of the White House holds scant protection from the onslaught of dehumanizing. Such degrading and hurtful images in the mainstream media and the social media indicate that such white racial framing remains a prominent fixture in this society.

## The Anti-Other Subframe: Latinos/as

Mainstream movie and other media images of Latinos/as include those of "illegal" immigrants, criminals, and sexualized Latino/a figures. For example, Latino male actors are regularly cast as gangsters, drug traffickers, or "illegal aliens" (Mastro and Behm-Morawitz 2005; Berg 2002). Such characterizations of Latinos were reprised in the successful animated children's film, *Despicable Me 2* (2013). It was one of Universal Studios' highest grossing films (IMDb 2014) and was so popular that spinoffs have been made (*Minions* and *Despicable Me 3*). The film *Despicable Me 2* follows the adventure of Gru, a white villain turned hero, as he tries to find the person responsible for a stolen mutagen, a potential weapon of mass destruction. The two Latino characters are Eduardo, a Mexican restaurant owner and father to the other Latino character, Antonio.

Three scenes illustrate how the contemporary anti-Latino subframe of the white racial frame works. One scene represents Antonio as a "Latin lover." He is the love interest of Gru's adopted daughter, Margo. However, this relationship is unrealistic. Antonio is a ladies' man (i.e., unfaithful), is a good dancer (i.e., a good lover), and has an indifferent but debonair persona. Gru's greatest fear as a white father is realized when he finds the pair on a date:

*Antonio:* "And my dream is to one day play video games for a living" [Spanish accent, grabs cookie nonchalantly]
*Margo:* "Wow you are so complicated" [smiling, leaning toward Antonio]
*Gru:* "Margo, what is going on here" [Margo quickly turns in fear]
*Margo:* "Oh Gru, se llama Antonio, mi llamo Margo"
*Gru:* "Me llama lama ding dong, who cares, let's go."

Audience members are supposed to find Gru's overreaction humorous, while sympathizing with his predicament. They should laugh but understand why Gru is visibly upset that things are moving progressively fast between the interracial young couple, Antonio and Margo. The white-oriented moviemakers are implying that Antonio only wants a sexual relationship. He is a threat to Margo's white purity and represents what white fathers fear in a boyfriend: mixed-race children and the threat to white racial purity in a racist system that operates on the "one-drop" rule. Gru uses mock Spanish to separate himself and his family from Antonio. This Spanish-mocking technique is very frequently used by a great many whites in numerous settings to emphasize their dominant racial position over Latinos (Hill 2008). This also reduces Spanish (as a language) and Spanish-speakers, who in the context of the US are predominantly Mexican, to unintelligible subjects. This is important not only in asserting the dominance of English as one marker of identity and signaling the superiority of white Americanness, but also because in a white racial frame that is constituted by a white–black binary, Latinos/as are symbolically, socially, and racially unintelligible.

A second notable scene takes place at the headquarters of the anti-villain league between Gru, Silas Ramsbottom, and Lucy Wilde. Gru tries hard to convince his partners Lucy and Silas, the director of the anti-villain league, that Eduardo is actually the villain El Macho. As the conversation continues, Antonio remains at the forefront of Gru's accusations. Playing the role of the protective father, Gru continues his case against Eduardo to Silas:

*Gru:* "Yes, but there has been a new development, and I'm telling you: This is the guy! You need to arrest him immediately and [raises voice] his deviously charming son! I'm pretty sure the son is involved too. The son . . . also, you got to get the son."

[Gru moves closer and whispers]: "I think that the son is the mastermind, there is a look, there's a devilish look in his eyes, and I don't like it."

Then, the two argue about the lack of evidence for Gru's concerns. Still, Gru remains fixated on Antonio, who has no evident connection to Eduardo's (El Macho's) intentions. Gru describes Antonio as creepy and devilish, suggesting that he deserves to be in prison in spite of a lack of evidence. Similar to the "black criminal" frame discussed previously, the Latino male is also a perpetual criminal suspect in the eyes of many whites, a figure that any white father should object to as a mate for his daughter. White supremacy, then, is maintained in large part by literally controlling the processes of reproduction. Furthermore, the fascination with (and fear of) mixed-race couples also corresponds to white-constructed myths about men of color and their "predisposition" to rape white women. Indeed, this white racial framing of the sex-crazed brown-black male Other has been used to gloss over many white men's sexual desires for, and illicit (often forced) sexual relationships with, women of color during slavery, the Jim Crow era, and even the contemporary time period. Thus, the white racial frame is constantly reinventing itself and repeatedly overlaps with multiple forms of oppression across various settings as evident in the *Despicable Me 2*'s updated animated version of Latinos/as as deviant working-class males (Feagin 2014). The film takes a dramatic twist when the identity of El Macho is finally revealed. The hardworking small business owner Eduardo is the international terrorist El Macho. The moniker El Macho tries to poke fun at the negative stereotype of hypermasculinity and patriarchy that the white racial frame ties "inherently" to Latino male identity to maintain white male rule as the "nicer" alternative. In this case "macho" or a hypermasculine Latino is the threat to humanity and Gru, as the alternative and representation of a "benign" white masculine "protector" is inherently superior.

The scene innocently takes place at Eduardo's house during a Cinco de Mayo party. Gru pursues Eduardo through an underground maze where El Macho suddenly appears:

| | |
|---|---|
| *El Macho:* | "You have not lost your tttoucchh my friend" [with mock Spanish accent, and dressed in a Mexican wrestler costume with beige lace pattern, red and black star cape, and face mask; costume allows for chest hair, mustache, and gold chain with the letter "M" to show] |
| *Gru:* | Haha, I knew it! You are El Macho! [mock Eastern European accent, fist pump, excited] |
| *El Macho:* | "That's right!" [in a loud voice, arms out, sound of the customary drum jingle] . . . |
| *El Macho:* | [Speaking to Doctor Nefario, Gru's former partner, but now his evil partner] "Haha . . . I merely faked my death, haha, but now it's time for me to make a spectaaacular return to evil! Doctor, I think it's time we show Gru what we're up to here." [smiling, arm around Gru, El Macho moves hands devilishly] |

Gru is ecstatic to confirm his view of the easy-going restaurateur as the evil mastermind that the anti-villain league has been tracking. More importantly, however, this scene sends several racially framed messages. First, there is the fear of the subversive brown immigrant, connoting that many Latinos/as, even businesspeople, are plotting against whites to inflict harm. The caricatures of the Latino wrestler as evil villain and the embellished fake Spanish accents are negative and racialized portrayals of all Latinos/as—even successful Latinos/as. Second, the racially framed narrative also concerns the extreme lengths that the villain El Macho takes to deceive his friends and community. He tricks Gru, relishes his faked death, and proudly presents his new crime partner, Doctor Nefario, Gru's former partner. In this scene the white-oriented moviemakers signify that El Macho has no moral compass and has an obsession with spreading terror. Ultimately the movie racially mocks Latinos/as and reinforces an anti-Other, anti-Latino frame.

Overall, anti-Latino frames in movies and other mass media are varied in terms of setting, nationality, class, and gender. *Despicable Me 2* covers only a few of the major contemporary racialized images foisted by whites onto Latinos/as including the sneaky immigrant, stateside terrorist, Latin lover, and dangerous foreigner. Perhaps the most shocking portrayal of *Despicable Me 2*'s anti-Latino frame is another scene in which Eduardo (El Macho) makes a mutagen-induced transformation on-screen. Desperate to defeat Gru, he drinks the mutagen and changes into a grotesque purple monster. At last, the movie suggests, the inner evil Latino is unleashed in full view; the metamorphosis is stunning as the restaurateur-turned-terrorist turns again into a monster. Eventually Gru prevails, and the movie ends on a positive note, as a children's story. Yet the racial damage is done. Children of all backgrounds around the world are exposed to a savagely racist framing that positions Latino males as sexually threatening, physically menacing, and violent or, simply, as "macho." These white racist impressions of Latinos/as are now implanted in the subconscious of viewers, young and old. At an early age, then, many children will learn that Latinos should be treated with suspicion, fear, and hostility.

## Conclusion

As a research paradigm, framing theory and the white racial frame can greatly inform social science scholarship by examining racialized representations of people of color in the mainstream media. The impact of explicit and implicit racist framing extends and reinforces existing racial inequalities. The centuries-old anti-black subframe and more recent anti-Latino/a subframe are often difficult to fully see because racialized assumptions about people of color are inherently part of the deeply ingrained popular white racial framing. Note that, in contrast, the pro-white subframe depicts whites as virtuous saviors, heroes, and controllers of individual and group destiny, yet the dominant white ownership of the mainstream media and the legacies of anti-Other framing remain powerful allies in keeping the white racial frame dominant in society.

As we have seen, the dominant group exhibits privilege through broad ways of media representation. White roles range from villains to heroes to saviors without serious repercussions, whereas nondominant groups are perceived in predictably stereotyped roles as criminals, comic relief, and sexual objects. The pro-white and anti-Other subframes therefore work in tandem to legitimize racial oppression and continue to separate whites from people of color. As a result, the images of whites and people of color become distorted fantasies of a dominant American society but with real consequences. What are the ramifications for whites? There are relatively none that are negative in comparison to the dehumanization people of color often simultaneously internalize and resist daily. Mainstream racialized images articulated in the framing of people of color promote distinct and deadly social dichotomies, not only white and others but also poor and rich, male and female, and heterosexual and homosexual. In the white racial frame, white men hold the normative "real American" status against which all others are judged. White hegemony over popular culture remains one of the dominant realities in the U.S. mass media.

Framing often works in multiple and intersecting ways. For example, both Latinos/as and blacks are often marked as threats to white America. Race, ethnicity, nationality, language, economics, and citizenship work in combination to exclude those deemed in the white racial frame to be inferior. Media framing is used in combination with other similar societal framing to explain racial dynamics and rationalize racial inferiority and discrimination. If we are ever to meet the standard of fairness and "justice for all," white media owners and associated media decision-makers must end the constant barrage of racist framing by implementing creative and accurate programming of people of color instead of lazily employing the old racist frames. Furthermore, counter-frames and reframing of current white racial framing should be inaugurated and emphasized across the country to combat racist white framing. We see this in the creative ways people use counter-frames on the Internet and in social media to challenge white racism through positive images, videos, blogs, and culture jamming. However, the negative racial framing of people of color, as chronicled through our white-controlled media examples, indicates that the anti-Other subframes of the white frame are very difficult to eradicate and effective remedies must be part of long-term change projects.

## Acknowledgment

The authors would like to acknowledge the many valuable suggestions made by José Navarro, Assistant Professor of English at Cal Poly San Luis Obispo.

## **References**

Bateson, G. (1955) "A Theory of Play and Fantasy," *Psychiatric Research Reports* 2: 39–51.
Berg, C. R. (2002) *Latino Images in Film: Stereotypes, Subversion, Resistance*. Austin, TX: University of Texas Press.
Bonilla-Silva, E. (2010) *Racism without Racists: Color-Blind Racism and the Persistence of Racial Inequality in the United States*. Lanham, MD: Rowman and Littlefield.
Cacciola, S. and Billy W. (2014, April 27) "N.B.A. Investigating Racial Remarks Tied to Clippers Owner," *New York Times*. Retrieved from http://www.nytimes.com/2014/04/27/sports/basketball/nba-clippers-owner-donald-sterling.html.
Carolyn, B. M. (2013) "Media Conglomeration is Women's Business: FCC Reports Female Broadcast Ownership Below 8%," *Media Report to Women* 41(1): 20–22.
Carragee, K. M. and Roefs, W. (2004) "The Neglect of Power in Recent Framing Research," *Journal of Communication* 54(2): 214–233.
Carrington, B. (2013) "The Critical Sociology of Race and Sport: The First Fifty Years," *Annual Review of Sociology* 39(1): 379–398.
Chen, J. (2012) "Gabby Douglas' Remarks on Racism and Bullying Prompt Backlash from Former Gymnastics Teammates and Training Gym," *New York Daily News*, August 28. Retrieved from http://www.nydailynews.com/entertainment/gossip/olympic-gymnast-gabby-douglas-remarks-oprah-racism-bullying-prompt-hurt-backlash-teammates-training-gym-article-1.1146321.
CNN. (2009, Feb. 19) "New York Post Apologizes for, yet Still Defends, Chimp Cartoon." Retrieved from http://www.cnn.com/2009/US/02/19/chimp.cartoon.apology/index.html#top_of_page.
Dávila, A. (2012) *Latinos Inc.: The Marketing and Making of a People*. 2nd ed. Berkeley, CA: University of California Press.
*Despicable Me 2*. (2013) Animated Film. Directed by Pierre Coffin and Chris Renaud. [DVD]. US: Universal Pictures.
de Vreese, C. H. (2012) "New Avenues for Framing Research," *American Behavioral Scientist* 56(3): 365–375.
Entman, R. M. (1993) "Framing: Toward Clarification of a Fractured Paradigm," *Journal of Communication* 43(4): 51–58.
Entman, R. M. and Rojecki, A. (2000) *The Black Image in the White Mind: Media and Race in America*. Chicago, IL: University of Chicago Press.
Feagin, J. R. (2006) *Systemic Racism: A Theory of Oppression*. New York: Routledge.
——. (2013) *The White Racial Frame: Centuries of Racial Framing and Counter-Framing*. 2nd ed. New York: Routledge.
Federal Communications Commission (FCC), United States. (2014) "Report on Ownership of Commercial Broadcast Stations," Washington, D.C.: Media Bureau, June 27. Retrieved from https://apps.fcc.gov/edocs_public/attachmatch/DA-14-924A1.pdf.
Gamson, W. A. (1989) "News as Framing: Comments on Graber," *American Behavioral Scientist* 33(2): 157–161.
——. (1992) *Talking Politics*. Cambridge, UK: Cambridge University Press.
Gamson, W. A. and Modigliani, A. (1989) "Media Discourse and Public Opinion on Nuclear Power: A Constructionist Approach," *American Journal of Sociology* 95(1): 1–37.
Gitlin, T. (2003) *The Whole World Is Watching: Mass Media in the Making and Unmaking of the New Left*. Berkeley, CA: University of California Press.
Goffman, E. (1974) *Frame Analysis: An Essay on the Organization of Experience*. New York: Harper & Row.
Hall, S. (1981) "The Whites of Their Eyes: Racist Ideologies and the Media," in G. B. Rodman (ed.), *The Race and Media Reader*. New York: Routledge, 37–51.
Hill, J. (2008) *The Everyday Language of White Racism*. Malden, MA: Wiley-Blackwell.
Hughey, M. W. (2014) "Survival of the Fastest?," *Contexts* 13(1): 56–58.
IMDb (Internet Movie Database). (2014) "Box Office/Business for *Despicable Me 2*." Retrieved from http://www.imdb.com/title/tt1690953/business?ref_=tt_dt_bus.
Iyengar, S., Peters, M. D., and Kinder, D. R. (1982) "Experimental Demonstration of the 'Not-So-Minimal' Consequences of Television News Programs," *American Political Science Review* 76(4): 848–858.

Joseph, A. (2014) "Hawks GM Danny Ferry Takes Indefinite Leave in Wake of Racism Controversy," *USA TODAY Sports*, September 13. Retrieved from http://www.usatoday.com/story/sports/nba/hawks/2014/09/12/danny-ferry-indefinite-leave-of-absence-atlanta-racist-scouting-report/15527829/.

Katzowitz, J. (2014) "Ted Wells Report: Jonathan Martin Appalled by Racist Messages," *CBS Sports*, February 14. Retrieved from http://www.cbssports.com/nfl/eye-on-football/24443157/ted-wells-report-jonathan-martin-appalled-by-racist-messages.

Mastro, D. E. and Behm-Morawitz, E. (2005) "Latino Representation on Primetime Television," *Journalism & Mass Communication Quarterly* 82(1): 110–130.

Matthes, J. (2009) "What's in a Frame? A Content Analysis of Media Framing Studies in the World's Leading Communication Journals, 1990–2005," *Journalism and Mass Communication Quarterly* 86(2): 349–367.

McCombs, M. E. and Shaw, D. L. (1972) "The Agenda-Setting Function of Mass Media," *Public Opinion Quarterly* 36(2): 176–187.

McCullagh, C. (2002) *Media Power: A Sociological Introduction*. New York: Palgrave.

Nederveen, P. J. (1995) *White on Black: Images of Africa and Blacks in Western Popular Culture*. New Haven: Yale University Press.

Paterniti, M. (2009) "Travis the Chimp: The Wild One," *New York Times*, December 23. Retrieved from http://www.nytimes.com/2009/12/27/magazine/27travis-t.html?pagewanted=all&_r=0.

Plaschke, B. (2014, Jan. 20) "It's Hypocritical to Rip Seahawks' Richard Sherman for Rant," *Los Angeles Times*. Retrieved from http://articles.latimes.com/2014/jan/20/sports/la-sp-seahawks-sherman-plaschke-20140121.

Powell, K. A. (2011) "Framing Islam: An Analysis of U.S. Media Coverage of Terrorism Since 9/11," *Communication Studies* 62(1): 90–112.

Rhoden, W. C. (2006) *Forty Million Dollar Slaves: The Rise, Fall, and Redemption of the Black Athlete*. New York: Random House.

Ryan, C., Carragee, K. M., and Meinhofer, W. (2001) "Theory into Practice: Framing, the News Media, and Collective Action," *Journal of Broadcasting & Electronic Media* 45(1): 175–182.

Saminaden, A., Loughnan, S., and Haslam, N. (2010) "Afterimages of Savages: Implicit Associations between Primitives, Animals and Children," *British Journal of Social Psychology* 49(1): 91–105.

Van Gorp, B. (2007) "The Constructionist Approach to Framing: Bringing Culture Back In," *Journal of Communication* 57(1): 60–78.

Vliegenthart, R. (2012) "Framing in Mass Communication Research – An Overview and Assessment," *Sociology Compass* 6(12): 937–948.

Vliegenthart, R. and van Zoonen, L. (2011) "Power to the Frame: Bringing Sociology Back to Frame Analysis," *European Journal of Communication* 26(2): 101–115.

## Further Reading

Feagin, J. R. (2013) *The White Racial Frame: Centuries of Racial Framing and Counter-Framing*. 2nd ed. New York: Routledge. (The dominant worldview and racial meanings white Americans and others consciously and unconsciously ascribe to people of color.)

Goffman, E. (1974) *Frame Analysis: An Essay on the Organization of Experience*. New York: Harper and Row. (The quintessential interactionist inquiry into frame analysis in relation to framing and human interactions.)

McCullagh, C. (2002) *Media Power: A Sociological Introduction*. New York: Palgrave. (An overview examining the complexities of power in the mass media, particularly production, content, and reception.)

Vliegenthart, R. and van Zoonen, L. (2011) "Power to the Frame: Bringing Sociology Back to Frame Analysis," *European Journal of Communication* 26(2): 101–115. (The article provides an in-depth review of frame and framing research across several academic fields including an investigation of mass media processes, distinctions, and effects.)

# 3
# CULTIVATION THEORY
## Gerbner, Fear, Crime, and Cops

*Valerie J. Callanan and
Jared S. Rosenberger*

In the summer of 2014, the town of Ferguson, Missouri exploded. Hundreds of demonstrators poured into the streets to denounce the killing of Michael Brown, an unarmed black teen, who lay in the street for over three hours after being shot dead by the local police. The police department responded with paramilitary force—riot gear, tanks, and tear gas. Night after night, American news focused on the angry black mobs and their destructive protests. Yet few Americans ever learned of the back story—decades of police harassment that focused on the poor blacks that traversed the tiny white enclaves surrounding Ferguson. These tiny towns resulted as whites fled from Saint Louis during the 1950s and 1960s when legal racial segregation was dismantled during the Civil Rights Movement. Each town has its own police department; each supported in part or whole by ticketing African Americans for such violations as jaywalking, moving violations, or vehicle problems, to such a degree that over 90 percent of individuals brought to court in these towns are non-residential blacks (Department of Justice 2015). Yet this story, which would have provided historical context to the demonstrations, was not covered by the mainstream media. Instead, Americans consumed an all too typical portrayal of African Americans as unruly, violent troublemakers.

The starkest example of institutional racial disparity in the United States is found in its criminal justice system. With over 7 million individuals under correctional control, the United States has an incarceration rate that far surpasses any other country in the world. The "tough on crime" policies of the 1980s and 1990s, such as the "War on Drugs," generated a massive build-up of the criminal justice system that disproportionately hurts the poor and people of color. For example, blacks are three times more likely to be arrested than whites; once arrested they are much more likely to be convicted, and once convicted they are more likely to receive a harsher sentence (Reiman 2013). The result: an incarceration rate for African-American males six times higher than whites with the lifetime odds of going to prison 1:3 and 1:17, respectively. The *Washington Post* (Kindy et al. 2016) reported that 40 percent of all the police shootings of unarmed individuals in 2015 were black men, although they only comprise 8 percent of the population. These racial differences are too widespread and too common to simply be explained away by individual-level prejudices.

Researchers have suggested that during times of racial threat, white backlash has surfaced, but in the form of social, not overt racial control. Beginning with Nixon's triumph over Southern white Democrats upset with the changes brought about by the Civil Rights Movement, to the recent Tea Party Movement upset with President Obama's win, racial politics have been tied to the politics of crime (for example, see Beckett 1997; Mendelberg 1997; Pickett, Tope, and Bellandi 2014). Thus, criminal justice policies and sentences that outwardly appear non-discriminatory have been disproportionately used over the last several decades against the poor and racial minorities. No better example is the long-running "War on Drugs," which escalated in the 1980s when crack cocaine hit the streets. The federal Anti-Drug Abuse Act of 1986 established lengthy mandatory sentencing for many drugs, such as five years for one gram of crack cocaine (which is disproportionately used by African Americans).

Crime coverage both changed and exploded during the 1970s and 1980s, which roughly corresponded to the rise in incarceration rates, especially for African-American males. Symbolic racism (the association of societal problems with specific race/ethnic groups) is fed by crime-related media, which has been documented to be very biased in its presentation of crime. For example, news media (Chermak 1995), newspaper accounts of homicide (Buckler and Travis 2005), and crime-reality shows (Oliver 1994) not only focus disproportionately on violent crimes and violent offenders, but more often on black offenders, especially when they commit violent crimes against whites. Thus, many white Americans, fed a steady diet of violent media, were only too content to support the various "wars" against social ills.

As a whole there is sufficient evidence to argue that some of the institutional racism in our criminal justice system may be attributable to how racial minorities are presented in the media. Research beginning in the 1970s recognized that messages about race are not only present in the media, but have an effect on individuals who consume them. In a sense, the media creates a self-fulfilling prophecy where depictions of minorities as criminals are widely presented and result in law enforcement agents, judges, lawyers, and the general public accepting the idea that minorities are more prone to crime. Television news, reality-programming, and primetime dramas tend to favor stereotypical, usually negative, views of racial minorities (Dixon, Azocar, and Casas 2003). This results in a public that subscribes to the cultural ideal of colorblindness while embracing the stereotypes they have been exposed to through media representations. This chapter summarizes the research on media cultivation of perceptions about race and crime in three areas: fear of crime, punitive attitudes, and attitudes toward law enforcement. We begin with a brief overview of cultivation theory.

## Gerbner and Cultivation Theory

In the 1970s George Gerbner and his associates began to study the effects of heavy, long-term television exposure. This project was not the first attempt to identify the effects of television, as social learning theorists were testing the effects of short-term exposure to violence on television on subsequent individual violent behavior (e.g., Bandura 1963). Gerbner, however, was not particularly concerned with how representations on television influence a person's behaviors, per se, but rather how repetitive patterns in television shape individuals' views of social reality (Shanahan and Morgan 1999).

This "Cultural Indicators Project" used a "three-pronged" research scheme: institutional process analysis, message system analysis, and cultivation analysis (Gerbner 1998).

Institutional process analysis studies how policies are designed to control the flow of media messages. Gerbner recognized that there are some differences in television messages based on the program, channel, or an individual's preference for certain types of television. However, he believes that it "is only repetitive, long-range, and consistent exposure to patterns common to most programming, such as casting, social typing, and the 'fate' of different social types, that can be expected to cultivate stable and widely-shared images of life and society" (Gerbner 1998: 181).

Institutional process analysis argues that many of the problems associated with television consumption are related to the way it is dominated by private corporations. Despite broadcasts being transmitted on public airways, the public has little control over television content. Because of the organizational imperative to turn a profit, television programming in the United States targets the mainstream (middle-class whites) and, thus, is relatively homogenous in content and narrative. Of interest, Gerbner was concerned about private control during a time period in which many more media companies existed. Sweeping deregulation throughout the 1980s and 1990s drastically reduced legal barriers for media corporations to merge. As a result, a small number of firms now control the majority of print, radio, and television media (Bagdikian 2014). In 1983, 90 percent of American media was produced by 50 companies, but only 6 by 2011 (Lutz 2012). This group of conglomerates now produces homogenized programs designed for the global market (Gerbner 1998). So, despite a drastic increase in consumption and production, these mergers have led to far less diversity in the content and messages of media produced.

The second prong of the analytical schema, message system analysis, examines the most common patterns and trends of media messages. Gerbner and his colleagues collected years of television programming data and used content analysis to identify the underlying messages. Their results found that violence was the most common denominator across television programming. They argued that the prevalence of violence in television transmits repeated messages that the world is a scary place where people cannot be trusted (Gerbner and Gross 1976).

Subsequent research has found television violence is disproportionately linked to specific demographic groups. Content analyses of local television news programs find that African Americans are overrepresented as criminals, often violent (Dixon and Linz 2000; Dixon, Azocar, and Casas 2003). Moreover, news stories about crime are more likely to be covered in the media when they involve black offenders and white victims (Dixon and Linz 2000). In addition, the way blacks are presented has been found to be qualitatively different from whites. Specifically, blacks are more likely to be shown in handcuffs or being combative with police (Entman 1990). Crime-based reality programs, such as *COPS*, also skew the presentation of crime. Like television news and crime dramas, blacks and Latinos are overrepresented as criminals, and they are more likely than white suspects to be physically attacked by the police (Oliver 1994; Welch 2007).

In contrast, whites make up the vast majority of television characters, as well as the victims of crime presented in the media (Britto et al. 2007; Chermak 1995; Prichard and Hughes 1997; Weiss and Chermak 1998). Additionally, whites are much more likely to be portrayed in positive roles and the ratio of positive roles to negative ones (such as an offender) is higher for whites than people of color (e.g., Dixon, Azocar, and Casas 2003; Romer, Jamieson and DeCoteau 1998). These racial typifications have led many scholars to claim that such misrepresentation cultivates not only higher levels of fear of crime, but more punitive attitudes toward black offenders and justification for questionable police practices, such as the use of force and racial profiling (Oliver and Armstrong 1998; Robinson 2000). However, very few studies have actually tested these ideas.

The third prong in Gerbner's research schema is the one most studied. Gerbner and Gross (1976) hypothesized that the inordinate amount of violence in television programming gives viewers an inaccurate and exaggerated perception of how much violence takes place in the real world. They coined this the cultivation hypothesis. Results from the Cultural Indicators Project showed support for the cultivation hypothesis and offered other insights on the effects of television consumption. Specifically, individuals who consume higher amounts of television were more likely to fear crime and believe it is much more prevalent than it is in the real world (Gerbner et al. 1977). Further, Gerbner and Gross (1976) suggested that heavy television consumers are less likely to trust people. They described the belief system that develops among heavy watchers as the "mean-world view."

The Cultural Indicators Project has done much to expand our knowledge on why certain representations are common in the media, what messages are sent by these representations, and how the representations affect individuals. Since this initial work, researchers have begun to consider how the effects of these representations might vary across audiences and, to a smaller degree, across media forms.

## Mainstreaming and Resonance

Later research conducted by Gerbner et al. (1980) found support for two important processes related to media cultivation: mainstreaming and resonance. The concept of mainstreaming suggests that television representations work in line with the mainstream values and beliefs of a given culture (Gerbner et al. 1986). Thus, mainstreaming is a process that involves the erosion of sub-cultural or group differences through media consumption. According to Gerbner et al. (1986), stories in the media (whether print, television, radio, internet, or film) serve as a mechanism that unites publics that come from tremendously diverse cultural, racial, educational, and socio-economic backgrounds. Media messages provide all Americans with what Gerbner refers to as "a packet of common consciousness—wherever they go" (Gerbner et al. 1986: 22). This allows diverse groups of individuals to live and work together with "some degree of cooperation" (22). The dominant theme of these messages is the reinforcement of the existing social and economic structure.

Resonance is the idea that individuals may be more likely to accept television representations if they can relate to the depiction (Gerbner et al. 1980). For example, a depiction of a violent assault against a young Caucasian woman may have a greater impact on a viewer who has had a similar experience or belongs to the same demographic group. Thus, Gerbner et al.'s (1980) research suggests that depictions have varying degrees of impact on viewers depending on how they resonate with the consumer.

The cultivation hypothesis and the work of Gerbner and his colleagues have not been accepted by the academic community without challenges. For example, Hughes (1980) critiqued the approach of Gerbner and his colleagues, arguing that the relationship between television consumption and "mainstream" could be explained by some third-party variable. Further, replications of Gerbner's research indicated that the relationship between television consumption and the cultivation of mainstream values was much more complicated than initially presented (Heath and Gilbert 1996). Essentially, as outlined by Hall et al. (1978) and Livingstone (1993), one's position in a given social structure conditions how media messages are received; moreover, those responses tend to be similar among members that occupy similar socio-demographic strata.

Current tests of the relationship between media consumption and the cultivation of beliefs, while controlling for a range of demographic and experiential factors, do exist. These studies suggest media consumption influences fear of crime (Madriz 1997; Chiricos, Padgett, and Gertz 2000; Romer, Jamieson, and Aday 2003), public opinion of the police (Eschholz et al. 2002; Dowler and Zawilski 2007; Callanan and Rosenberger 2011), and views about criminal sentencing (Roberts and Doob 1990; Dowler 2003; Callanan 2005).

## Media Formats

As technology has evolved, so has the number of different types of media outlets that permeate our lives. Some may argue that since news and entertainment have been expanded to various media formats, the messages may be very different. However, the process of mainstreaming suggests that even these alternative media formats are oriented to the widest possible audience. Further, it has been argued that while numerous media formats exist, the same messages are being repackaged to fit a different medium, a process referred to as "looping" (Surette 2001). As Gerbner (1998) suggests, mainstreaming represents "a relative homogenization, an absorption of divergent views, and an apparent convergence of disparate outlooks on the overarching patterns of the television world" (183). Certainly individuals can seek out alternative viewpoints, and representations that diverge from the mainstream, but these are typically singular and short-lived experiences for the consumer. Cultivation analysis suggests that the pervasive and overriding messages sent through the mass media, no matter the format, are the ones that will ultimately influence a consumer's view of the social world.

One of the most important factors in criminal punishment is race/ethnicity. Study after study has documented the huge racial inequality in the criminal (in)justice system, especially among black males. Blacks have historically held lower punitive attitudes than whites. This difference has traditionally been explained as a consequence of white racial animus and fear of black threat, which elevates punitive attitudes among whites, and distrust of the criminal injustice system among blacks, who have been or know of people who have been unfairly targeted and harmed by the system. Yet little is known about the correlates of black punitiveness outside of studies that contrast these sentiments with whites. With respect to media and cultivation, one would assume that blacks, who on average are more likely to live in high-crime areas than whites, would be more influenced by crime-related media consumption. Yet the little research that has examined race/ethnic differences in the effects of crime-related media consumption has found that very few media forms influence blacks' fear of crime, their beliefs about crime and/or the criminal justice system, or their punitive attitudes (Callanan 2005). In contrast, there is plenty of evidence to suggest that crime-related media consumption among whites cultivates fear of crime, belief that crime is rising, confidence in the criminal justice system, and higher punitive attitudes.

A few explanations of these differences have been presented in the literature. First, media may not have as strong an influence on minority viewers because its effects are moderated by personal experience. Previous research has suggested that the media is most influential when the viewer has little or no personal experience with the subject matter. Gerbner et al. (1980) called this idea the "substitution thesis" or, simply stated, the idea that media representations fill the consumer's voids in knowledge (Graber 1980; Surette 2007). This lack of first-hand knowledge may be disproportionately experienced by white viewers, as minorities are more likely to have direct or indirect interactions (through friends and family members) with the criminal justice system. While media representations "substitute" for the lack of real-world experiences of whites, they most likely conflict with the experiences of minority viewers. An additional explanation of the disproportionate effect of media representations on white viewers has become known as the "affinity thesis" (Dowler and Zawilski 2007). The mainstream media tends to produce programs geared toward middle-class whites, their widest and most profitable consumers. Thus, characters (especially victims) in crime-related media tend to reflect the demographic makeup of this audience. The "affinity thesis" posits that when viewers share socio-demographic characteristics with characters portrayed in the media, they are more likely to relate to their stories. In support of this, research has found that when viewers share racial and gender backgrounds with victimized characters on television, they themselves are more likely to fear being victimized (Chiricos et al. 1997).

## Cultivation and Fear of Crime

There are a number of areas that test the effects of media consumption on various forms of public opinion. The most substantial body of research is on the cultivation of fear of crime (e.g., Callanan 2012; Callanan and Rosenberger 2015; Chiricos, Eschholz, and Gertz 1997; Doob and MacDonald 1979; Gerbner, Morgan, and Signorielli 1980; Lane and Meeker 2003; Weitzer and Kubrin 2004). Early tests of Gerbner's work established support for the "mean and scary world" hypothesis, which argues that the more television someone consumes, the more likely they are to be fearful and believe no one can be trusted. However, the research was criticized on the measures used to represent "fear" (see LaGrange and Ferraro 1989). Later researchers were careful to test the influence of television consumption on cognitive perceptions of crime victimization and emotive fear of crime separately (see Eschholz et al. 2003; Ferraro 1995, 1996). Studies have found support for the notion that heavy television consumption increases both of these measures. In addition, Callanan and Rosenberger (2015) found that media consumption increases perceived risk, which in turn increases fear of crime. Thus, television has the potential to cultivate the mean and scary worldview both directly and indirectly (also see Box, Hale, and Andrews 1988; Callanan 2012; Taylor and Hale 1986).

Researchers have also expanded the scope of cultivation analysis to more than just television consumption. Many researchers now include measures for multiple media forms, such as newspapers, radio, video games, the Internet, and video streaming services. Moreover, researchers often evaluate the relative impact of different crime-related television genres (e.g., Callanan and Rosenberger 2015; Chiricos et al. 1997; Weitzer and Kubrin 2004), although Gerbner argued the specific genre mattered less than the cumulative hours spent viewing television. The explosion of multiple media forms may give the appearance of more options to viewers. However, the same companies that produce television produce additional forms of media as well (Morgan, Shanahan and Signorelli 2009). Thus, researchers expect messages that cultivate fear of crime and risk of victimization to be present in most types of media. Research finds that in addition to television consumption in general, television news (Chiricos et al. 2000; O'Keefe and Reid-Nash 1987), crime reality-based shows (Callanan 2012; Chiricos et al. 1997), and newspapers (Heath 1984) have all been linked with the cultivation of fear.

However, the effects of media consumption on fear of crime do not appear to be equal across race and ethnicity. In one of the few studies to test for differences in the relationship between media consumption and fear of crime across race, Callanan (2012) found that consumption of local television news and crime-based reality programs increased fear of crime for whites, blacks, and Latinos. However, there was some variability in the effects of crime dramas and newspapers across race/ethnic groups. Callanan and Rosenberger (2015) found that consumption of crime-reality programs increased white women's fear but had no effect on women of color. In addition, they found newspaper consumption makes white women more fearful but has no effect on both Hispanic and African-American women. The results suggest that the impact of media consumption is felt differently across race and ethnicity.

## Cultivation and Public Opinion of the Police

Another area of cultivation research that touches on race and media is how viewers may cultivate opinions of legal authorities, especially law enforcement (Callanan and Rosenberger 2011; Dowler 2002; Dowler and Zawilski 2007; Eschholz et al. 2002). As Gerbner's research initially pointed out, television representations are saturated with violence and crime, and where there is violence, there is law enforcement. Issues of crime and criminal justice are consistently one of the most covered topics in the news (McCall 2007). While crime dramas have been around for quite some time, there has been an increase in the number of crime dramas in primetime television. As a specific example, *Law and Order* ran for 20 years and produced four additional spinoffs, including the very popular *Law and Order: SVU*. In 2008, the average viewer could choose from as many as 19 crime dramas on a given night (Rhineberger-Dunn, Rader, and Williams 2008). In addition, there has been an increase in crime reality-based programming over the last 30 years. Building from the initial success of the television series *COPS*, shows like *The Forensic Files*, *The F.B.I Files*, *Cold Case Files*, and *The First 48* rank among the most popular crime-related programs (IMDb 2016). Although these programs are highly edited and dramatized, studies find that most viewers perceive them as a realistic view of crime (Oliver and Armstrong 1998). This perceived realism helps to explain why crime-reality shows (in addition to local television news) are found to have a more powerful effect on viewers' attitudes than other crime genres (e.g., Eschholz et al. 2002).

The "substitution thesis" suggests that television representations fill gaps of knowledge that viewers have. The likelihood that messages related to the police will cultivate viewers' perceptions is driven by the fact that most people have very limited real-world experience with the police or the criminal justice system (Surette 2007). The average American's interactions with law enforcement do not go beyond the inconvenience of an occasional traffic ticket (Surette 2001). Given that research finds that personal experience tends to reduce the impact of media representations (Chiricos, Padgett, and Gertz 2000; Gerbner et al. 1980), there is great potential for media representations of the police to have a significant impact on most consumers.

A number of studies have supported the idea that media consumption cultivates various types of positive attitudes toward the police (Dowler 2002; Eschholz et al. 2002; Callanan and Rosenberger 2011). These include confidence in the police, police effectiveness, police fairness, and perceptions of police misconduct and the excessive use of force. Dowler (2002) found that consumption in general at least slightly increases the perception that the police are effective. A study conducted by Eschholz et al. (2002) found that viewers who consume higher amounts of television news and crime reality-based programming are more likely to have confidence in the police. Callanan and Rosenberger (2011) tested the relationship between consumption of various types of media (crime dramas, crime reality, newspaper, television news, and total hours consumed) and multiple measures of attitudes toward the police. Their work found that crime-related media consumption increases confidence in the police and the perception that they are fair but has no impact on the belief that they use excessive force. However, these effects were not consistent across race; media consumption increased confidence in the police for white respondents, but had little to no significant effect on Latinos or blacks. They argue that this finding is also explained by the relationship between race/ethnicity and personal experience with the police. While whites may have limited interactions with the police so that media representations substitute for this lack of experience, black respondents are more likely to have been, or know someone who has been, the victim of police discrimination. As an example, statistics from New York City's Stop and Frisk program show that of the 4.4 million stops conducted by the NYPD between 2004 and 2012, 83 percent of those stopped were black or Hispanic (*New York Times* 2013).

## Cultivation and Punitive Attitudes

Evidence suggests that viewers cultivate opinions of the criminal justice system through media representations. These opinions have been shown to manifest themselves into higher levels of fear of crime, more support for the police, and misconceptions about the prevalence of crime. In addition, research has connected media consumption with more punitive attitudes toward offenders (Callanan 2005; Demker et al. 2008; Roberts and Doob 1990). Theoretically these works suggest that the way crime is presented in the media evokes harsh blame and condemnation of the individual. Crime is often framed in a way that suggests crime is a massive public issue that threatens all people (Sacco 1995). The criminal justice system, which is rife with procedure, is often portrayed as an impediment to "real" justice and puts the public at risk. This is commonly called the "faulty criminal justice frame" (Surette 2007). This frame lends itself to a simple solution; we need harsher laws and more punitive sentencing to protect the public from the real threat that criminals pose to us all (Rosenberger and Callanan 2011).

On one hand, the research suggests that media consumption cultivates positive attitudes toward the police and support for a more punitive justice system. On the other hand, research suggests that minorities disproportionately make up the criminal element that the public should fear in media representations (Dixon and Linz 2000). It seems then that media representations of the criminal justice system suggest that crime primarily committed by minorities, and despite the best efforts of the police, is a threat that demands action in the form of punitive laws and sentencing. Despite the connections of these separate lines of inquiry, and the fact that researchers have identified racial prejudice as an important predictor of punitiveness (Johnson 2001; Young 1985), very few researchers have attempted to determine how the media's effect on punitiveness differs across racial groups.

Given what has been established in research on media and public opinion of the criminal justice system, it is logical to posit that punitiveness is disproportionately cultivated in white viewers. Racial typifications have a heavy presence in crime-related media (Entman 1990, 1992); Chiricos, Welch, and Gertz (2004) and individuals who believe these racial typifications are more likely to be punitive. Callanan (2005) found that crime-related media had no direct effect on support for "three-strikes" sentencing (in which life-long terms are imposed on repeat offenders), irrespective of race/ethnicity; however, there were significant race/ethnicity differences in the effects of media consumption on other attitudes and beliefs about crime that were linked to greater support for three-strikes. Her research suggests that punitiveness among whites is tied to the messages they receive about racial minorities in crime-related media. The fear and concern over crime is driven both by their misconceptions of its prevalence and the skewed racial presentation of offenders and victims. The result is white viewers who are more likely to prefer punitive sentencing laws as a means to protect themselves and the public.

## Conclusion

To sum, it appears that cultivation effects vary across race/ethnicity depending on the belief, attitude, or perception that is being explored. The existing empirical evidence, although scant, suggests significant support for Gerbner's cultivation theory. Local television news and crime-based reality programs, which are perceived as realistic portrayals of crime, appear to have similar effects on fear of crime irrespective of race/ethnicity. As Gerbner argued decades ago, consumption of mainstream media does cultivate a "mean-world" view and fear in consumers, no matter what their personal characteristics.

Cultivation effects on attitudes toward the police, however, are only found among whites. This supports Gerbner's later work on substitution effects. When crime coverage is focused on lethal violence perpetrated by inner-city gang members and drug users who happen to be black or Hispanic, it is not surprising that white viewers would support police responses, no matter how egregious. When we portray crime in simple moral and racialized terms—dark evil-doer versus the white heroic crime fighter—it invokes simple responses to a complex issue. What these three lines of research show us is that media cultivates fear of crime and support for the police and perpetuates whites' perceptions of "the criminal justice system as an institution that should protect their interests by keeping minorities 'in their place'" (Unnever, Gabbidon, and Higgins 2011: 39). But African Americans, who live with constant reminders of police brutality, know better.

## References

Bagdikian, B. H. (2014) *The New Media Monopoly*. Boston, MA: Beacon Press.
Bandura, A., Ross, D., and Ross, S. (1963) "Imitation of Film-Mediated Aggressive Models," *Abnormal and Social Psychology* 66(1): 3–11.
Beckett, K. (1997) *Making Crime Pay: Law and Order in Contemporary America*. New York: Oxford.
Box, S., Hale, C., and Andrews, C. (1988) "Explaining Fear of Crime," *British Journal of Criminology* 28(3): 340–356.
Britto, S., Hughes, T., Saltzman, K., and Stroh C. (2007) "Does 'Special' Mean Young, White and Female? Deconstructing the Meaning of 'Special' in *Law & Order: Special Victims Unit*," *Journal of Criminal Justice and Popular Culture* 14(1): 39–57.
Buckler, K. and Travis, L. (2005) "Assessing the Newsworthiness of Homicide Events: An Analysis of Coverage in the Houston Chronicle," *Journal of Criminal Justice and Popular Culture* 12(1): 1–25.
Callanan, V. J. (2005) *Feeding the Fear of Crime: Crime-related Media and Support for Three Strikes*. New York: LFB Scholarly Publishing LLC.
——. (2012) "Media Consumption, Perceptions of Crime Risk and Fear of Crime: Examining Race/Ethnic Differences," *Sociological Perspectives* 55(1): 93–115.
Callanan, V. J. and Rosenberger, J. S. (2011) "Media and Public Perceptions of the Police: Examining the Impact of Race and Personal Experience," *Policing and Society* 21(2): 167–189.

——. (2015) "Media, Gender, and Fear of Crime," *Criminal Justice Review* 40(3): 322–339.
Chermak, S. M. (1995) *Victims in the News: Crime and the American News Media*. Boulder, CO: Westview Press Inc.
Chiricos, T., Eschholz, S., and Gertz, M. (1997) "Crime, News and Fear of Crime: Toward an Identification of Audience Effects," *Social Problems* 44(3): 342–356.
Chiricos, T., Padgett, K., and Gertz. M. (2000) "Fear, TV News, and the Reality of Crime," *Criminology* 38(3): 755–785.
Chiricos, T., Welch, K. and Gertz, M. (2004) "Racial Typification of Crime and Support for Punitive Measures," *Criminology* 42: 358–390.
Demker, M., Towns, M., Duus-Otterstrom, G., and Sebring, J. (2008) "Fear and Punishment in Sweden: Exploring Penal Attitudes," *Punishment and Society* 10(3): 319–332.
Department of Justice. (2015) *Investigation of the Ferguson Police Department*. Retrieved from https://www.justice.gov/sites/default/files/opa/pressreleases/attachments/2015/03/04/ferguson_police_department_report.pdf.
Dixon, T. L., Azocar, C. L., and Casas, M. (2003) "The Portrayal of Race and Crime on Television Network News," *Journal of Broadcasting and Electronic Media* 47(4): 498–523.
Dixon, T. L. and Linz, D. (2000) "Overrepresentation and Underrepresentation of African Americans and Latinos as Lawbreakers on Television News," *Journal of Communication* 50(2): 131–154.
Doob, A. N. and Macdonald, G. E. (1979) "Television Viewing and Fear of Victimization: Is the Relationship Causal?," *Journal of Personality and Social Psychology* 37(2): 170–179.
Dowler, K. (2002) "Media Influence on Citizen Attitudes toward Police Effectiveness," *Policing and Society* 12(3): 227–238.
——. (2003) "Media Consumption and Public Attitudes toward Crime and Justice: The Relationship between Fear of Crime, Punitive Attitudes, and Perceived Police Effectiveness," *Journal of Criminal Justice and Popular Culture* 10(2): 109–126.
Dowler, K. and Zawilski, V. (2007) "Public Perceptions of Police Misconduct and Discrimination: Examining the Impact of Media Consumption," *Journal of Criminal Justice* 35(2): 193–203.
Entman, R. M. (1990) "Modern Racism and the Images of Blacks in Local Television News," *Critical Studies in Mass Communications* 7(4): 332–345.
——. (1992) "Blacks in the News: Television, Modern Racism, and Cultural Change," *Journalism and Mass Communication Quarterly* 69(2): 341–361.
Eschholz, S., Blackwell, B. S., Gertz, M., and Chiricos, T. (2002) "Race and Attitudes toward the Police: Assessing the Effects of Watching 'Reality' Police Programs," *Journal of Criminal Justice* 30(4): 400–420.
Eschholz, S., Chiricos, T., and Gertz. M. (2003) "Television and Fear of Crime: Program Types, Audience Traits, and the Mediating Effect of Perceived Neighborhood Racial Composition," *Social Problems* 50(3): 395–415.
Ferraro, K. F. (1995) *Fear of Crime: Interpreting Victimization Risk*. Albany: State University of New York Press.
——. (1996) "Women's Fear of Victimization: Shadow of Sexual Assault?," *Social Forces* 75(2): 667–690.
Gerbner, G. (1998) "Cultivation Analysis: An Overview," *Mass Communication and Society* 1(3/4): 175–194.
Gerbner, G. and Gross, L. (1976) "Living with Television: The Violence Profile," *Journal of Communication* 26(2): 172–194.
Gerbner, G., Gross, L., Eleey, M. F., Jackson-Beeck, M., Fox, S., and Signorielli, N. (1977) "TV Violence Profile No. 8: The Highlights," *Journal of Communication* 27(2): 71–180.
Gerbner, G., Gross, L., Morgan, M., and Signorielli, N. (1980) "The 'Mainstreaming' of America: Violence Profile No. 11," *Journal of Communication* 30(3): 10–29.
——. (1986) "Living with Television: The Dynamics of the Cultivation Process," in J. Bryant and D. Zillmann (eds.), *Perspective on Media Effects*. Hillsdale, NJ: Lawrence Erlbaum, 17–40.
Graber, D. A. (1980) *Crime News and the Public*. New York: Praeger Publishers.
Hall, S., Critcher, C., Jefferson, T., Clarke, J., and Roberts, B. (1978) *Policing the Crisis: Mugging, the State and Law and Order*. London: Macmillan.
Heath, L. (1984) "Impact of Newspaper Crime Reports on Fear of Crime: Multimethodological Investigation," *Journal of Personality and Social Psychology* 47(2): 263–276.

Heath, L. and Gilbert, K. (1996) "Mass Media and Fear of Crime," *American Behavioral Scientist* 39(4): 379–386.

Hughes, M. (1980) "The Fruits of Cultivation Analysis: A Reexamination of Some Effects of Television Watching," *Public Opinion Quarterly* 44(3): 287–302.

IMDb (Internet Movie Database). (2016) "Most Popular Crime TV Series." Retrieved from http://www.imdb.com/search/title?genres=crime&sort=moviemeter,asc&title_type=tv_series.

Johnson, D. (2001) "Punitive Attitudes on Crime: Economic Insecurity, Racial Prejudice, of Both?," *Sociological Focus* 34(1): 33–54.

Kindy, K., Fisher, M., Tate, J., and Jenkins, J. (2016, Dec. 26) "A Year of Reckoning: Police Fatally Shoot Nearly 1,000." *Washington Post*.

LaGrange, R. L. and Ferraro, K. F. (1989) "Assessing Age and Gender Differences in Perceived Risk and Fear of Crime," *Criminology* 27(4): 697–720.

Lane, J. and Meeker, J. W. (2003) "Ethnicity, Information Sources and Fear of Crime," *Deviant Behavior* 24(1): 1–26.

Livingstone, S. (1993) "The Rise and Fall of Audience Research: An Old Story with a New Ending," *Journal of Communication* 43(4): 5–12.

Lutz, A. (2012, June 14) "These Corporations Control 90% of the Media in America," *Business Insider*.

Madriz, E. (1997) "Images of Criminals and Victims: A Study on Women's Fear and Social Control," *Gender and Society* 11(3): 342–356.

McCall, Jeffery M. (2007) *Viewer Discretion Advised: Taking Control of Mass Media Influences*. Lanham, MD: Rowman and Littlefield.

Mendelberg, T. (1997) "Executing Hortons: Racial Crime in the 1988 Presidential Campaign," *Public Opinion Quarterly* 61(1): 134–157.

Morgan, M., Shanahan, J., and Signorelli, N. (2009) "Growing Up with Television," in J. Bryant and M. B. Oliver (eds.), *Media Effects: Advances in Theory and Research*. New York: Routledge, 34–49.

*New York Times*. (2013, Aug. 12). "Racial Discrimination in Stop-and-Frisk," p. A-22.

O'Keefe, G. J. and Reid-Nash, K. (1987) "Crime News and Real-world Blues: The Effects of the Media on Social Reality," *Communication Research* 14(2): 147–168.

Oliver, M. B. (1994) "Portrayals of Crime, Race, and Aggression in 'Reality-Based' Police Shows: A Content Analysis," *Journal of Broadcasting and Electronic Media* 38(2): 179–192.

Oliver, M. B. and Armstrong, G. B. (1995) "Predictors of Viewing and Enjoyment of Reality-Based and Fictional Crime Shows," *Journalism and Mass Communication* 72(3): 559–570.

Pickett, J. T., Tope, D., and Bellandi, R. (2014) "Taking Back our Country: Tea Party Membership and Support for Punitive Crime Policies," *Sociological Inquiry* 84(2): 167–190.

Prichard, D. and Hughes, K. D. (1997) "Patterns of Deviance in Crime News," *Journal of Communication* 47(3): 49–67.

Reiman, J. (2013) *The Rich Get Richer and the Poor Get Prison: Ideology, Class, and Criminal Justice*. New York: Routledge.

Rhineberger-Dunn, G. M., Rader, N. E., and Williams, K. D. (2008) "Constructing Juvenile Delinquency through Crime Drama: An Analysis of *Law & Order*," *Journal of Criminal Justice and Popular Culture* 15(1): 94–116.

Roberts, J. V. and Doob, A. N. (1990) "News Media Influences on Public Views of Sentencing," *Law and Human Behavior* 14(5): 451–458.

Robinson, M. (2000) "The Construction and Reinforcement of Myths of Race and Crime," *Journal of Contemporary Criminal Justice* 16(2): 133–156.

Romer, D., Jamieson, K. H., and Aday, S. (2003) "Television News and the Cultivation of Fear of Crime," *Journal of Communication* 53(1): 88–104.

Romer, D., Jamieson, K. H., and DeCoteau, N. J. (1998) "The Treatment of Persons of Color in Local Television News: Ethnic Blame Discourse or Realistic Group Conflict?," *Communication Research* 25(3): 286–305.

Shanahan, J. and Morgan, M. (1999) *Television and Its Viewers: Cultivation Theory and Research*. Cambridge, UK: Cambridge University Press.

Surette, R. (2001) "Public Information Officers: The Civilianization of a Criminal Justice Profession," *Journal of Criminal Justice* 29(2): 107–117.

——. (2007) *Media, Crime, and Criminal Justice: Images, Realities, and Policies*. Belmont, CA: Thomson Wadsworth.

Taylor, R. B. and Hale, M. (1986) "Testing Alternative Models of Fear of Crime," *Journal of Criminal Law and Criminology* 77(1): 151–189.

Unnever, J. D., Gabbidon, S. L., and Higgins, G. E. (2011) "The Election of Barack Obama and Perceptions of Criminal Injustice," *Justice Quarterly* 28: 23–45.

Young, R. (1985) "Perceptions of Crime, Racial Attitudes, and Firearms Ownership," *Social Forces* 64(2): 473–486.

Weiss, A. and Chermak, S. M. (1998) "The News Value of African American Victims: An Examination of the Media's Presentation of Homicide," *Journal of Crime and Justice* 21(1): 71–88.

Weitzer, R. and Kubrin, C. E. (2004) "Breaking News: How Local TV News and Real World Conditions Affect Fear of Crime," *Justice Quarterly* 21(3): 497–519.

Welch, K. (2007) "Black Criminal Stereotypes and Racial Profiling," *Journal of Contemporary Criminal Justice* 23(3): 276–288.

## Further Reading

Callanan, V. J. (2005) *Feeding the Fear of Crime: Crime-related Media and Support for Three Strikes*. New York: LFB Scholarly Publishing LLC. (Explores the link between crime-related media consumption and support for punitive criminal sentencing, providing a robust test of Gerbner's cultivation hypothesis.)

Entman, R. M. and Rojecki, A. (2000) *The Black Image in the White Mind: Media and Race in America*. Chicago, IL: University of Chicago Press. (Explores the way in which media representations serve as the primary source of information about African Americans for many white viewers; provides insight into the effect that these images have on the attitudes of whites toward blacks.)

Shanahan, J. and Morgan, M. (1999) *Television and Its Viewers: Cultivation Theory and Research*. Cambridge, UK: Cambridge University Press. (Gerbner's longtime co-authors explore the way in which television consumption impacts viewers' beliefs and how these beliefs differ on issues of sex, politics, and violence.)

Surette, R. (2015) *Media, Crime, and Criminal Justice: Images, Realities, and Policies*. 5th ed. Stamford, CT: Cengage. (Explores the way in which crime-related media representations shape consumers' reality; highlights the relationship between media consumption, opinions, and policy creation.)

# 4
# HISTORICAL MEDIA ANALYSIS

## Oppression and Resistance

*Vanessa Murphree*

Historians and other scholars widely acknowledge that the media has helped to create dialogue and shift attitudes surrounding race in the US Some even suggest that the powerful effects of American media coverage of racial issues have contributed to and even caused ethnic and racial hatred, injustice, and violence. Even so, there is also a powerful social change component when considering the scholarship that has examined media history, race, and ethnicity. Instead of, and sometimes in addition to, looking at how minorities have been portrayed in the white press, scholars have researched media organizations that helped to inspire and propel social movements and consequent social change. The story of how these opposing forces used the same tool—the mass media—is essential to our understanding of our broader history and the important influence of both the media and minorities in defining our society. The media history scholarship reflects both sides of the story—the story of racism in the mainstream white media and the story of empowerment in the alternative minority media. In this chapter, through an examination of the scholarship surrounding the history of media and race, we discover many perspectives that help to explain how some white American media organizations have oppressed minority groups and how these same groups have employed the media to advance their causes and positions in society.

Naturally, the media have provided ample material for these scholarly perspectives, as racism has been a constant in American media history. Certainly, our earliest newspapers attacked Native Americans, referring to them as beasts and savages in need of religious reform or eradication. Over the years, as our history unfolded and new groups of immigrants entered the country, the media publicly disparaged, undervalued, and dismissed each group. But with time, these groups formed their own newspapers and communication strategies (and later broadcast outlets) that would serve and strengthen their own communities. In fact, much recent media history focuses on the hard-working and talented minority leaders who launched newspapers and other media organizations. These media outlets provided minority groups with a sense of self and purpose while serving as a source of social advancement as they raised awareness and helped to change attitudes and behaviors. The argument that the media has contributed to both positive and negative attitudes regarding race is widely accepted. As historian Jane Rhodes explained in her 1993 analysis, "This struggle between the transmission of racist ideology . . . and the efforts of oppressed groups to claim control over their own image, is part of the legacy of the American mass media" (185).

Though scholars are still interested in exploring how the mainstream press covered minorities and minority issues, as mentioned, much of today's scholarship tends to address minority media organizations and leaders, particularly black organizations and leaders. In recent years, however, historians have expanded the body of literature to include research addressing Native Americans, Asian Americans (generally during WWII and in the American West), and Mexicans. This scholarship, however, is limited. Several books, generally edited volumes, contain broad-based summaries of many ethnic publications and stories of their leaders (see, for example, Miller 1987; Ireland 1990; Rhodes 2010; Hutton and Reed 1995). Though these books don't provide in-depth analysis, they do offer tremendous perspective regarding the significance of the ethnic press as well as providing researchers with context for many media outlets, including publications that were printed in foreign languages.

An important example of a broad-based historical approach to media and minorities is *News for All the People*, by Juan González and Joseph Torres (2012), who present a review of mainstream press components while chronicling a number of minority news organizations. They describe how mainstream newspapers and radio/television stations "played a pivotal role in perpetuating racist views among the general population" (2). More importantly, the authors present illuminating stories of dedicated African-American, Native American, Latino, and Asian journalists who challenged the existing narrative and worked to replace it with new narratives for their respective audiences. They describe how the press knowingly "misled the public and inflamed racial bias . . . [while also creating a] deeply flawed national narrative" that described Europeans as overcoming "an array of backward and violent non-white people" (2–3). Gonzales and Torres explain how members of the minority press "waged heroic battles with their papers and over the airwaves to tell a different story—to assure fair and accurate news accounts of their communities" (12).

Historians began examining the black press as early as the 1890s, but these efforts were few and infrequent until the late 1900s. The topic of race and the media received significantly more attention beginning in the 1960s, but still could not be viewed as attracting widespread interest among historians. The next major wave of articles on minority media emerged in the 1980s. Over the following two decades, the topic of media and minorities would become the most popular topic in *American Journalism* and *Journalism History*, the pre-eminent media history journals. The initial focus was on newspapers and magazines, but contributors eventually published articles on minority images in advertising, film, broadcasting, and public relations. According to Jean Folkerts (1991), studies of minorities and women that started to appear in general history periodicals in the late 1980s reflected changing enrollment patterns and curriculums in journalism schools as well as the job market. She specifically notes two media history texts published in 1989: her own (written with Dwight Teeter), *Voices of a Nation: A History of Media in the United States*, and David Sloan's edited collection, *The Media in America*. She describes these books (which are widely used and have numerous editions) as deliberate attempts to include minorities and a broad range of media enterprises.

Despite the expansion of research into other media-related professions, the scholarship is still limited when looking at minorities in expanded professional areas. At least four researchers have examined the important role of public relations in advancing black causes such as the 1920s Black Nationalist Movement, the 1920 NAACP Conference, and the 1960s Civil Rights Movement (Cutlip 1994; Hon 1997; Mislan 2013; Murphree 2006; Straughan 2004). Conversely, at least two others—Cutlip (1994) and Walton (2009)—have examined how public relations was used to advance the causes of racist organizations such as the White Citizens Councils in Mississippi and the Ku Klux Klan.

Analyzing stereotypes and content is a common method in studies of advertisements, especially pre-1960s images (Kern-Foxworth 1994). Leslie (1995) compares occurrences of light- and dark-skinned models, and Zinkhan et al. (1990) looks at the number of blacks appearing in mainstream advertisements. Similar patterns can be seen in research on minorities in films. For example, Donald Bogle (1996) describes five character types for blacks between 1900 and the 1990s: toms (servile), coons (cowardly), mulattoes (tragic, mixed-race), mammies (dark-skinned, motherly), and bucks (oversexed and violent men who desire white women). The authors in Daniel Bernardi's (1996) edited volume discuss representations of Native Americans, African Americans, and Eskimos in films produced as early as the silent era. They show how non-white men were generally depicted as weak, unlikable, and emasculated.

One important exception to the stereotype identification approach to media research is a two-volume series written by Thomas Cripps (1993, 1999). While he does address stereotypes, he also provides broader cultural analyses. His first book focuses on how WWII helped liberalize the United States, thus giving blacks more opportunities to appear in films and eventually to portray less stereotypical characters. The second volume focuses on the period between the end of the war and the 1960s Civil Rights Movement.

Cedric Robinson's 2007 book examines depictions of race in American theater and film before WWII. Taking an economic approach, he suggests that capitalism helped to maintain black stereotypes on both stage and screen. Other researchers have analyzed stereotypes from a censorship perspective—for example, Douglas Smith's (2002) examination of the state of Virginia's use of censorship to sustain racial separation. He describes how the efforts of filmmakers from all parts of the country to present positive images of African Americans failed in Virginia due to the state's power to control what was shown on movie screens.

Similar to public relations, radio and television broadcasting has been used as an important organizational and entertainment tool in black communities; however, very few efforts have been made to address this topic from a historical perspective. One important example, however, is Barbara Dianne Savage's 1999 book, *Radio, War, and the Politics of Race, 1939–1949*, which discusses how African Americans influenced national radio network content during WWII. Savage notes that the federal government produced many black-oriented programs that encouraged racial tolerance. Deborah Heitner's *Black Power TV* (2013) chronicles the emergence of black public affairs television beginning in the late 1960s, and shows how both national and local shows provided venues for black expression and the dissemination of black culture.

As is generally the case when examining broader American historiographies, earlier efforts to analyze race and journalism tended to be biographical or focused on organizational history. As the topic of media and race attracted more research attention, perspectives expanded to include examinations of media coverage of specific events and theoretical analyses. James Carey's 1974 (reprinted in 1985) article "The Problem of Journalism History" criticizes media historians for focusing too much on two narrow themes: "The expansion of individual rights . . . [and the] growth of the public's right to know" (Carey 1985: 51). He instead calls for "an emphasis on cultural history" (51) or "historical consciousness" (52) with a focus on the minority press and the general topic of race and media—especially in the defining cultural context of the Civil Rights Movement.

Arguably the most important theoretical approach among media historians today is collective or public memory analysis. In the 1990s, scholars began to embrace this method, which is typically used to understand how the media influences or defines public memory of historical events, based on the assumption that the media prescribes our understanding of the past, at times encouraging false belief systems. Janice Hume (2010), a prominent collective memory historian, asserts that the press plays a historical role "in building American collective consciousness and memory" (187) simply because it reaches so many people, and therefore exerts significant impacts that far exceed those of textbooks and museums. Public memory scholar Carolyn Kitch (2005) notes that minority media organizations were often charged with "telling the truth and challenging truth at the same time" (107). She observes that black magazines "invoke memory so that past successes and outrages are not forgotten . . . [and] also create 'new' memory . . . asking readers to use the past in order to question the politics of the present" (108). Kitch also notes that the black press provided a platform for blacks to construct a new identity, with black magazines acknowledging the essential role of the past in influencing the present, since "history is a living presence [in black American] lives" (92). To support her assertion that black magazines have helped to redefine memory by documenting the past from a black perspective, she devotes a chapter to race coverage in *Ebony* (the country's oldest consumer-oriented black magazine) and *American Legacy* (a magazine founded in 1995 with a focus on black history). According to Kitch, "These magazines reveal how African Americans have used journalism as one means by which to become a part of the official American historical narrative while also challenging and changing that narrative through 'counter-memory'" (107). Another example of public memory analysis is Romano and Raiford's *The Civil Rights Movement in American Memory* (2006), in which they analyze how media portrayals of the Civil Rights Movement distorted collective memory by overlooking efforts outside the South, and by failing to look in depth at any leaders other than the Rev. Dr. Martin Luther King, Jr.

While these kinds of theoretical analyses have become increasingly common over the past two decades, most historians writing on both broad and specific media topics continue to use traditional historiographic methods for evidence collection, interpretation, and investigation. Certain narratives have increasingly emphasized cultural approaches that focus on how environments influence the media. These cultural histories often reflect progressive perspectives of how minority media organizations and leaders have supported and advanced minority causes and helped to break down long-standing obstacles to civil rights and first-class citizenship. Media historians have also tended to interweave biographical and developmental perspectives into their scholarly efforts, with developmental historians emphasizing professional changes and advancements. Other media and minority historians use an economic perspective to explain finances as a defining factor in minority media history.

## Media History and African Americans

By far the most frequently examined minority group in historical media analysis is African Americans, with the earliest scholarship published in 1891, but with the vast majority of studies published since 1990. African-American-related media history is currently at or near the top of the list of topics of papers published in *American Journalism* and *Journalism*

*History*. In the specific area of the black press (as opposed to the topic of depictions of blacks in the mainstream media), the majority of studies examine the media profession from a black perspective. In her 1991 analysis, historian Bernell Tripp observes that the black press is frequently analyzed in terms of "evolutionary stages" of black people using the media to advance their "cultural and moral outlook" and to "communicate the shortcomings of American society" (173). She notes that after WWII, historians began to look at the black press in the contexts of "political protest and social and cultural reform. . . . These historians pictured the Black media as having succeeded only after confronting a particularly hostile White press and American society" (176–7). According to Tripp, until the late 1980s historians relied on two fundamental approaches to analyzing the black press as an instrument of change: "minimizing the struggles" and "emphasizing obstacles" (173).

Such positive recognition is a central component of a large number of biographies of major figures in the black press, including Frederick Douglass, Marcus Garvey, Ida B. Wells, P. B. Young, and W. E. B. DuBois (as well as several lesser-known regional media professionals). Since these biographical books and articles frequently serve as secondary sources for studies of more narrow topics, they can be viewed as foundational for historical research on race and media. Biographical sketches of lesser-known individuals, especially women media pioneers, have been published as collections. For example, Jinx Broussard's 2004 volume, *Giving a Voice to the Voiceless*, examines the lives of four black women journalists, while Roger Streitmatter's 1994 collection, *Raising Her Voice: African-American Women Journalists Who Changed History*, looks at the contributions of 11 black women journalists from 1831 through the early 1990s. Three years earlier he published an article on the career of Ethel Payne, a Washington correspondent for the *Chicago Defender* and later a CBS radio and television national correspondent and commentator (Streitmatter 1991). James McGrath Morris's 2015 biography of Payne provides an in-depth analysis of her career and influence.

Comprehensive descriptions of black periodicals are found in several books published in the late nineteenth and early twentieth centuries. It is likely that the first scholarship addressing the black press was Garland Penn's *The Afro American Press and Its Editors*, which appeared in 1891 and presents profiles of editors and their newspapers. In 1929, Charles S. Johnson published an article on "The Rise of the Negro Magazine," in which he describes what he perceived as a shift in those periodicals from promoting unity to providing needed information. More recently, the topic of early black magazines (1838–1909) is also the focus of a 1981 book written by Penelope Bullock. Armistead S. Pride's 1968 book contains an updated list and description of black newspapers and magazines published at that time, but offers little in the way of analysis. Significantly more detailed analysis in terms of fighting racism, maintaining economic viability, and building community can be found in Roland Wolseley's 1971 book, *The Black Press, USA*. In 1997 Clint Wilson II published a comprehensive study of black newspapers from 1827 through the 1990s, *Black Journalists in Paradox: Historical Perspectives and Current Dilemmas*. The book also contains discussions of black-owned or oriented magazines, trade journals, radio and television stations, and advertising. Three books and a journal article published in the early 1990s by Domke (1994), Hutton (1993), Tripp (1992), and Wilson (1991) describe the development of selected black newspapers and the economic, political, and social conditions that supported black alternative publications. These texts represent a new trend in analyzing black periodicals as community builders, political tools, and instructional platforms.

One of the earliest analyses of a specific periodical was written by Bella Gross in 1932. Her subject was the first black-owned and black-operated newspaper, *Freedom's Journal*, which appeared in 1827 and lasted for two years. According to Gross, it bore "the stamp of high seriousness and moral earnestness" (247), and she credits the publisher with giving power and prestige to blacks and stimulating racial pride. Other scholars, including Barrow (1977), Burrowes (2001), and Nordin (1977), have written detailed analyses of the *Journal*; Jacqueline Bacon's 2006 book is the most comprehensive.

One of the most important publications in African-American history is the *Chicago Defender*, a weekly newspaper founded in 1905 that was published daily from 1956 until 2003, when it once again became a weekly. Published in Chicago, it was considered the best national source of African-American news. Arguably it is most famous for advocating the migration of blacks from the South to other parts of the country. In his 2006 book on the black press, Patrick Washburn devotes a significant portion to the role that the *Pittsburg Courier* and *Chicago Defender* played during the early days of the Civil Rights Movement. Other detailed analyses of the *Defender* include Thornton's (2014) work on editorial positions and their relationship to opinions expressed in letters to the editor, Cooper's (2014) discussion of Rebecca Stiles Taylor's women's column (published from 1939 to 1945), Kornweibel's (1994) review of government suppression of the paper during WWI, and Desantis's (1997) and Grossman's (1985) article on the *Defender*'s advocacy of the Great Migration.

Some researchers have emphasized economic factors in their analyses of the black press. In his study of the *Atlanta World*, another important black paper with a national audience, Leonard Ray Teel (1989) concludes that William Alexander Scott, the founding editor, put finances first and social concerns second. Other authors have given examples indicating that finances were paramount for most black publishers, and for good reason—without adequate capital, they could not use their forums to promote black causes and black culture. Publishers and editors of black newspapers with the largest circulations gathered much of their own news, but also relied heavily on black and white-owned wire services. The Associated Negro Press (ANP), a wire service founded in 1919 by Claude Barnet that focused specifically on black-oriented news, is the topic of a book written by Lawrence Hogan (1984). The ANP appears to have been a successful enterprise—it lasted for 24 years—but Hogan suggests that Barnett sold out to political interests, giving up objectivity in return for financial support.

America's participation in two world wars presented black editors and publishers with a unique challenge: how to continue advancing the interests of black citizens regarding topics such as lynching, segregation, and disenfranchisement while expressing patriotic support and advocating global democracy. William Jordan (2001) looks at these dilemmas from the perspective of WWI, but most other scholars focus on WWII. Snorgrass (1984) and Ross (1993) look at censorship and the relationship between Franklin D. Roosevelt and black newspaper editors.

The largest black-owned newspapers based in Chicago and east coast cities have received the most research attention, but there are examples of scholars discussing the significance of smaller periodicals operating in other parts of the United States. The authors in Henry Sugg's 1996 edited volume look at black newspapers in Iowa, Kansas, and Minnesota. Kimberly Mangun has published three studies of two Pacific Northwest newspapers, *The Advocate* and *New Age* (2006, 2008, 2009).

In her examination of black frontier editors in Oklahoma, Mary Cronin (2002) describes how they moved between protest and accommodation when responding to late nineteenth and early twentieth-century civil rights issues. Her focus in an earlier study was on black editors and their support for black westward migration from 1891 to 1915 (Cronin 2000). According to her findings, the editors emphasized the themes of "self-help, group solidarity, and race pride, along with the promise of a safe haven, as promotional devices to attract and keep settlers" (81).

The large body of work addressing the black press and the 1960s Civil Rights Movement can be divided into two categories: the ways that the black press addressed the movement, and the methods used by black advocacy organizations to manipulate or convince local and national media to advance their causes. Gene Roberts and Hank Klibanoff (2007) examine both white and black press coverage of the Civil Rights Movement from 1944 to 1968. Their primary focus is on the mainstream national media, but they also provide a survey of regional newspapers and some individual black reporters. David Davies' 2001 collection of articles looks at white Mississippi editors and identifies those who supported and those who fought against civil rights for black Americans.

Sports stories have long played a central role in black media and civil rights coverage. Again, there are many studies comparing stories on black sports figures published in white and black publications, especially on individuals involved in integration efforts. Brian Carroll (2007, 2006, 2011), a media history scholar whose primary focus is on baseball, has written on the ways that black newspapers addressed relationships among the sport, community pride, and sponsorship; on Jackie Robinson's column that appeared in the *Pittsburg Courier* and the public relations strategy behind it; on media themes associated with the integration of major league baseball; and on the history of the Negro leagues from their inception to the 1940s. In his book on black and white left-leaning sportswriters and baseball desegregation in the 1930s and 1940s, Chris Lamb (2012) describes how sportswriters worked for over 10 years to pave the way for Jackie Robinson's 1945 signing with the Brooklyn Dodgers organization.

## Media History and Other Minority Groups

The literature on media histories associated with Hispanics, Asian Americans, and Native Americans is fairly limited. In each case, research can again be divided into studies of how each group has been covered and described in the mainstream press over time, and portrayals of individual press leaders and their publications.

Two themes emerge when looking at the literature on Hispanic publications: immigration and labor. Articles on each topic show how the Hispanic press played a significant role in legitimizing the Hispanic-American experience and validating Hispanic-American contributions. As with other minority publications, the Hispanic press strove to eliminate negative stereotypes and replace them with positive images. Victoria Goff's 1995 book chapter presents a general overview of Spanish-language newspapers in terms of discrimination, politics, society, assimilation, the arts, and other themes. Felix Gutierrez's 1977 article for *Journalism History* summarizes the work of Hispanic publishers and their products in the American Southwest. Herminio Rios and Guadalupe Castillo made an important contribution in the form of a bibliography published in two parts (1970 and 1972), in which they identify 372 Mexican-American newspapers that operated between 1848 and 1942. Similarities are noted between portrayals of Mexicans and Native Americans in the mainstream press during the last century. Fuhlhage (2013, 2014) provides detailed examples of Mexicans being described as low class, uncultured, and unable or unwilling to improve themselves. Conversely, European Spaniards were generally portrayed as intelligent and exotic.

A significant number of studies on media history involving Asian Americans concentrate on coverage during WWII, especially the treatment of Japanese Americans, who were held in detention camps for the duration of the war. Based on his review of articles published in mimeographed newsletters produced by Japanese living in two of the 16 WWII internment camps, Takeya Mizuno (2003) shows how editorial control, government censorship, and other breaches of First Amendment rights were part of America's mass incarceration policy. In her analysis of magazine photographs of Japanese Americans interned during WWII, Dolores Flamiano (2010) suggests that the main purpose of the images was to convince other Americans that the internment camps were necessary. She also discusses how the images projected ideas about race, gender, and citizenship. Thomas Heuterman's 1995 article looks at local newspaper coverage of Japanese Americans living in the Yakima Valley of Washington State during the 1920s and 1930s. While he concludes that the main Yakima newspaper actually provided objective coverage of many Japanese activities, its editors failed to address the issue of hostility aimed at Japanese immigrants during times of economic difficulty.

Regarding media coverage of Chinese immigrants in the nineteenth century and first half of the twentieth century, Herman B. Chiu (1999) examined stories published in four Oregon newspapers during the 1870s and 1980s, and found a surprising lack of stories on Chinese immigrants, despite their large numbers in gold mining and as railroad laborers. He notes that when Chinese people were mentioned in news stories, they were almost always vilified. Andrew Kirk's 2007 article discusses how Mormon and non-Mormon journalists in Ogden, Utah covered a local boycott of vegetables grown by Chinese farmers in 1865. While he notes the strong current of racism in newspaper coverage, he also emphasizes the strong discouragement of violence against Chinese that was expressed in newspaper editorials, as well as the slow acceptance of Chinese workers in local press coverage over time.

Other researchers have looked at the large topic of Asian stereotypes in films and television programs. One example is Jane Naomi's 2011 book comparing real-life and fictional "oriental monk" characters shown in television programs produced between 1950 and 1975. She asserts that television screenwriters and producers hijacked Asian religion to create patently false images that have determined to a great extent what Americans know and understand about Asian culture.

Scholarship on the media history of Native Americans also tends to address either stereotypes or Native American-owned publishing businesses. General themes that emerge include debate over "good" versus "bad" Indians; the likelihood that most Americans get their ideas about Native Americans from television; and the focus on tribal sovereignty in the Native American press (see, for example, Loew and Mella 2005; Murphy and Murphy 1981). The general conclusion is that tribal journalists have been instrumental in bringing more freedom, rights, and resources to Native Americans.

Studies of Native American coverage in the mainstream press give many examples of predispositions held during various periods in American history. In his examination of portrayals of Native Americans in newspapers from 1820 through 1890, John Coward (1999) describes how clichés and stereotypes were based on journalists' beliefs in the simplicity of Native American culture and experiences. Coward suggests that these stereotypes, which are still observable today, were less about overt biases or racism than a confluence of social and professional pressures and norms during a period when Americans were consumed by the socio-cultural concept of manifest destiny, which combined elements of Protestantism and capitalism with the rush for westward expansion. He identifies other factors as standardized news-gathering and dissemination processes (e.g., wire services) and the rise of "adventure journalists" who created images of Native Americans. Mary Ann Weston (1996) examines stereotypes in news coverage involving Native Americans between 1920 and 1990, and argues that journalists were incapable of fully understanding the Native American experience because it was far too complex for them to deal with in their deadline-driven work environments. Last, Adare (2005), Fitzgerald (2014), Kilpatrick (1999), Raheja (2010), and Tahamahkera (2014) have all researched Native American stereotypes in film and television productions.

## The Future of Historical Media Analysis of Race

Media history scholars have employed a broad range of approaches to address questions regarding social change, the dominant power structure, community building, and racism. Their efforts allow for a better understanding of the significance of media in race relations, as well as the pivotal role that media have played in the communities of America's ethnic groups. Their studies of marginalized people are significant in terms of the history of all Americans, a history that is often defined by the media. For the most part, the media history literature underscores how minority media outlets have served as a supportive force for change in all of society, not just for minority groups, while at the same time reminding us of America's record of denying minority groups media access. Clearly there are many gaps that need to be filled, especially in the media histories of minority groups other than African Americans. Researchers are discovering that each group operated scores of newspapers at any given time, establishing them within a surprisingly short time frame following their emigration to North America. Twentieth-century media histories need to include more broadcasting, publishing houses, and advertising and public relations agencies. Finally, there is still a great deal of research to be done regarding coverage by the mainstream press of less prominent armed conflicts and civil rights movements.

## References

Adare, S. (2005) *Indian Stereotypes in TV Science Fiction*. Austin, TX: University of Texas.
Bacon (2007) *Freedom's Journal: The First African-American Newspaper*. Lanham, MD: Lexington.
Barrow, L. (1977/78) "'Our Own Cause:' Freedom's Journal and the Beginnings of the Black Press," *Journalism History* 4(4): 118–122.
Bernardi, D. (1996) *The Birth of Whiteness: Race and the Emergence of U.S. Cinema*. New Brunswick, NJ: Rutgers.
Bogle, D. (1996) *Toms, Coons, Mulattoes, Mammies and Bucks: An Interpretive History of Blacks in American Films*. New York: Continuum.
Broussard, J. (2003) *Giving a Voice to the Voiceless: Four Pioneering Black Women Journalists*. New York: Routledge.
Bullock, P. (1981) *The Afro-American Periodical Press, 1838–1909*. Baton Rouge, LA: Louisiana State University.
Burrowes, C. (2001) "Caught in the Crosswinds of the Atlantic," *Journalism History* 37(3): 130–141.
Carey, J. (1974) "The Problem of Journalism History," *Journalism History* 1(1): 3–5, 27. Partial reprint: (1985) *Journalism History* 12(2): 51–53.
Carroll, B. (2006) "Early Twentieth-Century Heroes," *Journalism History* 32(1): 34–42.
———. (2007) *When to Stop the Cheering? The Black Press, the Black Community, and the Integration of Professional Baseball*. New York: Routledge.
———. (2011) "'This is It!: Jackie Robinson and Wendell Smith in Brooklyn, 1947," *Journalism History* 37(3): 151–162.

Chiu, H. (1999) "How Newspapers in Four Communities Erased Thousands of Chinese from Oregon History," *American Journalism*, 16(1): 59–77.

Cooper, C. (2014) "Selling Negro Women to Negro Women and to the World," *Journalism History* 39(4): 241–249.

Coward, J. (1999) *The Newspaper Indian: Native American Identity in the Press 1820–90*. Urbana, IL: University of Illinois.

Cripps, T. (1993 and 1999) *Making Movies Black: The Hollywood Message Movie from World War II to the Civil Rights Era*. New York: Oxford University Press.

Cronin, M. (2000) "Black Press Boosterism in Oklahoma, 1891–1915," *Journalism History* 26(2): 71–81.

———. (2002) "Mixing Protest and Accommodation: The Response of Oklahoma's Black Town Newspaper Editors to Race Relations, 1891–1918," *American Journalism* 19(2): 45–64.

Cutlip, S. (1994) *The Unseen Power: Public Relations, a History*. Hillsdale, NJ: Lawrence Erlbaum & Associates.

Davies, D. (2001) *The Press and Race: Mississippi Journalists Confront the Movement*. Jackson, MS: University Press of Mississippi.

Desantis, A. (1997) "A Forgotten Leader," *Journalism History* 23(2): 63–72.

Detweiler, F. (1922) *The Negro Press in the United States*. Chicago, IL: University of Chicago.

Domke, D. (1994) "The Black Press in the 'Nadir' of African Americans," *Journalism History* 20(3 and 4): 131–140.

Fitzgerald, M. (2013) *Native Americans on Network TV: Stereotypes, Myths, and the "Good Indian."* New York: Rowman & Littlefield.

Flamiano, D. (2010) "Japanese American Internment in Popular Magazines," *Journalism History* 36(1): 23–35.

Folkerts, J. (1991) "American Journalism History: A Bibliographic Essay," *American Studies International* 29(2): 4–27.

Folkerts, J. and Teeter, D. (1989) *Voices of a Nation: A History of Media in the United States*. New York: Macmillan.

Fuhlhage, M. (2013) "The Mexican Image through Southern Eyes: De Bow's Review in the Era of Manifest Destiny," *American Journalism* 30(2): 182–209.

———. (2014) "Brave Old Spaniards and Indolent Mexicans," *American Journalism* 31(1): 100–126.

Gitlin, T. (1980) *The Whole World Is Watching*. Oakland, CA: University of California.

Goff, V. (1995) "Spanish-Language Newspapers in California," in F. Hutton (ed.), *Outsiders in 19th-century Press History: Multicultural Perspectives*. Bowling Green, OH: Bowling Green State, 55–70.

González, J. and Torres, J. (2012) *News for All the People: The Epic Story of Race and the American Media*. New York: Verso.

Gross, B. (1932) "Freedom's Journal and the 'Rights of All,'" *Journal of Negro History* 17(July): 241–286.

Grossman, R. (1985) "Blowing the Trumpet: The Chicago Defender and Black Migration during World War I," *Illinois Historical Journal* 78(2): 87–88.

Gutierrez, F. (1977) "Spanish-Language Media in America: Background, Resources, History," *Journalism History* 4(2): 44–31.

Heitner, D. (2013) *Black Power TV*. Durham, NC: Duke University.

Hon, L. (1997) "'To Redeem the Soul of America': Public Relations and the Civil Rights Movement," *Journal of Public Relations Research* 9(3): 163–212.

Heuterman, T. (1995) *The Burning Horse: Japanese-American Experience in the Yakima Valley, 1920–1942*. Cheney, WA: Eastern Washington University.

Hogan, L. (1984) *The Associated Negro Press and Claude Barnet*. Rutherford, NJ: Fairleigh Dickinson University.

Hume, J. (2010) "Memory Matters: The Evolution of Scholarship in Collective Memory and Mass Communication," *The Review of Communication* 10(3): 181–196.

Hutton, F. (1993) *The Early Black Press in America, 1927 to 1860*. Westport, CT: Greenwood.

Hutton, F. and Reed, B. (1995) *Outsiders in 19th-Century Press History*. Bowling Green, OH: Bowling Green State University Popular Press.

Ireland, S. (1990) *Ethnic Periodicals in Contemporary America*. Westport, CT: Greenwood.

Johnson, C. (1928) "The Rise of the Negro Magazine," *Journal of Negro History* 12(January): 7–21.

Jordan, W. (2001) *Black Newspapers and America's War for Democracy, 1914–1920*. Chapel Hill, NC: University of North Carolina.

Kanellos, N. and Martell, H. (2000) *Hispanic Periodicals in the United States, Origins to 1960s*. Columbus, OH: Ohio State University.

Kearn-Foxworth, M. (1994) *Aunt Jemima, Uncle Ben, and Rastus: Blacks in Advertising, Yesterday, Today, and Tomorrow*. New York: Greenwood Press.

Kilpatrick, J. (1999) *Celluloid Indians: Native Americans and Film*. Lincoln: University of Nebraska.

Kirk, A. (2007) "Radical Labor, Racism, and the Preservation of Hegemony in Ogden, Territorial Utah, 1885–1886," *American Journalism*: 149–173.

Kitch, C. (2005) *Pages from the Past: History and Memory in American Magazines*. Chapel Hill, NC: University of North Carolina.

Kornweibel, T. (1994) "'The Most Dangerous of All Negro Journals': Federal Efforts to Suppress the Chicago Defender during World War I," *American Journalism* 11(2): 154–168.

Lamb, C. (2012) *Conspiracy of Silence: Sportswriters and the Long Campaign to Desegregate Baseball*. Lincoln, NE: University of Nebraska.

Leslie, M. (1995) "Slow Fade To? Advertising in Ebony Magazine, 1957–1989," *Journalism & Mass Communication Quarterly* 72(2): 426–435.

Loew, P. and Mella, K. (2005) "Black Ink and the New Red Power: Native American Newspapers and Tribal Sovereignty," *Journalism & Communication Monographs*, Columbia, SC: Association for Education in Journalism and Mass Communication.

Mangun, K. (2006) "The (Oregon) Advocate: Boosting the Race and Portland, Too," *American Journalism* 23(1): 7–34.

——. (2008) "Boosting the Bottom Line: Beatrice Morrow Cannady's Tactics to Promote the Advocate, 1923–1933," *American Journalism* 25(3): 31–69.

——. (2009) "Editor A.D. Griffin: Envisioning a New Age for Black Oregonians (1896–1907)," *American Journalism* 26(3): 55–92.

Miller, S. (1987) *The Ethnic Press in the United States*. New York: Greenwood Press.

Mislan, C. (2013) "An 'Obedient Servant,'" *Journalism History* 39(3): 115–125.

Mizuno, T. (2003) "Journalism under Military Guards and Searchlights: Newspaper Censorship at Japanese American Assembly Camps during World War II," *Journalism History* 29(3): 98–106.

Morris, J. (2015) *Eye on the Struggle: Ethel Payne, the First Lady of the Black Press*. New York: HarperCollins.

Murphree, V. (2006) *The Selling of Civil Rights: The Student Nonviolent Coordinating Committee and the Use of Public Relations*. New York: Routledge.

Murphy, J. and Murphy, S. (1981) *Let My People Know: American Indian Journalism, 1929–1978*. Norman, OK: University of Oklahoma.

Naomi, J. (2001) *The Oriental Monk in American Popular Culture: Race, Religion, and Representation in the Age of Virtual Orientalism*. Berkeley, CA: University of California.

Nordin, K. (1977/8) "In Search of Black Unity: An Interpretation of the Content and Function of Freedom's Journal," *Journalism History* 4(4): 118–122, 123–128.

Penn, G. (1891) *The Afro-American Press and Its Editors*. Springfield, MA: Wiley.

Pride, A. (1968) *The Black Press: A Bibliography*. Minneapolis, MN: University of Minnesota.

Pride, A. and Wilson, C. (1997) *A History of the Black Press*. Washington, D.C.: Howard University.

Raheja, M. (2010) *Reservation Reelism: Redfacing, Visual Sovereignty, and Representations of Native American in Film*. Lincoln, NE: University of Nebraska.

Rhodes, J. (1993) "The Visibility of Race and Media History," *Critical Studies in Mass Communication* 10(2): 181–190.

Rhodes, L. (2010) *The Ethnic Press: Shaping the American Dream*. New York: Peter Lang.

Rios, H. and Castillo, G. (1970) "Toward a True Chicano Bibliography: Mexican-American Newspapers, 1848–1942," *El Grito* 3(4), 384–387; Part II (1972), *El Grito* 5(4): 172–174.

Roberts, G. and Klibanoff, H. (2007) *The Race Beat: The Press, the Civil Rights Struggle, and the Awakening of a Nation*. New York: Alfred A. Knopf.

Robinson, C. (2007) *Forgeries of Memory and Meaning: Blacks and the Regimes of Race in American Theater and Film before World War II*. Chapel Hill, NC: University of North Carolina.

Romano, R. and Raiford, L. (2006) *The Civil Rights Movement in American Memory*. Athens, GA: University of Georgia.

Ross, F. (1993) "The Cleveland Call and Post and the New Deal: A Change in African-American Thought," *Journalism History* 19(3): 87–91.

Savage, B. (1999) *Radio, War, and the Politics of Race, 1939–1949*. Chapel Hill, NC: University of North Carolina.

Sloan, D. (1989) *The Media in America*. Northport, AL: Vision Press.
Snorgrass, J. (1984) "The Baltimore Afro-American and the Election Campaigns of FDR," *American Journalism* 1(2): 35–60.
Smith, D. (2002) *Managing White Supremacy: Race, Politics, and Citizenship in Jim Crow Virginia*. Chapel Hill, NC: University of North Carolina.
Straughan, D. (2004) "'Lift Every Voice and Sing': The Public Relations Efforts of the NAACP, 1960–65," *Public Relations Review* 30(1): 49–60.
Streitmatter, R. (1994) *Raising Her Voice: African-American Women Journalists Who Changed History*. Lexington, KY: University of Kentucky.
Suggs, H. (1988) *P. B. Young Newspaperman: Race Politics and Journalism in the New South, 1910–1962*. Charlottesville, VA: University of Virginia.
Tahmahkera, D. (2014) *Tribal Television*. Chapel Hill, NC: University of North Carolina.
Teel, L. (1989). "W.A. Scott and the Atlanta World," *American Journalism* 6(3): 158–178.
Thornton, B. (2014) "The 'Dangerous' Chicago Defender," *Journalism History* 40(1): 40–50.
Tripp, B. (1991) "The Black Media, 1865–Present: Liberal Crusaders or Defenders of Tradition?," in W. Sloan (ed.), *Perspectives in Mass Communication*. New York: Routledge, 172–182.
——. (1992) *Origins of the Black Press: New York, 1827–1847*. Northport, AL: Vision.
Walton, L. (2009) "Organizing Resistance: The Use of Public Relations by the Citizens' Council in Mississippi, 1954–1964," *Journalism History* 35(1): 299–342.
Washburn, P. (2006) *The African American Newspaper: Voice of Freedom*. Evanston, IL: Northwestern University.
Weston, M. (1996) *Native American in the News: Images of Indians in the Twentieth Century Press*. Westport, CT: Greenwood Press.
Wilson, C. (1991) *Black Journalists in Paradox: Historical Perspectives and Current Dilemmas*. Westport, CT: Greenwood.
Wolseley R. (1971) *The Black Press, U.S.A.* Ames, IA: Iowa State University.
Zinkhan, G., Quails, W., and Biswas, A. (1990) "The Use of Blacks in Magazine and Television Advertising: 1956–1986," *Journalism and Mass Communication Quarterly* 67(3): 547–553.

## Further Reading/Viewing

Broussard, J. (2013) *African American Foreign Correspondents: A History*. Baton Rouge, LA: Louisiana State University. (Provides information about how and why African Americans reported foreign wars, including the black international experiences.)
Gonzales, J. and Torres, J. (2012) *News for all the People: The Epic Story of Race and the American Media*. New York: Verso. (An examination of the impact of coverage of minorities in white newspapers as well as the role of minority media leaders.)
Loew, P. and Mella, K. (2005) "Black Ink and the New Red Power: Native American Newspapers and Tribal Sovereignty," *Journalism & Communication Monographs*, Columbia, SC: Association for Education in Journalism and Mass Communication. (Explores the relationship between Native American newspapers and tribal sovereignty.)
Riggs, M. (director, co-producer) (1992) *Color Adjustment*. Northampton, MA: Media Education Foundation. (An extraordinary documentary that examines the history of African-American representations on prime-time television; director Marlon Riggs makes extensive use of archival footage and interviews many of the important cultural studies scholars, including sociologist Herman Gray, whose work has framed scholarship on race and media.)
Romano, R. and Raiford, L. (2006) *The Civil Rights Movement in American Memory*. Athens, GA: University of Georgia. (Explores how the media and other institutions have influenced memory of the Civil Rights Movement.)
Washburn, P. (2006) *The African American Newspaper: Voice of Freedom*. Evanston, IL: Northwestern University. (Chronicles the growth of the black press from 1910 through 1950.)

# 5
# PRIMING
## Memory, Media, and Minorities
### *Francesca R. Dillman Carpentier*

Much of what we understand about media priming is based on how we believe memory is structured (Roskos-Ewoldsen, Roskos-Ewoldsen, and Dillman Carpentier 2008; see Roskos-Ewoldsen, Klinger, and Roskos-Ewoldsen 2007 for a meta-analysis of media priming). Memory can be thought of as being episodic or semantic (Tulving 1972). Whereas episodic memory is tied to episodes, or experiences, that we live and remember, semantic memory consists of all the concepts, or otherwise general information, that are not expressly tied to a particular experience yet are still stored in our memory.

Concepts in semantic memory are thought to be connected (some concepts more strongly than others), and these connections form networks of ideas (e.g., Collins and Loftus 1975; Meyer and Schvaneveldt 1971). Connections between concepts can be forged and strengthened based on what we observe over time; the more we find two concepts in concert (e.g., "black" and "aggression"), the more we connect them in our semantic memory (see McNamara 2005; Herring et al. 2013 for reviews). As such, media depictions that repeatedly link blacks with aggression, for example, can be problematic. Each time we are exposed to the combination of these two concepts, the association we make between "black" and "aggression" grows stronger (e.g., Dixon and Maddox 2005; Johnson, Bushman, and Dovidio 2008; Oliver and Fonash 2002).

Unfortunately, there is a wealth of examples of the co-occurrence of race and negative concepts in media. In primetime entertainment programming, minority characters constitute a minimal proportion of the television world compared to their representation in the population (Mastro and Greenberg 2000). Most of the minority characters are black; of concern, these black characters depict more negative traits (e.g., lazy, objectified, aggressive) than their white counterparts (Mastro and Greenberg 2000). The scant minority characters in videogames are largely represented as hypermasculine, aggressive, and competitive, yet lacking in strategy or honor (Burgess, Dill, Stermer, Burgess, and Brown 2011). In television news, there is an overrepresentation of blacks as criminals, compared with Justice Department reports of the true breakdown of criminals by race/ethnicity (Dixon and Linz 2000).

Once concepts become strongly linked to one another, referencing one concept can call up, or rather increase the accessibility of, its closely related concepts in memory (see McNamara 2005). Thus, *priming* a concept not only makes that initial concept more accessible, but the activation also spreads throughout the concept's interconnected network to activate associated concepts (e.g., Anderson, Deuser, and DeNeve 1995; Berkowitz 1984;

see also Higgins 1996; McNamara 2005). For example, if the idea of "black" is closely associated with the idea of "aggression," simply activating "black" via an image of a black face can make various concepts associated with violence, e.g., guns, more easy to retrieve from memory (Payne 2001; also Burgess et al. 2011). Ease of retrieval is often tested by examining how quickly (in milliseconds) people respond that they recognize what an object or word is; accessibility is operationalized in these cases as reaction times to stimuli (see Bargh and Chartrand 2000).

The implication of having a memory structure that locates attributes of a minority group within a network of negative concepts is that priming any concept within that network (e.g., black, Latino, gun, violence, poverty, crime, sex, migrant) negatively influences the way we think about a person we categorize as representing the minority group (e.g., Higgins, Bargh, and Lombardi 1985). Although the dual race and negative cues need not be integrated for priming effects to occur (Northup and Dillman Carpentier 2016), negative evaluations are certainly intensified if the trigger expressly contextualizes race within a negative and stereotype-congruent framework (see Mendelberg 2008 for a review). For example, depicting blacks as criminals in news engenders agreement with the triggered stereotype and worsens perceptions of the depicted race (Abraham and Appiah 2006; Dixon 2006; Dixon and Azocar 2007; Dixon and Maddox 2005; Domke 2001; Mastro, Lapinski, Kopacz, and Behm-Morawitz 2009; Oliver and Fonash 2002; Peffley and Shields 1996). Similar effects are found with depictions of black criminals in entertainment (Ford 1997; Johnson et al. 2008; Johnson, Olivo, Gibson, Reed, and Ashburn-Nardo 2009), as well as in entertainment that incorporates aggression without criminality into the race depiction (Bresnahan and Lee 2011; Burgess et al. 2011; Johnson, Trawalter, and Dovidio 2000). Negative effects of black criminal portrayals can also spread to evaluations of others by racializing those evaluations or by facilitating the (mis)attribution of stereotype-congruent characteristics to the others (entertainment: Dill and Burgess 2013; news: Dixon 2007; Dixon and Azocar 2007; Oliver and Fonash 2002; Valentino 1999). Findings are similar in vein when the media depictions connote race with promiscuity (Brown-Givens and Monahan 2005; Johnson et al. 2008; Johnson et al. 2009; Monahan, Shtrulis, and Givens 2005) or with social problems/issues (Abraham and Appiah 2006; Banks and Bell 2013; Cho, Gil de Zuniga, Shah, and McLeod 2006; Monahan et al. 2005; Valentino, Hutchings, and White 2004; Valentino, Traugott, and Hutchings 2002).

To test this phenomenon, Dixon and Maddox (2005) asked 130 participants to watch a 15-minute news program and then fill out a questionnaire at the end. Participants were primarily white ($n = 95$); 15 of the participants were black. All of the participants received a 22-second crime story among the other stories of their news program. However, depending on the condition to which they were randomly assigned, some participants received a crime story in the newscast that featured a photograph of a white criminal, others received the same crime story featuring a photo of a light-skinned black criminal, others saw a medium-skinned black criminal, and still others saw a dark-skinned black criminal.

After watching the news program, they completed a questionnaire that assessed their memory for the crime story, their feelings (e.g., concern) about the crime story, and their perceptions of both the criminal and the victim featured in the story. Participants were also asked what they felt was the proper prison sentence for this criminal, as well as whether the death penalty was appropriate in this case. Once these assessments were completed, a second experimenter entered the room to purportedly begin another study with the participants. This experimenter asked them to help with pre-testing a questionnaire, which assessed the participants' television consumption habits. By doing this, the researchers provided a mental break between the assessments of the news story and perceptions of participants' own news use.

The results indicated that participants, on average, found the dark-skinned criminal to be more memorable than the white criminal. The victim was also more memorable when the criminal was black compared to when the criminal was white. Recall that the large majority of participants were white.

Among the participants who reported heavy viewership of news, those heavy viewers who saw the crime story with the dark-skinned criminal were most worried by that story compared to the level of concern reported by heavy viewers who received the other crime stimuli. Also, among these heavy news viewers, perceptions of the victim were much more positive for those who saw the light-skinned, medium-skinned, or dark-skinned criminal; by comparison, heavy viewers who received the white criminal photo did not show as much bias toward the victim. Interestingly, participants who reported only light news viewing did not exhibit any of these effects.

These findings by Dixon and Maddox (2005) suggest that the more people are exposed to media predisposed to linking blacks with crime, the easier it is for these people to access the combined concepts in memory, along with other associated negative ideas, or feelings in this case. Their study is a compelling example of the availability heuristic at work—the availability heuristic being the tendency for us to rely on information that is easy to remember when we are making judgments (Tversky and Kahneman 1974; see also Shrum 1996; Shrum, Wyer, and O'Guinn 1998). Use of the availability heuristic in evaluations is also an example of automatic cognitive processing.

Cognitive processing of information can be categorized as being automatic or controlled (Uleman and Bargh 1989). Whereas controlled processing refers to thinking that occurs in full consciousness, with purpose, or with deliberation, automatic processing refers to cognitive activity that occurs with little express awareness, effort, or intentionality. Priming effects tend to attract a minimal amount of our awareness; we tend not to recognize when a prime activates a relevant concept in our memory (e.g., Higgins, Bargh, and Lombardi 1985; Neely 1977). It is under these circumstances when depictions of race, especially negative depictions of race, most influence our judgments (e.g., Gordon and Anderson 1995).

In the first of three studies, Devine (1989) observed first that white participants shared a common knowledge of the negative black stereotype. Regardless of how anti-black they reported themselves to be, most participants recognized poor, aggressive, criminal, unintelligent, uneducated, lazy, sexualized, athletic, rhythmic, and ostentatious as negative black-associated characteristics. This finding indicates a pervasiveness of the linkage between race and negative concepts.

In Study 2, white participants were given a pretest that assessed their level of prejudice against blacks, among other assessments of personality and demographics. Later in the academic year, participants returned to assist in a purportedly different study, where they were first primed with the dual triggering of neutral (buffer) and stereotype-relevant concepts by showing participants words, each of which appeared for a mere 80 milliseconds in the participants' peripheral view. This tactic is tantamount to a subliminal prime, as participants would not be expressly aware of the words (e.g., Africa, afro, basketball, blues, ghetto, Harlem, jazz, lazy, musical, Negroes, poor, slavery, unemployed) they saw. Based on random assignment, some participants viewed words that were primarily stereotype-relevant and other participants viewed words that were largely neutral.

After the priming event, participants read a short 12-sentence story that featured a character, Donald, who engaged in several behaviors that might or might not be considered hostile (taken from Srull and Wyer 1979). Purposely, Donald was not well described; he was left ambiguous, and therefore any judgments about Donald's hostile nature were due to readers' interpretations of the story. After reading this story, participants rated Donald on a number of characteristics, including hostility. Regardless of their reported levels of prejudice, participants who received the strong prime, in which 80 percent of the words in the initial task were stereotype-relevant, interpreted Donald as being more hostile compared to the participants who received the weaker prime. Ratings on other characteristics were unaffected by the priming condition. This finding corroborates previous evidence that primes are most influential on judgments of ambiguous targets (e.g., Srull and Wyer 1979; see also Higgins 1996). This finding also corroborates evidence that assimilation is the typical outcome of priming, in that subsequent evaluations reflect or are biased toward the primed concept (e.g., Higgins 1996).

In Study 3, Devine asked white participants to write down labels they might use to describe black Americans. Next, participants were asked to list their thoughts, positive or negative, about the social group, black Americans. These exercises required the participants to be very aware of their pre-existing beliefs. Importantly, participants were told their responses would be anonymous, thus helping negate possible influences of social desirability or personal accountability for listing negative content. Finally, participants completed the anti-black sentiment measure used in the prior two studies. As might be expected, high-prejudice participants listed more negative than positive thoughts, whereas low-prejudice participants listed more positive than negative thoughts.

Reviewing the extant literature, it appears that stereotype activation is automatic; concepts that reflect stereotypical thoughts are activated in memory whether or not we are motivated to inhibit these thoughts (see neural signal evidence by Amodio et al. 2004 and Ofan, Rubin, and Amodio 2011). This automatic activation affects numerous social judgments, even when we do not openly endorse prejudice. For example, regardless of prejudice level, people might misremember seeing a black perpetrator in a news story featuring a non-black criminal suspect if they are primed with the associated idea of violence (Oliver and Fonash 2002). People with high and low levels of prejudice might also assume greater culpability of an unidentified criminal after being primed subliminally with words associated with a particular race (Graham and Lowery 2004). However, low-prejudice viewers are less likely than high-prejudice viewers to support the death penalty—an explicit measure that is both relevant to the priming event and likely encourages deliberation—whether they are exposed to news that features unidentified criminals or suspects identified as black (Dixon 2006). Exposure to violent and misogynous rap music can increase the accessibility of the negative black stereotype in memory for both low- and high-prejudice people, yet low-prejudice people will not endorse the stereotype when explicitly asked (Rudman and Lee 2002).

Together, this evidence suggests three challenges to priming effects. First, stereotype activation might not lead to manifestations of stereotype acceptance if we find our cognitions might be inappropriately biased (see also Ford and Kruglanski 1995 about correcting for bias). Second, we will likely inhibit tendencies toward overt stereotype endorsement if we are cognizant of the prime, as our awareness might highlight potential bias and motivate controlled processing (Gilbert, Tafarodi, and Malone 1993; see White 2007 about explicit race cues). Third, a prime is only likely to bias our social judgments toward the cue if we interpret that cue as being in agreement with or relevant to the judgment (e.g., Domke, Shah, and Wackman 1998; Herr, Sherman, and Fazio 1983). A prime that activates a political ideology that we reject, for example, will likely yield evaluations that contrast rather than echo the ideology (e.g., Dillman Carpentier, Roskos-Ewoldsen, and Roskos-Ewoldsen 2008).

Valentino and colleagues (Valentino et al. 2002) explored how subtle race cues embedded in political advertisements might influence perceptions of social policy that can be associated with racial stereotypes (e.g., affirmative action, crime, welfare), as well as policy issues that are not race-typified (e.g., abortion, education, health care). In both a traditional laboratory experiment and in interviews conducted with people in a large metro setting, the researchers noted that people tended to think more centrally within their political ideology when race was connected with stereotype-congruent issues. Political conservatives, for example, were more likely to affirm conservative ideals, and their party affiliation became a stronger criterion explaining their support for President Bush. A similar observation was made by Banks and Bell (2013), who found that activating stereotypical portrayals in anger-inducing political messages led political conservatives to dispute social policies that might assist minorities, yet these same messages led political liberals to favor these policies.

Moreover, a prime that triggers a negative racial stereotype for people who do not identify with the primed racial group might trigger other associations for people who do identify with that race. The majority of the studies showing bias of social judgments toward negative stereotypes have been performed with white participants. However, explicit racial cues likely trigger thoughts of ingroup or ethnic membership among people who identify with the race being cued; their subsequent perceptions of an issue consider race as a result (White 2007). Subtle cues, such as an image of a minority embedded into the content, might also emphasize ethnic identity in the memories of fellow minority group members (Forehand and Deshpande 2001), but fall short of encouraging racialized interpretations of an issue (White 2007). Rather, triggering ethnic identity might spread to other positive associations held by members of that minority group. For example, rap music videos that trigger negative thoughts for white participants (e.g., Rudman and Lee 2002) might instead trigger cultural identity and collective self-esteem in black listeners (Dixon, Zhang, and Conrad 2009). Unfortunately, when negative or stereotype-congruent ideas are triggered in tandem with minority group identity, members of the minority group exhibit thinking that suggests racialized or pessimistic outlooks (Oyserman, Fryberg, and Yoder 2007; White 2007).

If priming effects primarily echo the associations we have in our current memory, then we have the opportunity to strengthen weak associations and change the way we categorize race. For instance, increasing the number of positive exemplars of minorities in media might help counteract the activation, if not reinforcement, of stereotypes. For example, exposing people to visuals of specific positive ethnic role models (i.e., Latino actor Jimmy Smits) and/or prototypes of positive ethnic models embodying positive values (i.e., family values) was shown to generate positive perceptions toward the represented ethnic group (Mastro and Tukachinsky 2011). Worthy of note, this finding was observed when examples were framed within an entertainment context; the celebrity exemplar was featured within a celebrity magazine, and the positive values were discussed within an article introducing a new sitcom. Portrayals that are positive and counterstereotypical can also encourage people to attribute negative actions or events involving minorities (e.g., participation in riots) to environmental reasons, whereas negative, stereotypical portrayals encourage blame of the person (Power, Murphy, and Coover 1996).

Minority exemplars suggesting success, however, might not always generate positive outcomes. Priming President Barack Obama or media icon Oprah Winfrey led to increased endorsement of judgments associated with symbolic racism, albeit the typical explicit and implicit racial biases found in other literature were not elevated (Lybarger and Monteith 2011). Symbolic racism judgments include ideas that blacks no longer experience discrimination, that blacks have gotten more than they deserve, and that blacks' primary barrier to success is their own lack of desire to work hard for their success. Thus, positive exemplars of success might provide counterexamples that suggest to people that success is attainable for those who work for it, as this success must not have been hindered by discrimination. This provision is complicated, however, by evidence that suggesting (in political ads) that blacks are deserving of government assistance can reduce negative assimilative effects on evaluations (Valentino et al. 2004). Correspondingly, portrayals that induce sympathy or empathy might yield favorable interpretations of minorities (Johnson et al. 2009; Power et al. 1996).

A combination of media literacy training and an increased prevalence of counterstereotypical media depictions might provide the most promising solution for harnessing media to inhibit race bias. Evidence of the effectiveness of this type of combined approach has shown a reduction in implicit attitudes toward minorities (Ramasubramanian 2007). For people who were primed with the idea of thinking critically and who were given news stories with stereotype-disconfirming depictions, positive descriptors were more accessible in memory than were hostile descriptors of the minority. Therefore, presenting media messages that confront the link between blacks and crime, for instance, might be effective in weakening stereotype-supporting associations, especially if we are made aware that we might be misattributing our fear of crime to our mental model of minorities (see Holt 2013).

An important caveat to media literacy efforts: The best lens for interpreting stereotypical depictions is currently unknown, crucial to discover, and likely not uniform across all members of the population. Multiculturalism, for example, is an approach that strives for equal treatment of cultural groups, celebrating cultural diversity rather than having acculturation (assimilation) into the dominant culture as its goal (see Wilson and Gutierrez 1995 about multiculturalism in media). Priming the idea of multiculturalism seems to facilitate favorable attitudes toward targets who embody stereotypes and who thus can be located within their ethnic boundaries (Gutierrez and Unzueta 2010). However, counterstereotypical portrayals might be less favored when primed with multiculturalism (Gutierrez and Unzueta 2010). More troubling, multiculturalism might emphasize outgroup categorization by virtue of its focus on ethnic identity and diversity. Given that people might have a tendency to act more elusively toward outgroup members (e.g., Rios, Ybarra and Sanchez-Burks 2013) and sympathize less with these members (e.g., Power et al. 1996), favoring multiculturalism over other approaches might lead to unintended, exacerbatory outcomes.

Priming the idea of colorblindness, in contrast, seems to facilitate favor toward counterstereotypical targets who traverse their ethnic boundary (Gutierrez and Unzueta 2010). Whereas the celebration of counterstereotypes might assist in redrawing semantic networks that include race, priming colorblindness might also lead to an increase in prejudicial treatment of minorities who appear to embody, or at least do not challenge, their ethnic stereotype (Gutierrez and Unzueta 2010). This prejudicial behavior, in turn, can detrimentally affect the minorities' cognitive functioning (Holoien and Shelton 2012; see also McCauley, Minsky, and Viswanath 2013 about negative behavioral effects of stigmatization on ethnic groups). This uncertainty about what depictions of race are best for combatting the formation and reinforcement of negative stereotypes constitutes an area ripe for study, with the promise to further our understanding of how priming effects can be harnessed to enhance our associations between favorable concepts and race.

## References

Abraham, L. and Appiah, O. (2006) "Framing News Stories: The Role of Visual Imagery in Priming Racial Stereotypes," *Howard Journal Of Communications* 17(3): 183–203.

Amodio, D. M., Harmon-Jones, E., Devine, P. G., Curtin, J. J., Hartley, S. L., and Covert, A. E. (2004) "Neural Signals for the Detection of Unintentional Race Bias," *Psychological Science* 15(2): 88–93.

Anderson, C. A., Deuser, W. E., and DeNeve, K. M. (1995) "Hot Temperatures, Hostile Affect, Hostile Cognition, and Arousal: Tests of a General Model of Affective Aggression," *Personality and Social Psychology Bulletin* 21(5): 434–448.

Banks, A. J. and Bell, M. A. (2013) "Racialized Campaign Ads: The Emotional Content in Implicit Racial Appeals Primes White Racial Attitudes," *Public Opinion Quarterly* 77(2): 549–560.

Bargh, J. A. and Chartrand, T. L. (2000) "The Mind in the Middle: A Practical Guide to Priming and Automaticity Research," in H. T. Reis and C. M. Judd (eds.), *Handbook of Research Methods in Social and Personality Psychology*. Cambridge, UK: Cambridge University Press, 253–285.

Berkowitz, L. (1984) "Some Effects of Thoughts on Anti- and Prosocial Influences of Media Events: A Cognitive-Neoassociation Analysis," *Psychological Bulletin* 95(3): 410–427.

Bresnahan, M. J. and Lee, C. (2011) "Activating Racial Stereotypes on Survivor: Cook Islands," *Howard Journal of Communications* 22(1): 64–82.

Brown-Givens, S. M. and Monahan, J. L. (2005) "Priming Mammies, Jezebels, and Other Controlling Images: An Examination of the Influence of Mediated Stereotypes on Perceptions of an African American Woman," *Media Psychology* 7(1): 87–106.

Burgess, M. R., Dill, K. E., Stermer, S., Burgess, S. R., and Brown, B. P. (2011) "Playing with Prejudice: The Prevalence and Consequences of Racial Stereotypes in Video Games," *Media Psychology* 14(3): 289–311.

Cho, J., Gil de Zuniga, H., Shah, D. V., and McLeod, D. M. (2006) "Cue Convergence: Associative Effects on Social Intolerance," *Communication Research* 33(3): 136–154.

Collins, A. M. and Loftus, E. F. (1975) "A Spreading-Activation Theory of Semantic Processing," *Psychological Review* 82(6): 407–428.

Devine, P. G. (1989) "Stereotypes and Prejudice: Their Automatic and Controlled Components," *Journal of Personality and Social Psychology* 56(1): 5–18.

Dill, K. E. and Burgess, M. R. (2013) "Influence of Black Masculinity Game Exemplars on Social Judgments," *Simulation and Gaming* 44(4): 562–585.

Dillman Carpentier, F. R., Roskos-Ewoldsen, D. R., and Roskos-Ewoldsen, B. (2008) "A Test of the Network Model of Political Priming," *Media Psychology* 11(2): 186–206.

Dixon, T. L. (2006) "Psychological Reactions to Crime News Portrayals of Black Criminals: Understanding the Moderating Roles of Prior News Viewing and Stereotype Endorsement," *Communication Monographs* 73(2): 162–187.

——. (2007) "Black Criminals and White Officers: The Effects of Racially Misrepresenting Law Breakers and Law Defenders on Television News," *Media Psychology* 10(2): 270–291.

Dixon, T. L. and Azocar, C. L. (2007) "Priming Crime and Activating Blackness: Understanding the Psychological Impact of the Overrepresentation of Blacks as Lawbreakers on Television News," *Journal of Communication* 57(2): 229–253.

Dixon, T. L. and Linz, D. (2000) "Overrepresentation and Underrepresentation of African Americans and Latinos as Lawbreakers on Television News," *Journal of Communication* 50(2): 131–154.

Dixon, T. L. and Maddox, K. B. (2005) "Skin Tone, Crime News, and Social Reality Judgments: Priming the Stereotype of the Dark and Dangerous Black Criminal," *Journal of Applied Social Psychology* 35(8): 1555–1570.

Dixon, T. L., Zhang, Y., and Conrad, K. (2009) "Self-esteem, Misogyny and Afrocentricity: An Examination of the Relationship between Rap Music Consumption and African American Perceptions," *Group Processes and Intergroup Relations* 12(3): 345–360.

Domke, D. (2001) "Racial Cues and Political Ideology: An Examination of Associative Priming," *Communication Research* 28(6): 772–801.

Domke, D., Shah, D. V., and Wackman, D. B. (1998) "Media Priming Effects: Accessibility, Association, and Activation," *International Journal of Public Opinion Research* 10(1): 51–74.

Ford, T. E. (1997) "Effects of Stereotypical Television Portrayals of African-Americans on Person Perception," *Social Psychology Quarterly* 60(3): 266–275.

Ford, T. E. and Kruglanski, A. W. (1995) "Effects of Epistemic Motivations on the Use of Accessible Constructs in Social Judgment," *Personality and Social Psychology Bulletin* 21(9): 950–962.

Forehand, M. R. and Deshpande, R. (2001) "What We See Makes Us Who We Are: Priming Ethnic Self-Awareness and Advertising Response," *Journal of Marketing Research* 38(3): 336–348.

Gilbert, D. T., Tafarodi, R. W., and Malone, P. S. (1993) "You Can't Not Believe Everything You Read," *Journal of Personality and Social Psychology* 65(2): 221–233.

Gordon, R. A. and Anderson, K. S. (1995) "Perceptions of Race-Stereotypic and Race-Nonstereotypic Crimes: The Impact of Response-Time Instructions on Attributions and Judgments," *Basic and Applied Social Psychology* 16(4): 455–470.

Graham, S. and Lowery, B. S. (2004) "Priming Unconscious Racial Stereotypes about Adolescent Offenders," *Law and Human Behavior* 28(5): 483–504.

Gutierrez, A. S. and Unzueta, M. M. (2010) "The Effect of Interethnic Ideologies on the Likability of Stereotypic vs. Counterstereotypic Minority Targets," *Journal of Experimental Social Psychology* 46(5): 775–784.

Herr, P. M., Sherman, S. J., and Fazio, R. H. (1983) "On the Consequences of Priming: Assimilation and Contrast Effects," *Journal of Experimental Social Psychology* 19(4): 323–340.

Herring, D. R., White, K. R., Jabeen, L. N., Hinojos, M., Terrazas, G., Reyes, S. M., Taylor, J. H., and Crites, S. L. (2013) "On the Automatic Activation of Attitudes: A Quarter Century of Evaluative Priming Research," *Psychological Bulletin* 139(5): 1062–1089.

Higgins, E. T. (1996) "Knowledge Activation: Accessibility, Applicability and Salience," in E. T. Higgins and A. W. Kruglanski (eds.), *Social Psychology: Handbook of Basic Principles*. New York: Guilford, 133–168.

Higgins, E. T., Bargh, J. A., and Lombardi, W. (1985) "Nature of Priming Effects on Categorization," *Journal of Experimental Psychology: Learning, Memory, and Cognition* 11(1): 59–69.

Holoien, D. and Shelton, J. (2012) "You Deplete Me: The Cognitive Costs of Colorblindness on Ethnic Minorities," *Journal of Experimental Social Psychology* 48(2): 562–565.

Holt, L. (2013) "Writing the Wrong: Can Counter-Stereotypes Offset Negative Media Messages about African Americans?," *Journalism and Mass Communication Quarterly* 90(1): 108–125.

Johnson, J. D., Bushman, B. J., and Dovidio, J. F. (2008) "Support for Harmful Treatment and Reduction of Empathy toward Blacks: 'Remnants' of Stereotype Activation Involving Hurricane Katrina and 'Lil' Kim,'" *Journal of Experimental Social Psychology* 44(6): 1506–1513.

Johnson, J. D., Olivo, N., Gibson, N., Reed, W., and Ashburn-Nardo, L. (2009) "Priming Media Stereotypes Reduces Support for Social Welfare Policies: The Mediating Role of Empathy," *Personality and Social Psychology Bulletin* 35(4): 463–476.

Johnson, J. D., Trawalter, S., and Dovidio, J. F. (2000) "Converging Interracial Consequences of Exposure to Violent Rap Music on Stereotypical Attributions of Blacks," *Journal of Experimental Social Psychology* 36(3): 233–251.

Lybarger, J. E. and Monteith, M. J. (2011) "The Effect of Obama Saliency on Individual-Level Racial Bias: Silver Bullet or Smokescreen?," *Journal of Experimental Social Psychology* 47(3): 647–652.

Mastro, D. and Greenberg, B. S. (2000) "The Portrayal of Racial Minorities on Prime Time Television," *Journal of Broadcasting and Electronic Media* 44(4): 690–703.

Mastro, D. and Tukachinsky, R. (2011) "The Influence of Exemplar Versus Prototype-Based Media Primes on Racial/Ethnic Evaluations," *Journal of Communication* 61(5): 916–937.

Mastro, D., Lapinski, M., Kopacz, M. A., and Behm-Morawitz, E. (2009) "The Influence of Exposure to Depictions of Race and Crime in TV News on Viewers' Social Judgments," *Journal of Broadcasting and Electronic Media* 53(4): 615–635.

McCauley, M., Minsky, S., and Viswanath, K. (2013) "The H1N1 Pandemic: Media Frames, Stigmatization and Coping," *BMC Public Health* 13(1): 1–30.

McNamara, T. P. (2005) *Semantic Priming: Perspectives from Memory and Word Recognition*. New York: Psychology Press.

Mendelberg, T. (2008) "Racial Priming Revived," *Perspectives on Politics* 6(1): 109–123.

Meyer, D. E. and Schvaneveldt, R. E. (1971) "Facilitation in Recognizing Pairs of Words: Evidence of a Dependence between Retrieval Operations," *Journal of Experimental Psychology* 90(2): 227–234.

Monahan, J. L., Shtrulis, I., and Givens, S. (2005) "Priming Welfare Queens and Other Stereotypes: The Transference of Media Images into Interpersonal Contexts," *Communication Research Reports* 22(3): 199–205.

Neely, J. H. (1977) "Semantic Priming and Retrieval from Lexical Memory: Roles of Inhibitionless Spreading Activation and Limited-Capacity Attention," *Journal of Experimental Psychology: General* 106(3): 226–254.

Northup, C. T. and Dillman Carpentier, F. R. (2016) "Michael Jordan, Michael Vick, or Michael Who?: Activating Stereotypes in a Complex Media Environment," *Howard Journal of Communications* 26(2): 132–152.

Ofan, R. H., Rubin, N., and Amodio, D. M. (2011) "Seeing Race: N170 Responses to Race and Their Relation to Automatic Racial Attitudes and Controlled Processing," *Journal of Cognitive Neuroscience* 23(10): 3153–3161.

Oliver, M. and Fonash, D. (2002) "Race and Crime in the News: Whites' Identification and Misidentification of Violent and Nonviolent Criminal Suspects," *Media Psychology* 4(2): 137–156.

Oyserman, D., Fryberg, S. A., and Yoder, N. (2007) "Identity-Based Motivation and Health," *Journal of Personality and Social Psychology* 93(6): 1011–1027.

Payne, B. K. (2001) "Prejudice and Perception: The Role of Automatic and Controlled Processes in Misperceiving a Weapon," *Journal of Personality and Social Psychology* 81(2): 181–192.

Peffley, M. and Shields, T. (1996) "The Intersection of Race and Crime in Television News Stories: An Experimental Study," *Political Communication* 13(3): 309–327.

Power, J., Murphy, S. T., and Coover, G. (1996) "Priming Prejudice: How Stereotypes and Counter-Stereotypes Influence Attribution of Responsibility and Credibility among Ingroups and Outgroups," *Human Communication Research* 23(1): 36–58.

Ramasubramanian, S. (2007) "Media-Based Strategies to Reduce Racial Stereotypes Activated by News Stories," *Journalism and Mass Communication Quarterly* 84(2): 249–264.

Rios, K., Ybarra, O., and Sanchez-Burks, J. (2013) "Outgroup Primes Induce Unpredictability Tendencies under Conditions of Distrust," *Journal of Experimental Social Psychology* 49(3): 372–377.

Roskos-Ewoldsen, D. R., Klinger, M. R., and Roskos-Ewoldsen, B. (2007) "Media Priming," in R. W. Preiss, B. M. Gayle, N. Burrell, M. Allen, and J. Bryant (eds.), *Mass Media Effects Research: Advances through Meta-Analysis*. Mahwah, NJ: Erlbaum, 53–80.

Roskos-Ewoldsen, D. R., Roskos-Ewoldsen, B., and Dillman Carpentier, F. R. (2008) "Media Priming: An Updated Synthesis," in J. Bryant and M. B. Oliver (eds.), *Media Effects: Advances in Theory and Research*, 3rd ed. New York: Routledge, 74–93.

Rudman, L. A. and Lee, M. R. (2002) "Implicit and Explicit Consequences of Exposure to Violent and Misogynous Rap Music," *Group Processes and Intergroup Relations* 5(2): 133–150.

Shrum, L. J. (1996) "Psychological Processes Underlying Cultivation Effects: Further Tests of Construct Accessibility," *Human Communication Research* 22(4): 482–509.

Shrum, L. J., Wyer, R. S., and O'Guinn, T. C. (1998) "The Effects of Television Consumption on Social Perceptions: The Use of Priming Procedures to Investigate Psychological Processes," *Journal of Consumer Research* 24(4): 447–458.

Srull, T. K. and Wyer, R. S. (1979) "The Role of Category Accessibility in the Interpretation of Information about Persons: Some Determinants and Implications," *Journal of Personality and Social Psychology* 37(10): 1660–1672.

Tulving, E. (1972) "Episodic and Semantic Memory," in E. Tulving and W. Donaldson (eds.), *Organization and Memory*. New York: Academic Press, 381–403.

Tversky, A. and Kahneman, D. (1974) "Judgment under Uncertainty: Heuristics and Biases," *Science* 185(4157): 1124–1131.

Uleman, J. S. and Bargh, J. A. (eds.) (1989) *Unintended Thought*. New York: Guilford Publications.

Valentino, N. A. (1999) "Crime News and the Priming of Racial Attitudes during Evaluations of the President," *Public Opinion Quarterly* 63(3): 293–320.

Valentino, N. A., Hutchings, V. L., and White, I. K. (2004) "Cues that Matter: How Political Ads Prime Racial Attitudes during Campaigns," *American Political Science Review* 96(1): 75–90.

Valentino, N. A., Traugott, M. W., and Hutchings, V. L. (2002) "Group Cues and Ideological Constraint: A Replication of Political Advertising Effects Studies in the Lab and in the Field," *Political Communication* 19(1): 29–48.

White, I. K. (2007) "When Race Matters and When It Doesn't: Racial Group Differences in Response to Racial Cues," *American Political Science Review* 101(2): 339–354.

Wilson, C. C. and Gutierrez, F. F. (1995) *Race, Multiculturalism, and the Media: From Mass to Class Communication*, 2nd ed. Thousand Oaks, CA: Sage Publications, Inc.

## Further Reading

Behm-Morawitz, E. and Ortiz, M. (2013) "Race, Ethnicity, and the Media," in K. Dill (ed.), *The Oxford Handbook of Media Psychology*. Oxford: Oxford Library of Psychology, 252–266. (Places priming studies of media depictions of race into the larger context of psychological studies of race and media.)

Li-Vollmer, M. (2002) "Race Representation in Child-Targeted Television Commercials," *Mass Communication and Society* 5(2): 207–228. (A study of the content in children's television advertising, specifically focusing on the frequency and type of representation of race and ethnicity in these messages aimed at the youngest audiences.)

Mastro, D. and Atwell Seate, A. (2012) "Group Membership in Race-Related Media Processes and Effects," in H. Giles (ed.), *The Handbook of Intergroup Communication*. New York: Routledge, 357–369. (Reviews multiple theoretical perspectives on the relationship between media exposure and perceptions of race, focusing on the idea of ingroup/outgroup designation.)

Timmerman, L. M., Allen, M., Jorgensen, J., Herrett-Skjellum, J., Kramer, M. R., and Ryan, D. J. (2008) "A Review and Meta-Analysis Examining the Relationship of Music Content with Sex, Race, Priming, and Attitudes," *Communication Quarterly* 56(3): 303–324. (An examination of the relative strength of effects of race depictions in popular music and perceptions of race compared to other media priming effects.)

Tukachinsky, R. (2015) "Where We Have Been and Where We Can Go from Here: Looking to the Future in Research on Media, Race, and Ethnicity," *Journal of Social Issues* 71(1): 186–199. (Contextualizes and synthesizes the larger body of work at the intersection of race and media and is featured in a special issue of *Journal of Social Issues* on "Media Representations of Race and Ethnicity: Implications for Identity, Intergroup Relations, and Public Policy.")

# 6

# CRITICAL RACE THEORY

## Everything Old is New Again

### *Kim M. LeDuff*

> It seemed like a mirage . . . as if awakening from a bad dream, we opened our eyes to find an African American in the White House . . .. But to quote Derrick Bell, "we are not saved." In the same way that the collapse of formal segregation did not dismantle racial power in the mid-20th century, President Obama's victory did not signal its defeat in 2008.
>
> *Williams Crenshaw,*
> Twenty Years of Critical Race Theory:
> Looking Back to Move Forward *(2011)*

Anyone looking at the media landscape in 2016 could clearly see that racial tension in America was running high. Since Obama's election in 2008, news in America had included a litany of stories that occasionally caused viewers to question whether they were watching contemporary news coverage or the History Channel. In light of news coverage that includes discord over the meaning of the Confederate flag; unarmed black men being killed by police; presidential candidate rallies that could easily be mistaken for Klan rallies; and the Black Lives Matter vs. All Lives Matter debate, critical race scholar Derrick Bell's words seem prophetic. When it comes to race and representation in mass media, the view in the mid-2010s is not hopeful or positive.

There is no doubt that mediated messages have played a major role in the current state of race relations in the United States. Critical Race Theory (CRT) is a useful tool that can help media and social scholars better understand how we have arrived at this place more than 60 years after the Civil Rights Movement. The critique Critical Race Theorists have outlined over the years described dire concerns about American racial attitudes. In many cases, their greatest fears have become our current reality. Media critics have used CRT (originally a legal theory) to better understand American audiences and the impact of mediated messages on their view of race in America. In *Twenty Years of Critical Race Theory: Looking Back to Move Forward*, Kimberlé Williams Crenshaw (2011) notes a major flaw in mainstream media coverage in the post-Civil Rights era. She argues,

> The media helped normalize a particular erasure of racial power in its coverage of racial disparities and conflict. By rarely situating affirmative action or any other race-conscious policies within a frame that pointed to the contemporary practices of racial discrimination, the media helped to frame racism as a thing of the past. Those who resisted this internment of race were increasingly positioned as outside the mainstream.
>
> *(1343)*

But today it is clear that racism is alive and well in America. It is not just a matter of racist practices and beliefs on behalf of a small group of individuals who remain on the outskirts of society. Institutional and systematic racism are present and evident in the stories presented to audiences on local television news. How is it possible that U.S. citizens (even those in leadership roles) can feel that it is socially acceptable to espouse racist remarks in public spaces? How is this possible in a country that elected an African American to serve as President of the United States? How is this possible 60 years after the end of the Jim Crow era? CRT posits multiple explanations. The purpose of this chapter is to examine how critics can use the theory to explore the meaning behind the images, messages, signs, and symbols that reflect racist beliefs and practices in contemporary culture.

## The History of Critical Race Theory

The roots of CRT extend back to the 1970s when a group of legal scholars and activists realized that the waves of change following the Civil Rights era of the 1960s were not having much impact in society. In some cases, America's justice system even appeared to revert back to its pre-Civil Rights state. Derrick Bell (often cited as the father of CRT), an African American, and Alan Freeman, who is white, were pioneers of CRT. According to Delgado and Stefancic (2001) in their book, *Critical Race Theory: An Introduction*, "Both were deeply distressed over the slow pace of racial reform in the United States and decided that new approaches were needed to expose and deal with the less obvious, though just as deeply entrenched, types of racism that characterized modern time" (xiii). They note that the theory "considers many of the same issues that conventional civil rights and ethnic studies discourses take up, but places them in a broader perspective that includes economics, history, context, group- and self-interest, and even feelings and the unconscious" (3). According to Tara Yasso (2002), CRT draws from "a large literature base in law, sociology, history, ethnic studies, and women's studies" (3). She also notes that "CRT is a framework that can address the racism, sexism, and classism embedded in media" (3).

Mass communication scholars have found the theory to be useful as it aligns with many of the mass communication theories we use, including cultivation theory, agenda setting, and framing. In my own research, *Tales of Two Cities, How Race and Crime Intersect on Local Television News* (LeDuff 2002) and *Race and News: Critical Perspectives* (Campbell, LeDuff, Brown, and Jenkins 2012), I used the theory to deconstruct narratives and imagery in local and national television news stories. In crime stories, the narrative style frequently results in black males being framed as dangerous suspects but rarely included as police officers or informative sources in stories even in cities with large populations of black people. After the terrorist attacks of 9/11, news organizations frequently manufactured stories that framed people of Middle Eastern descent as terrorists. They searched local communities and universities for the possibility that students or citizens might have connections to Al Qaeda. As a result, some viewers were likely to equate ethnicity and/or religious beliefs with terrorism.

The news also covered stories in which people who were perceived as Middle Eastern or Muslim (even when they were not) were victims of hate crimes because American citizens viewed them as terrorists. Just as legal theorists found that court cases resulted in the same outcome because judges and juries had preconceived notions about defendants based on their race, mass communication scholars find that audiences are quick to place judgment. They have observed similar stories and have preconceived "pictures in their heads" when it comes to race, guilt, and innocence while reading or watching news. As Crenshaw (2011) argues,

The opportunity presented now is for scholars across disciplines not only to reveal how disciplinary conventions themselves constitute racial power, but also to provide an inventory of the critical tools developed over time to weaken and potentially dismantle them. . . . In short, the next turn in CRT should be decidedly interdisciplinary, intersectional and cross-institutional.

*(1262)*

What follows are three examples of how media coverage of events potentially shaped the perception of people of color and race relations in the minds of audiences. While scholars have identified a number of important tenets when it comes to CRT, three will be examined in an effort to illustrate the application of CRT to media studies.

## The Important Tenets of Critical Race Theory

In "What's Race Got to Do with It? Critical Race Theory's Conflicts with and Connections to Qualitative Research Methodology and Epistemology," Laurence Parker and Marvin Lynn (2002) characterize CRT as incorporating three main goals:

a) to present storytelling and narratives as valid approaches through which to examine race and racism in law and society; b) to argue for the eradication of racial subjugation while simultaneously recognizing that race is a social construct; c) to draw important relationships between race and other axes of domination.

*(10)*

The theory also allows researchers to examine race by acknowledging the inherent privilege of "whiteness" and analyzing race from a perspective that recognizes that privilege.

Three contemporary storylines will be critically analyzed to illustrate the goals of CRT as defined by Parker and Lynn (2002). These examples will illustrate that CRT is still an applicable theory when it comes to understanding how audiences may interpret the status of race relations in America if they are frequent consumers of mediated news messages. The examples also show how the news media as an institution is often more concerned with the sensational than telling a story from a perspective that educates audiences about the real issues at hand. Finally, these examples illustrate how media contributes to the perception of America as a nation that is increasingly polarized along racial and political lines.

### *Storytelling Narratives*

Mass media audiences are accustomed to narrative style when they read or watch news stories. After all, news reporting is a form of storytelling. When it comes to certain topics, audiences are often accustomed to there being two sides to the story (in the case of crime, a victim and a suspect; in the case of politics, two or more political parties). They have also been trained to anticipate (even if subconsciously) certain groups playing the same roles in those stories.

An example of this in contemporary news narrative might be found in the 2016 presidential election coverage. Looking at the presidential primaries in 2016, it was difficult to remember that less than a decade before many around the world paused with a sense of hope for race relations in America with the election of its first black president.

Derrick Bell's observation that "we are not saved" seems visionary as audiences watched the showdown that was the 2016 primaries. When compared to Obama's initial election in 2008, the 2016 election coverage illustrates just how quickly, and how far, the political pendulum can swing in the opposite direction. While racial tension in America had become more and more evident over the course of Obama's time in office, coverage of the 2016 election indicated that the tension was at a new high. An article on the alternative website thedailybeast.com was headlined, "GOP's 2016 Festival of Hate: It's Already the Most Racist Presidential Campaign Ever." Reporter Dean Obeidellah (2015) explained, "It's no longer code; it's now in our face. The GOP's 2016 platform is that Latino immigrants are coming to rape you, blacks want handouts, gays are waging a holy war versus Christians, and Muslims are not loyal to America."

After Obama's election it appears that a new form of racism raised its ugly head in America. Political party affiliation became a signal of much more than politics for many, thanks to media coverage and the polarization that was reflected on television and cable network news, newspapers, and social media. The characters took sides and the narrative was similar in story after story. As a result, an individual's political affiliation could be interpreted as a sign of personal beliefs about race and power in America. For many, "Democrat" has come to mean someone who sympathizes with minorities and non-traditional values. "Republican" has become synonymous with a preference for white-over-minority ascendency and traditional American values. American media coverage since Obama's election is partially responsible for this interpretation.

As Crenshaw (2011) observed, "The post-reform trajectory of civil rights discourse has long revealed that modest victories are inevitably appropriated as ammunition by those seeking to limit the scope of racial reform" (1315–16). While many would have predicted that Obama's election might have been a win for race relations in the country, Critical Race Theorists predicted otherwise. According to Delgado and Stefancic (1997):

> Literary and narrative theory holds that we each occupy a normative universe or "nomos" from which we are not easily dislodged. Talented storytellers nevertheless struggle to reach audiences with their message (everyone loves a story). The hope is that well-told stories describing the reality of black and brown lives can help readers bridge the gap between their worlds and those of others.
>
> *(41)*

Unfortunately, those who create the news have not always used the power of media to empower. Just as there are good guys and villains in the fairytales and fables we read as children, the narrative style of telling news stories has resulting in stereotypes of those on either side of the story being ingrained in our psyches. Based on the stories we are told over and over again, black and brown people are often the bad guys and society is protected from them by white heroes. This narrative is not a fair or accurate depiction of reality for those on either side of the story.

### *Race and Power*

According to Delgado and Stefancic (2001), one paradigm held by Critical Race Theorists may be defined as realism or economic determinism. They believe that "though attitudes and words are important, racism is much more than having an unfavorable impression of members of other groups. For realists racism is a means by which society allocates privilege and status" (17). In the 1990s, a common theme examined in mass media research was the criminalization of black people in the news. Over-reporting of black-on-black crime (particularly black men killing black men) and negative depictions of African-American life and culture in both entertainment and new programming were common themes in mass communication research. Christopher P. Campbell's *Race, Myth and the News* (1995) was filled with examples of such negative news coverage of minorities from across the country. Audience members with little real-world exposure to black people might be led to perceive African Americans as dangerous. But the true danger enters the picture when these perceptions affect people's treatment in the real world.

The stories of black men's deaths have taken a strange twist in the mid-2010s. The following lives ended under similar circumstances in a relatively short period of time: Trayvon Martin in 2012; Eric Garner, Michael Brown, and Tamir Rice in 2014; Eric Harris and Freddie Gray in 2015. All these unarmed black males died at the hands of white police officers. In many cases, no charges were initially filed against the officers and even when they were, some were curiously found innocent. These black men were perceived as dangerous and threatening and, in the name of the police officers' perceived self-preservation, they were killed. Though some of these men were completely innocent, others may have been guilty of minor crimes, but none were guilty of crimes that should have resulted in the death sentences they received without trial.

Protestors flooded city streets and in cities like Ferguson, Missouri and Baltimore, Maryland. The protests occasionally turned violent and media coverage was reminiscent of coverage of protests and riots in the pre-Civil Rights era. The #BlackLivesMatter movement was born as a response to the series of senseless killings and was quickly countered by smaller and white-led campaigns, including "#BlueLivesMatter" in support of police officers and "All Lives Matter," suggesting that #BlackLivesMatter includes an implied "only" before it. Perhaps Corey Robin summarizes it best in a June 2015 article for Salon.com:

> Since the 1960s, when law and order became the rallying cry of the country's rightward turn, particularly around issues of racial inequality, the notion that safety and security are the primary political goods has migrated across the ideological spectrum. People of comfort get freedom and security. . . . People of color and the poor get neither. . … Not only has the discourse of protection contributed to the racist practices and institutions of our overly policed and incarcerated society, but it also prevents us from seeing, much less tackling, the broader, systemic inequalities that might ultimately reduce those practices and institutions.

When Civil Rights activist and prominent African-American judge A. Leon Higginbotham (1996) identified "The Ten Precepts of American Slavery Jurisprudence," which included "Inferiority" and "Powerlessness," he argued that mainstream America seeks to "keep blacks—whether slave or free—as powerless as possible so that they will be submissive and dependent in every respect, not only to the master but to whites in general." In addition, he says, the goal is to "limit blacks' accessibility to the courts and subject blacks to an inferior system of justice with lesser rights and protections and greater punishments" and to "utilize violence and the powers of government to assure the submissiveness of blacks."

The stories of the killing of black men by white police officers rose to prominence in American media in 2015 and 2016, but was it the result of a sudden influx of such events? No. Situations similar to these have been happening for decades. But with a few of these stories reaching national prominence in close succession, the media latched on and the stories found a primary place in the minds of viewers. How the media told the stories sometimes depended on the political leanings of networks on which they aired. While conservative media outlets like Fox criminalized the victims, more liberal outlets like MSNBC focused on the outrage and protest. The vast difference in the way mainstream media outlets covered the stories suggests a schism among viewers they attempt to appeal to. Conservative and predominately white audiences gravitated to the coverage that framed the victims as guilty and the officers as simply fulfilling their roles: to protect and serve. Liberal media outlets sympathized with the victims, their families, and the fact that black and brown Americans now have to live in fear of those who are supposed to protect them. American journalists continue to look for "the big scary story" that will attract viewers and readers. CRT suggests that in this case the black male has been vilified and feared for many years in the news narratives that filled local and national news. But now the black male is sometimes portrayed as the victim and the white male the villain, leaving audiences grappling with the pictures and narratives in their heads after the stories they have been told for years are suddenly challenged—unless they choose to stick with ultra-conservative news sources.

### *Race and Other Axes of Domination*

News is not the only place in the mass media where CRT is a useful tool. The 2016 Super Bowl half-time show served as an example of how CRT is applicable in places where entertainment and news collide. The Saturday before Super Bowl 2016, mega pop star Beyoncé, who was set to be one of the half-time show attractions, released a new video for her song "Formation." The words and imagery featured in the video alone elicited an interesting response from audiences and media critics alike. The backdrop for the video was New Orleans and more specifically New Orleans post-Hurricane Katrina. The city and the disaster served as a reminder of the inequity that exists in America between black and white, rich and poor. The lyrics in the song and images in the video address a number of issues, including racism, police brutality, skin color politics within the black community, sexuality, and gender. In the *Washington Post*, Jeff Guo observed that "Formation" was "a late entry into the dialogue about black lives, and it largely sidesteps the politics. Still it feels essential. After grief comes anger, and after anger comes action—and here comes a literal rallying cry from the queen of empowerment anthems. The release of its music video this weekend sent shockwaves of glee through social media." But not everyone had a positive response.

Beyoncé chose the moment to make a political statement and it was not necessarily complimentary, especially in the eyes of white America. It was not by sheer coincidence that Beyoncé chose the Super Bowl, an event that attracts those that cultural critic bell hooks might define as America's "white supremacist capitalist patriarchs" in droves. Beyoncé realized that she would have a captive audience that dedicated time and resources to watch the game and see her. Her message in the songs suggests her greatest revenge as a black woman is the money she makes while entertaining the same people who oppress poor black Americans. Her reference to being a "Texas Bama" and having "hot sauce in my bag swag" suggests that audiences should not be fooled by her fame; that in essence she is just the same as the average black American being discriminated against and stereotyped by the media. For those who may have missed the actual music video, the message was reiterated loud and clear during the Super Bowl half-time show.

To add fuel to the virtual fire, Beyoncé made her Super Bowl half-time appearance dressed in all black and followed by an entourage of black women in dress reminiscent of what members of the Black Panther Party wore in the 1960s. In response to this display, audiences were again polarized and the media was quick to point it out. While many black viewers watched the display with pride, many white viewers were outraged. According to BET.com, "Ever since Beyoncé's Black Panther-themed Super Bowl 50 halftime performance, some white conservatives have been up in arms, saying that the superstar is promoting violence against the police." There appeared to be an assumption in the coverage and the buzz on social media that Beyoncé spoke for all of black America as she made her statement during Super Bowl 50. While some applauded her actions, Sean Trainor of Salon.com wrote, "Is 'Formation' the last word on anti-racist feminism? Of course it is not. . . . To demand Beyoncé be a 'spokesperson' is among the most insidious forms of racism. When we start pillorying Toby Keith or the Insane Clown Posse for misrepresenting white America, please get back to me."

As an African-American woman from the South, Beyoncé chose to make a political statement about the status of race relations in America. As a result she was criticized for her actions. Only time will tell how this move will impact her celebrity and sales of her music. But what was most interesting was how the dividing lines were drawn when it came to those who supported her message and those who were against it. There was a clear mix of interpretation, depending upon how audiences and commentators interpreted her and her message. A quick search of responses to the video and her Super Bowl appearance indicates that people saw Beyoncé speaking on behalf of blacks and black feminists, while some went as far as to see her message as anti-police. It is difficult to imagine that viewers would dissect a message from a white male on so many levels. This is an example of the complicated intersectionality that Critical Race Theorists identify.

## Conclusion

How did we arrive at this place in America? A place where a Republican Presidential nominee can publicly humiliate black and brown people and garner cheers and ultimately votes from potential voters? A place where protests in response to the senseless murders of unarmed black men led to protestors being handled by police in a manner that is eerily reminiscent of the way protestors were handled during the Civil Rights Movement? As Crenshaw (2012) explains, "Although the celebration prompted by Obama's victory was indeed monumental, his breakthrough did not open up a raceless space beyond the glass ceiling" (1312). We as a society cannot say that we were not forewarned. Critical Race Theorists saw the writing on the wall early on. In some ways the initial response of society and media coverage of life in the early years after the Civil Rights Movement gave the false impression that racism was over. The media perpetuated the myth by avoiding the stories that indicated the true price of oppression. Instead they focused on sensational stories to increase their viewership and for ratings. Unfortunately, hegemonic thoughts and practices in relation to race persisted and festered, and today it seems that many of the old challenges that society faced in pre-Civil Rights America are coming back to haunt us with a new and different twist.

During Obama's presidential campaign, the media focused on the narrative that many in this country were excited because we were on the verge of "change" and had "hope" in a post-racial America. But it wasn't long before the counter-narrative of racist backlash entered the picture. This is not to suggest that this is the fault of the president, but instead the magnification of the lack of effort on behalf of our society and American media to address the true ills that are so ingrained in our society when it comes to race relations. Those in the media profession continue to make the same old mistakes. The recent incidents described here are indeed reminiscent of the struggle that those who fought during the pre-Civil Rights era faced more than half a century ago. Today there is a new platform, social media, which allows huge audiences to voice their thoughts, opinions, and ideas. It is a platform where we see discussions play out in response to many of the stories that audiences across America first learn about through mainstream media. This technology, which was once touted as being almost utopian, has instead become one of the places where we can witness first-hand the great divides among race and class in modern society.

## References

Campbell, C., LeDuff, K. M., Jenkins, C. D., and Brown, R. A. (2012) *Race and News: Critical Perspectives*. New York: Routledge.

Crenshaw, K. W. (2011) "Twenty Years of Critical Race Theory: Looking Back To Move Forward," *Connecticut Law Review* 43(5): 1253–1352.

Cummings, M. (2016, Feb. 13) "Killer Mike: Beyoncé's Formation Critics Need to Pick up a History Book," BET.com. Retrieved from http://www.bet.com/news/music/2016/02/13/killer-mike-beyonce-formation-critics-need-to-pick-up-a-history-book.html.

Delgado, R. and Stefancic, J. (1997) *Critical White Studies: Looking Behind the Mirror*. Philadelphia, PA: Temple University Press.

Delgado, R. and Stefancic, J. (2001) *Critical Race Theory: An Introduction*. New York: New York University Press.

Guo, J. (2016, Feb. 9) "The Strange Contradiction in Beyoncé's New Song 'Formation,'" *Washington Post*. Retrieved from https://www.washingtonpost.com/news/wonk/wp/2016/02/09/the-strange-contradiction-in-beyonces-new-song-formation/.

Higginbotham, L. A. (1996) "The Ten Precepts of American Slavery Jurisprudence: Chief Justice Roger Taney's Defense and Justice Thurgood Marshall's Condemnation of the Precept of Black Inferiority," racism.org. Retrieved from http://academic.udayton.edu/race/02rights/precepts.htm.

LeDuff, K. M. (2009) *Tales of Two Cities: How Race and Crime Intersect on Local TV News In New Orleans and Indianapolis*. Saarbrücken, Germany: Lambert.

Obeidellah, D. (2015, Sept. 9) "GOP's 2016 Festival of Hate: It's Already the Most Racist Campaign Ever," *The Daily Beast*. Retrieved from (http://www.thedailybeast.com/articles/2015/09/29/2016-s-festival-of-hate-it-s-already-the-most-racist-presidential-campaign-ever.html.

Parker, L. and Lynn, M. (2002) "What's Race Got to Do with It? Critical Race Theory's Conflicts with and Connections to Qualitative Research Methodology and Epistemology," *Qualitative Inquiry* 8(1): 7–22.

Robin, C. (2015, June 21) "The Racist Disease We Never Discuss: Dylann Roof, Overpolicing and the Real Story about Safety in America," *Salon*. Retrieved from http://www.salon.com/2015/06/21/the_racist_disease_we_never_discuss_dylann_roof_over_policing_and_the_real_story_about_safety_in_america/.

Trainor, S. (2016, Feb. 11) "Dear Liberal White Guys: Before You Offer Your Critique of Beyoncé's 'Formation,' Read This," *Salon*. Retrieved from http://www.salon.com/2016/02/11/dear_liberal_white_guys_before_you_offer_your_critique_of_beyonces_formation_read_this/.

Yosso, T. J (2002) "Critical Race Media Literacy: Challenging Deficit Discourse about Chicanas/os," *Journal of Popular Film and Television* 30(1): 52–62.

## Further Reading

Crenshaw, K., Gotanda, N., Peller, G., and Thomas, K. (1996) *Critical Race Theory: The Key Writings that Informed the Movement*. New York: The New Press. (Edited by leading theoreticians of the CRT movement, this book gathers together some of the movement's most important essays.)

Delgado, R. and Stefancic, J. (1997) *Critical White Studies: Looking Behind the Mirror*. Philadelphia, PA: Temple University Press. (Describes white studies as the next step in CRT, inviting whites to examine themselves more searchingly and to "look behind the mirror.")

——. (2001) *Critical Race Theory: An Introduction*. New York: New York University Press. (An introduction to the field that explains the origins, principal themes, leading voices, and directions of CRT.)

Wise, T. (2015) *Under the Affluence: Shaming the Poor, Praising the Rich and Sacrificing the Future of America*. San Francisco, CA: City Lights. (Discusses race, whiteness, economic inequality, and the demonization of those in need.)

# Part II

# RACE, THE MEDIUM, THE MESSAGE

# 7

# PRIMETIME TELEVISION

## Portrayals and Effects

*Dana Mastro, Andrea Figueroa-Caballero, and Alexander Sink*

Decades of content analyses examining portrayals of race and ethnicity on primetime television indicate that this programming offers little in the way of equitable characterizations of racial/ethnic minorities (Mastro 2009). Of course variations in depictions exist across racial/ethnic groups and types of programs (e.g., genres); however, in the main these groups are underrepresented compared with U.S. population statistics and often limited to a restricted set of narrow and/or stereotypical roles. Exposure to these media messages is not without consequence. Effects studies consistently reveal that viewing the content offered on television influences the cognitions, attitudes, and behaviors of audiences, in a manner consistent with the media messages (varying based on individual difference features of the consumers). Accordingly, understanding how different racial/ethnic groups are portrayed on television, and the range of possible individual and societal-level implications that may result from exposure, is socially and theoretically significant. To this end, the current chapter: (a) documents the frequency and nature of depictions of racial and ethnic groups on primetime television, (b) details both the harmful and constructive outcomes known to result from exposure, and (c) suggests areas for further consideration.

## Why Focus on Television?

Calls for improvements in the representation of racial/ethnic groups on television have been present since the earliest days of TV and have remained a persistent criticism of the medium (Mastro and Greenberg 2000). From boycotts and protests of the *Amos n' Andy* show in the early 1950s to FCC Chair Newton Minow's 1961 condemnation of television programming as culturally vacuous to the U.S. Commission on Civil Rights' 1977 declaration that racial/ethnic groups appear as stereotypical "window dressing," television has been criticized for its failure to offer a respectable array of diverse characters. Although some are quick to dismiss the relevance of television in our contemporary media and technology-rich environment, evidence indicates that television continues to be the dominant media outlet for consumers, with U.S. adults viewing approximately five hours per day, not including exposure on computers or other screens (Nielsen 2012).

Thus, early admonitions regarding the role and responsibility of television in U.S. society ring just as true today as they did when offered by the U.S. Commission on Civil Rights in 1977:

> Television does more than simply entertain or provide news about major events of the day. It confers status on those individuals and groups it selects for placement in the public eye, telling the viewer who and what is important to know about, think about, and have feelings about. Those who are made visible through television become worthy of attention and concern; those whom television ignores remain invisible.
>
> *(1)*

## Primetime Portrayals and Effects of Exposure

Despite headlines in the popular press declaring a new era of racial/ethnic diversity on contemporary television (e.g., "Broadcasting the Big Strides in TV Diversity," *Los Angeles Times* 2014), current quantitative content analytic evidence tells a somewhat different story. In some regards (and for some groups) today's TV landscape marks a notable improvement over previous decades; however, in many ways the absence and/or marginalization of several racial/ethnic groups remains an ongoing reality. In the following sections, the history and current state of TV depictions of racial and ethnic groups are documented. It should be noted that the small number of occurrences of many groups means that little (beyond the sheer number) is known about the manner in which they are depicted.

### *Black Americans*

**Quantity.** Prior to the 1970s, few images of blacks were seen on primetime television (Wilson, Gutierrez, and Chao 2013). Analyses of the programming on television in the 1970s indicate that blacks comprised approximately 12 percent of the U.S. population at the time but a mere 6 percent of television characters (Greenberg and Brand 1994; U.S. Census Briefs 2010). The presence of blacks on primetime TV had increased to 8 percent in the 1980s and to 11 percent by the early 1990s (Mastro and Greenberg 2002). By the mid-1990s, blacks had achieved numeric parity on TV (at about 12 percent of the U.S. population and 13 percent of the TV population). Today, this rate has been sustained and even improved, with blacks making up approximately 16 percent of primetime characters and 13 percent of the U.S. population (Children Now 2004; Mastro and Greenberg 2000; Mastro and Tukachinsky 2010; Monk-Turner, Heiserman, Johnson, Cotton, and Jackson 2010). Equity in terms of the rate of representation is an important marker; however, a closer examination of how these representations vary across genres reveals a more complex picture.

Signorielli et al. (2004), in their sample of primetime television programs from 1997 through 2003, found that the numeric equality of blacks on TV masked the fact that they were isolated based on program type and channel. Specifically, black characters were largely presented in situation comedies and on networks with lower overall viewership— UPN and The WB. Harwood and Anderson (2002) noted a similar trend, reporting that although there had been an increase in black characters, half were found in only 7 of the 61 shows sampled. More recent data from Signorielli (2009a) indicate that whereas almost half of black characters are found in situation comedies, just 29 percent of white characters appear in sitcoms. Moreover, although over one third of black characters are found in programming primarily centered on minority characters, only 14 percent of other racial/ethnic characters (e.g., Latinos) are found in minority-centered shows. Thus, as Signorielli (2009a) points out, if these programs with "mostly minority characters" were not aired, the number of black characters on television would drop drastically—bringing to light the continued segregation of black characters on primetime.

Such genre disparities are noteworthy considerations as "genre conventions and constraints inevitably result in differing race-based presentations . . . [and] this tendency leaves open the possibility that depending on TV viewing preferences, a viewer may be exposed to one-sided images of Blacks, or simply not see them at all" (Mastro 2009: 326). For example, whereas dramas (as a genre) may present more multifaceted and complete characters, situation comedies are less likely to provide such character development. Thus, the relegation of black characters to a single genre of programming (sitcoms in particular) is problematic for three reasons: (a) they may be depicted as one-note (i.e., stereotypical) characters, (b) they may not be seen by a wide range of viewers, and (c) they may prompt negative perceptions of the group as a whole, if these depictions are stereotypical and/or unfavorable. As such, the question becomes: what do these portrayals look like when they do occur?

**Quality.** Television depictions of blacks in the 1950s revolved around unfavorable archetypes presented previously in radio serials and films of the early twentieth century, including the loyal mammie (e.g., Beulah from *The Beulah Show*) and ridiculed buffoon (Greenberg, Mastro, and Brand 2002; Wilson, Gutierrez, and Chao 2013). More broadly, roles for blacks centered on amusing, entertaining, and serving their white counterparts on TV. By the end of the 1960s, a subset of programming began to emerge which offered idyllic and overly idealized representations of blacks in the form of shows such as *Julia* (1968) which presented the perfectly integrated lifestyle of a single mom (a nurse) raising her son. Although idealistic in terms of the realities of the era, such programming was a positive change from many of the more unflattering messages about blacks offered on TV up to that point. The 1970s ushered in a number of sitcoms centered on the experiences of black families across varying backgrounds. Programs like *Good Times* (1974–9) and *What's Happening* (1976–9), among others, with predominantly black casts, helped bring black Americans to the small screen but their depictions were still often stereotypical, commonly depicting blacks as lazy or unemployable (Ford 1997; Greenberg, Mastro, and Brand 2002). Moreover, modified versions of the mammy and buffoon stereotypes persisted. For example, shows like *The Jeffersons* (1975–85), and later *Gimme a Break* (1981–4), portrayed "updated" mammy characters who, unlike their heavier, darker-complected counterparts from previous decades (who worked exclusively for affluent white families), these figures were lighter skinned, thinner, and served affluent white *or* black families. These new sitcoms were also considerably more likely to portray blacks as fun-loving or happy-go-lucky, often leaving their characters largely underdeveloped (Ford 1997). Overall, the content analytic work from the 1970s indicates that blacks were predominately characterized as lazy, poor, and/or jobless (Ward 2004) and in supporting roles (Gerbner and Signorielli 1979).

With the introduction of *The Cosby Show* in the 1980s, blacks were presented as more successful, professional, and authoritative (Harwood and Anderson 2002; Mastro and Behm-Morawitz 2005). This trend has continued to today, with the typical black character on primetime being a middle-class male, most commonly found in either law enforcement or some other professional-level occupation (Mastro and Behm-Morawitz 2005).

By focusing attention on attributes such as occupation and appearance, findings from several recent content analyses help provide a more nuanced understanding of the portrayal of blacks on primetime (see Mastro and Greenberg 2000; Mastro and Behm-Morawitz 2005; Monk-Turner et al. 2010; Signorielli 2009a; Signorielli 2009b). This research reveals blacks to be less well groomed, less respected, and more unprofessional (i.e., disheveled) than their racial/ethnic counterparts on television (Mastro and Greenberg 2000). Unsurprisingly then, black characters (women, specifically) are less likely than other racial/ethnic groups to be cast in professional jobs (Signorielli 2009b). On the other hand, blacks on primetime television are also less aggressive than their on-screen peers. Collectively, these content analyses illustrate the current state of black characters on television as highly isolated in terms of programming and still reliant on some problematic stereotypes (at least in some cases), despite reaching a level of parity with regard to overall quantity of portrayals.

**Implications of Exposure.** Communication theory suggests that both long and short-term exposure to mass media, television in particular, meaningfully contribute to public perceptions of diverse groups (Punyanunt-Carter 2008). As Entman (1994) notes, viewing depictions of racial/ethnic minorities on television is capable not only of distorting what information about these groups is known but also why certain groups should be viewed in these ways. Accordingly, the consequences of consuming negative, stereotypical content are argued to have far-reaching implications. Indeed, empirical evidence indicates that exposure to such depictions among white audiences prompts unfavorable views about blacks in society (e.g., Ford 1997; Fujioka 1999; Punyanunt-Carter 2008) as well as unsympathetic positions on diversity-related policy issues such as affirmative action (e.g., Busselle and Crandall 2002; Tan, Fujioka, and Tan 2000). More specifically, this research finds that consuming negative characterizations of blacks in the media leads to more unfavorable beliefs regarding criminality, intelligence, work ethic, socio-economic status, and values (Dixon 2007; Fujioka 1999; Mastro and Kopacz 2006; Peffley, Shields and Williams 1996; Tan, Fujioka, and Tan 2000). Alternatively, under certain conditions exposure to positive messages about blacks in the media can encourage more favorable evaluations and policy positions among white audiences (e.g., Fujioka 1999; Mastro and Kopacz 2006) and improve esteem among black viewers (e.g., Ward 2004).

### *Latino Americans*

**Quantity.** Latinos constitute the largest racial/ethnic minority group in the United States, with the U.S. Census Bureau estimating that roughly 16 percent of the population is of Latino origin (U.S. Census Briefs 2010). Despite the large and growing prevalence in the U.S. population, Latino characters are seen only infrequently on television. In fact, Latinos have suffered from persistent underrepresentation on television for nearly six decades (Mastro and Behm-Morawitz 2005; Mastro and Sink 2016). Only during the 1950s were Latinos presented on television at a rate comparable with their proportion of the real-world population, at 3 percent of TV characters and approximately 2.4 percent of the U.S. population. Since that time, the Latino population has grown rapidly, only to see the number of images on TV stagnate and even drop. For example, in the 1980s, Latinos comprised only 1 percent of television characters (Gerbner and Signorielli 1979; Greenberg and Baptista-Fernandez 1980) but represented approximately 8 percent of the nation's population by the end of that decade (*New York Times* 1988, September).

The 1990s saw only negligible increases in the sheer number of Latinos on television—at between 1.1 percent and 1.6 percent of the primetime television world but approximately 11 percent of the U.S. population at that time (Mastro and Behm-Morawitz 2005).

The premieres of situation comedies like *Luis* (2003), *The Ortegas* (2003), and *The George Lopez Show* (2002–7) in the early 2000s seemed to suggest the beginning of a shift in programming featuring Latino characters. Although the first two programs were canceled within weeks of their premieres, *The George Lopez Show* saw commercial success (alongside some criticism) and remained on the air for five seasons. With the exception of ABC's critically acclaimed *Ugly Betty* (2006–10), few other promising Latino-oriented shows were offered on primetime television. In terms of the number of Latinos appearing across the primetime landscape during this decade, research indicates that between 3.8 percent and 6.5 percent of the TV population was Latinos (Children Now 2004; Mastro and Behm-Morawitz 2005). Although this represents an increase over previous decades, it still falls far below their proportion of the U.S. population at the time, at approximately 13 percent (U.S. Census Briefs 2010).

The most recent analyses of Latinos on primetime television indicate that the number of portrayals is abysmally low when compared to U.S. Census data (at 16 percent), with Latino characters comprising less than 3 percent of the primetime population in the Fall 2013 season (Mastro and Sink 2016). Moreover, Latino men have nearly disappeared in recurring roles on television (Negrón-Muntaner 2014). Indeed, Latinas are more likely than Latino men to be featured in both lead and supporting roles on primetime. This shows little improvement (if any) in the overall quantity of Latinos on television. It should be noted, however, that the 2014 to 2015 television season included two new programs (*Cristela* and *Jane the Virgin*) on major networks (ABC and The CW) that both focused on Latino lead characters with predominately Latino casts.

**Quality.** When Latinos are depicted on primetime television, they appear primarily in secondary and nonrecurring roles (Mastro and Behm-Morawitz 2005). These televised Latino characters have historically been confined to a limited set of stereotypic and negative characterizations (Greenberg and Baptista-Fernandez 2005), including buffoons, criminals or law enforcers, and objects of sexual desire (Mastro and Behm-Morawitz 2005). The buffoon character is designed to provide comic relief. This humor is based largely on ridiculing or otherwise demeaning these characters based on their lazy and unintelligent disposition, thick accent, and inferior status (Mastro and Greenberg 2000). The criminal is typically a young, aggressive male with an unkempt appearance and a dishonest nature (Berg 1990). In stark contrast, the law enforcer is a well-groomed, honest, articulate, and respected authority figure (Mastro and Behm-Morawitz 2005). Finally, Latino characters appearing as objects of sexual desire are marked not only by their sensuality but also by their hot tempers and sexual aggressiveness (Berg 1990). Very few Latino characters are seen in high-status jobs, and out of all other racial/ethnic groups on television, they are most likely to be portrayed in service roles (Children NOW 2000). Anecdotally, it is easy to think of current/recent examples of these stereotypical archetypes, including the sexualized 'Gloria' character from ABC's *Modern Family* (2009–) and the buffoon-like character 'Fez' from Fox's syndicated *That '70s Show* (1998–2006).

In a more recent content analysis of Latinos on primetime television, Mastro and Behm-Morawitz (2005) concluded that some of these stereotypes appear to be fading from the television landscape, as their sample of Latino characters had comparable incomes, intelligence, and cleanliness to their white and black counterparts. However, compared to other characters, they held the most conversations about crime and violence.

Additionally, Mastro and Sink (2016) found that Latino characters were overrepresented as accented and inarticulate. Despite being a phenotypically diverse group, Latinos are presented as homogenized on primetime television and distinct ethnic backgrounds are rarely made apparent. These findings suggest that restrictive and unfavorable messages may still be perpetuated in television portrayals of Latinos.

**Implications of Exposure.** Effects studies have consistently demonstrated that exposure to unfavorable depictions of Latinos on television can have a harmful influence on both Latino and non-Latino audiences. Among non-Latinos, long and short-term exposure to negative portrayals of Latinos have been liked with stereotypic evaluations of Latinos in society, negative feelings and judgments toward Latinos, dispositional attributions, and decreased support for race-related policy issues among certain white audience members (Mastro 2003; Mastro, Behm-Morawitz, and Kopacz 2008; Mastro, Behm-Morawitz, and Ortiz 2007; Mastro and Kopacz 2006; Tukachinsky, Mastro, and Yarchi 2015). Moreover, increased television consumption strengthens the influence of television's messages on judgments of Latinos in society, especially for those who have limited contact with Latinos in everyday life (Mastro, Behm-Morawitz, and Ortiz 2007). Among Latino viewers, exposure to such content is associated with perceptions of discrimination against Latinos in U.S. society, negative affective, shame, and anger (Ortiz and Behm-Morawitz 2015; Schmader, Block, and Lickel 2015).

Importantly, television's influence in this context is not limited to harmful outcomes. Exposure to positive media representations of Latinos can have prosocial effects, including promoting egalitarian beliefs and favorable intergroup attitudes. Even a single exposure to positive and likable Latino characters has been found to improve white audience members' attitudes about Latinos, at least temporarily (Mastro and Tukachinsky 2011).

## *Asian Americans*

Although Asian Americans comprise approximately 4.8 percent of the U.S. population (U.S. Census Briefs 2010), so few Asians are presented on primetime television that little beyond the sheer number of appearances is known about these characters (see Mastro and Greenberg 2000). Prior to the 1970s, images of Asians on television were infrequent, at best (Mastro and Greenberg 2000; Wilson, Gutierrez, and Chao 2013). From the late 1960s into the 1980s the number of Asian Americans on television modestly increased, owing in part to the popularity of a handful of programs set in Hawaii (the state with the largest proportion of Asian Americans in the total population). With only a few exceptions, however, these characters were primarily in minor or background roles. From the 1990s through the early 2000s, Asian Americans constituted between 1 percent and 3 percent of the characters on primetime TV (Children Now 2001; Children Now 2004; Mastro and Behm-Morawitz 2005; Mastro and Greenberg 2000), compared with 4 percent of the U.S. population (U.S. Census 2000).

With such a limited number of Asians on television, one must look outside the realm of primetime to get a general sense of the depictions associated with this group. Much like Latinos, Asians are typically presented as a single, homogenous group, with distinctive ethnic and cultural differences ignored (Mok 1998). When seen, they are often represented in a manner consistent with the "model minority" stereotype, linking Asian Americans with a number of desirable qualities such as intelligence, strong family values, and strong worth ethic (Taylor and Stern 1997). Yet despite this high status, Mok (1998) notes that Asians are most often assigned minor or background (i.e., token) roles in entertainment programs, such as waiters, cooks, servants, laundry workers, peasants, or gardeners. Little more is known about the manner in which Asians are depicted on television or the implications of exposure to this content.

## *Native Americans*

Native Americans are perhaps the most chronically invisible group on primetime television. A recent analysis of 12 separate primetime seasons spanning the years 1987 to 2009 identified only three regularly occurring Native American characters, two of whom were accounted for by the same character whose show (*Northern Exposure*) appeared in two of the seasons included for analysis (Tukachinsky, Mastro, and Yarchi 2015). This means that only two unique Native American characters appeared across their sample of 2,336 regular characters.

Because of the near/complete absence of Native Americans on television, the manner in which they have been characterized has not been documented in quantitative content analysis. What little is known about their depictions on TV suggests that they are also presented as a homogenous group. That is, despite the fact that there are over 500 federally recognized Native American tribes, the media nearly entirely ignores this cultural and linguistic diversity (Tan, Fujioka, and Lucht 1997). Featured perhaps most prominently in the "Western" genre, popular in film and television during the early to mid-1900s, Native Americans were seen predominately as historical figures and characterized as barbarians, vicious, cruel, lazy, unintelligent, intoxicated, and in "traditional" garments and headdresses (Tan, Fujioka, and Lucht 1997).

Empirical studies on non-Native audiences have not linked television viewing with stereotyping of Native Americans, but this may simply reflect the scarcity of any Native American exemplars on television (see Tan, Fujioka, and Lucht 1997). For Native American audiences, exposure to images of American Indian mascots (e.g., the Washington Redskins, Cleveland Indians) and other common media characterizations of Native Americans (e.g., Disney's *Pocahontas*) has been found to have a harmful effect on evaluations of personal esteem and community worth (Fryberg et al. 2008). Certainly, to fully understand the implications of exposure to TV depictions of Native Americans on both Native and non-Native audiences, the impact of "invisibility" will need to be considered (Leavitt, Covarrubias, Fryberg, and Perez 2015).

## *Arab/Middle Eastern*

Very little is known about representations of Arab/Middle Eastern or Arab American/Middle Eastern American characters on primetime television. An analysis of the 2003–4 TV season reveals that Arab/Middle Eastern characters comprise 0.5 percent of the total characters on primetime and 0.3 percent of the characters appearing in the opening credits of the show (Children Now 2004). Nearly half of these roles (46 percent) are as criminals.

## *Indian/Pakistani*

Although the most recent analysis documenting depictions of Indians/Pakistanis or Indian Americans/Pakistani Americans is a decade old, this research indicates that Indians/Pakistanis make up 0.4 percent of the total primetime population and 0.3 percent of characters appearing in the opening credits (Children Now 2004). Anecdotally, the number of South Asians appearing as regular or recurring characters on primetime television today seems to be on the rise; specifically Indians and Indian Americans. Perusing the 2014–15 primetime lineup reveals a number of Indian/Indian American characters in lead and recurring roles including Mindy Kaling (character Mindy Lahiri), star of *The Mindy Project*, Kunal Nayyar (character Rajesh Koothrappali) on *The Big Bang Theory*, and Aziz Ansari (character Tom Haverford) on *Parks and Recreation*, among others. What is notable about these roles is that they are not defined by the character's ethnicity. However, absent systematic analysis of depictions of Indians on television, such assessments are purely speculative.

## Concluding Thoughts

As the evidence from content analyses and effects studies addressed here clearly indicates, the quality and quantity of media representations of race/ethnicity on television have significant social implications for all audience members. These media depictions create a shared version of what race/ethnicity represents in society and have the potential (under certain circumstances) to encourage an array of race/ethnicity-based outcomes related to both self and other. Notably, this means that the media's influence is not limited to harmful effects. Instead, it underscores the importance of a wide range of auspicious representations of diverse groups. Of course, media are not the sole contributors to racial/ethnic cognitions and interethnic behaviors; however, the meaningful role that media play in shaping and maintaining the public's racial/ethnic cognitions cannot be denied. Accordingly, a number of questions require more thorough attention. For example, additional research is needed to help flesh out the mechanisms through which television use contributes to the formation of stereotypes of diverse groups. Additionally, future research must consider more ecologically valid media exposure patterns to better understand possible effects. That is to say, how does both single and long-term exposure to a collection of competing messages (both positive and negative) influence audiences? Although viewers are likely to have preferred content to which they are likely to attend (e.g., certain genres, etc.), there is little doubt that TV audiences are exposed to a variety of (possibly distinct) characterizations of race/ethnicity. As such, understanding what messages win out and why is essential. Given the potential for television exposure to prompt both favorable and unfavorable psychological and societal effects, the consequences of use and the mechanisms underlying these outcomes should remain on the agenda of current media research and theorizing.

## References

Berg, C. R. (1990) "Stereotyping in Films in General and of the Hispanic in Particular," *Howard Journal of Communications* 2(3): 286–300.

Busselle, R. and Crandall, H. (2002) "Television Viewing and Perceptions about Race Differences in Socioeconomic Success," *Journal of Broadcasting & Electronic Media* 46(2): 265–282.

Children Now. (2000, Sept. 20) "Latinowood and TV: Prime Time for a Reality Check." Retrieved from http://www.hispanicarts.org/Media/REPORT1.pdf.

——. (2004, April) "Fall Colors 2003–2004: Prime Time Diversity Report." Retrieved from http://www.childrennow.org/uploads/documents/ fall_colors_2003.pdf.

Dixon, T. (2007) "Black Criminals and White Officers: The Effects of Racially Misrepresenting Law Breakers and Law Defenders on Television News," *Media Psychology* 10: 270–291.

Entman, R. M. (1994) "Representation and Reality in the Portrayal of Blacks on Network Television News," *Journalism & Mass Communication Quarterly* 71(3): 509–520.

Ford, T. E. (1997) "Effects of Stereotypical Television Portrayals of African-Americans on Person Perception," *Social Psychology Quarterly* 60(3): 266–275.

Fryberg, S. A., Markus, H. R., Oyserman, D., and Stone, J. M. (2008) "Of Warrior Chiefs and Indian Princesses: The Psychological Consequences of American Indian Mascots," *Basic and Applied Social Psychology* 30(3): 208–218.

Fujioka, Y. (1999) "Television Portrayals and African-American Stereotypes: Examination of Television Effects when Direct Contact is Lacking," *Journalism & Mass Communication Quarterly* 76(1): 52–75.

——. (2005) "Black Media Images as a Perceived Threat to African American Ethnic Identity: Coping Responses, Perceived Public Perception, and Attitudes Towards Affirmative Action," *Journal of Broadcasting & Electronic Media* 49(4): 450–467.

Gerbner, G. and Signorielli, N. (1979) *Women and Minorities in Television Drama 1969–1978*. Philadelphia, PA: Annenberg School of Communication, University of Pennsylvania.

Gerbner, G., Gross, L., Morgan, M., and Signorielli, N. (1982) "Charting the Mainstream: Television's Contributions to Political Orientations," *Journal of Communication* 32(2): 100–127.

Greenberg, B. S. and Baptista-Fernandez, P. (1980) "Hispanic-Americans: The New Minority on Television," *Life on Television: Content Analysis of U.S. TV Drama*, 3–12.

Greenberg, B. S. and Brand, J. E. (1994) "Minorities and the Mass Media: 1970s to 1990s," in J. Bryant and D. Zillmann (eds.), *Media Effects: Advances in Theory and Research*. Hillsdale, MI: Lawrence Erlbaum Associates, 273–314.

Greenberg, B. S., Mastro, D., and Brand, J. E. (2002) "Minorities and the Mass Media: Television into the 21st Century," in J. Bryant and D. Zillmann (eds.), *Media Effects: Advances in Theory and Research*. Hillsdale, MI: Lawrence Erlbaum Associates, 333–351.

Harwood, J. and Anderson, K. (2002) "The Presence and Portrayal of Social Groups on Prime-Time Television," *Communication Reports* 15(2): 81–97.

Leavitt, P., Covarrubias, R., Fryberg, S., and Perez, Y. A. (2015) "'Frozen in Time': The Impact of Native American Media Representations on Identity and Self-Understanding," *Journal of Social Issues* 71(1): 39–53.

*Los Angeles Times*. (2014, March 29) "Broadcasting the Big Strides in TV Diversity." Retrieved from http://articles.latimes.com/2014/mar/29/entertainment/la-et-st-broadcast-tv-diversity-20140329.

Markert, J. (2004) "*The George Lopez Show*: The Same Old Hispano?," *Bilingual Review/La Revista Bilingüe* 28(2): 148–165.

Mastro, D. E. (2003) "A Social Identity Approach to Understanding the Impact of Television Messages," *Communication Monographs* 70(2): 98–113.

——. (2009) "Effects of Racial and Ethnic Stereotyping," in J. Bryant and D. Zillmann (eds.), *Media Effects: Advances in Theory and Research*. Hillsdale, MI: Lawrence Erlbaum Associates, 325–341.

Mastro, D. E. and Behm-Morawitz, E. (2005) "Latino Representation on Primetime Television," *Journalism & Mass Communication Quarterly* 82(110): 110–130.

Mastro, D. E., Behm-Morawitz, E., and Kopacz, M. A. (2008) "Exposure to Television Portrayals of Latinos: The Implications of Aversive Racism and Social Identity Theory," *Human Communication Research* 34(1): 1–27.

Mastro, D. E., Behm-Morawitz, E., and Ortiz, M. (2007) "The Cultivation of Social Perceptions of Latinos: A Mental Models Approach," *Media Psychology* 9(2): 347–365.

Mastro, D. E. and Greenberg, B. S. (2000) "The Portrayal of Racial Minorities on Prime Time Television," *Journal of Broadcasting & Electronic Media* 44(4): 690–703.

Mastro, D. E. and Kopacz, M. A. (2006) "Media Representations of Race, Prototypicality, and Policy Reasoning: An Application of Self-Categorization Theory," *Journal of Broadcasting & Electronic Media* 50(2): 305–322.

Mastro, D. E. and Sink, A. C. (2016) "Phenotypicality Bias on Television? A Quantitative Content Analytic Examination of Primetime Programming," in M. Cepeda and D. Casillas (eds.), *The Routledge Companion to Latina/o Media*. New York: Routledge Press, 72–87.

Mastro, D. E. and Tukachinsky, R. (2011) "The Influence of Exemplar Versus Prototype-Based Media Primes on Racial/Ethnic Evaluations," *Journal of Communication* 61: 916–937.

Mok, T. A. (1998) "Getting the Message: Media Images and Stereotypes and Their Effect on Asian Americans," *Cultural Diversity and Mental Health* 4(3): 185–202.

Monk-Turner, E., Heiserman, M., Johnson, C., Cotton, V., and Jackson, M. (2010) "The Portrayal of Racial Minorities on Prime Time Television: A Replication of the Mastro and Greenberg Study a Decade Later," *Studies in Popular Culture* 32(2): 101–114.

Negrón-Muntaner, F. (2014) "The Latino Media Gap. A Report on the State of Latinos in U.S. Media," the Center for the Study of Ethnicity and Race at Columbia University, the Hispanic Foundation for the Arts, and the National Association of Latino Independent Producers. Retrieved from http://www.columbia.edu/cu/cser/downloads/Latino_Media_Gap_Report.pdf.

*New York Times*. (1988, Sept. 7) "U.S. Hispanic Population is up 34% Since 1980." Retrieved from http://www.nytimes.com/1988/09/07/us/us-hispanic-population-is-up-34-since-1980.html.

Nielsen (2012, Aug.) "How People Watch: A Global Nielsen Consumer Report," the Nielsen Company. Retrieved from http://www.nielsen.com/content/dam/corporate/us/en/reports-downloads/Global%20Video%20Report%20How%20People%20Watch.pdf.

Oritz, M. and Behm-Morawitz, L. (2015) "Latinos' Perceptions of Intergroup Relations in the U.S.: The Cultivation of Group-Based Attitudes and Beliefs from English and Spanish-Language Television," *Journal of Social Issues* 71(1): 90–105.

Peffley, M., Shields, T., and Williams, B. (1996) "The Intersection of Race and Crime in Television News Stories: An Experimental Study," *Political Communication* 13: 309–327.

Punyanunt-Carter, N. M. (2008) "The Perceived Realism of African American Portrayals on Television," *The Howard Journal of Communications* 19(3): 241–257.

Schmader, T., Block, K., and Lickel, B. (2015) "Social Identity Threat in Response to Stereotypic Film Portrayals: Effects on Self-Conscious Emotion and Implicit Ingroup Attitudes," *Journal of Social Issues* 71(1): 54–72.

Signorielli, N. (2009a) "Minorities Representation in Prime Time: 2000 to 2008," *Communication Research Reports* 26(4): 323–336.

———. (2009b) "Race and Sex in Prime Time: A Look at Occupations and Occupational Prestige," *Mass Communication and Society* 12(3): 332–352.

Tan, A., Fujioka, Y., and Lucht, N. (1997) "Native American Stereotypes, TV Portrayals, and Personal Contact," *Journalism & Mass Communication Quarterly* 74(2): 265–284.

Tan, A., Fujioka, Y., and Tan, G. (2000) "Television Use, Stereotypes of African Americans and Opinions on Affirmative Action: An Affective Model of Policy Reasoning," *Communication Monographs* 67(4): 362–371.

Taylor, C. R. and Stern, B. B. (1997) "Asian-Americans: Television Advertising and the 'Model Minority' Stereotype," *Journal of Advertising* 26(7): 47–61.

Tukachinsky, R., Mastro, D., and Yarchi, M. (2015) "Documenting Portrayals of Race/Ethnicity on Primetime Television Over a 20-Year Span and Their Association with National-Level Racial/Ethnic Attitudes," *Journal of Social Issues* 71(1): 17–38.

U.S. Census Briefs. (2010) "Overview of Race and Hispanic Origin: 2010." Retrieved from https://www.census.gov/prod/cen2010/briefs/c2010br-02.pdf.

U.S. Commission on Civil Rights. (1977) *Window Dressing on the Set: Women and Minorities in Television*. Washington, D.C.: U.S. Government.

Ward, L. M. (2004) "Wading Through the Stereotypes: Positive and Negative Associations between Media Use and Black Adolescents' Conceptions of Self," *Developmental Psychology* 40(2): 284–294.

Wilson, C., Gutierrez, F., and Chao, L. (2013) *Racism, Sexism, and the Media*. Thousand Oaks, CA: Sage.

# Further Reading

Behm-Morawitz, E. and Ta, D. (2014) "Cultivating Virtual Stereotypes?: The Impact of Video Game Play on Racial/Ethnic Stereotypes," *Howard Journal of Communications* 25(1): 1–15. (Survey that assesses the relationship between white college students' frequency of video game play and attitudes toward blacks and Asians.)

Dixon, T. L. and Williams, C. L. (2014) "The Changing Misrepresentation of Race and Crime on Network and Cable News," *Journal of Communication* 65(1): 24–39. (Quantitative content analysis of U.S. news coverage examining problematic representations of blacks, Latinos, and Muslims between 2008 and 2012.)

Holtzman, L. and Sharpe, L. (2014) *Media Messages: What Film, Television, and Popular Music Teach Us about Race, Class, Gender, and Sexual Orientation*. New York: M.E. Sharpe, Inc. (Includes a comprehensive examination of the development of film, TV, and pop music as genres, and summarizes relevant effects studies pertaining to race, class, gender, and sexual orientation.)

Mastro, D. E. and Stern, S. R. (2003) "Representations of Race in Television Commercials: A Content Analysis of Prime-Time Advertising," *Journal of Broadcasting & Electronic Media* 47(4): 638–647. (Results from a comprehensive content analysis of depictions of race/ethnicity in primetime television commercials indicating both progress and stagnation for different racial groups.)

# 8
# FILM
## Race and the Cinematic "Machine"
### *Gerald Sim*

As summer began in 2015, the American news media were abuzz, deconstructing Rachel Dolezal. NBC's *The Today Show* scored a scoop by landing the first interview with the former president of the National Association for the Advancement of Colored People (NAACP) chapter in Spokane, Washington. It followed a week of bemusement, trips through the political press's partisan spin cycle, and reflection by prominent black voices. The controversy ignited when Dolezal was outed as a white woman passing as African American with the aid of dark foundation make-up and creative hairstyling. The utter originality of this affair confounded many, and yet no more than a fortnight earlier, the movies were the setting for an analogous brouhaha. Film director Cameron Crowe struggled to answer questions about his choice to cast the phenotypically unambiguous white actress Emma Stone for the romantic comedy, *Aloha* (2015), in the lead role of "Allison Ng," a character who is quarter Hawaiian and quarter Chinese (Jung 2015; Lee 2015). These two news items force us to address some crucial issues of racial epistemology related to essentialism, representation, and history. Is race biologically defined or socially constructed? Rejecting biological essentialism on political and intellectual grounds is strategically understandable, but defining race in purely discursive terms renders Dolezal and Crowe's decisions unproblematic, when according to many, they are plainly not. More importantly, these cases demonstrate how uncannily and often cinema, of all the arts, presents us with a parallel cultural realm to work through social and political dilemmas.

Hollywood was sensitive to the critiques associated with *Aloha*'s casting controversy, which occurred not long after the 2015 Academy Awards, where nominees of color were controversially absent in the major categories (Bakare 2015). The practice of "whitewashing" possesses a long tradition among the industry's most successful and venerated productions. Film history is replete with ignominious examples of white actors portraying characters of color. Cases that seem especially absurd and distasteful these days are the most memorable, including practices of blackface (*The Birth of a Nation*, 1915), brownface (*West Side Story*, 1961), redface (*The Searchers*, 1956) and yellowface (*Breakfast at Tiffany's*, 1958). Questions about "whitewashing" almost always turn on the issue of representation, which can be examined in two respects: participation and accuracy. Casting becomes politicized when hiring decisions discriminate, deny economic opportunity, and impinge on minorities' rights to self-representation (Leab 1975; Shohat and Stam 2014). The phenomenon of white actors playing minority roles also recapitulates whiteness as the hegemonic, race-less norm (Dyer 1997)—the feature of white privilege that emboldened Dolezal's attempt to pass.

We can also understand the need for a more inclusive mode of production as a means to ensure verisimilitude. Another recent controversy suggests that having a say behind the camera is inextricable from ensuring proper representation in front of the lens. Approximately 12 Native American actors walked off the set of a Western, *The Ridiculous Six*, alleging that the script affronted Native women and elders, used make-up to darken Native actors, and misrepresented Apache culture (Schilling 2015; Gardner 2015). While the producers in this case chose not to apologize, Crowe defended himself from the furor surrounding *Aloha* by stating that the project had "employed many Asian-American, Native-Hawaiian and Pacific-Islanders, both before and behind the camera . . . and many other locals who worked closely in our crew and with our script to help ensure authenticity" (Crowe 2015). His claims of cultural realism were an attempt to assuage critics piqued at how a story set in Hawaii features a paucity of ethnic faces. Crowe's public statement and the outcry itself correspond with the terms of public discourse about race, for which the most pressing objectives remain social equality and cultural diversity.

Those political parameters circumscribe cinema as an economic enterprise and cultural mirror. But although the "cinema" refers literally to a motion picture theater, the expression has taken on figurative and metaphorical value. Cinema is also a technological commodity, spectacle, and social institution. Classical film theorists define the medium by its unique power to realistically and objectively capture the world (Arnheim 1957; Bazin 1960; Kracauer 1960). These adherents of "realism" rest their position on the mechanical nature of the camera and projector, as well as the chemical base of the filmstrip. The most notable, André Bazin, lauds how "an image of the world is formed automatically, without the creative intervention of man" (Bazin 1960: 7). However, at a historical juncture when digital cameras and projection systems are steadily pushing film stock into obsolescence, a period when mobile devices are joining television as acceptable alternatives to theatrical spectatorship, the foundations of what we understand cinema or film to be are rapidly shifting and even disappearing. Francesco Casetti, a theorist charting these changes, believes that the medium is "no longer necessarily tied to a single 'machine'" (2015: 5). Rather, it is an idea that persists in new venues, on new screens, and through new platforms.

As discourses and definitions of race shift, so do those that delineate cinema. Within the irresistible gusts of technological development, we are more than ever before cognizant of cinema's multiple and contingent identities, which provide different cultural or social contact points with race. This chapter surveys how each facet of cinema—base and apparatus; stereotypes; textual form; genre; and spectator—has been scrutinized by critical race film studies scholars. Casetti argues that parts of the cinematic "machine," such as the theater, screen, audience, and film, are breaking down and being reassembled elsewhere (68–9). In other words, instead of presenting itself in traditional form, cinema increasingly reincarnates itself partially, psychologically, everywhere, and on all types of screens. If Casetti is right, if our current and future experience of cinema involves only portions of cinema as we still know it, then it would be vital to understand how racial ideology infuses itself into each heterogeneous element.

## Base and Apparatus

"Film," of course, refers to the medium's material base, a celluloid strip of sequential images, and optical soundtracks that run along the edge. In spite of the value Bazin placed in cinema's mechanical and chemical make-up, the technology is never free from human subjectivity. Richard Dyer (1997) explains that cinema is an aesthetic technology, which at key moments of innovation, variation, and refinement assumed whiteness as a norm. Developments in the chemical composition of film stock, processing, aperture adjustments, lighting methods, and make-up practices used the white face as a touchstone. As Dyer observed, "Getting the right image meant getting the one which conformed to the prevalent ideas of humanity . . . of what colour—what range of hue—white people wanted white people to be" (90–1). Dark complexions hence require departures from standard practices deemed as "problems," especially in shots containing both black and white faces (97). It has always been possible to shoot dark faces "properly," as it were, but it only underlines the hierarchy of illumination that allows some people into culture more readily than others (103). The digital transition promises to break that hegemony, however. The ubiquitous use of digital intermediates—a post-production process where color and other image characteristics are digitally adjusted—provides flexibility. Cinematographers working with diverse casts are also discovering that sensors in digital cameras are better able to hold contrasting skin tones simultaneously (Hornaday 2013).

Presumptions carried over from photographic portraiture are not the only part of cinema that conforms to Eurocentric conceptions of humanity. The Renaissance perspective of the camera's image may also be considered ideological. An eminent essay by Jean-Louis Baudry traces the perspective and aspect ratio of the film image back to the camera obscura and Western painting (Baudry 1974/5). He argues that the single vanishing point sets up the viewer as a transcendental subject, an "active center and origin of meaning" (40). Reinforced through centuries of artistic practice over the style of, say, Chinese and Japanese painting, the interpellation has normalized vision and perspective in animated films and videogames. Baudry adds that subjectivity is specifically strengthened in cinema by the illusion of movement created by projection, and classical continuity editing that prioritizes narrative unity and cohesion (42–4). Baudry's critique is not directly concerned with race, and to interpret the essay as such requires us to lasso together the Renaissance, the Enlightenment, Eurocentrism, and white supremacy. But that conflation is not uncommon in critical race film theory, namely those rooted in postcolonial studies such as Homi Bhabha's (1983) that values split or mixed subjectivity over the unified subject of the Enlightenment.

## Stereotypes

Studying race through each constitutive part of cinema inverts the more familiar strategy with which Anglo-American film studies navigates the relationship between race and films. The field usually approaches the question through race, and subdivides the inquiry into sections devoted to different social groups' encounters with movies, to wit, "according to the formation of race and ethnicity in U.S. culture more widely, . . . the discrete histories and political projects of specific identity sites: African American, Asian American, Chicano-Latino American, Native American, Jewish American, Italian American, and

Irish American" (Wiegman 1998: 158). The limits of this methodology come from how it complies with identity politics and strengthens ethnic disciplinary boundaries at the expense of cultivating collective consciousness and action (Sim 2014: 44–56). Some see multiculturalism as an antidote to the drawbacks to identity-driven criticism (Wiegman 1998: 166–7; Shohat and Stam 2014), but I contend that the ideology actually facilitates sectarian divisions. In any event, despite the occasional exception, identitarian studies also tend to treat cinema too simplistically. Their focus dwells on how films reinforce stereotypes—when they depict racial minorities in negative, regressive, disrespectful ways. The importance of "image studies" remains undiminished because stereotypes evolve and ideology finds new ways to perpetuate prejudice and vice versa. And the widespread readiness by the public to condemn derogatory characterizations is without question a credit to that fruitful and longstanding mode of racially conscious film criticism. Following this chapter, I direct interested readers to a useful selection of such work for "Further Reading." But there is much more to think about than how a race is represented in one film or another.

Perhaps the earliest and most lucid declaration of film studies' need to develop more sophisticated methods for race comes from a 1979 essay in *Screen Education*, where Steve Neale lays out a case on theoretical, practical, political, and textual grounds. Negative stereotypes are most commonly criticized for being reductive and not matching up with the complexities of reality. But Neale points out that critiques of inaccuracy presume, against the theoretical trends in the humanities, that reality is empirically knowable. One could easily, for instance, take exception to the Black Panthers caricatured in *Forrest Gump* (1994), but we must also be prepared to offer a different history and more progressive account without insisting on definitiveness. Paradoxically, stereotype analysis usually implies that films should replace negative images with positive ones that are equally reductive, in effect thrusting onto cinema a responsibility to depict reality not as it is, but as it should be (Neale 1979). Moreover, positive images are usually influenced by bourgeois ideals or capitalist ideology (Neale 1979; Shohat and Stam 2014). For example, Sidney Poitier's iconic role as Dr. John Prentice in *Guess Who's Coming to Dinner* (1967) embodies those values. Finally, Neale finds that image analysis expends too much "concentration on character and characterization at the expense of attention to textual systems and modes of address" (35). That is to say, it may examine specific images in isolation when film meaning invariably emerges from many formal elements interacting with each other in a textual assembly of images and sounds.

Simplistic image analysis becomes less useful to critics more familiar with the complexity in film language. Consider the difference between two seminal works in the field, Edward Said's *Orientalism* (1978) and Ella Shohat and Robert Stam's *Unthinking Eurocentrism* (1994). *Orientalism*, a foundational book in postcolonial studies, is a product of Michel Foucault's intellectual influence on ideas about power and discourse. When Said links colonial projects to the racially inflected art and literature produced by colonizing powers, his textual readings evince sensitivity to discursive nuance as well as his background in comparative literature. But when discussing cinema, Said does not interpret films with the depth that Neale believes is necessary. Shohat and Stam, who draw direct connections between racial ideology in cinema, the function of Otherness in colonial narratives, and the economic and political base of imperial rule, agree with Said on the material context for racism. But as film scholars, they complement an extensive global survey of postcolonial media culture with an impetus to expand Said's premise, and succeed in accommodating "the multiplicity of [film] systems and operations" (Neale 1979: 33).

## Textual Form

Characters in film function in a visual and narrative context. They are framed with other characters and within the "diegesis," an analytical term used in film studies to refer to the world of the film. Multiple images are edited together, then layered with sound and music, to advance a plot. Through these means, filmmakers manufacture a film's intellectual or emotional tone, which can shift rapidly from one moment to the next. Each of these aspects of film form—shot composition, shot relations, sound, and music—follows a rather distinct discursive structure. The narrative text that results from their intermingling produces what Shohat and Stam summarize as "point-of-view"—how spectators grasp a character. They describe these variables contributing to the film's ideological message as "the question of perspective and the social positioning both of the filmmakers and the audience" (Shohat and Stam 2014: 205).

As a hermeneutic component, film music is ideologically tinged. Scoring conventions that establish location frequently borrow from cultural associations. But while rhythmic, harmonic, tonal, and instrumentational differences exist between cultures, musical codes are often simplistic and stereotypical. Few among us would "misinterpret" mariachi music or Oriental riffs even if we recognize their crudeness as narrative devices. Race is further implicated in film music's emotional significations. Jazz, for instance, represents "the urban, the sexual, and the decadent in a musical idiom perceived in the culture at large as an indigenous black form" (Kalinak 1992: 167). Hugo Friedhofer's music for *The Young Lions* (1958) illustrates this racial coding lucidly. The jazzy waltz associated with actor Marlon Brando's encounter with a provocative seductress contrasts with the fuller, more harmonic music signifying deeper emotions for his scenes with a woman he loves (Burt 1994: 18–21).

Music and montage (or editing) position spectators within the narrative geographically and socially. The camera's location and point of view places audiences in specific spots in the diegesis. When the Comanches raid the Edwards homestead in the introductory act of *The Searchers* (1956), the camera is within the house. As a result, we view the attack as a member of the Edwards family. The audience only sees the Comanches at a great distance, from inside the home and alongside the people under attack. Viewers also take on an emotional perspective. Atonal musical notes convey fear of the unknown. We witness panic start to grip the family, and are cued to feel their terror. Spectators thus develop a clear rooting interest in the situation. By the time we finally see the villainous chief Scar at the end of the scene, it is difficult to come away from his visage without feeling the Edwards family's visceral fear of the violent, sexual threat presented by the Other.

This is the sort of social positioning that Gillo Pontevcorvo contravenes in his famous anti-colonial film about the French-Algerian war, *The Battle of Algiers* (1967). The director, according to Engelhardt (1971), inverts an "imagery of encirclement" and, as Stam and Spence have observed, "the identificatory mechanisms of cinema on behalf of the colonised rather than the coloniser" (1983: 12–13). He relocates the camera to take a socially opposite viewpoint. Shohat and Stam spotlight a key scene where a group of Algerian women, colonized racial Others, are framed in close-up as they prepare a terrorist action. Underneath, images that install our point of view with them through spatial proximity, off-screen voices of French soldiers uttering sexist slurs impose a point of audition. Even without political context, the sequence is constructed to engender sympathy with killers and a reverse-Eurocentric perspective. As Shohat and Stam write, "It makes us *want* the women to complete their task" (2014: 253).

## Mode of Address: Genre

Cinema also affects perspective and positioning through its mode of address, a term derived from semiotics for the relationship that a film constructs for spectators. A powerful and noteworthy determinant of mode of address is genre, a bone of contention in a few recent controversies. In comedies and science fiction, for example, generic adjustments to normal expectations of realism can serve to defend against racism accusations. Netflix, the company that released the controversial *The Ridiculous Six*, defended the 2015 film in a news release: "The movie has 'ridiculous' in the title for a reason—because it's ridiculous. It is a broad satire of western movies and the stereotypes they popularized, featuring a diverse cast that is not only part of—but in on—the joke" (Gardner 2015: n.p.). Indeed, comedy theory broadly accepts the wisdom that critical if not emotional distance is a prerequisite condition for humor. The racial stereotyping in a satirical film such as *Blazing Saddles* (1974) is clearly not supposed to be taken literally. A film can also modify its address abruptly. In Spike Lee's drama, *Bamboozled* (2000), the commercial spoofs for "Da Bomb" malt liquor and "Timmy Hilnigger" clothes wield a sharp satirical edge, but the jokes require viewers to reset the terms of their narrative engagement with very little warning. In short, mode of address is an important determinant of what constitutes satire, but its subjectivity can absolve filmmakers of ideological responsibility.

Science fiction imposes a similar effect on cinematic realism. Spectatorial willingness to suspend disbelief abets the genre's reliance on fantasy. It liberates writers wishing to explore contemporary dilemmas from the limits of earthly reality, including those constraining open racial discourse. According to Ed Guerrero, race is a matter of "ongoing construction and contestation" that science fiction often works through "in many symbolic, cinematic forms of expression, but particularly in . . . abundant racialized metaphors and allegories" (1993: 41, 55–6). However, critics also point out that bodies of color are often mired in films "as a nexus of difference and danger." The eponymous monster in *Predator* (1987), for example, wears dreadlocks, evokes colonial ethnographic imagery, and is accompanied by African drumming on the soundtrack (Nama 2008: 75–6). At the same time, sci-fi realism affords creators plausible deniability. More than one installment of *Star Wars*, arguably the most profitable film series in history, has been charged with racial stereotyping. The customary defense mounted by both creator George Lucas and his production company Lucasfilm is that the fantasy films have no basis in reality (Okwu 1999; Hodges 2002).

That rhetorical parry does not nullify criticism, but it enjoys traction among skeptical publics. Indeed, commercial cinema itself has economic and institutional reasons to resist change. It will always be more tempting and convenient not to challenge ideological status quos because film productions are risk-averse business ventures that rely on institutions with great inertia. It is therefore understandable that radical material finds refuge in alternative genres such as avant-garde and independent cinema. Non-narrative films, experimental documentaries in particular, are often the most welcoming venues for filmmakers to question racial assumptions and epistemologies. Poststructuralist redefinitions of race's political, discursive, and performative contingencies inform the work of Marlon Riggs, Tracy Moffatt, Trinh T. Minh-Ha, and others (see Nichols 1993; Morris 2006; Trinh 1989). And in between mainstream cinema and experimental film sit the independent work of Julie Dash and Wayne Wang.

## Spectators

Regardless of how a film crafts its mode of address, in the end it can only provide interpretive cues because meaning is ultimately generated by spectators in the act of reading. Although ideology most insidiously interpellates subalterns into accepting the underpinnings of their own subjugation, audiences of color inevitably bring to their film experiences knowledge and awareness of their own Otherness. Reception studies posit that socially marginalized groups with life experiences incongruent with the ideal spectator's do not passively accept racist or colonialist representations of the world. Uncommon cultural awareness alienates spectators from the text, and lead to "a complex process of negotiation" (Bobo 1995: 3), whereby they generate "aberrant" (Shohat and Stam 1983: 352; Stam and Spence 1983: 18), "oppositional" (Reid 1995: 25), or resistive (Diawara 1988: 66) readings. These studies' conclusions are either hypothetical (based on a scholar's own analysis of film texts) or empirically driven (using audience surveys and interviews). The latter was motivated by the need to explore "how nonacademic readers actually make sense of texts" (Bobo 1995: 23), beyond merely assuming how readers use the cultural product (Shively 1992: 726).

Real readers invariably reveal that they respond to racial ideology ambivalently, and often in surprising and counterintuitive ways. For example, sociologist JoEllen Shively's research discovers that Native Americans, a group whose embodiment of uncivilized savagery in the Western originates from the genre's roots in Frederick Jackson Turner's "frontier thesis," in fact identify with the films' fantasy of freedom, independence, and affinity with the land (1992: 733). Donald Bogle similarly believes that African-American spectators appreciated the skill and subversive nous that black performers brought to denigrating roles (Bogle 1973). And while curiosity toward African-American reception of African-American films seems somewhat natural, it is equally productive to think about why black audiences gravitated to the martial arts genre in the 1970s (Desser 2000; Cha-Jua 2008).

As a whole, reception studies attempt in one form or other to establish cultural or political agency within a media landscape marked by Eurocentrism and white supremacy. The impetus drives the narrative of Jacqueline Stewart's *Migrating to the Movies* (2005), an account of early twentieth-century black film culture that shows how African-American audiences politicized their experiences in all-black movie theaters and translated that engagement into film production. The conditions of film spectatorship are, of course, currently in a radical phase of transformation. For now, theatrical exhibition is still far from extinct and remains a vital part of most films' economic life, but audiences are becoming increasingly accustomed to watching movies at home or on mobile platforms. The trend is reflected in recent work on virtual communities of film viewers, who gather online to discuss topics such as the Asian identities of biracial actors (Nishime 2005). Desire for agency unites audience research and historical work about minority film production.

The digital era offers optimism to those who believe that controlling the creative process is a critical precondition of agency, or that filmmakers' relationships to the mode of production define their creative identity (Reid 1993; Feng 2002: 7–8). In the minds of many, digital cinema democratizes film culture, since it makes all phases of cinema—production, distribution, and exhibition—cheaper and more accessible. The mournful eulogies emanating from traditionalists for the death of film are often overwhelmed by the celebratory discourse of others who embrace digital cinema and new media. Consider the criticism of the whitewashed casting in *Aloha*, which was amplified by the Internet and drew the filmmaker to respond online. Those frustrations were alleviated, somewhat ironically, through the idealistic promises of posthumous cinema.

## References

Arnheim, R. (1957) *Film as Art*. Berkeley, CA: University of California Press.
Bakare, L. (2015, Feb. 19) "Oscars Whitewash: Why Have 2015's Red Carpets Been so Overwhelmingly White?," *The Guardian*. Retrieved from http://www.theguardian.com/culture/2015/feb/19/the-great-awards-whitewash-diversity-loses-out-on-the-red-carpets.
Baudry, J. L. (1974/5) "Ideological Effects of the Basic Cinematographic Apparatus," trans. A. Williams, *Film Quarterly* 28(2): 39–47.
Bazin, A. (1960) "The Ontology of the Photographic Image," trans. H. Gray, *Film Quarterly* 13(4): 4–9.
Bhabha, H. (1983) "The Other Question . . ." *Screen* 24(6): 18–36.
Bobo, J. (1995) *Black Women as Cultural Readers*. New York: Columbia University Press.
Bogle, D. (1973) *Toms, Coons, Mulattoes, Mammies, and Bucks: An Interpretive History of Blacks in American Films*. New York: Viking Press.
Burt, G. (1994) *The Art of Film Music*. Boston, MA: Northeastern University Press.
Casetti, F. (2015) *The Lumiere Galaxy: 7 Key Words for the Cinema to Come*. New York: Columbia University Press.
Cha-Jua, S. K. (2008) "Black Audiences, Blaxploitation and Kung Fu Films, and Challenges to White Celluloid Masculinity," in P. Fu (ed.), *China Forever: The Shaw Brothers and Diasporic Cinema*. Chicago and Urbana, IL: University of Illinois Press, 199–223.
Crowe, C. (2015) "A Comment on Allison Ng," *The Uncool: The Official Website for Everything Cameron Crowe*, June 2. Retrieved from http://www.theuncool.com/2015/06/02/a-comment-on-allison-ng/.
Desser, D. (2000) "The Kung Fu Craze: Hong Kong Cinema's First American Reception," in P. Fu and D. Desser (eds.), *The Cinema of Hong Kong: History, Arts, Identity*. Cambridge, UK: Cambridge University Press, 19–43.
Diawara, M. (1988) "Black Spectatorship: Problems of Identification and Difference," *Screen* 29(4): 66–79.
Dyer, R. (1997) *White*. New York: Routledge.
Engelhardt, T. (1971) "Ambush at Kamikaze Pass," *Bulletin of Concerned Asian Scholars* 3(1): 65–84.
Feng, P. X. (2002) *Identities in Motion: Asian American Film and Video*. Durham, NC: Duke University Press.
Gardner, C. (2015, May 1) "Adam Sandler's 'Ridiculous Six': Makeup Pros Darkening Actors' Skin to Make Them Appear Native American, Says Source," *The Hollywood Reporter*. Retrieved from http://www.hollywoodreporter.com/news/adam-sandlers-ridiculous-six-makeup-792582.
Guerrero, E. (1993) *Framing Blackness: The African American Image in Film*. Philadelphia, PA: Temple University Press.
Hodges, M. H. (2002, May 18) "Critics Say 'Clones' has Racial Stereotypes," *The Detroit News*. Retrieved from http://www.screamingpickle.com/members/SW/detroit_racist_panel_episode_II.htm.
Hornaday, A. (2013, Oct. 17) "'12 Years a Slave,' 'Mother of George,' and the Aesthetic Politics of Filming Black Skin," *The Washington Post*. Retrieved from http://wapo.st/H6NsBi.
Jung, E. A. (2015, June 1) "Casting Emma Stone as Allison Ng in *Aloha* Should Have Been a Great White *Nope*," *Vulture*. Retrieved from http://www.vulture.com/2015/06/emma-stone-played-an-asian-american-in-aloha.html.
Kalinak, K. (1992) *Settling the Score: Music and the Classical Hollywood Film*. Madison, WI: University of Wisconsin Press.
Kracauer, S. (1960) *Theory of Film: The Redemption of Physical Reality*. New York: Oxford University Press.
Leab, D. J. (1975) *From Sambo to Superspade: The Black Experience in Motion Pictures*. Boston, MA: Houghton Mifflin.
Lee, C. (2015, May 29) "I'm Not Buying Emma Stone as an Asian-American in *Aloha*," *Entertainment Weekly*. Retrieved from http://www.ew.com/article/2015/05/29/im-not-buying-emma-stone-asian-american.
Morris, M. (2006) *Identity Anecdotes: Translation and Media Culture*. London: Sage Publications.

Nama, A. (2008) *Black Space: Imagining Race in Science Fiction Film*. Austin, TX: University of Texas Press.
Neale, S. (1979/80) "The Same Old Story: Stereotypes and Difference," *Screen Education* 32/3: 33–7.
Nichols, B. (1993) "'Getting to Know You. . .,' Knowledge, Power, and the Body," in M. Renov (ed.), *Theorizing Documentary*. New York: Routledge, 49–54.
Nishime, L. (2005) "Guilty Pleasures: Keanu Reeves, Superman, and Racial Outing," in S. Davé, L. Nishime, and T. G. Oren (eds.), *East Main Street: Asian American Popular Culture*. New York: New York University Press, 273–291.
Okwu, M. (1999, June 14) "Jar Jar Jarring," *CNN*. Retrieved from http://www.cnn.com/SHOWBIZ/Movies/9906/09/jar.jar/#3.
Reid, M. (1993) *Redefining Black Film*. Berkeley, CA: University of California Press.
Said, E. (1978) *Orientalism*. New York: Vintage Books.
Schilling, V. (2015, April 23) "Native Actors Walk off Set of Adam Sandler Movie after Insults to Women, Elders," *Indian Country Today*. Retrieved from http://ictmn.com/4ZpU.
Shively, J. (1992) "Cowboys and Indians: Perceptions of Western Films among American Indians and Anglos," *American Sociological Review* 57(6): 725–734.
Shohat, E. and R. Stam (2014) *Unthinking Eurocentrism: Multiculturalism and the Media*. New York: Routledge.
Sim, G. (2014) *The Subject of Film and Race: Retheorizing Politics, Ideology, and Cinema*. New York: Bloomsbury Academic.
Stam, R. and Spence, L. (1983) "Racism, Colonialism and Representation," *Screen* 24(2): 2–20.
Stewart, J. N. (2005) *Migrating to the Movies: Cinema and Black Urban Modernity*. Berkeley, CA: University of California Press.
Trinh, T. M. (1989) *Woman, Native, Other*. Bloomington, IN: Indiana University Press.
Wiegman, R. (1998) "Race, Ethnicity, and Film," in J. Hill and P. C. Gibson (eds.), *The Oxford Guide to Film Studies*. New York: Oxford University Press, 158–175.

## Further Reading

Berg, C. R. (2002) *Latino Images in Film: Stereotypes, Subversion, Resistance*. Austin, TX: University of Texas Press.
Cripps, T. (1977) *Slow Fade to Black: The Negro in American Film, 1900–1942*. New York: Oxford University Press.
Rollins, P. (2011) *Hollywood's Indian: The Portrayal of the Native American in Film*. Lexington, KY: University Press of Kentucky.
Xing, J. (1998) *Asian America Through the Lens: History, Representations, and Identity*. Walnut Creek, CA: AltaMira Press.
(As their titles suggest, these four books offer overviews of racial stereotypes in film.)

# 9
# POPULAR MUSIC
## Translating Race and Genre from Ethnic to Epic

*Paul Linden*

> Singers and songs are like seeds; they follow a large migration. When people leave their country and go on migrations, usually they take their stock of seeds and songs with them. I like the idea of people singing a song and then putting their own stamp on it and then passing it on like a tool.
>
> Tom Waits (1993)

To this point in the development of the scholarly study of the popular music industry, the most compelling, complete, and focused treatment of race and the music business remains a collection of chapters from Keith Negus' two books, *Popular Music in Theory* and *Music Genres and Corporate Cultures*. Negus' position relies on two points: that meaning in popular music is mediated by identity and that identity is subject to constant social negotiation. While the idea of identity as social performance dates back to the 1950s (Goffman 1959), Negus' analysis of race and music also benefits from the subsequent development of social construction theory (Berger and Luckman 1966; Romàn-Velàzquez 1996; Stokes 1994). Negus considers race and genre as categories that mediate between individual, ready-made social constructs on one hand and the variability of socio-cultural contexts on the other. It is from this position that Negus attacks essentialism as one of the traditional, ethno-musicological approaches to race. If essentialism seeks to locate specific musical elements or motifs as authentically "black" or "Latino," etc., Negus conversely argues that blues, salsa, or reggae are genres that support the social construction of musical as well as racial identities.

In this chapter, Negus' position is an important starting point due to its assertion that meaning in music is negotiable and therefore not fixed. The following pages consider the corporate production and reproduction of popular music as a process of translation. The concept of translation serves as a way to articulate various forces driving and informing this core issue of music's ability to acquire new significance based on its socio-cultural context. Just as the Tom Waits quote above points to the impact of migration upon the meaning or value of a given community's musical stock, the economic interests of corporate entities such as the radio industry and record companies inscribe new meaning into music. For example, how does Jamaican reggae music prior to 1970 mean something different from the global version found later in the decade? If, as Georgina Born and David Hesmondhalgh (2000) assert, "a music's construction of its own identity may involve the exclusion or repudiation of another music," we will ask how developing genres exclude or repudiate some part of themselves. As a given genre is pushed to grow from ethnic to epic, what is lost in translation?

## Rebranding of Black Music in America

In this section, we will look at the birth of rock 'n' roll and the rebranding of rap as hip-hop as instances in the development of what has been labeled "black music" in America. The plight of black forms of popular music (such as the blues and r&b) at the dawn of the rock 'n' roll era reveals a great deal regarding race and power in the music business. The movement of these musical forms from the margins to the mainstream of the music business signifies the role of record labels as mediators of provincial music trends and larger socio-cultural norms. As Mike Rowe explains in his book *Chicago Blues: The Music and City*, the story of the great migration grounds the figurative development in the historical reality of migrant communities.[1] The cultural and artistic implications of this exodus support the generally accepted claim that Chicago blues is the electrified permutation of Delta blues that, in turn, contributed to the formation of rock 'n' roll (George 1998; Marcus 2008; Peterson 1990). Initially grounded in the experience of oppression and poverty shared by rural laborers, the blues now boasts its own iconography within the wider entertainment industry. Contemporary Hollywood movies like *Crossroads* and *O Brother Where Art Thou?* use the icon of the nomadic bluesman hoboing with his stock of songs to convey grassroots yet streetwise authenticity across a wide demographic. While the story of the blues locates migration as an element of cultural translation, how does it respond to our larger inquiry regarding how the music business works to rearrange the meaning of the music?

In the case of rock 'n' roll and its debt to the blues, the coronation of rock's king—Elvis Presley—is an important moment of cultural translation. A major division exists in the scholarly appraisal of Elvis with respect to black music in particular. Bound by a predominant black–white binarism, one group criticizes Elvis as a representative of opportunistic white artists who achieved success by virtue of re-recording or "covering" black artists (Altschuler 2003; George 1998; Jefferson 1973; Southern 1971). In contrast, a second group uses socio-economic and musicological perspectives to re-appraise this earlier position (Bertrand 2000; Garofalo 1993; Linden 2012; Marcus 2008). This latter group uses social caste and hegemony to critique the idea that disenfranchisement in the music business is primarily a racial issue. Instead, these studies consider the primacy of power relationships separating creative from corporate communities. From this perspective, Elvis joins a host of other artists of various races and genres all united by record company mismanagement of artist royalties. In other words, as I've argued, "The lines of division are not drawn strictly by race, but by the location of an individual within the hierarchy of power, ownership, and control" (Linden 2012: 46). Paraphrasing George Lipsitz, Michael Bertrand adds, "If the popular music establishment had to accept the fad, it would ensure that only one 'Rock and Roll' revolutionary from outside the mainstream received corporate clout and a national forum from which to articulate the music's working-class message" (Bertrand 2000: 80). Within a year following his record deal with RCA, Elvis' interviews show an active and focused whitewashing of his image:

> I don't smoke and I don't drink, and I love to go to movies. Maybe someday I'm gonna have a home and a family of my own, and I'm not gonna budge from it. I was an only child but maybe my kids won't be.
>
> *(Presley 1957)*

Despite Bertrand's argument that Elvis' affinity for blues music was more a reflection of his social caste than of some pre-meditated posturing, his major-label makeover leaves little doubt that the image of "the king" was in fact the result of strategic forethought. While the above quote signifies wholesome values, it is also an effort to overwrite or erase the troublesome image mixing gyrating hips with the sounds of black music. As such, it is a commercial re-packaging of the artist designed for mainstream appeal.

Even in its repackaged form, rock 'n' roll remained disruptive to the music business as it impacted labels, broadcasters, and concert promoters. Over the course of the 1950s, the major labels' decision to pass on what they saw as the new fad of rock 'n' roll resulted in their loss of control of the record market. By the end of the decade, the majors had gone from owning 78 percent of record sales to 24 percent, ceding their dominance to independent labels like Chess, VeeJay, and Specialty (Hull 2004: 123). Given that handling rock 'n' roll in the 1950s implicated the dual taboos of sex and race, the majors' need to quickly regain control was risky. Prior to Elvis, it was convenient for mainstream 1950s America to write off sexually suggestive music as a sort of black aberration. With the loss of their market share, the recording industry establishment began to use radio and concert programming to reach out to the previously overlooked black community. By 1960, scandals involving prominent DJs, concert promoters, TV producers, and record companies revealed the corporate structures overseeing the mainstream recording industry were unable to keep from abusive exploitation, including that of the "race" market.[2]

While the issue of race clearly takes a back seat to the larger issue of profit, it is important to recognize the hegemonic subjugation of the working class—including its significant minority population—as a component of mainstream success. In the case of rock 'n' roll, there are numerous of examples of black authors whose compositions were overshadowed after being covered and re-released by white mainstream artists. Examples include "Shake, Rattle and Roll" (Bill Haley, 1954 from Jesse Stone, 1953); "Rocket 88" (Bill Haley, 1952 from Ike Turner, 1951); "A Little Bird Told Me" (Evelyn Knight, 1948 from Paula Watson, 1947); and "Sh-Boom" (the Crew Cuts, 1954 from the Chords, 1952). In all of these instances, the cover version would place near the top of the more lucrative pop music charts while the original versions might reach the less lucrative r&b charts. In these cases, authorship, royalties, and the visibility of the original artist's brand would suffer as the musical form crossed over from r&b into the mainstream.

## From Rap to Hip-Hop

Many of these same forces resurface in Byron Hurt's documentary that examines rap music, *Hip Hop: Beyond Beats and Rhymes*. This documentary indicates how rap's movement from an independent distribution network to subsequent incorporation into major record labels impacts its overall message. Not unlike the example of blues/r&b and rock 'n' roll, Hurt shows that majors also repackaged rap as a mainstream genre. To better understand this as a process of translation, consider the shifting lyrical content of songs within the genre. In the 1980s and early 1990s, rap conveyed a diversity of messages including the anti-violence of "Self Destruction" (Stop the Violence Movement) and the cautionary "Children's Story" (Slick Rick) to the gritty "Message" (Grand Master Flash) and misogynist "Wild Thing" (Ton Loc). Collecting testimonies of young black rappers in Chicago, Hurt shows that the transition from early rap to mainstream gangsta-rap mirrors the transition from rap as an independent label product to the corporate buyout of those labels by the majors. One of the young hopefuls interviewed by Hurt puts it like this: "They don't give us deals when we speak righteously, they think we don't want to hear that" (Hurt 2006). Cultural critic Mark A. Neal offers another summary:

> When you're talking to these young rappers, the most important thing for them is to get a record deal . . . and what they're hearing from the record companies is that "there are only certain examples of blackness that we're going to let flow through this space."
>
> *(Quoted in Hurt 2006)*

Hurt's exposé reveals that the takeover of rap by major media outlets resulted in a narrowing of the lyrical content to heavily misogynistic and violent themes. As former Def-Jam President Carmen Ashurst Watson puts it, "The time when we switched to 'gangsta' music is the same time that the majors bought up all the [independent] labels; and I don't think that's a coincidence" (quoted in Hurt 2006). Hurt's interviews are powerful indicators of how popular music forms can be subject to a semantic overhaul in the course of their commercial development.

Given that major-label affiliation means mainstream circulation, the shift to "gangsta" rap also coincides with the fact that the music was selling to mainstream consumers. This equation is clearly suggestive of how sex and violence can be used to construct a version of what rappers are supposed to be like that would entice the suburban white imagination. Hurt shows that connecting to mainstream white audiences coincides with a degree of disconnection with the experiences of young rappers on the street, its original community. The "gangsta" identity is thus a corporate construct ostensibly used by major labels to increase sales, but with the added result of alienating blacks as well. Negus shows how majors maintain corporate hegemony by tactics that amount to differential treatment of their hip-hop divisions either through violent corporate rhetoric or a general lack of resources. A case in point is Capitol records' decision to name their rap promotion unit "Capitol Punishment" as well as their use of other war-like metaphors like "snipers," "commanders," and "wardens" to describe their rap unit or its associated "street teams." Combined with under-investment in rap divisions, these metaphors constitute a mode of address that pre-figures a particular type of relationship linking major labels, rap music, and ultimately the perception of the consumers (Negus 1999: 97).

The example of translating rap deviates from that of rock 'n' roll and blues in that black artists remain visibly associated with the music, but their creative control is stripped and reduced to only singing about a limited number of themes.

### *Salsa*: Immigration and Translation

In his study, "Popular Music in Puerto Rico: Toward an Anthology of *Salsa*," Jorge Duany argues for a Puerto-Rican, as opposed to Cuban, reference point for the provenance of *salsa*. According to Duany, *salsa* has profound ties to the communal identity of working-class Puerto-Rican immigrants he refers to as a "semi-nomadic population, perpetually in transit between its homeland and exile" (Duany 1984: 197). To speak of *salsa* as a form of popular music in translation, then, it is necessary to bear in mind the ties that *salsa* articulates between this migrant community and its homeland. In this context, the music does not signify the homeland as such, but the experience of being uprooted, the continuous loss of homeland. It follows that *salsa* lays greater claim on the identity of this migrant community than we find in the other groups and genres in this study. This stronger tie works to resist *salsa*'s translation into the mainstream. Without endorsing an essentialist perspective, reading *salsa* in this way benefits from extra focus on the particularities of its native context. In the absence of a stable geographical reference point for generating an identity, immigrant Puerto-Rican communities use *salsa* as an assertive, self-affirming declaration of identity.

From this perspective, the effects of migration upon cultural art forms include new opportunities that did not exist in the homeland, such as the ability to voice political concerns. In the case of *salsa*, both Duany and Felix Padilla reveal tensions that arise from this scenario (Padilla 1990; Duany 1984). While the music industry has interest in the effort to reconfigure *salsa* for commercial exploitation, the migrant Puerto-Rican musicians responsible for bringing the music to the US understand an additional, political significance. These musicians maintain a vital relationship with the live performance as a public platform to directly address Latino consciousness and their own geographic and social mobility. As Negus indicates, "During the late 1960s and early 1970s, *salsa* became integral to the cultural political agenda of activists struggling for social, economic and political recognition in the Americas and Caribbean" (Negus 1999: 131).

While not exclusively bound to either the commercial or political context, it is useful to see the malleability of the status of *salsa* music as a signifying cultural artifact as it shifts in translation. From the transplant Puerto-Rican perspective, the commercial and artistic levels are largely conflated by the need to speak to the sorrows and dreams of a working-class barrio life. However, the commercial effort to re-package *salsa* by record labels has been described as removing the proletarian aggression from the earlier form (*salsa caliente*) and replacing it with a sentimental, feminized version (*salsa romantica*) also referred to as "ketchup" or "*salsa* lite" (Manuel 1995: 283). While it stands to reason that members of the original, migrant community tend to dismiss the modernized version of what they once claimed as their music, Margaret Ramirez reminds us that corporate co-optation also results in new audiences. In the case of *salsa romantica*, the genre's reception develops—at least from a financial perspective—"from an older, blue collar, Spanish-speaking population to a younger, bilingual market" (Ramirez 1996: B5).

Standard major-label distribution models demonstrate the tensions inherent in trying to translate the meaning of *salsa* between the native and corporate contexts. As Negus indicates, there is a frequent breakdown in these U.S. labels' ability to re-constitute or even reach *salsa*'s original, blue-collar communities. Labels attempting to distribute Latin music the way they distribute their mainstream records suffer from many of the differences separating Latin and U.S. cultures. Negus finds that the majority of Latin divisions at major labels are unable to communicate with the distribution division that, in turn, lacks the specialist knowledge of the target culture needed when approaching Latin music retailers. He shows how Sony records successfully avoided this situation "as the only major record company which has, for many years, maintained a separate Latin distribution system, Sony Discos" (Negus 1999: 143). This rare, functional model reveals corporate co-optation of distribution as one stumbling block for U.S.-based major labels trying to reach Latin markets. Just as we have seen with hip-hop divisions, major labels typically marginalize their Latin ones. In the case of *salsa*, however, problems of translation are quite literal as demands for greater support and investment result in the standard response to "sing in English."

POPULAR MUSIC

## **Mainstreaming Reggae**

Reggae music provides another example of a genre whose signification shifts as migrant Jamaican communities bring their stock of songs to the UK in the post-WWII rebuilding effort. In this context, reggae music is imported as part of the larger Jamaican culture and subsequently incorporated into the growing British recording industry. Stuart Watts' 2009 documentary *Keep On Runnin': 50 Years of Island Records* shows how Island Records laid its foundation in selling Jamaican music to Jamaican transplants. Watts uses interviews with artists and businessmen to show how Island developed its niche. Jamaican ex-patriot Count Prince Miller recounts, "Can you imagine? You just leave Jamaica, you leave the Ska, and when it came, it was like a godsend! Every house had it." British music executive Tom Hayes echoes that thought: "Music to Jamaicans was the same as groceries to us . . . . Whatever their weekly wage was, part of [it] was for music." Between 1960 and 1964, Island Records continued to gain market share, most dramatically following Millie Smalls' hit "My Boy Lollipop." Island founder Chris Blackwell's account of Smalls' return to Jamaica after her first international tour provides some perspective on her success:

> I recall when Millie's motorcade came to the hotel where her mother was waiting for her, and Millie came out and walked towards her mother and her mother curtsied to her. When I saw that, I thought "oh my lord!" Her mother felt so far away from her. Up to that moment, I thought I had done a great job for her, but then I wasn't sure.
>
> (Watts 2012)

This anecdote reveals that the effect of "othering" imparted by the machinery of the music business was powerful enough to reverse the order of the nuclear family. Instead of demanding the respect of her daughter, Millie's mother abandons it as if the daughter had come from another, royal family. In the current context, this observation suggests an analogy between family relationships and those at work on a wider social level. In so doing, it helps us recognize how commercial success can be disruptive to identity on the levels of the individual, the family, and larger social communities.

In less than a decade, Island Records entered into direct competition with the major labels. By 1970, it had grown into the largest independent label in the UK with artists like Cat Stevens and Bob Marley selling more records than many major-label artists. As one of Island's top acts of the 1970s, Bob Marley exemplifies the translation of reggae from a provincial to a mainstream music genre. In the hands of Island Records, Marley's traditional reggae sound was updated. As Island artist representative Richard Williams put it, "It's very hard now to conceive how unfashionable reggae was with the rock audience in the 1970s, it's not exaggerated to say it was despised, really, really loathed, and clearly Blackwell and Island were interested in changing that perception" (Watts 2009). In many ways, Blackwell's career up to the mid-1970s was an investment in bringing positive visibility to reggae culture, through records, film, and artist development.[3] With Marley, however, Blackwell drew on his earlier success introducing the electric guitar as a lead instrument into the context of reggae for the first time.[4] This innovation not only sonically re-imagined the Wailers as a black rock group, it also helped move the group from the provincial market of reggae music onto the lucrative rock charts.

So how far had reggae come? What was this antecedent, underground form of the music, its social context, and the meaning of the music in that context? Andrew Kopkind responds to these questions with his definition of reggae:

> [Reggae is] a percussive beat and a melodic line of music, but by extension a social and artistic movement that expressed the Jamaican mood of suffering, blackness and heavenly peace. [Its] lyrics say something about the pain of the world and the hope for a sunnier future. They replicate perfectly the visual tones of Jamaican shantytown poverty against the agonizing beauty of the Caribbean sky.
> *(Kopkind 2012: 149)*

Jimmy Cliff echoes this with his own equation: "Sixty percent of it is the frustration of oppressed people . . . . Forty percent is fantasy. We sing a happy melody but it is sad underneath" (Kopkind 2012: 150). Kopkind's understanding of Jamaican suffering includes the Anglo-American exploitation of the island nation's resources. To this end, he cites the film *The Harder They Come* as an ironic sign of reggae's integration into what he calls the "imperial entertainment industry." Kopkind's irony comes from the film's focusing on black and poor Jamaicans juxtaposed against what he refers to as the "pervasive Anglo-American penetration of the island" and "the American music monster . . . making plans for the biggest cultural rip-off since Calypso" (Kopkind 2012: 151). As Jamaicans, Cliff and Kopkind ground reggae's cultural meaning in a basic and communal experience of suffering and fantasy. Just as Cliff calls reggae the "only true people's music," prior to Bob Marley, reggae was strongly associated with a provincial experience that did not translate to the mainstream.

To support its crossing over to widespread audiences, reggae needed a slight adjustment—the addition of electric guitar. As we have seen, however, commercial success is not always a positive experience, especially according to members within the genre's original community. In his "Roots and Rock: The Marley Enigma," Linton Kwesi Johnson criticizes Blackwell's handling of Marley as "a truly capitalist affair" (Johnson 2012. 154). Johnson recognizes the mainstream translation of reggae as being intimately involved with the construction of a marketable image, that of the "Rasta rebel":

> The "image" is derived from Rastafarianism and rebellion, which are rooted in the historical experience of oppressed Jamaica. It then becomes an instrument of capital to sell Marley and his music, thereby negating the power which is the cultural manifestation of this historical experience. So, though Marley is singing about "roots" and "natty," his fans know not. Neither do they understand the meaning of dread . . . . The dread has been replaced by the howling rock guitar and the funky rhythm and what we get is the "enigma" or "roots" and rock.
> *(Johnson 2012: 154)*

For the study at hand, this quote demonstrates how translation works to cover the distance between image and reality. Johnson recognizes that music is tethered to the experience of a community when he says reggae is "rooted" in a history of oppression. But post-translation, that history is no longer embodied by the Rasta rebel. Similar to the irony Kopkind describes above, the enigma of roots and rock is the juxtaposition of imperialist Anglo-American rock dressing itself in the authenticity of the experience of oppression, while also creating more oppression through imperialistic disenfranchisement (i.e., Kopkind's "cultural rip-off"). From a semiotic point of view, the Rasta rebel is a sign emptied of its historical content and open for association with defiance as a vaguely defined idea, one with which mainstream teens are able to more easily identify. In this sense, the "howling guitar" marks the absence of the history of oppression, a history that is erased in the process of reggae's commercial ascension.

## Conclusion

The preceding pages provide an overview of how specific music genres develop from the popular (an identity based on the experience of a specific community) to the professional (as identity based on profitability and the marketplace). Though popular music may be subject to the essentialist claim that ties it indelibly to the idea of a homeland, such music also exhibits a degree of plasticity. As noted in the introduction, Negus reformulates the issue of race and music away from using music to look for signs of racial authenticity and toward locating the wider context in which "musical expression is appropriated as a sign system for the creation of specific socio-cultural identities" (Negus 1996: 122). The use of cultural translation as an interpretive methodology allows readers to follow popular music forms across a "before" and "after" structure. Scholarship dedicated to reggae, rock, *salsa*, and rap reveals how the signification of provincial music forms becomes untethered from its original situation. As such, popular music forms are very much like the seeds or tools from Tom Waits' introductory quote; they are developed and used in an initial cultural context and then passed on and subject to further articulations bound to reconfigure their semantic content. As noted in the introduction, Negus reformulates the issue of race and music away from using music to look for signs of racial authenticity and toward locating the wider context in which "musical expression is appropriated as a sign system for the creation of specific socio-cultural identities" (Negus 1996: 122). The concept of "différance" as elaborated by Jacques Derrida in his *Of Grammatology* offers a useful theoretical support by addressing semiology as a fundamental and recurrent disjunction of sign and referent. From this perspective, the relationship between musical genre and any ultimate cultural "signified" or "referent" is subject to constant disruption, renegotiation, and deferral.

In the early 1950s, the upbeat blues music of the pre-rock 'n' roll era was reaching the mainstream white American kids, and that was a problem for the conservative, pre-civil rights establishment. It didn't need to be rebranded and given a white "king of rock 'n' roll" to be successful on its own terms. But it was co-opted, whitewashed, and re-framed to satisfy the market-driven needs of its then disenfranchised handlers. Looking at this as an instance of translation, it was not the small labels but the black creators, songwriters and performers, who were temporarily forgotten. Forty years later, in the midst of the major-label buyout of independent rap labels, this instance of cultural appropriation has a short-lived but interesting analog, the Black Rock Coalition (BRC). An intentional effort by black musicians to subvert the stereotype of rock as a predominantly white genre, the BRC reveals a broadening formal signification as black artists reclaimed their original tie to the birth of rock. Despite its short-lived success, the black rock movement is important to our conclusion because it speaks directly to the predominant loss of agency by black artists since rock 'n' roll went mainstream. Amidst issues of erasure, marginalization, or corporate redefinition of artistic image, the ability to control artistic identity stands out as the predominant legacy associated with the mainstreaming of black popular music forms over the last half-century.

Looking at ethnic music forms originating outside of the US, *salsa* and reggae present an opportunity for comparing and contrasting the effects of mainstreaming. While reggae experienced a degree of success that cannot be claimed by *salsa*, both had to be stripped of their specific historical legacies of political oppression to engage large-scale distribution systems. As we have seen with rap music's translation into hip-hop, both *salsa* and reggae underwent a shift in artistic reference that is legible on the level of lyrical content. However, while gangsta-rap focused narrowly on songs asserting sex and violence as an appeal to the suburban white imagination, *salsa* and reggae sacrificed their defiant political stance to gain widespread distribution. In these cases, overt revolutionary messages are overwritten by pacified images of sensuality, unity, or perhaps a vague sense of angst. Economically speaking, the greater success of reggae may also be located in its strategy of translation. The incorporation of electric guitar as a lead instrument allowed for reggae to make sense within the rock aesthetic as it was defined by the radio and record industry. Compared to reggae, *salsa*'s resistance to translation included the language barrier, a stronger tie to communal identity, and a comparatively disorganized integration into the Anglo-American "music monster."

Because music conveys the same "discursive instability" attributed to race (Radano and Bohlman 2000), the use of translation to mark shifts in geographical, economic, and semantic contexts may be evaluated positively or negatively. In most cases, it results in the creation of new and larger audiences. However, the issue of translating a musical genre from the context of its native community across corporate structures such as record labels or other mass distribution platforms reveals significant pitfalls in articulation. This study has shown alienation of core fan bases, loss of artistic control, and loss of perceived authorship as associated ills suffered by multiple ethnic communities whose musical stock has been picked up by mass media business entities.

## Notes

1 Rowe's estimates of the immigration of blacks from the southeastern US range from approximately 453,800 in the decade spanning 1910–20 to over 1.5 million per decade between 1940 and 1960.
2 Alan Freed's fall from grace and Dick Clark's interrogation by the U.S. Senate are well-known examples. For an overview of these as well as the "month's worth of chicken dinner" scam perpetrated by Nashville radio DJ John Richbourg see Linden, P. (2012) "Race, Hegemony and the Birth of Rock and Roll," *MEIEA Journal* 1(12): 56.
3 After struggling to break Jimmy Cliff onto the charts, Blackwell redoubled his focus on Jamaican music, notably by working on the film *The Harder They Come*.
4 Blackwell's experimentation adding distortion to Steve Winwood's guitar and the Spencer Davis Group's "Keep on Running" was part of a formula that momentarily displaced the Beatles' "Day Tripper" as the #1 song in 1966.

## References

Alper, G. (2005) "How the Flexibility of the Twelve-Bar Blues Has Helped Shape the Jazz Language," *College Music Symposium* 45: 1–12.
Altschuler, G. (2003) *All Shook Up: How Rock 'n' Roll Changed America*. New York: Oxford University Press.
Baker, H. A. (1993) *Black Studies, Rap and the Academy*. Chicago, IL: University of Chicago Press.
Berger, P. L. and Luckman, T. (1966) *The Social Construction of Reality: A Treatise in the Sociology of Knowledge*. Garden City, NY: Double Day.
Bertrand, M. (2000) *Race, Rock, and Elvis*. Chicago, IL: University of Illinois Press.
Bilby, K. (1985) "The Caribbean as a Musical Region," in S. Mintz and S. Price (eds.), *Caribbean Contours*. Baltimore, MD: Johns Hopkins University Press.

Born, G. and Hesmondhalgh, D. (eds.) (2000) *Western Music and Its Others: Difference, Representation and Appropriation in Music*. Berkeley, CA: University of California Press.
Brown, J. (ed.) (2007) *Western Music and Race*. Cambridge, UK: Cambridge University Press.
Chandler, D. (1998) *The Construction of Reality in TV News Programmes*. Retrieved December 29, 2014, from http://www.aber.ac.uk/media/Modules/TF33120/news.html.
Cohen, S. and Young, J. (eds.) (1981) *The Manufacture of News: Social Problems, Deviance and the Mass Media*. London: Constable.
Derrida, J. (1997) *Of Grammatology*. Baltimore, MD: Johns Hopkins University Press.
Duany, J. (1984) "Popular Music in Puerto Rico: Toward an Anthology of *Salsa*," *Latin American Music Review* 5: 186–216.
Garofalo, R. (1993) "Black Popular Music: Crossing over or Going under?," in T. Bennett et al. (eds.), *Rock and Popular Music: Politics, Policies, Institutions*. New York: Routledge, 231–248.
George, N. (1998) *The Death of Rhythm and Blues*. New York: Penguin.
Gilroy, P. (1993) *The Black Atlantic: Modernity and Double Consciousness*. Cambridge, MA: Harvard University Press.
Goffmann, E. (1959) *The Presentation of Self in Everyday Life*. New York: Doubleday.
Hull, G. (2004) *The Recording Industry*. New York: Routledge.
Hurt, B. (2003) *Hip Hop: Beyond Beats and Rhymes* [DVD]. United States: Media Education Foundation.
Jefferson, M. (1973) "Ripping off Black Music," *Harper's* January: 40–45.
Johnson, L. K. (2012) "Roots and Rock: The Marley Enigma," in T. Cateforis (ed.), *The Rock History Reader*. New York: Routledge, 153–154.
Kellner, D. (1995) *Media Culture: Cultural Studies, Identity and Politics between the Modern and the Postmodern*. New York: Routledge.
Kopkind, A. (2012) "Reggae: The Steady Rock of Black Jamaica," in T. Cateforis (ed.), *The Rock History Reader*. New York: Routledge, 149–152.
Kun, T. S. (2005) *Music, Race and America*. Berkeley, CA: University of California Press.
Lightfoot, W. E. (2003) "The Three Doc(k)s: White Blues in Appalachia," *Black Music Research Journal* 23(1): 167–193.
Linden, P. (2007) "Les écoles du Blues: Delta Blues," *Blues & Co* September: 40–42.
——. (2012) "Race, Hegemony and the Birth of Rock and Roll," *MEIEA Journal* 12(1): 43–67.
Lipsitz, G. (2007) *Footsteps in the Dark: The Hidden Histories of Popular Music*. Minneapolis, MN: University of Minnesota Press.
Manuel, P. (1995) "Latin Music in the New World Order: *Salsa* and Beyond," in R. Sakolsky and F. Wei-Han Ho (eds.), *Sound Off: Music as Subversion/Resistance/Revolution*. New York: Autonomedia, 278–286.
Marcus, G. (2008) *Mystery Train: Images of America in Rock 'n' Roll Music*, 5th ed. New York: Plume.
Miller, K. H. (2010) *Segregating Sounds: Inventing Folk and Pop Music in the Age of Jim Crow*. Durham, NC: Duke University Press.
Narváerez, P. (1994) "The Influences of Hispanic Music Cultures on African-American Blues Musicians," *Black Music Research Journal* 14(2): 203–224.
Negus, K. (1996) *Popular Music in Theory: An Introduction*. Middletown, CT: Wesleyan University Press.
——. (1999) *Music Genres and Corporate Cultures*. New York: Routledge.
Padilla, F. (1990) "Salsa: Puerto Rican and Latino Music," *Journal of Popular Culture* 24: 87–104.
Peterson, R. (1990) "Why 1955? Explaining the Advent of Rock Music," *Popular Music* 9(1): 97–116.
Presley, A. (1991 [1957]) *Elvis Presley: The 1950s Interviews* [CD]. United Kingdom: Magnum Force.
Radano, R. (2012) "Music, Race, and the Fields of Public Culture," in M. Clayton et al. (eds.), *The Cultural Study of Music: A Critical Introduction*. New York: Routledge, 309–316.
Radano, R. and Bohlman, P. V. (eds.) (2000) *Music and the Racial Imagination*. Chicago, IL: University of Chicago Press.
Ramirez, M. (1996) "Joining the Party: Multinational Giants See Great Potential in Latin Music," *Los Angeles Times* (Washington Edition), March 12, B5.
Romàn-Velàzquez, P. (1996) *The Construction of Latin Identities and Salsa Music Clubs in London: An Ethnographic Study*. Ph.D. thesis, Leicester University.
Rowe, M. (1975) *Chicago Blues: The City and the Music*. Cambridge, MA: De Capo Press.
Southern, E. (1971) *The Music of Black Americans: A History*. New York: Norton.
Stokes, M. (1994) "Introduction: Ethnicity, Identity and Music," in M. Stokes (ed.), *Ethnicity, Identity and Music: The Musical Construction of Place*. Oxford, UK: Berg.

Troutman, J. W. (2013) "Steelin' the Slide," *Southern Cultures* 19(1): 26–52.
Waits, T. (1993) Interview in "Visions d'Alice," TV documentary by Thierry Thomas. France, Germany: La Sept/ARTE.
Watts, S. (2009) *Keep On Runnin': 50 Years of Island Records* [DVD]. United Kingdom: Double Jab Productions.

## Further Reading/Viewing

Bertrand, M. (2000) *Race, Rock, and Elvis*. Chicago, IL: University of Illinois Press. (An excellent critique of accepted interpretations of the racial significance of Elvis' rise to stardom, followed by Bertrand's own, convincing assessment.)
Born, G. and Hesmondhalgh, D. (eds.) (2000) *Western Music and Its Others: Difference, Representation and Appropriation in Music*. Berkeley, CA: University of California Press. (A collection of 11 essays informed by new musicology and locating the issue of race and music within a global context.)
Cateforis, T. (ed.) (2012) *The Rock History Reader*. New York: Routledge, 153–154. (A decade-by-decade collection of articles and interviews by popular music critics and practitioners addressing major events shaping the industry of their day.)
Clayton, M. et al. (eds.) (2012) *The Cultural Study of Music: A Critical Introduction*. New York: Routledge. (Large collection of essays using sociological approaches to interrogate the relationship between music and cultural anthropology.)
Hurt, B. (2003) *Hip Hop: Beyond Beats and Rhymes* [DVD], United States: Media Education Foundation. (In this documentary, Hurt interviews a wide selection of music consumers, artists, and professionals to reveal the constructed nature of gangsta-rap's hyper-masculinity.)
Sakolsky, R. and Wei-Han Ho, F. (eds.) (1995) *Sound Off: Music as Subversion/Resistance/Revolution*. New York: Autonomedia, 278–286. (Collection of 38 articles by music critics, professionals, and political activists exploring race as part of the larger anti-establishment thrust of popular music forms.)

# 10
# THE INTERNET

## Oppression in Digital Spaces

*Kishonna L. Gray*

"On the Internet, nobody knows you're a dog." This adage, which has been around since the advent of the Internet, has become an important contextual framework used to examine the medium. The implication is that when one traverses into virtuality, our physical bodies have no bearing on our experiences and outcomes because, often, no one knows who we are. Early Internet scholars theorized that virtual environments would provide an outlet to exist beyond the parameters of the body (Daniels 2012). In its early days, the liberating potential of the Internet had extreme lure; however, this lure existed in a realm of assumed whiteness, as the Internet was traditionally a domain of the privileged. "Cyberfeminists" argued that the Internet had liberating qualities that could free women from the confines of their gendered bodies (Bromseth and Sunden 2010). The premise, however, has been criticized as both utopian and irrelevant to marginalized circumstances in new technologies (Bromseth and Sunden 2010). We cannot just forgo our bodies in virtual spaces, because much of our real-world selves are emitted into these spaces. The discussion must move beyond the confines of the digital and be reexamined for its potential to mobilize the oppressed in both digital and physical spaces.

The purpose of this chapter is to provide a contemporary context for the Internet as it relates to race and ethnicity. By examining the racialized dynamics in access (i.e., the "digital divide"), Internet usage (i.e., Black Twitter), and control (i.e., the lack of diversity and inclusion in Internet industries), this chapter will examine just how unequal the Internet still is along racial lines.

### Hegemonic Identities and the Internet

Internet technologies and virtual communities are assumed to be white and masculine (Daniels 2013; Gray 2012; Kress 2009). These unequal power relationships are accepted as legitimate and are embedded in the cultural practices of digital technology, and the Internet is an important site to examine the production and reproduction of culture. Giroux (1997) contends that

> the emergence of mass visual productions in the United States requires new ways of seeing and making visible the racial structuring of White experience. The electronic media—television, movies, music, and news—have become powerful

pedagogical forces, veritable teaching machines in shaping the social imaginations of students in terms of how they view themselves, others, and the larger society.

*(12)*

Giroux recognizes the power and impact that electronic media have on culture, especially because of how widespread these technologies are disseminated. This pervasiveness deems the Internet a site worthy of exploration in the production of culture, especially as it is increasingly interactive, with user-generated content now constituting a large portion of the web (Jenkins 2008). The continued growth and expansion of the Internet requires that we develop the context in examining its ability to maintain whiteness.

Examining whiteness is an important part of examining race and the Internet. As a hegemonic entity, whiteness is the thing that has become too normalized to be able to see. This is the paradox of whiteness, being both assumed and in need of constantly being re-asserted. And its normalness makes it difficult to be analyzed. Chidester (2008), in an analysis of the rhetorics of whiteness, contends,

> Whiteness uses the visual both to assert itself and to recede into the background when necessary. It is a rhetorical tool that can claim immense range and influence precisely because it is so difficult to affix to any single communicative text or set of discourses.
>
> *(159)*

But there is growing awareness of whiteness in popular culture (Carr and Lund 2009; Giroux 1997), especially in relation to the Internet. For example, the popular Twitter hashtag "#CrimingWhileWhite" exploded in the days after the death of Eric Garner, an African-American man who was killed by New York police, one of a series of racially polarizing police killings in 2014. Those reposting this hashtag quickly recognized the privileges associated with being white in sharing their tweets:

> Played with realistic toy guns my entire childhood, wherever we wanted. #CrimingWhileWhite
>
> My 13yo son and his friends were loitering at Walgreens recently. Only his black friend got searched for shoplifting. ~ #CrimingWhileWhite ~
>
> Ticket for going 120. No license. Judge let me off. "You go to too good a school to be so dumb so I assume you aren't." #CrimingWhileWhite
>
> Exhaled blunt smoke in a cop's face as I opened my door and then told him he couldn't come in without a warrant. He left. #CrimingWhileWhite

While the tweets do highlight recognition of privilege, inserting them into the #BlackLivesMatter conversation didn't seem timely and only furthered the significance of white privilege: look at what we get away with! The point of the "CrimingWhileWhite" hashtag was not about the privilege afforded to whiteness, but rather the lack of privilege afforded blacks or the perpetual state of oppression for some over others. There was no movement to dismantle the power that led to this privilege.

What this acknowledgment of privilege does add to the conversation is that it increases the visibility of discourses of whiteness; further, this could indicate an important shift in the way race operates, especially online. Citing Foucault, Fraser (2007) says "discourse is tied to the systems of power found in any given social formation at any given moment in time" (203). Thus, it seems an important moment to examine the current shape and variety of discourses of whiteness. Although whiteness is assumed in virtual spaces, it becomes apparent in not only creating the "other" online; it also informs the experiences of the "other." While the Internet has aided in shaping marginalized communities by increasing their participation in civic society, a manifestation of real-world inequalities in virtual spaces exists and influences their virtual realities. Even in a liberatory space such as the Internet, racial and ethnic minorities are still marginalized.

## Theories of Marginality

Theories of marginality focus on both the oppressive and constructive aspects of belonging and not belonging to multiple and opposing communities at the same time. Most of Michel Foucault's theorizing of human identity focused on the ways in which the self is objectified through scientific inquiry (1988). Within this line of investigation, he examined the relationship between power and the production of knowledge and the discursive development of various disciplinary processes such as the gaze, which seeks to categorize, identify, and control society's individuals. In particular, he examined how discursive formations were defined in large part by identifying that which lay outside its boundaries. Such boundaries and boundary-making are, however, areas of contestation and arenas for expressing domination in the production of knowledge. Marginalized users of Internet technologies have identified innovative ways to still participate within Internet culture, as this chapter will outline.

Discourse on identity is not only defined in terms of binaries, but is also shaped by hierarchical relationships of power. Black identities, for example, have been defined not only in contrast to white ones, but have also been shaped by various forms of power that have historically failed to acknowledge the voice of those identified as black in defining the parameters of the black and white binary. Before his death in 1984, Michel Foucault (1988) had been working on a set of ideas he termed *technologies of the self*. The work represented a shift in his focus away from the objectification of the self and toward the question of how a human being turns him/herself into a subject. As this chapter will explore, there are discursive realities of technology of the self that are both objectifying and subjectifying as racial and ethnic identity are approached using discursive terms constituted in the margins of objectivity/subjectivity, outsider/insider, and domination/liberation.

Latino studies scholars have also closely examined the category of marginality. In the seminal work of Gloria Anzaldúa, Latino identity is situated within the borders, in the in-between spaces. She writes: "The struggle is inner: Chicano, indio, American Indian, mojado, mexicano, immigrant Latino, Anglo in power, working class Anglo, Black, Asian—our psyches resemble the bordertowns and are populated by the same people" (Anzaldua 1999: 109). Even though we may be working toward a postborder world (Dear and LeClerc 2003), where new cultural hybridities co-exist and mutate to form new possibilities, the Internet can be seen as recreating the physical border in virtual spaces by deeming some worthy of participation and others not. The hashtag #Yamecanse (I am tired) began dominating the online conversation in 2014 in the wake of 43 Mexican students disappearing, and the protesters began to declare their exhaustion and exasperation with state-sponsored violence and corruption that has seemingly become the norm (BBC Trending 2014).

The tweets revealed much more than just a rally to find missing students or a call to justice in Mexico; this hashtag led to the massive solidarity of Mexicans and Mexican Americans and led to more protests and demonstrations on the conditions of Mexican and Mexican Americans within our social institutions. Activists within the movement stated they wanted changes in our social institutions from education to health, and they used social media to help spread that message. It is also a direct indictment of how the Internet can transcend borders to reach the masses, but the reactions and backlash reveal to marginalized users that they still exist within the parameters of their bodies. Extending beyond social media, many activists used YouTube to highlight their frustration with the current method of justice. The quote below by filmmaker Natalia Beristain reflects the anger:

> Senor Murillo . . . , I, too, am tired . . . . I'm tired of vanished Mexicans, of the killing of women, of the dead, of the decapitated, of the bodies hanging from bridges, of broken families, of mothers without children, of children without fathers.
> *(Associated Press 2014)*

The appropriation of this comment made by the Mexican Attorney General, Jesus Murillo, in his failure to fully explain what happened, reflects the impact that social media has on coopting the narrative traditionally in the hands of the privileged.

Nakamura (2002) uses the lens of the remediation circuit to examine the contemporary design, production, dissemination, and consumption of racial formations. She begins her monograph by describing the proliferation of the Internet as inextricably linked to technological developments that put America on a graphical, rather than purely textual, interface of the Internet. Further, the racialized shape and content of the Internet's visuality must also be understood as emerging alongside the neoliberal, colorblind politics of the 1990s. In this way, the universally equal citizens of cyberspace were imagined within the colorblind paradigm, behind the veil of ignorance, a raceless population. The Internet offered a space in which race and other identifying markers could remain hidden or ambiguous. However, rather than as technology, which allows its users to avoid race identification, the Internet, argues Nakamura, has largely remediated offline racial formations (Nakamura 2002).

## Control

Internet scholarship illustrates a picture of a race-neutral creation and development of the Internet; nonetheless, race is directly implicated in the very structure of the design of Internet technologies. Daniels cites this example:

> Everett (2002) observes that she is perpetually taken aback by DOS-commands designating a "Master Disk" and "Slave Disk," a programming language predicated upon a digitally configured "master/slave" relationship with all the racial meanings coded into the hierarchy of command lines.
> *(2)*

The early design of the Internet stems from this racialized discourse and it is hard to disconnect the implicit meanings behind the dichotomous phrase, master/slave. Although many would contend no racist intent, the history of this country was built upon the master/slave relationship and for the descendants of this relationship, black Americans, it is even more problematic.

Moving beyond the foundational language, the bodies on which the foundation was built are even more problematic. Many of the technological advances of the Internet rose out of an industry with significant disparities along race, gender, and class. Although the Silicon Valley may tout itself as diverse, these tech firms were and still are controlled by elite, white males. And as Daniels (2012) highlights, those who assemble the circuit boards and clean the offices are largely immigrant laborers. Other examples reveal a privileging of default whiteness, thus becoming the norm: the white hand pointer (White 2006), the default white avatar (Kafai, Cook, and Fields 2010), and the default white voice, among others. Sadly, when racial minorities challenge this prevailing notion of assumed whiteness, it is often they who are blamed for perpetuating racial inequalities. An example from videogame culture will illustrate this point. Virtual gaming communities are spaces that often dramatize certain aspects of identity, such as gender and class. Unfortunately, ethnicities are often absent. As Kolko (2000) argues, the Internet is far from liberatory but rather a space that sanctions a "cultural map of assumed whiteness" (225). And when there is an attempt to make race and ethnicity present, it is met with resistance. I will illustrate with the example of Leeroy Jenkins.

Leeroy Jenkins was a video created to promote guild play in World of Warcraft, the wildly popular online role-playing game (Gray 2011). The character Leeroy was an attempt to show what not to do during gameplay. Leeroy did not take the game seriously, he did not collaborate with his teammates, and he basically led to his team's demise. This is a traditional racialized cybertype, as Nakamura (2002) explains, deploying traditional stereotypes of blacks as the inferior other, further legitimizing whiteness. The fact that World of Warcraft has a small number of black avatars shows that blackness seems to be allowed in sporadically, in small doses, and in a manner that fulfills the desires of the dominant, white other (Higgin 2009). For players and game designers, the deployment of this type of narrative confirms that "blackness is not an appropriate discourse of heroic fantasy" (Higgin 2009: 3). When bloggers began commenting on Leeroy Jenkins, any mention of racially stereotypical imagery enflamed many users within the space. In response, one user replied that Leeroy was merely a character within a game without a race. Comments such as these confirm what people of color already know—in virtual reality, everyone finally gets to be white (Gray 2011: 8). As Higgin (2009) observed,

> The White dominance of gamespace has been recast as a racially progressive movement that ejects race in favor of a default, universal whiteness and has been ceded, in part, by a theoretical tendency to embrace passing and anonymity in cyberspace. When politically charged issues surface that reveal the embedded stereotypes at work amid an ostensibly colorblind environment, they are quickly de-raced and cataloged as aberrations rather than analyzed as symptomatic of more systemic trends.
>
> *(2009: 7–8)*

There is an almost complete lack of interest in discussing racialized content and experiences within digital spaces. As Eduardo Bonilla-Silva would suggest, it's racism without racists.

According to Bonilla-Silva (2003), colorblind racism reproduces inequality and perpetuates white privilege because its practices are subtle, institutional, and apparently nonracial. Importantly, colorblind ideology is a political tool that is used by the dominant group (consciously or unconsciously) to maintain the racial order and preserve white privilege (as cited in Gray and Raza 2012).

Colorblind ideology is a pervasive belief system that rationalizes and gives power to the existing social structure—or rather, the racialized social system (Bonilla-Silva 2001, 2003). Bonilla-Silva (2001, 2003) contends that the new racism is difficult to detect because colorblind ideology camouflages racial practices. In fact, colorblind racism reproduces inequality and perpetuates white privilege because its practices are subtle and embedded in the operation of institutions. Whites exercise colorblind ideology to rationalize the disadvantaged minority status as a product of the market, natural phenomena, and the cultural limitations of persons of color. The controversy that surrounded police shootings of racial minorities in 2014 and 2015 revealed similarly colorblind/racist stances of many individuals. Conservatives suggested that neither the race of the police officers nor the race of the victims mattered, and that those who brought race into the discussion were race-baiters. Comments and blog posts that reflected these ideas were abundant on the Internet, as were the critical analyses of policing in the twenty-first century. However, in our "colorblind" era, it could become difficult to decipher which commentary is rooted in a true examination of the reality in differential policing and which is just rooted in colorblind rhetoric. But without digital literacy, there are still permeations of racist discourse perpetuated online. Sadly, those who are victims of lagging behind the technological curve are often portrayed as marginalized members of our community.

## The Digital Divide

The digital divide is broadly defined as the concern that certain groups in the population might not have access to information technology, which could impede their opportunities. Race has always been an important factor for predicting access and use of computers (Daniels 2012). A study conducted by the Census Bureau in the 1990s highlighted that African Americans had lower rates than whites in computer ownership and telephone service (Daniels 2012). This study led to the phenomenon known as the digital divide. Since then, blacks have been touted as poster children for the digital divide (Everett 2009). But an additional factor that this chapter will concern itself with centers on how having access alone does not close the digital gap. Scholars are now acknowledging that media literacy skills are equally important in closing the digital divide (Hargittai 2002; Lenhart 2003). Additionally, some research suggests that a lack of relevant content on the Internet influences blacks' engagement in the medium (Hoffman, Novak, and Schlosser 2000; Lazarus and Lipper 2000; Kretchmer and Carveth 2001).

The most significant factor within the digital divide is the income gap, but when other identities intersect with income (race, gender, education, ability, etc.), outcomes are drastically influenced. Specifically looking at race, Attewell (2001) suggests that the racial digital divide exists mainly due to income and educational inequalities, rather than race alone (253). Poor and minority children are less likely to have access to computers and the Internet at home and school, while their parents are less likely to have access to them at home and work (Natriello 2001: 260). This is more than likely due to racial employment discrimination, which keeps minorities in the lower-income brackets and out of more technical occupations. In a study conducted by Hoffman and Novak, it was found that at the same income level (more than $40,000), African Americans in fact had a higher percentage of home computer owners. Although education levels can help explain why a higher percentage of African Americans earn an income of less than

$40,000, whites are twice as likely to have a home computer compared to their black counterparts, and slightly more likely to have access to computers at work (Hoffman and Novak 1998: 390).

As there are differences in access, there are also racial differences in use. As Yardi and Bruckman (2012) found, whites have Internet access and broadband Internet at higher rates than African Americans. On the other hand, African Americans use mobile phones more often than whites do, including for Internet use, to play games, and to use social networking sites. So although there may be some differences in use, rates of access, and adoption, the most significant differences are the types of devices used and the purposes they serve. A 2010 study by the Pew Research Center found that black, Latino, and low-income users were more likely to go online using smartphones than desktop or laptop computers. Nearly 20 percent of African-American smartphone subscribers use only their phones to go online, along with 16 percent of Latinos. The same is true of only 10 percent of white mobile phone subscribers. But no matter the medium employed, rates of Internet use are comparable.

The digital divide is a conceptual framework for understanding the historical and contemporary impacts on the diffusion of Internet technologies among marginalized groups and the adoption of those technologies within these populations. As Warschauer (2007) suggests, the concept of the digital divide is complex and represents a particular point in the chain of social inequity. The term digital divide represents the gap in information communication technology usage between social groups as classified by various identifiers (Gorski 2003). The digital divide can also be examined along the lines of race, educational achievement, disability status, citizenship, and English language proficiency. Wynn (2005) has identified three reasons for the continuation of the digital divide: (1) poor economic conditions lead to an inability to afford certain information technology apparatuses, including computers and connectivity mediums; (2) the progression of technology to more advanced stages could leave those at a further disadvantage; and (3) the state of disadvantage leaves these digitally divided groups incapacitated from educating and exposing themselves to opportunities within the digital world. Kvasny (2006) expands upon the concept of the digital divide and discusses digital inequality. This process links socio-economic factors such as poverty, discrimination, inconsistent employment, and education with the diffusion and usage of information and communication technology that perpetuate social inequity.

Another way to examine digital inequalities is to examine the experiences and realities of people of color after they gain access to Internet technologies. One such example stems from danah boyd's (2011) work on teen social media use. In her research, she identified a trend among the racialized practices of a cohort of youth. As one participant revealed, MySpace, an early social networking site, became a ghetto with the increased presence of minority users. As a trend that exists in physical spaces, virtual spaces are also witnessing the flight of white users to other, less "urban" spaces. Teens in school self-segregate on the basis of social categories like race, ethnicity, and socio-economic status, and social media is not exempt from this trend.

On the other hand, the presence of racialized others may compel some users to treat the minority intruder in a hostile manner so they will leave the space. In Xbox Live, Microsoft's online multi-player gaming device, the presence of black-sounding gamers has led to significant racial harassment, and many black gamers self-segregate into private party chats on the Xbox Live system to avoid this type of treatment (Gray 2012). As minority gamers contend, their private spaces are virtual ghettoes, as they have been redlined to these areas.

The use of the term ghetto has historical signifiers that reveal a larger connection to the intersection of race and class. It also refers to a "set of tastes that emerged as poor people of color developed fashion and cultural artifacts that proudly expressed their identity" (boyd 2011: 205). By using "ghetto" in the sense that the participants in this study employed, it relegated certain users to the margins of the Internet. Because of the adoption of colorblind ideology by many mainstream Internet users, there is a complete lack of awareness in how this leads to racism. But this factor influences racial minorities' full access and adoption of Internet technologies.

Racial segregation on the Internet is also apparent in how it is used by white supremacist groups. The day after Barack Obama was elected as the first black President of the United States in 2008, Stormfront, the white Nationalist website, crashed due to the number of individuals visiting the site (Daniels 2012). This seems to run contrary to the idealized notion of racial equality and highlights the continued systemic racism that constitutes our reality. Hate groups who use the Internet to disseminate their ideological stances are savvy in the manner they present themselves. Using Stormfront as an example, they don't employ terms like "racist" or "bigot" as the KKK might. Instead, they opt for less aggressive language and their homepage states that their "mission is to provide information . . . to build a community of White activists working for the survival of our people" (Black 2001). The Internet has provided a new outlet for hate groups to supplement their offline efforts. Even more disturbing, the Internet provides a level of anonymity—a kind of virtual KKK hood—that many members within these organizations seek.

There are others on the Internet who may not be organized in the manner that hate groups are, but they still engage in similar racist acts toward perceived racial minorities based on how they sound. Scholars have found that in virtual communities that rely on voice-based communications, a great deal of racism emerges. Linguistic profiling occurs when auditory cues are used to identify the identity of another person in a setting where they are not visible (Gray 2014). Similar to racial profiling, which uses visual cues, linguistic profiling relies on accent, slang, voice pitch, and other auditory markers to identify racial or ethnic backgrounds. Usually, this kind of voice discrimination does not warrant a hostile response. But in some cases, linguistic profiling may lead to avoidance, discrimination, harassment, and racism.

Researchers have documented this type of toxic environment for those with linguistic patterns that deviate from Standard American English in virtual gaming communities (Gray 2012). This "white" speech pattern has been defined as the norm by many within Xbox Live, while those who deviate quickly fall victim to harassment and racism. Black and Latino gamers in particular reveal that they are constantly harassed when the default gamer hears how they sound. They are told that they sound "too black" or that they use "too much Spanglish" for the space. This leads to the marginalization of a segment of gamers that constitute a huge portion of the gaming industry. As research indicates, these gamers are forced to segregate, leading to more ghetto-ization of virtual spaces (Gray 2012).

## The Future

Scholars have warned against the "unproblematized" views of perceiving the Internet as a utopian space where all individuals and all groups have equal access to the production, dissemination, and consumption of information (Wei and Kolko 2005). Recent examples within popular culture reveal the innovative ways that the Internet can be used to mobilize racial minorities. The 2014 hashtag and subsequent movement, #BlackLivesMatter, exposed the extent of the lack of understanding of the lived experiences of blacks within the criminal justice system. Racial minorities defy the stereotype as the poster children for the digital divide. They engage in Internet technologies in innovative ways that disrupt the hegemonic narrative of people of color as laggards in technology. Fortunately, criticism has called attention to these issues. Recognition of inequities in both technology use and representation has shifted the contemporary attitude toward the fluidity of identity and progressive signification through race.

If we are to truly dissect and transform how race is communicated within Internet culture, we need to focus our attention on the industry, on access, on Internet use, on experiences within virtual settings, on representations, and even on the politics of technological production. Without examining the underlying causes of the inequities, our critiques will be severely limited. Examining the perpetual state of whiteness within Internet culture allows us to extend the conversation of not only who maintains the Internet but also for whom it is maintained. Users must be sensitized to the performance of race online and to the filters through which they perceive race.

## References

Anzaldua, G. (1987) *Borderlands la Frontera: The New Mestiza*. San Francisco, CA: Aunt Lute.
Associated Press (2014, Nov. 8) "'I've had Enough,' says Mexican Attorney General in Missing Students Gaffe," *The Guardian*. Retrieved from http://www.theguardian.com/world/2014/nov/09/protests-flare-in-mexico-after-attorney-generals-enough-im-tired-remarks.
Attewell, P. (2001) "Comment: The First and Second Digital Divides," *Sociology of Education* 74(3): 252–259.
BBC Trending (2014, Dec. 9) "'I am Tired': The Politics of Mexico's #Yamecanse Hashtag," BBC. Retrieved from http://www.bbc.com/news/blogs-trending-30294010.
boyd, d. (2012) "White Flight in Networked Publics: How Race and Class Shaped American Teen Engagement with MySpace and Facebook," in L. Nakamura and P. Chow-White (eds.), *Race after the Internet*. New York: Routledge, 203–222.
Bromseth, J. and Sunden, J. (2011) "Queering Internet Studies: Intersections of Gender and Sexuality," in M. Consalvo and C. Ess (eds.), *The Handbook of Internet Studies*. Oxford: Wiley-Blackwell, 270–299.
Carr, P. R. and Lund, D. E. (2009) *The Great White North: Exploring Whiteness, Privilege, and Identity in Education*. Rotterdam, The Netherlands: Sense Publishers.
Chidester, P. (2008) "May the Circle Stay Unbroken: Friends, the Presence of Absence, and the Rhetorical Reinforcement of Whiteness," *Critical Studies in Media Communication* 25(2): 157–174.
Daniels, J. (2013) "Race and Racism in Internet Studies: A Review and Critique," *New Media and Society* 15(5): 695–719.
Dear, M., Leclerc, G., and Leclerc, G. (2003) "The Postborder Condition: Art and Urbanism in Bajalta California," in M. Dear (ed.), *Postborder City: Cultural Spaces of Bajalta California*. New York: Routledge, 1–30.
Everett, A. (2009) *Digital Diaspora: A Race for Cyberspace*. Albany, NY: State of New York University Press.
Foucault, M. (1988) *Technologies of the Self: A Seminar with Michel Foucault*. Amherst, MA: University of Massachusetts Press.
Fraser, N. (2007) "Creating Model Citizens for the Information Age: Canadian Internet as Civilizing Discourse Policy," *Canadian Journal of Communication* 32(2): 201–218.
Giroux, H. A. (1997) "White Squall: Resistance and the Pedagogy of Whiteness," *Cultural Studies* 11(3): 376–389.
Gorski, P. C. (2003) "Privilege and Repression in the Digital Era: Rethinking the Sociopolitics of the Digital Divide," *Race, Gender, and Class* 10(4): 145–176.
Gray, K. L. (2011) *Deviant Bodies Resisting Online: Examining the Intersecting Realities of Women of Color in Xbox Live* (Doctoral dissertation, Arizona State University).
——. (2012) "Deviant Bodies, Stigmatized Identities, and Racist Acts: Examining the Experiences of African-American Gamers in Xbox Live," *New Review of Hypermedia and Multimedia* 18(4): 261–276.

Higgin, T. (2009) "Blackless Fantasy: The Disappearance of Race in Massively Multiplayer Online Role-Playing Games," *Games and Culture* 4(1): 3–26.

Hoffman, D. L. and Novak, T. P. (1998) "Bridging the Racial Divide on the Internet," *Science* 280 (April 17): 390–391.

Jenkins, H. (2008) *Convergence Culture: Where Old and Mew Media Collide*. New York: New York University Press.

Kafai, Y. B., Cook, M. S., and Fields, D. A. (2010) "'Blacks Deserve Bodies Too!': Design and Discussion about Diversity and Race in a Tween Virtual World," *Games and Culture* 5(1): 43–63.

Kress, T. M. (2009) "In the Shadow of Whiteness: (Re)exploring Connections between History, Enacted Culture, and Identity in a Digital Divide Initiative," *Cultural Studies of Science Education* 4(1): 41–49.

Kvasny, L. (2006) "Cultural (Re)production of Digital Inequality in a U.S. Community Technology Initiative," *Information, Communication and Society* 9(2): 160–181.

Nakamura, L. (2002) *Cybertypes: Race, Ethnicity, and Identity on the Internet*. New York: Routledge.

——. (2008) *Digitizing Race: Visual Cultures of the Internet*. Minneapolis, MN: University of Minnesota Press.

——. (2009) "Don't Hate the Player, Hate the Game: The Racialization of Labor in World of Warcraft," *Critical Studies in Media Communication* 26(2): 128–144.

Omi, M. and Winant, H. (1994) *Racial Formation in the United States: From the 1960s to the 1990s*. 2nd ed. New York: Routledge.

Warschauer, M. (2007) "A Teacher's Place in the Digital Divide," *Yearbook of the National Society for the Study of Education Annual Yearbook* 106(2): 147–166.

Wei, C. Y. and Kolko, B. E. (2005) "Resistance to Globalization: Language and Internet Diffusion Patterns in Uzbekistan," *New Review of Hypermedia and Multimedia* 11(2): 205–220.

West, C. (1982) *Prophecy Deliverance!: An Afro-American Revolutionary Christianity*. Philadelphia, PA: Westminster Press.

Wynn, C. A. (2005) *Control, Alt, Delete: African Americans Escaping the Digital Divide*. Washington DC: American University.

Yardi, S. and Bruckman, A. (2012) "Income, Race, and Class: Exploring Socioeconomic Differences in Family Technology Use," *Proceedings of the SIGCHI Conference on Human Factors in Computing Systems*, New York: Association for Computer Machinery: pp. 3041–3050.

## Further Reading

Daniels, J. (2013) "Race and Racism in Internet Studies: A Review and Critique," *New Media and Society* 15(5): 695–719. (Interrogates race and racism as researched within media and Internet studies; employs racial formation theory and urges the need for a critical examination of whiteness in Internet studies.)

Everett, A. (2009) *Digital Diaspora: A Race for Cyberspace*. Albany, NY: SUNY Press. (Explores historical and contemporary instances of Internet usage among the African diaspora; situates black Internet users as innovators as opposed to laggards and victims of the digital divide.)

Nakamura, L. (2013) *Cybertypes: Race, Ethnicity, and Identity on the Internet*. New York: Routledge. (Interrogates how the Internet shapes and reshapes our perceptions of race, ethnicity, and identity, labeling them as cybertypes, similar to stereotypes.)

Rauch, S. M. and Schanz, K. (2013) "Advancing Racism with Facebook: Frequency and Purpose of Facebook Use and the Acceptance of Prejudiced and Egalitarian Messages," *Computers in Human Behavior* 29(3): 610–615. (Examines the persistence of racism, racist ideology, and racist practices using the social media outlet Facebook as the catalyst.)

van Deursen, A. J. and van Dijk, J. A. (2014). "The Digital Divide Shifts to Differences in Usage," *New Media and Society* 16(3): 507–526. (As the digital divide shifts to more focus on usage difference than racial difference, this article provides a much-needed interrogation of how cultures group-employ the Internet.)

# 11
# SOCIAL MEDIA

## From Digital Divide to Empowerment

*Gina Masullo Chen*

Social media erupted after the death of Michael Brown, an unarmed black teenager shot by a white police officer in suburban St. Louis in August 2014 (Southall 2014; Deutsch and Lee 2014). Within days, 6 million tweets were posted (Axelrod 2014) about the shooting and its turbulent aftermath, which included protests, the National Guard being called in, and reporters being arrested (Davey, Eligon, and Blinder 2014). Photographs, videos, and often misinformation about the case rocketed through Twitter, Facebook, Vine, Snapchat, and other social media channels (Bilton 2014). In many ways, this frenzy was nothing new. Other high-profile news stories, from Hurricane Irene in 2011 to the Boston Marathon bombing two years later, have played out in real time over social media (Davis, Alves, and Sklansky 2014; Frebert, Saling, Vidoloff, and Eosco 2013). However, what sets the shooting in Ferguson, MO, apart is that it offers a vivid example of the potential for civic engagement and empowerment through social media for people of color. As Jim Axelrod wrote in a piece for CBS news online: "But what is new about Ferguson is the role of social media in spreading the message wider and more quickly, particularly for African Americans" (2014: 1). Social media in the Ferguson case played a galvanizing role: It united people of color and gave them a voice heard around the world. In a way, this experience was similar to how social media introduced speed and interactivity into traditional forms of social mobilization in the 2011 Egyptian Revolution (Eltantawy and Wiest 2011). As such, it demonstrates the interplay between social media and race and how technology offers new avenues of communication for people who may have lacked a means to express themselves in more traditional media channels.

This chapter will examine social media and race, drawing on Critical Race Theory and exploring the role of the Internet in the lives of people of color. First, I will discuss how traditional media and the digital divide historically have left people of color with less of a voice. Then I will propose how social media have—perhaps in a small way—changed that experience in some cases, providing a means for civic engagement and empowerment for people of color. Finally, I will conclude with what the future may hold for the intersection of social media and race. For this discussion, social media are defined as websites where people create profiles about themselves and converse with others (boyd and Ellison 2007; Thelwall 2008). The definition includes platforms such as Twitter, Facebook, and Instagram.

Historically, traditional media, including television, newspapers, and movies, have offered two avenues for people of color—invisibility or marginalization. Critical Race Theory argues that the reason for this is that racism is not an aberration but is embedded in our culture as a means of reinforcing the power structure of the dominant white group (Delgado and Stefanic 2012). Stuart Hall (1998) argues persuasively that this point of view was bolstered in part when the media became mass in an effort to appeal to the growing audience at the close of the nineteenth century. Hall (1992) further posits that the media do not merely inaccurately portray race, but construct and distort race to create a "media-mediated" (14) version that does not reflect reality. Some argue that this so-called "old-fashioned" (Sears, Hetts, Sidanius, and Bobo 2000: 18) or overt racism has been eradicated. However, studies of news reports, newspapers, television shows, and movies suggest that is not the case (e.g., Campbell 1995; Campbell, LeDuff, Jenkins, and Brown 2012; Johnson, Dolan, and Sonnett 2011; Liebler 2010; Merskin 1998; Ono and Pham 2009). For example, the stereotypical "mammy" character that has plagued media depictions of African-American women for decades (Collins 2000) has gained new energy as male actors don dresses and re-create this portrayal in movie characters, such as Madea in Tyler Perry's films, Rasputia in Eddie Murphy's *Norbit*, and Martin Lawrence as Big Momma (G. Chen, Williams, Hendrickson, and L. Chen 2012). Similarly, time has done little to diffuse the media overrepresentation of African Americans and Latinos as law-breakers (Dixon and Linz 2000; Campbell et al. 2012), Asian women as exotic and Asian men as asexual and nerdy (Ono and Pham 2009), or Latinas as maids (Soto 2008). Even reality shows and YouTube videos perpetuate these stereotypical depictions (Tyree 2011; Guo and Harlow 2014).

In other cases, people of color are symbolically annihilated (Strinati 2004) in the media by not being represented at all (Campbell et al. 2012; Johnson et al. 2011; Liebler 2010; Merskin 1998; Ono and Pham 2009). This further marginalizes these groups by giving them no voice. In addition a *myth of marginality* persists, as people of color are portrayed as the "other" to the dominant white society (Chuang 2012; Liebler 2010). Hall (2000) notes that this *inferential racism* is "more widespread—and in many ways, more insidious—because it is largely *invisible* even to those who formulate the world in its terms" (274). Adding to this problem is the fact that journalists and other media professionals historically have not been racially diverse, and efforts to dismantle this reality have largely failed (Melinger 2013). This norm has fostered media that perpetuate a more subtle racism that reflects the "preferred meaning of a still dominant white society" (Jenkins 2012: 24) in such aspects as news story source and topic selection (Owens 2008). Discussions of race end up as problems that need to be solved (Hall 2000), and journalistic routine practices reinforce a "mediated reality" (Shoemaker and Reese 2014: 39) that promotes the dominant society, rather than an accurate view.

## Internet as "Great Equalizer"?

In the early days of the World Wide Web, some trumpeted the Internet as a solution to the divisions between the races and other groups. It was thought that the Web offered a way for people to connect across boundaries in virtual communities (Rheingold 2000). Many hoped the Internet would diminish hierarchies between groups, giving the Web the power to "redefine dominant relationship patterns that are culturally instigated" (Ebo 1998: 3). Online communication fosters *weak ties* (Granovetter 1973; Chen 2011) between people, and these weak ties were thought to encourage diverse relationships

(Rheingold 2000). The relative anonymity of the Internet suggested the potential for cohesion among divergent groups that had been traditionally separated, paving the way, proponents argued, for a more egalitarian society. In addition, the Web can de-emphasize visual identities, so the characteristics of a person may be less apparent (Ebo 1998). Certainly, in some cases, this proved true. For example, Mehra, Merkel, and Bishop (2004) found the Internet could be empowering for marginalized groups including African-American women, low-income families, and sexual minorities. Blogging in particular promised a digital democracy because almost anyone could do it, for free (Gilmor 2004; Schradie 2012). However, another viewpoint proposed that virtual communities would mimic the biases of race, class, and gender in the offline world. This "cyberghetto" perspective suggested that hegemonic powers that fostered inequitable divisions offline would hold sway online, creating a hierarchical virtual world (Ebo 1998). Differences in access to computers and the Internet furthered this view, leading to a digital divide between those who have technology and those who do not. These differences break down on various overlapping social categories, including race, class, geographic location, and education (Schradie 2012; Warren 2007). The result was a digital inequality that mirrored the inequities perpetuated by the norms of society as a whole.

Against this backdrop, social media's invention offered a glimmer of hope for greater equanimity in media. Whites initially dominated social media, much as they had other forms of media. Early on, racial differences were found in which platforms people used (Hargittai 2008). However, shifts began to take place as the smartphone—rather than a laptop or desktop computer—became the tool of choice for social media use. For example, a Pew Research survey of 6,010 American adults found that African Americans continue to be less likely than whites to use the Internet and have high-speed broadband access at home, but these differences have largely disappeared when it comes to mobile platforms (Smith 2014). In fact, African Americans are the most active mobile Internet users, and their numbers are growing faster than any other group (Horrigan 2009). Among Internet users, social media adoption rates are nearly identical for whites (72 percent) and blacks (73 percent), and almost ubiquitous for those in the 18–29-year-old category of both racial groups (Smith 2014). African-American rates of Twitter use (22 percent) exceed those of whites (16 percent), and younger blacks have particularly high Twitter user rates (40 percent; Smith 2014). Similarly, 68 percent of Latino Internet users say they use social media, compared with 58 percent of all Americans online, and this percentage climbs to 84 percent for 18–29-year-old Latinos (Lopez, Gonzalez-Barrera, and Patten 2013). Conversely, Asian Americans have always been the most wired segment of the U.S. population, exceeding all other racial groups in terms of percentage of Internet users (Spooner 2001). Of course, it is important to note that people of color using social media still comprise a small percentage of the overall population of that group. However, as social media usage grows among people of all racial groups, these platforms offer some opportunities for expression that were missing in earlier media forms.

## Social Media Offers Public Voice

In the Ferguson shooting of an unarmed black man, for example, social media gave African Americans a channel to challenge or add to the discourse about the incident that traditional news outlets were reporting. Citizens were able to shift the discussion from the shooting itself to a dialogue about how law enforcement responds to unarmed black men. To make this point, one young black man posted two pictures of himself on

Twitter (Vega 2014). One picture showed him dressed in a tuxedo with a saxophone around his neck, and the other depicted him wearing a black T-shirt and a bandana with his finger pointing toward the camera. The *New York Times* reported on the pictures and interviewed the man, Tyler Atkins. Atkins noted in the article that he felt Brown's identity in the Ferguson case was distorted by negative stereotypes, and the same would have happened to Atkins if he had been wearing the T-shirt versus the tuxedo (Vega 2014). This example is instructive because without social media Atkins would not have had the power to communicate about the shooting in a way that shifted the discourse and garnered him coverage from arguably the most powerful newspaper in America. Twitter gave him a platform to express his views that led to coverage of this issue. Certainly, Atkins was not unique in his argument that stereotypes about race may have played a role in the shooting. However, his viewpoint became part of a drumbeat of sentiments on social media and "helped propel and transform a local shooting into a national cause" (Vega 2014: 1).

In many ways, the Brown shooting mirrors how social media played a role in the 2012 Trayvon Martin case. In that case, George Zimmerman, a Hispanic neighborhood watch volunteer, was accused of shooting Martin, an unarmed black teenager, as Martin walked to a Florida house where he was staying as a guest (Alvarez 2012). Zimmerman reported he shot Martin in self-defense and was later acquitted of second-degree murder, sparking a furor on social media about whether the verdict was fair (Ehrlich 2013; Williams-Harris 2013). People used their Facebook feeds to comment on the case. Some replaced their profile pictures with a black square or a silhouette depicting Martin in a hoodie, the garment he had been wearing when he was shot (Williams-Harris 2013). Protestors used social media to express their views on the case—in support of both Zimmerman and Martin. Traditional media sources then covered these online protests, tweets, and Facebook posts, adding legitimacy to the discourse and extending their reach. In a very real way, these examples show how African Americans were able to disrupt the "distorting mirror" that Hall (1992: 14) argues traditional media hold up to reality and replace that mirror with messages they felt needed to be added to the public debate. Certainly, it would be misguided to attribute to a tweet or a status update the power to overturn decades of inferential or overt racism. Yet clearly social media offered a new avenue to proclaim concerns for those who previously had few options.

## Power of the #Hashtag

Another means by which social media may offer a voice to people of color is through the use of the *hashtag*, a hash or pound symbol that is used to label tweets on Twitter (Brock 2012; Chang 2010; Small 2011). Hashtags began as a means to help sort information on Twitter, but they have morphed into a "user-created meta-discourse convention" (Brock 2012: 534) that allows people to imbue emotion in their tweets. Papacharissi and Oliveira (2012) note that hashtags point to Twitter's role as a stream of social awareness and present a way for users to highlight what they think is news. On Twitter and other forms of social media, people imagine an audience in their heads (Marwick and boyd 2011), and then they target that audience with their messages. As a result, the hashtag can provide a powerful means for people of color to highlight their messages as a way to engage with their imagined audience and share what they see as valuable. For example, in both the Trayvon Martin and Michael Brown shootings, hashtags developed organically around specific content related to the topic. After Martin's death, #JusticeForTrayvon gained traction on Twitter, Instagram and Facebook (Williams-Harris 2013). In addition, #IfTheyGunnedMeDown and #DontShoot were used to raise concerns about police officers' use of force against people of color after Brown died (Deutsch and Lee 2014).

In a more global sense, the hashtag #BlackTwitter has gained prominence as a rallying virtual place for African-American Twitter users (Florini 2014; Brock 2012). #Black Twitter is used for a variety of topics, but its power is how it creates a "social public" (Brock 2012: 530) as users generate culturally relevant content and disseminate it to their imagined audience, the online black community. As such, #BlackTwitter—and more recently #BlackLivesMatter—has become a means of *signifyin'*—a term Florini defines as a "marker of black racial identity that indexes black popular culture" (2014: 227). Brock (2012) suggests that using this hashtag can be "understood as a discursive, public performance of black identity" (537). Brock (2012: 539) explains further:

> The signifyin' hashtag invites an audience, even more so than the publication of a Tweet to one's followers, by setting the parameters of the discourse to follow. It's also a signal that the Twitterer is part of a larger community and displays her knowledge of the practice, the discourse, and the group's worldview.

Much of the power of social media to give people of color a voice is because it costs nothing, and ideas can rapidly gain currency across a large group of people. For example, when a soccer play at Syracuse University in Upstate New York was videotaped using racial slurs, students at that university responded on Twitter by creating the hashtag #ITooAmSU to share their stories of inequity and stereotypes (Polino 2014). The effort began as a form of self-expression, but it has grown to an effort to bring people together and even organize formal events to combat racism (Polino 2014). As such, social media has provided a technological method for people of color from across the world to unite virtually and share ideas with the larger public. The technology itself provides a wider audience than any individual could have captured alone.

## Social Media and an Informed Electorate

Social media may also have an influence on giving people of color a say in politics. Research has shown that the Internet and other technologies have the power to invigorate political discourse (Papacharissi 2004). Social media became a hallmark of the campaign for President Obama's election to his first term in 2008 (Katz, Barris, and Jain 2013; Garcia-Castañon, Rank, and Barreto 2011). President Obama's use of digital media is credited in part with attracting African Americans and Latinos to register and vote, particularly in Southern states (Stern and Rookey 2013). It also illustrated a means by which candidates could spread a message without the filter of traditional media, offering, perhaps, a more level playing field for future candidates of color (Ford, Johnson, and Maxwell 2010).

At the same time, online participation in politics skyrocketed in 2008, as more than half of American adults turned to the Internet to learn about the campaign or the political process, including 66 percent of black Internet users and 64 percent of Hispanic Internet users (Smith 2009). Garcia-Castañon and colleagues' (2011) analysis of telephone survey data from 4,563 registered voters found that across all racial groups, people who used the Internet to gain political information were more likely to participate politically, but the effect was strongest for African Americans. Certainly, it would be myopic to attribute too much power to social media. Other research suggests (e.g., Yamamoto and Kushin 2014) that turning to social media for campaign information is also positively related to cynicism and apathy, at least among college students. However, clearly from the 2008 presidential election onward, social media has offered a means by which anybody—and particularly groups historically left out of the media conversation—can join and become more informed members of the electorate.

## Conclusion

In summary, social media provides some form of technological solution to the lack of voice that people of color have encountered in traditional media for decades. Because social media are not tied to broadband access or desktop and laptop computers, they offer a means to bridge—in a small way—the digital divide. Those who cannot afford or gain access to a computer can still disseminate their opinions using social media on smartphones. This provides a new opportunity for those previously left out of the public debate by traditional media to both spread their messages and gain a larger audience through the virality of social media that was unheard a mere decade ago. Linguistic tools that have developed on social media, such as the hashtag, offer a means for people of color to gather together virtually, providing a stronger outlet through sheer numbers. In particular, virtual communities that have developed around specific hashtags, such as #BlackTwitter and #BlackLivesMatter, offer a promise of civic engagement through social media. However, despite these positives, clearly much of the societal racial division offline is apparent online as well. The "cybertopia" (Ebo 1998: 2) dreamed of in the early days of the Internet has not transpired, but social media offers fertile ground for a more egalitarian media reality in the future. Whether that will happen will depend on how much people seize the opportunity that social media offers for providing a voice and how strongly social media can resist falling prey to the social norms that led to the traditional inequities based on race in society.

## References

Alvarez, L. (2012, Nov. 6) "Social Media, Growing in Legal Circles, Find a Role in Florida Murder Case," *New York Times*. Retrieved from http://www.nytimes.com/2012/11/07/us/social-media-finds-a-role-in-case-against-zimmerman.html?pagewanted=all.

Bilton, N. (2014, Aug. 27) "Ferguson Reveals a Twitter Loop," *New York Times*. Retrieved from http://www.nytimes.com/2014/08/28/fashion/ferguson-reveals-a-twitter-loop.html.

boyd, d. and Ellison, N. (2007) "Social Network Sites: Definition, History, and Scholarship," *Journal of Computer-Mediated Communication* 13(1): 210–230.

Brock, A. (2012) "From the Blackhand Side: Twitter as a Cultural Conversation," *Journal of Broadcasting & Electronic Media* 56(4): 529–549.

Campbell, C. (1995) *Race, Myth, and the News*. Thousand Oaks, CA: Sage.

Campbell, C., LeDuff, K. M., Jenkins, C. D., and Brown, R. A. (2012) *Race and News: Critical Perspectives*. New York: Routledge.

Chang, H. (2010) *A New Perspective on Twitter Hashtag Use: Diffusion of Innovation Theory*. Proceedings of the ASIST, Pittsburg, PA.

Chen, G. M. (2011) "Tweet This: A Uses and Gratifications Perspective on How Active Twitter Use Gratifies a Need to Connect with Others," *Computers in Human Behavior* 27: 755–762.

Chen, G. M., Williams, S., Hendrickson, N., and Chen, L. (2012) "Male Mammies: A Social-Comparison Perspective on How Exaggeratedly Overweight Media Portrayals of Madea, Rasputia, and Big Momma Affect How Black Women Feel about Themselves," *Mass Communication and Society* 15: 115–135.

Chuang, A. (2012) "Representations of Foreign Versus (Asian) American Identity in a Mass Shooting Case: Newspaper Coverage of the 2009 Binghamton Massacre," *Journalism & Mass Communication Quarterly* 89(2): 244–260.

Collins, P. H. (2000) *Black Feminist Thought: Knowledge, Consciousness, and Politics of Empowerment*. 2nd ed. New York: Routledge.

Davey, M., Eligon, J., and Blinder, A. (2014, Aug. 18) "Missouri Tries Another Idea: Call in National Guard," *New York Times*. Retrieved from http://www.nytimes.com/2014/08/19/us/ferguson-missouri-protests.html.

Davis, E. F., Alves, A. A., and Sklansky, D. A. (2014) "Social Media and Police Leadership: Lessons from Boston," *New Perspectives in Policing Bulletin*. Washington, D.C.: U.S. Department of Justice National Institute of Justice.

Delgado, R. and Stefanic, J. (2012) *Critical Race Theory: An Introduction*. New York: New York University Press.

Deutsch, L. and Lee, J. (2014, Aug. 19) "No Filter: Social Media Show Raw View of #Ferguson," *USA Today*. Retrieved from http://www.usatoday.com/story/news/nation-now/2014/08/14/social-media-ferguson-effect/14052495/.

Dixon, T. and Linz, D. (2000) "Overrepresentation and Underrepresentation of African Americans and Latinos as Lawbreakers on Television News," *Journal of Communication* 50(2): 131–154.

Ebo, B. (1998) *Cyberghetto or Cybertopia: Race, Class, and Gender on the Internet*. Westport, CT: Praeger Publishers.

Ehrlich, B. (2013, July 15) "Trayvon Martin: How Social Media Became the Biggest Protest," *MTV News*. Retrieved from http://www.mtv.com/news/1710582/trayvon-martin-social-media-protest/.

Eltantawy, N. and Wiest, J. B. (2011) "Social Media in the Egyptian Revolution: Reconsidering Resource Mobilization Theory," *International Journal of Communication* 5: 1207–1224.

Florini, S. (2014) "'Tweets, Tweeps, and Signifyin': Communication and Cultural Performance on 'Black Twitter,'" *Television & New Media* 15(3): 223–237.

Ford, P. K., Johnson, T. A., and Maxwell, A. (2010) "'Yes We Can' or 'Yes We Did'? Prospective and Retrospective Change in the Obama Presidency," *Journal of Black Studies* 40(3): 462–483.

Freberg, K., Saling, K., Vidoloff, K. G., and Eosco, G. (2013) "Using Value Modeling to Evaluation Social Media Messages: The Case of Hurricane Irene," *Public Relations Review* 39(3): 185–192.

Garcia-Castañon, M., Rank, A. D., and Barreto, M. A. (2011) "Plugged In or Tuned Out? Youth, Race, and Internet Usage in the 2008 Election," *Journal of Political Marketing* 10: 115–138.

Gilmor, D. (2004) *We the Media*. Santa Rosa, CA: O'Reilly Media.

Granovetter, M. S. (1973) "The Strength of Weak Ties," *American Journal of Sociology* 78(6): 1360–1380.

Guo, L. and Harlow, S. (2014) "User-Generated Racism: An Analysis of Stereotypes of African Americans, Latinos, and Asians in YouTube Videos," *Howard Journal of Communications* 25: 281–302.

Hall, S. (1992) "Race, Culture, and Communications: Looking Backward and Forward at Cultural Studies," *Rethinking Marxism: A Journal of Economics, Culture, & Society* 5(1): 10–18.

——. (1998) "Notes on Deconstructing 'The Popular,'" in J. Storey (ed.), *Cultural Theory and Popular Culture: A Reader*. Upper Saddle River, NJ: Prentice Hall, 443–453.

——. (2000) "Racist Ideologies and the Media," in P. Marris and S. Thornham (eds.), *Media Studies: A Reader*. New York: New York University Press, 271–282.

Hargittai, E. (2008) "Whose Space? Differences among Users and Non-Users of Social Network Sites," *Journal of Computer-Mediated Communication* 13: 276–297.

Horrigan, J. (2009, July 22) "Wireless Internet Use," *Pew Research Internet Project*. Retrieved from http://www.pewinternet.org/2009/07/22/wireless-internet-use/.

Jenkins, C. (2012) "Newsroom Diversity and Representations of Race," in C. Campbell, K. M. LeDuff, C. D. Jenkins, and R. A. Brown (eds.), *Race and News: Critical Perspectives*. New York: Routledge, 22–42.

Johnson, K. A., Dolan, M. K., and Sonnett, J. (2011) "Speaking of Looting: An Analysis of Racial Propaganda in National Television Coverage of Hurricane Katrina," *Howard Journal of Communications* 22: 302–318.

Katz, J. E., Barris, M., and Jain, A. (2013) *The Social Media President: Barack Obama and the Politics of Digital Engagement*. New York: Palgrave.

Liebler, C. (2010) "Me(dia) Culpa: The 'Missing White Woman Syndrome' and Media Self Critique," *Communication, Culture, & Critique* 3(4): 549–565.

Lopez, M. H., Gonzalez-Barrera, A., and Patten, E. (2013, March 7) "Closing the Digital Divide: Latinos and Technology Adoption," *Pew Research Hispanic Trends Project*. Retrieved from http://www.pewhispanic.org/2013/03/07/vi-social-networking/.

Marwick, A. E. and boyd, d. (2011) "I Tweet Honestly, I Tweet Passionately: Twitter Users, Context Collapse, and the Imagined Audience," *New Media & Society* 13(1): 113–140.

Mehra, B., Merkel, C., and Bishop, A. P. (2004) "The Internet for Empowerment of Minority and Marginalized Users," *New Media & Society* 6(6): 781–802.

Melinger, G. (2013) *Chasing Newsroom Diversity: From Jim Crow to Affirmative Action.* Chicago, IL: University of Illinois Press.

Merskin, D. (1998) "Sending Up Signals: A Survey of Native American Media Use and Representation in the Mass Media," *Howard Journal of Communications* 9: 333–345.

Ono, K. A. and Pham, V. (2009) *Asian Americans and the Media.* Malden, MA: Polity Press.

Owen, L. C. (2008) "Network News: The Role of Race in Source Selection and Story Topic," *Howard Journal of Communications* 19: 355–370.

Papacharissi, Z. (2004) "Democracy Online: Civility, Politeness, and the Democratic Potential of Online Political Discussion Groups," *New Media & Society* 6: 259–283.

Papacharissi, Z. and Oliveira, M. D. (2012) "Affective News and Networked Publics: The Rhythms of News Storytelling on #Egypt," *Journal of Communication* 62: 266–282.

Polino, A. (2014, Sept. 22) "SU Students Unite Under Twitter Hashtag," *NCC News Online*. Retrieved from https://nccnews.expressions.syr.edu/uncategorized/su-students-unite-under-twitter-hashtag/.

Rheingold, H. (2000) *The Virtual Community: Homesteading on the Electronic Frontier.* Cambridge, MA: The MIT Press.

Schradie, J. (2012) "The Trend of Class, Race, and Ethnicity in Social Media Inequality: Who Still Cannot Afford to Blog," *Information, Communication, & Society* 15(4): 555–571.

Sears, D. O., Hetts, J. J., Sidanius, J., and Bobo, L. (2000) "Race in American Politics," in D. O. Sears, J. Sidanius, and L. Bobo (eds.), *Racialized Politics: The Debate about Racism in America.* Chicago, IL: University of Chicago Press, 1–43.

Shoemaker, P. J. and Reese, S. (2014) *Mediating the Message.* 3rd ed. New York: Routledge.

Small, T. A. (2011) "What's the Hashtag? A Content Analysis of Canadian Politics on Twitter," *Information, Communication & Society* 14(6): 872–895.

Smith, A. (2009, April 15) "Online Politics in 2008," *Pew Research Internet Project*. Retrieved from http://www.pewinternet.org/2009/04/15/online-politics-in-2008/.

——. (2014, Jan. 6) "African Americans and Technology Use," *Pew Research Internet Project*. Retrieved from http://www.pewinternet.org/2014/01/06/african-americans-and-technology-use/.

Soto, R. E. (2008) "'Made to Be the Maid?' An Examination of the Latina as Maid in Mainstream Film and Television," in M. Meyers (ed.), *Women in Popular Culture: Representation and Meaning.* Cresskill, NJ: Hampton Press, 85–100.

Southall, A. (2014, Aug. 18) "Social Media on Ferguson: Autopsy Reactions and Scenes of Unrest," *New York Times.* Retrieved from http://www.nytimes.com/2014/08/18/us/more-clashes-with-police-in-ferguson-and-reaction-to-autopsy-report.html?_r=1.

Spooner, T. (2001, Dec. 12) "Asian Americans and the Internet," *Pew Research Internet Project.* Retrieved from http://www.pewinternet.org/2001/12/12/asian-americans-and-the-internet/.

Stern, M. J. and Rookey, B. D. (2012) "The Politics of New Media, Space, and Race: A Socio-Spatial Analysis of the 2008 Presidential Election," *New Media & Society* 15(4): 519–540.

Strinati, D. (2004) *An Introduction to Theories in Popular Culture.* New York: Routledge.

Thelwall, M. (2008) "Social Networks, Gender, and Friending: An Analysis of MySpace Member Profiles," *Journal of the American Society for Information Science and Technology* 59(8): 1321–1330.

Tyree, T. (2011) "African American Stereotypes in Reality Television," *Howard Journal of Communications* 22: 394–413.

Vega, T. (2014, Aug. 12) "Shooting Spurs Hasthag Effort on Stereotypes," *New York Times.* Retrieved from http://mobile.nytimes.com/2014/08/13/us/if-they-gunned-me-down-protest-on-twitter.html?_r=3&referrer=.

Warren, M. (2007) "The Digital Vicious Cycle: Links between Social Disadvantage and Digital Exclusion in Rural Areas," *Telecommunications Policy* 31: 374–388.

Williams-Harris, D. (2013, July 12) "Social Media 'Blackout' as Jury Gets Trayvon Martin Case," *Chicago Tribune.* Retrieved from http://articles.chicagotribune.com/2013-07-12/news/chi-trayvon-martin-social-media-20130712_1_george-zimmerman-trayvon-martin-rip-trayvon.

Yamamoto, M. and Kushin, M. J. (2014) "More Harm Than Good? Online Media Use and Political Disaffection among College Students in the 2008 Election," *Journal of Computer-Mediated Communication* 19(3): 430–445.

## **Further Reading**

Harfoush, R. (2009) *Yes We Did! An Inside Look at How Social Media Built the Obama Brand.* Berkeley, CA: New Riders. (A closer look at the role of social media in the 2008 presidential election.)

Harp, D., Bachman, I., Rosas-Moreno, T. C., and Loke, J. (2010) "Wave of Hope: African American Youth Use Media and Engage More Civically, Politically than Whites," *Howard Journal of Communication* 21: 224–246. (Results of a multi-wave panel survey of media use and political and social attitudes among 12–17-year-olds that shows Africans Americans are more likely than whites to engage in civic and political activities online and offline.)

Nakamura, L. and Chow-White, P. A. (2012) *Race after the Internet.* New York: Taylor & Francis. (Examination of how social inequity along racial lines persists despite the equalizing force of the Internet.)

Rightler-McDaniels, J. L. and Hendrickson, E. M. (2014) "Hoes and Hashtags: Construction of Gender and Race in Trending Topics," *Social Semiotics* 24(2): 175–190. (A content analysis and critical discourse analysis of Twitter hashtags that relate to the construction of race and gender.)

# 12
# JOURNALISM AND AFRICAN AMERICANS

## Diversity and Perspective

### Cheryl D. Jenkins

Media coverage of alleged police brutality, the shooting deaths of unarmed African-American men and women by police, and the subsequent protests in response to those actions again in 2014 and 2015 brought to the forefront the failures of mainstream journalism to report critically on issues concerning race in America. Mainly relying on episodic rather than thematic perspective in their reporting, most journalists still seem to lack the ability to provide appropriate context to explain the complexities surrounding issues of race in this country. *Quill*, a magazine published by the Society of Professional Journalists, in 2015 observed:

> We live in what is supposed to be a post-racial era. As a result, many reporters seem to have accepted the ideology that the best way to be even-handed is to ignore race altogether. . . . Even as protestors continue to take to the streets, we still see relatively little reporting on documented racial gaps in education, health, employment and accumulated wealth. . . . Journalists have a responsibility to do more than report on the latest news developments, relying on whatever sources are handy. We should weave a web of information that ties people together across the demographic spectrum, supporting everyone's involvement in the democratic process.
>
> *(Lehrman 2015: 31)*

Mainstream news coverage of race-related events follows a pattern. In early 2012 Americans began to see reports about the fatal shooting of 17-year-old Trayvon Martin in Sanford, Florida by neighborhood watchman George Zimmerman. As the coverage of this incident continued, so did the implication that Martin himself played a hand in his own demise and that his "threatening" attire and "questionable" background should play a role in the outcome of the case. The Martin tragedy set the stage for a larger moral discussion of how the media handles issues related to race, how victims are covered and portrayed in the media, and how the framing of this tragic event falls in line with journalists' tendency to present stories as one-dimensional struggles between good and evil.

The overly simplistic coverage of the Martin incident as well as other racialized events helps to strengthen the argument that a more diverse news media, with viewpoints that reflect the actual makeup of the communities being covered, would serve a true democracy better. As such, this chapter focuses on journalistic representations of African Americans as it examines the current efforts of the mainstream media industry to incorporate a more diverse workforce, the effects of limited diverse perspectives and voices on news content, and the influence of alternative news media on coverage of complex topics like race in the twenty-first century.

Efforts by the American mainstream media to recruit and hire more minority journalists have traditionally garnered minimal results, unfortunately. Although data show an increase in hiring numbers over the years, the fact is most newsrooms across the country do not reflect the demographic makeup of the communities they cover (Wilson, Gutierrez, and Chao 2003; Porter 2004; Fleming-Rife and Proffitt 2004; Dedman and Doig 2005). The Kerner Commission challenged the news media to "diversify their workforces, news agendas, and reporting" over 40 years ago. Released in March 1968, the Commission's report, officially titled the *Report of the National Advisory Commission on Civil Disorders*, addressed the role of mass media in the violence that erupted in dozens of U.S. cities the previous year. The commission recommended in its extensive report that the news media should "take a leadership role" in helping to reverse the lack of understanding in the general public about the plight of black America during the late 1960s. This, according to the commission, could be accomplished by "news organizations engaging in voluntary self-studies of their own news content, developing sources within the black community, and by assigning regular beat reporting within African American neighborhoods" (Byerly and Wilson 2009: 212).

The results and ultimate fallout from the commission's report affected the broadcast industry as well. According to Hollifield and Kimbro (2010), following the release of the Kerner report, the Federal Communication Commission adopted Equal Employment Opportunity (EEO) rules as part of broadcast-station regulation on the argument that stations discriminating in employment did not serve their audiences. The FCC stated:

> Beginning in 1971, stations with more than five employees were required to file an annual employment form (Form 395-B) reporting the race and gender of all employees in each of nine job categories, with station employment practices evaluated during license renewal. In the decade following, employment of minorities in U.S. commercial television stations rose from 9 percent to 16 percent of all jobs, and from 6 percent to 14 percent of "Top 4" positions. Research suggested, however, that much of the change was "window dressing," with minorities and women reclassified into Top 4 positions but without real decision-making authority.
> *(Hollifield and Kimbro 2010: 231)*

Newspaper hiring data published in a study by the Pew Research Center in 2013 stated that, overall, minority journalists accounted for 12 percent of the total newspaper newsroom workforce in 2012. Smaller newspapers were less likely to employ minority journalists and women were often underrepresented in newspaper newsrooms. The study concluded that in the past two decades, there has been little overall change in the percentage of minorities in the newsroom. Subsequently, on a positive note, the number of minority journalists in daily newspaper newsrooms increased by a couple of hundred in 2013 even as newsroom employment declined by 3.2 percent, according to the annual census released in 2014 by the American Society of News Editors and the Center for Advanced Social Research.

ASNE's 2014 census also found that 63 percent of the news organizations surveyed have at least one woman among their top three editors. The percentage of minority leaders is lower, with 15 percent of participating organizations saying at least one of their top three editors was a person of color. This was the first year the questions about women and minorities in leadership were asked. Overall, the survey found that there were about 36,700 full-time daily newspaper journalists at nearly 1,400 newspapers in the United States. That's a 1,300-person decrease from 38,000 in 2012. Of those employees, about 4,900, or 13.34 percent, are racial and ethnic minorities. That's up about 200 people, or one percentage point, from the previous year's 4,700 and 12.37 percent. It is nearly as high as the record of 13.73 percent in 2006. The percentage of minority journalists has remained between 12 and 14 percent for more than a decade. In 1978, when ASNE launched its Newsroom Employment Census of professional full-time journalists, only 3.95 percent were minorities (Minorities in newsrooms increase, 2014).

The table below illustrates the divide between white and minority workers in the newspaper industry by job category in 2014.

The table below shows the racial makeup of newspaper workers in 2013. As noted, supervisory or leadership positions decreased between 2013 and 2014.

The vast divide between the numbers of whites compared to minorities in the newsroom has been a point of contention for media scholars and practitioners for years.

*Table 12.1* Whites and minorities by job category

| 2014 | Total Work Force | Minorities | | Whites | |
| --- | --- | --- | --- | --- | --- |
| | | No. | Pct. | No. | Pct. |
| Supervisors | 8,991 | 1,015 | 11 | 7,976 | 89 |
| Reporters/Writers/Bloggers | 16,743 | 2,231 | 13 | 14,513 | 87 |
| Copy Editors | 4,722 | 578 | 12 | 4,144 | 88 |
| Producers/Designers | 3,043 | 514 | 17 | 2,530 | 83 |
| Photographers/Artists/Videographers | 3,223 | 550 | 17 | 2,673 | 83 |
| **Totals** | **36,722** | **4,887** | **13** | **31,835** | **87** |

*Source*: ASNE 2014 Census http://asne.org.

*Table 12.2* Whites and minorities by job category

| 2013 | Total Work Force | Minorities | | Whites | |
| --- | --- | --- | --- | --- | --- |
| | | No. | Pct. | No. | Pct. |
| Supervisors | 9,087 | 943 | 10 | 8,144 | 90 |
| Reporters/Writers/Bloggers | 17,422 | 2,199 | 13 | 15,223 | 87 |
| Copy Editors | 4,778 | 506 | 11 | 4,272 | 89 |
| Producers/Designers | 3,202 | 494 | 15 | 2,709 | 85 |
| Photographers/Artists/Videographers | 3,493 | 573 | 16 | 2,920 | 84 |
| **Totals** | **37,982** | **4,715** | **12** | **33,267** | **88** |

*Source*: ASNE 2013 Census http://asne.org.

In 2010, Dori J. Maynard, president of the Robert C. Maynard Institute for Journalism Education and an expert on the subject of newsroom diversity, stated in *Editor and Publisher*:

> At this point the industry and the country are going in two different directions. The industry is getting whiter while the country is getting browner. As legacy media struggles to remain relevant, it's imperative that we step up our efforts to ensure that all news organizations have the staffing culturally competent to accurately and fairly reflect all segments of our society.
>
> *(12)*

According to Jenkins (2012), the idea of diversifying newsrooms and covering complex issues with more diverse perspective and insight has been an objective of American media for almost half a century. This aspect of the news organization has a theoretical basis and implications. First, the notion of a more complex or inclusive media stems from this institution's historical tendency to portray African Americans and other marginalized groups as either inferior to the dominant class in society or to not include their perspectives at all. Second, journalists determine the approach to the coverage of news events and issues in the media, and the way they frame their stories affects how readers and viewers comprehend those events and issues. Framing provides a way to make sense of relevant events and dramatically shapes the way issues are viewed. And, since "framing" can be influenced by a journalist's personal values in addition to ideological constraints imposed on the medium (Kraeplin 2008), cultural background is a relevant predictor of news value judgment and source selection that journalists make each day.

Most industry leaders today acknowledge the media's shortcomings in covering minority communities, issues of race and racism, and ideological and political divides between racial and ethnic groups. Research suggests that mass media can contribute to sustaining and even strengthening prejudicial attitudes through different forms of bias, stereotypes, and frames (Jenkins and Cole 2012). The obvious aspects of cultural influence and differences affect interpretations of media frames in a way that media scholars have highlighted in varying degrees. In particular, the treatment of race and issues of racism when covered by the media reveals intrinsic attitudes of media professionals that are inherent in societal ideologies. Journalists all have their own personal identities that can become a part of how or what they write. This can be troubling as research suggests that a person's own ideology and previously held beliefs can be the strongest factor for negative racial attitudes (Gans 1979).

Moreover, racial identity is a frame that one uses to categorize another person, typically based on skin color; it seems most often to be a frame in which individuals identify consciously or unconsciously with those with whom they feel a common bond because of similar traditions, behaviors, values, and beliefs (Ott 1989). The subtle framing of news stories using racial cues can have a great impact on the representation of a given race. And, as racial framing found its way into media coverage of controversial stories like the Trayvon Martin tragedy, the 2014 shooting of Michael Brown by Officer Darrin Wilson in Ferguson, Missouri, and the 2015 death of Baltimore resident Freddie Gray at the hands of the Baltimore City Police, it becomes central in the argument for a more nuanced discussion about the inclusion of more minorities with views reflective of their own identities and cultures in mainstream newsrooms.

Dolan (2011) argues that American mainstream journalism "consistently serves white racial interests and the racial status quo despite its push for diversity and improvement in the coverage of nonwhite communities" (31). The study reexamined the relationship between white journalists' self-identity and self-understanding and their journalistic identifications. The researcher interviewed 60 white mainstream journalists to evaluate how the way they see themselves (as neutral, fair, and above politics) affects the stories they choose to tell (or not), as well as the way those identifications keep them from seeing their news choices as the result of their racial, class, sexual, or gender interests, among others. This is a departure from other works in critical journalism studies that have focused more on what journalists think of others and how that affects the journalism they produce (Gans 1980; Gitlin 1980; Heider 2000; Tuchman 1978).

The majority of the respondents interviewed saw being white as inconsequential, which led Dolan to theorize that they were unlikely to see themselves as members of a "racial interest group." The researcher considered this finding problematic in relation to how the reporters covered news concerning race and other sensitive topics. Dolan's study found,

> When asked how they try to be fair and avoid bias, many journalists said they do their best to recognize their biases and then account for them or put them aside while reporting and editing stories. But not knowing—and often never even considering—what it means to be white can lead to white journalists believing they are more neutral when evaluating whether race is an element of story—or the degree to which it's an element of a story—because they have no racial interests to put aside. They may expect nonwhites to put their racial interests aside—or at the very least not let them have an undue influence in making news judgments—and may suspect nonwhite journalists of "having an agenda," being "ideological," or being "overly sensitive" when arguing race is an element in a story or raising concerns about news coverage.
>
> *(23)*

Dolan concluded that the tendency of whites not to think about whiteness, or about norms, behaviors, experiences, or perspectives that are white-specific, can lead to news judgments that unintentionally reinforce white incumbency, such as missing or avoiding racial aspects of various stories. Although journalists demonstrate a number of often contradictory identifications and self-understandings about themselves and their work, such as commitments to diversity and not taking sides, these conflicts are almost always resolved in favor of the racial status quo. Further, it is not only important to study the structures of journalistic conventions and practices, but also "the cultural factors (journalistic identifications, color-blind discourses, professionalism, Enlightenment ideals) that maintain allegiances to those structures even as they are routinely criticized from all directions and their usefulness and viability are questioned as the business models for mainstream news media continue to collapse" (4).

This argument further illustrates the notion that personal beliefs and values are reflected in the way stories are told by journalists and the types of stories that are actually being told. It also substantiates the need not only for journalism with multiple points of view, but also for journalism with structures and procedures that can adequately accommodate those views. According to Deggans (2012), greater diversity in the media equals greater accuracy and fairness, and U.S. history is filled with stories journalists got wrong because they excluded the perspectives of anyone who wasn't a white male. Further, he argues that a diverse newsroom better reflects the population, which enables fairer, more accurate, or incisive reporting. These tenets of journalism have helped to maintain the integrity of this constitutionally protected estate and are integral components of the formal structure of journalism that are considered norms of the craft.

Most media scholars argue that a diversified newsroom will improve media coverage of minority communities and issues, but others think that the power of journalistic norms will constrain minority journalists so they will be unable or unwilling to enhance the news coverage of minorities. According to Nishikawa et al. (2009), through training, journalists are taught to adhere to universally recognized "newsgathering norms." Scholars have identified and critiqued the norms of objectivity, accuracy, balance, and fairness because these norms limit what journalists deem as news and influence how that news is presented.

The Nishikawa study found that objective and fair reporting demands that journalists report two sides of an issue regardless of the nature or complexity of the issue. This can be problematic as research has shown that when the press covers complex topics that involve issues of race, ethnicity, and culture in general, taking an interpretive approach to news coverage can provide "a more truthful, comprehensive, and intelligent account of the day's events in a context which gives them meaning" (Davies 2005: 208), compared to a more objective approach. The benefits of news being reported and interpreted for clarity, value, and cultural significance may be a more useful need of journalism than just repeating facts that have no intrinsic meaning or value to everyday citizens. Further, mainstream journalists consistently rely on authoritative sources, particularly political and government leaders, rather than non-official or dissident voices. Nishikawa et al. (2009) concluded that "this dependency on official sources leads to the exclusion and marginalization of minority voices, hindering democracy as a result" (3).

As a result, mainstream news organizations may seek to hire minority journalists, but, through the routine use of journalistic norms, minority journalists are expected to "act" like traditional journalists, not like minorities. As the study observes:

> Minority journalists are forced to back away from their racial identity and lived experiences and conform to the professional norms and values of the organization and the individuals who hired them. This results in an "illusion of inclusion" in the mainstream newsroom. That is, "true diversity" becomes an illusion as minority journalists find themselves marginalized in newsrooms, encouraged only to report stories that reinforce white stereotypes or further a one-sided political agenda. As a result, a diverse newsroom does not always equal better coverage of minorities and stronger readership from a multicultural community.
> 
> *(4)*

Deggans (2012) also argues that there are potential problems journalists may face when adhering to the traditional norms of journalism, especially when covering issues of race. He does suggest, however, that ethical decision-making be at the core of any successful strategy for media diversity and that "real success in covering race comes when perspectives are tempered by a clear strategy for preserving fairness and accuracy." The issue, he says, is that the coverage of such sensitive topics often falls into four categories:

> Reflex – We cover issues a certain way because we've always done it that way. Trusting police reports too much or failing to see the news in a teenager killed could be a result.

Fear – We fear being criticized for injecting race into a story, particularly if it isn't the central issue.

Lack of history – We don't understand the community we're covering and their specific issues. Black resident in Sanford (Florida) had specific gripes about how police treated them that many national media outlets didn't discuss (when covering the Trayvon Martin tragedy).

Avoidance – When a newsroom is diverse, sometimes staffers of color are expected to provide the bulk of coverage on issues relating to race. That's not fair to the staffers or to the community, which deserves news outlets where every journalist is attentive to such stories and issues.

While traditional media continue to grapple with the complexities of creating a more diverse and inclusive media, particularly with questionable results when reporting on issues of race, many subjective and alternative sources of news continue to provide space for more critical reporting and dialogue. "Ethnic media" often fill that gap for people of color. For instance, many black Americans have often found issues that affect their community to be more prominently featured and critically reported and discussed in the black press. Jenkins (2011) says that, historically, black newspapers have filled in the gaps on discussions about race that need context and perspective to be useful in decision-making. And although some minority columnists at mainstream papers have attempted to tackle such a complex topic, particularly when mainstream America is directly affected, these newspapers have fared worse in covering the issues that affect minorities in this country and this is mainly because of the lack of diversity in newsrooms and the professional norms of the journalists themselves.

Moody et al. (2008) asserted that black and mainstream newspaper content normally differ due to the varied missions addressed by the two newspaper types: "Mainstream media aims to serve the general population, while the black press targets the black community. In addition, black press newspapers often cover specific issues important to the black community from a black perspective that is often overlooked by the mainstream media" (6). Additionally, Ratzlaff and Iorio (1994) found that while both newspaper types often focused on the same issues, they did not use the same frames. Their study also found that positions advocated by the black and mainstream newspapers tended to follow party lines, with the mission statements of the individual newspapers serving as a key factor that influenced how journalists framed those issues.

Deggans (2012) used the example of how the Trayvon Martin tragedy was covered by mainstream media to point out problems with the reporting of a story clouded with racial overtones. His analysis of the coverage suggests that initial mainstream news reports left out important aspects of the case that would have directly connected it to more racialized themes that ultimately affected the black community. Laying out his points chronologically, Deggans stated:

One of the first reports on the shooting, an 86-word piece printed in the *Orlando Sentinel* Feb. 27, noted simply that "two men were arguing before shots were fired." The next day, the newspaper published another 152-word story naming Martin, citing his age and noting his Facebook page listed Miami as his hometown, quoting a local TV station's report that there had been a fistfight before the shooting. But the newspaper didn't name Zimmerman, it wrote, "because he has not been charged."

By March 2, the *Miami Herald* had published a report noting erroneously that Martin was shot dead at a convenience store, quoting the teen's uncle. It did name Zimmerman, but understated the 28-year-old's age by three years. None of these stories, however, had the detail which would turn Martin's case into an international media tsunami: Martin was black and the shooter who killed him was not.

Race was the engine which turned Trayvon Martin's death into the first story to briefly eclipse the presidential race in coverage during 2012; sparking "million hoodie" marches across the country . . . and eventually costing Sanford police chief Bill Lee his job.

With the race difference, police reticence to arrest Zimmerman took on a new light, raising fears of a Southern town's good ol' boy network in action.

And journalists had an angle which could elevate the unfortunate shooting of a young boy into a story with implications about racial profiling, small town justice and the struggle for a working class, black family to get fair treatment from a mostly white police force and criminal justice system.

The black press in both online and print formats used the Martin tragedy to highlight systemic issues of racial profiling and the criminalization of young African Americans, particularly African-American men. The controversial story, as Tracy Powell (2012) pointed out in an article published on the Poynter Institute's media wire, "galvanized the black press and its audience." The story also ushered in new guards of black media, with online news sites and bloggers sprouting up to provide much-needed insight and perspective to coincide with the more traditional reporting of the mainstream media.

Jeff John Roberts (2012), a writer for the African-American news site theGrio, stated that the site helped drive major network NBC's coverage of the Trayvon Martin tragedy. Roberts wrote,

> Since its first piece on March 8 (2012), theGrio has published more than 250 stories on Martin and many of its videos have landed on shows like the "Today" show and "NBC Nightly News." theGrio's success reflects the rise of a new generation of African American news as well as a new symbiosis between niche and mainstream media outlets.

Powell (2012) says that the black press has the freedom to stay on top of stories like Trayvon Martin's, even when other news happens, a freedom that may not exist at other types of publications. Powell's piece quoted Nisa Muhammad, chairwoman of the National Association of Black Journalists' Black Press Task Force and staff writer for *The Final Call* newspaper, who observed,

> Black audiences, in particular, are not going to get everything they need to know about this story from the mainstream media. Passion and commitment to the story to the end is what readers get from the black press. We're going to stay on this story until justice is done.

The limitations present in mainstream media to adequately serve communities of color have pushed more journalists from that community to create alternative modes of disseminating news information deemed significant to them. The black press has traditionally been known to take a more interpretive and sometimes subjective approach when reporting on events that affect African Americans; subsequently, the nuance that has been achieved from this type of journalism seems to transition well into the digital age in which the media now exists. A great lesson from the Trayvon Martin coverage is that black websites and bloggers helped bring attention to a story that almost never saw the front pages of the American mainstream press. Powell (2012) stated about the coverage:

> While mainstream publications debate whether the hoodie Martin wore led to his death or whether racism played a role in his killing, black publications see an opportunity to fulfill a greater mission. They are also more focused on the specifics of Martin's case than more mainstream news organizations. For the black press and its audience: They recognized this story as an opportunity to say that sometimes there is a suspicion that the institutions in society don't work for people of color the way they work for white people. The central concern here was maybe the police and prosecutors who were initially involved didn't do as thorough a job as they should have.

*Washington Post* editor Milton Coleman (2011) has observed that nearly half a century after rioters in Los Angeles took to the streets to protest racial and economic injustice in the US, the entire notion of newsroom diversity is up for grabs, starting with what the words mean in the digitized and fragmented environment that is journalism today. He argues that most mainstream media outlets see the issue of newsroom diversity close to, if not completely, settled. Coleman argues that this sentiment exists even though data show that the number of minority journalists who can help provide a more comprehensive account of the day's news is still woefully low:

> Diversity fatigue has been alive and well in America's news industry for many years. Even before ASNE started to experience a steady decline in its membership, the diversity sessions at its annual convention were sparsely attended. In the minds of some people, diversity had gone far enough. They viewed it as an unaffordable luxury during a time of financial difficulties that signaled the need to hold on to high-value customers and newsroom employees, most of whom were white.
>
> (34)

The measured steps mainstream journalism has taken to increase diversity in its newsrooms have not been lost upon young journalists who are completely comfortable with the online and digital platforms news outlets must now use. Many are taking advantage of the more autonomous method of media production to create their own mode of message dissemination.

According to Hayes (2012), reporters like Danielle C. Belton represent a new breed of journalists-turned-entrepreneurs who are carving out their own niches after working in the old paradigm of print media. Belton is a former newspaper reporter and columnist for the *Bakersfield California* and launched her own blog in 2007 after leaving the newspaper. She told Hayes:

> Daily newspapers are struggling, so it's not shocking that there is a decline. Whenever things get narrow, newspapers are not as open to diversity. The reality is that you don't make a lot of money starting out in the middle of nowhere, in small towns and the rural South. It's harder to be a minority uprooted from your community and thrust into a sink-or-swim situation.
>
> *(7)*

Belton has proven that there are alternatives to a traditional career in print journalism. Hayes (2012) stated that with two million readers in less than two years, Belton's satirical look at politics in her blog *The Black Snob* has earned recognition on CNN, *The Daily Beast*, ABC's *Good Morning America* and *Nightline*, and in *Time* magazine, the *New York Times*, and the UK's *The Observer*. She also appeared on NPR's "Tell Me More" with Michel Martin and PBS's "To The Contrary" with Bonnie Erbe. As Hayes writes,

> As the new reality continues for newspapers, some minority reporters are re-emerging by creating their own voice and filling voids that have not been captured through traditional news media. They represent a paradigm shift that may not be easily captured in media surveys and they are deciding how and in what capacity they will participate in the news arena.
>
> *(7)*

Roberts (2012) stated that the emergence of these outlets shows that African-American media is sharing a similar experience to news media overall—one in which "digital natives" are best poised to succeed and the new guards in black media are being made online.

## Concluding Thoughts

Minority groups have historically found alternative ways to have their voices heard when faced with little to no inclusion in mainstream media outlets. And although those alternative methods have had major impacts on message dissemination in this country, they are still homogenous in nature and only serve to address the unique needs and concerns of one particular group. Media outlets that purport to serve an entire democratic society cannot afford such homogeneity. As columnist Riva Gold wrote in a 2013 article for *The Atlantic*, that standard "can lead to news coverage that is incomplete, tone-deaf, or biased." The troubling trend in mainstream media is that it is less inclusive of voices outside of dominant power structures in society. With over 30,000 journalists covering the news in American mainstream media, the industry continues to fail in its efforts to diversify its newsrooms with fewer minorities getting the opportunity to work in news, and news organizations suffering in their ability to report on minority populations in their community.

Moreover, with the newspaper industry in particular losing thousands of positions over the past decade, the media business can no longer afford not to cater to the needs of the society it actually serves. As such, the industry must be more responsive to diverse audiences and advertisers. Additionally, the limitations are not specific to the coverage or inclusion of one particular ethnic or racial group in America. In addition to reports on diversity mentioned earlier from ASNE, data from the Radio Television Digital News Association (2014) show that minority groups only accounted for 22.4 percent of television journalists and 13 percent of radio journalists. African Americans, Hispanics, Asians, and Native Americans were the groups included in the overall count of minority workers.

That means the numbers are collectively low across minority groups who together make up 37.9 percent of the U.S. population, according to 2015 census data.

Finally, as noted in research conducted by Vercellotti and Brewer (2006), many minorities often combine their consumption of mainstream news with alternative forms of media to get a more thorough and inclusive view of important events in society. This is indicative of a subpar effort by mainstream media to incorporate more diverse perspectives and voices in its news content and may also influence the rise in the popularity of alternative news media in this country. The issue has not been lost on many industry leaders. After recent reports from ASNE indicated continued misses in newsroom diversity, Karen Magnuson, editor of the *Rochester Democrat and Chronicle* and co-chair of the ASNE Diversifying the News Committee, stated:

> The fact that our industry isn't making progress continues to be frustrating. As the makeup of our nation changes, our news reports must change, as well. Our newsrooms and coverage must be inclusive to tell the real story of what is really happening in our communities. How can we do that well if our newsrooms lack diverse voices and perspectives? We editors can and should do better.
>
> *(Quoted in Hebbard 2015)*

## References

American Society of Newspaper Editors (2014, July 29) "Minorities in Newsrooms Increase; 63 Percent of Newspapers Have at Least One Woman among Top-Three Editors," Asne.org. Retrieved from http://asne.org/content.asp?pl=121andsl=387andcontentid=387.

Byerly, C. and Wilson C. (2009) "Journalism as Kerner Turns 40: Its Multicultural Problems and Possibilities," *Howard Journal of Communications* 20: 209–221.

Coleman, M. (2011) "Diversity in Newsrooms: Fresh Strategies, New Goals," *Nieman Reports* 65(3): 34–35.

Davies, D. (2005) "The Challenges of Civil Rghts and Joseph McCarthy," in S. R. Knowlton and K. L. Freeman (eds.), *Fair and Balanced: A History of Journalistic Objectivity*. Northport, AL: Vision Press, 206–220.

Dedman, B. and Doig, S. K. (2005, June 1) "Newsroom Diversity has Passed Its Peak at Most Newspapers, 1990–2005 Study Shows," Knight Foundation Power Reporting. Retrieved from http://www.powerreporting.com/knight/.

Deggans, E. (2012, Oct. 23) "Why Ethics and Diversity Matter: The Case of Trayvon Martin Coverage," Poynter Institute Media Wire. Retrieved from http://www.poynter.org/news/mediawire/192604/mostly-white-and-sometimes-brown-media-people-in-a-mostly-brown-and-sometimes-white-world/.

Dolan, K. (2011) "Journalistic and White Identifications and the Failures of Diversity." Paper presented at the annual meeting of the International Communication Association, Boston, MA.

Fleming-Rife, A. and Proffitt, J. M. (2004) "The More Public School Reform Changes, the More It Stays the Same: Framing Newspaper Coverage of Brown v. Board of Education at 50," *Journal of Negro Education*, 73(3) (Summer).

Gitlin, T. (1980) *The Whole World Is Watching*. Berkeley, CA: University of California Press.

Gross, R., Curtin, P. A., and Cameron, G. T. (2001) "Diversity Advances both Journalism, Business," *Newspaper Research Journal* 22(2): 14–27.

Hayes, D. (2012) "Newsroom Diversity: An Online Paradigm Shift," *Diverse: Issues In Higher Education* 29(10): 7.

Hebbard, D. B. (2015, July 28) "ASNE Census Shows Large Job Losses for U.S. Journalists, Little Progress in Minority Hiring," *Talking New Media*. Retrieved from http://www.talkingnewmedia.com/2015/07/28/asne-census-shows-large-job-losses-for-us-journalists-little-progress-in-minority-hiring/.

Heider, D. (2000) *White News: Why Local News Programs Don't Cover People of Color*. Mahwah, NJ: Lawrence Erlbaum Associates.

Hollifield, C. A. and Kimbro, C. W. (2010) "Understanding Media Diversity: Structural and Organizational Factors Influencing Minority Employment in Local Commercial Television," *Journal of Broadcasting and Electronic Media* 54(2): 228–247.

Jenkins, C. (2012) "Newspapers and Representations of Race," in C. Campbell, K. LeDuff, C. Jenkins, and R. Brown (eds.), *Race and News: Critical Perspectives*. London: Routledge, 22–42.

Jenkins, C. and Cole, H. (2012) "Nappy-headed Hos: Media Framing, Blame Shifting and the Controversy of Don Imus' Pejorative Language," in C. Campbell, K. LeDuff, C. Jenkins, and R. Brown (eds.), *Race and News: Critical Perspectives*. London: Routledge, 177–198.

Kraeplin, C. (2008) "Two Tales of One City: How Cultural Perspective Influenced the Framing of a Pre-civil Rights Story in Dallas," *American Journalism* 25(1): 73–98.

Lehrman, S. (2015, April 3) "Weave Web of Diverse Sources across Demographics," *Quill* 103(2): 31.

Moody, M., Dorries, B., Blackwell, H., and Sutton, A. (2008) "Missing Pretty Girl Syndrome: How Mainstream and Black Press Framed the Phenomena of Missing Women in the Mid-2000s." Paper presented at the annual meeting of the *International Communication Association*, Montreal, Quebec, Canada.

Moynihan, S. (2010) "Newsroom Diversity Still an Attainable Goal?," *Editor and Publisher* 143(6): 12–15.

Nishikawa, K. A., Towner, T. L., Clawson, R. A., and Waltenburg, E. N. (2009) "Interviewing the Interviewers: Journalistic Norms and Racial Diversity in the Newsroom," *Howard Journal of Communications* 20(3): 242–259.

Papper, B. (2014, July 29) "Women, Minorities Make Newsroom Gains," Radio Television Digital News Association. Retrieved from http://www.rtdna.org/article/women_minorities_make_newsroom_gains.

Porter, T. (2004, April 21) "ASNE's Diversity Study: Looking for Answers," message posted to http://www.timporter.com/firstdraft/archives/000298.html.

Powell, T. (2012, April 23) "Trayvon Martin Story Revitalizes Black Press, Mobilizes 'Newguard,'" pointer.org. Retrieved from http://www.poynter.org/news/mediawire/169798/trayvon-martin-story-revitalizes-black-press/.

Ratzlaff, A. and Iorio, S. H. (1995) "Political Issues in the Early Black Press: Applying Frame Analysis to Historical Contexts," paper presented to the Association for Education in Journalism and Mass Communication annual meeting in Washington, DC, 1995.

Roberts, J. J. (2012, April 12) "Trayvon Martin, theGrio and 'New Guards' of Black Media," Retrieved from https://gigaom.com/2012/04/12/trayvon-martin-thegrio-and-new-guards-of-black-media/.

Vercellotti, T. and Brewer, P. R. (2006) "'To Plead Our Own Cause': Public Opinion toward Black and Mainstream News Media among African Americans," *Journal of Black Studies* 37(2): 231–250.

White, G. (2015, July 24) "Where Are All the Minority Journalists?," *The Atlantic*. Retrieved from http://www.theatlantic.com/business/archive/2015/07/minorities-in-journalism/399461/.

Wilson, C., Gutierrez, F., and Chao, L. M. (2003) *Racism, Sexism and the Media*. Thousand Oaks, CA: Sage Publications.

## Further Reading

Byerly, C. and Wilson C. (2009) "Journalism as Kerner Turns 40: Its Multicultural Problems and Possibilities," *Howard Journal of Communications* 20: 209–221. (Examination of the state of news media 40 years after the Kerner Report and the industry's demonstrated stagnation in the area of diversity.)

Heider, D. (2000) *White News: Why Local News Programs Don't Cover People of Color*. Mahwah, NJ: Lawrence Erlbaum Associates. (An ethnographic study that provides insight into how the local news coverage of people of color is perceived by the people involved in the coverage.)

Mellinger, G. (2013) *Chasing Newsroom Diversity: From Jim Crow to Affirmative Action*. Urbana, Chicago, and Springfield: University of Illinois Press. (Explores the complex history of the decades-long American Society of Newspaper Editors' diversity initiative, which culminated in the failed Goal 2000 effort to match newsroom demographics with those of the U.S. population.)

Newkirk, P. (2002) *Within the Veil: Black Journalists, White Media*. New York: New York University Press. (Examines the ways in which race influences news reporting, both overtly and covertly, and how African-American journalists have influenced and been denied influence to the content, presentation, and nature of news.)

Nishikawa, K. A., Towner, T. L., Clawson, R. A., and Waltenburg, E. N. (2009) "Interviewing the Interviewers: Journalistic Norms and Racial Diversity in the Newsroom," *Howard Journal of Communications* 20(3): 242–259. (Results of a study using face-to-face interviews with African-American and Latino journalists working at mainstream papers to examine journalistic norms and racial diversity in those newsrooms.)

# 13
# JOURNALISM AND LATINOS

## Stereotypes, Underrepresentation, and Ignorance

*Raul Reis*

On February 10, 2015, Antonio Zambrano-Montes, a Mexican national who had settled 10 years earlier in Pasco, a city of 70,000 people in Washington state, died after being fatally shot by police officers after a frantic chase in a busy intersection. The 30-second video of the chase and shooting was seen and shared by millions of viewers in the United States and abroad in the days after the incident, prompting many to speculate that Pasco, Wash., would enter the national consciousness and debate about race and police brutality much in the same way Ferguson, Mo., had managed to do half a year before (Oliver Laughland, *The Guardian*, February 17, 2015). Despite some significant street protests in Pasco and elsewhere in the weeks that followed, somehow the "Pasco moment" never really solidified, and the collective conversation about human rights, which these days seems to be mostly taking place on (and being steered by) social media, moved on to other topics, such as the so-called "religious freedom" laws in Indiana, Mississippi, and other states.

The shooting by police officers of an unarmed Mexican-American man in Pasco packed all the punch of a significant race/media/human rights event. Pasco's population is 56 percent Hispanic (Census Quick Facts 2010), and yet only one of the seven elected city council members is of Hispanic descent, with Hispanics making up only 22 percent of the local police force at the time of the incident (Laughland 2015). The shooting was captured by an amateur photographer and widely disseminated over the Internet and social media, much in the same way the video capturing the death of Eric Garner during a confrontation with the New York City police had been in July 2014. Additionally, NBC News reported on February 16 that Zambrano-Montes' fatal shooting was the fourth police shooting incident in Pasco in 6 months, prompting Latino leaders to ask the U.S. Department of Justice to investigate the case (NBC News 2015). A similar pattern had been observed in the aforementioned confrontations and court cases involving shootings of African-American citizens in Missouri, Florida, Ohio, New York, and elsewhere, with the Ferguson incident prompting a scathing report from the U.S. Department of Justice. And yet the Pasco shooting was all but forgotten by the public sphere after a few weeks.

When the Pasco case resurfaced again in early September 2015, news organizations across the country reported that the Franklin County prosecutor had declined to pursue criminal charges against the three police officers involved in the fatal Zambrano-Montes shooting (Helsel 2015). Once again, the public reaction was a deafening silence.

Communication researchers who have studied the representation of Latinos in both news and entertainment U.S. media have been arguing for decades that this portrayal is characterized by negative stereotyping, severe underrepresentation, and general ignorance about the community (Fujioka 2011). If that assessment still holds true, the Zambrano-Montes case would be highly emblematic of a decades-long phenomenon, which could in turn help to explain why the incident failed to galvanize a larger national audience in the same way the Trayvon Martin, Michael Brown, and Eric Garner cases did.

Indeed, an academic discussion about Latinos and the media could hardly fail to acknowledge how scholars have dealt with three main issues: stereotyping and its effects on popular perception; underrepresentation and its pitfalls; and ignorance about the group and the potentially negative consequences of that ignorance. This chapter aims to discuss those issues by examining data gathered in previous research studies as well as scholarly and professional articles and books that have discussed the topic.

## Stereotyping and Its Effects

In their book *Racism, Sexism, and the Media*, Wilson, Gutierrez, and Chao (2013) give a compelling and vivid account of how stereotypes surrounding the portrayal of Latinos and Latinas in U.S. entertainment media have changed along the decades. From "greasy" Latin lovers to quick-tempered "banditos"; from sensual dancers and temptresses to spit-fire home wreckers; Latinos and Latinas have often been portrayed as people lacking honorable values, stable relationships, or even meaningful professional careers (74–5). Similarly to what happened to other minorities, such as the heroes (and villains) from Middle Eastern and Asian backgrounds, throughout the twentieth century, the portrayal of Latinos on large and small screens was often conveniently linked to the political and economic alliances of the day. When it comes to Latinos specifically, the worst stereotypes of the 1930s (when it was convenient to scapegoat "others" for the Great Depression and economic problems) gave way to more positive portrayals in the 1940s and 1950s, when Latin Americans became big U.S. allies in WWII and the ensuing Cold War against communism. At their most benign, however, those images still portrayed Latinas and Latinos as exotic bombshells and Latin lovers (Lupe Velez, Carmen Miranda, Cesar Romero), or bumbling, heavily accented comic relief (Cantinflas, Desi Arnaz).

Perhaps more troubling, since most people rely on the news media to help them make sense of the world, is the way Latinos and Latinas are portrayed in the news. As media scholar Michael Schudson pointed out, mass media news is "a dominant force in the public construction of common experience and a popular sense of what is real and important" (2003: 3 and quoted in Santa Ana 2013: 24). As a dominant force creating our collective understanding of the world, news media have also become perhaps the dominant way in which most citizens come into contact with Hispanic culture in the US.

In his study of the representation of Latinos on network news (2013), Santa Ana focused on the "immigrant" as a metaphor employed by news organizations to talk about Latinos, showing how that metaphor morphed from "immigrant as animal" up to the 1990s to "immigrant as criminal" in the early 2000s (159).

By consistently referring to unauthorized immigrants as *illegal immigrants*, Santa Ana noted, network anchors and correspondents used a crucial adjective to semantically alter the original meaning of the word *immigrant*, painting immigrants as lawbreakers and creating the prevalent metaphor "immigrant as criminal." As shown by decades of research on the cultural and political power of discourse, news frames and metaphors carry a lot of weight in determining how we form our opinions around people, groups, and issues. That is particularly true (and devastatingly more powerful) when the metaphor is widely adopted and disseminated by mass media:

> Now portrayed as criminals, immigrants remain the lowest form of humans. In one sense, it is an improvement, since immigrants are no longer characterized as lower forms of life. For anti-immigration partisans, however, it was also a shift of political tactics, because while over the previous century they had been able to publicly excoriate immigrants with racist terms without repercussion, in the late 1990s their language increasingly diminished their moral standing in the eyes of the general public.
>
> *(Santa Ana 2013: 159)*

Media stereotypes can also have much more serious consequences, which go beyond creating a general negative sentiment around an ethnic group and specific political tactics. Examining the 1943 Los Angeles "zoot suit riots," Wilson, Gutierrez, and Chao (2013) showed how the violent mob attacks by WWII servicemen on mostly Hispanic youths in downtown L.A. were perhaps triggered (or at least implicitly justified) by a barrage of negative news coverage of Mexican Americans in Southern California in the previous decade (41–2). Analyzing the coverage of Mexican Americans by the *Los Angeles Times* between 1933 and 1943 (and how it could have contributed to create a negative view of Mexican youths), Turner and Surace (1956) found a steady decline in the use of the term "Mexican," which had tended to be employed in a more favorable or at least neutral way, and a corresponding increase in the use of the expression "zoot suiters," which became an unambiguously negative term describing Mexican youths wearing baggy, oversized, striped dark suits.

Most of those articles portrayed "zoot suiters" as delinquents and young criminals. Turner and Surace hypothesized that the steady decline in positive portrayals of downtown Los Angeles' "romantic" Mexican past, combined with the increase in negative stereotyping of Mexican-American zoot suiters, especially in the three years prior to the beatings, could indeed have become the "basis for unambivalent community sentiment supporting hostile crowd behavior" toward the group (quoted in Wilson, Gutierrez, and Chao 2013: 44). That analysis of events and media coverage that took place more than 70 years ago brings to mind the negative stereotyping of African-American youths for their affinity for baggy jeans and other apparel associated with hip hop music and fashion—which has been around at least since the 1980s and 1990s—and extended in recent years to their preference for hooded sweatshirts, which became a notorious (and somewhat media-generated) pejorative signifier in the aftermath of the Trayvon Martin case. Likewise, 2016 presidential candidate Donald Trump's inflamed rhetoric around Mexican immigrants—as of this writing, he had not yet apologized for characterizing them as "murderers" and "rapists" during his official campaign launch event—may have contributed to a general rise in anti-immigrant sentiment around the country, since it may have tapped into an existing fear of immigrants and immigration, stoked by decades of negative stereotyping and the widespread media use of negative metaphors such as the one described by Santa Ana in his study (Lind 2015).

In their study comparing official crime statistics with the results of a content analysis of cable and network news programs, Dixon and Williams (2014) hypothesized that Latinos suspected of committing a crime would be overrepresented in the news as undocumented immigrants. After analyzing 146 cable and network news programs between 2008 and 2012, they found that Latino suspects were indeed significantly more likely to be seen as immigrants on television news (97 percent of the time) compared to the official statistics from "real life" (47 percent of the cases, according to data from the U.S. Department of Justice for the same period). Using a quantitative methodology, the researchers arrived at the same "immigrants as criminals" metaphor reached by Santa Ana via discourse analysis.

## Severe Underrepresentation

Negative stereotyping of Hispanics is just one of the facets in the complex ways the country's largest and fastest-growing ethnic minority is portrayed in the media. Severe underrepresentation of Latinos in news and entertainment media, coupled with the underrepresentation of the group in newsrooms and production companies, has also contributed to define how we perceive this ethnic group. The American Society of News Editors (ASNE) has been tracking the ethnic and gender diversity in U.S. news organizations since 1978, and the results of ASNE's annual diversity census provide valuable insight into the ethnic and gender composition of newsrooms across the country. In 2000, for example, Hispanic journalists represented only 3.68 percent of all journalists working in U.S.-based newsrooms, a dismal number if compared to the 12.5 percent of Latinos among the general U.S. population, according to the 2000 U.S. Census (ASNE 2000; U.S. Census 2000). The numbers had improved slightly for Latinos by 2003—to 4 percent of all U.S. journalists—and that was also the year ASNE stopped listing the percentages for each race or ethnicity in its annual summary of the survey findings.

The 2015 ASNE diversity newsroom census revealed that only 12.7 percent of all U.S. journalists belonged to *any* ethnic or racial minority, still a minuscule number compared to the numbers for the general U.S. population: 37.4 percent of U.S. residents were estimated by the U.S. Census to belong to a racial or ethnic minority in December 2015, with 17.2 percent of them being of Hispanic descent (ASNE 2015; U.S. Census 2015).

Does it matter that Hispanics (and other racial or ethnic minorities) are so underrepresented in U.S. newsrooms? Along the past decades, some media scholars have tried to establish a connection between the predominantly negative (or inexistent) coverage of racial minorities by the media to the dearth of minority journalists and decision-makers in news organizations.

Borrowing concepts from political theory, Coffey (2013) showed the importance of descriptive, proportional, and physical representation, echoing previous scholars' assertion that the presence of members of underrepresented groups—both in political and media contexts—has a positive effect on the way those communities see themselves, also providing salience and a voice to their concerns and interests. Ultimately, seeing your group represented in media reports—as on-camera sources and/or reporters, for example—might have the effect of stimulating democratic participation for members of those groups, while contributing to the perception by the general public that those groups and their issues and concerns are worth listening to. In her study, Coffey found that television's designated market areas (DMAs) that had larger percentages of African-American, Hispanic, and Asian populations tended to have a greater presence of members of those groups as on-air personnel, a positive recent development if compared with similar studies done by Campbell (1995), Heider (2000), Poindexter et al. (2003), and other researchers in previous decades. Coffey also found that the representation of some racial categories (Native Americans, Hawaiians, and other Pacific Islanders) in television newsrooms was still lower than the percentages for those groups within the actual population. She pointed out that future studies should focus on the impact of that higher representation on news content and on the communities themselves.

Similarly, in his book *White News: Why Local News Programs Don't Cover People of Color*, Heider (2000) showed that even in a state as ethnically diverse as Hawaii, people of color are only sporadically represented in local television news.

In his seminal book *Race, Myth and the News*, Campbell (1995) examined 40 hours of television news programming (900 stories total) and found that African-American journalists made up 11 percent of the news anchors and reporters that appeared in those shows, while other studies showed that 13.3 percent of all TV journalists were members of ethnic minorities in the late 1980s (Campbell, citing Stone 1988b). Putting aside for a second the shocking fact that, by that logic, only 2.3 percent of television journalists belonged to other ethnicities (presumably Hispanic and Asian American), Campbell notes that although the percentage of on-camera African-American TV journalists was close to the percentage of blacks in the general population, the numbers were "probably misleading in terms of the overall representation of minority journalists and of their impact news coverage," since other "[studies have found that minorities are largely employed either in high profile, on-camera positions or as camera operators, rather than in editorial decision-making capacities" (Campbell 1995: 38, citing Schultz 1988; Stone 1988a). As also pointed out by Campbell, at the time only 4 percent of local television news directors were people of color, with whites then holding 92 percent of the supervisory jobs that usually lead to managerial positions (38).

In the early to mid-1990s, the ASNE newsroom diversity surveys found that more than half of all daily newspapers in the US still did not employ *any* journalists of color, with African-American journalists making up less than 5 percent of all newspaper journalists in 1992. As we pointed out above, almost 24 years later, that overall number is still stuck in the low two digits (12.7 percent for *all* ethnic minorities in 2015). Why is it relevant to discuss these numbers in such detail? As Campbell (1995) observed, leading up to (and in the aftermath of) the Rodney King riots in Los Angeles, news organizations themselves had used "scarcity of minority journalists in the newsroom" as an explanation for the severe under-coverage of minority communities and neighborhoods (31). Despite placing an extra burden on minority journalists to cultivate sources and come up with story ideas focusing on ethnic communities, there seems indeed to be some truth to the claim that those communities are perhaps more accurately covered by reporters whose ethnicity provides them easier access and better rapport with the sources they cover. That has been confirmed anecdotally through interviews done by Reis, Sheerin, and MacMillin with *Miami Herald* journalists for their book *Writing and Reporting for Digital Media* (2015).

However, in his study of those 900 stories broadcast by 29 television stations in small, medium, and large markets across the country, Campbell found that "although the stations devoted differing amounts of coverage to the [Martin Luther] King Jr. holiday, few covered any stories about minorities or minority communities on the following day's broadcasts," with minorities rarely serving as on-camera sources and news reports focusing by and large on "white people and activities in white communities" (39). Perhaps more shockingly yet, Campbell found that minorities were absent even from feature stories (profiles, community activities and events, etc.) aired during the newscasts he analyzed. Of hundreds of feature stories aired by those 29 stations in the period studied, only one highlighted a person of color: a well-regarded African-American prison warden who was retiring. What all the other stories had in common, Campbell wrote, was that they "appeared to exhibit the same pattern that has been found in content analysis research—little coverage of the nonwhite community and the consistent use of white sources in stories on topics that affect audience members of all colors" (39).

In his extensive ethnographic study of two television newsrooms, one in Honolulu, Hawaii, and the other in Albuquerque, New Mexico, Don Heider (2000) was interested in finding out "what goes wrong" between 9 a.m. and 5 p.m., so that even in heavily multicultural and ethnically diverse markets such as those two, newscasters still end up covering mostly white folks in their news and feature stories. Using a critical-cultural theoretical framework, Heider wanted to find the ultimate answer to his question by examining how story ideas are selected, how news is gathered and produced, and how news decisions are made. The lack of diversity in their newscasts, as well as the lack of consistent coverage of minority communities in general, was acknowledged by journalists and news decision-makers in both newsrooms, with a managing editor in Honolulu admitting that journalists sometimes shied away from those stories for fear of digging deeper into underlying racial tensions in the community, and a reporter in Albuquerque admitting to being troubled by the fact that the station was focusing on "traditional" stories and ignoring the richness and complexity of life in some of the communities they were covering.

## Ignorance of Minority Communities

These last observations lead us to the third main issue mentioned by previous analyses of race, ethnicity and media: a general ignorance of minority communities, including entire Hispanic groups and neighborhoods, by journalists and media organizations. When he conducted his ethnographic study in those Hawaii and New Mexico television newsrooms, what Heider (2000) found—both in his direct observation of how those newsrooms worked and in conversations with his informants—was that coverage of minority communities tended to fall into two broad camps: festivals and crime. Coverage of racial and ethnic festivals and celebrations made for good television, portraying "colorful" human-interest events that stayed far removed from anything deemed controversial. However, members of those ethnic communities complained that the only other time they were "seen on the news was in crime reporting," with a Chicano community leader in Albuquerque complaining that the news was too "focused on the negative" (39). That characterization was disputed by the television station's assignment editor, who noted that they covered crime stories as they came through the police scanner: "The [police] scanner is color blind," he told the researcher (40). In Heider's study, community leaders "had no trouble naming a myriad of issues that received little, if any, coverage from the local television news operations," (44) including gentrification of ethnic neighborhoods, education, and even environmental racism. That observation by community leaders reinforces the general claim that years of focus on "festivals and crime" may have blinded journalists and their news organizations to the richness and complexity of the positive and negative issues that really matter to and affect minority groups.

Besides confirming what the literature in the field already predicted—that ethnic minorities would be underrepresented in broadcast news and in the newsrooms that produced them—Heider tried to provide some explanations to help us understand the causes of this phenomenon. Those ranged from geography (difficult access by media workers to some areas of Hawaii where minority communities lived) to a lack of political/historical/contextual knowledge about those communities. Heider also focused on the already mentioned lack of ethnic representation among news decision-makers, as well as on the lack of resources, access, and public relations savvy, all factors that may hinder those communities' ability to "sell" their concerns and interests to news organizations. However, even when minority journalists "make it" into newsrooms across the country, there is no guarantee that their previous knowledge and engagement with those communities will directly translate into their daily coverage. Through in-depth interviews with black and Latino journalists working for mainstream newspapers, Nishikawa et al. (2009) found a "widespread acceptance of traditional journalistic norms," such as accuracy, balance, and neutrality by those professionals, with minority journalists going out of their way to avoid anything that smacked of "advocacy" in their stories (248).

In their study of misrepresentation of race and crime on network and cable news, Dixon and Williams (2014) found that while "blacks were actually 'invisible' on network news, being underrepresented as both violent perpetrators and victims of crime," Latinos were "greatly overrepresented as undocumented immigrants" (24). More than two decades of research studies have confirmed that, when it comes to the coverage of Latino communities and Hispanic citizens, by over-focusing on crime and immigration, news media are by implication ignoring most other issues that affect or are relevant to those groups. In her book *Media and Minorities: The Politics of Race in News and Entertainment* (2006), Stephanie Larson echoes those claims that the story of Hispanics in mainstream news is one of exclusion and selective exclusion (119). Even in places where larger Latino populations require news organizations to dedicate more of their coverage to Hispanic communities, stories still tend to focus on crime and conflict, ignoring all other issues of importance to them. The invisibility of Hispanics as news sources gets to be almost bizarre—Larson mentions findings in the National Association of Hispanic Journalists' (NAHJ's) annual report, "Network Brownout," indicating that Hispanics are used as sources in only half of network stories about Hispanics (120–1).

Larson also reiterated an observation made by other researchers that mainstream media stories tend to ignore the diversity *within* the Hispanic community itself:

> The terms "Hispanic" or "Latino" are used to represent a multitude of people: legal and illegal aliens, the native born and the foreign born, Mexican Americans and Puerto Ricans. Although this projects a greater national presence and image of solidarity, it overlooks the uniqueness of the subgroups.
>
> *(121)*

That generic grouping of disparate communities under one big umbrella might have the effect of producing other types of distortions and stereotyping by the news media, as well as what Larson calls "selective exclusion," whereby communities such as Cuban Americans in South Florida end up receiving much more national coverage and attention than other Hispanic groups (121).

The results of a study done by Marchi (2008) seem to buck this trend in an interesting and promising way. Starting with the premise established by previous studies that the coverage of multicultural festivals by the media tended to fall under the "journalistic realm of the *sphere of consensus*," where ethnic communities were presented in apolitical and exotic ways (925, citing the work of Hallin 1994; Campbell 1995; Entman and Rojecki 2000; Wilson et al. 2003), the researcher chose to examine news coverage of two large representatives of those celebrations, Martin Luther King Jr. Day and Day of the Dead (*Dia de los Muertos*), to find out if overtly political or controversial issues—such as racial inequality, immigration, and racism—were included in the coverage of those events. Examining the coverage of those two events by two large California newspapers (*San Francisco Chronicle* and *Los Angeles Times*) over a 10-year period, Marchi found that those news organizations *did* devote a significant number of Martin Luther King Jr. and Day of the Dead-related stories to discuss issues such as racial inequality, affirmative action, migrant deaths, violence, and labor struggles. In the case of Latino communities and *Dia de los Muertos* celebrations, for example, a significant number of stories focused on issues such as environmental racism, exploitative labor conditions, anti-immigrant violence, gang violence, and other "forms of death that disproportionately affect low-income, minority populations" (933).

Observing that "the mass media have played an important role in popularizing the Day of the Dead within mainstream America through coverage ranging from the Associated Press and NPR, to local TV stations," Marchi also noted that, besides having an inherent cultural aspect, Day of the Dead celebrations have assumed a markedly political tone among Chicano and Latino communities in the US, reflecting the most immediate concerns of those groups (932). As promising as these results are, it is important to remember that the study only analyzed the news coverage of the two most prominent daily newspapers in California, a more politically liberal state that is home to the second largest Latino population in the country (38.1 percent of the general population, behind only New Mexico's 46.7 percent), according to a 2013 Pew Research Center tabulation of the 2011 U.S. Census results.

## Conclusion

When it comes to the portrayal of Latinos in the news and entertainment media (and the presence of Hispanics in those industries), is it all bad news? As we just saw above, there seems to be some light at the end of the tunnel. As the Latino population grows in the country, and as the group starts to exercise more overall political influence, it is only natural that changes in media attitudes may start to accelerate. Negative stereotypes, ignorance, and underrepresentation of Latinos and their communities in the media are still problems that news and entertainment companies will have to remedy. Recent media events such as the vitriolic rhetoric within the Republican presidential camp and the police shooting event that opened this chapter show that those issues are still a significant part of the national media and popular discourse around Hispanics and their communities. It is possible to anticipate, however, that similarly to the way in which media coverage and popular discourse around other minority groups has shifted over the years, the same process may occur very soon with Hispanics. It may be a more gradual process, starting, for example, in cities and states that have significant percentages of Latino populations, and slowly spreading around the rest of the country. In this context, it is also possible to anticipate the day in which different groups within the larger "Hispanic community" umbrella will receive coverage—and be portrayed—in a way that respects their uniqueness, while also letting the good (and the not-so-good) shine through in all their colors and possible combinations.

# References

ASNE. (2000, April 12) "Minority Journalists Make Small Gains in Daily Newspapers," American Society of News Editors. Retrieved from http://asne.org/content.asp?pl=121andsl=172andcontentid=172.

ASNE. (2015, July 28) "Percentage of Minorities in Newsrooms Remains Relatively Steady; 63 Percent of Newspapers Have at Least One Woman among Top-three Editors," Asne.org. Retrieved from http://asne.org/content.asp?pl=121andsl=415andcontentid=415.

Brown, A. and Lopez, M. H. (2013, Aug. 29) "Mapping the Latino Population, By State, County and City," Pew Research Center. Retrieved from http://www.pewhispanic.org/2013/08/29/mapping-the-latino-population-by-state-county-and-city/.

Campbell, C. P. (1995) *Race, Myth and the News*. Thousand Oaks, CA: Sage Publications.

Coffey, A. J. (2013) "Representing Ourselves: Ethnic Representation in America's Television Newsrooms," *Howard Journal of Communications* 24(2): 154–177.

Dixon, T. L. and Williams, C. L. (2014) "The Changing Misrepresentation of Race and Crime on Network and Cable News," *Journal of Communication* 65(1): 24–39.

Entman, R. M. and Rojecki, A. (2000) *The Black Image in the White Mind: Media and Race in America*. Chicago, IL: University of Chicago Press.

Fujioka, Y. (2011) "Perceived Threats and Latino Immigrant Attitudes: How White and African American College Students Respond to News Coverage of Latino Immigrants," *Howard Journal of Communications* 22(1): 43–63.

Hallin, D. C. (1994) *We Keep America on Top of the World: Television Journalism and the Public Sphere*. London: Routledge.

Heider, D. (2000) *White News: Why Local News Programs Don't Cover People of Color*. Mahwah, NJ: L. Erlbaum Associates.

Helsel, P. (2015, Sept. 9) "No Charges for Pasco Police Officers Who Killed Antonio Zambrano-Montes," NBC News. Retrieved from http://www.nbcnews.com/news/us-news/no-charges-pasco-police-officers-who-killed-antonio-zambrano-montes-n424571.

Larson, S. G. (2006) *Media and Minorities: The Politics of Race in News and Entertainment*. Lanham, MD: Rowman and Littlefield.

Laughland, O. (2015, Feb. 17) "Pasco Police Shooting: Victim's American Dream Ends in Violent Reality," *The Guardian*. Retrieved from http://www.theguardian.com/us-news/2015/feb/17/pasco-fatal-police-shooting-zambrano-montes-hispanic.

Lind, D. (2015) "Donald Trump's Anti-immigrant Demagoguery Works because It's Not about Jobs. It's about Fear," Vox. Retrieved from http://www.vox.com/2015/7/29/9060427/nativism-research-immigration-trump.

Marchi, R. M. (2008) "Race And The News," *Journalism Studies* 9(6): 925–944.

NBC News. (2015, Feb. 16) "Pasco Latino Leaders: Feds Need To Investigate Fatal Police Shooting," NBC News. Retrieved from http://www.nbcnews.com/news/latino/pasco-latino-leaders-feds-need-investigate-fatal-police-shooting-n307026.

Nishikawa, K. A., Towner, T. L., Clawson, R. A., and Waltenburg, E. N. (2009) "Interviewing the Interviewers: Journalistic Norms and Racial Diversity in the Newsroom," *Howard Journal of Communications* 20(3): 242–259.

Poindexter, P. M., Smith, L., and Heider, D. (2003) "Race and Ethnicity in Local Television News: Framing, Story Assignments, and Source Selections," *Journal of Broadcasting and Electronic Media* 47(4): 524–536.

Reis, R., MacMillin, K., and Sheerin, M. (2015) *Writing and Reporting for Digital Media*. Dubuque, IA: Kendall Hunt.

Santa Ana, O. (2012) *Juan in a Hundred: The Representation of Latinos on Network News*. Austin, TX: University of Texas Press.

Schudson, M. (2003) *The Sociology of News*. New York: Norton.

Schultz, E. (1988) "Toward the Challenge of Change," *RTDNA Communicator*, 91.

Stone, V. A. (1988a) "Pipelines and Dead Ends: Jobs Held by Minorities and Women in Broadcast News," *Mass Comm Review* 15(2 and 3): 10–19.

Stone. V. A. (1988b) "Trends in the Status of Minorities and Women in Broadcast News," *Journalism Quarterly* 65(2): 288–293.

Turner, R. H. and Surace, S. J. (1956) "Zoot-Suiters and Mexicans: Symbols in Crowd Behavior," *American Journal of Sociology* 62(1): 14–20.

U.S. Census. (2000) The United States Census Bureau. Retrieved from http://www.census.gov/main/www/cen2000.html.

U.S. Census. (2015) The United States Census Bureau. Retrieved from http://www.census.gov/2015censustests.

U.S. Census Quick Facts. (2010) The United States Census Bureau. Retrieved from https://www.census.gov/quickfacts/table/PST045215/00.

Wilson, C. C., Gutierrez, F., and Chao, L. M. (2013) *Racism, Sexism, and the Media: Multicultural Issues into the New Communications Age*. Thousand Oaks, CA: Sage Publications.

## Further Reading

Campbell, C. (1995) *Race, Myth and the News*. Thousand Oaks, CA: Sage. (An analysis of television news coverage and how it helps perpetuate racial myths and stereotypes.)

Heider, D. (2000) *White News: Why Local News Programs Don't Cover People of Color*. Mahwah, NJ: Lawrence Erlbaum. (An analysis of local television news coverage that focuses on how ignorance and omission also work to reinforce racial myths.)

Marchi, R. M. (2008) "Race and the News: Coverage of Martin Luther King Day and Dia de los Muertos in Two California Dailies," *Journalism Studies* 9: 925–944. (An analysis of newspaper stories that contradicts some earlier studies, showing more nuanced and in-depth coverage of minority groups in San Francisco and Los Angeles.)

Santa Ana, O. (2013) *Juan in a Hundred: The Representation of Latinos on Network News*. Austin, TX: University of Texas Press. (Comprehensive semiotic and textual analyses of network news stories focused on Hispanic groups.)

Wilson, C. C., Gutiérrez, F., and Chao, L. M. (2013) *Racism, Sexism, and the Media*. 4th ed. Thousand Oaks, CA: Sage. (Includes a major survey that examines several decades of the complicated relationship between mass media and the largest racial and cultural minorities in the United States.)

# 14
# ADVERTISING
## A Window to Race and Culture
*Anthony J. Cortese*

Why study images of ethnic minorities in advertising? These images shape cultural attitudes about racial minorities and are very powerful agents of socialization. Advertising reflects social stratification—a barometer of the willingness of whites to share mainstream culture with people of color. Finally, studying these images fosters critical media literacy and empowers us to become more autonomous, capable of liberating ourselves from power arrangements and toward positive social change (Cortese 2016).

This chapter examines how ethnic images and race relations have historically been presented in advertising and how such portrayals correlate with patterns of intergroup relations and tensions. Advertising gives us a window to such social relations and ideological challenges to them. Over the years, stereotypes of African Americans and other ethnic minorities have not been eliminated but have changed in character, taking subtler and more symbolic or underhanded forms (Jackman 1994; Karins, Coffman, and Walters 1969; Pettigrew 1985). When social norms that characterize white–black relations are disputed and unresolved, portrayals of black people may not mirror this decreasing subordination but rather may employ more qualified or subtler stereotypes or retreat from challenges to norms completely by limiting images, creating greater social distance (Jackman 1994). Advertising images, as cultural commodities and social constructions, have long been sites of struggle along racial fault lines in the United States' cultural landscape (Erikson 1976; Gamson et al. 1992).

In the early twentieth century, popular cultural objects caricatured blacks, echoing their second-class citizenship and assisting as an instrument of social control. Prior to the Civil Rights Movement of the 1960s, the mass media world was nearly all white. The "mammy" and other stereotypes of African Americans assured whites of a "natural" racial hierarchy. Predominantly white media industries produced overtly racist images during an era of customary and legal segregation in employment, residential housing, public transportation, and education.

The Civil Rights Movement successfully challenged the racist ideology that had resulted in discrimination, legal segregation, and the social, economic, and political oppression of blacks in the US. As educational and occupational attainment and voter registration increased for people of color, the symbolic trappings of domination were also challenged. Traditional stereotypes dwindled or died. Consciousness-raising on issues of racial imagery also resulted in the appearance of many more black characters in mainstream advertising than in the past.

There are also more blacks employed as cultural producers within mainstream media industries (see, for instance, Cassidy and Katula 1990). With increased numbers come efforts to produce more culturally authentic imagery of the black community. Nevertheless, minority-owned advertising agencies must walk a fine line between creating positive imagery out of a sense of community responsibility and securing the bottom line—making money. Unless there is profit, the agencies will not be creating any images, let alone positive ones.

## Symbolic Vestiges of Domination

How much progress have we made in ethnic relations since the early part of the twentieth century? Are we a "color-blind" society or do we remain polarized by race? Social scientists generally posit steadily improving racial attitudes of white Americans, especially in terms of their attitudes toward African Americans. More tangible indicators corroborate such attitudinal changes, most notably the rise of a black middle class. Yet there continues to be negative stereotyping of ethnic minorities, evidence of widely divergent views of the extent and importance of racial discrimination to modern race relations, and evidence of deepening feelings of alienation among black Americans. White openness to integration at the personal level is also very limited. Blacks and Latinos continue to have low college attendance and graduation rates, high unemployment rates, and high rates of intraethnic violent crime. There are also new and subtle ethnic stereotypes.

As the twentieth century ended, stereotypes of African Americans were not removed from cultural products but altered in character, taking subtler and more indirect forms (Jackman 1994; Karins, Coffman, and Walters 1969; Pettigrew 1985). In a commercial produced for Ziploc bags, for instance, all actors had speaking parts except a sturdy black woman, whose reaction to the product was expressed with an excited "Ooh-wee!" Although ostensibly not blatantly racist, the commercial actually carried on the stereotype of the black mammy—subservient, dark, heavy, asexual, and inarticulate (Woods 1995). Hollywood films like *Imitation of Life* and *Gone with the Wind* have been famously criticized for mammy characters who used outbursts instead of grammatical sentences to communicate.

Perhaps the most well-known mammy image in advertising is Aunt Jemima, with her signature bandana. The original Aunt Jemima, Nancy Green (1831–98), displayed acute business acumen in an era when few blacks or women operated businesses. This former slave from Montgomery County, Kentucky, was the world's first living trademark. She made her debut at age 59 at the Columbian Exposition in Chicago, where she served pancakes in a booth. The Aunt Jemima Mills Company distributed a souvenir lapel button that bore her photograph. The slogan later became the motto for the company's promotional campaign. Green was the official trademark for three decades, and the mammy image—as in the Ziploc commercial—can still be seen in advertising.

These ethnic images are closely related to power relations through economic, classificatory, artistic, and judicial factors (Gans 1979; Griswold 1981; Peterson 1976). During turbulent times with intense resentment, as social movements skirmish to gain momentum, caretakers show cultural icons among the conflicts and crises of social norms (Dubin 1987; Swidler 1986; Wuthnow, and Witten 1988). When norms are challenged, images may not directly mirror this sudden shift. Rather, advertising uses subtler or more limited stereotypes. Symbolic annihilation may also be used—eliminating ethnic images altogether. Restricting images of interethnic contact may result in greater social distance between whites and people of color. In the 1950s and early 1960s, advertisers did not use ethnic minority models because of unsubstantiated fears of economic backlash from white consumers (Gould et al. 1970). For example, despite tremendous popularity as an entertainer with cross-over appeal, Nat King Cole could not contract a national sponsor for his 1956 television show (Woods 1995).

Though ethnic minority representation in advertising has clearly increased, how black people are depicted and what they contribute to the product's image remains questionable. Some advertisers appear to lack awareness of or regard for sensitive cultural issues or ethnic stereotypes related to watermelons and the black child as a "pickaninny." Academic research on ethnic stereotypes in advertising has slowed considerably in the 2000s. But as late as 1990, only 3 percent of people featured in national advertising were black (New York City Department of Consumer Affairs in Guy 1991). *GQ*, *Vogue*, and *Esquire* featured the fewest black models; *Sports Illustrated*, the most. When blacks did appear in ads, they tended to be athletes, entertainers, laborers, or children. The incidence of black women was even lower than that of black men. Less than 20 percent of all ads with blacks used black women (New York City Department of Consumer Affairs in Guy 1991). One study (Wilkes and Valencia 1989) found that blacks were featured in 17 percent of the 904 commercials seen but had major roles in only 31 percent of all ads with blacks. Blacks tended to be cast marketing beer or malt liquor, cigarettes, hair care, automobiles, and electronic products.

Connecting ethnic images to periods of social change highlights the social norms and cultural ideologies of a particular age (Williams 1981). A 1903 Pears Soap ad with a before-and-after visual sequence suggests the soap is strong enough to "clean" a black child, symbolizing a cultural ideology that blacks were unclean and being black carried a negative social identity. Inspecting cultural continuities and changes that are an integral part of critical periods in history furthers our understanding of the interconnections between symbolic and social relations (Pescosolido et al. 1997).

## Three Models of Racial and Ethnic Minorities in Advertising

There are three possible explanations for the way minorities are presented in ads: equal presentation, social reality, and cultural attitudes (Cortese 2015).

### *Equal Presentation Model*

In the equal presentation model, whites and minorities are shown in exactly the same way, regardless of any cultural, economic, or physical differences. If whites are presented predominantly as middle-class persons in middle-class settings, African Americans are portrayed similarly, regardless of actual differences in the class distribution. Copycat and racial assimilation ads also support the equal presentation model.

**Copycat.** Minorities prefer to see images of people like themselves in advertising (Woods 1995). Consequently, advertising targeted at ethnic markets that uses ethnic models lends an aura of trustworthiness to the product or service. But this naive approach is risky if the marketer does not understand the nuances of ethnic culture.

In the early 1980s, advertisers began to replace white models with black or Latino models and translate English into Spanish to capture ethnic markets. The copycat, ethnocentric and uncreative, duplicates an ad but uses a model of different race/ethnicity.

The copycat mistakenly assumes blacks are simply dark-skinned white people. Some concepts and representations are not transferable across cultures (Lockhart 1992). Blacks and Latinos are diverse and large enough groups to necessitate distinctive and separate campaigns. The copycat denies the uniqueness of ethnic subcultures and reveals a failure to understand important socio-historical, racial, and cultural differences that affect the buying power of ethnic minorities. The behavior, attitudes, motivations, and mindsets of blacks, Latinos, and Asians are grounded in their particular socio-historical backgrounds.

Advertisers must understand black or Latino identity. Ethnicity has repercussions for consumption patterns, responses to particular advertising, and buying behavior. Effective advertising campaigns aptly demonstrate cultural differences. A mass marketing ad may emphasize scenery, wildlife, and mountainous landscapes. To target blacks, however, that same advertiser may refocus on style, fashion, and images central to an urban environment. Ostensibly, copycat ads tell us that minorities and whites are the same, there is racial equality, and acculturation is highly desirable. Beneath the surface, however, the message is that whites might not buy a product used by minorities. If it were not problematic, there would be no need to use both white and ethnic versions of the same ad. Why not use just one version, ethnic or white?

Copycat ads are a targeting afterthought. Mainstream marketing research tries to help advertisers reach the white, middle- to upper-class market. As ethnic minorities become socially mobile, they too are targeted, but often through copycat ads instead of those that play on unique subcultural images and symbols. The copycat technique often misreads Latino consumers, for example. A marketing campaign for fabric softener, for example, targeted at Latinas who are recent arrivals to the United States is ineffective if they do not grasp the notion of two-step (wash and soften) laundry.

Which ad is the original and which is the copycat? They appear in print at approximately the same time. The difference is the target audience for the magazine or newspaper. The issue is not which is the copycat, but the bending of ethnic images into a utopian assimilated social context instead of using actual, unique subcultural values, images, and symbols. Despite the widespread use of copycat ads, their absence from advertising textbooks is notable. This may be due to a fear of facing the controversial nature of ethnic advertising (O'Guinn et al. 1998).

***Racial Assimilation.*** Through casting, print advertising exalts white standards of beauty: light skin, straight or wavy hair, and blue or green eyes. In other words, one must be as white as possible. When minority women appear in ads, they also conform to the provocateur: young, beautiful—as defined by white standards—perfect, and sexually seductive. They are sometimes shown with light skin, straight hair, hazel or green eyes, and Euro-American features. The racial assimilation model in advertising also applies to ethnic minority men.

## *Social Reality Model*

The social reality model presents minority life as it is, not as a copy of white life. For instance, McDonald's displays a single black mother whose young son is not especially fond of his mother's date (Burrell 1992). Representations of ethnic minority subculture include extended families, urban settings, and parents with multiple jobs. Minorities are more likely to be poor or in lower-status occupations than whites. Ads reflect educational, socio-economic, and cultural differences between lower to lower-middle-class minorities and middle to upper-middle-class whites in American society. This model draws attention to social inequality, much of which has its historical roots in racial segregation. The social reality model also explains ethnic marketing. Advertisers recognize the disproportionately large increase in the population and buying power of ethnic and racial minorities.

### *Cultural Attitudes Model*

The cultural attitudes of whites toward blacks influence the way blacks are portrayed in advertising. These cultural attitudes reflect:

1. a history of slavery, lynching, threats, and other forms of racist intimidation;
2. state-legislated and court-ordered segregation and educational and occupational discrimination;
3. judicial and court biases in the application of the death penalty and jury selection; and
4. the denial of basic human rights.

The remnants of that history are visible in contemporary social stratification based on race, which is reflected in advertising. American society is highly stratified by race, ethnicity, gender, and social class. Advertising becomes an indicator of the readiness of influential groups to accept or tolerate the mainstreaming of ethnic minorities in society. In short, advertisements are signs of ethnic secondary and primary assimilation.

Williams (1970) identifies 10 values that are central in U.S. culture. In addition to freedom, democracy, science, progress, and the like, they include racism and group superiority. These values, including the negative ones, are passed to the next generation through cultural transmission (Macionis 1996). Cultural beliefs favor whites over people of color, males over females, and the privileged over the disadvantaged. There are privileges that attach to white skin color that are often latent, invisible, or unnoticed. Although we would like to think of ourselves as a society where everyone is equal, like George Orwell's successful revolutionaries in *Animal Farm*, there is no doubt that some of us are "more equal than others."

The stereotypes and racist ideologies of dominant groups toward ethnic minorities in advertising are very revealing (Perkins 1979). These stereotypes depend on a connection of patterns that can be explained only in relation to each other (Carby 1987). Survey data indicate whites are most willing to accept integration and equal treatment in the area of employment, less so in the area of close social contact and residential integration, and least so in the area of interracial relationships and marriage.

## Secondary Assimilation

Advertising displays employment integration, residential integration, and interracial relationships. Humphrey and Schuman (1984) compared the frequency and social characteristics of African Americans and whites in ads from *Time* and *Ladies' Home Journal* in 1950 and 1980. During that 30-year span, the occupational level of blacks portrayed had risen considerably. Accordingly, ads reflect the finding whites are willing to accept occupational integration.

Despite positive reactions to minority representations in advertising, marketers have not been willing to feature them on a regular basis. In 1985, the Lawyers Committee for Civil Rights Under Law assailed *The Washington Post* for a sharp underrepresentation of ethnic minorities featured in its real estate section ads. From January 1985 through April

1986, minorities were featured in less than 2 percent of the *Post*'s ads (*Advertising Age* 1986). At the time, the population of Washington, D.C. was 90 percent black. The Post replied by establishing a 25 percent target for blacks in real estate ads. The paper further said it would refuse advertising that did not comply with the policy. This acute underrepresentation of blacks mirrors survey data that indicate resistance to residential integration (Humphrey and Schuman 1984).

## Primary Assimilation

Before 1970, the rates of interracial marriage in the US were less than 2 percent. By 1980, the rates slightly increased to 3.2 percent. By 2010, rates rose to 8.4 percent (Wang 2012), reflecting a noteworthy increase in social acceptance. (Nevertheless, whites are the least likely to marry outside of their race.) There has been an increase of ads with interracial intimate relationships, including a much-discussed Cheerios ad that ran in the 2014 Super Bowl. This reflects a reduction of social distance in the closest form of primary racial assimilation. There has also been a recent trend in advertising to show interracial friendships and interracial socializing.

Not all differences between representations of African Americans and whites in ads can be readily explained by either of the first two models. Research on consumer responses to integrated advertising is inconclusive (Reid and Vanden Bergh 1980), perhaps because cultural attitudes toward ethnic minorities are contextually conditioned. Moreover, these cultural attitudes are mirrored in print advertising.

## Ethnic Stereotyping

White cultural attitudes about racial and ethnic minorities are often closely linked to cultural stereotypes. Another strategy in using minorities in advertising is to go completely in the other direction from equal presentation and play up or exaggerate the cultural and racial uniqueness of the role or the model.

### *African-American Stereotypes*

One of the prevailing and enduring stereotypical images of ethnic minorities in the mass media has been that of the ruthlessly aggressive predator, someone who injures or exploits others for one's own gain. A predator preys, plunders, destroys, or devours. Mass media have incessantly portrayed people of color as predators through their ethnicity or phenotypic features. The predator image has been around since at least the 1880s when American Indians were showed preying on stagecoaches in advertising for Buffalo Bill's Wild West shows (Cortese 2016).

Black men have also been stereotyped as predators or thugs as a means of social control. This image can be seen in contemporary advertising, including political advertising. President H. W. Bush famously used an ominous image of Willie Horton, a furloughed African-American convict who was convicted of a brutal murder, to paint his opponent, Massachusetts Gov. Michael Dukakis, as soft on crime. Similarly stereotypical images—of African Americans and Latinos—were used during the 2015–16 Republican primary elections in ads run by candidates Donald Trump and Ted Cruz (Roller 2015).

Black women have been stereotyped as seductresses—a sexual predator of sorts. The Jezebel is promiscuous and sexually irresponsible. This stereotypical image has been around since at least 1929 with Nina Mae McKinney's portrayal of a seductress who marries a revivalist in the feature film *Hallelujah*. The image of the sexual predator continues in contemporary advertising. Black women are routinely portrayed as predatory, primitive, wild, or animal-like (Jhally and Kilbourne 2010).

## *The Luscious Latina*

Latinos are even more underrepresented than African Americans in advertising. They were virtually nonexistent in ads prior to 1980 (Woods 1995). Even in the late 1980s, Latinos were featured in only 5.8 percent of all television commercials and as only 1.5 percent of the speaking characters on network television ads (Wilkes and Valencia 1989). When they do appear, Latinos are in background roles as part of a group. They are seen more often in commercials for food products, entertainment, alcohol, and furniture. Latinos typically are not represented in mainstream advertising hosting dinner parties, washing dishes, or drinking coffee (Woods 1995). An exception to the vast underrepresentation of Latinos in mass media is the Latina sex object or seductress. "The Luscious Latina" stereotype in film, television, and advertising has endured because of its marketability (Fregoso 1993; Woll 1980). The alcohol industry especially reinforces representations that exploit and demean women.

The amalgam of genetic features characteristic of Latino populations provides an exotic and attractive look. At the same time, cultural factors and social stratification based on race have helped prevent Latinas from being assertive and self-confident. The passive role of Latinas corresponds to the complementary and active role of Latino men. The logic seems to be that since Latino men are macho, Latinas must be passive. This has resulted in a stereotype that portrays Latinas as inarticulate, subservient, passive, and gullible. This negative stereotype tends to limit mass media portrayals of Latinas to roles as either maids or sex objects.

Actresses in the past, such as Rita Hayworth and Delores Del Rio, and today, such as Salma Hayek, sometimes present an image with both positive (e.g., powerful and sensuous) and negative (e.g., boisterous and oversexed) characteristics. Historically, Del Rio broke the color barrier for Latinas in Hollywood in the 1920s. The exotic woman had her niche in movies. Lupe Velez, another breakthrough Latina actress, fell into the role of the comedic spitfire by "speaking with a heavy accent and resorting to rapid-fire Spanish when annoyed" (Menard 1997). The spitfire, oversexed, and overly emotional woman is not a flattering image. These images are present in today's media, including advertising.

Hayworth did not become popular in the 1930s and 1940s until she assimilated to Anglo standards. She dropped her image as a raven-haired, oversexed Latina and transformed herself into an auburn-haired love goddess. Carmen Miranda, a contemporary of Hayworth, on the other hand, was never able to shake her image as a spitfire and was always typecast accordingly. Other Latinas pursued the trail blazed by these pioneers—Rita Moreno in the 1950s, Raquel Welch in the 1960s and 1970s, Charo in the 1970s, Sonia Braga in the 1980s, Jennifer Lopez and Hayek in the 1990s and the new millennium—though never quite breaking out of the sexually charged roles still retained for Latinas.

Advertisers recognize and capitalize on the allure and popularity of Latinas. Typecasting and stereotypes are the core of the modeling and film industries. Advertising agencies and Hollywood producers have always looked for "types." Unfortunately, Latinas are limited to roles as Luscious Latinas, maids, or illegal immigrants. Young Latina models and actors, looking for visibility and a means to survive, are forced to accept jobs that cast them in these stereotypical roles.

Moreover, Latinas may also sometimes accept stereotypes because a role that requires physical attractiveness enhances notions of self-worth and self-esteem. The problem with this is that only a small proportion of Latinas are able to take advantage of this stereotype. Working-class Latinas are not afforded the opportunities to advance their careers or personal lives with this privilege. It is not always wise to stake one's self-regard on an attribute as ephemeral as physical attractiveness. It is crucial that Latina models and actors have access to playing everyday people, ranging from hard-working mothers to professional women.

### *American Indian Stereotypes*

American Indian imagery has historically been culturally insensitive (e.g., a rifle marketed as the "Savage Code"). Among the most visible and controversial popular culture stereotypes of Native Americans is the nickname of the NFL's Washington Redskins. The Federal Communications Commission views the name as "offensive and derogatory." Native American symbolism has been used often in advertising. One popular use is the Jeep Cherokee. A representation of an Indian woman remains on the logo for Land O'Lakes dairy products. In 1991, much to the consternation of the Lakota (Sioux) tribe, a brewer introduced a new type of malt liquor dubbed "Crazy Horse" (Woods 1995). The namesake for the product was obviously the legendary war chief. In fact, the Crazy Horse label features a Sioux war chief headdress. Nevertheless, his descendants argue Crazy Horse condemned alcohol because he understood how destructive it was to his people.

Highly stylized images were inspired by American Indian symbolism. Ads feature a backdrop of cabins built for tourists in the 1930s by the Civilian Conservation Corps. The shelters stand open for viewing the beauty of the red rock that inspired the Anasazi tribe to religious ceremony nearly 2,000 years ago. American Indian symbolism often markets cigarettes, making an odd link between Indian life and the natural qualities of tobacco. American Indian imagery in advertising is often exploited or misused, suggesting cultural insensitivity and ethnic ignorance on the part of advertisers.

### *Asian Stereotypes*

Representations of Asian Americans in advertising, radio, film, and television are infrequent, notwithstanding a sharp 43 percent increase (from 2000 to 2010) in the number of Asian Americans who now comprise 5.6 percent of all people in the United States—either alone or in combination with one or more other races (Hoeffel et al. 2012). At the close of the twentieth century, only a small fraction of TV characters were Asian Americans; most of those roles were minor (Gerbner 1998). Asian characters comprised 3 percent of prime-time characters, but only 2 percent were recurring (Children Now 2001). Even though the presentation of Asian characters has increased in recent years, the underrepresentation and stereotyping of Asians continue (Sun 2002). Perhaps the main difficulty associated with these data is the lack of non-stereotypical role models for Asian-American children and teens. While some contemporary ads sometimes feature Asian women who are articulate, commanding, and acculturated, they break sharply with the lotus blossom, geisha, or China doll image of Asian women as submissive, frail, passive, and quiet.

Sadly, the typical Asian female in contemporary advertising is old wine in a new bottle. She conforms to the Dragon Lady—an Asian woman who is seductive and desirable but untrustworthy (Espiritu 1997a). Films in the early twentieth century (e.g., *Daughter of Fu Manchu*) portrayed this stereotypical scheming, treacherous, dangerous Dragon Lady—a female version of the Asian bad guy. She hypnotizes her male enemy, gains trust by seducing him, and when he least expects it, she disposes of him through sabotage or backstabbing (Espiritu 1997a).

The stereotype of the Dragon Lady can be traced back to the late 1800s when Chinese men immigrated to America typically for manual labor. Americans viewed them with animosity because of perceived competition for jobs. They feared mass immigration would result in sudden reproduction of Asians in the US. Americans suffered from "Yellow Peril," a belief the Chinese would overpopulate and eventually take over and destroy American civilization. During this era, many states—including California—prohibited racial mixing through the passage of anti-miscegenation laws. Consequently, Chinese women were shipped to America to serve as prostitutes for Chinese men (Yung 1999). Chinese prostitutes were accused of being demoralizing, tainting the blood of white American youth, spreading sexually transmitted diseases, and being sexually corrupt (Uchida 1998). The perception of Chinese women as indecent and shameful helped to justify the enactment of anti-Chinese legislation. Anti-Chinese prejudice was reflected in Hollywood films that further perpetuated this depiction of the Dragon Lady.

Anna Mae Wong, a famous Chinese actress in the early twentieth century, is well known for playing villainous Asian women in films such as *Thief of Baghdad*, where she plays a Mongol slave girl who helps an evil ruler take over the world and *Daughter of the Dragon*, where she plays the daughter of malevolent villain, Fu Manchu. In both roles, she is untrustworthy, dangerous, and manipulative. If we consider this sexualization of Asian women over the past century, it is evident contemporary roles are simply an adaptation or contemporary version of the Dragon Lady—built on an ultra-sexualized appearance. Add tough, rude, candid, aggressive, sarcastic, and manipulative; remove submissive and selfless.

The Dragon Lady stands in stark contrast with a history in advertising that virtually never displays Asian men as sexually desirable. This image is controversial in Asian-American communities. The new Dragon Lady is popular among Asian-American female college students who enjoy how that image refutes the submissive and quiet Asian female stereotype. Future research should focus on how Asian-American representations influence Asian Americans and other racial groups. Ethnographic interviews and focus groups could be gainfully applied to address the tension between media hegemony and individual viewer autonomy. The media political economy affects Asian-American media representations and disrupts the status quo to produce regulatory and systematic changes. Ads stereotype the Asian woman as a passive sex object or a hyper-sexualized subject. Asian women continue to be reduced to one-dimensional caricatures in Western representations (Espiritu 1997b). In advertising, the Asian woman is eroticized as exotic, sensuous, and promiscuous, but untrustworthy.

## Contemporary Images of Ethnic Minorities in Advertising

Social change in the US gradually reversed images of ethnic minorities in advertising. People of color have become more visible and portrayed more favorably. Four points about images of ethnic minorities in advertising are notable (Cortese 2016):

1   Until the 1980s, there were virtually no ethnic minority fashion models on the runways or in mainstream print media. This historical omission of positive ethnic minority images in advertising represents opposition to social change in which minority equality is viewed as threatening to whites (Humphrey and Schuman 1984).
2   Ads are becoming an ethnic rainbow. The saturation of ethnic minority images in mainstream broadcast and print media tracks racial advances; higher educational and occupational attainment; recent black economic, political, and social empowerment; and a retreat of traditional racial stereotypes.
3   Despite the large increase in ethnically diverse models, problems remain with how their images are marketed to the public. Ethnic minority models in ads often conform to standards of white beauty.
4   Models remain exploited through ethnicity or phenotypic features. This trend of playing up unique ethnic characteristics is a form of symbolic racism seen in books in which minorities are portrayed with distant images, commemorating particular cultural heritage, but without contact with whites.

Perhaps multicultural ads are now popular because they reflect social reality as a global village. Ads using only white models risk appearing stiff or dated. Similarly, using only one token person of color in a white crowd or group is a thinly veiled attempt to appear sensitive to ethnic minorities. Now minorities are used to sell products and services to all people. The use of black models in advertising grabs the attention of both black and white viewers (Burrell 1992).

The use of minorities in ads emerged in Europe. Couturiers, notably Givenchy, began using black women as runway fashion models (Scott 1989). Negative responses followed; some felt jobs should not be given to "immigrants." *Elle*, a top French fashion magazine, championed the development of the multicultural look in its editorial pages. The global-village look entered the US in 1985 when the American version of *Elle* was introduced.

One of the original advertisers to adopt the global-village look was Benetton. The Italian knitwear producer initiated its United Colors of Benetton campaign in 1984 (Scott 1989). The ads show ethnically diverse, attractive teens and youngsters, often arm in arm. Benetton's goal is to project a sense of brotherhood and sisterhood as well as appeal to ethnic consumers. Also in the 1980s, *Esprit*, a San Francisco-based sportswear enterprise, took a step further in this direction by using actual employees in ads. Today Wal-Mart does the same with its ethnically diverse workforce.

Advertising across the globe has become increasingly ethnically diverse. Japan, a country whose advertising has reflected an obsession with blond hair, blue or green eyes, long legs, and narrow noses is now using more Latinos, blacks, and Asians. Ethnically diverse advertising images provide a unique alternative to sterile white ones and are more representative of the real world. Modeling agencies now recruit internationally to meet the ever-increasing demand for fresh faces and an ethnic look. The shift toward more ethnically diverse fashion models is a big step and offers a cultural opening to a previously closed arena. Multiculturalism represents cultural strength instead of racial division. The multiracial look is in vogue in advertising. The process of changing racial definitions continues, and dramatic developments are on the horizon. These potential changes may be attributable to increasing rates of interracial marriage and a census that finally recognizes multiracial identities.

There has been a considerable increase in ethnic representations in advertising. However, sometimes advertisers merely "color" mainstream ads. Copycat ads are prevalent.

Ethnic stereotypes remain. In other marketing campaigns, ethnic themes are tastefully done. Sometimes explicit reference is made to phenotypical differences such as skin color. Ethnic representations in advertising have increased and improved. Some break racial stereotypes. Through visual imagery and text deconstruction, ethnic representations in advertising provide the tools to understand how mainstream culture views ethnic subcultures (Cortese 2016).

## References

Burrell, T. (1992, March 12) Interview by Gail Baker Woods. Burrell Building, Chicago.
Carby, H. (1987) *Reconstructing Womanhood: The Emergence of the Afro-American Woman Novelist*. New York: Oxford University Press.
Cassidy, M. and Katula, R. (1990) "The Black Experience in Advertising: An Interview with Thomas J. Burrell," *Journal of Communication Inquiry* 14(1): 93–104.
Cortese, A. (2016) *Provocateur: Images of Women and Minorities in Advertising*. 4th ed. Boulder, CO: Rowman and Littlefield.
Dubin, S. (1987) "Black Representations in Popular Culture," *Social Problems* 34: 122–140.
Erikson, K. (1976) *Everything in Its Path*. New York: Simon & Schuster.
Espiritu, Y. L. (1997a) *Ideological Racism and Cultural Resistance: Constructing Our Own Images*. Thousand Oaks, CA: Sage.
———. (1997b) *Asian American Women and Men: Labor, Laws, and Love*. New York: Sage.
Fregoso, R. L. (1993) *The Bronze Screen: Chicana and Chicano Film Culture*. Minneapolis, MN: University of Minnesota Press.
Gamson, W. A., Croteau, D., Hoynes, W., and Sasson, T. (1992) "Media Images and the Social Construction of Reality," *Annual Review of Sociology* 18: 373–393.
Gans, H. (1979) *Deciding What's News*. New York: Random House.
Gerbner, G. (1998) *Casting and Fate in '98. Fairness and Diversity in Television: An Update and Trends Since the 1993 SAG Report* (A Cultural Indicators Project report to the Screen Actors Guild). Philadelphia, PA: Temple University.
Gould, J. W., Sigband, N. B., and Zoerner Jr., C. E. (1970) "Black Consumer Reactions to 'Integrated' Advertising," *Journal of Marketing* 34(July): 20–26.
Griswold, W. (1981) "American Character and the American Novel: An Expansion of Reflection Theory in the Sociology of Literature," *American Journal of Sociology* 86(4): 740–765.
Guy, P. (1991, July 24) "Study Says Ads Overlook Minorities," *USA Today*.
Hoeffel, E. M., Rastogi, S., and Kim, M. O. (2012) "The Asian Population: 2010," 2010 Census Briefs. Retrieved from http://www.census.gov/prod/cen2010/briefs/c2010br-11.pdf.
Humphrey, R. and Schuman, H. (1984) "The Portrayal of Blacks in Magazine Advertisements: 1950–1982," *Public Opinion Quarterly* 48: 551–563.
Jackman, M. (1994) *The Velvet Glove: Paternalism and Conflict in Gender, Class, and Race Relations*. Berkeley, CA: University of California Press.
Jhally, S. and Kilbourne, J. (2010) *Killing us Softly 4: Advertising's Image of Women*. Northampton, MA: Media Education Foundation.
Karins, M., Coffman T. L., and Walters, G. (1969) "On the Fading of Social Stereotypes: Studies in Three Generations of College Students," *Journal of Personality and Social Psychology* 13: 1–16.
Lockhart, K. (1992, July 30) Interview by Gail Baker Woods. Lockhart and Pettus, New York.
Macionis, J. J. (1996) *Society: The Basics*. Englewood Cliffs, NJ: Prentice-Hall.
O'Guinn, T. C., Allen, C. T., and Semenik, R. J. (1998) *Advertising*. Cincinnati, OH: South-Western College Publishing.
Perkins, T. E. (1979) "Rethinking Stereotypes," in M. Barrett, P. Corrigan, A. Kuhn, and J. Wolf (eds.), *Ideology and Cultural Production*. New York: St. Martin's, 135–159.
Pescosolido, B. A., Grauerholz, E. and Milkie, M. A. (1997) "Culture and Conflict: The Portrayal of Blacks in U.S. Children's Picture Books through the Mid- and Late-Twentieth Century," *American Sociological Review* 62: 443–464.
Peterson, R. (1976) *The Production of Culture*. Beverly Hills, CA: Sage.
Pettigrew, T. F. (1985) "New Black-White Patterns: How Best to Conceptualize Them?," *Annual Review of Sociology* 11: 329–346.

Rohmer, S. (1931) *Daughter of Fu Manchu*. London: Cassell.
Roller, E. (2016, Jan. 12) "Willie Horton's Heirs," *New York Times*. Retrieved from http://www.nytimes.com/2016/01/12/opinion/campaign-stops/ads-from-donald-trump-and-ted-cruz-play-to-racist-fears.html?_r=0.
Scott, S. (1989, Sept. 25) "It's a Small World after All," *Time*: 56.
Swidler, A. (1986) "Culture in Action: Symbols and Strategies," *American Sociological Review* 51: 272–286.
Uchida, A. (1998) "The Orientalization of Asian Women In America," in *Women's Studies International Forum*. Atlanta, GA: Elsevier Science Ltd.
Wang, W. (2012) "The Rise of Intermarriage Rates, Characteristics Vary by Race and Gender," Pew Research Center. Retrieved from http://www.pewsocialtrends.org/2012/02/16/the-rise-of-intermarriage.
Wilkes, R. E. and Valencia, H. (1989) "Hispanics and Blacks in Television Commercials," *Journal of Advertising* 18: 19–25.
Williams, R. (1981) "The Analysis of Culture," in T. Bennett, G. Martin, C. Mercer, and J. Wollacott (eds.), *Culture, Ideology, and Social Process*. London: Open University Press, 43–52.
Williams, Jr., R. M. (1970) *American Society: A Sociological Interpretation*. 3rd ed. New York: Knopf.
Woll, A. L. (1980) *The Latin Image in American Film*. Los Angeles, CA: UCLA Latin American Center Publications.
Woods, G. B. (1995) *Advertising and Marketing to the New Majority*. Belmont, CA: Wadsworth Publishing.
Wuthnow, R. and Witten, M. (1988) "New Directions in the Study of Culture," *Annual Review of Sociology* 14: 49–67.
Yung, J. (1999) *Unbound Voices: A Documentary History of Chinese Women in San Francisco*. Berkeley, CA: University of California Press.

# Further Reading

Cortese, A. (2016) *Provocateur: Images of Women and Minorities in Advertising*. 4th ed. Boulder, CO. and Lanham, MD: Rowman and Littlefield. (Offers an up-to-date, critical analysis of race and modern advertising.)
Kean, L. G. and Prividera, L. D. (2007) "Communicating about Race and Health: A Content Analysis of Print Advertisements in African American and General Readership Magazines," *Health Communication* 21(3): 289–297. (A content analysis conducted to investigate advertisements for consumption products in major magazines indicating that marketing of consumption products differs based on the magazine's target population in regard to race.)
"20 Ads that Changed How We Think about Race In America," *Business Insider*, 2013. Available at http://www.businessinsider.com/20-ads-that-changed-how-we-think-about-race-in-america-2013-2#ixzz3jF7pXtYB. (This slideshow contains the tale of race in the US, as told through its visual ads.)

# 15
# ETHNIC MEDIA
## Moving Beyond Boundaries
### Sherry S. Yu

The mediascape in multicultural societies is transforming. Aside from increasing transnational migration, forces of globalization (both cultural and economic) and digitalization allow media to transcend their formal national boundaries. Ethnic media are no exception. Formerly confined to the domain of ethnic or diasporic communities, these media go beyond not only geographic, but also ethnic boundaries. What is lagging behind this shift is the social perception and academic approach toward ethnic media, which consider ethnic media as media *by* and *for* immigrants, ethno-racial groups, and linguistic minorities only. This brief discussion traces the evolution of ethnic media by examining various aspects—terminologies, historical trajectories, and trends in production and consumption—and suggests that new critical approaches to understanding ethnic media are needed.

## Terminologies and Definitions

There are many terms that describe media *by* and *for* immigrants, ethno-racial groups, and linguistic minorities. Among those terms, "ethnic media" has been used most widely in the field of ethnic media studies as well as in the public realm. Although not unanimously supported for various reasons, this blanket term helps even non-users understand instantly what these media are. Variations of the term reflect an emphasis on different aspects of ethnic media. Some scholars propose user-oriented terms that highlight specific projects pursued by these media for "ethnic" or "minority" groups, whether cultural or language retention, subaltern political struggles, or identity politics and community bonding. These terms include "ethnic media" (Husband 1998; Kosnick 2007; Matsaganis, Katz, and Ball-Rokeach 2011; Murray, Yu, and Ahadi 2007), "ethnic community media" (Tsagarousianou 2002), "ethnic minority media" (Browne 2005; Downing 1992; Husband 2005), "minority media" (Dayan 1999; Riggins 1992; Rigoni 2005; Sreberny 2005; Silverstone and Georgiou 2005), "minority language media" (Guyot 2007), and "multicultural media" (Ahmed, Veronis, Feng, Jaya, and Charmarkeh 2014). It is this emphasis on "ethnicity" or "minority" that sets these media apart from so-called "mainstream media." Mainstream is defined, in relation to "ethnic," as that "part of society *within* which ethnic and racial origins have at most minor impacts on life chances or opportunities" (Alba and Nee 2003: 12). Similarly, in the US, mainstream refers to "individuals with European heritage"

(Matsaganis et al. 2011: 10). Does this mean that "mainstream media" are media *by* and *for* those who belong to these groups, mainly people of European heritage? Yes and no. Yes, the underrepresentation of ethnic minorities in production and content in mainstream media is one of the main factors that motivated minorities to develop media *by* and *for* themselves (Gandy 2000). No, because while "ethnic media" are produced and consumed primarily or almost entirely *by* ethnic minorities, "mainstream media" are consumed by all, regardless of ethnicity.

What "constitutes" ethnic media varies as well. In *Understanding Ethnic Media*, Matsaganis, Katz, and Ball-Rokeach (2011: 10) define "ethnic media" as "media produced *by* and *for* (a) immigrant, (b) ethnic, racial, and linguistic minorities, as well as (c) indigenous groups living in various countries across the world," a definition in which media for indigenous people are considered as part of "ethnic media." In contrast, media for indigenous people—which are also referred to by various terms—"indigenous media" (Alia 2010), "first people's media" (Roth 2010), or "aboriginal media" (Fleras 2011; Knopf 2010)—are *officially* not considered ethnic media in countries such as Canada. The Canadian Radio-television and Telecommunications Commission (CRTC) defines ethnic media—or more specifically, ethnic programs—as media "directed to any culturally or racially distinct group *other than* one that is Aboriginal Canadian, or from France or the British Isles" (emphasis added) (Public Notice CRTC 1999a-117).

The emphasis on ethnicity is less significant when it comes to the production-oriented term, "diasporic media" (Georgiou 2005, 2006; Karim 2009; Naficy 2003). Georgiou (2005) uses a broader definition of "diasporic media," which encompasses local, national, and transnational media that are *available* to diasporic communities. In understanding the multi-locality of media production and consumption, a broader conceptual approach focusing on the availability of media to local diasporic communities is considered. Karim (2009), on the other hand, distinguishes "ethnic" from "diasporic" by focusing on the *origin* of production: the former is produced in the local ethnic community in the host country, whereas the latter is produced in the country of origin. If the former connects the local community members, the latter connects geographically dispersed members of the same diaspora across many national jurisdictions. In a much narrower sense, the term "diasporic media" can also be considered as media locally produced by exiles. Naficy (2003: 51–52) establishes the following three categories: Ethnic television (programs produced in the host country by local minorities); transnational television (programs imported into or by the host country or multinational/transnational media); and diaspora television (programs produced in the host country by "liminars and exiles"; for instance, the diaspora television Naficy examines is Iranian media in Los Angeles).

The multiplicity and diversity of the terms reflect the efforts to capture the continually evolving nature of the mediascape for immigrants, ethno-racial groups, and linguistic minorities. It is, however, this fundamental nature that necessitates further revision of the existing terms, considering not only the ever-multiplying multi-local production and consumption of media, especially in the digital era, but also cross-ethnic media production and consumption among demographically diverse and increasingly transnational individuals. The Canadian mediascape, for example, is constituted of various multilingual options originating at various geographic levels and produced by cross-ethnic groups: "Multicultural media" (mainstream media that offer multilingual services such as Roger's OMNI and Shaw Multicultural Channel); "third-language media" (established by local ethnic communities such as *Vancouver Chosun*, *Indo-Canadian Voice*, and *Shahrvand*); "pan-ethnic media" (established by local ethnic communities targeting broader audiences such as the *Asian Pacific Post* and *Canadian Immigrant*); and "transnational media" (imported from the country of origin or produced locally by local branch offices such as Z-TV, CCTV, and *Sing Tao*). Enormous changes have been seen in the broadcasting sector alone in which these services are available on terrestrial, cable, satellite, and online (in the form of streaming services). The US also demonstrates how the old containment of the term ethnic media as relating to a particular group or territory is being left behind by the particularly strong cable and satellite sectors, which are also expanding into online services. Companies such as Time Warner, Dish Network, and DirecTV offer a variety of multilingual services including programs/channels both locally produced and internationally imported. Online streaming services such as hulu.com (est. 2007) also offer non-English programs, such as Latino and Korean programs with English subtitles, thereby reaching out not only to "ethnic" but also broader audiences.

The emergence of the "digital diaspora"—"diasporas organized on the Internet" (Brinkerhoff 2009: 2)—which facilitates diasporic communication over space rather than geographic place further confirms multi-local production and consumption and reinforces a trans-local sense of belonging (Cheng 2005; Georgiou 2005). Free from possible restrictions that may have been placed on home-bound online space, diasporic communities engage in a variety of spaces, whether online forums organized for overseas Chinese students, scholars, and professionals (e.g., *Chinese News Digest*, *Hua Xia Wen Zhai*) or the BBC World Service, which is offered in 31 languages, including Persian, Arabic, and Chinese, and facilitates bonding within and dialogue beyond diasporic communities (Ding 2007; Gillespie 2009; Andersson, Gillespie, and Mckay 2010).

The members of diasporas in general and digital diasporas in particular are not only technologically moving forward but are also demographically transformative and call for more attention to hybridity than the previously focused "ethnicity." Indeed, in the process of adoption of the new while retaining the old culture through interaction with the *other* in multiple localities, their identity is constantly a work in progress, although in varying degrees and over different timescales. Take the example of socio-economically empowered "new Asian Americans" who lack the "stereotypical Chineseness" which has "settled comfortably in the mind of the West" (Ong 1999: 98) or "the multiple-passport holder" (Ong 1999: 1) who identifies with multiple nationalities, citizenship, ethnicities, and cultures, and who enjoys the benefits of each country. All of these different social groups constitute what outsiders assume as homogenous "ethnic" groups. It is, after all, the eyes of the beholder that reinforce or challenge perceptions and social categorization of the ethnicity of the *other*. In fact, such essentialization of ethnicity is a barrier to ethnic media studies by dismissing the coexistence of multiple identities, which leads to equally diverse media consumption and production patterns (De Leeuw and Rydin 2007; Dohest, Cola, Brusa, and Lemish 2012; Georgiou 2006; Sreberny 2005) and makes ethnic media projects equally diverse. Certainly, ethnic media projects have never been linear and generalizable: some pursue subaltern counter-public projects against the country of origin (such as the aforementioned *Hua Xia Wen Zhai*), while others pursue entertainment (such as mvibo.com which used to offer Korean entertainment programs, among others, with English subtitles). All of these examples suggest that the mediascape formerly confined to immigrants, ethno-racial groups, and linguistic minorities is evolving, and so should the existing terms that describe these media.

## Historical Perspectives

Such conceptual complexity is part and parcel of the complex history of ethnic media. One of the important factors that motivated the creation of ethnic media was, as Gandy (2000) argued, continued underrepresentation of ethno-racial minorities in mainstream media production and content. Examples are not hard to find. Georgiou's study on London's ethnic media (2002) found that there were even fewer blacks and Asians at the management level of the BBC, Channel 4, and ITV in 2000 than in 1990. Similarly, in Canada, visible minorities accounted for less than 7 percent of the Canadian public broadcasting workforce (Canadian Broadcasting Corporation) in 2010 (CBC 2010). In the US, the Federal Communication Commission (FCC) adopted the Equal Employment Opportunity (EEO) regulations in 1971; however, these regulations have not led to any substantial improvement (Hollifield and Kimbro 2010). In the case of media content, the situation is not so different. Studies continue to find examples of underrepresentation of ethnic minorities (see, for example, Awad 2012; Mahtani and Mountz 2002; Phillips 2011; Tator and Henry 2006).

As a response, coupled with ever-increasing global migration and the advancement of media technologies, ethnic media have proliferated around the globe over the past few decades. Especially in the two most-favored destinations for immigration, the US and Canada, a record number of ethnic media outlets—3,000 (broadcast and print combined) and 300 (print only) outlets respectively—have been documented (see New America Media and the National Ethnic Press and Media Council of Canada). The level of development tends to depend on, but is not limited to, the demographic profile of ethnic groups (e.g., socio-cultural capital), the history of migration, and perhaps most importantly, the host country's policy directives for immigration, multicultural integration or assimilation, and foreign relations. International policies concerning minority media are not absent, but rather broad in scope and limited in impact. Articles 17 and 19 in the U.N. Declaration of Human Rights only broadly mention freedom of opinion and expression and participation in cultural life (Browne 2005). UNESCO also looks into media usage in general, but rarely that of ethnic minorities in particular (Browne 2005). Media policies are rather an outcome of national self-determination than international governance, as is evident in the case of the UNESCO Convention on the Protection and Promotion of the Diversity of Cultural Expression, to which the US is not a signatory (Parliament of Canada).

Riggins proposes five models for the nation-state's structural support for minority media (1992: 8–10), which helps us understand the relationship between policy directives on immigration and ideological perspectives on ethnic media at the national level: (1) the integrationist model, which supports minority media with an intention to strategically and easily monitor minorities; (2) the economic model, which supports minority media to help multicultural groups assimilate into the dominant culture; (3) the divisive model, which encourages ethnic rivalry as a mechanism of social control; (4) the preemptive model, which encourages the state to establish its own minority media to prevent minorities from establishing their own; and (5) the proselytism model, which mobilizes minority media to promote state values.

Classic immigrant countries such as the US, Canada, and Australia oscillate between the integrationist and economic models. Similar patterns of U.S. and Canadian immigration policies demonstrate the phases of discrimination (the late 1800s and the early 1900s), phasing-out of discriminatory practices (1940s–50s) and neoliberal (1960s and onwards) approaches (Abu-Laban and Gabriel 2002; Burnet and Palmer 1988; James 2000; Min 2006). The discriminatory policies in the early years of immigration in the US—such as the Chinese Exclusion Act of 1882 and the Immigration Act of 1917—continued until the 1940s, when the US began to ease immigration and naturalization for its WWII allies (James 2000: 18). During this period, the high correlation between the US's foreign relations and the development of ethnic media is exemplified in the case of German media, which suffered during WWI when the US entered the war against Germany (Wittke 1957). On the other hand, neoliberal policies such as the Immigration and Nationality Act of the US (1990) and the Business Immigration Programme of Canada (1986)—both of which focused on recruiting "quality" immigrants who would not only be self-sufficient socio-economically but also contribute to the economy of the new country (Kobayashi, Li, and Teixeira 2011; Li 2007; Li and Skop 2007)—facilitated the growth of ethnic media in North America since the early 1990s. The influx of affluent investor/entrepreneur-class immigrants started to establish ethnic media much like other ethnic enclave businesses (Zhou, Chen, and Cai 2006).

Canada's commitment to multiculturalism as a political philosophy since the 1970s, however, makes Canada lean more toward the integrationist model, with an emphasis on the recognition of cultural diversity and assistance for the social integration of immigrants. As part of this multicultural mandate, media policies such as the Policy Framework for Canadian Television (Public Notice CRTC 1999b-97) and Ethnic Broadcasting Policy (Public Notice CRTC 1999a-117) ensure fair and accurate representation of ethnicity and ethnic programs in Canadian broadcasting. Such explicit policies are absent in the US, consistent with its opposition to the UNESCO Convention on the Protection and Promotion of the Diversity of Cultural Expression since 2005 (Parliament of Canada). Nevertheless, the absence of such policies is compensated to a certain extent by strong grassroots initiatives such as New America Media (a network of over 3,000 ethnic media organizations) and the American Society of Newspaper Editors, which drive ground-level interaction within and across ethnic and mainstream media organizations (Roy and Close 2007).

Australia has followed a similar path. Australia's "White Australia policy" has persisted so strongly in Australian politics that the notorious Immigration Restriction Act 1901, for example, required a dictation of a passage of 50 words in length in a European language (Joppke 2005). A move toward liberalization, such as the "good neighbor policy," emerged in the late 1940s and led to neoliberal immigration policies between 1983 and 1996, which aimed to integrate into the Asia Pacific region (Castles 2000). Australia's Special Broadcasting Service (SBS) is regarded as a prime example of state support for multiculturalism, although it was supported primarily because the station could be non-commercial and self-supporting and could mobilize minority support for the Labour Party in the 1972 election (Davies in Browne 2005).

Ethnic media in Europe, on the other hand, evolved historically to provide media for "guest workers." The guest-worker programs in Europe—for example, Britain's European Voluntary Worker, France's guest worker recruitment through *Office National d' Immigration*, and Germany's *Gastarbeiter* recruited through *Bundesanstalt für Arbeit*—invited foreign labor migrants and supported them while they resided in the country; however, none of these programs was intended to allow permanent settlement of the workers (Castles 2000). The development of ethnic media thus reflects this sentiment that ethnic programming targeting these groups—such as West Germany's weekly television magazine program, *Nachbarn* (neighbors), in the mid-1960s—aimed to facilitate the return of migrant workers to their home countries rather than settlement and integration in the host country (Browne 2005). The growth of ethnic media, however, took place during the intense commercialization, deregulation, and privatization of European public service media in the 1950s through the early 1990s (Curran 2000). Ethnic media were promoted as "eminently marketable" and media outlets such as London's Sunrise Radio and Greek Radio emerged during this period (Tsagarousianou 2002: 219). The momentum for growth was further accelerated during the Civil Rights Movements in the 1970s and 1980s, which necessitated more venues for the expression of diverse voices (Browne 2005). In the broader spectrum of policy support for ethnic media, however, Europe has been rather inconsistent. For Britain, Georgiou's study (2002) found that its broadcasting law of 1996 contained no clauses concerning the reality of a multicultural society, and the Department of Culture, Media, and Sport lacked policy support for cultural diversity in media production on the ground.

## Current Contributions and Research

Aside from the history of ethnic media in the context of these important structural policy initiatives, various aspects of ethnic media have been studied, ranging from mapping of the sector to the trend in consumption and production. Some of the leading international mapping projects in the US, Canada, and Europe include: *The Metamorphosis Project* (1998–2002) by the Annenberg School of Communication at the University of Southern California (www.metamorph.org) and *The Ethnic Media Project* (2004) by the Center of Media and Society at the University of Massachusetts (www.umb.edu/cms) in the US; *The Cultural Diversity and Ethnic Media in B.C.* study (2006–7) by Simon Fraser University and Canadian Heritage (www.bcethnicmedia.ca) and *The Ottawa Multicultural Media Initiative* (2010–13) by the University of Ottawa and the City of Ottawa (artsites.uottawa.ca/ommi/en) in Canada; and *Mapping Minorities and their Media* (2002–5) by the London School of Economics of the UK (www.lse.ac.uk/media@lse/ research/EMTEL/minorities/project_home.html) and *Mediam'Rad: Ethnic and Diversity Media* (2005–7) by the Panos Institute of France in Europe. These widely cited projects contributed to increasing the visibility of the formerly underrepresented media sector by mapping ethnic media organizations active in the region and initiating debates on issues concerning cross-ethnic media collaboration, intercultural dialogue across communities, and policies that govern media practices.

Beyond media mapping, studies have also addressed how these media are consumed and produced. Ethnic media play various roles depending on, but not limited to, production by media genre (e.g., news versus entertainment) and orientation to different media users (e.g., new immigrants, matured immigrants, transnationally mobile immigrants). In general, ethnic media are known to contribute to creating culturally friendly communicative spaces (Couldry and Dreher 2007; Georgiou 2005) that help fuel a sense of community (Ball-Rokeach, Kim, and Matei 2001; Cheng 2005; Karim 2002; Lin and Song 2006; Murray et al. 2007; Ojo 2006) or build identity and shared "consciousness" (Bailey 2007; Georgiou 2002, 2006; Kosnick 2007; Sinclair, Yue, Hawkins, Pookong, and Fox 2001; Sreberny 2000, 2005; Sun 2006). Such values are also found to be important for younger generations, as manifested in media led by hyphenated populations (e.g., Korean-Americans' *Kore Asian Media*, formerly known as *KoreAm* journal) or ethno-culturally hybrid populations with multiple identities (e.g., Vancouver's *Schema Magazine*).

Ethnic media also serve to further the social, political, and economic integration of ethnic communities. Theoretical approaches in media studies of the range of socio-political roles adopted by ethnic media are rather extreme. Ethnic media are seen pessimistically as fragmenting "sphericules" (Gitlin 1998: 173) or "parallel societies" (Hafez 2007: 136) that are disconnected from the public sphere, or more optimistically as reforming a part of a "multi-ethnic public sphere" (Husband 1998: 134). To this end, Ball-Rokeach's Communication Infrastructure Theory (2001) suggests the possibility for creating a well-functioning civil society, if ethnic residents, community organizations, and media are properly connected to their counterparts in broader society on different geographic levels. Examples of how ethnic media may mobilize communities to push for social and political recognition within broader society include Britain's London Greek Radio, which is mandated to play a mediatory role by delivering "mainstream information" (e.g., social benefits, training, job opportunities) to those whose low language skills prohibit them from economic, cultural, and political participation in European societies (Georgiou 2005: 494). By contrast, ethnic media may be expected to create "a forum for intercultural dialogue" in response to spreading anti-immigration sentiments, as evident in the case of Germany's Radio MultiKulti for Turkish people in Berlin (Kosnick 2007: 155). Younger-generation Muslims are also active in this mission in France by going "beyond the post-colonial ideologies . . . [to] emphasise dialogue with national [French] and European institutions" (Rigoni 2005: 566).

News content produced by ethnic media is expected to serve this end by providing space for expression, adaptation, and resistance. However, studies simultaneously find—although varying by community—significant emphasis on news about the country of origin rather than the country of settlement, and raise a self-alienation hypothesis (Lin and Song 2006; Murray et al. 2007; Lindgren 2011). On this note, it is important to ask whether such a skewed focus toward the country of origin truly reflects genuinely higher interest in the home-country news or something else, given socio-cultural, economic, and generational divides within the community and equally varied information needs among members: immigrant vs. ethnic; old vs. new immigrants; old vs. younger generations; local vs. transnational migrants; and socio-economically privileged vs. under-privileged.

The economic role of ethnic media explains why, at least to a certain extent. Ethnic media serve not only as an information hub for enclave businesses to advertise and connect with customers, but also as ethnic businesses themselves. Aside from transnational media branches such as *Sing Tao*—a leading Chinese-language daily found across major cities in North America—a majority of ethnic media are primarily mom-and-pop-style print media (Murray et al. 2007; Matsaganis et al. 2011), since sole proprietorships are easier to launch given the reduced cost of entry to digital distribution. The downside of such small-scale operational models is higher vulnerability in the market, which complies with the logic of political economy in the media industries. Indeed, it is predicted that minority media owners are more likely to face bankruptcies as they tend to be "under-collateralized and therefore vulnerable to economic downturns" (Waldman and the Working Group 2011). Thus, limited financial resources, let alone equally limited socio-cultural capacity, increase dependency on home-country news, which helps fill the daily "news hole" (Bennett 2012: 172) and, more importantly, creates ad space to attract advertising. The consequence is that the higher the emphasis on financial sustainability, the higher the portion of home-country news in the overall news output.

## Critical Issues

Underrepresentation of ethno-racial minorities in media production and content was one of the factors that underpinned the growth of ethnic media. However, the pattern continues: ethnic media organizations and the discourse they produce daily are equally underrepresented in the broader media system. The record shows that in the US, African and Latino Americans—the two largest ethno-racial groups, which account for over 12 percent and 17 percent of the U.S. population respectively—own only 0.33 percent and 1 percent of television stations respectively (U.S. Census 2013; Waldman and the Working Group 2011). Studies also continue to find disconnects between ethnic media and broader society. Couldry and Dreher's study of Australia's emerging communicative spaces (2007) identified potential contributions to intercultural dialogue with mainstream media, but also a simultaneous lack of media strategies that enable substantive outcomes. Consequently, ethnic discourse produced by these media outlets is circulated only within their respective communities without reaching a broader audience. As Karim's study on South Asian media in Vancouver (2002: 239) confirmed, "Even though civic discourse disseminated through ethnic media may not be as fragmented as Gitlin (1998) fears, the situation is also far from Husband's (1994) idea of the multi-ethnic public sphere, where a multitude of voices reach a larger audience."

Interestingly, however, while such a pattern of underrepresentation continues when the ethnic community is the "public" (Gandy 2000), a reverse pattern is observed when the ethnic community becomes important potential strategic "consumers" and "voters." Mainstream media have been making efforts to tap into the ethnic market by publishing in different language editions (e.g., *The Vancouver Sun*'s former Chinese-language edition, *taiyangbao.com*) or developing cross-ethnic partnerships (e.g., Black Entertainment Television and Viacom, Telemundo and NBC, *Sing Tao* and Star Media Group). Such joint ventures are more attractive if the solid financial records of leading ethnic media have made them a desirable "commodity" (Jin and Kim 2011). What is of more concern is the "instrumentalization of ethnic media"—the strategic use of ethnic media as an instrument to serve the needs of interest groups rather than to pluralize public discourse (Yu 2016). Disturbing cases found in Canada include the silent monitoring of ethnic media content for partisan purposes by Citizenship and Immigration Canada in 2012 and the "ethnic vote scandal" by the BC Liberals in 2013, which attempted to use ethnic media as channels to ethnic voters (Yu 2016).

Such marginalization of ethnic media and discourse has to do largely with a narrowed understanding of ethnic media in society in general and academia in particular. Whether the term "ethnic media" is officially *defined* (as in the case of Canada) or unofficially shared as a blanket term, it is generally *understood* as media *by* and *for* the *other* rather than media for *all* members of broader society as a potential option to consider in their daily media repertoire. As a result, policy frameworks concerning ethnic broadcasting (see, for example, the aforementioned Canada's Policy Framework for Canadian Television and Ethnic Broadcasting Policy) tend to focus on fair and accurate representation or creation of space for ethno-racial minorities, rather than *accessibility* to these available ethnic resources for members of broader society. Equally, in academia, ethnic media studies have focused on varying aspects of ethnic media yet predominantly *within* the domain of ethnic communities rather than *as part of* the broader media system. However, given the rapid demographic changes in metropolitan centers—such as Los Angeles where over

60 percent of the population is non-white (U.S. Census Bureau 2010)—access to ethnic discourse for the proper exercise of citizenship and functioning democracy becomes more salient. That said, the notion of ethnic media as media only *by* and *for* the *other* requires a critical reassessment. Such a narrow conceptualization of ethnic media stands as a barrier to the proper production, integration, and distribution of ethnic discourse in places where minorities have overtaken the majority of the population. In an ideal multicultural society and the media system that it develops, multiple narratives from diverse communities must be produced and widely circulated, contested, and eventually integrated into the public discourse.

## The Future of Ethnic Media and Ethnic Media Studies

To this end, more research efforts and grassroots initiatives are needed to explore the ways in which public discourse in a multicultural society can be pluralized. A potential solution suggested in Europe is to promote ethnic-mainstream media coproduction, such as the cases of Beur FM and Temoignage (France) and El Gringo and Metro (Sweden) (Matsaganis et al. 2011). In North America, what is more commonly seen instead is a tendency to create multicultural, multiethnic, and multilingual spaces. Grassroots initiatives by media professionals such as New America Media and LA Beez aggregate ethnic news in collaboration with ethnic media to create a platform for "voices of the marginalized" (newamericamedia.org), while more localized efforts among local residents, academics, and journalists (such as the Alhambra Source) attempt to build cross-ethnic dialogue. What is unknown, however, are the success and failure factors that influence these initiatives, and, more importantly, the impact on broader society. Bailey and Harindranath (2006: 307) argue that ethnic media may help promote "differentiated citizenship" but their impact on broader society is still unclear. This same question about the broader impact needs to be extended to these emerging spaces to maximize the benefit of intercultural efforts, or to find new directions.

This brief discussion of ethnic media attempted to further ongoing debates on various aspects of ethnic media: terminologies and definitions, historical trajectories, trends evolving in production and consumption, and areas for future studies. All of these aspects seem to suggest that ethnic media are continually evolving—even more rapidly in the digital era—by going beyond geographic and ethnic boundaries. Ethnic media grow as a result of social changes and market forces, despite limited policy support. As Browne argues (2005), the development of ethnic media is after all the result of an interplay among social climate, lobbyists, legislature, political parties, regulatory agencies, and personal involvement. How these factors will come into play in transforming the understanding of ethnic media from media only *by* and *for* the *other* to media for *all* remains a question. However, the critical role of ethnic media as an important tool for a functioning democracy in a multicultural society seems to be no longer in question.

## References

Abu-Laban, Y. and Gabriel, C. (2002) *Selling Diversity*. Peterborough, Ontario: Broadview Press.
Ahmed, R., Veronis, L., Feng, J., Jaya, P. S., and Charmarkeh, H. (2014) *OMMI 2012 Survey: Demographic Profiles of Ottawa's Four Participating Ethno-Cultural Communities*. Ottawa Multicultural Media Initiative, University of Ottawa, Ottawa, Canada.
Alba, R. and Nee, V. (2003) *Remaking the American Mainstream: Assimilation and Contemporary Immigration*. Cambridge, MA: Harvard University Press.

Alia, V. (2010) *The New Media Nation: Indigenous Peoples and Global Communication*. New York: Berghahn Books.

Andersson, M., Gillespie, M., and Mckay, H. (2010) "Mapping Digital Diaspora @ BBC World Service: Users and Uses of the Persian and Arabic Websites," *Middle East Journal of Culture and Communication* 3: 256–278.

Awad, I. (2012) "Desperately Constructing Ethnic Audiences: Anti-immigration Discourses and Minority Audience Research in the Netherlands," *European Journal of Communication* 28(2): 168–182.

Bailey, O. G. (2007) "Transnational Identities and the Media," in O. G. Bailey, M. Georgiou, and R. Harindranath (eds.), *Transnational Lives and the Media: Re-imagining Diaspora*. Basingstoke, UK; New York: Palgrave Macmillan, 212–230.

Bailey, O. G. and Harindranath, R. (2006) "Ethnic Minorities, Cultural Difference and the Cultural Politics of Communication," *International Journal of Media and Cultural Politics* 2(3): 299–316.

Ball-Rokeach, S. J., Kim, Y. C., and Matei, S. (2001) "Storytelling Neighborhood: Paths to Belonging in Diverse Urban Environments," *Communication Research* 28(4): 392–428.

Bennett, L. (2012) *News: The Politics of Illusion*. Boston, MA: Longman.

Brinkerhoff, J. M. (2009) *Digital Diasporas: Identity and Transnational Engagement*. Cambridge; New York: Cambridge University Press.

Browne, D. R. (2005) *Ethnic Minorities, Electronic Media, and the Public Sphere: A Comparative Study*. Cresskill, NJ: Hampton Press.

Burnet, J. R. and Palmer, H. (1988) *Coming Canadians: An Introduction to a History of Canada's Peoples*. Toronto, Ontario: McClelland and Stewart.

Canadian Broadcasting Corporation. (2010) *CBC/Radio-Canada 2010 Annual Employment Equity Report to Human Resources Skills Development Canada*. Retrieved from http://www.cbc.radio-canada.ca/_files/cbcrc/documents/equity/ee-exec-2010-en.pdf.

Canadian Radio-television and Telecommunications Commission. (1999a) Public Notice CRTC 1999–117, Ethnic Broadcasting Policy. Retrieved from http://www.crtc.gc.ca/eng/archive/1999/PB99-117.HTM.

Canadian Radio-television and Telecommunications Commission. (1999b) Public Notice CRTC 1999–7, Building on Success – A Policy Framework for Canadian Television. Retrieved from http://www.crtc.gc.ca/eng/archive/1999/PB99-97.htm#t6.

Castles, S. (2000) *Ethnicity and Globalization: From Migrant Worker to Transnational Citizen*. London; Thousand Oaks, CA: Sage Publications.

Cheadle, B. and Levitz, S. (2012, Nov. 13) "Government Paid for Media Monitoring of Immigration Minister's Image," *The Globe and Mail*. Retrieved from http://www.theglobeandmail.com/news/national/government-paid-for-media-monitoring-of-immigration-ministers-image/article5249773/.

Cheng, H. L. (2005) "Constructing a Transnational, Multilocal Sense of Belonging: An Analysis of Ming Pao (West Canadian Edition)," *Journal of Communication Inquiry* 29(2): 141–159.

Couldry, N. and Dreher, T. (2007) "Globalization and the Public Sphere: Exploring the Space of Community Media in Sydney," *Global Media and Communication* 3(1): 79–100.

Curran, J. (2000). "Rethinking Media and Democracy," in J. Curran and M. Gurevitch (eds.), *Mass Media and Society*. 3rd ed. London: Arnold; New York: Oxford University Press, 120–154.

Dayan, D. (1999) "Media and Diasporas," in J. Gripsrud (ed.), *Television and Common Knowledge*. London: Routledge, 18–33.

De Leeuw, S. and Rydin, I. (2007) "Diasporic Mediated Spaces," in O. G. Bailey, M. Georgiou, and R. Harindranath (eds.), *Transnational Lives and the Media: Re-imagining Diaspora*. Basingstoke, UK; New York: Palgrave Macmillan, 175–194.

Ding, S. (2007) "Digital Diaspora and National Image Building: A New Perspective on Chinese Diaspora Study in the Age of China's Rise," *Pacific Affairs* 80(4): 627–648.

Dohest, C., Brusa, M. M., and Lemish, D. (2012) "Studying Ethnic Minorities' Media Use: Comparative Conceptual and Methodological Reflections," *Communication, Culture and Critique* 5: 372–391.

Downing, J. (1992) "Spanish-language Media in the Greater New York Region during the 1980s," in S. H. Riggins (ed.), *Ethnic Minority Media: An International Perspective*. Newbury Park, CA: Sage Publications, 256–275.

Fleras, A. (2011) *The Media Gaze: Representations of Diversities in Canada*. Vancouver, British Columbia: UBC Press.

Gandy, O. (2000) "Race, Ethnicity and the Segmentation of Media Markets," in J. Curran and M. Gurevitch (eds.), *Mass Media and Society*. London: Arnold, 44–69.

Georgiou, M. (2002) *Mapping Minorities and Their Media: The National Context – The UK*. EU Project on Diasporic Minorities and their Media in the EU. London School of Economics. Retrieved from http://www.lse.ac.uk/media@lse/research/EMTEL/minorities/papers/ukreport.pdf.
——. (2005) "Diasporic Media across Europe: Multicultural Societies and the Universalism-Particularism Continuum," *Journal of Ethnic and Migration Studies* 31(3): 481–498.
——. (2006) *Diaspora, Identity and the Media: Diasporic Transnationalism and Mediated Spatialities*. Cresskill, NJ: Hampton Press.
Gillespie, M. (2009) "Anytime, Anyplace, Anywhere: Digital Diasporas and the BBC World Service," *Journalism* 10(3): 322–325.
Gitlin, T. (1998) "Public Sphere or Public Sphericules?," in T. Liebes and J. Curran (eds.), *Media, Ritual and Identity*. London; New York: Routledge, 168–174.
Guyot, J. (2007) "Minority Language Media and the Public Sphere," in M. Cormack and N. Hourigan (eds.), *Minority Language Media: Concepts, Critiques and Case Studies*. Clevedon, Ontario; Buffalo, NY: Multilingual Matters, 34–51.
Hafez, K. (2007) *The Myth of Media Globalization*. Cambridge, UK: Polity Press.
Hollified, C. A. and Kimbro, C. W. (2010) "Understanding Media Diversity: Structural and Organizational Factors Influencing Minority Employment in Local Commercial Television," *Journal of Broadcasting and Electronic Media* 54(2): 228–247.
Husband, C. (1998) "Differentiated Citizenship and the Multi-ethnic Public Sphere," *Journal of International Communication* 5(1–2): 134–148.
——. (2005) "Minority Ethnic Media as Communities of Practice: Professionalism and Identity Politics in Interaction," *Journal of Ethnic and Migration Studies* 31(3): 461–479.
James, A. (2000) "Demographic Shifts and the Challenge for Planners: Insights from a Practitioner," in M. A. Burayidi (ed.), *Urban Planning in a Multicultural Society*. Westport, CT: Praeger, 15–35.
Jin, D. Y. and Kim, S. (2011) "Sociocultural Analysis of the Commodification of Ethnic Media and Asian Consumers in Canada," *International Journal of Communication* 5: 552–569.
Joppke, C. (2005) *Selecting by Origin: Ethnic Migration in the Liberal State*. Cambridge, MA: Harvard University Press.
Karim, K. H. (2002) "Public Sphere and Public Sphericules: Civic Discourse in Ethnic Media," in S. D. Ferguson and L. R. Shade (eds.), *Civic Discourse and Cultural Politics in Canada: A Cacophony of Voices*. Westport, CT: Albex Publishing, 230–242.
——. (2009) "The National-global Nexus of Ethnic and Diasporic Media," in L. Regan Shade (ed.), *Mediascapes*. 3rd ed. Toronto, Ontario: Thomson Nelson, 259–270.
Knopf, K. (2010) "Sharing our Stories with All Canadians: Decolonizing Aboriginal Media and Aboriginal Media Politics in Canada," *American Indian Culture and Research Journal* 34(1): 89–120.
Kobayashi, A., Li, W., and Teixeira, C. (2011) "Introduction," in C. Teixeira, W. Li, and A Kobayashi (eds.), *Immigrant Geographies of North American Cities*. Don Mills, Ontario: OUP Canada, xv–xxxviii.
Kosnick, K. (2007) "Ethnic Media, Transnational Politics: Turkish Migrant Media in Germany," in O. G. Bailey, M. Georgiou, and R. Harindranath (eds.), *Transnational Lives and the Media: Re-imagining Diaspora*. Basingstoke, UK; New York: Palgrave Macmillan, 49–172.
Lindgren, A. (2011) "Interpreting the City: Portrayals of Place in a Toronto-area Ethnic Newspaper," *Aether: The Journal of Media Geography* VIII(A): 66–88.
Li, W. (2007) "Chinese Americans: Community Formation in Time and Space," in I. M. Miyares and C. A. Airriess (eds.), *Contemporary Ethnic Geographies in America*. Lanham, MD: Rowman and Littlefield, 213–232.
Li, W. and Skop, E. (2007) "Enclaves, Ethnoburbs, and New Patterns of Settlement among Asian Immigrants," in M. Zhou and J. V. Gatewood (eds.), *Contemporary Asian America: A Multidisciplinary Reader*. 2nd ed. New York: New York University Press, 222–236.
Lin, W. and Song, H. Y. (2006) "Geoethnic Storytelling: An Examination of Ethnic Media Content in Contemporary Immigrant Communication," *Journalism* 7(3): 362–388.
Mackin, B. (2013) "Ministry Mired in 'Quick Wins' Scandal Got $1-million Boost ahead of Election and More Revelations Found in Newly-released Government Docs," *The Tyee*. Retrieved from http://thetyee.ca/News/2013/06/12/Quick-Wins-Docs/print.html.
Mahtani, M. and Mountz, A. (2002) "Immigration to British Columbia: Media Representation and Public Opinion," *Research on Immigration and Integration in the Metropolis*, Working paper series No. 02–15.

Matsaganis, M., Katz, V., and Ball-Rokeach, S. J. (2011) *Understanding Ethnic Media: Producers, Consumers, and Societies*. Los Angeles, CA: Sage.

Min, P. G. (2006) "Major Issues Related to Asian American Experiences," in P. G. Min (ed.), *Asian Americans: Contemporary Trends and Issues*. 2nd ed. Thousand Oaks, CA: Pine Forge Press, 80–107.

Murray, C., Yu, S., and Ahadi, D. (2007) *Cultural Diversity and Ethnic Media in British Columbia*. Centre for Policy Studies on Culture and Communication, Simon Fraser University. Retrieved from http://www.bcethnicmedia.ca/Research/cultural-diversity-report-oct-07.pdf.

Naficy, H. (2003) "Narrowcasting in Diaspora: Middle Eastern Television in Los Angeles," in K. H. Karim (ed.), *The Media of Diaspora*. London; New York: Routledge, 51–62.

Ojo, T. (2006) "Ethnic Print Media in the Multicultural Nation of Canada," *Journalism* 7(3): 343–361.

Ong, A. (1999) *Flexible Citizenship: The Cultural Logics of Transnationality*. Durham, NC; London: Duke University Press.

Parliament of Canada. (2015) UNESCO Convention on the Protection and Promotion of the Diversity of Cultural Expressions. Retrieved from http://www.parl.gc.ca/Content/LOP/researchpublications/prb0564-e.html.

Phillips, G. (2011) "Reporting Diversity: The Representation of Ethnic Minorities in Australia's Television Current Affairs Programs," *Media International Australia* 139: 23–31.

Riggins, R. H. (1992) *Ethnic Minority Media: An International Perspective*. London: Sage.

Rigoni, I. (2005) "Challenging Notions and Practices: The Muslim Media in Britain and France," *Journal of Ethnic and Migration Studies* 31(3): 563–580.

Roth, L. (2010) "First Peoples' Television in Canada," in S. B. Hafsteinsson and M. Bredin (eds.), *Indigenous Screen Cultures in Canada*. Winnipeg, Manitoba: University of Manitoba Press, 17–34.

Roy, S. and Close, S. (2007) "Ethnic Media in USA: Giant Hidden in Plain Sight," in O. Bailey, G. Olga, M. Georgiou, and H. Ramaswami (eds.), *Transnational Lives and the Media: Re-imagining Diaspora*. Basingstoke, UK; New York: Palgrave Macmillan, 263–267.

Silverstone, R. and Georgiou, M. (2005) "Editorial Introduction: Media and Minorities in Multicultural Europe," *Journal of Ethnic and Migration Studies* 31(3): 433–441.

Sinclair, J., Yue, A., Hawkins, G., Pookong, K., and Fox, J. (2001) "Chinese Cosmopolitanism and Media Use," in S. Cunningham and J. Sinclair (eds.), *Floating Lives: The Media and Asian Diaspora*. Lanham, MD: Rowman and Littlefield, 35–90.

Sreberny, A. (2000) "Media and Diasporic Consciousness: An Exploration among Iranians in London," in S. Cottle (ed.), *Ethnic Minorities and the Media*. Buckingham, UK; Philadelphia, PA: Open University Press, 149–163.

——. (2005) "'Not Only, but Also': Mixedness and Media," *Journal of Ethnic and Migration Studies* 31(3): 443–459.

Sun, W. (2006) "Introduction: Transnationalism and a Global Diasporic Chinese Mediasphere," in W. Sun (ed.), *Media and the Chinese Diaspora*. London; New York: Routledge, 178–199.

Tator, C. and Henry, F. (2006) *Racial Profiling in Canada: Challenging the Myth of a Few Bad Apples*. Toronto, Ontario: University of Toronto Press.

Tsagarousianou, R. (2002) "Ethnic Community Media, Community Identity and Citizenship in Contemporary Britain," in N. W. Jankowski (ed.), *Community Media in the Information Age: Perspectives and Prospects*. Cresskill, NJ: Hampton Press, 209–230.

U.S. Census Bureau. (2010) 2010 "American Community Survey 1-Year Estimate: Selected Population Profile in the United States." Retrieved from http://factfinder2.census.gov/faces/tableservices/jsf/pages/productview.xhtml?pid=ACS_10_1YR_S0201&prodType=table.

——. (2013) "2013 American Community Survey 1-Year Estimate: Hispanic or Latino Origin by Race." Retrieved from http://factfinder.census.gov/faces/tableservices/jsf/pages/productview.xhtml?pid=ACS_13_1YR_B03002&prodType=table.

Waldman, S. and Working Group on Information Needs of Communities. (2011) *Information Needs of Communities – The Changing Media Landscape in a Broadband Age*. Retrieved from http://www.fcc.gov/info-needs-communities.

Wittke, C. (1957) *The German-language Press in America*. Lexington, KY: University of Kentucky Press.

Yu, S. (2016) "Instrumentalization of Ethnic Media," *Canadian Journal of Communication* 41(2): 341–349.

Zhou, M., Chen, W., and Cai, G. (2006) "Chinese-language Media and Immigrant Life in the United States and Canada," in W. Sun (ed.), *Media and the Chinese Diaspora*. London; New York: Routledge, 42–74.

## Further Reading

Bailey, O. G., Georgiou, M., and Harindranath R. (eds.) (2007) *Transnational Lives and the Media: Re-imagining Diaspora*. Basingstoke, UK; New York: Palgrave Macmillan. (A collection of theoretical approaches to and empirical case studies of the media and diaspora.)

Browne, D. R. (2005) *Ethnic Minorities, Electronic Media, and the Public Sphere: A Comparative Study*. Cresskill, NJ: Hampton Press. (Examination of structural and community factors that influence the participation of ethnic minorities in the public sphere through ethnic media.)

Karim, K. H. (ed.) (2003) *The Media of Diaspora*. London; New York: Routledge. (A collection of case studies on ethnic media in traditional and online formats.)

Matsaganis, M., Katz, V., and Ball-Rokeach, S. J. (2011) *Understanding Ethnic Media: Producers, Consumers, and Societies*. Los Angeles, CA: Sage. (A comprehensive overview of the production and consumption of ethnic media in a global context.)

Siapera, E. (2010) *Cultural Diversity and Global Media: The Mediation of Difference*. Chichester, UK; Malden, MA: Wiley-Blackwell. (Examination of theoretical approaches to and empirical findings on the media and multiculturalism.)

# 16
# SPORTS MEDIA IN THE UNITED STATES

## Trivializing Race

*Daniel Sipocz*

On Sunday January 19, 2014, National Football League player Richard Sherman, cornerback for the Seattle Seahawks, was interviewed on live television by Erin Andrews on the field immediately following a physical playoff win over the San Francisco 49ers. Rather than focusing on the thrill of victory or the Seahawks' berth to the Super Bowl, Sherman shouted excitedly about an opponent he had just gotten the better of to clinch the win. He said, "I'm the best corner[back] in the game! When you try me with a sorry receiver like Crabtree, that's the result you're going to get. Don't you ever talk about me." When Andrews asked who was talking about Sherman, he responded equally enthusiastically, "Crabtree. Don't you open your mouth about the best, or I'll shut it for you real quick. LOB [Legion of Boom]!" The interview caught Andrews off guard and created a stir among fans and media alike.

The media reaction following Sherman's interview did not focus on what he said, but how he said it. Much of the media, including sports and mainstream news media, asked if Sherman was a "thug" and concentrated on his socio-economic status growing up in Compton, California (Rogers 2014). His educational background, including studying communication while attending Stanford University, did not play a strong role in the discussion of Sherman's interview. The subtext of asking if Sherman was a *thug* played upon dominant stereotypes about his race, intelligence, socio-economic background, and athletic ability. In press conferences following the interview and leading up to the Super Bowl, Sherman had to respond to the media stories asking if he was a thug rather than focusing on the championship game itself. Such a focus by the media marginalized Sherman, diminishing his team's accomplishments and distracting from the reason why the press conference was occurring to begin with: the Seahawks were playing in the Super Bowl. The racially based coverage also marginalized the sports journalism profession by focusing on the stereotypes rather than producing a serious and substantial discussion of the stereotypes and their impact on society. Sherman questioned the racially based media discussion about his status as a "thug," telling those same media members, "The reason it bothers me is because it seems like it's an accepted way of calling somebody the N-word now. It's like everybody else said the N-word and then they say 'thug' and that's fine" (Wilson 2014). The comparison by Sherman of the N-word and thug raised important questions about the use of racial stereotypes in sports media that reinforce negative connotations based on the color of one's skin.

This contemporary, prominent example highlights the difficulty sports media in the US have in offering any insightful substance in discussing the role race plays in sports coverage. The lack of substance in media coverage of sports should not be the case, however. The coverage could act as a spotlight to help guide national conversation on important topics. Hall (1981) argued, "The media construct for us a definition of what race is, what meaning the imagery of race carries and what the 'problem of race' is understood to be" (35). Because the media establishes definitions, imagery, and the meaning audiences are supposed to understand, as described by Hall, the media also has the task of discussing the significance of race and the problems that come with coverage as seen in Sherman's case. Hall (1981) noted that race, a social construct, is part of a "cultural map" (31). These cultural maps "provide the frameworks through which we represent, interpret, understand and 'make sense' of some aspect of social existence" (Hall 1981: 31). Therefore, sports and sports media as institutions contribute to our sociological understanding of the world around us, especially regarding social relationships and learning how to interact within those relationships (Brooks and Rada 2002; Bruce 2004). The Sherman coverage portrayed black NFL players as thugs who lack intelligence, and it played into other racial stereotypes as well. However, sports coverage rarely discusses or examines on a substantial level the impact it has on society when it disseminates these types of stereotypes.

The lack of substance in sports media coverage is hardly a problem limited to the US, though. Whannel (2008) critiqued the media coverage of race in sports media in England, describing a lack of "reflective philosophy of sport" resulting in sports stereotypes being taken for granted. The same critique can be applied to the U.S. sports media. Whannel (2008) noted, "The media report sport with great professional skill but discuss it with a crass lack of seriousness" (112). By asking if Sherman was a thug, the U.S. sports media lacked the seriousness that Whannel noted was necessary to discuss race in sports and society. The difficulty in discussing race in sports media reflects the difficulty mainstream news media and society in the US have in approaching a sensitive and conflict-inducing topic. Despite society's difficulty to construct a significant, serious discussion about race and how it is covered, scholars across many fields of study have compiled a large body of knowledge about race in sports media.

The body of scholarship surrounding sports and sports media has grown quickly over the last two decades. The use of racial stereotypes in sports coverage is among the most frequently studied topics by scholars (Birrell 1989; Davis and Harris 1998; Eastman and Billings 2001; Hartmann 2000; McChesney 1988; Riess 2014; Wenner 1988; Whannel 2008). Scholars have examined the practice of racial stereotyping in many sports, from football (Bruce 2004; Rada 1996; Rainville and McCormick 1971), to basketball (Denham, Billings, and Halone 2002) and professional golf (Eastman and Billings 2001) to the Olympics (Billings and Eastman 2002). Each found that sports media played a significant role in the way minorities were represented, usually through racial stereotypes. As the body of scholarship grows in breadth and depth, there remains a need to study race in sports media as society, sports, and the media change. Scholarship encompasses many interests beyond the scope of stereotypes in the messages and meanings disseminated in the production of sport coverage. Other popular topics of study include, but are not limited to, ideological content of sports coverage, the process of producing content, the meanings of the content, and how the coverage reflects and reinforces dominant values of society.

This chapter will outline why sports are significant in society, why there is a need to study sports media, and the sports media's role in reinforcing stereotypes, through previous scholarship and the Sherman example. This chapter will also give an overview of the scholarship produced and outline the difference of quantitative and qualitative studies and their findings that have contributed significantly to the body of scholarship in regards to race in sports coverage.

Sports are increasingly televised, covered by a variety of media organizations and influential in the US. Athletic competition serves as a proving ground that unites the athletes and fans alike through a shared experience of victory, defeat, and big plays. Those who view sporting events experience the spectacle of the event and are often entertained by the live, unscripted drama and unpredictability. However, until the last two decades, scholarship all but ignored sports. Consequently, formal study of sports, media and their impact on society has been limited. Wenner (1988) noted, "It is ironic that sports programming has eluded the scrutiny of mass communication researchers. Indeed, research is often initiated by that which is obviously visible in the marketplace" (16). Sports coverage is increasingly visible on television with more than 30,000 hours of live event and studio programming airing on ESPN, the self-proclaimed "Worldwide Leader in Sports," alone in 2012 (ESPN Fact Sheet 2015). According to Riess (2014), one of the reasons why scholars generally ignored sports media was the perception of sports as only a game. Riess (2014) noted, "The prevailing view that sports is the 'playground of the newspaper' contributed to the trivialization of the history of sports media" (552). Even legendary sports broadcaster Howard Cosell trivialized sports media, referring to sports as the toy department of human life (Thomas 1995).

The trivialization of sports media began to change in the late 1980s as technology changed the capabilities of broadcast companies in the US. The expansion of sports broadcast on television in the late 1980s was in large part because of ESPN's increasing popularity with fans as the network brought an increasing quantity of athlete competitions into the homes of millions of Americans.

As sports became more prominent in media, they also became more commercialized. According to McChesney (1989), the media made sport into the institution we know today. Television brought the personalities of athletes and the journalists who covered them to the forefront. These personalities changed the culture surrounding sports and its coverage from just an activity to commercialized, must-see spectacles available on countless channels. Mass media also exposed racial and cultural problems that were rooted in the coverage of sports. According to Wenner (1988), "The mass-communicated and highly commercialized sports culture is easily related to a myriad of issues concerning socialization, interpersonal communication, value formation, racial and gender assessments, and the balance of political and economic power" (16). With the increase in commercialization, the sports media's focus has centered on generating revenue and creating a spectacle and spending less time discussing the issues that are presented in the coverage. The emphasis of spectacle only further increased the lack of serious coverage and the inability to talk about sensitive and controversial topics. In other words, the spectacle once again trivializes sports and its coverage back to the toy store of life. Consequently, sports function as a means to reinforce and celebrate the dominant beliefs of a culture which help to form identity (Wenner 1988). However, few gave critical thought to the ways in which the media cover sports and reinforce dominant beliefs of a society, and what the dominant beliefs say about society until something, such as the Sherman interview and its fallout, forces sports media and society to confront the issues head on.

Even though sports have not been studied much until recently in academia, sports are often viewed as a place where equality exists. In the US, much of society believes that the athletic realm is a racial equalizer, but sport is actually the site of struggle. Sports are a contested racial landscape that serves as a reflection of white male hegemony in the context of society in general. White men own teams and media companies, manage leagues, and generally have control over the rules that govern the black athletes. For example, more than 80 percent of the athletes in the National Basketball Association (NBA) are African American (Associated Press 2009). The athletes, consequently, are the focal point of the "product" of the NBA. As the focal point of the NBA's product, there is an overabundance of representation of black athletes which creates impressions and assumptions about the athletes, league, product, and roles in society that black athletes have. These representations in sports media legitimize racially based assumptions that blacks are well suited for careers, especially in the NBA, in sports but not for other occupations (Artz and Murphy 2000; Sabo and Jansen 1998). Consequently, the belief is that sports equal the playing field. Prominent ESPN sports commentator Chris Berman (1999) furthered the belief when he wrote that sports help break down barriers and bring people together. Sports may provide opportunities to individuals based on their talent and skill rather than appearance as Berman wrote, but sports can do even more than symbolically standing for equality. Human rights activist Nelson Mandela emphasized the ability of sports to unite the world and provide opportunities to overcome discrimination. Mandela said in a speech in 2000, "Sport has the power to unite people in a way little else can. Sport can create hope where there was only despair. It breaks down racial barriers. It laughs in the face of discrimination. Sport speaks to people in a language they can understand" (Mandela 2000; Muir 2007). Despite the beliefs that sports are played on a level playing field, media coverage is not. The media rely upon stereotypes in their coverage to tell stories and sell the spectacle of the event to society. Consequently, sport's ability to level the playing field may be limited. Hartmann (2000) pointed out that the belief of a level playing field often leads to specific assumptions regarding the benefits sports offer to racial minorities in the US:

> Dominant cultural conceptions of sport's racial impact can be stated easily enough. Sport is seen by most Americans as a positive and progressive racial force, an avenue of racial progress, and an arena of racial harmony. It is understood as a "way out of the ghetto," the general racial "equalizer," and a leader in Civil Rights, if not a literal "model" for race relations in the United States.
>
> *(232)*

Such racial assumptions could reinforce stereotypes on a mass scale, affecting society, without producers or audiences recognizing it (Campbell 1995; Entman and Rojecki 2000). For example, the media coverage surrounding Sherman was that football was his way "out of the ghetto." Although football presented Sherman with opportunities to get out of the bad neighborhood he grew up in, his intellect and academics also helped him. He achieved success in the classroom and attended Stanford because he was intelligent and applied himself in academics just as he did in football. Sherman's intelligence and success challenge the sports media's use of two stereotypes—sports as a means to escape the ghetto and the dumb jock—used in covering his post-game interview. This also showed that stereotypes trumped the outcome of the game, further trivializing sports media back into the toy store. Wenner (1988) noted, "A good portion of mediated sports consumption has little to do with information about who is winning or losing a game that is broadcast live" (42). The information provided often depends on the context surrounding the sporting event and athletes involved. In Sherman's case, the context the media focused on was the ghetto and not the academics or his intelligence. Consequently, information provided in commentary and storylines can be based on and reinforce racial stereotypes that further the "commonsense" belief in equality (Campbell 1995).

Despite this commonsense belief that all Americans are equal, stereotypes undermine the equality argument in sports and society as a whole. Hartmann (2000) noted the need for continued study of race in sports because the coverage in sports media (and media in general) does not often reflect reality. The disconnection between reality and what is actually covered is one of the reasons why scholars study race in sports coverage. According to Pease (1989), "Minorities seem to have made little progress since 1965 in terms of having their voices and concerns heard, their problems discussed, their triumphs and sorrows reported and their opinions considered" (34). Findings such as these continue to be supported in research examining race in the media. According to Campbell (1995), the lack of progress in minorities having their voices and concerns heard or represented in media is "evident in news coverage that reflects a common sense that is decidedly white and that contributes to an understanding of minorities as a peripheral part of mainstream American society" (42). The same commonsense culture that reflects white hegemony in mainstream news media is also reflected in sports media. Black athletes are sometimes pigeonholed into certain types of athleticism, reinforcing specific stereotypes of minorities, limiting cultural understanding, and creating social tension. Often the focus of such pigeonholing is about an athlete's intelligence, socio-economic background, and pure athletic ability as evidenced in the coverage surrounding Sherman. When media singles out racial differences as it did in Sherman's case, it reinforces prejudice by the majority (Entman and Rojecki 2000).

Reinforcing prejudices becomes a societal problem as large numbers of people who pay close attention to sports are convinced the prejudices are appropriate. Sports and sports media coverage are studied to confront the social values promoted by the media as worthy of being reinforced and maintained in society (Carrington 2009; Coakley 2009; Giacobbi and DeSensi 1999; Gruneau 1983; Hartmann 2000; Juffer 2002; Nichols 2011). Studying sports media and the coverage it produces can help attack racial stereotypes and societal structures that promote differences that support white hegemony and privilege in hopes of incrementally changing those structures and the stereotypes that support them.

Racial difference, like other differences based on outward appearance, presents socially and culturally constructed differences as natural or common sense (Brooks and Rada 2002; Campbell 1995). Many (Barth 1969; Gorham 1999; Hall 1981; Hartmann 2000; Lipmann 1922) agree that stereotypes based on racial and ethnic groups are humanly created social constructs that serve as a cultural map for society. Therefore, stereotypes contain cultural knowledge, beliefs, or expectancies about differences between groups of people (Hamilton and Trolier 1986)—all of which help make sense of the world. Seiter (1986) added that stereotypes help people make evaluations that justify social differences and norms, which paves the way for coverage that asks if someone is a "thug." Kellner (2003) noted specifically the media's role in the reinforcement of stereotypes: "The media are a profound and often misperceived source of cultural pedagogy: They contribute to educating us how to behave and what to think, feel, believe, fear, and desire—and what not to" (7). Because the media help society learn what is accepted and what is not in culture, the media is a powerful entity; the media can also redefine stereotypes and cultural norms.

The power of the media is not often thought about consciously by the average audience member, making critical engagement with the messages disseminated even more important. Because the average person does not think consciously about the power of the media or the messages disseminated and what the messages are telling society, there is a need to critically think about the media's power. According to Long and Hylton (2002), there is a definite need to examine race in the media because, "wherever there are structured differences and privilege because of whiteness and blackness we need to establish a critical gaze to emphasize and then challenge these powerful inequalities" (100). Confronting the differences and stereotypes and attempting to redefine accepted societal commonsense definitions of race can help turn the focus of sports media coverage into something more substantial and promote the equality U.S. citizens feel exists. Instead of asking whether Sherman is a thug, the sports media could have shifted its focus toward the ways in which Sherman reflects a twenty-first-century America.

Thinking about the media's scope of influence on society can be a challenging task. There is much to consider and all of it can be studied. Everything from reporters and editors, the word choices, organization of stories, photographs or videos used in the stories, the sources quoted and attributed, and the placement of stories on the page (print or online) should be subject to scrutiny in addition to the message disseminated. Sports provide a rich body of content, sometimes referred to as *text*, to study because of the audio, visual, commentary, and context (storylines) elements that go into covering each event. All of these elements are part of the text that can be consumed, shared, and studied. Each element makes up a piece of a puzzle that a scholar assembles to describe the significance of the story and the context it was created in and exists in, as well as deconstructing the cultural definitions the story establishes. Stangor and Schaller (1996) described the elements in media products as follows:

> The tangible artifacts of consumable mass media thus comprise an "information highway" for the transmission of social stereotypes. These representations of stereotypes are bought, sold, traded, checked out, and otherwise shared by millions, even billions of people across boundaries of distance and time untraveled by ordinary interpersonal communication.
>
> *(12)*

Each artifact, whatever it may be—a newspaper article, radio broadcast, television program, online stories and videos, tweets, vines, Instagram photos—contains information which is disseminated to and consumed by a mass audience. These are the artifacts, or texts, that scholars study. In studying the text, scholars examine not just the message and meaning, but also the context of the message. This includes how and why the text was created and disseminated as well as the public reaction to the text; each piece of text, whether physical newspaper clippings, video footage, or digitally rendered, are engaged with and consumed by an audience. The text can be studied in two different ways: qualitatively and quantitatively.

Qualitative research methods help to answer "how and why questions" regarding the topic of study. In sports scholarship, qualitative researchers often focus their attention on using theory or concepts to help explain how the text and society interact with each other. It is important to consider the research questions in determining if qualitative methods are appropriate in studying the chosen text. In the realm of race and sports, scholars address the cultural meanings constructed by the media coverage, what the meanings reinforce or challenge, and the significance of the meanings. Qualitative studies usually employ a variety of methods in the same study to examine the text closely with the purpose of addressing the meanings generated in and outside of the text. When studying race in sports, qualitative methods help to study the context and meanings created around specific media coverage, the importance of stereotypes in the media as well as what they signify in understanding the power relations within a society. Solomos and Back (1996) further explain why race and stereotypes are studied:

> Race and ethnic categories are ideological entities that are made and remade through struggle. In this sense, race can be seen as a discursive category through which differences are accorded social significance. But it is also more than just a discursive category since it carries with it material consequences for those who are included within, or excluded from, a particular racial identity. Stereotypes are studied because of what they mean and how they shape society.
>
> *(xiv)*

Like the Sherman example at the beginning of this chapter, there are many other anecdotal examples of racial stereotypes in sports media coverage.

Former NFL player-turned-announcer Amad Rashad described his experiences as a black athlete through the narrative of his autobiography. Rashad's experiences are explained in a qualitative examination of sports commentary of announcers as it relates to the racial makeup of athletes. He noted that there was a significant and distinguishable difference in the way commentators described black and white athletes in the 1980s:

> If you close your eyes and listen, you can tell whether a commentator is discussing a white or a black athlete. When he says that somebody is a "natural," so fluid and graceful, you know he's talking about a black performer. When you hear that this other guy's a hard worker, or that he comes to play every day on the strength of guts and intelligence, you know that the player in question is white. Just open your eyes.
>
> *(83)*

Rashad was not the only one to take note of racial stereotyping in sports. Doc Rivers, former National Basketball Association player-turned-coach of the Los Angeles Clippers, expressed concern for the way in which race was depicted in basketball. According to Rivers, there were multiple racial stereotypes used regularly in teams' scouting reports while he played in the NBA during the 1990s. In these scouting reports black players were described as "athletically gifted," "explosive," and having great instincts. Simultaneously, white players were described as "determined," "floor generals," and as having strong work ethic (Rivers and Brooks 1993). That type of anecdotal evidence supports the findings of qualitative research and differs from quantitative research that often simply counts the occurrences of such descriptors.

The evidence presented through the Sherman, Rashad (1988), and Rivers (1993) examples illustrates that stereotypes are retransmitted by media. The stereotypes are not limited to professional athletes, however. Washington and Karen (2001) noted that college-level athletes also see racial stereotypes in coverage. There is hope that some progress is being made, though. A 2001 study of commentary during collegiate basketball games found some progress in the media's portrayal of race between athletes. Despite more positive and less stereotyped descriptions, African-American players were still presented most often in regards to their athletic ability while white players were described as hard working and students of the game (Eastman and Billings 2001). Murrell and Curtis (1994) summarized decades of racial stereotyping that qualitative researchers find in their studies: "Performance was a function not of what the player does, but what the player is: a natural athlete" (230). The athletic ability ultimately hinges on race and that is one of the issues critical and cultural researchers take aim at.

Many quantitative studies about race in sports coverage use content analysis as the primary way in which researchers examine race in sports quantitatively. These studies provide empirical evidence that racial stereotyping existed in the media artifacts and discuss the statistical significance of the findings relating to racial aspects in sports media coverage. Rainville and McCormick (1977), one of the first to examine race in sports coverage, conducted a content analysis investigating ethnic stereotyping in college football broadcasts. In doing so, Rainville and McCormick noted the difference in descriptors used in broadcasters' explanations of players' skills and established a foundation for future studies to follow. Their approach was rooted in numbers and counting the actual occurrences of specific stereotypical descriptions rather than the anecdotal evidence that Rashad and Rivers produced in their autobiographies.

Rainville and McCormick (1971) found that white players were significantly more likely to be praised than black athletes while black players were found to be more likely to be criticized for making poor plays. Rainville and McCormick also noted blacks were described as "naturally gifted" athletes who should automatically succeed because of this, as have many others over the years (Rainville and McCormick 1977; Rushton 1995; Herrnstein and Murray 1994; Entine 2000). Rivers (1993) and Rashad (1988) added to the findings, but through qualitative methods. Rainville and McCormick (1971) also found that white football players were described as overcoming the odds when succeeding at football while being praised for their work ethic.

One of the most popular ways to study race in sports media is to examine how the media represents an athlete. *Framing*, the concept of how information is presented to an audience by the media—usually through omission—is an important one to draw upon when examining media coverage (Goffman 1974; Iyengar 1991). By framing information, the media can make some aspects of reality more salient while obscuring other aspects (Entman 1993). Frames used by the media serve as a central theme or idea in which information is built around and disseminated to an audience. Using framing in media studies can help to reveal patterns in how information is presented to the public and what beliefs, values, or definitions are worthy of being part of the dominant culture. This reinforces the status quo. Entman (1993) described how the status quo can be reinforced through the influence of frames on the public: "Frames, which are manifested by the presence or absence of certain keywords, stock phrases, stereotyped images, sources of information, and sentences that provide thematically reinforcing clusters of facts or judgments" (15). The existence of framing in media coverage, however, does not guarantee an influence on how the audience thinks, but rather what to think about. Consequently, McCombs and Shaw (1972) contend that framing is an extension of agenda-setting theory which posits that the media provide audiences limited windows on the world. Framing and agenda setting are popular theoretical foundations for studying race in sports media.

Giacobbi and DeSensi (1999) analyzed the frames in the media coverage of Tiger Woods as he became a household name as a professional golfer in the late 1990s. Much like Rainville and McCormick (1971), the authors found marginalization of Woods through framing practices that excluded him or used racial stereotypes to emphasize racial difference to explain how Woods did not fit in with the Professional Golfers Association. Similarly, Major League Baseball player Sammy Sosa, from the Dominican Republic, was initially framed out of media coverage during the 1998 homerun chase in favor of white baseball player Mark McGwire (Juffer 2002). Only when it became apparent McGwire and Sosa were contenders to break the record for most homeruns in a season was Sosa included in the coverage (Juffer 2002). The frames in the Sosa and McGwire homerun case could also be broken down by nationalism. According to Juffer (2002), Sosa and McGwire were also framed by country with McGwire being depicted as the rugged American, which had similar effects as framing by race had with McGwire being the hero and Sosa being the outsider intruding on a heroic story.

Whether examining race in sports media coverage quantitatively or qualitatively, racial and ethnic stereotypes will continue to play important roles in the findings. However, there is much more to studying race and the sports media. Sports and sports media's influence on society must be taken into account as well, as noted by previous scholarship in this chapter. Stereotypes help scholars earmark the beliefs of society and have a benchmark with which to compare previous sports coverage. As sports media grows as a field of study, the findings will continue to become more sophisticated and demonstrate the significance of sports in American culture.

Sports are more than just a toy store of newspapers and media organizations, although the lack of substance in discussing race, as in the case of Sherman, does trivialize sports journalism as a profession. The coverage of sports can reinforce or challenge racial stereotypes that both reflect and define culture in a society. Previous scholarly work has described the racial issues in sports coverage. Those same issues continue to be present in the sports media coverage today. Whether it was NBA stars Rivers or Rashad in the late 1980s and early 1990s, professional golfer Tiger Woods in the late 1990s and early 2000s, college sports, the Olympics, NBA stars LeBron James and Jeremy Lin, or NFL star Sherman in the 2010s, race plays a prominent and regular role in the sports coverage produced.

The reinforcement of the current status quo within sports media coverage will not improve the situation. As Campbell (1995) noted, the current environment creates a commonsense definition of what is to be expected regarding race. These commonsense stereotypes do not reflect the reality and need to be challenged. Lin, for example, should not have been stereotyped as the serious, academically centered Asian during the "Linsanity" coverage of 2012 (Sipocz 2015). The sports coverage of Lin, which emphasized puns on his Asian ancestry and name, supported commonsense definitions about Asians and their athletic ability. The same can be said about black athletes. Previous scholarship has shown that while some progress has been made in how black athletes are described, they are still stereotyped as natural athletes. Until recently, the quarterback position in football fell into these commonsense definitions of race that told society that black football players could not be quarterbacks. It was common sense that white football players led the offense and the team in general. Consequently, the commonsense definitions disseminated by the sports media reinforced the stereotypes in society at large.

It is these very commonsense definitions, described by Hall (1981) as cultural maps that help society make sense of the world around them, that betrayed the sports media in its coverage of Sherman leading up to the Super Bowl in 2014. The attention of the sports media reinforced significant racial stereotypes following Sherman's interview. By asking if he was a thug, the sports media supported racial stereotypes that tell society that black athletes are not as intelligent as white athletes and also come from the ghetto.

The implications of such assumptions and use of racial stereotypes by the sports media continue to trivialize sports coverage, perpetuating the idea that the sports section is nothing more than a toy store.

## References

Artz, L. and Murphy, B. O. (2000) *Cultural Hegemony in the United States*. Thousand Oaks, CA: Sage.
Associated Press. (2009, June 10) "NBA Gets High Marks for Diversity in New Study," *NBA.com*. Retrieved from http://www.nba.com/2009/news/06/10/NBA.diversity.ap/index.html.
Barth, F. (1969) *Ethnic Groups and Boundaries: The Social Organization of Cultural Difference*. London: George Allen and Unwin.
Berman, C. (1999) "Foreword," in M. MacCambridge (ed.), *ESPN SportsCentury*. New York: Hyperion, 17–19.
Billings, A. C. and Eastman, S. T. (2002) "Gender, Ethnicity, and Nationality: Formation of Identity in NBC's 2000 Olympic coverage," *International Review for the Sociology of Sport* 37: 349–368.
Birrell, S. (1989) "Racial Relations Theories and Sport: Suggestions for a More Critical Analysis," *Sociology of Sport* 6: 212–227.
Brooks, D. and Rada, J. (2002) "Constructing Race in Black and Whiteness: Media Coverage of Public Support for President Clinton," *Journalism and Communication Monographs* 4(3): 115–156.
Bruce, T. (2004) "Marking the Boundaries of the 'Normal' in Televised Sports: The Play-By-Play of Race," *Media, Culture, and Society* 26(6): 861–879.
Campbell, C. P. (1995) *Race, Myth and the News*. Thousand Oaks, CA: Sage Publications.
Carrington, B. (2009) "Sport without Final Guarantees: Cultural Studies/Marxism/Sport," in B. Carrington and I. McDonald (eds.), *Marxism, Cultural Studies and Sport*. New York: Routledge, 15–32.
Coakley J. J. (2009) *Sport in Society: Issues and Controversies*. Boston, MA: McGraw-Hill.
Davis, L. and Harris, O. (1998) "Race and Ethnicity in U.S. Sports Media," in L. Wenner (ed.), *Mediasport*. London: Routledge, 154–169.
Dines, G. and Humez, J. M. (2003) "Cultural Studies, Multiculturalism and Media Culture," in their edited book, *Gender, Race, and Class in Media: A Text-Reader*. Thousand Oaks, CA: Sage, 9–20.
Denham, B. E., Billings, A. C., and Halone, K. K. (2002) "Differential Accounts of Race in Broadcast Commentary of the 2000 Men's and Women's Final Four Basketball Tournaments," *Sociology of Sport Journal* 19: 315–332.
Eastman, S. T. and Billings, A. C. (2001) "Biased Voices of Sports: Racial and Gender Stereotyping in College Basketball Announcing," *Howard Journal of Communications* 12(4): 183–202.
Entine, J. (2000) *Taboo: Why Black Athletes Dominate Sports and Why We Are Afraid to Talk about It*. New York: Public Affairs.
Entman, R. M. (1993) "Framing Toward Clarification of a Fractured Paradigm," *Journal of Communication* 43(4): 51–58.
Entman, R. M. and Rojecki, A. (2000) *The Black Image in the White Mind*. Chicago, IL: University of Chicago Press.
ESPN Fact Sheet. (2015) *MediaZone*. Retrieved from http://espnmediazone.com/us/espn-inc-fact-sheet/.
Giacobbi, P. and DeSensi, J. (1999) "Media Portrayals of Tiger Woods: A Qualitative Deconstructive Examination," *Quest* 51(4): 408–417.
Goffman, E. (1974) *Frame Analysis: An Essay on the Organization of Experience*. New York: Harper and Row.
Gorham, B. (1999) "Stereotypes in the Media: So What?," *The Howard Journal of Communications* 10: 229–247.
Gruneau R. S. (1983) *Class, Sports, and Social Development*. Boston, MA: University of Massachusetts Press.
Hall, S. (1981) "The Whites of Their Eyes: Racist Ideologies and the Media," in G. Bridges and R. Brunt (eds.), *Silver Linings: Some Strategies for the Eighties*. London: Lawrence and Wishart, 28–52.
Hamilton, D. L. and Trolier, T. K. (1986) "Stereotypes and Stereotyping: An Overview of the Cognitive Approach," in J. F. Dovidio, J. F. Gaertner, and S. L. Gaertner (eds.), *Prejudice, Discrimination, and Racism*. Orlando, FL: Academic Press, 127–163.
Hartmann, D. (2000) "Rethinking Relationships between Sport and Race in American Culture: Golden Ghettos and Contested Terrain," *Sociology of Sport Journal* 17: 229–253.
Herrnstein, R. and Murray, C. (1994) *The Bell Curve: Intelligence and Class Structure in American Life*. London: Free Press.

Iyengar, S. (1991) *Is Anyone Responsible? How Television Frames Political Issues.* Chicago, IL: University of Chicago Press.
Juffer, J. (2002) "Who's the Man? Sammy Sosa, Latinos and Television Redefinitions of the 'American' Pastime," *Journal of Sport and Social Issues* 26(4): 337–359.
Kellner, D. (2011) "Cultural Studies, Multiculturalism, and Media Culture," in G. Dines and J. M. Humez (eds.), *Gender, Race, and Class in Media: A Critical Reader.* Thousand Oaks, CA: Sage, 7–18.
Lippmann, W. (1922) *Public Opinion.* New York: Harcourt, Brace and Co.
Long, J. and Hylton, K. (2002) "Shades of White: An Examination of Whiteness in Sport," *Leisure Studies* 21(2): 87–103.
Mackie, D., Hamilton, D. L., et al. (1996) "Stereotypes and Stereotyping," in C. N. Macrae, C. Stanor, and M. Hewstone (eds.), *Psychological Foundations of Stereotype Formation.* New York: Guilford Press, 41–78.
Mandela, N. (2000) *Speech by Nelson Mandela at the Inaugural Laureus Lifetime Achievement Award, Monaco 2000.* Nelson Mandela Foundation. Retrieved from http://db.nelsonmandela.org/speeches/pub_view.asp?pg=item&ItemID=NMS1148.
McCarthy, D. and Jones, R. (1997) "Speed, Aggression, Strength and Tactical Naivete," *Journal of Sport and Social Issues* 21: 348–362.
McChesney, R. W. (1989) "Media Made Sport: A History of Sports Coverage in the United States," in L. A. Wenner (ed.), *Media, Sports and Society.* Newbury Park, CA: Sage, 49–69.
McCombs, M. E. and Shaw, D. L. (1972) "The Agenda Setting Function of the Mass Media," *Public Opinion Quarterly* 36: 176–187.
Muir, H. (2007) "Show Red Card to Racism," *The Guardian.* Retrieved from http://www.guardian.co.uk/society/2007/sep/26/societyguardian.societyguardian6.
Murrell, A. J. and Curtis, E. M. (1994) "Causal Attributions of Performance for Black and White Quarterbacks in the NFL," *Journal of Sport and Social Issues* 18: 224–233.
Nichols, L. (2011) "A Skate Park in the Pentagon's Likeness: Militarism, Hegemony, and Skateboarding on the Web," *International Journal of Sport and Society* 2: 17–28.
Pease, E. (1989) "Kerner Plus 20: Minority News Coverage in the Columbus Dispatch," *Newspaper Research Journal* 10(3): 17–38.
Rada, J. (1996) "Color Blind-Sided: Racial Bias in Network Television's Coverage of Professional Football Games," *The Howard Journal of Communications* 7: 231–240.
Rainville, R. and McCormick, E. (1977) "Extent of Covert Racial Prejudice in Profootballers, Announcer's Speech," *Journalism Quarterly* 54: 20–26.
Rashad, A. and Bodo, P. (1988) *Rashad: Vikes, Mikes, and Something on the Backside.* New York: Viking.
Riess, S. A. (2014) *A Companion to American Sport History.* Hoboken, NJ: John Wiley and Sons Inc.
Rivers, G. and Brooks, B. (1993) *Those Who Love the Game: Glenn "Doc" Rivers on Life in the NBA and Elsewhere.* New York: H. Holt.
Rogers, D. (2014, Jan. 28) "Seattle Seahawks: Is Richard Sherman a Thug?," *The Huffington Post.* Retrieved from http://www.huffingtonpost.com/dexter-rogers/richard-sherman-thug_b_4705030.html.
Rushton, P. J. (1995) *Race, Evolution, and Behaviour: A Life History Perspective.* London: Transaction Publishers.
Sabo, D. and Jansen, S. C. (1998) "Prometheus Unbound: Constructions of Masculinity in the Sports Media," in L. Wenner (ed.), *MediaSport.* New York: Routledge, 202–217.
Seiter, E. (1986) "Stereotypes and the Media: A Re-Evaluation," *Journal of Communication* 36: 16–26.
Sipocz, D. (2015) "Race in the Kingdom," in J. McGuire, G. Armfield, and A. C. Earnheardt (eds.), *The ESPN Effect: Academic Studies of the Worldwide Leader in Sport.* New York: Peter Lang.
Solomos, J. and Back, L. (1996), *Racism and Society.* Basingstoke, UK: Macmillan.
Stangor, C. and Schaller, M. (1996) "Social Psychological Foundations of Stereotype Formation," in C. Stangor (ed.), *Stereotypes as Individual and Collective Representations.* New York: Guilford Press.
Thomas, R. (1995, April 23) "Howard Cosell, Outspoken Sportscaster on Television and Radio, is Dead at 77," *New York Times.* Retrieved from http://www.nytimes.com/1995/04/24/obituaries/howard-cosell-outspoken-sportscaster-on-television-and-radio-is-dead-at-77.html.
Washington, R. and Karen, D. (2001) "Sport and Society," *Annual Review of Sociology* 27: 187–212.
Wenner, L. A. (1989) *Media, Sports, and Society.* Newbury Park, CA: Sage Publications.
Whannel, G. (1992) *Fields in Vision: Television Sport and Cultural Transformation.* London: Routledge.
——. (2008) *Culture, Politics and Sport: Blowing the Whistle, Revisited.* London: Routledge.
Wilson, R. (2014, Jan. 22) "Richard Sherman: 'Thug' Is Accepted Way of Calling Someone N-Word," *CBSSports.com.* Retrieved from http://www.cbssports.com/nfl/eye-on-football/24417234.

## Further Reading

Anderson, E. and Mccormack, M. (2010) "Intersectionality, Critical Race Theory and American Sporting Oppression: Examining Black and Gay Athletes," *Journal of Homosexuality* 57(8): 949–967. (Explores the intersection of race, sexuality, gender, and sport, noting the coding of black and gay athletes in coverage.)

Billings, A. C. (2012) "Talking Around Race: Stereotypes, Media, and the Twenty-First Century Collegiate Athlete," *Wake Forest Journal of Law and Policy* 2(1): 199–213. (Argues that sports media, perceived to be in a racially enlightened era, still relies upon racial stereotypes to cement the stories.)

Hawkins, B. (2013) *The New Plantation: Black Athletes, College Sports, and Predominantly White NCAA Institutions*. New York: Palgrave Macmillan. (Compares the NCAA to Southern plantations and slavery, focusing on both economic and racial factors.)

Hylton, K. and Morpeth, N. D. (2012) "London 2012: 'Race' Matters and the East End," *International Journal of Sport Policy and Politics* 4(3): 379–396. (Examines the London 2012 Olympic Development Program, specifically the belief that the program was designed to lead to the regeneration of communities; they argue that policies stemming from a single mega-event cannot alter the racial inequalities entrenched in a culture.)

McGuire, J., Armfield, G., and Earnheardt, A. C. (eds.) (2015) *The ESPN Effect: Examining the Worldwide Leader in Sport*. New York: Peter Lang. (Collection of studies examines ESPN's cultural impact on society from a variety of perspectives, including looking at race, gender, sexuality, and economics.)

# 17
# SPORTS MEDIA IN EUROPE

## An International Context

*Jacco van Sterkenburg*

Ideas about multiculturalism, race, and ethnicity are under discussion in many countries in Europe. There is a strong call upon racial/ethnic minority groups to assimilate to hegemonic norms and values (Essed and Trienekens 2008), and right populist groups in countries such as Greece, Hungary, and France (but also others) question the rights and status of immigrant groups. Taking the Netherlands, the country I live in and know best, as a reference point for a moment: Discussions about racial and ethnic inclusion and exclusion and multicultural society have dominated much of the national debate in the past 15 years. A variety of international organizations as well as the media have pointed to and discussed extensively the existence of various forms of racial/ethnic exclusion and discrimination in the Netherlands. The Council of Europe, for instance, suggested that minority ethnic groups in Dutch society experience disproportionate levels of racism; Amnesty International spoke of racial profiling by the Dutch police; heated debates took place over alleged racism evident in the Dutch labor market and in the meanings of Dutch symbolic figures like Black Pete. The pronounced debate around everyday (explicit and implicit) racisms shows that racism is not a thing of the past despite the general tendency in many Western European countries to discredit talk about possible racisms as outdated and no longer relevant (Essed and Trienekens 2008).

Little reflection by opinion makers seems to occur, however, on dominant and often implicit assumptions about race and ethnicity that are embedded in the current debates. One of the critical but often neglected social domains in which the meanings associated with race and ethnicity are (re)produced and manifest themselves in contemporary Western societies is sport (Carrington 1998). Sport is usually seen as having a positive function for racial and ethnic relations in current multicultural societies. Sport, the argument goes, appeals to a variety of ethnic groups and makes a fundamental contribution to the forming of social capital and to processes of social bonding and integration in multicultural societies (e.g., Verweel 2007). Contrary to other social domains, sport is often seen as a race-less arena in the sense that social distinctions do not play a major role and chances for everyone are equal regardless of racial/ethnic background (Tamir and Bernstein 2015).

In contrast to this perspective, however, stands the common scholarly recognition that sport also (re)produces and strengthens racialized ideologies. This is evident in incidents in soccer stadiums across Europe, which function not only as a place where bonding mechanisms take place, but also as a platform for racist outbursts and chanting, including jungle noises, gorilla gestures, or the throwing of bananas toward black players (e.g., Müller, van Zoonen, and De Roode 2007; van Sterkenburg, Janssens, and Rijnen 2005). Other sports are not free of racism or racial/ethnic discrimination; on the contrary, the Fundamental Rights Agency (2010), for instance, has identified expressions of explicit and more implicit and institutionalized forms of racism and racial/ethnic discrimination in a great variety of sports across European countries, including basketball, handball, amateur football, and ice hockey.

Given such continued evidence of racial discrimination in sport, it is not surprising that European sport governing bodies like UEFA (Union of European Football Associations) and FARE (Football Against Racism in Europe) and related stakeholders have engaged in anti-racist campaigns and pro-diversity projects. Nevertheless, both organizers and observers are skeptical about the broader and long-term effects of these projects (e.g., FRA 2010; Müller, van Zoonen, and De Roode 2008). More specifically, anti-racism and pro-diversity projects seem to be directed at combating explicit forms of racism but tend to miss everyday forms of racial/ethnic prejudice and stereotyping that constitute an important background context for more explicit/outright forms of discrimination (van Zoonen and van Sterkenburg 2012). One of the places where such everyday racialized discourse is most prominent and acquires its everyday "naturalness" is *sport in the media*. Mediasport is a very popular and visible source and platform of mixed ethnic practices. As such, sport media and their representations can be considered a key site for the reproduction of dominant (and alternative) ideas concerning race/ethnicity (Hylton 2009).

## The Social Power of Sport Media

The social power of sport in the media is perhaps illustrated best by the popularity of sport celebrities who offer sources for identity formation for diverse youth audiences worldwide. Previous research has shown that young viewers use celebrities and/or TV programs to negotiate among each other what is acceptable behavior to themselves and to other people (Duits and Romondt Vis 2009; Gillespie 1995). Sport in the media also offers such points of reference for the viewer, especially given its dramatization of events and continuous emphasis on key sportspersons (De Leeuw 2003; Hermes 2005; Lines 2000; van Sterkenburg 2011a). Sportspersons function as role models but at the same time invoke discourses surrounding social dimensions such as race and ethnicity. They are, in other words, not only persons but discursive constructions as well, which represent what it means to be black or white, male or female, abled or disabled, etc. (Duits and Romondt Vis 2009; Rowe 2013). "Media talk" about sport can thus be considered a *pedagogic* site since it confronts young people in particular with possible ways of seeing themselves and others (Azzarito and Harrison 2008). Sport media *representations* of sportspersons are important here as they are "the means by which we think and feel" (Dyer 1997: xiii) about the athletes and about the markers of race/ethnicity they represent. In the next section I will therefore turn to sport media representations of race and ethnicity. Throughout the chapter I will use race and ethnicity as conflated concepts ("race/ethnicity"). Although I acknowledge that analytic distinctions can be drawn between "race" and "ethnicity," the concepts are often used in conflated ways in everyday discourse where the references to skin color and phenotype usually associated with "race" are never wholly absent from culturally informed discourses of ethnicity and vice versa (Essed and Trienekens 2008; Hall 2000; Gunaratnam 2003).

## Representations of Race/Ethnicity in the International Sport Media

One of the first sports media studies examining racial patterns in sport commentators' descriptions of sportspeople was conducted by Rainville and McCormick in 1977. Rainville and McCormick hypothesized that the race of the (football) players influenced U.S. sports media commentary. Their hypothesis was based on subjective observations by the blind author Rainville, who discovered that he was able to identify a player's race by listening to live broadcasts even though the player's race was not mentioned explicitly. Their results indicated that commentators gave white players more play-related praise, representing them in a more positive light and as being aggressive (in a positive way). Black players were more often depicted as the recipient of aggression and compared unfavorably to other players (Rainville and McCormick 1977). The classic study by Rainville and McCormick has been replicated and extended by more recent studies in the realm of mediasport. Substantially, these studies have taken a critical, discursive approach toward mediasport, focusing on the relationship between sport media discourses surrounding race and ethnicity and power relations in wider society. Generally, these studies show that the sports media are fascinated with the supposed natural physical abilities of black (usually male) athletes. Most typically, sports media describe black athletes as "natural" sportsmen with great, "animal-like" physical power (e.g., Hylton 2009; McCarthy, Jones, and Potrac 2003). The vast majority of this research has been conducted by U.S. and U.K. researchers who generally categorized race and ethnicity as a two-level variable: "black" or "white." This overemphasis on the physical capacities of black athletes marginalizes implicitly the mental capacities required for sports performances, thus constructing a "mind–body split" in which the black sportsman is associated with a superb body, but with a lack of cognitive abilities (Bradbury, Amaria, Garcia, and Bairner 2011; Carrington 2001). A different but related narrative comes from more ethnographically informed case studies that examined discourses surrounding individual male sport celebrities. Those studies concluded that the sport media not only represent black masculinity as physically superior but also relatively often as dangerous, animalistic, and criminal (Andrews and Silk 2010; Bradbury et al. 2011). Andrews and Silk (2010) coined this discourse *ghettocentric logic* as it associates black athletes with the urban, ghettocentric spaces of "poverty, drugs and crime-ridden streets" (1636; also see van Sterkenburg 2011a).

### *Representations of White Athletes*

The analytic focus on media representations of black male athletes contrasts with the scholarly attention for the media representation of *white* athletes. As Carrington (2008) and Hylton and Lawrence (2015) argued, sport sociologists have usually not considered white bodies "raced" bodies and white athletic bodies have, as a consequence, been under-researched. Nevertheless, sport and media scholars have increasingly recognized the importance of studying whiteness and representations of white athletes in recent years (Andrews 2013; Hylton and Lawrence 2015). Analyses of media content show that white athletes belonging to the racial/ethnic majority group are relatively often described in terms of their hard work, perseverance, and intellectual and organizational qualities (e.g., Bradbury et al. 2011; Hylton 2009; McCarthy et al. 2003). At the same time, white athletes are *not* represented as hyper-physical or aggressive/criminal like their black counterparts and they can thereby become the human "norm" against which non-whites are (re)constructed as deviant and the "Other."

Critical scholars like Müller et al. (2007) have referred to this discourse as *processes of racialization/ethnization*: routine and everyday practices of racial/ethnic categorizing and stereotyping through which everyday racism becomes normalized and unacknowledged (also see van Sterkenburg, Knoppers, and De Leeuw 2012). Other scholars speak of "enlightened racism," referring to a discourse in which the success of black athletes is framed in terms of natural athletic qualities while the success of white athletes remains associated with cognitive capacities and management/leadership abilities (Hylton 2009; Sabo and Jansen 1998). This racialized discourse may not be a conscious process or a product of individual intent. White sport commentators often react to events that happen ad-hoc and tend to draw on widely circulating hegemonic discourses that are readily available to them and that contain commonly held racial/ethnic stereotypes. The challenge for sport media researchers is, as Hylton (2009) argued, to identify how and when such racialized media practices occur and are being reproduced in everyday messages. This is especially important since commentators themselves—many of them white males (but not necessarily so)—are usually not aware of these stereotypes and instead tend to see themselves as objective, race-neutral professionals for whom race is no longer an issue (Spencer 2004; van Sterkenburg 2011a). They use, in other words, a *rhetoric of colorblindness* (Bonilla-Silva and Forman 2000: 70), perceiving racial discrimination as not so relevant anymore and "as sporadic and declining in significance."

In practice, the end result of such colorblind rhetoric is the (re)production of unreflexive, stereotypical, and one-sided representations of race and ethnicity that can have meaning and consequences beyond the boundaries of sport, for instance in framing unconscious thinking about hiring individuals in positions of leadership and coaching. Recent internationally comparative research confirms this. A study by Bradbury, Mignon, and van Sterkenburg (2014), for instance, shows that hegemonic racial stereotypes are widespread and commonly used in the football sector and may have limiting effects on the careers of minority ethnic coaches; these coaches' experience is that they are perceived primarily as good athletes instead of good leaders/managers, which creates an obstacle for their coaching career. Likewise, Danish research reveals tendencies among white club coaches to associate black, African young players with possessing speed, power, and individuality (Agergaard and Sorenson 2009) and lacking in tactical understanding. Such skewed representations may additionally strengthen hierarchies in society at large, since it is especially the characteristics associated with being white such as leadership, intellect, and perseverance that are usually associated with positions of power and leadership in society (Rada and Wulfemeyer 2005; van Sterkenburg 2011a).

## *Intersections with Gender*

These racialized representations may take gender-specific forms as well. Whereas white women are associated with dependence, elegance, and weakness, African-American women are more often associated with characteristics such as aggressiveness, dominance, and independence (Azzarito and Solomon 2005). Both black male and female athletes have often been portrayed as strong, quick, and athletic, but with "unpredictable" and "wild" moments when they supposedly lack the cognitive capabilities—unlike their white peers—to have composure at "critical moments" (Carrington 2001: 94). The vast majority of sport media studies focus, still, on male sportspersons. There are some notable exceptions but much work is still to be done to reduce this gender bias in sport and media research (Andrews 2013; for studies that *do* focus on representations of female sportspersons in diverse countries, see, for example: Elling and Luijt 2009 for the Netherlands; Wensing and Bruce 2003 for Australia; Pfister 2015 for Germany).

## *Other Ethnicities*

In addition to the substantial focus on "black" and "white" athletes in sport media studies, international studies have explored sport media coverage of other minority ethnic athletes. These studies confirm the perception of sport commentary as a local manifestation of discourses and stereotypes that circulate broadly in society (Lindlof and Taylor 2011). Sabo, Jansen, Tate, Duncan, and Leggett (1996) concluded, for instance, that sport commentators stereotypically represented Asian athletes as "machinelike" and "unemotional," while British studies have shown Asian athletes to be relatively often represented as self-disciplined, effeminate, and physically weak (Bradbury et al. 2011; Burdsey 2004; Coakley and Pike 2009). A variety of scholars have argued that Latin-American athletes are relatively often portrayed as passionate, hot-tempered, and/or selfish, and thus as lacking in cool headedness and psychological self-control (Coakley and Pike 2009; Hoose in Davis and Harris 1998; Juffer 2002; van Sterkenburg, Knoppers, and De Leeuw 2012). Such discourses seem part of a wider, globalized discourse surrounding these racial/ethnic groups (van Sterkenburg et al. 2012). In addition to this, East-Asian and Muslim athletes have been represented as irrational and threatening in the British press (Malcolm, Bairner, and Curry 2010), while various studies have shown that the Australian sport media construct Aboriginal athletes as the ultimate racial/ethnic Other: as fast and instinctive but also as unreliable and lacking in discipline and mental capacities (e.g., Coakley, Hallinan, Jackson, and Mewett 2008; Coram 2007). An exploratory content analysis of soccer commentary in the Dutch context concluded that "Surinamese-Dutch" soccer players were associated with their physicality (van Sterkenburg et al. 2012).

## *Contradictory Evidence*

There is some contradictory evidence as well showing that sport journalists increasingly try to avoid prejudicial and stereotypical treatment of minority racial and ethnic groups (Billings 2004; Byrd and Utsler 2007; van Sterkenburg 2011a). This finding reflects Hall's (1995) assertion that the media are not only a site where hegemonic discourses are reproduced but can also be a place where such discourses can be challenged and subverted (see also van Sterkenburg 2011a). However, these studies seem to be exceptions rather than a trend until recent years, pointing to the continued urgency for those concerned with racialized sport media reporting to continue to do critical empirical research on sport media reporting (Hylton 2009). Of similar importance is the question of how such reporting is then received and negotiated by *media audiences*. As mentioned earlier, sport programs invite their audiences to talk about them, often in a social setting (Peeters and van Sterkenburg 2016). Such sport talk is (inter)active and productive but also bounded by the discursive parameters set by the text and the discursive competences of the audiences (Costera, Meijer, and De Bruin 2003). As an experiment, I often show images of black and white athletes to groups of media students I am teaching, asking them how they would explain the overrepresentation of white athletes in sports like skiing or weightlifting and of black athletes in a sport like sprinting. Usually, students draw on a limited reservoir of discourses for their explanations. These reflect to an important extent the hegemonic discourses (re)produced by the sport media explaining black success in sprinting by reference to natural speed and strength and white success in skiing or weightlifting by reference to "culture." (They argue weightlifting or skiing are major sports in white-dominated *cultures*.) Such an overlap between audience discourses and sport media discourses has also been found in various other audience reception studies in the field. I will turn to those in the next section.

## Audiences and Race

Most studies exploring audience receptions of race/ethnicity in media have focused on news programs, soap operas, celebrity culture, and police series (e.g., Costera Meijer and De Bruin 2003; Duits and Romondt Vis 2009; Liebes and Katz 1990; Gillespie 1995) but they have often ignored sports in the media. The audience studies that *did* focus on race and sport media have often used qualitative methodology like individual or focus group interviews (e.g., Hermes 2005; Hylton and Lawrence 2015; Rowe 2015; McCarthy et al. 2003). Such qualitative methodology has been considered an appropriate method to reveal individual or group-based assumptions about race and ethnicity (van Sterkenburg 2011b). Some of these studies concluded that media users, regardless of their racial/ethnic origin, tend to adopt the hegemonic media discourse surrounding race and ethnicity. Most notably, media users mainly tended to apply a so-called "natural physicality discourse" to give meaning to black athletes by associating black athletes with "natural" speed and physical prowess (Hermes 2005; Hylton and Lawrence 2015; van Sterkenburg and Knoppers 2004). A "natural" *mentality* discourse connecting white athletes with cognitive abilities was less evident among audiences, although it did occur in some instances as well, in implicit or more explicit forms (see for research in the Dutch and English context: Hermes 2005; van Sterkenburg 2013; van Sterkenburg and Knoppers 2004).

A variety of other scholars, however, have shown the matter is more complex. They found that the discourses used by media sport users do not necessarily overlap with dominant race/ethnicity discourses in the media (van Sterkenburg 2011b). This confirms the argument made by media scholars such as Boyle and Haynes (2000) who emphasize that sport media audiences do not passively absorb and accept the ideas (re)produced by the sport media but that audience discourses also depend on the repertoire of prior experiences and the social location that individuals bring to the media experience (like their racial/ethnic positioning). (Also see Buffington and Fraley 2008; McCarthy et al. 2003; van Sterkenburg 2011b.) British scholars McCarthy, Jones, and Potrac (2003), for instance, concluded in their audience reception study of British football that black viewers experienced the discourses surrounding black footballers as naturally fast and athletic as stereotypical and offensive. The white viewers, on the other hand, did recognize the racial stereotype but tended to accept the stereotype as reflecting reality or reflecting the requirements for a certain position in the field. As McCarthy et al. (2003: 234) stated, only "a small discursive space existed [among the White audiences] between awareness of the Black athletic stereotype and acceptance of that stereotype." Likewise, Knoppers and Elling (2001) concluded that minority ethnic interviewees tended to challenge hegemonic sport media discourses surrounding race and ethnicity more often than their (white) majority ethnic counterparts. This confirms the argument made by various scholars that in Western societies it is especially the majority population of white people—white males in particular—who are ideally positioned to read the text in line with its "referred meaning" (Bruce 2013; Peeters and van Sterkenburg 2016).

Knoppers and Elling (2001) and Hermes (2005) additionally found that white *male* youths were more likely than white *female* youths to draw on the black athletic stereotype. Hermes (2005) argued that *the type* of sport content matters as well. Whereas male viewers of football in her study discussed international (club) football players in terms of their technical qualities with hardly a link to discourses about race or ethnicity, these media users used nationalist discourses when watching matches of the Dutch national team. Nationalist discourses often functioned as an entry into racialized types of talk in which the white football players were implicitly or explicitly considered to be more "Dutch" than the non-white players who played for the Dutch national team (Hermes 2005). Rowe (2015) also concluded that majority ethnic populations use mediated sport as a tool to monitor immigrants' loyalty to the nation. In the interviews he conducted, Rowe found that immigrants felt greater pressure to prove their loyalty to the national sport teams than Australian citizens or permanent residents of British origin did. For immigrant populations it was important to "pass this sporting loyalty test" (22) to feel accepted and included.

Despite the relevant insights these audience reception studies give us about sport media-based audience discourses and processes of inclusion and exclusion, they have one major drawback: they are relatively limited in their scope and number. Future research should therefore continue to address interpretations of race/ethnicity by sport media audiences. Such research should focus not only on race but also on its intersections with other social dimensions like gender and social class. Such research is still relatively rare and would add to our understandings of how race and ethnicity gain meaning in and through popular culture. This type of intersectional research would, furthermore, be relevant for a wide range of related academic disciplines like media studies, race/ethnicity studies, gender studies, and sport studies, and could provide—if it is done carefully—a useful framework for future research in the field. To conclude this chapter, I will now turn to two other avenues of future research in the field.

## Future Strands of Research

In identifying future strands of research I draw in part on what various expert scholars have suggested in a collection on sport media representations and audience perceptions of race, ethnicity, nation, and gender that I edited with Ramon Spaaij for the journal *Soccer and Society* (2014/15). In that special issue, Hylton and Lawrence (2015) called upon scholars to explore more in-depth the different whitenesses that are represented and perceived in the sport media. Specifically, they argued that some white players are part of the "we," the norm in the popular imagination, while audiences shift other white players to the peripheries of whiteness due to their "otherness" in terms of geography, culture, sexuality, or masculinity. An example of such a player who is central in Hylton and Lawrence's study is the white Portuguese football celebrity Cristiano Ronaldo. The authors stress, however, that "otherness" in the case of such white sportsmen is never only signaled by their whiteness but always through its intersections with other dimensions like gender or sexuality (contrary to non-white athletes whose otherness is signaled by their skin color only). The authors' exploration of the representations and audience interpretations of Ronaldo reveals the "plurality of whiteness," and indicates the need for "future explorations of whiteness as contingent and problematic" and for "dismantling the black–white binary which shapes overwhelmingly popular discourses of racism" (14). A last strand of future research that I want to address here is the significance of social media like online reader comments or Twitter messages for meanings given to sport media coverage and its constructions of race and ethnicity. Until now, relatively little has been written about audience perceptions of mediated sport events in and through online media products and comments (Tamir and Bernstein 2015). Bruce and Stewart (2015: 16) argue, therefore, that sport media researchers should "move beyond the traditional focus solely on media texts and enter the messy, contradictory, and ever changing online public sphere, for it is here that truths are actively produced and struggled over." Combining textual analysis with audience research, Bruce and Stewart themselves focused on media representations and online audience interpretations of the New Zealand football team during the 2010 football World Cup. While their content analysis of media *representations* revealed a predominantly nationalist framing of the New Zealand football team as "our boys," their additional focus on online reader comments provided valuable additional information revealing the range of ways the public actually took up this nationalist discourse. More specifically, it appeared it was primarily the hard-playing style of the New Zealand team that the public appreciated and turned the players into "our boys," while the role of football itself in New Zealand sporting culture remained a matter of debate despite the extensive media coverage of the football event. Likewise, Billings et al. (2015) and Tamir and Bernstein (2015) showed that Twitter messages and online reader comments provide sport media researchers with rich and valuable information about public perceptions of the relationship between sport and race. Tamir and Bernstein's analysis of online comments on the Israeli national football team confirms to an important extent previous findings that revealed the difficulties minority ethnic athletes have in being accepted and valued by the public as representing the nation. Billings et al. (2014), on the other hand, in their analysis of Twitter reactions during the 2014 football World Cup, did not find as many nationalist and ethnocentric responses as they expected on the basis of previous studies of major international sport events like the Olympics. These findings show that the relatively under-explored area of the sport–social media–race axis deserves further scholarly attention. Such research should include online reader comments and Twitter messages but also fan-generated weblogs and YouTube videos (van Sterkenburg 2011a). They all constitute an increasingly important component of public discourse in contemporary societies and reflect the increasingly significant role fans and media users play in the transmission and localized translations of globalized sport media discourses, including those about race/ethnicity in sport (Tamir and Bernstein 2015; van Sterkenburg 2011a).

## References

Agergaard, S. and Sorensen, J. K. (2009) "The Dream of Social Mobility: Ethnic Minority Players in Danish Football Clubs," *Soccer and Society* 10: 766–780.
Andrews, D. L. (2013) "Reflections on Communication and Sport: On Celebrity and Race," *Communication and Sport* 1: 151–163.
Andrews, D. L. and Silk, M. L. (2010) "Basketball's Ghettocentric Logic," *American Behavioral Scientist* 53: 1626–1644.
Azzarito, L. and Harrison, L. (2008) "'White Men Can't Jump': Race, Gender and Natural Athleticism," *International Review for the Sociology of Sport* 43: 347–364.

Azzarito, L. and Solomon, M. (2005) "A Reconceptualization of Physical Education: The Intersection of Gender, Race, Social Class," *Sport Education and Society* 1: 25–47.

Billings, A. C. (2004) "Depicting the Quarterback in Black and White: A Content Analysis of College and Professional Football Broadcast Commentary," *Howard Journal of Communications* 15: 201–210.

Billings, A. C. and Eastman, S. T. (2002) "Selective Representation of Gender, Ethnicity, and Nationality in American Television Coverage of the 2000 Summer Olympics," *International Review for the Sociology of Sport* 37: 351–370.

Billings, A. C., Burch, L. M., and Zimmerman, M. H. (2015) "Fragments of Us, Fragments of Them: Social Media, Nationality, and U.S. Perceptions of the 2014 FIFA World Cup," *Soccer and Society* 16(5–6): 726–744.

Bonilla-Silva, E. and Forman, T. A. (2000) "'I Am Not a Racist but. . .': Mapping White College Students' Racial Ideology in the USA," *Discourse and Society* 11: 50–85.

Boyle, R. and Haynes, R. (2000) *Power Play. Sport, the Media and Popular Culture*. Harlow, UK: Pearson Education Limited.

Bradbury, S., Amara, M., Garcia, B., and Bairner, A. (2011) *Representation and Structural Discrimination in Football in Europe: The Case of Minorities and Women*. Loughborough, UK: Loughborough University, School of Sport, Exercise and Health Sciences.

Bradbury, S., Mignon, P., and van Sterkenburg, J. (2014) *The Glass Ceiling in Football: Levels of Representation of Visible Ethnic Minorities and Women in Leadership Positions, and the Experiences of Elite Level Ethnic Minority Coaches*. London: FARE.

Bruce, T. and Stewart, A. (2015) "As Kiwi As? Contestation over the Place of Men's Football in New Zealand Culture," *Soccer and Society* 16(5–6): 710–725.

Carrington, B. (1998) "Sport, Masculinity and Black Cultural Resistance," *Journal of Sport and Social Issues* 22: 275–298.

Buffington, D. and Fraley, T. (2008) "Skill in Black and White: Negotiating Media Images of Race in a Sporting Context," *Journal of Communication Inquiry* 32: 292–310.

Burdsey, D. (2004) "Obstacle Race? 'Race', Racism and the Recruitment of British Asian Professional Footballers," *Patterns of Prejudice* 38: 279–299.

Byrd, J. and Utsler, M. (2007) "Is Stereotypical Coverage of African-American Athletes as 'Dead as Disco'?: An Analysis of NFL Quarterbacks in the Pages of Sports Illustrated," *Journal of Sports Media* 2: 1–28.

Carrington, B. (2001) "Fear of a Black Athlete: Masculinity, Politics and the Body," *New Formations* 45: 91–110.

——. (2008) "'What's the Footballer Doing Here?': Racialized Performativity, Reflexivity, and Identity," *Critical Methodologies* 8: 423–452.

Coakley, J. and Pike, E. (2009) *Sports in Society: Issues and Controversies*. Maidenhead, UK: McGraw-Hill.

Coakley, J., Hallinan, C., Jackson, S., and Mewett, P. (2008) *Sports in Society: Issues and Controversies in Australia and New Zealand*. Sydney: McGraw-Hill.

Coram, S. (2007) "Race Formations (Evolutionary Hegemony) and the 'Aping' of the Australian Indigenous Athlete," *International Review for the Sociology of Sport* 42: 391–408.

Costera Meijer, I. and de Bruin, J. (2003) "The Value of Entertainment for Multicultural Society: A Comparative Approach towards 'White' and 'Black' Soap Opera Talk," *Media, Culture and Society* 25: 695–703.

Davis, L. R. and Harris, O. (1998) "Race and Ethnicity in U.S. Sport Media," in L. Wenner (ed.), *MediaSport*. London: Routledge, 154–169.

De Leeuw, S. (2003). "Hoe Komen wij in Beeld? Cultuurhistorische Aspecten van de Nederlandse Televisie" [*How are we Being Portrayed? Culture-historic Aspects of Dutch Television*]. Inaugural lecture held at Utrecht University, The Netherlands, on November 6, 2003.

Duits, L. and Romondt Vis, P. (2009) "Girls Make Sense: Girls, Celebrities, and Identities," *European Journal of Cultural Studies* 12: 41–58.

Dyer, R. (1997) *White*. London/New York: Routledge.

Elling, A. and Luijt, R. (2009) "Different Shades of Orange? Media Representations of Dutch Women Medalists," in P. Markula (ed.), *Olympic Women and the Media: International Perspectives*. Basingstoke, UK: Palgrave Macmillan, 132–149.

Essed, P. and Trienekens, S. (2008) "'Who Wants to Feel White?' Race, Dutch Culture and Contested Identities," *Ethnic and Racial Studies* 31: 52–72.

Fundamental Rights Agency. (2010) *Racism, Ethnic Discrimination and Exclusion of Migrants and Minorities in Sport: A Comparative Overview of the Situation in the European Union*. Vienna, Austria: FRA.
Gillespie, M. (1995) *Television, Ethnicity and Cultural Change*. London/New York: Routledge.
Gunaratnam, Y. (2003) *Researching Race and Ethnicity: Methods, Knowledge and Power*. London; New York; New Delhi: Sage.
Hall, S. (1995) "The Whites of Their Eyes. Racist Ideologies and the Media," in G. Dines and J. M. Humez (eds.), *Race and Class in Media: A Text Reader*. Thousand Oaks/London/New Delhi: Sage, 18–22.
Hall, S. (2000) "Conclusion. The Multi-Cultural Question," in B. Hesse (ed.), *Unsettled Multiculturalism: Diasporas, Enlightenments, Transruptions*. London: Zed Books, 209–241.
Hermes, J. (2005) "Burnt Orange: Television, Football, and the Representation of Ethnicity," *Television and New Media* 6: 49–69.
Hylton, K. (2009) *'Race' and Sport: Critical Race Theory*. London/New York: Routledge.
Hylton, K. and Lawrence, S. (2015) "Reading Ronaldo: Contingent Whiteness in the Football Media," *Soccer and Society* 16(5–6): 639–656.
Juffer, J. (2002) "Who's the Man? Sammy Sosa, Latinos, and Televisual Redefinitions of the 'American' Pastime," *Journal of Sport and Social Issues* 26: 337–359.
Knoppers, A. and Elling, A. (2001) *Gender, Etniciteit en de Sportmedia: Productieprocessen en Publieksinterpretatie* [Gender, ethnicity and the sport media: Production processes and public interpretation]. Arnhem, The Netherlands: NOC*NSF Breedtesport.
Liebes, T. and Katz, E. (1990) *The Export of Meaning: Cross-cultural Readings of Dallas*. New York/Oxford: Oxford University Press.
Lindlof, R. and Taylor, B. (2011) *Qualitative Communication Research Methods*. Thousand Oaks, CA: Sage.
Lines, G. (2000) "Media Sport Audiences – Young People and the Summer of Sport '96: Revisiting Frameworks for Analysis," *Media Culture and Society* 22: 669–680.
Malcolm, D., Bairner, A., and Curry, G. (2010) "'Woolmergate': Cricket and the Representation of Islam and Muslims in the British Press," *Journal of Sport and Social Issues* 34: 215–235.
McCarthy, D., Jones, R. L., and Potrac, P. (2003) "Constructing Images and Interpreting Realities: The Case of the Black Soccer Player on Television," *International Review for the Sociology of Sport* 38: 217–238.
Müller, F., van Zoonen, L., and De Roode, L. (2007) "Accidental Racists: Experiences and Contradictions of Racism in Local Amsterdam Soccer Fan Culture," *Soccer and Society* 8: 335–350.
Müller, F., van Zoonen, L., and De Roode, L. (2008) "The Integrative Power of Sport: Imagined and Real Effects of Sport Events on Multicultural Integration," *Sociology of Sport Journal* 25: 378–401.
Peeters, R. and van Sterkenburg, J. (2016) "Making Sense of Race/Ethnicity and Gender in Televised Football: Reception Research among British Students," *Sport in Society*, 1–15. doi: 10.1080/17430437.2016.1158472.
Pfister, G. (2015) "Sportswomen in the German Popular Press: A Study Carried Out in the Context of the 2011 Women's Football World Cup," *Soccer and Society* 16(5–6): 639–656.
Rada, J. A. and Wulfemeyer, K. T. (2005) "Color Coded: Racial Descriptors in Television Coverage of Intercollegiate Sports," *Journal of Broadcasting and Electronic Media* 49: 65–85.
Rainville, R. E. and McCormick, E. (1977) "Extent of Covert Racial Prejudice in Pro Footballers Announcers' Speech," *Journalism Quarterly* 54: 20–26.
Rowe, D. (2013) "Reflections on Communication and Sport: On Nation and Globalization," *Communication and Sport* 1: 18–29.
Rowe, D. (2015) "The Mediated Nation and the Transnational Football Fan," *Soccer and Society* 16(5–6): 693–709.
Sabo, D. and Jansen, S. C. (1998) "Prometheus Unbound: Constructions of Masculinity in Sports Media," in L. Wenner (ed.), *MediaSport*. London: Routledge, 202–220.
Sabo, D., Jansen, S. C., Tate, D., Duncan, M. C., and Leggett, S. (1996) "Televising International Sport: Race, Ethnicity, and Nationalistic Bias," *Journal of Sport and Social Issues* 20: 7–22.
Spencer, N. E. (2004). "Sister Act VI: Venus and Serena Williams at Indian Wells: 'Sincere Fictions' and White Racism," *Journal of Sport and Social Issues* 28: 115–135.
Tamir, I. and Bernstein, A. (2015) "Do They Even Know the National Anthem? Minorities in Service of the Flag – Israeli Arabs in the National Football Team," *Soccer and Society* 16(5–6): 745–764.
van Sterkenburg, J. (2011a) *Race, Ethnicity and the Sport Media*. Amsterdam, The Netherlands: Amsterdam University Press/Pallas Publications.

———. (2011b) *Come on Orange! National Bonding and Identification among Viewers of Various Ethnic Origins during the 2010 Football World Cup on Dutch TV*. Zürich, Switzerland: FIFA and CIES (internal FIFA report).

———. (2013) "National Bonding and Meanings Given to Race and Ethnicity: Watching the Football World Cup on TV," *Soccer and Society* 14: 386–403.

van Sterkenburg, J. and Knoppers, A. (2004) "Dominant Discourses about Race/Ethnicity and Gender in Sport Practice and Performance," *International Review for the Sociology of Sport* 39: 301–321.

van Sterkenburg, J. and Spaaij, R. (2015) "Mediated Football: Representations and Audience Receptions of Race/Ethnicity, Gender and Nation," *Soccer and Society* 16(5–6): 993–603.

van Sterkenburg, J., Janssens, J., and Rijnen, B. (2005) *Football and Racism: An Inventory of the Problems and Solutions in Eight West European Countries in the Framework of the Stand Up Speak Up Campaign*. Nieuwegein, The Netherlands: Arko Sports Media.

van Sterkenburg, J., Knoppers, A., and De Leeuw, S. (2012) "Constructing Racial/Ethnic Difference In and Through Dutch Televised Soccer Commentary," *Journal of Sport and Social Issues* 36(4): 422–442.

van Zoonen, L. and van Sterkenburg, J. (2012) "Male and Female Audiences of Televised Football: How do they Negotiate Processes of Racialization in Televised Football?" (unpublished research proposal).

Wensing, E. and Bruce, T. (2003) "Bending the Rules: Media Representations of Gender during an International Sporting Event," *International Review for the Sociology of Sport* 38: 387–396.

## Further Reading

Andrews, D. L. (1996) "The Fact(s) of Michael Jordan's Blackness: Excavating a Floating Racial Signifier," *Sociology of Sport Journal* 13: 125–158. (A study that explores the mediated celebrity Michael Jordan as a discursive site that reproduced specific U.S. discourses surrounding race.)

Billings, A. C. and Eastman, S. T. (2002) "Selective Representation of Gender, Ethnicity, and Nationality in American Television Coverage of the 2000 Summer Olympics," *International Review for the Sociology of Sport* 37: 351–370. (This study looks into representations of ethnicity, gender, and nationality in American (NBC) TV coverage of the 2000 Olympics.)

Carrington, B. (2011) "'What I Said Was Racist – But I'm Not a Racist': Anti-Racism and the White Sports/Media Complex," in J. Long and K. Spracklen (eds.), *Sport and Challenges to Racism*. Basingstoke, UK: Palgrave Macmillan, 83–99. (Carrington explores the operation of whiteness and institutionalized white privilege within the sport media and discusses future challenges in anti-racism work.)

Hylton, K. (2009) *'Race' and Sport: Critical Race Theory*. London/New York: Routledge. (Takes Critical Race Theory as a theoretical framework to discuss racial/ethnic prejudices, stereotypes, and the operation of whiteness in sport and sport media.)

van Sterkenburg, J. and Spaaij, R. (2016) *Mediated Football: Representations and Audience Receptions of Race/Ethnicity, Nation and Gender*. London/New York: Routledge. (Articles from different disciplines that together offer insight into the dynamic interplay between football media representations, production processes and audience receptions in relation to race/ethnicity, nationality and gender.)

# Part III

# RACE, ETHNICITY, AND INTERSECTIONALITY

# 18
# AFRICAN AMERICANS
## From Minstrelsy to Reality TV
### *Rockell A. Brown*

Historically, African Americans have had a tumultuous relationship with mass media. This history has been well documented by scholars (Bogle 2001a; Bogle 2001b; Campbell 1995; Campbell, LeDuff, Jenkins, and Brown 2012; Dates and Barlow 1993; Gray 1995; Haggins 2008; Hunt 2005; Jackson 2006). Many of the images that populated early popular culture were primitive and stereotypical. The images were found in books, newspapers, magazines, and cartoons, and they were prevalent during the nineteenth century in minstrel shows and vaudeville performances—two of the more common forms of popular entertainment of that era. These caricatures set the tone for how blacks were ultimately depicted in film, radio, advertising, and television news and entertainment programming, and can largely be characterized as negative. These portrayals have often reflected the attitudes held about blacks in American society (Nelson 2008). According to Campbell and Giannino, "The ruling class has a long history of using exaggerated media images to demean marginal groups and bolster its privileged status within the existing power structure" (2011: 110). In essence, the use of historical, controlling images reaffirms dominant ideology and maintains the status quo.

While the quantity of representation of African Americans has fluctuated over the years, the quality of the images remains an area of concern. Harper (1998) suggests that a primary reason that the representation of African Americans has been a concern is because it is thought to have an impact "that extends beyond the domain of signs as such and into the realm of African Americans' material well-being, which comprises, among other factors, the social relations through which black people's status in the country is conditioned" (62). Thus, media representations of African Americans can have residual effects in their everyday lived experiences beyond popular culture in the form of discrimination and the establishment of public policies aimed at controlling black and brown bodies (Collins 2004; Harper 1998; Harris-Perry 2011; Pozner 2010).

Despite changes in contemporary mass media and, especially, the televisual landscape (which has more outlets as a result of cable/satellite, niche programming, and more content being created by people of color), in many instances, the themes and characters continue to reinforce hegemonic ideas and stereotypes. It can be argued that television is distinguishable from other media with regard to its ability to disseminate harmful stereotypes. Nelson (2008) noted that compared to film and other media, television dispersed images "more rapidly—and more democratically, because audiences chose what to watch" (194). Furthermore, according to Dates and Barlow (1990), "American commercial television is a clear reflection of the split in the African American image in popular culture, and of empowered groups' rigid control of most images presented on the television screen" (267). Gray (1995) and Nelson (1998) suggest that the representations of African Americans have been greatly impacted by the politics of the television production process, which is rooted in dominant ideology. In many instances, this dominant ideology privileges a white, male, middle-class perspective even when African Americans are involved in the process as writers, directors, and producers because they typically "operate under the creative control and direction of white studio and network executives" (Gray 1995: 71). Even though African Americans may be involved at various stages of the production process, they do not always have the final say and can have their ideas rejected or overruled by executives who hold more power.

This chapter examines African-American representations in the mass media, primarily by exploring how they have been portrayed in reality television, a quintessential form of contemporary pop culture. First, an overview of categories of African-American television representation based on the work of Herman Gray and Angela M. S. Nelson is provided. Next, media stereotypes of African Americans and the reality television genre are discussed. Then, literature examining reality television shows featuring diverse casts, predominantly African-American casts, and African-American families are reviewed. The chapter concludes by discussing the implications and possibilities for the future of African-American media representations.

## Categories of African-American Media Representations

Nelson (1998/2008), influenced by Gray's (1995) analysis of discursive practices in media representations of African Americans, classifies four significant racial humor categories that characterize that representation in television sitcoms: Hybrid Minstrelsy and Black Employment (1948–65); Assimilationist Minstrelsy and Black Glamour (1961–1973); Assimilated Hybrid Minstrelsy (1972–1983); and Multiculturalism, Simultaneity, and Diversification (1984–2008). According to Nelson (2008), the hybrid minstrelsy and black-employment era (1948–1965) featured "black sitcom characters in stereotypical and subservient roles" (194). She cites five prevalent stereotypes associated with this period: sambo (happy, lazy men), coon (subhuman men), mammy (servant/mother), oriole (similar to the dumb blond), and sapphire (domineering woman). The assimilationist minstrelsy and black glamour category (1961–1973) cited by Nelson included shows that treated "the social and political issues of black presence in particular, and racism in general, as individual problems" (196). These shows featured "acceptable Negroes" who were comfortable in white worlds and who reinforced and reflected mainstream values. The black lady and black buddy images Collins (2004) identifies are representative of the images that emerged during this period that were in large part "based on Julia Baker, from *Julia* and Chet Kincaid, from *The Bill Cosby Show*" (Nelson 2008: 197). The assimilated hybrid minstrelsy era (1972–1983) described by Nelson concerns shows that featured "black and white characters that are just alike, except for minor differences of habit and racial perspective" (Nelson 2008: 197). Nelson indicates that this period featured recycled minstrel era caricatures as well as some new and updated versions of the old negative images. Nelson writes that the representations that fall within the multicultural, simultaneity, and diversification category (1984–2008) provide an African-American take on what it means to be American and does so by offering multiple African-American identities and perspectives; in essence, it features multidimensional characters and is inventive in its approach to the medium. However, Nelson also acknowledges that some of the programming prevalent during this era also featured historical arch stereotypes as well as updated stereotypes.

## Stereotypes, African Americans, and Reality Television

Arch stereotypes such as the mammy, jezebel, and sapphire have commonly been associated with African-American women while the tom, sambo, coon, and buck/brute have been associated with African-American men (Boggle 2001; Dates and Barlow 1990; Nelson 2008). The tropes and archetype caricatures that have been associated with African Americans historically are also prevalent within the reality television genre, in programs created by non-blacks and blacks alike. The cast members embody characteristics of arch stereotypes, modified stereotypes, and stereotypes that possess qualities of more than one arch or modified stereotype. Scholars have noted the legacy of minstrelsy and controlling images in a number of reality television programs (Orbe 1998; Orbe and Hopson 2002; Andrejevic and Colby 2006; Bell-Jordan 2008; Dubrofsky and Hardy 2008; Goldman 2012; Harris and Goldman 2014; Piriano 2013; Tyree 2011; Smith 2013; Bennett 2014). Prevalent tropes and stereotypes of African Americans that are present in reality television programming include both (1) violent, hypersexual, materialistic, angry, aggressive, and unstable black men and women, and (2) the savage/brute, coon, sambo, pimp, hustler, jezebel, gold-digger, freak/hoochie, sapphire, diva, homo thug (Stephens and Phillips 2003; Andrejevic and Colby 2006; Bell-Jordan 2008; Campbell and Giannino 2011; Collins 2004, Dubrofsky and Hardy 2008; Orbe 1998; Orbe and Hopson 2002; Piraino 2013; Tyree 2011). Pozner (2010) indicates that reality television is ideologically persuasive as well as entertaining. As such, Campbell and Giannino maintain that it perpetuates "ruling-class ideologies that value men's power over women, white sensibilities over marginalized ways of knowing and opulence over modesty" (2011: 104).

Even though there have been attempts to produce something different, or in the case of reality television show reality or how real people handle real situations, negative representations continue to permeate because beliefs and perceptions are steeped in an ideology that is difficult to break away from. These beliefs and perceptions are inevitably influenced by the experiences those involved in the production process have had with television and other forms of mass media. Thus, it is possible that what some believe or think about African Americans is based on how they have been portrayed in media.

## Reality TV Shows Featuring Diverse Casts

Pozner (2010) indicates the casts of early reality television programs (in the 1990s through the early 2000s) were mostly white, and when persons of color were featured they were marginalized, portrayed as a token character, and/or were in recurring roles. For instance, she contends that they tended to portray African-American women in stereotypical roles she described as black bitches, entitled divas, angry black women, hoochie mamas, ghetto girls, and mammies (Pozner 2010). Research has found that reality programs with diverse casts tend to privilege whiteness and African-American cast members tend to reinforce hegemonic notions of blackness (Andrejevic and Colby 2008; Dubrofsky and Hardy 2010; Pozner 2010). Dubrofsky and Hardy (2010) indicate that whiteness is understood as that which is normal or familiar and that it is privileged because it is often void of obvious signifiers. They submit that within reality television shows with predominantly white casts, black cast members are expected to claim an identity, which often involves embodying a stereotypical representation of blackness and, if they do not, they are deemed inauthentic.

Orbe and Hopson (2002) examined MTV's *The Real World* and indicated that "the signifiers associated with Black men on the show reflect general stereotypes found in all aspects of U.S. popular culture" (220). They found that black males portrayed on the show fell into one of four categories: inherently angry, emotionally unstable or unpredictable, a violent threat, or sexually aggressive. All of these signifiers or character traits can be traced back to the historically controlling image of the African-American man as the savage brute. Later representations might be closer to what Collins (2004) refers to as the criminal, thug, and/or player. These representations reinforce hegemonic notions that imply that black men are inherently violent, dangerous, and hypersexual and should be feared. Additionally, Andrejevic and Colby (2008) argue that Gladys, the only black cast member of the 1999 season of MTV's *Road Rules*, was cast with the expectation that she would "perform a certain racial stereotype": that of the "angry black woman" (200). They suggest that she was depicted as rough, urban, and almost always defensive, and that "she always posed the threat of violence" (203). Moreover, Tyree (2011) found that in reality programming featuring mostly white casts, African Americans "were often triggers or catalysts in arguments, disagreements, and physical altercations . . . and were more likely than not to be stereotyped" (408). Likewise, Goldman (2012) indicated that African-American women featured in reality shows with diverse casts were, in large part, featured less often and in the background unless they were exhibiting stereotypical qualities such as the mean black woman or the sexualized black woman; in these instances, Goldman found, they were given more camera time.

Bell-Jordan (2008) also examined reality television shows with diverse casts. She asserts that the shows reinforce ideological assumptions about race in ways similar to television news:

> The narratives about race on these shows can be understood as similar in five prevailing ways to how race is mediated in television news: (1) they dramatize race and racial issues by juxtaposing opposing viewpoints; (2) they promote conflict in the framing of race and racial issues, specifically in terms of interracial conflict and intra-racial conflict; (3) they perpetuate hegemonic representations of race by emphasizing violence and anger; (4) they personalize racism by privileging individual solutions to complex social problems; and (5) they leave conflict and contradictions unresolved.
> 
> *(357)*

Bell-Jordan contends that race is used as a textual device on the programs and that the portrayals seem to strengthen hegemonic "reductive thinking about African Americans as either 'hood' or 'integrated' (that is 'acceptable or 'unacceptable')" (360). Within this framework, there is little room for audiences to imagine or recognize the diversity among African Americans. In essence, white cast members' poor behavior is characterized or perceived as situational or specific to the individual whereas black cast members' behaviors are seen (and constructed) as natural or innate. Bell-Jordan's observations regarding the similarities between television news and reality television shows and their construction of race are quite telling, particularly the notion that they perpetuate hegemonic representations of race by emphasizing violence and anger.

Andrejevic and Colby (2006) suggest one of the draws of reality television is that ideally it offers audiences who are also potential cast members the opportunity to challenge stereotypes and determine how they will be represented. They argue that shows such as MTV's *The Real World* and *Road Rules* have largely been unsuccessful in debunking stereotypes in their depictions of black cast members as they have "tended to reinforce a litany of caricatures" (198). Like much of what is seen on television, reality programming featuring diverse (but majority-white) casts tends to reduce complex social and widespread problems to one of the individual, which supports the notion that problems related to race or racism are mostly isolated incidents and ignores the systemic and institutional racism that remains prevalent and impacts the life experiences of many people of color (Andrejevic and Colby 2006; Gray 1995). Thus, systemic racism and the continued oppression it causes are largely and conveniently ignored, as this would contradict the notion of a post-racial society. In this regard, these types of reality shows fit within the assimilationist minstrelsy and black glamour category in that they seem to treat "the social and political issues of black presence . . . and racism in general, as individual problems" (Nelson 2008: 196). However, the African-American cast members in these shows are not always accepted or made to feel comfortable in the manufactured environment.

## Reality Television Featuring Predominantly Black Casts

Jennifer Pozner (2010) suggests the arrival of VH1's *Flavor of Love* (2006) ushered in a paradigm shift in reality television programming, particularly where African Americans are concerned. She indicates non-whites became more visible within reality television; however, she maintains that shows featuring majority African-American casts were more like modern-day minstrel shows that included jezebels, pimps, and thugs. Additionally, Smith (2013) contends that stereotypes of African Americans found in reality television usually pertain to "sexuality (e.g., The Brute, The Jezebel), physical prowess (e.g., The Brute/The Criminal/The Nat/The Buck, The Athlete). They might also be presented as aggressive (e.g., The Matriarch/The Sapphire, The Brute/The Criminal/The Nat/The Buck), while others are described as docile (e.g., The Tom, The Sister Savior)" (41–42).

A litany of unflattering images has been identified in *Flavor of Love*. For example, Dubrofsky and Hardy (2008) found that rapper Flavor Flav, the show's star, as well as the women featured on the show perform notions of blackness that are in alignment with dominant ideology, such as being hypersexual, overly emotional, angry, loud, and out of control, and that those representations ultimately reaffirmed long-held stereotypes of African Americans. Likewise, Campbell and Giannino (2011) draw parallels between the portrayal of Flavor Flav in *Flavor of Love* and the historically controlling image of the coon. They indicate that Flavor Flav embodied multiple characteristics of the coon and that he depicted a new-age coon, "the super coon." According to Campbell and Giannino, "The gestation of the twenty-first century coon included an evolution whereby the caricature is objectified and commodified by the hegemonic strata which ultimately leads to the recreation/rebirth of today's super-coon Flavor Flav" (106). Campbell and Giannino cite everything from his gaudy mansion, his attire, the foods he eats, and the manner in which he eats to his poorly articulated thoughts and ideas as examples of how he has elevated the coon and reinvented the minstrel tradition. Furthermore, they maintain that his hyperbolic persona merely offers the illusion of power whereas he is actually powerless. This is demonstrated through his misogynistic treatment of the women appearing on the show, especially renaming them based on some aspect of their appearance (Campbell and Giannino 2011). The renaming ritual is particularly problematic as it harkens back to slavery and how slaves' names were changed. In essence, he mimics the oppressors. Campbell and Giannino explain that this "not only highlights the powerlessness of the women . . . but also elucidates the pseudo power ascribed to the super coon who can oppress others by rendering them nameless but cannot engage in the kind of intellectual and critical discourse necessary to confront a system that simultaneously renders him powerless" (109). *Flavor of Love* can be situated in Nelson's assimilated hybrid minstrelsy category because it imitates *The Bachelor* thematically, yet it clearly features recycled minstrel era caricatures such as the coon, sapphire, and the hypersexual jezebel.

Goldman (2012) indicates that African-American women are portrayed positively and negatively in reality shows in which they are the majority (i.e., *The Real Housewives of Atlanta*, *Basketball Wives*, and *Love & Hip Hop*). In terms of positive depictions, she found that they portray professionals and good mothers, that they are physically attractive (outside of mainstream standards), in healthy relationships, and not always hypersexual. However, Goldman maintains that the amount of negative portrayals prevalent in the shows she analyzed generally outweighed the positive ones. Negative characteristics exhibited by the cast members included being mean, aggressive, and hypersexual. Furthermore, Goldman (2012) observed that some of the positive attributes that were found were featured in the cast biographies and not necessarily emphasized within the storylines. Additionally, Bennett (2014) examined *Love & Hip Hop Atlanta* to interrogate reality television's representation of black women and men, the manner in which black men employ male privilege, and how black women subvert male privilege in the context of the show. He found that the representations reinforce and reproduce harmful stereotypes of African Americans. Bennett indicates that female cast members embody characteristics of the sapphire and jezebel, and male cast members support the mythological notions of black men as hypersexual, violent, emotionally unstable, and uneducated/irresponsible (Hopson and Orbe 2002; Jackson 2006). On the other hand, Bennett found that the women on the show were also depicted as "caring mothers, compassionate friends, and strong independent women" (55). He further suggests that there are positive qualities attached to the black men on the show that might be overlooked as well:

> At times, Black men embody vulnerability by expressing their emotions, such as love, in relationships with the women in their lives. This space of emotional vulnerability and communal bonding is where *Love & Hip Hop Atlanta* deviates from traditional representations of Black femininity and Black masculinity on television.
>
> *(Bennett 2014: 55)*

Goldman (2012) and Bennett (2014) seem to read against the encoding of the dominant ideology present in reality television. Their analysis reveals that African Americans are being depicted with more complexity, particularly when the cast is composed mostly of African Americans. Given the multidimensional personas of some of the cast members in the shows they examined, it is plausible to situate those programs in Nelson's (2008) multicultural, simultaneity, and diversification category. On the other hand, the shows also promote mainstream values and sensibilities while reaffirming hegemonic notions of African Americans being aggressive and hypersexual black men and women (particularly on *Love & Hip Hop Atlanta*), in alignment with Nelson's (2008) assimilated hybrid minstrelsy category.

## The Black Family in Reality TV: From Black Fatherhood to Black Motherhood

Smith (2011) examined reality television's portrayal of black fathers by juxtaposing *Run's House* and Snoop Dogg's *Father Hood* with *The Cosby Show*. Among the similarities she aptly highlights are that none of the three shows outwardly addresses racism, classism, or societal ills; instead, the shows revolve "around family success, humor, and harmony" (470). The most notable contrast observed among the three shows concerned the fathers' approach to disciplining their children. Smith notes that *The Cosby Show* and *Run's House* were similar in that they both operated from a more traditional parenting paradigm and both the parents and the children expressed their feelings during family discussions. On the other hand, Snoop was much more laidback and was not much of a disciplinarian; however, his wife, like the wives on *The Cosby Show* and *Run's House*, was. Fatherhood also distinguished itself as real-life issues such as sex were addressed, and the show purposefully highlighted the ties the Broadus family maintained with Snoop's old neighborhood. Smith indicates that *Run's House* and *Father Hood* are prone to reinforcing enlightened racism, similar to *The Cosby Show* (Jhally and Lewis 2005). She writes,

> First, all three shows display professional and material success in environments void of race-based obstacles. Two, the two reality sitcoms, viewed as more "real" than traditional sitcoms, lend credence to the belief of the [raceless] American Dream. Third, reality TV—like *The Cosby Show*—has proven its ability to attract diverse audiences, which increases opportunities for White exposure to Black fathers/families.
>
> *(Smith 2011: 477)*

She also observes that both shows reinforce the stereotype that success or achievement for African Americans is most acceptable through entertainment—such as music or sports—that affirms hegemonic ideals. It seems worth noting that Calvin Broadus (Snoop) has a criminal background and, although it has not seemingly hindered his success or earning potential, it does reinforce the myth that black men are inherently criminal. However, his success is not a likely outcome for the countless African-American men and women whose lives have been permanently changed due to criminal convictions and the associated stigma. Likewise, during one of the episodes, his sons have a run-in with the law after illegally parking one of Snoop's cars they did not have permission to drive (Smith 2011). It is possible that without the protection of Snoop's celebrity status, there could very well have been a different outcome. This was a teachable moment missed by Snoop and the show's other producers.

Goldman (2014) examined reality television portrayals of African-American female celebrities that revolved around their families: *Braxton Family Values* and *Mary Mary*. Her analysis revealed that both shows featured professional, family-oriented women and, while both contained elements of anger and sexuality, these were neither over-the-top nor a primary characteristic of the cast members. Instead, Goldman indicates that their behavior was displayed purposefully and in context, particularly in their attempts to resolve conflict, which they often did successfully. She concluded:

> The shows present Black women who are ambitious and successful. They possess strong mothering skills and know the difference between hypersexuality and acceptable sexuality. In addition, their use of aggression is purposeful and to protect others. The women are not solely presented as one specific stereotype. Instead, they are featured as multifaceted women who experience several highs as well as lows. Thus, more positive images of Black women in reality television can and do exist.
>
> *(Goldman 2014: 49)*

Goldman points to these shows as evidence that television can still entertain audiences without exploiting black women, depicting them as angry and hypersexual.

The reality shows revolving around African-American families seem to be situated within Nelson's multicultural, simultaneity, and diversification category by offering multiple African-American identities and perspectives. However, like *The Cosby Show*, they "operate in a world that parallels that of whites" and appeal to mainstream values such as "mobility and individualism" as well as privileging "the upper-middle-class black family" (Gray 1995: 89). In this regard, the shows also fit within assimilationist and pluralist discourses described by Gray (1995).

## Reality TV and the Future of African-American Media Representations

Reviewing the literature concerning African-American representation on reality television reveals that both historical and revised media stereotypes are reinforced and reproduced through this genre. With this in mind, much of reality television bears a striking resemblance to the "Blaxploitation" films and ghetto sitcoms of the 1970s. They are largely enjoyed by black audiences and simultaneously reinforce hegemonic ideas and beliefs about African Americans. Much like the sitcom, reality television is formulaic and has a tendency to reinforce dominant beliefs rather than challenge them. Thus, "the excessive sexualized discourse and hyperbolic ghetto attitude is personified as authentically black and far removed from the normative nature of Whiteness, erecting the parameters of Blackness in the space" of reality TV (Dubrofsky and Hardy 2008: 386). Furthermore, Bennett (2014) posits that reality television shows—like many mass media artifacts—"offer opportunities to exploit marginalized communities for ratings and drama" in an attempt to maximize profits (1). He goes on to suggest that reality television has treated the black body as a commodity while reinforcing dominant ideology, as many of the shows "center intersecting privileged and marginalized identities to promote conflict surrounding Black cast members at the expense of offering humanizing representations of Black culture" (19).

According to Pozner, reality television

> has the power to influence our notions of normalcy versus difference, convince us that certain behaviors are "innate" for different groups of people, and present culturally constructed norms of gender, race, class and sexuality as "natural" rather than performances we've learned to adopt through societal education and expectation.
>
> *(2010: 98)*

Tyree suggests that even though much of reality television is staged, some perceive the performances as authentic and this could potentially impact interactions audience members have with African Americans in real life (2011: 409). Additionally, Smith maintains that though reality TV "might offer the possibility for those featured to construct their own identities, editing techniques and producers' decisions often override these potentialities" (2013: 47).

What might be most troubling about this, however, is that this is the case even when the executives behind the shows—and behind many problematic media representations—are African-American men and women. This underscores the pervasiveness of dominant ideology and the interlocking forces of white supremacy and capitalism. When African Americans reproduce these damaging images, internalized racism in conjunction with the financial rewards made possible by capitalist enterprises are the likely cause. For some African Americans, becoming a part of the media elite ultimately leads to continuing the negative media legacy. In some instances, when African Americans are in charge of creating and circulating their own images, all too often the images reinforce hegemonic racist and sexist notions about black women and men (Stephens and Phillips 2003).

Although some progress has been made, as illustrated by the reality shows featuring African-American families, there is still a way to go as the positive portrayals are often overshadowed by the negative imagery prevalent in the media landscape. Ultimately, the goal should be to have more television programming and other media products that align with Nelson's (2008) multicultural, simultaneity, and diversification category, and there is evidence of that as discussed above; however, it is difficult for content creators to avoid falling back on the familiar, as illustrated with the shows that continue to recycle stereotypes in the minstrelsy tradition.

This chapter reviewed literature concerning mass media representations of African Americans through the lens of reality television. It did not attempt to address all mass media (or even all reality television programming) but used reality television as a lens through which to view the problematic representations of African Americans throughout the history of popular culture. Much work is still needed in producing better, well-rounded, and realistic—not perfect—media images of African Americans, and this is possible, as seen occasionally in reality television and in other forms of mass media.

## References

Andrejevic, M. and Colby, D. (2006) "Racism and Reality TV: The Case of MTV's *The Real World*," in D. Escoffery (ed.), *How Real is Reality TV? Essays on Representation and Truth*. Jefferson, NC: McFarland and Company, 195–211.

Bell-Jordan, K. E. (2008) "Black. White. And a Survivor of *The Real World*: Constructions of Race on Reality TV," *Critical Studies in Media Communication* 25(4): 353–372.

Bennett, P. D. (2014) *Love, Drama, and Tears: Hip Hop Feminism, Blackness, and Love & Hip Hop Atlanta*. Master's Thesis, Southern University Illinois Carbondale.

Bogle, D. (2001a) *Toms, Coons, Mulattoes, Mammies, and Bucks: An Interpretive History of Blacks in American Films*. New York: Continuum.

——. (2001b) *Primetime Blues: African Americans on Network Television*. New York: Farrar, Straus and Giroux.

Campbell, C. (1995) *Race, Myth, and the News*. Thousand Oaks, CA: Sage.

Campbell, C., LeDuff, K. M., Jenkins, C. D., and Brown, R. A. (2012) *Race and News: Critical Perspectives*. New York: Routledge.

Campbell, S. and Giannino, S. S. (2011) "Flaaaavooor-flaaav: Comic Relief or Super-Coon?," in R. Jackson and M. Hopson (eds.), *Masculinity in the Black Imagination: Politics of Communicating Race and Manhood*. New York: Peter Lang Publishing, 103–112.

Collins, P. H. (2004) *Black Sexual Politics: African Americans, Gender, and the New Racism*. New York: Routledge.
Dates, J. L. and Barlow, W. (1993) *Split Image: African Americans in the Mass Media*. Washington, D.C.: Howard University Press.
Dubrofsky, R. E., and Hardy, A. (2008) "Performing Race in *Flavor of Love* and *The Bachelor*," *Critical Studies in Media Communication* 25(4): 373–392.
Goldman, A. Y. (2012) *Constructing a Woman's Reality: Examining Images of African American Women in Six Selected Reality Docusoaps*. Ph.D. Dissertation, Howard University.
———. (2014) "Meet the Braxtons and the Marys: A Closer Look at Representations of Black Female Celebrities in WE TV's *Braxton Family Values* and *Mary Mary*," in A. Y. Goldman, V. S. Ford, A. A. Harris, and N. R. Howard (eds.), *Black Women and Popular Culture: The Conversation Continues*. Lanham, MD: Lexington Books, 33–54.
Gray, H. (1995) *Watching Race: Television and the Struggle for Blackness*. Minneapolis, MN: University of Minnesota Press.
Haggins, B. (2008) "The Black Situation Comedy," in T. Boyd (ed.), *African Americans and Popular Culture*. Westport, CT: Praeger Publishers, 217–243.
Hall, S. (2003) "The Whites of Their Eyes: Racist Ideologies and the Media," in G. Dines and J. M. Humez (eds.), *Gender, Race, and Class in Media: A Text-Reader*. Thousand Oaks, CA: Sage Publications, 89–93.
Harper, P. B. (1998) "Extra-Special Effects: Television Representation and the Claims of 'The Black Experience,'" in S. Torres (ed.), *Race and Television in the United States*. Durham, NC: Duke University Press, 62–81.
Harris-Perry, M. V. (2011) *Sister Citizen: Shame, Stereotypes, and Black Women in America*. New Haven, CT: Yale University Press.
Hunt, D. (2005) *Channeling Blackness: Studies on Television and Race in America*. New York: Oxford University Press.
Jackson, R. (2006) *Scripting the Black Masculine Body: Identity, Discourse, and Racial Politics in Popular Media*. Albany, NY: State University of New York Press.
Jhally, S. and Lewis, J. (2005) "White Responses: The Emergence of 'Enlightened' Racism," in D. Hunt (ed.), *Channeling Blackness: Studies on Television and Race in America*. New York: Oxford University Press, 74–88.
Nelson, A. M. S. (1998) "Black Situation Comedies and the Politics of Television Art," in Y. R. Kamalipour and T. Carilli (eds.), *Cultural Diversity and the U.S. Media*. New York: State University of New York Press, 79–87.
Nelson, A. M. S. (2008) "African American Stereotypes in Prime-Time Television: An Overview, 1948–2007," in T. Boyd (ed.), *African Americans and Popular Culture*. Westport, CT: Praeger Publishers, 185–216.
Orbe, M. P. (1998) "Constructions of Reality on MTV's 'The Real World': An Analysis of the Restrictive Coding of Black Masculinity," *Southern Communication Journal* 64(1): 32–47.
Orbe, M. P. and Hopson, M. (2002) "Exploring Images of the Black Male on MTV's *The Real World*," in J. Martin, T. Nakayama, and L. Flores (eds.), *Readings in Intercultural Communication Experiences and Contexts*. New York: Routledge, 219–226.
Piraino, A. B. (2013) "Bitches, Pimps, and Hoes Abound: Riesman's 'The Lonely Crowd' and the Development of the Reality Television Persona," *Journal of Communications Media Studies* 5(1): 59–70.
Pozner, J. (2010) *Reality Bites Back: The Troubling Truth about Guilty Pleasure TV*. Berkeley, CA: Seal Press.
Smith, D. C. (2011) "Critiquing Reality-Based Televisual Black Fatherhood: A Critical Analysis of *Run's House* and *Snoop Dogg's Father Hood*," in G. Dines and J. M. Humez (eds.), *Gender, Race, and Class in Media: A Critical-Reader*. Thousand Oaks, CA: Sage Publications, 469–480.
Smith, S. (2013) "And Still More Drama!: A Comparison of the Portrayals of African-American Women and African-American Men on BET's *College Hill*," *Western Journal of Black Studies* 37(1): 39–49.
Stephens, D. P. and Phillips, L. D. (2003) "Freaks, Gold Diggers, Divas, and Dykes: The Sociohistorical Development of Adolescent African American Women's Sexual Scripts," *Sexuality and Culture* 7: 3–49.
Tyree, T. (2011) "African American Stereotypes in Reality Television," *Howard Journal of Communications* 22: 394–413.

## Further Reading

Bogle, D. (2001) *Primetime Blues: African Americans on Network Television*. New York: Farrar, Straus and Giroux. (Chronicles the history of African Americans in prime-time television entertainment programming.)

Gray, H. (1995) *Watching Race: Television and the Struggle for Blackness*. Minneapolis, MN: University of Minnesota Press. (Examines the politics of the television production process and the representation of African Americans; presents three kinds of discursive practices in which African-American representations on television are grounded.)

Nelson, A. M. S. (2008) "African American Stereotypes in Prime-Time Television: An Overview, 1948–2007," in T. Boyd (ed.), *African Americans and Popular Culture*. Westport, CT: Praeger Publishers, 185–216. (Presents Nelson's four significant racial humor categories in which African-American television representation can be situated historically.)

Pozner, J. (2010) *Reality Bites Back: The Troubling Truth about Guilty Pleasure TV*. Berkeley, CA: Seal Press. (Offers a comprehensive look at how reality television programming reinforces hegemonic notions of race, class, and gender.)

# 19
# LATIN@S

## Underrepresented Majorities in the Digital Age

*Celeste González de Bustamante and Jessica Retis*

In 2014, Alfonso Cuarón became the first Latino in the more than eight-decade history of the Academy Awards to win an Oscar for Best Director. The following year, Alejandro González Iñárritu was presented with the same award. During the ceremony, actor Sean Penn, right before announcing the award, "jokingly" stated, "Who gave this son-of-a-bitch a green card?" González Iñárritu, who is reportedly a friend of Penn, joked, "Maybe next year the government will inflict some immigration rules to the Academy. Two Mexicans in a row, that's suspicious, I guess" (Iñárritu 2015). During his acceptance speech he dedicated the award to:

> My fellow Mexicans. The ones who live in Mexico, I pray that we can find and build the government that we deserve. And the ones that live in this country who are part of the latest generation of immigrants in this country, I just pray that they can be treated with the same dignity and respect as the ones who came before and built this incredible immigrant nation.
>
> *(Iñárritu 2015)*

The exchange between Penn and Iñárritu ignited a firestorm of opinions on Twitter and other social media. Latin@s were able to deplore and denounce Penn's comments as being, at best, in "bad taste," and, at worst, blatantly racist and nativist. The events at the 2014 and 2015 Academy Award ceremonies also brought to the fore two themes that this chapter seeks to address: (1) Hollywood's and mainstream media's continuation of stereotypical and derogatory depictions of Latinos and Latinas—the disconnect with, disregard for, and discomfort with the demographic realities of a growing Latino population in the United States, and (2) the new ways in which Latin@s choose to represent themselves in the digital age or, in other words, social networks and new media are creating new opportunities for Latin@s to represent themselves through the creation of counter-narratives.

Aside from serving as an introduction into the field of race, ethnicity, and the media, paying specific attention to representations of Latinos and Latinas in the media in the digital age, this chapter presents some of the major theoretical lenses through which scholars have analyzed Latin@s,[1] media, and representation. Beyond creating a snapshot of the state of the field, the chapter provides some examples of how mainstream media represent (or misrepresent) Latin@s in the United States, as well as discusses how Latin@s choose to portray and depict themselves, along with some of the possibilities and challenges in so doing in a twenty-first-century digital landscape.

## The Majority–Minority Context

Since the nineteenth century, Latino communities have evolved as a result of transnational processes: while U.S. capital flowed south, people headed north.[2] Throughout the second half of the twentieth century, the effects of industrialization, the dismantling of traditional agriculture, armed conflicts, and the pressures of social exclusion and political instability exacerbated the factors that pushed the emigration of Latin Americans, while economic conditions in the United States increasingly pulled immigrants north (Retis 2006); further, as Juan González (2011) points out, in contrast to what tends to be portrayed in popular media discourse, these movements were not caused by a surprise collective desire for material benefits of U.S. society, but were rather the result of civil wars and social chaos generated by the processes of military and economic interventions and in many cases were backed and influenced by U.S. imperialistic policies in the region.

Throughout the last five decades the U.S. Census has noted the growth and diversification of Latino communities, conceived, however, as a supposedly homogeneous group to incorporate in the category of Hispanics in official records and promoted by media and marketing discourses (Dávila 2001; Yúdice 2009). Despite their diversity, as Yúdice reminds us, Latin@s are still perceived as a homogeneous group, assumed to share the same culture based on the language (Spanish) and religion (Catholicism). Therefore, similar to the case of Asians, Latinos end up being treated as a separate "race," especially in everyday life. This is due not only to their cultural difference from blacks and whites, but also to their designation by the government, police, and education (e.g., schools), and categorization by the labor market, media, advertising, and medical institutions (Yúdice 2009: 17).

General media tend to overlook the fact that most Latino immigrants arrived during the 1990s[3] and frequently ignore the geopolitical and economic contexts of these influxes. While critical theories interpreted the 1980s as the "Lost Decade" when analyzing the effects of structural adjustment programs in Latin American countries (Retis 2006), American public discourse designated it as the "Hispanic Decade" to refer to the growing Latino presence (Yúdice 2014). During those years, more than 4 million arrived, double the amount of the previous decade and quadruple the number during the 1960s (Retis 2014). If during the "Hispanic Decade," population growth was based upon the Anglo population, during the 1990s a change in process started and intensified during the next decade. For the first time the contribution of population growth came from those who up until that time were considered the second largest minority in the country: Latinos comprised 34 percent of total U.S. population growth (Canales 2011).

The most recent demographic studies noted new rearrangements and processes of geographical concentration and dispersion of Latin@s in the United States. Hispanic groups now make up 55.4 million, 17.4 percent of the population (Krogstad and Lopez 2015), almost 400 percent more than in 1980 (14.8 million, 6.5 percent of the total population). In some states such as California (15 million, 38 percent), Texas (10 million, 38 percent), New Mexico (1 million, 47 percent), and Arizona (2 million, 30 percent), or some counties such as Los Angeles (5 million, 48 percent), Harris County, Texas (1.7 million, 41 percent), Miami-Dade County, Florida (1.6 million, 65 percent), Cook County, Illinois (1.2 million, 24 percent), Maricopa County, Arizona (1.1 million, 30 percent), or Bexar County, Texas (1 million, 59 percent), where they are referred to as minorities, Latino groups now make up the majority of the population. They are part of what the U.S. Census has identified as states or equivalents with majority–minority populations (Hawaii, District of Columbia, California, New Mexico, and Texas), or the 11 percent of the counties with majority–minority in 2014 (U.S. Census Bureau 2015). Yet, despite the demographic shifts, as will be discussed below, mainstream media has largely ignored the new majority–minority reality.

## Conceptual Frameworks for Analyzing and Understanding Latin@s and Representation

To understand issues of representation of ethnic and racial groups in the United States, historical and demographic realities must be considered. These social and cultural contingencies have influenced the ways in which dominant media construct various groups of people and have had and continue to have real social, cultural, and economic impacts on people of color in the US (Báez and Castañeda 2014).

In the midst of and partly as a response to a growing Latino population in the United States, various states have passed legal measures that specifically seek to exclude and diminish this group from civic engagement and social mobility. Some of the most exclusionary measures have been passed in states such as Arizona, where Latinos make up more than one-third of the population, and in Georgia, where the Latin@ population has grown dramatically in recent years (Santa Ana and González de Bustamante 2012). Further, the condition of exclusion for heritage speakers in academic and social environments (Schreffler 2007; Harklau 2009) has been considered as a way of re-segregating Latino groups in secondary and college education systems (Chao 2012; Yosso and Solorzano 2006) and demonstrates how language proficiency becomes a barrier to social mobility (Spence, Rojas, and Straubhaar 2011).

It is essential to understand these processes at the local, national, regional, and transnational levels. Research requires interdisciplinary approaches and more comprehensive analyses of social stratification and socioeconomic inequalities that transcend the prism of immigration, race, and ethnicity. Critical researchers discuss whether we are confronting the *mass media* or the *class media* when analyzing the composition, structure, and behavior of the mainstream media in the United States (Wilson, Gutiérrez, and Chao 2003) or how stereotypes allow the mental organization of collective perceptions about other groups as different from the in-group or reference group (Fiske and Taylor 1991). Other scholars have analyzed how the general market media characterized Latin@ communities and Latinidad incorporating two inter-related ideological processes: genderization and racialization (Molina Guzman 2005; Valdivia 2011, 2000; Fregoso 2003) or how contemporary media representations simultaneously feminize the racial Other and racialize the feminine Other (Molina Guzman 2006; Valdivia 2011; Molina Guzman, and Valdivia 2010).

At first glance, it might seem obvious that the topic of Latin@s, media, and representation would fit squarely with Critical Race Theory (CRT), which looks at studying and transforming the relationships among race, racism, and power (Delgado and Stefancic 2012). Yet while there has been work in that area, Anguiano and Castañeda (2014) illustrate that communication researchers have not been overly exuberant in connecting their work within this tradition. In this globalized world of digital media, Anguiano and Castañeda propose a confluence of the subfields of CRT and Latino CRT or LatCrit to create "Latina/o Critical Communication Theory," in an effort to "contribute to critical communication studies and its commitment to investigate inequality in order to foster social change" (Anguiano and Castañeda 2014: 109). The explanatory power of a communication framework that focuses on Latina/o discursive and performance strategies is not meant to be exclusive, but rather seeks to avoid the dichotomization of racial identities to which Orbe and Allen have referred and have called upon scholars to consider (2008).

## Structural Inequalities and the Media

There are several structural factors that help to explain why and how Latino groups have been and continue to be represented and underrepresented in news and entertainment media. First, they are made "invisible" or, as Tuchman (1978) stated, "silently annihilated" in media coverage. Second, when they are included in general media content, they tend to be portrayed as sources of societal problems. Third, the lack of diversity of producers in entertainment and news media serves to exacerbate historical tendencies in Latino media portrayals and representation. Fourth, while Hollywood and general news media have remained reluctant to include Latino groups in content, they have been and continue to pursue Latino communities as consumers.

### *Invisibility in the News*

Research has demonstrated that Latin@s are made invisible in the mainstream media discourse, and when they do appear they are represented in a misinformed way and with greater negative connotations than other ethnic minorities (National Council of La Raza 1997; Santa Ana 2013). In the 1990s, the amount of national news concerning Hispanics represented 1 percent of all news produced (National Council of La Raza 1994), which was even less than the amount of news covering African Americans or Asians (Entman and Rojecky 2000). Two decades later a study by the National Association of Hispanic Journalists (NAHJ 2006) showed that in the case of TV news, the representation margin was less than in the printed news media outlets. Only 0.83 percent of broadcast stories by ABC, CBS, and NBC in 2005 covered Hispanics. This low percentage was, paradoxically, an increase from the previous year, when the average was 0.72 percent. Santa Ana (2013) analyzed over 12,000 stories broadcast in 2004 by the four top American networks (ABC, CBS, NBC, and CNN) and found that less than 1 percent of these stories addressed Latino issues, and that "given that Latinos comprised 14 percent of the United States population at the time, the nation's understanding of Latinos from network news programs was and remains wholly inadequate" (Santa Ana 2013: xvii).

### *Social Conflict as Newsworthy*

Vargas (2000) views newsmaking as key to the (re)production of knowledge, and she argues that the power/knowledge perspective postulates that professional journalistic practices help to legitimize the discourse necessary to construct power relations that come to be seen as natural. In that sense, news media contribute to the social construction of the perception of Latin@s in the United States. So what Latin@ stories do make the news? The NAHJ Report (2006) found that there were five predominant topics: those related to national government (19 percent), crime (18.1 percent), human-interest issues (17 percent), immigration (14.3 percent), and sports (11.4 percent). NAHJ's report also found that Hispanics were non-existent in those stories that were not "overtly" related to Hispanics. Santa Ana (2013) identified the two criteria that made a Latino event newsworthy in 2004: "Either it was an 'inside-the-Beltway' topic or it was a story about death and mayhem. It follows that the networks still did not consider Latinos to be an integral part of the American social fabric" (2013: xviii). Vargas (2000) argues that newspapers, perhaps despite editors' and reporters' efforts to do otherwise, reproduce a racializing discourse that constructs Latinos as an underclass.

Despite changing demographics, in mainstream media Latin@s continue to be portrayed in stereotypical and distorted ways in a post-9/11 media landscape (Chavez 2008). Most analyses have involved the main broadcast TV networks, but Dixon and Williams' work moves beyond network television to include cable news networks. They found that "Latino perpetrators were significantly more likely to be seen as immigrants (97 percent) on network and cable news than to actually be immigrants in U.S. society (47 percent), according to official reports" (2015: 31). The continued distortion of perceptions-versus-realities fosters misunderstandings about various ethnic groups, including Latin@s.

In their study of English-language and Spanish-language media coverage of the 2008 economic crisis, Báez and Castañeda (2014) found that framing of Latin@s has resulted in a new form of redlining (28), and that "low income racial and ethnic minorities were framed as irrational and irresponsible in mainstream and conservative media for taking on subprime mortgages and, thus, are one of the primary reasons for the mortgage meltdown." English-language media portrayed Latin@s within a victim/threat binary, and generally depicted Latin@s through the use of statistics in lieu of personal stories. This is similar to what González de Bustamante (2012) found regarding coverage of undocumented immigrants in Arizona during the 1970s.

## *Less Diversity in the Newsroom*

Examining news production from a "sociology of news media" perspective is useful when considering current trends in newsrooms, as journalists have increasingly fewer opportunities to specialize on issues of social and human interest (Retis and Sierra 2011). And, while diversity has increased in newsrooms over the past decades (from 3.95 percent in 1978 to 12.76 percent in 2015), Hispanics only make up 4 percent of the journalists working in American newsrooms (ASNE 2015). A recent survey among Latino journalists found that 42 percent reported downsizing or cutbacks in staff hours at work, and more than 75 percent agreed that they have been forced to do more with less resources (NAHJ 2014), and a large percentage (40.2 percent) are concerned about job security (NAHJ 2015).

## *Entertainment Media Exclusion*

By sheer numbers, entertainment media are only slightly better than news media when it comes to representation of Latino groups and issues. A 2014 report titled "The Latino Media Gap" summarized eight principal findings: (1) Latino participation in programming and movies is extremely limited; (2) Latino men have disappeared as leading actors, though the percentage of Latinas and Afro-Latino actors is rising; (3) Latinos are still missing behind the scenes; (4) stereotypes restrict opportunities and perceptions; (5) news is worse than fiction; (6) Latino content and audiences expand viewership; (7) consumer pressure creates impact; (8) Latinos drive new media production and innovation (Negrón-Muntaner et al. 2014).

Statistics regarding representation make it somewhat remarkable that in both 2014 and 2015, films of two Hollywood directors of Mexican origin won "Best Picture." Aside from some exceptional successes, inclusion of Latinos in entertainment media has not improved in dramatic ways, but the political economy of representation is complex. The 2015 Hollywood blockbuster *San Andreas* is somewhat illustrative. The main plot of the movie, directed by Canadian-born Brad Peyton, centers on a massive earthquake that jolts the entire state of California from Los Angeles to San Francisco. The subplot surrounds a dysfunctional and divided family, led by its patriarch, Raymond (Ray) Gaines, played by Dwayne "the Rock" Johnson.

While some ethnic and racial minorities figure into the screenplay (Johnson is black, Nova Scotian, and Samoan) none of the central characters is Latin@. There is a scene in which Ray Gaines helps a Latino "pedestrian" (E. Ambriz DeColosio) and his son avoid getting crushed by falling debris from a building (IMDb 2015). The real diversity in the cast is seen in the overrepresentation of actors from outside of the United States, including a Canadian (The Rock), two Australians, a young Irish actor, and an English actor of Indian descent who plays a reporter. The only real "characters" of Latino origin are the places in which the movie transpires, such as San Francisco, Los Angeles, and of course, San Andreas, the great fault line that runs through the entire state. Viewers/consumers are left with a historical reference to what was once part of the Spanish colonial empire, and later, part of Mexico, but almost no present-day reference to the state's demographic realities are featured in the film (Nelson 2015). Latin@s are quite literally made almost invisible. Given that California has the largest Latino population in the country (15 million), and that Latin@s make up the largest ethnic/racial group in the state, the lack of representation of any Latin@s as central characters is staggering and somewhat stupefying.

Entertainment media are attempting to approximate Latin@s through the production of some content. In 2014, the U.S. television network CW released *Jane the Virgin*, a comedy-drama that was adapted from the original Venezuelan soap opera, *Juana la virgen*. Members of the main cast of the series are Latin@s. Written and produced by Jennie Snyder Urman, the series has won Peabody and Golden Globe awards, proving that a program with primarily Latin@ characters can draw a consistent audience and does not always have to reaffirm gender and ethnic stereotypes to gain acclaim and an audience.[4] In accepting the award for "Best Actress in a Comedy Series" in 2015, Gina Rodriguez stated, "This award is so much more than myself. It represents a culture that wants to see themselves as heroes" (Zeilinger 2015). The series *Jane the Virgin*, and *Ugly Betty* before it, which was also an adaptation from the Colombian *Betty la fea*, include attempts to market programming to Latino audiences.

### *Consumers, But Not Producers*

In the world of entertainment media, Latino groups are pursued as a market, but less so as actual producers of content. In some cases, their presence on camera has increased slightly in corporate media channels, but Hollywood, cable, and other corporate entertainment media have a far less stellar record in providing avenues for Latinos to be in decision-making positions such as producers, directors, and managers. In other words, the powers that control mainstream entertainment media are willing to target programming to Latinos, but less willing to give up control and enable Latinos and Latinas to create programs and represent/present themselves.

Among mainstream television entertainment producers, Latinos represented only 1.1 percent of producers, 2 percent of writers, and 4.1 percent of directors, according to the Latino Media Gap report. Data show that there is an overrepresentation of Latin@s in the box office: they constitute 17 percent of the total population, but include 32 percent of viewers who went to the movies in 2013 (Negrón-Muntaner et al. 2014).

## The "Hispanic Market"

While the growth of Hispanics as consumers has been substantial (1.5 trillion, according to Nielsen 2014b), it has been barely significant when examining the participation of Latin@s in media production or management roles. The growing buying power of Latinos has been recognized by major corporations who decided to invest in the Hispanic market, particularly in the Spanish-language broadcast media. According to Nielsen (2014a), the Hispanic radio audience grew by more than 500,000 listeners in 2013. Nearly 40 million Hispanics use the radio every week, with a slight male majority (53 percent), 67 percent mostly outside home, and in the morning between 6 a.m. and 10 a.m. Hispanic consumers spend about $135 a year on music (above the average, $105) and $72 on concerts and festivals (above the average, $48). There are more than 500 Spanish-language radio stations around the country. These stations are heavily geared toward entertainment programming, with only 30 out of the 500 stations offering news and talk radio programs (Pew Center Research 2014). The latest data on Latino-oriented TV also reflect a growing pattern in the industry. In 2000, there were only 17 Spanish-language TV stations on cable, by 2010 there were already over 70, and in 2015 there were 134 (Retis and Badillo 2015).

## Self-Representation in the Digital Age: Challenges and Opportunities

The digital era has brought with it a new set of opportunities and challenges for Latin@ representation in news and entertainment media. Advances in technology have facilitated production of content. At the same time, audiences are fragmented, and past scholarship has demonstrated that people tend to watch and gravitate toward programming and information that fits within and reinforces their worldviews (Abrams and Giles 2007; Katz, Blumler, and Gurevitch 1974). In other words, through new media and technology, more members of Latino groups are creating their own programming but, in general, the impact of these program forms on mass audiences has been limited. At the same time, while the Hollywood film industry and mainstream media have not kept up with demographic realities, the digital media picture has improved somewhat. Of the 50 most-watched channels on YouTube.com, 18 percent are produced either by Latin@s or feature Latino-oriented content. The digital media landscape has opened doors for an increase in entertainment and informational programs about Latinos/as that are produced by Latinos/as (Negrón-Muntaner 2014).

When consumer behaviors are taken into consideration, the possibilities are bright for Latin@s who are poised to produce digital programming for Latin@ groups. Recent surveys indicated that Latin@s displayed the largest increase in Internet usage, greater than that of non-Hispanic blacks or non-Hispanic whites. The rapid growth of Latino homes with access solely to cellular telephones and not landlines reveals an increase in other forms of technology (Livingstone, Parker, and Fox 2009). A 2013 study found that Hispanics are more likely than non-Hispanics to consider a cell phone a necessity as opposed to a luxury (59 percent), a figure that is significantly higher than that of non-Hispanic whites (46 percent) and non-Hispanic blacks (46 percent). Forty-nine percent of all Hispanic mobile telephone users send and receive text messages (López, Barrera, and Patten 2013).

Hispanic consumers are ahead in the digital curve as they have quickly adopted multi-screen practices in video consumption, represent 47 million traditional viewers, and continue to grow. They spend more time watching videos on digital devices, with an average of 8 hours per month, which is 90 minutes more than the U.S. average. Latino consumers are acquiring smart-phones at a faster rate than any other demographic group; almost three out of four Hispanics have a smart-phone (72 percent), 10 percent above the U.S. average (10 million watch videos on their phones, with an average of 6 hours per month) and play videogames about 8 hours per month, almost an hour more than the general population (Nielsen 2014b). These data speak of active digital consumers and a growing trend, data that have already been noted by private companies that are producing new synergies in the production and distribution of cultural goods and services (Retis and Badillo 2015).

## *The Significance of Spanish-Language Media*

As they have in the past, Spanish-language media continue to play an important role in shaping and reflecting the identity of Latin@ communities throughout the United States. Báez and Castañeda (2014) found that Spanish-language media portrayals of Latin@s involved in the mortgage crisis included voices of those affected and, thus, provided alternative perspectives. In other words, those most directly involved in the crisis were not mere numbers, but were depicted as human beings who were struggling through a challenging time. The advocacy role of Spanish-language media has been noted in other studies (Casillas 2014; Vigon, Bustos-Martinez and González de Bustamante 2012).

In 2014, audiences grew for the nation's second largest Spanish-language network, Telemundo, while they dipped a bit for the largest Spanish-language network, Univision (Pew Research Center 2015). At the same time, revenue for Spanish-language media saw growth in 2014. The same study showed that the behavior of Spanish-language media consumers is changing, in that more often they use their mobile devices instead of desktops to access information and content produced by Univision and Telemundo (Pew Research Center 2015). Despite the important role of Spanish-language media in presenting and representing Latin@ voices in the media, there has been a decline in audiences. Part of this trend relates to demographic shifts that demonstrate that much of the growth of Latin@s in the United States since 2000 is the result of U.S. births of Latin@s rather than new immigrants. Further, about six out of ten adult Latinos/as speak English or are bilingual (Pew Research Center 2015).

## *Emerging Avenues for Latin@ Representations and Research*

English-language outlets such as Fusion.net target millennials, presenting a variety of news content, including "news and views from the other Americas" (fusion.net). The network also features programs such as "America with Jorge Ramos," designed to attract young Latino/a viewers. Other news and informational websites such as New America Media, AJ+, and Huffingtonpost.com are creating journalism that includes voices of various ethnic and racial groups, but their reach is limited. They offer a counter-narrative, but those watching these newcomers to the net are often familiar with the issues related to Latin@s. They tend not to attract viewers who are watching mainstream television and those who could benefit from hearing and seeing alternative points of view. In other words, what ends up happening is a sort of "preaching to the choir" type of media pattern and behavior that does little to further the diversity of representation of ethnic groups. Over time, as media consumers continue to shift away from the small screen (television) to mobile devices, the full picture of representation could change, but for now, some groups continue to be largely underrepresented.

The Internet and YouTube allow almost anyone with a connection and the right digital equipment to produce their own content for people around the world to see. Further, according to some experts, the future of high-quality programming is on the Internet and this is where Latin@s can be included in a larger part of the media landscape in terms of both representation and production. Latin@ producers are making their mark in a variety of online and digital platforms, individually, in joint ventures, and through Latin@-focused media associations.

In 2013, Robert Rodriguez created El Rey Network, a 24-hour English-language cable venture that offers programming to about 40 million U.S. cable subscribers to Comcast and Time Warner Cable and to DirecTV customers. The Texas-based network has a distinctly Latino point of view, and its programming includes a wrestling series, "Lucha Underground," based on the Mexican lucha libre sport, a variation of wrestling (Spangler 2015). In addition, Rodriguez has moved beyond traditional methods of casting; the creator of the Spy Kids series has gone online to search for talent (Spangler 2015). He has also teamed up with Jeff Gomez, CEO of Starlight Runner and a leader in transmedia approaches to content, to produce a host of multiplatform products around the *Lucha Libre* series.

Organizations such as the National Association of Latino Independent Producers (NALIP) have worked to support the development of Latin@ producers and directors. According to NALIP, since its creation in 1999, the organization has grown to more than 40,000 members online. The group supports up-and-coming directors through training and development programs such as the Latino Producers Academy and the Latino Writers Lab. In 2015, NALIP created LatinoLens, which concentrates on the following four areas: narrative, digital/tech, documentary, and TV/streaming (NALIP 2015). While the examples discussed above are viewed as positive steps, and perhaps they are harbingers of what could come in the future, at present, they remain exceptions to the general media landscape.

Given the challenges and structural factors that have excluded Latin@s from fully participating in the media landscape, the authors reaffirm a call for further research. We find valuable the suggestion made by Anguiano and Castañeda (2014) to approach the subject from an interdisciplinary and CRT perspective. The authors also suggest that, given the geopolitical factors that have influenced migration patterns, scholarship should examine the topic of representation from a transnational perspective. There are numerous questions and areas of import that remain unanswered or unclear, such as: the grand paradox between targeting Latin@s as consumers, but not as producers; the continued lack of diversity in newsrooms; the exclusion and symbolic annihilation of Latin@s on the big and small screens; and analyses of content produced by general media, alternative media, and by Latin@s themselves. Without continued and further research on the subject, students and scholars alike are left scratching their heads about the disconnect between the demographic realities and contemporary patterns of Latin@ media production and (mis)representation.

## Notes

1 The authors opt for the terms Latin@s (Latinos/as) and Hispanics interchangeably to refer to U.S.-born men and women of Latin-American origin, as well as immigrants from nations in Latin America and the Caribbean. Both terms are used throughout the United States, although the term Hispanic is more frequently used in the eastern part of the US, while Latino/a is used more frequently in the western US, even though the majority (54 percent) tend to identify with their country of origin and only 24 percent prefer the usage of these panethnic labels (Taylor et al. 2012).
2 The annexation of more than half of the country of Mexico and the Puerto Rican territory resulted in the incorporation of major Latin@ groups, and after WWII, the Bracero Program brought around 100,000 workers a year. The guest-worker program would last in one form or another until 1965, when it ended (González 2011: 103). During the latter half of the twentieth century, the expansion of U.S. economic and political intervention in Latin America led to population flows in the opposite direction of U.S. capital interests in the region (Retis 2006, 2014).
3 The groups that arrived during the second half of the twentieth century settled in "ethnic enclaves" (Portes and Wilson 1980) formed in previous decades by other Latin@s due to strengthening of transnational immigrant networks (Menjivar 1997; Hodagneu-Sotelo 1994) consolidating initial processes of geographical concentration.
4 It should be noted that while in some cases the series breaks from some ethnic stereotypes, it continues to reinforce a somewhat stereotypical gendered image of the "hot" and highly sexualized Latina.

## References

Abrams, J. R. and Giles, H. (2007) "Ethnic Identity Gratifications Selections and Avoidance by African Americans: A Group Vitality and Social Identity Gratifications Perspective," *Media Psychology* 9: 115–134.
Anguiano, C. and Castañeda, M. (2014) "Forging a Path: Past and Present Scope of Critical Race Theory in Communication Studies," *The Review of Communication* 14(2): 107–124.
ASNE. (2015) "American Society of News Editors Newsroom Census (various years)." Retrieved from http://asne.org/.
Báez, J. and Castañeda, M. (2014) "Two Sides to the Same Story: Media Narratives of Latinos and the Subprime Mortgage Crisis," *Critical Studies in Media Communication* 31(1): 27–41.
Canales, A. (2011) "Las Profundas Contribuciones de la Migración Latinoamericana a los Estados Unidos," in J. Martínez (ed.), *Migración Internacional en América Latina y el Caribe. Nuevas Tendencias, Nuevos Enfoques*. Santiago de Chile, Chile: CEPAL, 257–331.
Chao, R. (2012) "Law, Social Policy, and the Latina/o Education Pipeline, Research Report," UCLA Chicano Studies Research Center, 1–5.
Dávila, A. (2001) *Latinos Inc.: The Marketing and Making of a People*. Berkeley, CA: University of California Press.
Delgado, R. and Stefancic, J. (2012) *Critical Race Theory: An Introduction*. 2nd ed. New York: New York University Press.
Dixon, T. L. and Williams C. L. (2015) "The Changing Misrepresentation of Race and Crime on Network and Cable News," *Journal of Communication* 65: 24–39.
Entman, R. and Rojecki, A. (2000) *The Black Image in the White Mind: Media and Race in America*. Chicago, IL: University of Chicago Press.
Fiske, S. and Taylor, S. E. (1991) *Social Cognition*. New York: McGraw-Hill.
Fregoso, R. L. (2003) *MeXicana Encounters: The Making of Social Identities on the Borderlands*. Berkeley, CA: University of California Press.
Gonzalez, J. (2011) *Harvest of Empire. A History of Latinos in America*. New York: Penguin.
Harklau, L. (2009) "Heritage Speakers' Experiences in New Latino Diaspora Spanish Classrooms," *Critical Inquiry in Language Studies* 6(4): 211–242.

IMDb (International Movie Database). (2015) *San Andreas*. Retrieved from http://www.imdb.com/title/tt2126355/.

Iñárritu, A. G. (2015) "On Stage Speech Transcript: Best Picture," Academy of Motion Picture Arts and Sciences, Beverly Hills, CA. Retrieved from http://www.oscars.org/press/onstage-speech-transcript-best-picture.

Katz, E., Blumler, J. G., and Gurevitch, M. (1974) "Utilization of Mass Communication by the Individual," in J. G. Blumler and E. Katz (eds.), *The Uses of Mass Communications: Current Perspectives on Gratifications Research*. Beverly Hills, CA: Sage, 19–32.

Molina Guzman, I. (2005) "Gendering Latinidad through the Elian News Discourse about Cuban Women," *Latino Studies* 3: 179–204.

———. (2006) "Mediating Frida: Negotiating Discourses of Latina/o Authenticity in Global Media Representations of Ethnic Identity," *Critical Studies in Media Communication* 23(3): 232–251.

Molina Guzman, I. and Valdivia, A. N. (2010) "Disciplining the Ethnic Body: Latinidad, Hybridized Bodies, and Transnational Identities," in L. Reed and P. Saukko (eds.), *Governing the Female Body: Science, Media and the Production of Femininity*. Albany, NY: SUNY Press, 206–231.

NAHJ. (2006) *The Portrayal of Latinos and Latino Issues on Network Television News, 2004, with a Retrospect to 2005*. Washington, D.C.: National Association of Hispanic Journalists.

———. (2014) *The 2014 State of Hispanic Journalists Report: Hispanic Journalists' Beliefs about Their Careers, Technology and Social Media*. Washington, D.C.: National Association of Hispanic Journalists.

———. (2015) *The 2015 State of Hispanic Journalists Report: Hispanic Journalists' Beliefs about Their Careers, Technology and Social Media*. Washington, D.C.: National Association of Hispanic Journalists.

NALIP. (2015) "A Year in Highlight for Latino Content Creators." National Association of Latino Independent Producers. Retrieved from http://www.nalip.org/a_year_in_highlight_for_latino_content_creators_nalip_2015.

National Council of La Raza. (1994) *Out of the Picture: Hispanics in the Media in the State of Hispanic America*. Washington, D.C.: NCLR.

Negrón-Muntaner, F. (2014) "The Latino Media Gap." Report on the State of Latinos in U.S. Media, National Association of Latino Independent Producers.

Nelson, J. (2015, June 10) "Dwayne Johnson Black? Hollywood Doesn't Seem to Think So," *Atlanta Blackstar*. Retrieved from http://atlantablackstar.com/2015/06/10/is-dwayne-johnson-black-hollywood-doesnt-seem-to-think-so/.

Nielsen. (2012) "State of the Hispanic Consumer: The Hispanic Market Imperative, Quarter 2." New York: The Nielsen Company.

———. (2013) "Latino Populations Are Growing Fastest Where We Aren't Looking," New York: The Nielsen Company. Retrieved from http://www.nielsen.com/us/en/insights/news/2013/latino-populations-are-growing-fastest-where-we-arent-looking.html.

———. (2014a) *Listen Up. Hispanic Consumers and Music*. New York: The Nielsen Company.

———. (2014b) *The Digital Consumer*. New York: The Nielsen Company.

Noriega, C. (2000) *Shot in America: Television, the State, and the Rise of Chicano Cinema*. Minneapolis, MN: University of Minnesota Press.

Orbe, M. P. and Allen, B. J. (2008) "'Race Matters' in the *Journal of Applied Communication Research*," *Howard Journal of Communications* 19: 201–220.

Pew Research Center. (2015) "A Majority of English Speaking Hispanics in US Are Bilingual," Pew Research Center. Retrieved from http://www.pewresearch.org/fact-tank/2015/03/24/a-majority-of-english-speaking-hispanics-in-the-u-s-are-bilingual/.

Ramirez Berg, C. (2009) *Latino Images in Film: Stereotypes, Subversion and Resistance*. Austin, TX: University of Texas Press.

Retis, J. (2006) "El Discurso Público Sobre la Inmigración Extracomunitaria en España: Análisis de la Construcción de las Imágenes de los Inmigrantes Latinoamericanos en la Prensa de Referencia." Doctoral dissertation, Universidad Complutense de Madrid.

———. (2013) "Immigrant Latina Images in Mainstream Media: Class, Race and Gender in Public Discourses of the United States and Spain," in M. Lirola (ed.), *Discourses on Immigration in Times of Economic Crisis: A Critical Perspective*. London: Cambridge Scholars Publishing, 28–58.

———. (2014) "Inmigrantes Territoriales/Inmigrantes Digitales: Latinoamericanos en Contextos Diaspóricos," in G. Carbone and O. Quezada (eds.), *Comunicación e Industria Digital*. Lima, Peru: Universidad de Lima.

Retis, J. and Badillo, A. (2015) *Los Latinos y las Industrias Culturales en Español en Estados Unidos*. Madrid, Spain: Real Instituto Elcano.

Retis, J. and Caballero, F. S. (2011) "Rethinking Latin American Communicology in the Age of Nomad Culture: Transnational Consumption and Cultural Hybridizations," *Westminster Papers in Communication and Culture* 8(1): 102–130.

Santa Ana, O. (2013) *Juan in a Hundred: The Representation of Latinos on Network News*. Austin, TX: University of Texas Press.

Santa Ana, O. and González de Bustamante, C. (2012) *Arizona Firestorm: Global Immigration Realities, National Media and Provincial Politics*. New York: Rowman and Littlefield.

Spangler, T. (2015, June 29) "Robert Rodriguez's El Rey Network Wants to Find Talent on the Internet," *Variety*. Retrieved from http://variety.com/2015/digital/news/robert-rodriguezs-el-rey-network-wants-to-find-talent-on-internet-1201530420/.

Spence, J., Rojas, V., and Straubhaar, J. (2011) "Generational Shifts in Language Use among U.S. Latinos: Mobility, Education and Occupation," *International Migration* 51(5): 172–191.

Taylor, P., Lopez, M. H., Martínez, J., and Velasco, G. (2012) *When Labels Don't Fit. Hispanics and Their Views of Identity*. Washington, D.C.: Pew Hispanic Center.

Tuchman, G. (1978) "Introduction: The Symbolic Annihilation of Women by the Mass Media," in G. Tuchman, A. K. Daniels, and J. Benet (eds.), *Health and Home: Images of Women in the Mass Media*. New York: Oxford University Press, 3–38.

U.S. Census Bureau. (2015) "Millennials Outnumber Baby Boomers and Are Far More Diverse, Census Bureau Reports." Retrieved from http://www.census.gov/newsroom/press-releases/2015/cb15-113.html.

Valdivia, A. (2000) *A Latina in the Land of Hollywood and Other Essays on Media Culture*. Tucson, AZ: University of Arizona Press.

——. (2010) *Latino/as and the Media*. Malden, MA: Polity Press.

——. (2011) "Building a Feminist Trajectory," *Communication, Culture and Critique* 4: 355–360.Vargas, L. (2000) "Genderizing Latino News: An Analysis of Local Newspaper's Coverage of Latino Current Affairs," *Critical Studies in Media Communication* 17(3): 261–293.

Wilson, C., Gutiérrez, F., and Chao, L (2004) *Racism, Sexism, and the Media: The Rise of Class Communication in Multicultural America*. New York: Sage.

Yosso, T. and Solórzano, D. (2006) "Leaks in the Chicana and Chicano Educational Pipeline, Latino Policy and Issues Brief," *UCLA Chicano Studies* 13: 1–4.

Yúdice, G. (2009) *Culturas Emergentes en el Mundo Hispano de Estados Unidos*. Madrid, Spain: Fundación Alternativas.

Zeilinger, J. (2015, Feb. 8) "6 Ways *Jane the Virgin* Is Destroying Latino Stereotypes," mic.com. Retrieved from http://mic.com/articles/110768/6-ways-jane-the-virgin-is-destroying-latino-stereotypes#.F1ipNZTHL.

# Further Reading

Dávila, A. (2001) *Latinos Inc. The Marketing and Making of a People*. Berkeley, CA: University of California Press. (Dávila's work is essential reading to understand the connections between marketing, consumerism, and ethnicity.)

Delgado, R. and Stefancic, J. (2012) *Critical Race Theory: An Introduction*. 2nd ed. New York: New York University Press. (An important introductory work on Critical Race Theory.)

Gonzalez, J. (2011) *Harvest of Empire: A History of Latinos in America*. New York: Penguin. (Describes and explains the long history of Latinos and Latinas in the United States and the important contributions they have made.)

Wilson, C., Gutiérrez, F., and Chao, L. (2004) *Racism, Sexism, and the Media: The Rise of Class Communication in Multicultural America*. New York: Sage. (This work should be required reading for anyone interested in understanding how race, gender, and class intersect in the media.)

# 20
# NATIVE AMERICANS
## The Denial of Humanity
### Debra Merskin

If you are among the 99 percent of Americans who are not Native American,[1] and know Indians[2] mostly through media representations, who do you think they are? Savages? Squaws? Princesses? Children of Nature? If you are Native, the few messages you do receive via the mass media and popular culture are either that you exist only in the past (*Dances with Wolves*, *500 Nations*) or, if shown more contemporarily, work almost exclusively in casinos (*The Killing*, *Big Love*) or in law enforcement (*Banshee*). The symbolic annihilation of Indian peoples is an ethical issue for communication scholars and practitioners. Stereotypical representations not only reinforce dehumanizing and limiting views of the capabilities, appearances, and cultures of Native people to themselves (internalized oppression) and to non-Indians, but also support "structural exclusions and cultural imagining [that] leave minority members vulnerable to a system of violence," both symbolically and actually (Perry 2002: 232). This chapter provides an overview of media portrayals of Native Americans. The first section contextualizes these representations by briefly discussing contemporary conditions of being Native in America. This is followed by a description of the history of representations of American Indians in several mass media forms (cinema, newspapers, television) and a discussion of debates related to research in this area, concluding with critical perspectives and debates in scholarship.

### Setting the Stage

What does it mean to be Native American in the twenty-first century? On one hand, there is the numerical designation and on the other, the symbolic. In the first case, if you are among the 5.2 million individuals who, according to the U.S. Census, self-identify as American Indian/Alaska Native or almost half of that number who indicate they are fully American Indian/Alaska Native, you likely belong to one of the more than 560 federally recognized tribes. The largest tribes are Navajo (Diné), Cherokee, Sioux, and Chippewa. Many (approximately 40 percent) people claiming American Indian/Alaska Native as race live in the Western region of the United States, followed by the South (33 percent), Midwest (17 percent), or North East (10 percent). The cities with the largest populations of American Indian and Alaska Native alone or in combination are New York and Los Angeles. The greatest concentration of an Indian population is in Anchorage, Alaska. In terms of lived experiences, Indians are subjects of higher rates of violence and higher incarceration rates than the general population (Freng 2007). The suicide rate among American Indian/Alaska Natives is more than double that of other groups, particularly during adolescence and young adulthood (Frieden 2011). There is more binge drinking, higher alcohol and tobacco use, and the highest poverty rates of any racial group. Long enduring, inaccurately informed, and poorly conceived representations of Native people also contribute to the way they are treated by the criminal justice system (Ross 1998). As Jackson (1992, cited in Ross: 184) points out: "The . . . stereotypical view of Native people . . . . being drunk and in prison . . . influence[s] decisions of the police, prosecutors, judges, and prison officials."

Relative to other U.S. minority groups, however, Indians are under 1 percent of the total U.S. population. Typically, because of small sample sizes, statistics about this group result in their being made invisible by assignment to the "Other" category of research findings (Frieden 2011). This means that they do not represent a significant target audience for advertisers in terms of numbers and spending power. In addition, although tribal gaming has economically helped, Native people living on reservations are among the poorest of all minority groups. Therefore, in terms of population, numbers of significance don't speak to advertisers and activism is often misconstrued as violent due in part to the very stereotypes that define them.

The other way of thinking about Native Americans is that being Indian is also a mediated representation. In North America, for more than 500 years, the symbolic construction of Indian-ness that has taken place in the minds and imaginations of outsiders is largely a result of media and popular press representations, the subject of the next section. As Berkhofer (1979) observed, "The idea and the image of the Indian must be a White conception. Native Americans were and are real, but the *Indian* was a White invention and remains largely a White image" (3).

## Smoke and Shadows

> You know the only thing more pathetic than Indians on TV? Indians watching Indians on TV.
>
> *(Thomas in Smoke Signals)*

How are Native Americans characterized in the contemporary, mainstream, popular imagination? Stereotypes, defined as over-generalized, one-dimensional "reductionist beliefs, are collections of traits or characteristics that present members of a group as being all the same" (Merskin 2011a: 142). These signifying mental practices persist today; their origins are in fear-based constructions of the past.

Images of Indians can be traced at least as far back as the arrival of Europeans on the North American continent. Excerpts from Columbus' 1492 journal present Native peoples as childlike, easily impressed, and naïve. At the time, "there were approximately ten to twelve million people" already living in the land that would become the United States (Ross 1998: 11). These were politically strong, independent, culturally complex peoples with distinctive histories and cultures. During days of Colonial America, a few accounts spoke positively about Native people and the sophistication of their cultures. For example, Francis Daniel Pastorius[3] wrote in 1700, "The natives, the so-called savages . . . have never in their lives heard the teaching of Jesus concerning temperance and contentment, yet they far excel the Christians in carrying it out" (contributing to the child-of-nature image). Most writings, however, were fueled by fears of the wilderness as a dark, unknown, dangerous, even demonic place (to which Native people belonged). Many white colonists and explorers saw First Nations people as less than human and as impediments to taking land they believed they were naturally entitled to. To justify removal, relocation, and eventually, extermination, it was therefore necessary to construct propagandist versions of Indian-ness. Captivity narratives, stories of abduction and assimilation of whites (usually women) by Indians, published in America in the eighteenth and nineteenth centuries, drew on an old English tradition. These tales were an essential part of the construction of Indians as thieves, marauders, and rapists. While hostage-taking is a usual part of war, captivity narratives such as *The History of Maria Kittle* (Bleeker 1793) mixed actual events with fictional fillers to create tales of trial, tribulation, and sometimes redemptions, but more times than not, depictions of Native masculinity were created specifically as threats to white womanhood.

In the 1800s, stereotypical images of Native Americans were constructed in children's games, magazines, and newspaper stories, on the covers of sheet music, and in theatrical performances. The cigar store Indian presents as one of the main stereotypes of Native men—the stoic noble savage who simultaneously guards the store entrance but also complies with white rules of "no dogs or Indians allowed." Similarly, the Indian "princess" is used to convey natural, wholesome virginity and freshness to products such as Land O'Lakes butter or Sue Bee Honey. The oppositional squaw/drudge is the "anti-Pocahontas":

> Where the princess was beautiful, the squaw was ugly, even deformed. Where the princess was virtuous, the squaw was debased, immoral, a sexual convenience. Where the princess was proud, the squaw lived a squalid life of servile toil, mistreated by her men—and openly available to non-Native men.
> (Francis 1995: 121–2)

These portrayals were widely distributed with the introduction and popularity of cinema. In 1890, at the same time as motion pictures were invented, the U.S. 7th Calvary, led by General George Armstrong Custer, killed hundreds of American Indian men, women, and children at Wounded Knee on the Pine Ridge Reservation in North Dakota. This genocide secured the place of Indians in the white European imagination as mythological, subsumed, tragic, and metaphorical in a romanticized view of the past. From 1883 until around 1913, Wild West Shows such as Buffalo Bill Cody's toured the nation with demonstrations by "wild" Indians, some of whom were survivors of the horrors of the expansionist genocide. Many of the extras were paid in tobacco and alcohol. The important leading roles were not played by Indians, but rather by whites in "redface." These onscreen betrayals continued throughout the twentieth century.

At the same time, however, Indian actors, directors, and producers started making their own movies, telling their own stories. James Youngdeer (of the Nanticoke tribe) was the first American Indian director/producer/actor/writer. He and Lillian St. Cyr (Winnebago) produced single-reel Westerns during the silent film era that positively portrayed Indians. *The Silent Enemy* (i.e., starvation) was a 1930 independent film that intentionally steered away from the war-whooping stereotypical depictions. The attempt was a more naturalistic, historically accurate documentary-style film shot in Northern Ontario. While the goal was to capture a "vanishing" way of life, the motivations were truer than in studio productions.

The population of Native Americans was at an all-time low (estimates of fewer than 250,000 individuals) and the idea of the vanishing Indian quite real. Several photographers

(John Throssel, Crow) and filmmakers made their own media and told different stories than their white counterparts. This auteurship continued through the 1930s.

Films of the 1930s–60s were created mostly through a non-Indian lens. They included I(i)ndians, but the only successful productions were those that reified the formulaic savage image, nowhere more evident than in the genre of Westerns. Cowboy and I(i)ndian movies such as *Stagecoach*, by director John Ford, typified the static story structure: innocent white people besieged by indians (who stand in the way of progress and are brutal, ruthless, and a threat to white women). "Tonto-speak" (broken English) was employed as a narrative device that contributed to the stereotype of Indians as unassailable, ignorant, naïve, and childlike. The typical film had a white hero encounter wild, untamable "savages." White men in "redface" also played indian roles. Charlton Heston, Victor Mature, Chuck Connors, Burt Reynolds, and others donned heavy make-up, wrapped a headband around their foreheads (Indians don't wear headbands), and pretended to be indians (redface). This is no less problematic than white actors in black or yellowface. The monolithic Plains Indian of Hollywood and advertising is often some combination of randomly assigned "indian" dress, i.e., beads, feathers, and headdresses regardless of gender, with little to no regard for the tribe to which the person might belong. Screen legend John Wayne stood in for the mythological loner hero who was tough, fearless, and above all else, justified in fulfilling Manifest Destiny no matter the price.

White women often played Native women as well. Except for the princess and a few abused older Indian women, Native American women have been largely invisible in films. The mythic princess image is particularly powerful as it often forms the basis for non-Indian children's image of Indian women. Thus, the desire Disney's highly historically inaccurate *Pocahontas* portrays is one of impossible-to-achieve female beauty wrapped up in buckskin and self-sacrificing for the white hero's life and liberty.

There is less research on news representations of Native Americans. News, "which purports to deal in fact, not fiction, which seeks to inform as well as entertain, plays by a different set of rules from popular culture or literature or advertising" (Weston 1996: 2). Whereas readers and viewers know that films, advertisements, and other popular representations might be fantasy based, there is an expectation that news represents an accurate view of the world. While today newspapers stories about Indians are mostly limited to powwows and casinos, the frontier press emphasized three major stereotypes we still see today: Noble Savage, Bad Indian, and Degraded Drunken Indian (Berkhofer 1979). The Noble Savage was "the good Indian [who] appears friendly, courteous, and hospitable to the invaders of his land" (28). The Bad Indian is the dark, sexually promiscuous, thieving, naked savage. Representations of Native Americans as savages, in whatever form, reduce an entire people to the status of object, and "within the traditional Western conceptualization of the world mere natural objects have no moral standing" (Green 1993: 323). Finally, the Degraded Drunken Indian is inassimilable, scorned, and pathetic. In his study of press coverage of eight "watershed events in Native American history from 1862–1891," Reilly (2010) concludes that the frontier press, which was closer to the conflicts, actually did a better job and had more accurate, less stereotypical coverage than did national newspapers.

What was different about Western United States frontier press coverage compared with that in the East was the "tyranny of distance" (Blainey 1968/2001) and that reporters couldn't interview "the other side," i.e., the Indians. For many readers, the encounters were not only geographically far away, but also emotionally and psychologically. The mythological narratives of frontier battles were influenced by legend: "To the open spaces of the West . . . journalism has added its own mystique" (Reilly

2010: xxi). In a study of mainstream twentieth-century newspaper and magazine coverage of Native Americans, Weston (1996) wrote not about Indians but rather about the coverage of them and the role coverage might have had in shaping views of Native peoples and influencing public policy.

News coverage is situated in historical moments and yet the "official view of how Native Americans should be treated shifted from forced assimilation to cultural pluralism to termination to limited self-determination" (4). As such, representations in the press remained relatively static.

> The very conventions and practice of journalism have worked to reinforce that popular and often inaccurate imagery—[stories of conflict, the unusual, the bizarre]. Stereotyping does not depend only on the use of crude language or factual inaccuracies. It also comes from the choice of stories to report, the way the stories are organized and written, the phrases used in the headlines.
>
> *(163)*

News media coverage of the occupation of Alcatraz Island by the American Indian Movement (AIM) (1969–71) put Indians in front of non-Indians, but the representation showed activism as violence. In 1973, another standoff with authorities took place in the community of Wounded Knee, South Dakota when U.S. federal officials seized land occupied for 71 days by 200 Oglala Lakota and AIM members on the Pine Ridge Reservation. The previous summer, members gathered to discuss the many (371) broken treaties, the high unemployment rate, poverty, and police brutality. On February 27, heavily armed federal troops surrounded the poorly supplied, cold, and hungry protestors who sought retribution for past and present dishonors and demanded an investigation into corruption in the Federal Bureau of Indian Affairs (BIA), misuse of tribal funds, strip mining of the land, and restoration of promises such as honoring the 1868 treaty that said the Black Hills of South Dakota belonged to the Sioux people.

Oddly, an inaccurate and somewhat absurd movie (*Billy Jack*) along with an act of civil disobedience at that year's Academy Awards helped restore hope and renew faith among the tribe. At the Academy Awards, when Marlon Brando was announced as the winner of the Best Actor award for *The Godfather*, Shasheen Littlefeather (Apache, Yaqui, Pueblo), dressed in full tribal regalia, spoke in his place, saying Brando declined the award, "because of the treatment of American Indians today by the film industry . . . . And also with recent happenings at Wounded Knee." The audience response was both cheers and boos. Littlefeather apologized for interrupting the evening, and then followed with it being her hope that "in the future . . . our hearts and our understandings will meet with love and generosity." According to the documentary *Reel Injuns* (Diamond 2009), the Sioux at Wounded Knee who saw this surprising act of resistance felt supported and heard.

Despite mediated moments of visibility, fictionalized and stereotypical notions of indian people persist in films, advertising, and popular culture. Appropriation continued of so-called Indian ways at summer camp reenactments, in Halloween costumes, Thanksgiving pageants, mock tribal naming and sweat lodge practices, ecstatic dancing, tribal games, and overall imitating Indian people as children of nature, and is still found today. Little in popular discourse serves to contradict these one-dimensional, inaccurate narratives. Imitating magical Indians is something non-Indians often do. The 1990s saw a revitalization of the nostalgia trope, "the reenacting and re-ritualizing . . . the imperialist, colonizing journey as narrative fantasy of power and desire, of seduction by the

Other" (hooks 1992: 25). The 1990s looked to be an era of setting the record right: Ted Turner's[4] mini-series *500 Nations* and films such as *Dances with Wolves* (1990) and *Last of the Mohicans* (1992) seemed like a step in that direction. However, these expressions solidified the indian as living only in the past. Native American director Chris Ayre's *Smoke Signals* (1998, based on the Sherman Alexie short story) was the first all-Indian starred-in, directed, produced, and written feature film in nearly 70 years. That same year two other Native-directed films also premiered at the Sundance Film Festival: *Tushka* (Ian Skorodin, Chocataw) and *Naturally Native* (Valerie Red-Horse, Cherokee/Sioux). However, in the 2000s, the blockbuster success of the *Twilight* franchise has overshadowed new representations of Native masculinity and perpetuated young Native men as animalistic and highly sexual.

Only the television series *Northern Exposure* (1990–5) offered a more realistic narrative about being Indian. The outsider perspective was still in place, by telling the story of a white doctor who is sent to a tiny Alaskan community. But the program sympathetically presented Indians as complex, everyday people, not a mass of undifferentiated types. Unfortunately it was and is the only television representation like this.

Since the early twentieth century, American Indian images, music, and names have also been incorporated into many American advertising campaigns, marketing efforts, and commercial labeling. These continue to demarcate and consume the indian as the exotic Other in the popular imagination (Ganje 2011; Merskin 2001, 2011a, 2011b, 2014). Today, products on grocery and department stores shelves still bear faces and names that are entirely fanciful, constructed by outsiders, or that rightly belong to American Indian individuals and tribes. The savage stereotype as mascot for the Florida State Seminoles football team or the University of Illinois Fighting Illini, for example, draws on portrayals of an evil, angry, generic indian pulled from literary and photographic sources of earlier times. The savage-as-signifier of death, vengeance, evil, and rage, when placed on a t-shirt, transfers meaning to the otherwise ambiguous product. Three primary representations of Native people, all derivations of the savage stereotype, persist today in brands, logos, and names: (1) Noble Savage—includes the image of a teary-eyed Native American chief who watches as the land is polluted and naming vehicles a (Jeep) Cherokee, Dakota, or Winnebago to associate it with qualities such as adaptability, ruggedness, and sense of adventure; (2) Enlightened Savage—the child-of-nature/first environmentalist stereotype; and (3) Bloodthirsty Savage—used as sports team mascots in name and image, such as the Atlanta Braves, Washington Redskins, Cleveland Indians, and Kansas City Chiefs (all of whom are still with us). These monikers are also applied to American military equipment such as Tomahawk Missiles and Black Hawk helicopters. As a result, the "savage" is thought of as an outsider, "merely an animal in human form" (Green 1993: 327); from which the Other developed in three representational directions that still apply today. The problem is that these representations are not contradicted by other information, or alternative views in mainstream media. Thus, the stereotypes persist, full of hegemonic potential. There is a consumer blind spot when it comes to these brand images and names because they are so long-standing and familiar. The red and white packaging of Big Chief Sugar, for example, alludes to red skin, as well as the company's Americana schema. Crazy Horse Malt Liquor, no longer available due to successful lawsuits by its descendants, combined the Noble Savage stereotype with a "proud, but ultimately defeated, Indian chief" (Merskin 2001: 168). While many of these products originated in what we might think of as less-enlightened times, the defense of a team name like Redskins remains. Furthermore, new products have been introduced that bear names, images, or associations: for example, the 1982 introduction of American Spirit cigarettes, owned by R. J. Reynolds. American Spirit visually, typographically, and symbolically brands itself by using the silhouette of a chief in full-feathered headdress, smoking a peace pipe (Merskin 2014).

## Critical Perspectives and Debates

Much of what is written, historically at least, about Native Americans is by non-Natives. Whether anthropological or historical, this literature has largely come from a non-Indian perspective. In a review of the book *The Invented Indian*, Vine DeLoria Jr. writes, "There never has been an objective point of view regarding Indians and there never will be. For most of the five centuries, whites have had unrestricted power to describe Indians in any way they chose," thereby creating "comfortable fictions" that veil the truth about what happened (1992: 397–98). Thus, "Indians were simply not connected to the organs of propaganda so that they could respond to the manner in which whites described them" (398). This includes a good deal of academic scholarship.

DeLoria further argues for reflexivity and that those writing in this area of scholarship with a social justice component should not pretend to be objective, but rather be open about their politics: "[A] political agenda is permissible—but just say so. Don't cloak the collection in a mist of piety, which purports to restore balance and objectivity to the modern scene" (398).

"Whites telling . . . other whites something about Indians" as if they know "the truth" is also problematic. Just as politics should be laid bare in reflexive writing, so should be one's genetics and lived experience (or lack thereof). This conflict speaks to an invented indian who is sometimes one's media-constructed self-image of Indian, and for others a sense of failed authenticity because the generated stereotype is so pervasive. For non-Indian others it is training that firmly implants stereotypes. Whoever speaks should speak from their heart—and do so reflexively. This perspective relates well to an ethics of representation that includes reflection upon who says what about whom and with what authority, not only in media representations but also scholarship. To declare some representations "bad," others good, chastise Native peoples for not stepping up and representing themselves the way the author thinks they should, or deciding that one knows the "right" representation is, in the end, not terribly productive. It might be more useful to think about what skills all researchers have, from insider knowledge to expertise on representation, social justice, semiotics, law, policy, and health. Participatory action research that draws on liberation psychology offers another useful path toward new knowledge.

What is at stake here not only concerns communication practices but also individual well-being. Children, Native American included, are perhaps the most important recipients of this information. If during the transition to adolescence, Native children internalize these stereotypical representations that suggest Indians are lazy, obligated to willingly provide their native/natural bounty to whites, alcoholic by nature, and violent, this misinformation can have a lifelong impact on perceptions of self and others.

To ignore history and continue presenting Native peoples in this limited way is a moral decision on the part of communications experts and corporations, "for, denying humanity to Native Americans, they thereby deny to them the possibility of receiving the moral standing and treatment that is due to them as human beings" (Green 1993: 329). Stereotyping communicates inaccurate beliefs about Natives not only to whites but also to Indians.

## Notes

1 The terms Indian, Native American, Indigenous North American, First Nations, American Indian, and Native are used interchangeably throughout this chapter in honor of individual preferences and histories.
2 Drawing on Klopotek, I use the uncapitalized term "indian" "which connotes the symbolic character of the white imagination, akin to a troll or an elf," and the upper-case term "Indian," to denote the people descended from the original human inhabitants of the Americas: "The purpose of making the distinction between indians and Native Americans in writing is to emphasize the extent to which the indian is truly a construction of the white imagination, having little resemblance to Native Americans. Of course the concept of any universal term or category for all the indigenous nations of the Americas is itself deeply rooted in colonialism, but such terms—for better or worse—have become more meaningful at the beginning of the 21st century" (Klopotek 2001: 20).
3 The founder of German Town, the first German settlement in Pennsylvania. http://nationalhumanitiescenter.org/pds/becomingamer/peoples/text3/indianscolonists.pdf.
4 Ironically, Turner owns the Atlanta Braves whose tomahawk-chopping fans celebrate the team with this racist gesture.

## References

Berkhofer, R. F. (1979) *The White Man's Indian*. New York: Vintage.
Blainey, G. (1968/2001) *The Tyranny of Distance: How Distance Shaped Australia's History*. Tuggerah, Australia: Pan Macmillan.
Bleeker, A. E. (1793/2009) *The History of Maria Kittle*. Gloucester, UK: Dodo Press.
DeLoria, V. Jr. (1992) "Comfortable Fictions and the Struggle for Turf," *American Indian Quarterly* 16(3): 397–410.
Diamond, N. (dir.) (2009) *Reel Injun*. [Motion Picture]. Rezolution Pictures and the National Film Board of Canada.
Francis, D. (1995) *The Imaginary Indian: The Image of the Indian in Canadian Culture*. 3rd ed. Vancouver, Canada: Arsenal Pulp Press.
Freng, A. (2007) "American Indians in the News: A Media Portrayal in Crime Articles," *American Indian Culture and Research* 31(1): 21–37.
Frieden, T. R. (2011, Jan. 14) "CDC Health Disparities and Inequalities Report: United States, 2011," Centers for Disease Control and Prevention. *Morbidity and Mortality Weekly Report* 60: 1–114.
Ganje, L. A. (2011) "Marketing the Sacred," in S. D. Ross and P. M. Lester (eds.), *Images that Injure*. New York: Praeger, 91–106.
Green, M. K. (1993) "Images of American Indians in Advertising: Some Moral Issues," *Journal of Business Ethics* 12: 323–330.
hooks, b. (1992) *Black Looks: Race and Representation*. New York: Routledge.
Jackson, M. (1989) "Locking Up Natives in Canada," *University of British Columbia Law Review* 23(2): 215–300.
Klopotek, B. (2001). "'I Guess Your Warrior Look Doesn't Work Every Time: Challenging Indian Masculinity in the Cinema," in M. Basso, L. McCall, and D. Garceau (eds.), *Across the Great Divide: Cultures of Manhood in the American West*. New York: Routledge, 251–274.
Merskin, D. (2001) "Winnebagos, Cherokees, Apaches, and Dakotas: The Persistence of Stereotyping of American Indians in American Advertising Brands," *Howard Journal of Communications* 12: 159–169.
——. (2011a) *Media, Minorities and Meaning: A Critical Introduction*. New York: Peter Lang.
——. (2011b) "The S-Word: Discourse, Stereotypes, and the American Indian Woman," *Howard Journal of Communications* 21: 345–366.
——. (2014) "How Many More Indians? An Argument for a Representational Ethics of Native Americans," *Journal of Communication Inquiry* 38: 184–203.
Pastorius, F. D. (1700/1912) "Circumstantial Geographical Description of Pennsylvania, 1700, Including Later Letters to Germany," in A. C. Myers (ed.), *Narratives of Early Pennsylvania, West New Jersey and Delaware, 1630–1707*. New York: Charles Scribner's Son, 384–385.
Perry, B. (2002) "From Ethnocide to Ethno Violence: Layers of Native American Victimization," *Contemporary Justice Review* 5: 231–247.
Reilly, H. J. (2010) *The Frontier Newspapers and the Coverage of the Plains Indian Wars*. Santa Barbara, CA: ABC-CLIO.

Ross, L. (1998) *Inventing the Savage*. Austin, TX: University of Texas Press.
Weston, M. A. (1996) *Native Americans in the News: Images of Indians in the Twentieth Century Press*. Westport, CT: Greenwood.

# Further Reading

Bird, S. E. (1999) "Gendered Construction of the American Indian in Popular Media," *Journal of Communication* 49(3): 61–83. (This is a historical study of how representations of Native Americans have become sexualized in relation to the white gaze, particularly the stud and the princess stereotypes.)

Carstarphen. M. G. and Sanchez, J. (eds.) (2012) *American Indians and the Mass Media*. Norman, OK: University of Oklahoma Press. (This edited collection contains chapters that examine mainstream media representations and how they have impacted Native communities, cultures, histories, and imaginations. Topics include early newspapers, *Life* magazine, the movie *Smoke Signals*, the squaw stereotype, and in particular, tribal voices are heard throughout, especially in entries on new media.)

King, C. R. (2009) *Media Images and Representation* (Contemporary Native American Issues). New York: Infobase Publishing. (This book covers a range of representations of Native Americans from mascots to news, television programs, Indigenous media, and the Internet.)

Strickland, R. (1997) *Tonto's Revenge: Reflections on American Indian Culture and Policy*. Albuquerque, NM: University of New Mexico Press. (Legal scholar Rennard Strickland's essays on law, literature, history, film, art, and culture reveals patterns of oppression and domination through representation as well as opportunities for self-redefinition.)

Yellowbird, M. (2004) "Cowboys and Indians: Toys of Genocide, Icons of American Colonialism," *Wicazo Sa Review* 19(2): 33–48. (This first-person essay describes the experience of a Native American academic who discovers cowboy and Indian figures at a convenience store and observes his nephews playing with them. Critical observations on the construction of Otherness are amplified as well as how these toys serve as symbols of genocide and colonialism.)

# 21
# ASIAN AMERICANS
## Model Minoritizing Digital Labor in a Post-Racial Age

*Vincent N. Pham and Kent A. Ono*

Perhaps there is no more powerful stereotype of Asian Americans than that of the "model minority." Harkening back to a 1966 *New York Times* article by William Petersen titled "Success Story: Japanese-American Style" and a *U.S. News and World Report* story on Chinese Americans titled "Success Story of One Minority in the US," the mainstream media has often characterized and depicted Asian Americans as the minority that fulfilled the American dream against all odds and without government assistance. According to Osajima's germinal article, "Asian Americans as the Model Minority: An Analysis of the Popular Press image in the 1960s and 1980s," the "overt racial comparisons between the success of Asians and the failures of other minorities are tempered and replaced . . . by a non-racial discourse that focuses primarily on differences between Asian American families and 'American' families" (1998: 169–70). This comparison of racial groups and its promotion of non-racial discourses, currently considered post-racial or "colorblind" (Bonilla-Silva) discourses, continues to be a vital part of how Asian Americans are configured and represented within media.

Asian Americans as model minorities arose within the context of the Civil Rights Movement and, among other things, this became a mode for disciplining other minorities, particularly African Americans and Latina/os, hence driving a wedge between racially disprivileged groups. Asian Americans became "model" in part because mainstream media constructed Asian Americans as being silent on social issues and choosing to work themselves out of their situation instead of asking for government aid.[1] Deborah Woo (2000) argued that model minority discourse constructed Asian Americans as being successful and highly educated, and that this success was made possible through hard work and a dedication to family, thus constructing Asian Americans as the penniless and poor characters who became successful by dint of their own hard work and accomplishment—essentially modern-day Horatio Algers.

Despite its significance during and after the Civil Rights Movement of the 1950s–70s, the model minority representation remains salient in the twenty-first century, relying on the Horatio Alger mythology that helped define the American dream during the late nineteenth century. Jachinson Chan (2001) argued that Charlie Chan—the intelligent, obedient, submissive, and non-threatening sidekick to the white main character—was one of the early precursors to the model minority. Asian-American model minorities appeared in the form of Asian Americans taking up specific "intelligent" and respectable jobs—Asian-American women journalists in the 1980s and medical doctors in the 2000s (Ono and Pham 2009).

Model minority discourse purports to provide a "positive" stereotype of Asian Americans, even as its effect is wholly negative on other racial groups, as it is ultimately on Asian Americans. The Asian American as model minority can also affect interpersonal relationships, where Asian Americans are seen as "nerdy" and socially inept and hence "left out" (Zhang 2010). Yet even as model minority discourse took up a variety of characters and representations that seemed positive on the surface, it also connected a variety of other historical representations of Asian Americans, particularly that of "Yellow Peril," where the Asian body and culture would threaten to invade, take jobs, and strip the US of its nationality and productivity. Shim (1998) and Kawai (2005) address the connectedness of Yellow Peril to the model minority stereotype, where it moves within a cycle or in dialectical tension, respectively. Thus, model minorities are always inevitably threatening (Ono and Pham 2009). This is evidenced in a *Wall Street Journal* article that characterizes a school in northern California as being too Asian and hence difficult for white students, who have to move to different school districts to increase their chance for college entry as well as a supposed holistic education that emphasizes arts and other subjects that Asians would not be interested in (Hwang 2005). The film *Akeelah and the Bee* highlights the danger of an overachieving Asian-American speller, who acts like a "robot," as opposed to a human, and thus threatens the integrity of the oral skills (Ono and Pham 2009). In these cases, Asian Americans are a danger because of their advanced academic skills, even as they are acceptable in their success.

Special attention has been given to Asian Americans within advertising and technology. Taylor and Stern (1997) found that advertisements overrepresented Asian Americans in background roles and in working professional roles, rather than in social or domestic ones—thus reinforcing the robotic aspects of hardworking Asian Americans. Paek and Shah's (2003) quantitative analysis revealed that Asian Americans were "depicted as highly educated, proficient with technology, and affluent" (225). Lee and Joo's (2005) analysis of print ads reinforced Paek and Shah's findings about Asian-American alignment with technology and the model minority and added that such representations could have negative effects on group members. Phua's (2014) study on media priming found that stereotypical aspects of the model minority, such as the idea that Asian Americans are hardworking, can also be transferred to brands but may come with negative aspects too, such as being passive or boring.

At this juncture, model minority discourse is widely known and circulated. Importantly, model minority discourse is not static but also evolves within the context in which it is deployed. Just as Osajima argued in the 1980s, when the model minority myth served to legitimate President Ronald Reagan's stress on the family, and his attacks on abortion, school busing, and other social programs "originally designed to benefit racial minorities" (170), current discourse about Asian Americans is couched within a logic generated by the model minority myth. Most recently, Shankar (2015) argues that this model minority discourse helped set the foundation for Asian Americans to be considered a "model consumer" for the advertising industry. In this case, the logic of model minority discourse for Asian Americans powers capitalism by constructing Asian Americans as a model consumer worthy of being targeted and also serves as the primary optic through which Asians and Asian Americans are understood in an area where questions about their relevance remain. Thus, the literature regarding Asian Americans as model minorities shows how model minority discourses reappear, sometimes purely as a reiteration of earlier representations, but in forms that reinforce particular aspects and logics of the discourse.

Such reappearance and recirculation of racial discourses occur because, as Ono and Pham (2009) argue, racial logics as they relate to Asians and Asian Americans are structurally embedded in media, where the model minority myth reappears repeatedly as one mode through which we understand Asians and Asian Americans. But discourse about the model minority discourse has evolved, and so has scholarly and popular engagement with it. Indeed, today, Asian Americans challenge the stereotype overtly, such as in videos on YouTube.[2] Asian-American apparel companies actively try to dispel it.[3] Moreover, rather than model minority discourse merely being about Asian and Asian-American students as "whiz kids" on television, the main way model minority characters appear is as scientists, technicians, or medical staff.[4] In short, the representation of Asian-American model minority has veered toward the "robotic." At this point, this chapter has briefly discussed the history of model minority myth scholarship and illustrated the expanse and limits of model minority discourse. The following sections will examine the contemporary media landscape by exploring how discourse about Asian and Asian-American digital and Internet builders and inventors—specifically the creators and founders of YouTube—rely on model minority imagery even when that image does not directly align. In doing so, we argue that the model minority trope can operate in an ambivalent way—complicating the simple way in which the trope is mapped onto new situations and stories while also reproducing its racially exceptional self-made success and intelligence aspects.

## Critical Economics of Internet Chief Economic Officer (CEO) Discourse

From the mid-1990s to the late 2000s and spurred by the onset of new technologies, the Internet transformed from military communication intra-net (i.e., DARPANET) focused primarily on internal communication into a mass media communication system able to support the dissemination of multi-media content (i.e., Web 1.0) and finally to our current social media-driven and user-generated created Internet (i.e., Web 2.0)—culminating in an Internet environment that allows for unprecedented social interactions and economic transactions without regard to time and space. Technologies like web browsers, search engines, and even free email permitted the widespread use of the Internet and its evolution to a site of information gathering and sharing and consumption practices, structuring our interaction with the Internet and helping us make our way through a complex network of information and media. While innovative at its time of creation, the now taken-for-granted technologies, software, and services allow for the easy navigation of the information-rich worldwide web and enable everyday people to use the Internet to quickly and easily communicate with others. Importantly, these technologies have contributed to an age of hyper-information, an increasingly globalized world, and the building of an unparalleled economic infrastructure.

This no small feat—the relative quick transition from the specialized internal communication function of the Internet to a widespread and multiple one that also allows for quick, inexpensive, and easy transnational communication and, importantly, capitalistic transactions. While we as a society are quick to recognize the quickly evolving technology that changed and reconfigured the utilization of the Internet, what remains unrecognized, hidden, or overlooked when thinking about media technologies are the very people who helped build these Internet start-ups and lead them into our everyday life. These automated, efficient, and ultimately fantastical technologies, built upon layers and layers of programming code, are developed by people in start-up companies, full of aspirations, goals, and identities not yet thrust into the public eye but that are in many ways racially constructed as Asian and Asian American. Thus, how does the mainstream media make sense of two unforeseen and mostly invisible subjects: technological innovation and the presence of Asians and Asian Americans as the creators, purveyors, leaders, and ultimately CEOs of Internet technology? This chapter attempts to answer this conundrum by considering the development of unforeseen Internet technologies in relation to news media coverage of Asian-American Internet CEOs—all while recognizing that model minority discourses existed prior to both and informed society's understanding of Asian Americans. By weaving together media coverage of Internet innovation and Asian-American visibility against the backdrop of model minority, we argue that contemporary model minority aspects are emphasized and reinforced while others may be contradicted or altogether absent.

Asians and Asian Americans have been crucial to the development of the Internet. Sociological and anthropological work has focused on Asian Americans in the Silicon Valley, elucidating the presence of Indian-American labor, youth, and identity and their struggles in the Silicon Valley (Shankar 2008) or South-Asian use of ethnic enclaves, employees that cut across class lines, and the resulting establishment of Internet start-ups (Saxenian 2000; Shankar 2008). While research on Asian and Asian-American Internet-related employees exists (Varmi 2002; Wong 2006; Rudruppa 2009–10), it largely examines line workers, outsourcing, and the transnational use of a "coolie" labor force.

Despite the popular news stories about the powerful contributions Asians and Asian Americans have made to the establishment of the Internet, very little research has been published on Asian-American Internet moguls, entrepreneurs, and CEOs. Academic scholarship, to our knowledge, has overlooked the increased presence and construction of Asian and Asian-American Internet CEOs. However, that is not to say that they are ignorant of a CEO's effects. Mainstream news media are familiar with reporting on CEOs, and companies recognize the public impact of CEOs. According to Park and Berger (2004), media coverage on CEOs is generally related to CEO changes or transitions, strategic directions, or a company's business-related performance and focuses on the competency and personal dimensions of the CEO. In addition, discourse produced by CEOs in the news stories may influence the CEO's image and affect the company's reputation and image, especially since CEOs "help define an organization's image with internal and external stakeholders" (Park and Berger 2004: 95). Although it is debatable whether CEOs can manage their image, they inevitably function on behalf of a company, producing and communicating symbols to the public for the benefit of the company (J. E. Grunig 1993).

Yet the critical research on CEO discourse is sparse. Much of the research highlights the public relations functions of CEOs without giving critical attention to the very representation of CEOs (Budd Jr. 2004; Marken 2004; Foster 1990; L. A. Grunig 1997; Marston 1993). However, Norander's (2008) analysis of Carly Fiorina, the female CEO of Hewlett Packard, provides a critical look at the gendered news construction and subject positioning of an Internet CEO, recognizing that "Fiorina's hiring was a significant moment in the history of U.S. business culture" (100) due to her gender, which countered the hegemonic masculinity of the American business CEO (Mumby 1998). While the aforementioned scholarship rightfully considers the public function of CEOs and its benefit, it is remiss in considering how news discourses about CEOs are racially framed or implicitly articulated. Norander's analysis centers on gender, while only mentioning race in relation to white male CEOs, the prevalence of white women in middle-management, and the dearth of women of color in any managerial roles. While Norander's analysis highlighted Fiorina's slow rise to the top of Hewlett Packard from other business experiences, such as Lucent Technologies, our case attempts to make sense of the rise of both youthful and Asian-American entrepreneurs into positions as CEOs in hurried time, especially as the very Internet technologies being developed have reshaped our understanding of and engagement with the Internet.

As yet, no mention has been made within critical scholarly literature, to our knowledge, about Asian and Asian-American Internet executives. In illustrating the primary issues regarding Asian-American media representations, we examine news discourse surrounding the creators of YouTube, using Lexis/Nexis and ProQuest searches with their names as search terms. By exploring news discourse about Asian and Asian-American Internet CEOs, we consider how the news media constructed the role of Asians and Asian Americans in building the Internet and its American technological dreams.

The characterization of the entrepreneurs-turned-CEOs, coupled with youth and race, posed a distinct problem in reporting the increased presence and news visibility of Asian-American Internet CEOs and their rapid rise in the technology industry. Through our study of discourse representing Asian and Asian-American Internet executive entrepreneurs, we argue that, in part, because of their shockingly fast success, media are unable initially to establish complex narratives of model minority status. A story of Horatio Alger "rags to riches" does not fully set in, even while haphazard mentions of that identity do appear. Rather, they are seen as expendable to the economics of the Internet, another fad to help the Internet evolve to increased efficiency for a changing economy. As a result, the story appears assumed and rushed, though it is seemingly necessary to construct a narrative of U.S. business and its acquisition of the technologies of the future, particularly at the expense of the very people who invented the technologies.

## Two Coders and a Designer

The online video streaming website, YouTube, remains one of the more public and recent examples of Asian-American Internet entrepreneurs-turned-multi-millionaire and upper-level management. YouTube's meteoric rise and eventual sale to Google mirrored Hotmail's rapid popularity and acquisition by Microsoft. However, the collaborative development of YouTube by three people and the controversial nature of YouTube technology and business set it apart from previous Internet start-ups. Articles tend to talk about the three founders together. Most stories focus on things showing on YouTube itself, its increased use, and business deals made regarding copyright. By October 6, 2006, articles reported YouTube's acquisition by Google for $1.6 billion, approximately 15 percent of Google's cash balance.

Former PayPal employees Steve Chen, Jawed Karim, and Chad Hurley founded YouTube in February 2005 and drew from many PayPal (the popular online payment system) staff members to help build YouTube in its early years (Terese 2006). Roughly a year and a half later, on October 26, 2006, Google purchased YouTube for $1.65 billion, making the founders millionaires.[5] The initial articles about YouTube rushed to describe their movement from obscurity to fame, often noting their limited finances before stardom and focusing on Chen and Hurley.

Initial articles focused mostly on the novelty of YouTube as it dominated the popular imagination in 2006, its upstart nature, and the changing media environment—hence on technologies, not the people behind them. YouTube was deemed *Time* magazine's 2006 "Invention of the Year," and was described by the *New York Daily News* as launching a "revolution by allowing Joe Schmoes everywhere to get their 15 nanoseconds of Web fame" as it beat out other inventions of a "super-economical car and a soldier-saving robot" (Hutchinson 2006: 4). An editorial in the *Chicago Tribune* ambivalently describes YouTube as an example of "American ingenuity" while stating that audiences might want to "kick yourself because it wasn't your idea (Wish it were your idea?)." Thus, the creation of YouTube (and its creators) is seen as blatantly obvious and uncreative yet an indication of the potential of America's promise and dream. The technology is seen as revolutionarily trivial—unimportant in saving lives or changing society for the better but rather a self-serving and self-centered technology that is changing the media environment. Consequently, the people behind YouTube might be viewed as not all that creative, impressive, or important if it wasn't for the large sums of money that purchased the site.

While the technology was being explained, the profiles of Chen, Karim, and Hurley began to appear. A short article in *Investor's Business Daily* tells such a story, titled, "YouTube video website founders: From pure geeks to media moguls." The article reads:

> A year ago, co-founders Chad Hurley and Steve Chen were in between jobs, a pair of twenty-something geeks running up big credit card debts as they tooled around a garage trying to develop an easy way for people to share homemade videos on the Web.
>
> Now, they're budding media moguls in a new entertainment era that relies on unconventional sites like YouTube—by some measures the top video-sharing site, one that's cultivated a huge audience while testing the bounds of creativity, monotony, copyrights and obscenity.
>
> *(Investor's Business Daily 2006)*

Here, the trope of the inventors in the garage, maxing out credit cards to make their dream happen, serves to establish small beginnings and a lack of resources. Yet this attempt to illustrate their "impoverishment" differs greatly from the poverty-stricken Horatio Algers who made themselves out of nothing. In this case, the inventors of the new media environment are still quite fortunate and privileged with college degrees from flagship land grant institutions known for their science, technology, engineering, and math programs.

David Greising's 2006 *Chicago Tribune* business piece titled "YouTube founder rides video clips to dot-com riches" tells a similar story of geek-to-media moguls, of struggling credit-card-maxed-out entrepreneurs that finally strike riches, and the simple idea of online streaming video clips as the vehicle to their success. However, this article focuses on Chen as the primary character. Chen's ability as a code writer and his aspirations to make "Silicon Valley fortunes" were evident as he left the University of Illinois two semesters early, bypassing graduation. Greising's article states that "Chen and Karim were exceptional code writers, and Hurley's gift for design could give a new Web site a compelling look" (2006: 1). Although they all came from the University of Illinois as engineers, Chen became the technology person (and became Chief Technology Officer of YouTube) while Hurley became designated design man. In addition, Karim was the influential coder in building YouTube and acted as the somewhat awkward subject of the first uploaded video. However, as Karim disappears from this narrative (most likely since he left the company to go to graduate school at Stanford), Chen and Hurley become the driving force of YouTube, propping up the Internet servers with their credit cards until venture capitalists came in, dealing with copyright issues, and eventually striking a deal with Google at a Denny's restaurant halfway between Google's and YouTube's offices. In this story, the trope of the Asian nerd as technology guru arises for Chen and Karim whereas the white partner, Chad Hurley, serves as the artistic design person and is attributed the design aspects of YouTube and hence its most visible and public presence.

These sudden rise to riches stories appear more frequently after Google's takeover of YouTube. Unsurprisingly, articles often refer to the subjects' relative youth. An article in the *Chicago Daily Herald* on October 11, 2006 (Kukec) begins by mentioning Chen's age, 27. People describe him in his high school days as smart, unmotivated, and wanting to have fun. In one article in *Advertising Age*, the title makes this reference explicit, "Steve Chen, 27, and Chad Hurley, 29" (Advertising Age 2006). In the *Chicago Tribune* article, a short paragraph starts with "at age 28" before listing Chen's affiliations with PayPal and Facebook (Greising 2006). The focus on age implies these people succeed despite their youthfulness and inexperience. Most importantly, their youthfulness and college-like demeanor are repeatedly articulated in discussions of legality, especially as they deal with issues of copyright that span from 2007 until 2010, following the sale to Google. In youthful slang, Karim wrote in an April 2005 email to Hurley and Chen, "It's all 'bout da videos, yo. We'll be an excellent acquisition target once we're huge" (Whitehouse 2010: 31). Chen is described as being hesitant and beckoned Karim to stop with "stolen videos on the site" (Whitehouse 2010). Age becomes an integral narrative to understanding the behaviors of the founders, one that disregards copyright issues as it unexpectedly reshapes our relationship to media content in a dynamic media environment.

In the backdrop of the story of YouTube are racial and immigrant-like narratives, especially in regards to Chen and Karim. The *Chicago Daily Herald* article concludes in a question-and-answer format in which Chen is asked about being born in Taiwan (Kukec 2006). Chen also went to the prestigious boarding high school, Illinois Math and Science Academy, only to leave the academy and finish at his local high school. Thus, Chen did not always excel academically. Karim, a son of German and Bangladeshi parents, born in East Germany, grew up in West Germany, immigrated to and went to high school in Minnesota, and left the riches of YouTube and Internet start-ups to complete a master's degree in computer science at Stanford University. He eventually started "Youniversity Karim Ventures," meant to help college students with their own start-up companies. Karim's endeavors focused on education and not purely the riches they might bring. The juxtaposition of Karim's educational endeavor with Chen's educational difficulties complicates the model minority narrative. Rather, their stories propose a narrative that emphasizes their youth, slacker ethos, ingenuity, and intelligence minus the work ethic associated with Horatio Algers, countering the media's model minority stereotype.

## A Complicated (Tech) Model Minority

These news media discourses highlight what we describe as the critical economics of Asian-American Internet executive discourses, which position Asian Americans as entrepreneurs and laborers who contribute to neoliberal systems of self-sufficiency, effectiveness, and capitalist economy. The narrative of the YouTube creators—Steve Chen and Jawed Karim—is that they developed a technology, burst onto the scene, and then quickly sold the company to Google before becoming venture capitalists or start-up mentors.

Such discourses inevitably frame and construct Asian Americans in the role of inventors constrained in their rhetorical agency when they sell their goods. Steve Chen and the YouTube founders become relegated to the background, invisible in discussions regarding the economic influence and impact of their beloved technology. They cannot be Steve Jobs, who is deemed as perpetually innovative. Rather, they occupy the position of Internet legend. Of course, their ability to speak and be heard and respected always relies on their ability to generate capital and refashion the Internet in inherently capitalistic ways. Indeed, Google's acquisition of YouTube served Google's attempt to get into online video, but for Chen it helped further develop the technology for better user experiences. In a sense, they sacrificed themselves to the larger project of the "Internet." The quickly transforming media and technological environment that has transformed the global economics by collapsing time (through efficiencies) and space (by crisscrossing geographies) has fundamentally transformed the economic and communicational terrain and era. Still, the ways of making sense of people remain relatively fixed, unable to adjust to the fast-changing technical processes.

To make sense of this highly evolving new media environment spurred by previously unseen Asian-American entrepreneurs, news media constructed narratives that emphasized the unlikely rise and their rational and profit-producing decisions to sell their technology to larger corporations while downplaying their dedication to creating new Internet technologies. Nonetheless, the discursive backdrop and widespread trope of Asian-American model minorities permeate these narratives. They are seen as lucky in creating, robotic in their actions, nerdy in their manner of work, and, hence, socially inept, but eventually successful.

Yet the model minority myth functions differently here by continuing to code Asians and Asian Americans as smart, educated, and successful while avoiding other aspects of the Horatio Alger legend. It particularly avoids the "hard work" aspect and assumes that is essentialized to Asians and Asian Americans as they progress through STEM fields and technology sectors. Thus, hard work is recoded as already part of the job to get to the point where the new model minority's job is to develop and sell the idea to lubricate the engine of capitalism through its relationship to large multinational companies. The narratives do not construct them as impoverished and in need of money or jobs; rather, they are in need of inspiration and entertainment and to create technology and not art.

As Asians and Asian Americans become more visible in the mainstream, the media attempt to make sense of their accomplishments and widespread visibility by circulating easily understood narratives that draw upon commonly used tropes. Yet these tropes, particularly the model minority myth, do not always easily align with the facts of the narrative and provide avenues in which the tropes can be challenged or complicated, while reproducing salient aspects of these racial tropes. In considering the model minority myth in the age of new media development, we illustrate how intelligence and hard work is already assumed and reinforced, yet the robotic nature of their work (and their nerdiness), without the glitz and glamour of stardom, complicate the model minority myth. In doing so, the flexibility of the model minority myth's continued relevance lies not only in its widespread representation of Asians as smart and successful but also how that is articulated with societal changes and how one makes sense of them. Just as the origins of the model minority myth were used to downplay civil rights concerns and make sense of civil rights movements, the use of the model minority myth here (and its relevant aspects) makes sense of the technological changes and breakthroughs and renders Asians and Asian Americans as exceptional post-racial entrepreneurs and inventors, but unappealing as CEOs.

## Notes

1 This narrative of Asian-American compliance, politeness, complacence, and passivity ignored the history of Asian-American activism, including the role of Asian Americans in the Civil Rights and Black Power Movements (see, for instance, Daryl Maeda 2005).
2 Many early Asian-American YouTube stars, like KevJumba and Nigahiga, created fan bases by directly addressing model minority stereotypes.
3 The Asian-American apparel company, Blacklava, sells shirts that display "I suck at Math" or "1 + 1 = 3" to disrupt stereotypes about "smart Asians."
4 See Ono and Pham (2009) for chapter on model minorities.
5 Additionally, venture capitalists, like Sequoia Capital, also made large profits off their initial investment in the early days of YouTube.

## References

Advertising Age. (2006, Aug. 6) "Steve Chen, 27, and Chad Hurley, 29," *Advertising Age*. Retrieved from http://adage.com/article/special-report-40-under-40/steve-chen-27-chad-hurley-29/110942/.
Bonilla-Silva, E. (2003) *Racism without Racists: Color-blind Racism and the Persistence of Racial Inequality in the United States*. Lanham, MD: Rowman and Littlefield.
Budd, Jr., J. F. (2004) "A Retrospective: Where's the Psychic Income? Of Myths, Mores and Myopia," *Public Relations Quarterly* 49(3): 44–45.
Chan, J. (2001) *Chinese American Masculinities: From Fu Manchu to Bruce Lee*. New York: Routledge.
Cho, J. (1998, Nov. 30) "How Green Is the Valley? How Asian Americans Should Interpret—and Exploit—the Job Boom in High-Tech," *A Magazine*.
Foster, L. G. (1990) "The CEO Connection: Pivotal for the '90s," *Public Relations Journal* 46(1): 24–25.
Greising, D. (2006, Oct. 15) "YouTube Founder Rides Video Clips to Dotcom Riches," *Chicago Tribune*.
Grunig, J. E. (1993) "Image and Substance: From Symbolic to Behavioral Relationships," *Public Relations Review* 19: 121–139.
Grunig, L. A. (1997) "Excellence in Public Relations," in C. L. Caywood (ed.), *The Handbook of Strategic Public Relations and Integrated Communications*. New York: McGraw-Hill, 286–300.
Hutchinson, B. (2006, Nov. 6) "YouTube is *Time*'s Invention of the Year," *New York Daily News*.
Hwang, S. (2005, Nov. 19) "The New White Flight: In Silicon Valley, Two High Schools with Outstanding Academic Reputations Are Losing White Students as Asian Students Move In. Why?," *Wall Street Journal*. Retrieved from http://www.wsj.com/articles/SB113236377590902105.
Investor's Business Daily. (2006, April 10) "YouTube Video Website Founders: From Pure Geeks to Media Moguls," *Investor's Business Daily*.
Jo, S. (2008) "How Organizations Want to Be Viewed: Public Relations Photographs in Online Wire Services," *Public Relations Review* 34(1): 74–76.
Kawai, Y. (2005) "Stereotyping Asian Americans: The Dialectic of the Model Minority and the Yellow Peril," *Howard Journal of Communication* 16: 109–130.
Kukec, A. M. (2006, Oct. 11) "From Suburban Teen to Multi-millionaire: YouTube Cofounder Steve Chen Talks about His Journey to Success," *Chicago Daily Herald*.
Lee, K. and Sung-Hee, J. (2005) "The Portrayal of Asian Americans in Mainstream Magazine Ads: An Update," *Journalism and Mass Communication Quarterly* 82: 654–671.
Maeda, D. J. "Black Panthers, Red Guards, and Chinamen: Constructing Asian American Identity through Performing Blackness, 1969–1972," *American Quarterly* 57(4): 1079–1103.
Marken, G. A. (2004) "CEO Still Sets the Tone, Agenda of Public Relations," *Public Relations Quarterly* 49(1): 16–17.
Marston, R. (1993) "CEOs Are a Breed Apart," *Public Relations Quarterly* 38(3): 29–33.
McCarthy, P. and Hatcher, C. (2004) "Reputation Building: The Public Communication Styles of Carly Fiorina and Rupert Murdoch," *Australian Journal of Communication* 31(1): 1–18.
Mumby, D. K. (1998) "Organizing Men: Power, Discourse, and the Social Construction of Masculinity(s) in the Workplace," *Communication Theory* 8: 164–182.
Norander, S. (2008) "Surveillance/Discipline/Resistance: Carly Fiorina under the Gaze of the *Wall Street Journal*," *Communication Studies* 59(2): 99–113.
Ono, K. A. and Pham, V. N. (2009) *Asian Americans and the Media*. Malden, MA: Polity Press.

Osajima, K. (1998) "Asian Americans as the Model Minority: An Analysis of the Popular Press Image in the 1960s and 1980s," in G. Okihiro et al. (eds.), *Reflections on Shattered Windows: Promises and Prospects for Asian American Studies*. Pullman, WA: Washington State University Press, 165–174.

Paek, H. J. and Shah, H. (2003) "Racial Ideology, Model Minorities, and the 'Not-So-Silent' Partner: Stereotyping of Asian Americans in U.S. Magazine Advertising," *Howard Journal of Communication* 14: 225–243.

Park, D. J. and Berger, B. K. (2004) "The Presentation of CEOs in the Press, 1990–2000: Increasing Salience, Positive Valence, and a Focus on Competency and Personal Dimensions of Image," *Journal of Public Relations Research* 16(1): 93–123.

Petersen, W. (1966, Jan. 9) "Success Story: Japanese-American Style," *New York Times*.

Pham, A. (2000, Feb. 14) "Pioneering Asians Find Land of Plenty," *Boston Globe*.

Phua, J. (2014) "The Influence of Asian American Spokesmodels in Technology-Related Advertising: An Experiment," *Howard Journal of Communications* 2(4): 399–414.

Rudrappa, S. (2009–10) "Cyber-Coolies and Techno-Braceros: Race and Commodification of Indian Information Technology Guest Workers in the United States," *U.S.F. Law Review* 353: 353–372.

Saxenian, A. (2000) "Silicon Valley's New Immigrant Entrepreneurs," Working Papers, Center for Comparative Immigration Studies, UC San Diego.

Schlender, B. (2006, March 6) "How a Virtuoso Plays the Web," *Fortune* 141(5): F79–F83.

Shankar, S. (2008) *Desi Land: Teen Culture, Class, and Success in Silicon Valley*. Durham, NC: Duke University Press.

———. (2015) *Advertising Diversity: Ad Agencies and the Creation of Asian American Advertising*. Durham, NC: Duke University Press.

Sharma, B. (2011) "Desis in Fashion Vouch for Customers as Advertisers," *India Abroad*.

Shim, D. (1998) "From Yellow Peril through Model Minority to Renewed Yellow Peril," *Journal of Communication Inquiry* 22(4): 385–409.

"Success Story of One Minority in the US" (1966, Dec. 26) *U.S. News and World Report*.

Taylor, C. R. and Stern, B. B. (1997) "Asian-Americans: Television Advertising and the 'Model Minority' Stereotype," *Journal of Advertising* 26(2): 47–61.

Terese, A. (2006, Feb. 3) "YouTube Offers Easier, Faster Video Uploads," *Daily Illini*.

Varmi, R. (2002) "High-Tech Coolies: Asian Immigrants in the U.S. Science and Engineering Workforce," *Science as Culture* 11(3): 337–361.

Whitehouse, K. (2010, March 19) "It's 'Bout Videos, Yo It's the Benjamins, Not Copyright: Founder's Emails," *New York Post*.

Wong, B. (2006) *The Chinese in Silicon Valley, Globalization, Social Networks, and Ethnic Identity*. Lanham, MD: Rowman and Littlefield.

Woo, D. (2000) *Glass Ceilings and Asian Americans: The New Face of Workplace Barriers*. Walnut Creek, CA: Alta Mira Press.

Zhang, Q. (2010) "Asian Americans Beyond the Model Minority Stereotype: The Nerdy and Left Out," *Journal of Intercultural and International Communication* 3(1): 20–37.

# Further Reading

Ono, K. A. and Pham, V. N. (2009) *Asian Americans and the Media*. Malden, MA: Polity Press. (An in-depth overview of mainstream media representations of Asians and Asian Americans and Asian-American attempts to posit alternative images via independent media and Internet activity.)

Osajima, K. (1998) "Asian Americans as the Model Minority: An Analysis of the Popular Press Image in the 1960s and 1980s," in G. Okihiro et al. (eds.), *Reflections on Shattered Windows: Promises and Prospects for Asian American Studies*. Pullman, WA: Washington State University Press, 165–174. (A historical and comparative analysis of the persistence of the "Asian Americans as model minority" image in the 1960s and 1980s.)

Shankar, S. (2015) *Advertising Diversity: Ad Agencies and the Creation of Asian American Advertising*. Durham, NC: Duke University Press. (A multi-year ethnographic study of Asian-American ad agencies and the intertwining logics of consumerism and the model minority.)

Shim, D. (1998) "From Yellow Peril through Model Minority to Renewed Yellow Peril," *Journal of Communication Inquiry* 22(4): 385–409. (A semiotic and ideological analysis of cinematic portrayals of Asians and Asian Americans from the mid-nineteenth century through the Reagan-Bush era.)

# 22
# ARABS, MUSLIMS, AND ARAB AMERICANS

## Constructing an Evil Other

*Evelyn Alsultany*

### Conflating Arab and Muslim Identities

Arab and Muslim identities have long been conflated in U.S. government and media discourses, as well as in popular culture. Since Arabs and Muslims are usually represented as one and the same, it is difficult to write about representations of Arab Americans without also addressing representations of Arabs and Muslims. All too often, representations of Arabs and Muslims have served to racialize Arab ethnicity and vilify the religion of Islam. In this chapter, I review the entangled U.S. media representations of all three groups—Arabs, Muslims, and Arab Americans—noting the history of these representations, their various manifestations in current popular culture, and their enduring, harmful effects. Throughout, I use the notation "Arab/Muslim" not to perpetuate the conflation of categories, but rather to highlight and critique it.

Though much scholarship has examined the racialization of Arabs and Muslims following the events of September 11, 2001 ("9/11") (e.g., Bayoumi 2006; Naber and Jamal 2007; Puar 2007; Razack 2008; Maira 2010; Cainkar 2011), the racialization of Arabs and Muslims did not begin with 9/11. Rather, such representations have a much longer heritage of government and media narratives that construct Arabs and Muslims as outside of the purview of Americanness. Well before 9/11, scholars of Arab-American Studies noted that Arab Americans are located within a racial paradox, in which they are simultaneously racialized as white and non-white. Not legally recognized by the United States government as a minority group, and unable to fit into the racial and ethnic categories used by the United States Census—black, white, Asian, Native, and Hispanic—Arabs have not been legally "raced" and are therefore "outside of the boxes" and presumably white (Naber 2000; Samhan 1999). Nonetheless, as Nadine Naber writes, the Arab-American racial paradox before 9/11 was constructed through a distinct process of racialization in which Arab Americans were racialized primarily according to religion (vis-à-vis Islam) and politics (vis-à-vis the Israeli/Palestinian conflict), as opposed to phenotype. After 9/11, Naber argues that "the post-9/11 backlash has been constituted by an interplay between two racial logics, cultural racism and nation-based racism" (Naber 2008: 279). Naber defines cultural racism as "a process of othering that constructs perceived cultural (e.g., Arab), religious (e.g., Muslim), or civilizational (e.g., Arab and/or Muslim) differences as natural and insurmountable" (Naber 2008: 279). In other words, justifications for discrimination and violence come to be based in culture, religion, or notions of civilization, as opposed to biology or phenotype. In contrast, nation-based racism is a process of othering based on notions of citizens versus foreigners, where foreignness is inscribed with criminality and therefore marked as undesirable and unassimilable in the US. Naber argues that a convergence of cultural racism and nation-based racism has enabled the resurgence of domestic policies targeting immigrant exclusion and foreign policies involving military deployment and war (Naber 2008: 280–1).

But if the racialization of Arabs and Muslims remains somewhat ambiguous in the legal-political realm, U.S. mass media and Hollywood films in particular have been far less equivocal. Ella Shohat, for example, demonstrates that Arabs have been racialized via Eurocentric narratives in terms of visual representations, troping, and narrative positioning (Shohat 1991) while Jack G. Shaheen examines Hollywood's creation of an Arab phenotype over the last century (Shaheen 2000). The on-screen Arab has dark features (skin, hair, eyes), a distinguished hook-nose, "exotic" clothing (veil, bellydancing outfits, keffiyeh, etc.), and conforms to a limited number of cultural tropes (greedy, rich, corrupt oil sheik, fanatical, violent, religious beliefs, terrorist, etc.) (Shaheen 2000). In reality, of course, Arab and Muslim "looks" span the racial spectrum and cannot be reduced to one "type." The ironic result is that the U.S. media has produced a conflated Arab/Muslim "look" that is both narrow enough to mark people for exclusion and discrimination yet also expansive enough to erroneously include Indians, Pakistanis, and Iranians—as evidenced by "mis-directed" hate crimes during the Gulf War and after 9/11.

Casting for TV dramas and films has historically contributed to this conflation and confusion. TV dramas participate in the construction of a phenotype and the fiction of an Arab or Muslim "race" and hence the notion that Arabs and Muslims can be racially profiled. In *Sleeper Cell*, the lead terrorist is Arab/Muslim but portrayed by an Israeli-Jewish actor, Oded Fehr, who has played Arab roles before, most notably in *The Mummy* films (1999 and 2001). In season 2 of *24*, the Arab terrorist is played by Francesco Quinn, who is Mexican American (his father, Anthony Quinn, also often played Arab characters). During the fourth season of *24*, the Arab/Muslim terrorist is Marwan Habib, played by Arnold Vosloo, a South African actor who also appeared (as an ancient Egyptian) in *The Mummy* (1999 and 2001). Terrorists on other shows have been portrayed by Nestor Serrano who is Latino, Tony Plana who is Cuban American, and Anil Kumar who is South Asian. *24*'s "good Arab-American" counter-terrorism agent, Nadia Yassir, is played by Marisol Nichols, who is Mexican-Hungarian-Romanian. Most of the actors who have played Arab/Muslim terrorists, at least in the last decade, are Latinos, South Asians, and Greeks. Junaid Rana examines how Pakistanis have been conflated as Middle Eastern in post-9/11 visual culture through the construction of a racialized Muslim that both produces and contains the threatening Muslim figure (Rana 2012). Through a critical analysis of visual technologies of racialization, Rana demonstrates how the figure of the Muslim is rendered as a geographically and historically legible racial target, which is then deployed to depict Pakistani migrants in the West as potential terrorists.

The point here is not that only Arabs should portray Arab characters, but rather that casting lends itself to the visual construction of an Arab/Muslim race that supports the conflation of Arab and Muslim identities. As a result, it is commonly assumed among the U.S. populace that Iranians and Pakistanis are Arab and that all Arabs are Muslim and all Muslims Arab, despite the fact that there are 1.2 billion Muslims worldwide and that only about 15–20 percent of them are Arab. This construction of a conflated Arab/Muslim "look" in turn supports (intentionally or not) policies like racial profiling by doing the ideological work of matching certain "looks" with categories deemed threatening and dangerous. Such representations make it difficult to disentangle the Arab/Muslim conflation and to speak with more precision.

Why are these categories interchangeable when most Muslims are not Arab? This conflation enables a particular racial othering that would not operate in the same way through another conflation, such as, for example, Arab/Christian, Arab/Jew, or Indonesian/Muslim. The result is particularly damaging because it flattens the inherent—and enormous—variety of the world's Muslim population, projecting all Muslims as one very particular type: fanatical, misogynistic, anti-American. This recurring conflation, advanced by United States government and media discourses, both historically and in the long aftermath of 9/11, constructs an evil Other that can be powerfully and easily mobilized during times of war. The Arab/Muslim conflation has been strategically useful to American empire building during the War on Terror precisely because it comes with historical baggage. It draws on centuries-old Orientalist narratives of patriarchal societies and oppressed women, of Muslim fundamentalism and anti-Semitism, of irrational violence and suicide bombings. This already-established conflation, in turn, makes possible the portrayal of the US as the inverse of everything that is "Arab/Muslim": the United States is thus equal and democratic, culturally diverse and civilized, home to progressive men and liberated women, and violent only when attacked or protecting democracy.

Regarding the overall impact of such representations, Tim Jon Semmerling argues in *'Evil' Arabs in American Popular Film* that portrayals of Arabs in U.S. cinema reveal more about American Orientalist fears than about actual Arabs (Semmerling 2006). Karin Gwinn Wilkins' *Home/Land/Security: What We Learn about Arab Communities from Action-Adventure Films* conducts focus groups to determine how Americans perceive Arab villains in action-adventure films, and particularly their perception of Arabs as threats to U.S. national security, fear of the Middle East, and U.S. heroes who conquer the Arab threat (Wilkins 2008). She reveals the undisputable link between media representations and their lived consequences in terms of discriminatory perceptions and practices.

## Representations in Hollywood Films, Television, and News: 1897–2000

Over the last century, Arab/Muslim men have most often been represented as romantic sheiks, rich oil sheiks, and most notably, terrorists. Arab/Muslim women have been portrayed as sultry belly dancers, harem girls, and oppressed women. Early silent films that represented the Middle East, such as *Fatima* (1897), *The Sheik* (1921), and *The Thief of Baghdad* (1924), portrayed the region as far away, exotic, and magical; a place of Biblical stories and fairy tales; a desert filled with genies, flying carpets, mummies, belly dancers, harem girls, and rich men living in opulent palaces (or equally opulent tents). In *Reel Bad Arabs: How Hollywood Vilifies a People*, Jack G. Shaheen documents nearly 1,000 Hollywood films and their representations of Arabs and Muslims. He describes the "fictional Arabia" projected by Hollywood in the 1920s–60s as consisting of deserts, camels, scimitars, palaces, veiled women, belly dancers, concubines held hostage, slave markets, and Arab men who seek to rape white women (Shaheen 2000: 8). Films during this period—notably, made while parts of the Middle East were colonized by European powers—reflect the fantasies of the colonizers and a logic that legitimizes colonialism (Shohat and Stam 1994). It was not unusual for both "good" and "bad" Arabs to be represented and for a white man to save the day by saving the good Arabs from the bad, freeing the female Arab slaves from their captors, and rescuing white women from Arab rapists.

The year 1945 was an important historical moment that marked the decline of European colonialism at the end of WWII, the beginning of the Cold War, the creation of Israel (in 1948) in the shadow of the Holocaust, and the emergence of the United States as a global power. As the United States began its geopolitical ascendancy, representations of the "foreign" contributed to the making of American national identity; the projection of erotic and exotic fantasies onto the Middle East began to shift to more ominous representations of violence and terrorism (Edwards 2005). Representations of Arabs/Muslims as terrorists emerge with the inauguration of the state of Israel in 1948, the Arab-Israeli war and subsequent Israeli occupation of Palestinian territories in 1967, and the formation of Palestinian resistance movements. As Jack G. Shaheen writes:

> The image began to intensify in the late 1940s when the state of Israel was founded on Palestinian land. From that preemptive point on—through the Arab-Israeli wars of 1948, 1967, and 1973, the hijacking of planes, the disruptive 1973 Arab oil embargo, along with the rise of Libya's Muammar Qaddafi and Iran's Ayatollah Khomeini—shot after shot delivered the relentless drum beat that all Arabs were and are Public Enemy No. 1.
>
> *(Shaheen 2001: 28–9)*

From the late 1940s into the 1970s and 1980s, images of Arab men shifted from romantic and dangerous sheikhs to new images of rich, flashy oil sheikhs who threaten the U.S. economy and dangerous terrorists who threaten national security (Shaheen 2001: 21). These images, Shaheen writes, "regularly link the Islamic faith with male supremacy, holy war, and acts of terror, depicting Arab Muslims as hostile alien intruders, as lecherous, oily sheikhs intent on using nuclear weapons" (Shaheen 2001: 9). As for representations of Arab women, before WWII, they were portrayed as alluring harem girls and belly dancers (Jarmakani 2008). After WWII, images of Arab women largely disappeared from the representational field, but in the 1970s they reemerged as sexy but deadly terrorists and in the 1980s as veiled and oppressed (Yunis and Duthler 2011). After the 1990–1 Gulf War, Arab women were rendered invisible once again in the U.S. media. Therese Saliba writes that this was effected in two ways: they were either not represented, or when they were, it was only to accentuate their invisibility and therefore to support "neocolonial interests of the new world order and the U.S. media's repression of the war's destruction" (Saliba 1994: 126).

As for primetime television, Jamie Farr on *M.A.S.H.* (1972–83) and Hans Conreid on *The Danny Thomas Show* (1953–71) are the only consistent and non-stereotypical Arab-American characters in the history of U.S. television (until more recently, as I will discuss at the end of this chapter). Arab-American actors, such as Wendy Malik, Kathy Najimy, F. Murray Abraham, and Tony Shalhoub, appear on television and film, but rarely in roles as Arab Americans. Representations in television mirror those in film and other mediums of popular culture. In *The TV Arab*, Jack Shaheen examines children's cartoons, police dramas, and comedy shows on U.S. television from 1975 through 1984, identifying depictions of Arabs as billionaires, bombers, and belly dancers. He writes, "Television tends to perpetuate four basic myths about Arabs: they are all fabulously wealthy; they are barbaric and uncultured; they are sex maniacs with a penchant for white slavery; and they revel in acts of terrorism" (Shaheen 1984: 4).

Significant shifts toward portraying Arabs and/or Muslims as terrorists in the 1970s are not only evident in Hollywood filmmaking and TV shows but also in the U.S. corporate news media. Melani McAlister in *Epic Encounters* argues that Americans' association of the Middle East with the Christian Holy Land or Arab oil wealth shifted to a place of Muslim terror through news reporting on the Munich Olympics (1972), the Arab oil embargo (1973), the Iran hostage crisis (1979–80), and airplane hijackings in the 1970s and 1980s (McAlister 2001). Between 1968 and 1976, Palestinians and Palestinian sympathizers led 29 hijackings, forming a central part of the U.S. news cycle and becoming a popular theme in Hollywood films in the 1970s and 1980s (McAlister 2001: 182). The news media came to play a crucial role in making the Middle East, and Islam in particular, meaningful to Americans as a place that breeds terrorism.

The Iran hostage crisis was a key moment in conflating Arab, Muslim, and Middle Eastern identities. Though Iran is not an Arab country, during the hostage crisis Iran came to stand for Arabs, the Middle East, Islam, and terrorism—all of which came to be used interchangeably. Edward Said's examination of how the news media reported the Iran hostage crisis demonstrates case after case of biased portrayal of Islam: "During the past few years, especially since events in Iran caught European and American attention so strongly, the media have therefore covered Islam: they have portrayed it, characterized it, analyzed it, given instant courses on it, and consequently they have made it 'known'" (Said 1997: i). "Knowing Islam" in the US came to mean knowing fundamentalism and terrorism. The monolithic portrayal of Islam as threatening reduces a diverse and dynamic Islam, including its varied followers and their experiences, into something unknown and unknowable.

This genealogy of the emergence of the Arab terrorist threat in the U.S. commercial media reveals that while 9/11 is a new historical moment, it is also part of a longer history in which viewers have been primed by the media for decades to equate Arabs and Muslims first with dissoluteness and patriarchy/misogyny and then with terrorism.

## Representations Post-9/11

Many authors note a more ambivalent portrayal of Arabs and Muslims post-9/11; specifically, some notable improvements on the one hand, but the continuation of harmful stereotypes on the other. In *Guilty: Hollywood's Verdict on Arabs after 9/11*, Jack Shaheen acknowledges some films (e.g., Babel (2006) and Rendition (2007)) for their relatively more complex portrayals of Arabs and Muslims, but also notes more ominous portrayals in Hollywood films and TV dramas in which Arabs and Muslims are turned into the new "bogeymen" (Shaheen 2008). He argues that such depictions have facilitated U.S. interventionist policies in the Middle East, such as going to war in Iraq in 2003. Brigitte Nacos and Oscar Torres-Reyna in *Fueling Our Fears: Stereotyping, Media Coverage and Public Opinion of Muslim Americans* show how the news media after 9/11 was responsible at times for promoting stereotypes and discriminatory policies (e.g., referring to torture at Abu Ghraib prison as "abuse" instead of "torture"), while at other times attempting to increase cultural understanding (e.g., emphasizing the need to protect Muslim-American civil rights and an increase in stories about everyday Muslim-American life) (Nacos and Torres-Reyna 2006).

My own book, *Arabs and Muslims in the Media*, explores how the multicultural movement of the 1980s and 1990s is a crucial turning point in the history of Orientalist representations of Arabs and Muslims. This period saw the introduction of sympathetic representations, a mode that has become standardized after 9/11 (Alsultany 2012). The post-9/11 shift is not one in which Arabs once represented solely as terrorists are now represented only sympathetically—far from it. Rather, the shift is from a few exceptional, sympathetic representations of Arabs and Muslims to a new strategy of making sympathetic representations a stock feature of media narratives. A few films in the 1990s—particularly *The Siege* (1998) and *Three Kings* (1999)—challenged the trend of representing Arabs and Muslims as one-dimensional stereotypes; these films offered a multidimensional terrorist character and included a "good" Arab or victimized Arab American for (almost) every "evil" Arab.[1] In *Three Kings*, the "good" Iraqi character was educated in the US; in *The Siege*, the "good" Arab American works as an FBI agent. A similar trend is spotted in *Not without My Daughter* (1991) in which a "good" U.S.-educated Iranian helps Betty escape Iran. Crucially, the "good" Arab or Muslim characters are always either American-educated or choose to dedicate their lives to helping the U.S. government fight terrorism. When these films were produced during the era of the multicultural movement, these strategies were considered "new" and as "exceptions."

After 9/11 these representational strategies, particularly including a "good" Arab/Muslim American to counteract the "bad" or terrorist Arab/Muslim, came to define the new standard when representing Arabs and Muslims. The TV drama, *24*, in particular, proved innovative in portraying the Arab/Muslim terrorist threat, while seeking not to reproduce the stereotype of the Arab/Muslim terrorist. *24* used a range of representational strategies to accomplish this, including portraying Arab and Muslim Americans as patriotic Americans or as innocent victims of post-9/11 hate crimes, humanizing portrayals of Arab/Muslim terrorists, and fictionalizing the country of the terrorist.

On the surface, such innovative strategies seem to effectively subvert stereotypes. However, a diversity of representations, even an abundance of sympathetic characters, do not in themselves "solve" the problem of racial stereotyping. As Ella Shohat, Robert Stam, Herman Gray, and other scholars have shown, focusing on whether a particular image is either "good" or "bad" does not address the complexity of representation (Shohat and Stam 1994; Gray 1995). Rather, it is important to examine the ideological work performed by images and the storylines beyond such binaries. If we interpret an image as simply positive or negative, then we can conclude that the problem of racial stereotyping is over because there have been sympathetic images of Arabs and Muslims during the War on Terror. However, an examination of such an image in relation to its narrative context reveals how it participates in a larger field of meaning about Arabs and Muslims. Despite such notable efforts, combating stereotypes is more complex than including positive and nuanced Arab/Muslim characters and storylines. In short, such efforts have a minimal impact so long as the underlying premise of the story hinges on an Arab/Muslim terrorist threat. While I acknowledge that shows like *24* and others seeking to balance negative representations with sympathetic ones took important steps to diversify their portrayal of Arabs and Muslims, we cannot go as far as assuming that such efforts actually solve stereotyping. Indeed, interpreted too rosily, such "positive" representational strategies can even become part of the problem if and when they suggest that racism is not tolerated in the US, despite the slew of policies that have targeted and disproportionately impacted Arabs and Muslims.

Many other post-9/11 TV shows use these strategies of sympathetic representation, from terrorist-themed shows like *Sleeper Cell* (Showtime, 2005–7) and *Homeland* (Showtime, 2011–present) to broader shows with occasional terrorist themes like *Law and Order* (NBC, 1990–2010) and *The Practice* (ABC, 1997–2004), reflecting the standardization of this representational practice. Still, representations of Arab and Muslim identities in contexts that have nothing to do with terrorism remain strikingly unusual in the US commercial media. There have been a few sitcoms and reality television shows that aim to break out of prevailing molds: *Whoopi* (NBC, 2003–4), *Aliens in America* (CW, 2007–8), *Community* (NBC, 2009–present), *Little Mosque on the Prairie* (2007–12), *All-American Muslim* (TLC, 2011–12), and *Shahs of Sunset* (2012–present) all offer broader portrayals of Arabs and Muslims. While the extent to which some of these shows challenge stereotypes has been debated, they are nonetheless examples of representations of Arabs and Muslims outside of the context of terrorism and homeland security.

What cannot be forgotten, however, is that at the same time that representations that challenge the stereotyping of Arabs and Muslims were being broadcast, circulated, and consumed, real Arabs and Muslims were being detained, deported, held without due process, and tortured by the US. According to the FBI, hate crimes against Arabs and Muslims multiplied by 1,600 percent from 2000 to 2001 (FBI 2001). Throughout the decade following 9/11, hate crimes, workplace discrimination, bias incidents, and airline discrimination targeting Arab and Muslim Americans have persisted. In addition to individual citizens taking the law into their own hands, the U.S. government passed legislation that targeted Arabs and Muslims (both inside and outside the US) and legalized suspending their constitutional rights.[2] The USA PATRIOT Act, passed by Congress in October 2001 and renewed multiple times since, legalized the following (previously illegal) acts and thus enabled anti-Arab and Muslim racism: monitoring Arab and Muslim groups; granting the U.S. Attorney General the right to indefinitely detain non-citizens suspected of having ties to terrorism; searching and wiretapping secretly, without probable cause; arresting and holding a person as a "material witness" whose testimony might assist in a case; using secret evidence, without granting the accused access to that evidence; trying those designated as "enemy combatants" in military tribunals (as opposed to civilian courts); and deportation based on guilt by association rather than actions (Council on American-Islamic Relations 2002). To put it mildly, the explicit targeting of Arabs and Muslims by government policies, based on their identity as opposed to their criminality, contradicts claims to racial progress.

Certainly not all Arabs and Muslims were subject to post-9/11 harassment. Nonetheless, these multiple representational strategies do not in themselves solve stereotyping and racism, and can actually perform the ideological work of producing the illusion of a post-race moment that obscures the severity and injustice of institutionalized racism as outlined above. Such TV dramas produce reassurance that racial sensitivity is the norm in U.S. society, while simultaneously perpetuating the dominant perception of Arabs and Muslims as threats to U.S. national security. Though some television writers certainly have humane motives, and though some producers honestly desire to create innovative shows, devoid of stereotypes, such efforts are overwhelmed by the sheer momentum of our current representational scheme. So long as Arabs and Muslims are represented primarily in the context of terrorism, our current crop of representational strategies—for all of their apparent innovations—will have a minimal impact on viewers' perceptions of Arabs and Muslims, and far worse, will perpetuate a simplistic vision of good and evil under the guise of complexity and sensitivity.

## Notes

1 For analysis and criticism of *Three Kings* and *The Siege*, see T. Semmerling (2006) *"Evil" Arabs in American Popular Film*; M. McAlister (2001) *Epic Encounters*, chapter 6; J. Shaheen (2001) *Reel Bad Arabs*; Wilkins and Downing (2002) "Mediating Terrorism: Text and Protest in Interpretations of *The Siege*," *Critical Studies in Media Communication* 19(4): 419–437; Lila Kitaeff (2003) "*Three Kings*: Neocolonial Arab Representation," *Jump Cut: A Review of Contemporary Media* 46: 1–16.

2 For reports on the government's practice of detaining and deporting Arabs and Muslims after 9/11, see, for example, American-Arab Anti-Discrimination (2002) "ADC Fact Sheet: The Condition of Arab Americans Post-9/11," March 27, http://www.adc.org/index.php?id=282 and A. Bakalian and M. Bozorgmehr (2009) *Backlash 9/11: Middle Eastern and Muslim Americans Respond*. Berkeley, CA: University of California Press.

# References

Alsultany, E. (2012) *Arabs and Muslims in the Media. Race and Representation after 9/11*. New York: New York University Press.

Bayoumi, M. (2006) "Racing Religion," *CR: The New Centennial Review* 6(2): 267–293.

Cainkar, L. (2011) *Homeland Insecurity: The Arab American and Muslim American Experience after 9/11*. New York: The Russell Sage Foundation.

Council on American-Islamic Relations. (2002) "The Status of Muslim Civil Rights in the United States 2002: Stereotypes and Civil Liberties," *Civil Rights Report*. Retrieved from http://www.cair.com/CivilRights/CivilRightsReports/2002Report.aspx.

Edwards, B. (2005) *Morocco Bound: Disorienting America's Maghreb, from Casablanca to the Marrakech Express*. Durham, NC: Duke University Press.

FBI. (2001) *Hate Crimes Statistics Report*. Retrieved from http://www.fbi.gov/about-us/cjis/ucr/hate-crime/2001.

Gray, H. (1995) *Watching Race: Television and the Struggle for Blackness*. Minneapolis, MN: University of Minnesota Press.

Jarmakani, A. (2008) *Imagining Arab Womanhood: The Cultural Mythology of Veils, Harems, and Belly Dancers in the US*. New York: Palgrave Macmillan.

Maira, S. (2010) *Missing: Youth, Citizenship, and Empire after 9/11*. Durham, NC: Duke University Press.

McAlister, M. (2001) *Epic Encounters: Culture, Media, and U.S. Interests in the Middle East, 1945–2000*. Berkeley, CA: University of California Press.

Naber, N. (2000) "Ambiguous Insiders: An Investigation of Arab American Invisibility," *Racial and Ethnic Studies* 23(1): 37–61.

——. (2008) "Look, Mohammad the Terrorist in Coming!: Cultural Racism, Nation-Based Racism, and the Intersectionality of Oppressions after 9/11," in N. Naber and A. Jamal (eds.), *Race and Arab Americans before and after 9/11: From Invisible Citizens to Visible Subjects*. Syracuse, NY: Syracuse University Press, 276–304.

Naber, N. and Jamal A. (eds.) (2008) *Race and Arab Americans before and after 9/11: From Invisible Citizens to Visible Subjects*. Syracuse, NY: Syracuse University Press.

Nacos B. and Torres-Reyna, O. (2006) *Fueling Our Fears: Stereotyping, Media Coverage and Public Opinion of Muslim Americans*. New York: Rowman and Littlefield.

Puar, J. (2007) *Terrorist Assemblages: Homonationalism in Queer Times*. Durham, NC: Duke University Press.

Rana, J. (2011) *Terrifying Muslims: Race and Labor in the South Asian Diaspora*. Durham, NC: Duke University Press.

——. (2013) "When Pakistanis Became Middle Eastern: Visualizing Racial Targets in the Global War on Terror," in E. Alsultany and E. Shohat (eds.), *Between the Middle East and the Americas: The Cultural Politics of Diaspora*. Ann Arbor, MI: University of Michigan Press, 176–192.

Razack, S. (2008) *Casting Out: The Eviction of Muslims from Western Law and Politics*. Toronto, Ontario: University of Toronto Press.

Said, E. (1997) *Covering Islam*, revised ed. New York: Vintage.

Saliba, T. (1994) "Military Presences and Absences: Arab Women and the Persian Gulf War," in S. Jeffords and L. Rabinowitz (eds.), *Seeing through the Media: The Persian Gulf War*. New Brunswick, NJ: Rutgers University Press, 263–284.

Samhan, H. (1999) "Not Quite White: Race Classification and the Arab American Experience," in M. Suleiman (ed.), *Arabs in America: Building a New Future*. Philadelphia, PA: Temple University Press, 209–226.

Semmerling, T. (2006) *'Evil' Arabs in American Popular Film*. Austin, TX: University of Texas Press.

Shaheen, J. (1984) *The TV Arab*. Bowling Green, OH: Bowling Green State University Popular Press.

——. (2001) *Reel Bad Arabs: How Hollywood Vilifies a People*. Northampton, MA: Olive Branch Press.

——. (2008) *Guilty: Hollywood's Verdict on Arabs after 9/11*. Northampton, MA: Olive Branch Press.

Shohat, E. (1991) "Gender and the Culture of Empire: Toward a Feminist Ethnography of the Cinema," *Quarterly Review of Film and Video* 13(1–3): 45–84.

Shohat, E. and Stam, R. (1994) *Unthinking Eurocentrism: Multiculturalism and the Media*. New York: Routledge.

Wilkins, K. (2008) *Home/Land/Security: What We Learn about Arab Communities from Action-Adventure Films*. Lanham, MD: Lexington Books.

Yunis, A. and Duthler, G. (2011) "Tramps vs. Sweethearts: Changing Images of Arab and American Women in Hollywood Films," *Middle East Journal of Culture and Communication* 4(2): 225–243.

## Further Reading

Alsultany, E. (2012) *Arabs and Muslims in the Media: Race and Representation after 9/11*. New York: New York University Press. (An examination of how positive representations of Arab and Muslim Americans after 9/11 can produce meanings that justify inequality.)

McAlister, M. (2001) *Epic Encounters: Culture, Media, and U.S. Interests in the Middle East, 1945–2000*. Berkeley, CA: University of California Press. (An examination of how popular culture has shaped American interest in the Middle East and the relationship between culture and U.S. foreign policy.)

Said, E. (1981) *Covering Islam. How the Media and the Experts Determine How We See the Rest of the World*. New York: Vintage. (Examines how U.S. journalists reporting on the Iran Hostage Crisis in 1979–80 disregarded historical and political factors in favor of a monolithic portrait of Islam.)

Shaheen, J. (2001) *Reel Bad Arabs: How Hollywood Vilifies a People*. Northampton, MA: Olive Branch Press. (An encyclopedia-style book that documents almost a thousand Hollywood films and their portrayal of Arabs from the late 1800s to 2000, revealing the overwhelmingly negative portrayal of Arabs and Muslims throughout Hollywood history.)

Shohat, E. and Stam R. (1994) *Unthinking Eurocentrism: Multiculturalism and the Media*. New York: Routledge. (Analyzes Eurocentrism and multiculturalism in popular culture and argues for the decolonization of global culture through an examination of indigenous and Third-World media.)

# 23
# MIXED RACE
## From Pathology to Celebration
### Ji-Hyun Ahn

Racial mixing is a longstanding topic of theory and empirical analysis in multiple disciplines, including literary criticism, postcolonial studies, and race and ethnic studies. Scholars address racial mixing in terms of in-betweenness, (racial) hybridity, and *mestizaje*, a Latin-American term that describes cultural blending (e.g., Ang 2001; Bhabha 1998; Bhabha 1994; Canclini 1995; Kraidy 2005; Anzaldúa 1987). Yet until recently, media studies have not focused on mixed raciality because audiences are not taught to read multiracial figures on-screen. However, the cultural meaning of multiraciality is changing as media representation becomes more diverse and inclusive. Media scholars note that the media/cultural representation of mixed-race people has shifted "from pathologization to celebration" (Parker and Song 2001) and "from tragic to heroic" (Beltrán and Fojas 2008).

This chapter addresses the causes of this shift and its significance for larger social transformation by critically examining the politics of mixed-race representation in the American media landscape. The chapter focuses on scholarly discussion in the United States, but it also encompasses transnational scholarship by introducing research on mixed-race representation in East Asia that takes a different historical trajectory from the West.

## Beyond Binary: Historical Context of Mixed-Race Studies in the US

The concept of mixed raciality is historically and culturally constructed, defined by particular boundaries in different societal contexts. Scholars use multiple concepts to radically re-theorize mixedness. In her inspiring book *Borderlands/LaFrontera: The New Mestiza*, Gloria Anzaldúa (1987), a feminist and Chicano studies scholar, uses the term "mestiza consciousness" to theorize new hybrid subjectivity. In the postcolonial studies tradition, theorists such as Stuart Hall (1978; 1995), Néstor García Canclini (1995), and Homi Bhabha (1994) use the terms "hybridity" and/or "Third Space" to produce a conceptual space that blurs boundaries and challenges the established categorizations of racial identities. Across these conceptual frameworks, one of the crucial theoretical implications of mixed-race categories is that they deconstruct formerly rigid binary oppositions such as black and white, colonizer and colonized, master and slave, and original and reproduced, illustrating that these binaries are not fixed but constructed.

The term "mixed-race" generally refers to a person born to differently racialized parents. Yet the term "multiracial" was introduced to reflect the constructed nature of the mixed-race category and has gained linguistic currency, complementing the use of the term mixed-race today. In current usage, "mixed-race, biracial, and multiracial all are used equally to refer to relationships and individuals of two or more of the socially constructed racial categories of the United States" (Beltrán and Fojas 2008: 4). Because the mixed-race category is culturally and historically specific, various names and terminologies indicate particular types of racial mixing: *mestizo* (racial mixing of indigenous Latin Americans with Europeans and others), Chicano (Latinos of mixed Mexican heritage), hapa (originally referred to a mixed Hawaiian heritage but more generally refers to individuals with mixed Asian or Pacific Islander and white), and Amerasian (historically used to describe the mixed-race population born to American soldier fathers and Asian mothers in postwar Asia).

This diversity of mixed-race categories and terminologies demonstrates that racial mixing has always been complex. Yet mixed-race identity in the United States is commonly perceived through the frame of black–white relations due to the country's long history of European colonialism and slavery. Throughout much of its history, America practiced a well-known racial categorization system of hypodescent called the "one-drop rule," under which anyone with even "one drop of black blood" was considered black. Scholars note that the notion of hypodescent perpetuated a notion of "pure blood" and "pure white" (Wilson 1992; Davis 1992; Nakashima 1992). In other words, the one-drop rule enforced the dominant class's desire to keep the American nation white (Squires 2007). In the meantime, the "strong reinforcement of the one-drop rule provided a firm black identity for most African Americans" (Davis 1992: 125) because it strengthened group cohesion within the black community (Kimberly 2009). In addition, until 1967, the year that *Loving vs. Virginia* ended anti-miscegenation laws, U.S. law prohibited interracial marriage as a threat to racial purity (Nakashima 1992). Such racial classification (e.g., the one-drop rule) as well as racial laws (e.g., anti-miscegenation law) vividly illustrate how American racial hierarchy is constructed in relation to blood, though Hawaii had an alternative racial categorization system that balanced egalitarian pluralism and assimilation (Davis 1992: 131). In short, scholarly discussion of mixed race points to the myth of a black and white racial binary system as a source of racism against mixed-race people (Valentine 2009).

## Early Hollywood Narrative on Miscegenation and Mixed-Race Identity

For decades, the Hollywood film industry has been one of the most powerful media institutions producing popular cultural texts that shape social norms and stereotypes about gender, race, class, and sexuality (Shohat and Stam 1994). One of the most lasting Hollywood stereotypes of mixed-race persons is the "tragic mulatto." Originating from the Spanish term *mulo* (mule in English), which literally refers to a hybrid offspring of a donkey and a horse, the term "mulatto" is derogatorily used to describe a black biracial person. In early literary tradition as well as in Hollywood films, mixed-race characters were described as "tragic, unnatural phenomena" and "psychologically damaged outcasts, angry at both parents' racial groups" (Squires 2007: 34). In the tragic mulatto trope, the characters were tragic "because the mixed race individual must die to restore order for white society" (Squires 2014: 107). This stereotype denigrates blackness as a "problem" to be gotten rid of. Angel (2007: 248) insists, "By continuously framing these stories [of mixed-race characters] as tragic, rigid categories of racial identity are reinforced, and the multiracial child is buried further under layers of racial essentialism."

This tragic mulatto character in early Hollywood was easily absorbed into the passing narrative. As Nerad (2014) observed, "Although there are incidences of white-to-black passing, because of the history of slavery, Jim Crow segregation, and racism in the United States, the most common iteration of racial passing has been black-to-white" (11). In other words, the practice of passing more typically occurred among light-skinned people of color by taking on white identities for the purpose of acquiring upwards social mobility. Yet those who passed for white "were subject to social, physical, and legal repercussions if whites discovered their masquerade" (Squires 2007: 55). As such, the passing characters were treated as deceitful and punished in Hollywood films made in the era of segregation.

In addition to the passing narrative, because colonialism and slavery are so deeply rooted in American racial imagination and politics, the fear and desire of miscegenation—interracial sex and marriage between black and white partners—emerged as a central theme among some African-American novelists in the early twentieth century (Daniel et al. 2014: 7). Since interracial marriage was illegal until 1967 in the United States, depictions of miscegenation were also restricted by the Production Code Administration (PCA) in early Hollywood. Yet miscegenation was not entirely absent from Hollywood films. Producers invented various techniques to visualize the desire for miscegenation without violating the Production Code. Films avoided showing "actual miscegenation" by casting white actors in non-white roles (Beltrán and Fojas 2008: 8), illustrating that miscegenation was a "forbidden fantasy/desire" in early Hollywood films.

In her analysis of Hollywood narrative and cinematic representation of miscegenation from the early 1900s to the late 1960s, Susan Courtney (2005) astutely demonstrates that Hollywood films projected a fantasy of black and white miscegenation to generate viewing pleasure for spectators. By examining how early Hollywood films, including *The Birth of a Nation* (1915), *Imitation of Life* (1934), *Pinky* (1949), and *Guess Who's Coming to Dinner* (1967), construct miscegenation narrative within the films in relation to the changes in the PCA's restriction on miscegenation, Courtney (2005) shows that the miscegenation narrative was gendered, sexualized, and raced, reinforcing white patriarchy.

As the first Hollywood film that cast a black actress as the passing character, John Stahl's *Imitation of Life* (1934) deserves elaboration. Stahl's choice of Fredi Washington to play the character Peola, a black biracial figure who decides to pass as white in the film, was a sensation at that time, given Hollywood's long tradition of casting whites as black characters (Bowdre 2014). Though Washington's screen time in the film was not substantial, her presence unnerved PCA members who "read Peola's light skin and her eventual passing as signifiers of miscegenation" (Courtney 2005: 144). In other words, while the film did not actually depict miscegenation, the PCA read Peola's fair skin (and her passing) on the screen as a *result* of miscegenation that fictionally happened outside the film narrative. Courtney (2005: 144) explains, "By conflating miscegenation and passing in this way, the censors attempt to extend the Code's ban on sex and desire across black and white racial boundaries to prohibit identification across them as well."

In 1967, the Supreme Court of the United States struck down all remaining anti-miscegenation laws in the United States in its *Loving vs. Virginia* ruling. This key moment in the history of American racial politics increased the visibility of mixed-race people in America's public consciousness and precipitated a "biracial baby boom" (Beltrán and Fojas 2008; Angel 2007; Root 1992). Though whether the actual number of interracial marriages increased *because of* the *Loving* decision is controversial, the case significantly reduced the stigma against interracial marriage (Daniel 2014). Released in the year of the *Loving* decision, *Guess Who's Coming to Dinner* (1967) was the first Hollywood film to locate interracial marriage at the center of its plot, and it still stands as one of the most popular and successful miscegenation Hollywood films. While the power of PCA had significantly declined by the 1960s, interracial sex and marriage were still considered taboo. Thus, though the plot of *Guess Who's Coming to Dinner* treated the conflicts and reunification of two main protagonists' families, the film contained no interracial sex scenes (Angel 2007).

## From Tragic to Heroic: Contemporary Mixed-Race Representation

After the *Loving* decision, social movements of the 1970s and 1980s including feminist movements, anti-racist movements, and gay right movements precipitated the rise of political correctness and multiculturalism in the 1990s. In this context, mixed-race studies scholarship burgeoned in the 1990s and into the 2000s. A few important early studies include Paul Spickard's *Mixed Blood* (1989), Maria Root's edited volume *Racially Mixed People in America* (1992), Naomi Zack's anthology *American Mixed Race* (1995), Parker and Song's anthology *Rethinking Mixed-Race* (2001), and Jayne Ifekwunigwe's *"Mixed Race" Studies: A Reader* (2004). Based on this founding scholarship in mixed-race studies, mixed-race media scholarship began to develop in the early twenty-first century. As the first media studies anthology devoted to the topic of mixed-race representation, Mary Beltrán and Camilla Fojas' *Mixed Race Hollywood* (2008) explores a range of themes regarding popular mixed-race representation in early Hollywood films and in contemporary television programs, celebrity image/culture, and Internet sites. As the book's topic implies, multiracials now appear in all forms of media, including magazines, ads, comics, matching websites, film, and TV.

Whereas early Hollywood miscegenation narratives and visual representations of mixed-race figures depicted the lives of mixed-race people as tragic, associating negative cultural meanings with racial mixing, contemporary popular representations of mixed-race people complicate racial lines and cultural meanings of biraciality. As Beltrán and Fojas (2008: 10–11) describe, contemporary Hollywood's representation of mixed-race characters has become "neutral, ordinary, positive, or even heroic," leading to an "overall boom of the casting of mixed-race actors in contemporary film and TV."

Analyzing mixed-race African-American characters in contemporary American popular culture, including best-selling novels, primetime TV dramas, and reality competition shows, Ralina Joseph (2013) demonstrates that the image of the tragic mulatto has been reconfigured in the contemporary setting. She describes two hegemonic representational modes of mixed-race African Americans in mainstream media: the "new millennium mulatta" and the "exceptional biracial." According to Joseph, the tradition of the tragic mulatto informs the new millennium mulatta in that new millennium mulatta characters are punished for playing a race card. For the new millennium mulatta, blackness is considered the "cause and effect of sadness and pain" that "must be surpassed to arrive at a state of health or success" (Joseph 2013: 6). In this sense, the new millennium mulatta iterates the "sad race girl" trope of the tragic mulatto.

By contrast, the exceptional multiracial typology prizes mixed-race blackness over "pure" blackness. The exceptional multiracial is celebrated for overcoming or transcending blackness (or even race), as in the case of model Tyra Banks as well as the participants on the reality competition show *America's Next Top Model* (see chapter 4 of Joseph's book). This exceptional multiracial trope is a part of recent discourses that assert a post-racial society and colorblindness by framing race as malleable and something that one can transcend through performance. Joseph insists that these two types of stereotype on mixed-race African Americans are not replacing each other. Instead, the new millennium mulatta "is functioning in tandem with it [exceptional multiracial], with both modes operating simultaneously in a dialectic" (Joseph 2013: 4).

Joseph's analysis of the exceptional biracial is resonant with what Mary Beltrán (2005) calls "new Hollywood racelessness." Beltrán (2005) argues that the action film genre in contemporary Hollywood now casts biracial or multiracial actors as protagonists. A few emblematic examples are Keanu Reeves in *The Matrix* trilogy, Russell Wong in *Romeo Must Die* (2000), and Vin Diesel in *The Fast and the Furious* (2001). These action heroes' biraciality (or multiraciality) is marked as a new ideal of Hollywood's raceless aesthetics. Yet these biracial action heroes' racial(ized) bodies are still "likely to be read as white," reinforcing Hollywood's longstanding tradition of white supremacy (Beltrán 2005: 64).

Beltrán's analysis raises the topic of racial visibility in visual culture. The textual meaning of the visual materials is not fixed but rather contested through audiences' interpretation and reinterpretation (Du Gay and Hall 1997). How audiences read the images of biracial figures on the screen indicates the level of racial visibility in visual culture. In her book *Undercover Asian*, LeiLani Nishime (2014) problematizes the visual absence of multiracial Asian Americans in American popular culture, revealing audiences' inability to read them as multiracial Asian Americans. Through her thorough analysis of emblematic multiracial Asian Americans—Keanu Reeves, Tiger Woods, and Kimora Lee Simmons—she argues that their (racialized) bodies serve as cultural sites where audiences' mis-reading and re-reading of race take place, offering both new possibilities and limits for reconsidering racial visibility in popular media. She notes, "The primary issue is not whether Reeves is 'really' Asian or white or even multiracial, but under what circumstances he is visible (or not visible) as multiracial Asian American—and why" (Nishime 2014: xv).

Like Hollywood action films, contemporary television is actively incorporating multiracial representations as well as diverse ethnic representations through so-called "multiculticasting" or "colorblind casting." Although not explicitly interracial/multiracial-themed shows, increasing numbers of dramas include more multiracial cast members for secondary roles or background characters for the purpose of setting up the post-racial world of the main protagonists. Examples are *Nip/Tuck* (2003–10), *Grey's Anatomy* (2005–present), *Glee* (2009–15), and *Modern Family* (2009–present), to name a few. In addition, some primetime TV dramas such as *Battlestar Galactica* (2004–9) and *Parenthood* (2010–15) have made interracial couples and their biracial children central to the show's narrative, reflecting increasing numbers of social issues around multiracial people in America. As Nilsen and Turner (2014: 4) assert, "While negative racial stereotypes do continue to circulate within the media, the dominant mode of televisual racialization has shifted to a colorblind ideology that foregrounds racial differences in order to celebrate multicultural assimilation."

It is certainly empowering for audiences, people of color in particular, to see more inclusive racial representation on TV. Yet scholars also critique the ideological implications of this inclusive casting practice, arguing that such casting is not necessarily progressive or inclusive. Erica Childs (2012) argues that "interracial relationships may be popping up more frequently on television but they do more to reinforce the current racial situation rather than challenge us to move beyond it." Pointing out that interracial inclusion in primetime TV dramas is mostly through the union between white men and women of color, Squires (2014: 131) insists that it is because "men of color are too threatening to become part of the extended family." Even with the multiracial family on the show, it is problematic that Asian mothers are largely missing from biracial TV families, whereas white fathers present and play an active role in the family dynamics (Day 2015). Critical scholarship is therefore needed to examine how current casting practices frame racial and cultural diversity.

## Mixed-Race People as a Marker of a Post-Racial Society?

One of the most contentious debates on mixed raciality in the contemporary era regards the discourse of a post-racial society. Barack Obama's election as the first black biracial president significantly changed the cultural and political landscape in the US (Kimberly 2009; Parameswaran 2009; Jolivétte 2012), triggering among some the idea that race and racism is no longer an issue in the United States. This idea took root in the popular discourse of a post-racial and colorblind society.

Since the early 1990s, the mainstream media has popularized the idea that the growing multiracial population in the US indicates a racially harmonious future in articles such as *Time* magazine's "New Face of America" in 1993, *Newsweek*'s special report on "Redefining Race in America" in 2000, and the *New York Times*' article on "Generation E.A.—Ethnically Ambiguous" in 2003. These claims were supported by statistical data on demographic change (e.g., the 2010 Census showing that America's multiracial population grew faster than any single-race population). In this aspiration toward the "new face of America," the mainstream media treated biracial/multiracial people as a marker of a utopian vision of post-racial society (Squires 2014). This treatment aligned with Hollywood's shift in mixed-race representation from the trope of the tragic mulatto to that of heroic, exceptional figures and the media's celebration of mixed-race beauties, which together romanticized mixed-race people as the harbingers of America's post-racial future. The visible increase in popular culture of emblematic "exceptional multiracial"—to use Joseph's (2014) term—celebrities such as Tiger Woods, Keanu Reeves, Jessica Alba, and Jennifer Lopez signifies a new level of racial diversity and integration in the United States.

Despite the mainstream media's enthusiastic embrace of mixed-race figures, scholars have expressed concern over the discourse that celebrates a supposed post-racial society through mixed raciality (see Elam 2011; Dawkins 2012; Mahtani 2014; Squires 2014). As a critical intervention in the production of mixed-race aesthetics and media rhetoric regarding post-racial society, Michelle Elam (2011) deconstructs the mixed-race mythology by interrogating the ways in which the mixed-race category (and identity) is framed, marketed, and celebrated in the post-Civil Rights era. Minelle Mahtani (2014) also resists the romanticization of multiraciality, questioning what type of (racial) mixing particularly matters to whom through an anti-colonial perspective. As such, even though popular media appropriates the image of the mixed-race figure as a utopian vision of a raceless society, "race remains prevalent *because* of biracial people, not *in spite* of it" (Ramon 2013: 100). Perhaps what current mixed-race celebration signifies is not the end of race/racism but a new departure for reimagining political action as we enter a seemingly problematic post-racial society.

JI-HYUN AHN

# Mixed-Race Representation in a Global Context

Research on mixed raciality is focused on the US and the UK, but some recent work has broadened (critical) mixed-race studies to include a more global scope. One of the first anthologies on mixed-race populations around the globe, *Global Mixed-Race Studies* (2014), reminds scholars that mixed-race experiences and identity politics must be understood in relation to historical context and national/regional politics. While the book is a meaningful first step toward globalizing mixed-race studies, it also requires critical intervention on what it means to set "North American experiences and histories as a backdrop" (King-O'Riain 2014: viii) when we discuss other nations' mixed-race experiences in different contexts. To wrap up our discussion, I will introduce current studies on mixed-race representation in East Asia, in South Korea and Japan in particular, to offer some useful insights into global mixed-race studies.

In the West, race has played an important role in shaping national politics. By contrast, few East Asian countries have a long history of racial politics due to their relatively homogenous racial/ethnic populations and their strong developmental nationalism in the postcolonial era. Thus, Asian mixed-race studies generally examine "Amerasians" because of America's heavy military presence in the region during and after WWII. Wherever the American army was based, including Seoul (South Korea), Okinawa (Japan), and Phuket (Thailand), Amerasians were considered a social problem and were ostracized because of their "racial impurity."

For this reason, media representations of mixed-race individuals have been rare in East Asia. In South Korean postwar films, mixed-race figures embodied the tragic national history of war and national anxiety over American military imperial power (Koh 2009). In this sense, Amerasian characters resembled the tragic mulatto trope: tragic, angry, helpless, poor, and pitiful, though their pain and social stigma was rooted in the historical context of war rather than slavery and segregation. This is also true of Japanese film. Analyzing cinematic representations of mixed-race children in Japanese films from the 1950s to the 1970s, Mika Ko (2014) argues that films rarely depicted the lives of mixed-race children but instead sexualized and objectified female biracial bodies under a heterosexual male gaze to illustrate emasculated (Japanese) masculinity.

Yet the transition from pathology to celebration in mixed-race representation is a global trend. Mixedness and (racial) otherness is now promoted and commercialized in the work of selling difference and diversity in East Asia in the era of neoliberal globalization (Ko 2010). Global migration has accelerated the increase of international/interracial marriages in East Asia, expanding a different mixed-race population (mixed-race children of Asian descent) and kindling a new fascination with racial mixing. In Japan, the rise of *hāfu* discourse contrasts with the earlier *konketsu*, the Japanese term for mixed-blood, which carries a negative connotation, signals a positive change in the cultural meaning of biraciality. Yet the *hāfu* discourse is highly gendered such that *hāfu* models in fashion and beauty industry are mostly white biracial females of European or American descent (Iwabuchi 2014). By contrast, in South Korean mainstream media, white biracial males are increasingly popular figures (Ahn 2015). As such, the cultural currency of whiteness in East Asia is highly contested and entails multiple ruptures. Yet this topic is understudied. The examination of biracial whiteness in the transnational context is a much-needed research program that has the potential to reshape the conceptual frame of global mixed-race studies by tracing how whiteness transforms as it travels across the globe, and to problematize white privilege at the global level.

# References

Ahn, J-H. (2015) "Desiring Biracial Whites: Cultural Consumption of White Mixed-race Celebrities in South Korean Popular Media," *Media, Culture and Society* 37: 937–947.

Ang, I. (2001) *On Not Speaking Chinese: Living between Asia and the West*. London; New York: Routledge.

Angel, N. (2007) "The Missing Bi-racial Child in Hollywood," *Canadian Review of American Studies* 37: 239–263.

Anzaldúa, G. (1987) *Borderlands: The New Mestiza = La Frontera*. San Francisco, CA: Spinsters/Aunt Lute.

Beltrán, M. (2005) "The New Hollywood Racelessness: Only the Fast, Furious, (and Multiracial) Will Survive," *Cinema Journal* 44: 50–67.

Beltrán, M. and Fojas, C. (2008) *Mixed Race Hollywood*. New York: New York University Press.

Bhabha, H. (1994) *The Location of Culture*. London: Routledge.

——. (1998) "Culture's in between," in D. Bennett (ed.), *Multicultural States: Rethinking Difference and Identity*. London: Routledge, 29–36.

Bowdre, K. M. (2014) "Passing Films and the Illusion of Racial Equality," *Black Camera: An International Film Journal* 5: 21–43.

Canclini, N. G. (1995) *Hybrid Cultures: Strategies for Entering and Leaving Modernity*. Minneapolis, MN: University of Minnesota Press.

Childs, E. C. (2012) "The Prime Time Color Line: Shades Of Grey: Interracial Couples On TV," *Flow: A Critical Forum on Television and Media Culture* 15. Retrieved from http://www.flowjournal.org/2011/12/shades-of-grey.

Courtney, S. (2005) *Hollywood Fantasies of Miscegenation: Spectacular Narratives of Gender and Race, 1903–1967*. Princeton, NJ: Princeton University Press.

Daniel, G. R., Kina L., Dariotis, W. M., and Fojas, C. (2014) "Emerging Paradigms in Critical Mixed Race Studies," *Journal of Critical Mixed Race Studies* 1(1): 6–65.

Davis, F. J. (1992) "The Hawaiian Alternative to the One-Drop Rule," in M. P. P. Root (ed.), *Racially Mixed People in America*. Newbury Park, CA: Sage, 115–131.

Dawkins, M. A. (2012) *Clearly Invisible: Racial Passing and the Color of Cultural Identity*. Waco, TX: Baylor University Press.

Day, L. (2015) "One-sided Biracial TV Families: Why Are So Many Asian Moms MIA?," *AsAmNews*. Retrieved from http://www.asamnews.com/2015/08/05/one-sided-biracial-tv-families-why-are-so-many-asian-moms-mia/.

Du Gay, P. and Hall, S. (1997) *Doing Cultural Studies: The Story of the Sony Walkman*. London: Sage, in association with The Open University.

Elam, M. (2011) *The Souls of Mixed Folk: Race, Politics, and Aesthetics in the New Millennium*. Stanford, CA: Stanford University Press.

Hall, S. (1978) "Racism and Reaction," in Commission on Racial Equality (ed.), *Five Views of Multi-Cultural Britain*. London: Commission on Racial Equality, 23–35.

Hall, S. (1995) "Introduction: Who Needs 'Identity'?," in S. Hall and P. Du Guy (eds.), *Questions of Cultural Identity*. London: Sage, 1–17.

Ifekwunigwe, J. O. (2004) *"Mixed Race" Studies: A Reader*. London; New York: Routledge.

Iwabuchi, K. (2014) "Introduction: Critical Mixed Race Studies and Japanese Experiences," *Journal of Intercultural Studies* 35: 621–626.

Jolivétte, A. (2012) *Obama and the Biracial Factor: The Battle for a New American Majority*. Chicago, IL: Policy Press.

Joseph, R. L. (2013) *Transcending Blackness: From the New Millennium Mulatta to the Exceptional Multiracial*. Durham, NC: Duke University Press.

Kimberly, D. (2009) "Interracial Intimacies, Barack Obama, and the Politics of Multiculturalism," *The Black Scholar* 39: 4–12.

King-O'Riain, R. C. (2014) *Global Mixed Race*. New York: New York University Press.

Ko, M. (2010) *Japanese Cinema and Otherness: Nationalism, Multiculturalism and the Problem of Japaneseness*. New York: Routledge.

——. (2014) "Representations of 'Mixed-Race' Children in Japanese Cinema from the 1950s to the 1970s," *Journal of Intercultural Studies* 35: 627–645.

Koh, D-Y. (2009) "Representing American GIs in Postwar Korean Cinema: From *The Flower in Hell* (1958) to *Address Unknown* (2001)," *American History* 30: 147–175. (In Korean.)

Kraidy, M. (2005) *Hybridity, or the Cultural Logic of Globalization*. Philadelphia, PA: Temple University Press.
Mahtani, M. (2014) *Mixed Race Amnesia: Resisting the Romanticization of Multiraciality*, Vancouver, British Columbia: University of British Columbia Press.
Nakashima, C. (1992) "An Invisible Monster: The Creation and Denial of Mixed Race People in America," in M. P. P. Root (ed.), *Racially Mixed People in America*. Newbury Park, CA: Sage, 162–178.
Nerad, J. (2014) *Passing Interest: Racial Passing in U.S. Novels, Memoirs, Television, and Film, 1990–2010*. Albany, NY: SUNY Press.
Nilsen, S. and Turner, S. E. (2014) *The Colorblind Screen: Television in Post-racial America*. New York: New York University Press.
Nishime, L. (2014) *Undercover Asian: Multiracial Asian Americans in Visual Culture*. Urbana, IL: University of Illinois Press.
Parameswaran, R. (2009) "Facing Barack Hussein Obama: Race, Globalization, and Transnational America," *Journal of Communication Inquiry* 33: 195–205.
Parker, D. and Song, M. (2001) *Rethinking Mixed Race*. London: Pluto Press.
Ramon, D. L. (2013) "Review Article: *Clearly Invisible* by Marcia Alesan Dawkins and *The Souls of Mixed Folk* by Michele Elam," *Philip Roth Studies* 9: 99–103.
Root, M. P. P. (1992) *Racially Mixed People in America*. Newbury Park, CA: Sage.
Shohat, E. and Stam, R. (1994) *Unthinking Eurocentrism: Multiculturalism and the Media*. London: Routledge.
Spickard, P. (1989) *Mixed Blood: Intermarriage and Ethnic Identity in Twentieth-Century America*. Madison, WI: University of Wisconsin Press.
Squires, C. R. (2007) *Dispatches from the Color Line: The Press and Multiracial America*. Albany, NY: State University of New York Press.
——. (2014) *The Post-racial Mystique: Media and Race in the Twenty-First Century*. New York: New York University Press.
Valentine, D. (2009) "Visualizing a Critical Mixed-Race Theory," *Stance* 2: 18–25.
Wilson, T. P. (1992) "Blood Quantum: Native American Mixed Bloods," in M. P. P. Root (ed.), *Racially Mixed People in America*. Newbury Park, CA: Sage, 108–125.
Zack, N. (1995) *American Mixed Race: The Culture of Microdiversity*. Lanham, MD: Rowman and Littlefield Publishers.

# Further Reading

Beltrán, M. and Fojas, C. (2008) *Mixed Race Hollywood*. New York: New York University Press. (The first anthology on mixed-race representation in American media and popular culture that ranges from early Hollywood to celebrity culture, TV programs, and online sites.)
Courtney, S. (2005) *Hollywood Fantasies of Miscegenation: Spectacular Narratives of Gender and Race, 1903–1967*. Princeton, NJ: Princeton University Press. (A thorough examination on miscegenation narrative in early Hollywood films in its relation to the larger historical context of American racial politics.)
Elam, M. (2011) *The Souls of Mixed Folk: Race, Politics, and Aesthetics in the New Millennium*. Stanford, CA: Stanford University Press. (A critical study of mixed-race aesthetics in a number of different forms, such as literary, artistic, media and popular culture, including comic strips, fiction, and drama.)
Joseph, R. L. (2013) *Transcending Blackness: From the New Millennium Mulatta to the Exceptional Multiracial*. Durham, NC: Duke University Press. (A close look at visual representations of biracial African Americans in contemporary American popular culture and media.)
Nishime, L. (2014) *Undercover Asian: Multiracial Asian Americans in Visual Culture*. Urbana, IL: University of Illinois Press. (Examines popular media images of multiracial Asian Americans and studies why and how audiences fail to recognize multiracial Asian Americans in visual culture.)

# 24
# EUROPE

## Representations of Ethnic Minorities and Their Effects

*Christian Schemer and Philipp Müller*

Public opinion surveys indicate that most people in European countries harbor negative attitudes toward ethnic minorities and favor policy programs intended to restrict immigration (Zick, Küpper, and Hövermann 2011; Zick, Pettigrew, and Wagner 2008). For instance, a recent analysis of data from six rounds of the European Social Survey (covering the period between 2002 and 2012) demonstrates that anti-immigrant attitudes are a relatively stable phenomenon across European countries that has not significantly increased or decreased during this period (Hjerm and Bohman 2014). Moreover, the data show that the general level of racial attitudes differs between countries. Many Eastern-European countries (e.g., the Czech Republic or Hungary) exhibit a higher perceived ethnic threat while especially Scandinavian countries (e.g., Sweden or Norway) show less negative views on ethnic groups. The key factors that lead to these differences seem to be a lack of familiarity with foreigners and the fear of conflict over values and culture rather than social and economic competition between ethnic minorities and the majority population (Schneider 2008).

Communication research in Europe (Ruhrmann 2002; ter Wal 2002) and the US (Mastro 2009) indicates that these attitudes may be in part due to biased depictions of ethnic minorities in the media. This chapter provides an overview of how ethnic minorities are portrayed in the media in European countries. First, we give a short sketch of how immigration and integration in Europe has developed. Second, we provide a summary of findings on media representations of ethnic minorities in Europe. Here we focus on commonalities and differences between countries. In addition to cross-cultural variation in media representations of ethnic minorities, we show that there is considerable variation in the coverage of ethnic groups across media and news genres. We also consider the discourse that prevails among political elites, e.g., in parliamentary speeches. We conclude by pointing to extant gaps in research and possible avenues for future studies.

## Historical Developments

In the present context, we use the term "ethnic minorities" when we mean people that migrate from one country to another with the intention to stay there. The term "race"—although widely used by scholars in the US—can rarely be found in a European context (Trebbe 2009: 24). It can be regarded as emphasizing biological differences between different groups of human beings while "ethnicity" rather seems to refer to cultural commonalities (Spencer 2004). To European ears, "race" bears a somewhat negative connotation due to the racial ideology of the Nazi regime. Ethnic minorities can be considered as a social construct that only makes sense against the background of a majority population in a given nation-state.

The immigration streams into Europe after WWII differ considerably between countries. Most of these differences are due to different historical routes that European countries have taken (Geddes 2003). For instance, in France immigrants have mainly been entering from former colonies in Northern Africa, while in the UK, most immigrants came from Pakistan or Bangladesh. In Germany, immigrants are mainly guest workers from Turkey, Italy, or Portugal who were hired in the post-war era to re-build the country. In most European countries the balance of immigrants to emigrants is positive; only in some Eastern-European countries is it negative (Zick, Pettigrew, and Wagner 2008).

In recent years, immigration is widely discussed in three different contexts: First, after the end of the Cold War, countries from the former Soviet Republics entered the European Union (EU). Since the EU grants its inhabitants unrestricted mobility across countries, this has resulted in streams of immigration from Eastern to Western Europe (Favell 2008). Second, the recent crises in the Middle East and Northern Africa have led to an increase in the number of refugees and asylum seekers that try to find shelter in Europe (Hatton and Williamson 2006). So-called "boat people" who are smuggled on board ships over the Mediterranean Sea have especially caught broad public (and also media) attention (Pugh 2001). Third, in the aftermath of the 9/11 terrorist attacks Muslims have been the focus of the political and media debate in the US and in most European countries. Often, Muslims are depicted in a negative light in the context of this debate (Poole 2002; Saeed 2007). Public discourse often simultaneously deals with current immigrants or refugees from the Middle East and second- or third-generation immigrants from states such as Turkey, Pakistan, or from Northern Africa who have found a home in Europe for decades.

## Media Representations of Ethnic Minorities

There is little comparative research on media representations of ethnic minorities across European countries (Bennett, ter Wal, Lipiński, Małgorzata, and Krzyżanowski 2011; Kolmer 2012; ter Wal 2002; ter Wal, D'Haenens, and Koeman 2005). Most of the studies are conducted in countries of which the immigration history dates back several decades, e.g., the UK, Germany, or the Netherlands. This history considerably stimulated academic research on intergroup relations and media coverage of ethnic groups. Systematic research is less common in European countries that lack a longer immigration history. The focus of most quantitative or qualitative studies is on the coverage of immigrants in the news. Less research deals with other media genres (but see Igartua, Barrios, Ortega, and Frutos 2014; Top 2000). In quantitative content analyses the range is from simple word counts (e.g., co-occurrence of ethnic group members and positive and negative words, Galliker, Herman, Imminger, and Weimer 1998) to the coding of topics, issues, and frames (Ruhrmann, Sommer, and Uhlemann 2006; Van Gorp 2005).

## Underrepresentation of Ethnic Minorities

Despite differences in research traditions or methodology, there are general patterns that can be observed in nearly all European countries (for an overview, see ter Wal 2002).

First, ethnic minorities are underrepresented in the news compared to official statistics. For instance, a study in the Netherlands found that ethnic minorities are underrepresented as a social group in press photographs (Top 2000). A content analysis of Belgian television news indicates the near absence of ethnic groups as part of society (Saeys and Coppens 2002). Additional research found evidence of a gender gap: Among the few members of ethnic groups that receive media attention, men are clearly overrepresented (Krüger and Simon 2005). Thus, female members of ethnic groups obviously suffer from double discrimination.

However, there are signs of improvement of news representations of ethnic minorities over time. Specifically, a study of British television programs indicated an increase of representations of ethnic minorities (Statham 2002). This is especially true for public broadcasting stations that are obliged to normative standards of diversity (for the UK, see Law, Svennevig, and Morrison 1997; for Germany, see Ruhrmann et al. 2006). Despite this improvement, ethnic minorities are still overrepresented in news stories on crime and violence (Sommer and Ruhrmann 2010; ter Wal et al. 2005). Similar to representations of minorities in the U.S. media (Oliver 1994), European ethnic minorities are especially overrepresented as criminal suspects or perpetrators as compared to the majority group, e.g., in German newspapers (Müller 2005), Austrian tabloids (Arendt 2010), Italian regional newspapers (Di Nicola and Caneppele 2004), Swiss quality newspapers (Galliker et al. 1998), and Spanish television news (Igartua et al. 2014).

## Ethnic Minorities as Passive Agents

Even if ethnic minorities are in the news, they often do not function as active agents, information sources, or interview partners. Most of the time they remain silent and are passive agents who are marginalized. On German television, asylum seekers appear most of the time as passive objects that are dealt with and seldom treated as active subjects (Hömberg and Schlemmer 1995). A more recent study from Belgium corroborates the image of asylum seekers as passive actors that suffer from persecution and disasters (Van Gorp 2005). Diachronic studies provide evidence of an improvement in the representations of ethnic minorities, e.g., in the UK (Statham 2002) and Germany (Müller 2005). Accordingly, ethnic minorities receive more attention in the press and are seen more often as active agents. For instance, a German study found that the share of airtime devoted to immigration issues or immigrants was 10 percent of the overall airtime during an average day (Krüger and Simon 2005). Nevertheless, this representation seems to vary considerably between different groups. As Buchanan et al. (2004) pointed out, asylum seekers or refugees still receive very little attention in the media.

## Negativity in Coverage of Ethnic Minorities

Overall, ethnic minorities are more often portrayed in an unfavorable light, e.g., as free-loaders, drug dealers, terrorists, or individuals who violate cultural values. In a study of news in the UK, negativity referred to (1) claims to reduce the rights of ethnic minorities, (2) statements that portrayed minorities as a burden to the welfare state, or (3) depictions of ethnic groups as being immoral, bogus refugees, or carriers of diseases, such as TB or AIDS (Law et al. 1997). In Swiss news coverage immigrants were more strongly associated with the issue of crime than any other issue (Galliker et al. 1998).

In Germany, more than one third of all television news items on ethnic minorities in 2003 dealt with terrorism (Ruhrmann et al. 2006). Another third of the broadcasts were related to crime. Findings from other European countries generally support the overall notion that ethnic minorities appear as a threat to the economy, security, and cultural values prevailing in European countries (ter Wal 2002; ter Wal et al. 2005).

A common pattern identified in European journalism is the association of ethnic minorities with metaphors. Specifically, immigrants or refugees are often portrayed using the language of natural disasters, such as flood, avalanche, or glut (Gardikiotis 2003; Ruhrmann 2002). In a similar vein, immigrants are depicted as "masses" that "pour" into or "swamp" European countries (Charteris-Black 2006). Through such metaphoric language, ethnic minorities are stigmatized as a social group that represents multiple threats to Europeans. Research in a discourse analytical tradition generally supports these findings (Bennett et al. 2011). This pattern of results is qualified by the finding that negativity in news reporting varies as a function of cultural distance. The more culturally distant and the less beneficial to the welfare state an ethnic group is, the higher the share of negativity (Lubbers, Scheepers, and Wester 1998; Ruhrmann 2002). Despite the negative representations of ethnic minorities that dominate European journalism, there are at least some that appear in a favorable light. Portrayals of foreign artists, athletes, or visiting guests are found to be generally positive (e.g., Ruhrmann 2002).

The image of ethnic minorities also varies between media genres and news outlets. Specifically, results from different European countries suggest that tabloid newspapers depict ethnic minorities in a more negative light as compared to up-market news (Lubbers et al. 1998; Statham 2002). Additionally, liberal newspapers exhibit more positive portrayals of ethnic minorities than conservative newspapers (Geißler 2000; Lubbers et al. 1998). A Dutch study demonstrates that the portrayals of ethnic minorities in television talk shows are more positive than in other genres, mainly due to the inclusion of ordinary people (ter Wal 2002). Studies from countries that have a longer research tradition suggest that the media image of ethnic minorities has improved over time. For instance, a study in the UK shows that concerns of minorities and contributions of immigrants to society receive more news attention (Law et al. 1997). Research form Germany (Müller 2005) and Switzerland (Galliker et al. 1998) also indicates that the number of negative portrayals of ethnic minorities has decreased over time. However, ethnic minorities that are perceived to cost more than they benefit the country still receive negative evaluations in the news (Ruhrmann 2002).

After 9/11 and the bombings in London and Madrid, Muslims received more attention as an ethnic group than other social groups (Sommer and Ruhrmann 2010). A recent content analysis in Germany showed that television news focused more on intergroup conflict than on intergroup dialogue. For instance, portrayals of the relationships between Muslims and non-Muslims emphasize conflict more frequently than dialogue between cultures. This was true for German television and Arab television broadcasts (Schurz et al. 2012). Another study found that German news coverage is more negative when it covered Muslims than other religious groups (Kolmer 2012). This research also showed that the image of Islam is more negative on U.S. and German television than on British, French, or Italian television news. In sum, there seems to be an ethnic hierarchy with some groups that are beneficial to a country receiving less negative news and more positive news coverage and with some groups ranging at the bottom that are stigmatized in the media (Lubbers et al. 1998).

## Episodic Framing of Ethnic Minorities

Most of the news stories about ethnic groups are event-driven and episodic and follow "emergency" situations, e.g., riots, protests, or the implementation of new immigration policies (ter Wal 2002). Thematic coverage or background information on ethnic minorities is scarce. Put differently, the audience receives little information about the conditions of immigrants in their home countries, the circumstances and problems that immigrants face in receiving countries, or the social causes of the problems (Ruhrmann 2002). The focus of news stories is primarily on the problems associated with ethnic minorities, with the social, cultural, religious, or economic context largely neglected. Thus, the repeated depictions of unrelated events, such as crime stories, riots, or terrorist attacks authored by ethnic groups, result in individual attribution of blame for these events and make it difficult for the audience to figure out the societal or systemic causes that may have contributed to these acts (Iyengar 1991; Sommer and Ruhrmann 2010). These general patterns of media coverage of ethnic groups in Europe are similar to typical reporting practices in the US (Dixon and Linz 2000).

## Representations of Ethnic Minorities in Political Discourse

In addition to the media, political authorities are important sources of information that can dominate the discourse about immigration or immigrants as social groups. How they deal with and talk about ethnic minorities in public can have a considerable influence on the general image of these groups—especially since politicians' public statements are broadly distributed in society through mass media channels (ter Wal 2002). A longitudinal analysis in the Netherlands demonstrated that the immigration discourse in parliament and the news media was highly interrelated (Vliegenthart and Roggeband 2007). Specifically, frames, such as "restriction" or "Islam-as-a-threat," often initially appear in the political arena. These frames are then adopted by journalists and used to contextualize a news story on a specific event or issue. This way, news media not only adopt political actors' statements about immigrants in terms of direct quotes, but such statements also seem to influence the subsequent news coverage. This perpetuation of prejudicial framing makes it important to consider the discourse on ethnic minorities in the political arena.

In several European countries, negative portrayals of ethnic groups as threats to security and cultural values (e.g., Romanians in Austria, Albanians in Italy, Roma in France) have contributed to legitimizing restrictive immigration policy programs (Parker 2012; Wodak 1996; Zinn 1996). In election campaigns, political actors often intentionally play the "race card" to mobilize voters. Such strategies have not only been employed by right-wing political parties such as Front National in France, Die Republikaner in Germany, and the Belgian Vlaams Blok (Jagers and Walgrave 2007), but have also been found in the campaigns of mainstream conservative parties such as CDU/CSU in Germany, the British Tories, and the French Gaullists (Thränhardt 1995). The use of a similar rhetoric has been demonstrated in Germany (Butterwege and Häusler 2002), the UK (Saggar 1998), and Switzerland (Schemer 2012).

Of course, the fact that political actors use xenophobic notions as a strategic tool in election campaigns is not unproblematic. It can be argued that especially mainstream political actors are applying a xenophobic rhetoric in a more subtle way than politically extreme parties do (Thränhardt 1995). At the same time, they possess a stronger degree of political authority, positive reputation, and general acceptance that comes with their governmental office. The expression of racial appeals by mainstream political actors may thus find resonance in a broad audience and can increase the acceptability of xenophobia in the public. Ultimately, political discourse might this way legitimize ethnic prejudice (van Dijk 2000, 2002).

## Conclusion

The present summary of research on ethnicity and race clearly shows that ethnic groups are still marginalized and stigmatized in European media. They are often underrepresented, are seldom active agents, and overwhelmingly appear in negative roles. The event-driven character of news reporting on ethnicity is unlikely to improve the knowledge of audience members and change their attitudes toward ethnic groups. Although research on ethnicity in Europe has considerably increased in terms of quantity and quality, there are still blind spots that deserve further inquiry. First, there is a lack of systematic monitoring of media representations of ethnic minorities over time and across cultures (Statham 2002). Thus, it would be interesting to study whether ethnic hierarchies of minority groups are invariant in terms of culture. It is also important to investigate whether increasing commercialization of media systems in Europe diminishes differences in coverage of ethnic groups across countries. Finally, the monitoring of news coverage of ethnic groups over time is an important endeavor for upcoming research. There are some hints that the media image of some ethnic groups has improved and their marginalization has decreased over time. However, these findings may also be only outliers that do not follow a continuous trend to a more favorable image of ethnic groups in Europe.

A second gap in research is the lack of studies that deal with portrayals of ethnic minorities in fictional media content and entertainment media. Content analyses focus on news coverage, less on entertainment media. To date, we cannot reliably infer from these studies whether there is a difference between entertainment media and news coverage. Also lacking is research on online depictions of ethnic groups, e.g., in blogs, forums, or social media (Bennett et al. 2011). There is evidence that online communication is more extreme than offline communication and that the anonymity of blogs, forums, or social networking sites facilitates the expression of hate against ethnic minorities (Tynes, Giang, Williams, and Thompson 2008).

Third, compared to research on media representations of ethnic minorities, there are fewer studies on the effects of portrayals of ethnic groups on stereotypes or racial attitudes in the public. Systematic research on media effects of biased media portrayals on audience members can be found in some countries, such as Germany (Boomgaarden and Vliegenthart 2009), Austria (Arendt 2010), Switzerland (Schemer 2014), the Netherlands (Boomgaarden and de Vreese 2007), and Spain (Igartua, Moral-Toranzo, and Fernández 2011). These studies clearly show that unfavorable depictions of ethnic minorities increase stereotypes, prejudice, and antipathy toward these groups. Some studies also suggest that news stories and media programming can be used to improve the image of ethnic minorities among the public (Müller 2009; Schemer 2014).

A fourth issue relates to the representation of ethnic minorities in media organizations (ter Wal 2002). If members of ethnic minorities take part in the production of media content, this might result in more balanced coverage. However, it has been noted that ethnic diversity in European news organizations is significantly lower than in the overall labor markets of the respective countries (e.g., Deuze 2002). Scholars and practitioners alike argue that in addition to the production of ethnic minority programming, an increase in the share of journalists from ethnic minority groups would facilitate a more balanced and informed news selection and coverage about ethnic minorities (Ruhrmann 2002).

Fifth, ethnicity also plays a role in the context of the current European integration process: People from various ethnic backgrounds share a supranational political system, i.e., the EU Ethnic boundaries seem to be an obstacle to the integration process (Carey 2002). Several researchers have stressed the role that media coverage could play in overcoming them (de Vreese 2002; Trenz 2008). The fact that there is no common European media system but rather a variety of distinct national media systems exacerbates this political goal. Some scholars have argued that the national media outlets in Europe emphasize the uniqueness of their respective countries instead of accentuating an integrative perspective (Firmstone 2008). However, systematic research on the role of ethnicity and national identities in media coverage about European integration is still lacking. This seems even more relevant since it directly relates to the perception of ethnic minorities: A stronger identification with a supranational concept of Europe can also reduce prejudice toward ethnic groups from outside Europe (Curtis 2014).

## References

Arendt, F. (2010) "Cultivation Effects of a Newspaper on Reality Estimates and Explicit and Implicit Attitudes," *Journal of Media Psychology* 22(4): 147–159.

Bennett, S., ter Wal, J., Lipiński, A., Małgorzata, F., and Krzyżanowski, M. (2011) *Media for Diversity and Migrant Integration. Thematic Report 2011/02: Media Content*. Florence, Italy.

Boomgaarden, H. G. and de Vreese, C. H. (2007) "Dramatic Real-world Events and Public Opinion Dynamics: Media Coverage and Its Impact on Public Reactions to an Assassination," *International Journal of Public Opinion Research* 19(3): 354–366.

Boomgaarden, H. G. and Vliegenthart, R. (2009) "How News Content Influences Anti-immigrant Attitudes: Germany, 1993–2005," *European Journal of Political Research* 48: 516–542.

Buchanan, S., Grillo, B., and Threadgold, T. (2004) *What's the Story: Results from Research into Media Coverage of Refugees and Asylum Seekers in the UK*. London: Article 19.

Butterwege, C. and Häusler, A. (2002). "Rechtsextremismus, Rassismus und Nationalismus: Randprobleme oder Phänomene der Mitte? [Right-wing Extremism, Racism, and Nationalism: Marginal Problems or Central Phenomena?]," in C. Butterwege, J. Cremer, A. Häusler, G. Hentges, T. Pfeifer, C. Reißlandt, and S. Salzborn (eds.), *Themen der Rechten – Themen der Mitte. Zuwanderung, demografischer Wandel und Nationalbewusstsein*. Opladen, Germany: Leske & Budrich.

Carey, S. (2002) "Undivided Loyalties. Is National Identity an Obstacle to European Integration?," *European Union Politics* 3(4): 387–413.

Charteris-Black, J. (2006) "Britain as a Container: Immigration Metaphors in the 2005 Election Campaign," *Discourse & Society* 17: 563–581.

Curtis, K. A. (2014) "Inclusive versus Exclusive: A Cross-national Comparison of the Effects of Subnational, National, and Supranational Identity," *European Union Politics* 15(4): 521–546.

Deuze, M. (2002) "National News Cultures: A Comparison of Dutch, German, British, Australian, and U.S. Journalists," *Journalism & Mass Communication Quarterly* 79(1): 134–149.

de Vreese, C. H. (2002) *Framing Europe: Television News and European Integration*. Amsterdam, The Netherlands: Aksant Academic Publishers.

Di Nicola, A. and Caneppele, S. (2004) *Media e criminalità: la rappresentazione della criminalità nei giornali della provincia di Padova [Media and Crime: The Representation of Crime in Regional Newspapers]*. Trento, Italy: Transcrime, Università degli Studi di Trento.

Dixon, T. L. and Linz, D. (2000) "Overrepresentation and Underrepresentation of African Americans and Latinos as Lawbreakers on Television News," *Journal of Communication* 50(2): 131–154.

Favell, A. (2008) "The New Face of East–West Migration in Europe," *Journal of Ethnic and Migration Studies* 34(5): 701–716.

Firmstone, J. (2008) "Approaches of the Transnational Press to Reporting Europe," *Journalism* 9(4): 423–442.

Galliker, M., Herman, J., Imminger, K., and Weimer, D. (1998) "The Investigation of Contiguity: Co-occurrence Analysis of Print Media Using CD-ROMs as a New Data Source, Illustrated by a Discussion on Migrant Delinquency in a Daily Newspaper," *Journal of Language and Social Psychology* 17(2): 200–219.

Gardikiotis, A. (2003) "Minorities and Crime in the Greek Press: Employing Content and Discourse Analytic Approaches," *Communications* 28(3): 339–350.

Geddes, A. (2003) *The Politics of Migration and Immigration in Europe*. London: Sage.

Geißler, R. (2000) "Bessere Präsentation durch bessere Repräsentation [Better Presentation through Better Representation]," in H. Schatz, C. Holtz-Bacha, and J.-U. Nieland (eds.), *Migranten und Medien. Neue Herausforderungen an die Integrationsfunktion von Presse und Rundfunk*. Wiesbaden, Germany: Westdeutscher Verlag.

Hatton, T. J. and Williamson, J. G. (2006) "Refugees, Asylum Seekers, and Policy in Europe," in R. J. Langhammer and F. Foders (eds.), *Labor Mobility and the World Economy*. Berlin, Germany: Springer.

Hjerm, M. and Bohman, A. (2014) "Is It Getting Worse? Anti-immigrant Attitudes in Europe during the 21st Century," in C. Sandelind (ed.), *European Populism and Winning the Immigration Debate*. Brussels, Belgium: ELF.

Hömberg, W. and Schlemmer, S. (1995) "Fremde als Objekt [Foreigners as Objects]," *Media Perspektiven* 1: 11–20.

Igartua, J.-J., Barrios, I. M., Ortega, F., and Frutos, F. J. (2014) "The Image of Immigration in Fiction Broadcast on Prime-time Television in Spain," *Palabra Clave* 17(3): 589–618.

Igartua, J.-J., Moral-Toranzo, F., and Fernández, I. (2011) "Cognitive, Attitudinal, and Emotional Effects of News Frame and Group Cues, on Processing News about Immigration," *Journal of Media Psychology* 23(4): 174–185.

Iyengar, S. (1991) *Is Anyone Responsible? How Television Frames Political Issues*. Chicago, IL: University of Chicago Press.

Jagers, J. and Walgrave, S. (2007) "Populism as Political Communication Style: An Empirical Study of Political Parties' Discourse in Belgium," *European Journal of Political Research* 46: 319–345.

Kolmer, C. (2012) "Gläubige Menschen – eine verdrängte Minderheit: Religion in den Medien 2007–2012 [Religious People – A Marginalized Minority: Religion in the Media, 2007–2012]," in D. Amaca and R. Schatz (eds.), *Integrationsindex*. Beirut, Lebanon: Innovatio.

Krüger, U. M. and Simon, E. (2005) "Das Bild der Migranten im WDR Fernsehen [The Image of Migrants on a Regional Television Channel]," *Media Perspektiven* 3: 105–114.

Law, I., Svennevig, M., and Morrison, D. (1997) *Privilege and Silence: 'Race' in the British News during the General Election Campaign, 1997. Research Report for the Commission for Racial Equality*. Leeds, UK.

Lubbers, M., Scheepers, P., and Wester, F. (1998) "Ethnic Minorities in Dutch Newspapers 1990–5: Patterns of Criminalization and Problematization," *Gazette* 60(5): 415–431.

Mastro, D. E. (2009) "Racial/Ethnic Stereotyping and the Media," in R. L. Nabi and M. B. Oliver (eds.), *The SAGE Handbook of Media Processes and Effects*. Los Angeles, CA: SAGE.

Müller, D. (2005) "Die Darstellung ethnischer Minderheiten in deutschen Massenmedien [The Portrayal of Ethnic Minorities in German Mass Media]," in R. Geißler and H. Pöttker (eds.), *Massenmedien und die Integration ethnischer Minderheiten in Deutschland*. Bielefeld, Germany: Transcript.

Müller, F. (2009) "Entertaining Anti-racism. Multicultural Television Drama, Identification and Perceptions of Ethnic Threat," *Communications* 34: 239–256.

Parker, O. (2012) "Roma and the Politics of EU Citizenship in France: Everyday Security and Resistance," *Journal of Common Market Studies* 50(3): 475–491.

Poole, E. (2002) *Reporting Islam. Media Representations of British Muslims*. London: I.B. Tauris.

Pugh, M. (2001) "Mediterranean Boat People: A Case for Co-operation?," *Mediterranean Politics* 6(1): 1–20.

Ruhrmann, G. (2002) "The Stranger: Minorities and Their Treatment in the German Media," in J. B. Atkins (ed.), *The Mission. Journalism, Ethics and the World*. Ames, IA: Iowa State University Press, 79–91.

Ruhrmann, G., Sommer, D., and Uhlemann, H. (2006) "TV-Nachrichtenberichterstattung über Migranten – Von der Politik zum Terror [Television Coverage of Migrants – From Politics to Terror]," in R. Geißler and H. Pöttker (eds.), *Integration durch Massenmedien. Medien und Migration im internationalen Vergleich*. Bielefeld, Germany: Transcript.

Saeed, A. (2007) "Media, Racism and Islamophobia: The Representation of Islam and Muslims in the Media," *Sociology Compass* 1(2): 443–462.

Saeys, F. and Copppens, T. (2002) "Belgium," in J. ter Wal (ed.), *Racism and Cultural Diversity in the Mass Media: An Overview of Research and Examples of Good Practice in the EU Member States, 1995–2000*. Vienna, Austria: European Research Centre on Migration and Ethnic Relations.

Saggar, S. (1998) "Smoking Guns and Magic Bullets: The 'Race Card' Debate Revisited in 1997," *Immigrants & Minorities* 17(3): 1–21.

Schemer, C. (2012) "The Influence of News Media on Stereotypic Attitudes toward Immigrants in a Political Campaign," *Journal of Communication* 62(5): 739–757.

Schemer, C. (2014) "Media Effects on Racial Attitudes: Evidence from a Three-wave Panel Survey in a Political Campaign," *International Journal of Public Opinion Research* 26(4): 531–542.

Schurz, K., Dietrich, N., Jirschitzka, J., Schott, C., Wolf, K., and Frindte, W. (2012) "Auswertung der Medienanalyse [Analysis of Media Coverage]," in W. Frindte, K. Boehnke, H. Kreikenbom, and W. Wagner (eds.), *Lebenswelten junger Muslime in Deutschland*. Berlin, Germany: Bundesministerium des Innern.

Sommer, D. and Ruhrmann, G. (2010) "Oughts and Ideals – Framing People with Migration Background in TV News," *Conflict & Communication Online* 9(2): 1–15.

Spencer, R. (2004) "Assessing Multicultural Identity Theory and Politics," *Ethnicities* 4(3): 357–379.

Statham, P. (2002) "United Kingdom," in J. ter Wal (ed.), *Racism and Cultural Diversity in the Mass Media*. Vienna, Austria: European Research Centre on Migration and Ethnic Relations.

ter Wal, J. (ed.) (2002) *Racism and Cultural Diversity in the Mass Media*. Vienna, Austria: European Research Centre on Migration and Ethnic Relations.

ter Wal, J., D'Haenens, L., and Koeman, J. (2005) "(Re)presentation of Ethnicity in EU and Dutch Domestic News: A Quantitative Analysis," *Media, Culture & Society* 27: 937–950.

Thränhardt, D. (1995) "The Political Uses of Xenophobia in England, France and Germany," *Party Politics* 1(3): 323–345.

Top, B. (2000) *Onderzoeksverslag Zwart-wit: onderbelicht?: Onderzoek naar multiculturele fotografie in Nederlandse kranten en jongerenbladen [Research Report Black-White: Under-highlighted?]*. Amsterdam, The Netherlands: Werkgroep Migranten en Media Nederlandse Vereniging van Journalisten.

Trenz, H.-J. (2008) "Understanding Media Impact on European Integration: Enhancing or Restricting the Scope of Legitimacy of the EU?," *Journal of European Integration* 30(2): 291–309.

Tynes, B. M., Giang, M. T., Williams, D. R., and Thompson, G. N. (2008) "Online Racial Discrimination and Psychological Adjustment among Adolescents," *Journal of Adolescent Health* 43: 565–569.

van Dijk, T. A. (2000) "New(s) Racism: A Discourse Analytical Approach," in S. Cottle (ed.), *Ethnic Minorities and the Media*. Milton Keynes, UK: Open University Press, 33–49.

——. (2002) "Discourse and Racism," in D. Goldberg and J. Solomos (eds.), *The Blackwell Companion to Racial and Ethnic Studies*. Oxford: Blackwell, 145–159.

Van Gorp, B. (2005) "Where is the Frame? Victims and Intruders in the Belgian Press Coverage of the Asylum Issue," *European Journal of Communication* 20(4): 484–507.

Vliegenthart, R. and Roggeband, C. (2007) "Framing Immigration and Integration: Relationships between Press and Parliament in the Netherlands," *International Communication Gazette* 69(3): 295–319.

Wodak, R. (1996) "The Genesis of Racist Discourse in Austria Since 1989," in C. R. Caldas-Coulthard and M. Coulthard (eds.), *Texts and Practices: Readings in Critical Discourse Analysis*. London: Routledge, 107–128.

Zick, A., Pettigrew, T. F., and Wagner, U. (2008) "Ethnic Prejudice and Discrimination in Europe," *Journal of Social Issues* 64(2): 233–251.

Zinn, D. L. (1996) "Adriatic Brethren or Black Sheep? Migration in Italy and the Albanian Crisis, 1991," *European Urban and Regional Studies* 3(3): 241–249.

## Further Reading

Bennett, S., ter Wal, J., Lipiński, A., Małgorzata, F., and Krzyżanowski, M. (2011) *Media for Diversity and Migrant Integration: Thematic Report 2011/02: Media Content*. Florence, Italy: Robert Schuman Centre for Advanced Studies. (Follow-up of ter Wal's 2002 book.)

Downing, J. and Husband, C. (2005) *Representing Race: Racisms, Ethnicity and the Media*. London: Sage. (Provides a conceptual framework for understanding the role of the media in the discourse on ethnicity and racism.)

ter Wal, J. (ed.) (2002) *Racism and Cultural Diversity in the Mass Media*. Vienna, Austria: European Research Centre on Migration and Ethnic Relations. (Synopsis of research reviews on the image of ethnic minorities in the media, representations of minorities in media institutions, and anti-racist activism in European countries.)

# 25
# EAST ASIA
## Looking In and Looking Out
### *Yasue Kuwahara*

The countries in East Asia, particularly China, Japan, and Korea, have maintained close relationships for over 2,000 years. While the bases of their societies, such as the values based on Confucianism and linguistic styles, are similar, and their historical experience with the West is also similar in that they have been under the influence of Western hegemony, their relationships were not always amicable, as attested to by Japan's colonization of Korea between 1910 and 1945 and recent territorial disputes among them. Such experiences are reflected in the relationship between race and mass media in East Asia.

There are two aspects to the issue of race and media in East Asia—internal and external. The internal aspect refers to how the countries use mass media to promote their views of one another that amend or aggravate their relationships. The external aspect, on the other hand, is about the countries' separate and collective perception and attitude toward the rest of the world. Needless to say, the internal and external aspects are significantly related, especially the increased global flux of popular culture since the 1980s, which has influenced both aspects of race and media. This chapter examines both aspects.

### Internal Aspect

According to the commonly accepted classification of race, the Chinese, Koreans, and Japanese all belong to the Asian race and the differences among them are considered ethnic differences. As research on existing scholarship on race and media reveals, however, ethnicities are often treated as race in East Asia due to the experience of Japanese Imperialism after the late nineteenth century until the end of WWII. The Chinese and Koreans who suffered from the aggression of the Japanese Imperial Army, it seems, regarded the discrimination against them as due to the Japanese view of themselves as the superior race. As Japan began to challenge the Anglo-American order in the 1930s, those in power sought an explanation for distinctive Japanese characters to justify the expansion of Imperialism in the West and Asia. Known as *Nihonjinron* (theories of Japanese cultural or racial uniqueness), this explanation assumed that Japanese society was "an integrated and harmonious whole" and that "all or most Japanese possess the same national character" (Mouer and Sugimoto 1986: 43–4). Although China and Korea considered Japan a member of the same race that shared a common language as represented by the idea of *Doubun Doushu* (the same language, the same race), the latter separated itself from the former. With the defeat in WWII, *Nihonjinron* was forgotten among the Japanese (until it came back in the 1970s). First too devastated by the aftermath of the war and then too busy to rebuild the country, the Japanese government never formally apologized to China or Korea who, in turn, never forgave Japan for its atrocities during the war. Partly due to historical memory and partly due to education, people in China and Korea have remained anti-Japanese and their relationship with Japan has remained antagonistic until this day, and mass media have reflected it. For instance, only those reports that looked down on Japan with disdain were allowed in Korean mass media prior to 1990. Similarly, Japanese mass media were responsible for the anti-Japanese images of Korea and China that became prevalent among the Japanese during the 1970s (Ko 2012).

The relationship entered a new phase when Japan began to experience high economic growth in the 1970s. *Nihonjinron* that had supported Japanese Imperialism came back with a new twist as Japan started its economic expansion in the global market. Even though the West thought Japan would forever remain a third-world country in the immediate aftermath of WWII, Japan proved them wrong by successfully rebuilding its economy. Such an economic miracle was possible because of distinctive Japanese characteristics. *Nihonjinron* was revived. As examined eloquently by Koichi Iwabuchi, Japan positioned itself away from the rest of Asia and created a trilateral relationship consisting of Japan, the West, and other Asian countries through self-Orientalism, which is "a strategy of inclusion through exclusion and of exclusion through inclusion" (1994: 4). Japan saw itself as superior to the rest of Asia because of its economic power. It is equivalent to or better than the West, yet its distinctive characteristics make it exotic to the West. As Japan's economy continued to grow, people from other Asian countries started moving to Japan with the hope of getting their share of prosperity. As the number of foreign residents increased, the Japanese who were not used to living with foreign "others" were not at ease and tended to discriminate against them. For instance, landlords were reluctant to rent to non-Japanese and some businesses banned them. The Japanese viewed them with suspicion and, when a crime was committed, blamed it on them. Witnesses to muggings in dark streets at night almost always said that the culprit was Chinese or Korean (but seldom Japanese). Mass media advocated such popular sentiment by associating residential foreigners, particularly non-Caucasians, with crime and danger and began to treat them as social problems (Iwabuchi 2007).

While the antagonistic relationships among the three countries continued, there was a positive change brought first by Japanese popular culture and then by Korean popular culture. In the 1990s, Japanese television drama, popular music, and animation began to get the attention of Hong Kong youth who, by the end of the decade, preferred Japanese popular culture to American popular culture. The same trend was observed in other Chinese cities like Beijing, Shanghai, and Guangzhou. Although Japanese cultural products were banned in South Korea after the end of WWII, President Kim Dae-jung's four-stage opening policy lifted the ban in 1998, thus starting a Japan boom (Otmazgin). On the other hand, *Hallyu*, which refers to the popularity of Korean popular culture outside of South Korea, began with the broadcast of Korean television drama in China in the 1990s and spread over Asia in a short period of time. *Hallyu* arrived in Japan when *Winter Sonata* was broadcast on an NHK (Japan's public broadcasting system) satellite channel in 2003. The archetypal melodrama unexpectedly became a mega hit among middle-aged women who made Bae Yung-joon, an actor who played the protagonist of the show, an international heartthrob and began the "Yonsama boom," a reference to the Japanese honorific title ascribed to Bae by his Japanese fans. *Winter Sonata* was broadcast a total of four times in Japan and opened the door to other Korean television dramas.

Positive experience the female fans gained from the exposure to Korean dramas clearly increased their interest in Korean culture as attested to by increased tourism to Korea as well as participation in Korean language and cooking classes, among other things (Mori 2008; Hirata 2008). The popularity of television drama was followed by K-pop, Korean popular music, which attracted younger generations of the Japanese. Groups, such as Girls Generation, Kara, and TVQX, made frequent visits to Japanese music television shows with songs that they sang in Japanese, thus functioning as cultural diplomats between the two countries. The success of their popular culture in Japan was taken seriously among Koreans who never forgot their colonized experience. According to Young Eun Chae's analysis of two major Korean newspapers, more than 90 percent of the article regarding *Hallyu* published in *Chosun Ilbo* and *Hangyure* dealt with their impact in Japan (2012: 205). Moreover, the rebroadcast of *Winter Sonata* in 2005, after its success in Japan, garnered higher ratings than any of the previous broadcasts. It was a triumphant moment for Koreans who had long suffered from the colonial memory (Chae). The positive effect of *Hallyu* in Japan, however, was met by anti-Korean agitation disseminated through books, comics, and message boards.

Unlike China and South Korea, Taiwan maintained an amicable relationship with Japan after WWII partly because older generations of Taiwanese had fond memories of Japanese governance in the early twentieth century, and partly because Japan unofficially accepted Taiwan as an independent state. Therefore, Japanese popular culture was easily accepted by the Taiwanese people, especially those in their teens to thirties, some of whom called themselves 哈日族 (har-lee zu), meaning Taiwanese Japanophiles. On the other hand, Taiwan's relationship with South Korea, let alone China, was in no way amicable. South Korea and Taiwan shared the same anti-Communist position against China until a diplomatic relationship between South Korea and China was established in August 1992. Taiwanese mass media began to paint a negative image of South Korea by focusing on accidents, natural disasters, and other problems in the Korean Peninsula. They especially offered emotional and negative coverage of Korean sports. It has been said that the Taiwanese media coverage of Korea is equivalent to the Korean coverage of Japan. In the meantime, with the rapid growth of the Chinese economy, South Korea increasingly lost its interest in Taiwan, and recent media coverage is limited to major political issues, such as regime changes. Thus, people in both countries must rely on social media, blogs, and television drama to find out about each other. There was a meeting between the representatives of Taiwanese and Korean media to discuss this situation and find a solution to their antagonistic relationship on December 19, 2014. Those who were in attendance reminded themselves of the importance of fair and objective reporting to serve the audience (Shiroyama 2014).

## External Aspect

As for the external aspect of race and media in East Asia, it is essential to understand Sinocentrism, which has formed the basis of Chinese self-perception throughout history. It is the perception that China is the center of the universe and all other countries are Chinese subjects and therefore not really its concerns. It has also formed a dichotomous view that Chinese are humans and foreigners are beasts (Ko). As old as the Han Dynasty (206 BC–AD 220), Sinocentrism still influences the Chinese mass media. For instance, villains in a crime film must not be Chinese and "the crime must not be initiated within China's borders, as if the land itself were somehow pure" (Vittachi 2015: SR7).

Max Fisher considers the 4-month-long campaign of China-based cyber attacks on the *New York Times* in 2012 as manifestation of new Sinocentrism. Fisher read a blog by Christopher Ford, a China expert who attended a conference in Beijing, and stated that Ford first thought the Chinese government's attempt to correct "biased" coverage by the Western media aimed to prevent unrest domestically and to eliminate any negative images associated with China internationally. But then Ford realized that such behavior was actually based on Sinocentrism:

> China's fixation upon shaping others' accounts of China, then, is arguably not necessarily "just" the result of insecurity or narcissism. Some of it may in fact grow out of a deeply-rooted conception of social order in which narrative control is inherently a strategic objective because it is assumed that status or role ascriptions and moral characterizations play a critical role in shaping the world they describe.
>
> *(Fisher 2013: n.p.)*

Thus, although it has not been proven, Fisher considers that it is reasonable to assume that the Chinese government was behind the hacking incidents which were observed in various parts of the world.

Korea and Japan were influenced by Sinocentrism, especially after the Sino-Japanese War (1894–5), when the East Asian countries fought against European imperialists, a period sometimes known as the White Peril. After WWII, however, as their relations with the West changed, their perception also changed. During the occupation by the Allied Forces (1945–52), Japanese society went through changes that included the political and economic systems as well as civil values. It is interesting to note that to propagate the value of democracy among the Japanese, the occupation government used magazines and newspapers that it controlled (Columbia University 2009). The West, especially the United States, changed from the enemy to a positive referent point during these years. Hollywood movies, television programs, and popular music, including rock 'n' roll, were increasingly and widely imported to Japan. American programs that dominated Japanese television in the early 1960s taught viewers the Western lifestyle. The rising popularity of Hollywood movies resulted in the decline of the domestic film industry: box office revenue from Japanese films remained lower than that of Hollywood movies between 1975 and 2000 (Suzuki 2015). Western popular music was regarded as more "authentic" than its Japanese counterpart among some youths, and some FM stations exclusively aired only Western songs. Increased consumption of Western popular culture coincided with Japan's transformation through self-Orientalism; Japan came to be regarded as the West in the East not only in its self-perception but also by other Asian countries (Iwabuchi 1994).

Furthermore, in the Japanese popular consciousness, only the West mattered, and the rest of the world was regarded as inferior to Japan and therefore unimportant. In terms of race, only white/Caucasians deserved attention and Asians and blacks were discriminated against. The first Japanese exposure to blacks took place in the sixteenth century when the Dutch merchants who came to meet Nobunaga Oda brought African servants with them. Commodore Matthew Perry of the U.S. Navy entertained the Japanese delegate with a minstrel show on his naval ship off the Uraga Bay. Through encounters like these as well as exposure to black images in the Western media, the Japanese perception of blacks came to reflect Western racism, as well documented by John Russell (1991) and

Michael Washington (2000). Such a perception is shared in other East Asian countries. In China and Taiwan, historically, lighter skin color is associated with status and wealth while darker skin indicates a lower social class, i.e., peasants. Discrimination against the black race intensified when the Maoist state invited Africans to study in China in the 1960s. Barry Sautman, a professor of social sciences at Hong Kong University, thinks that mass media are largely responsible for shaping the Chinese negative perception of blacks: "In the media, Africa is portrayed as a house of horrors, with a huge number of people dying from diseases, wars and extremely high crime rates" (Jaffe 2012: n.p.). Koreans who have had limited exposure to blacks have a stereotypical perception: Black people are uneducated, underclass, and often criminal. This perception manifested itself during the Los Angeles riot in 1992 when Korean shop owners who thought black residents would loot their stores fought violently against them. Moreover, it is astonishing to see "blackface"—non-black actors in dark make-up posing as blacks, a remnant of the American minstrel shows in the nineteenth century—on Korean television as recently as 2014 (Jung 2014).

Perceptions of race in East Asia began to change in the 1990s with the change in economic power and subsequent increased cultural flow. As the Japanese economy expanded the market in developing countries, Japan experienced an ethnic boom in the 1980s. When the Persian Gulf War (1990–1) broke out, Japanese weary of U.S. imperialism began to identify with Asia. The Japan that had disassociated itself from Asia had returned to the region even though it maintained the view that it was "in but above Asia" (Iwabuchi 2002: 8). Other East Asian countries, with their rising economic power, increasingly began to purchase Japanese popular culture until finally Japanese popular culture beat American popular culture in the consumer market. East Asians prefer Japanese products to American products because of the former's cultural familiarity/proximity. According to Koichi Iwabuchi, East Asians are attracted to Japanese popular culture because it is Westernized/Americanized and they are interested in American popular culture, yet Japanese popular culture contains elements of Asia that are familiar to them. In Iwabuchi's words, the success of Japanese popular culture is due to "asianization of the West" as opposed to "westernization of Asia" (2012). The changing perception of race is reflected in the mass media. Whereas foreigners who frequented on Japanese TV known as *Gaijin Tarento* (foreign celebrities) prior to 2000 were almost exclusively Caucasian, African Americans (Bob Sapp, Billy Blanks, Jero), a Nigerian (Bobby Ologun), Koreans (Bae Yong-joon, Hyun Bin), and a Samoan (Konishiki) started getting media attention after the turn of the century (Kuwahara 2008). Also, a television program, *Koko ga Hen da yo Nihonjin* (roughly translated as *Hey Japanese: This is Strange*), in which foreign residents compared Japan to their home countries, became popular. As rap music found its way to East Asia, some youth developed an interest in hip hop culture and began to appropriate and remake rap music as represented by "yellow B-Boys" of Japan and Korean "rap dance" by Seo Teiji and the Boys, Hyun Jin Young, and Wawa (Condry 2006; Song 2014). While underground rappers use their music as a means to voice their opinions about society, others, including "idol groups" (acts manufactured by the music industry), merely appropriate black culture and thus perpetuate stereotypes. At an amateur rap concert held in a shopping mall in Seoul in 2011, many performers imitated gangsta rap both in songs and dance, singing and acting out violence. African-American youth who are fans of K-pop often deplore this. Many Japanese youth merely copy African-American styles by, for instance, changing their straight hair to Afros and then locking it, because African Americans are "cool." Even idol groups appropriate races to their advantage as Girls' Generation manipulated the "hegemonic notion of whiteness" and TVQX exhibits identifiable characteristics of African-American masculinity (Oh 2014; Anderson 2014). Such efforts on their part increase their appeal amid the growing global cultural flow, yet do not change the existing perception of race. (As mentioned above, KBS, Korea's state-run television, allowed blackface to appear on the show in 2014.) While blacks seldom appear on Japanese television dramas, *Money War* aired in February 2015 had two black actors as bouncers. It seems that a positive stereotype of Caucasians has lost influence in East Asia in recent years but a negative stereotype of blacks lingers on.

## Conclusion

Since the end of WWII, the countries in East Asia have experienced changing relationships among themselves from animosity stemming from their colonial memory to alliances for economic gain. Mass media have played an important role, shaping the popular perception of one another. While mainstream media, especially under communist and dictatorial leadership, endorsed the governmental views until the 1980s, the increased influx of popular culture, such as TV dramas, anime, and popular music for the past three decades, has created different perceptions among people in these countries. It will be interesting to see how the continuously increasing exchange of popular culture products will impact the relationships among the East Asian countries. Compared to Westerners, people in East Asia have had limited experience with racial "others" historically. Their perception of "others" was, thus, largely shaped by the Western hegemony which places Caucasians on the top of the racial hierarchy and blacks on the bottom. While the recent global situations as well as the increased global cultural exchange have changed the view of "others," the traditional perception is still easily observed in the mass media. This clearly shows the strong grip that the mass media hold on the East Asian public.

## References

Anderson, C. (2014) "That's My Man! Overlapping Masculinities in Korean Popular Music," in Y. Kuwahara (ed.), *The Korean Wave: Korean Popular Culture in Global Context*. New York: Palgrave-Macmillan, 117–132.

Chae, Y. E. (2014) "*Winter Sonata* and Yonsama, Ideal Love, and Masculinity: Nostalgic Desire and Colonial Memory," in Y. Kuwahara (ed.), *The Korean Wave: Korean Popular Culture in Global Context*. New York: Palgrave-Macmillan, 191–212.

Columbia University. (2009) "The American Occupation of Japan, 1945–1952," *Asia for Educators*. Retrieved from http://afe.easia.columbia.edu/special/japan_1900_occupation.htm.

Condry, I. (2006) *Hip-Hop Japan: Rap and the Paths of Cultural Globalization*. Durham, NC: Duke University Press.

Fisher, M. (2013, Feb. 1) "New Sinocentrism: The Ideology that May Be Driving China to Hack Foreign Media," *The Washington Post*. Retrieved from http://www.washingtonpost.com/blogs/worldviews/wp/2013/02/01/new-sinocentrism-the-ideology-that-may-be-driving-china-to-hack-foreign-media/.

Hirata, Y. (2008) "Touring 'Dramatic Korea': Japanese Women as Viewers of *Hanryu* Dramas and Tourists on *Hanryu* Tours," in C. B. Huat and K. Iwabuchi (eds.), *East Asian Pop Culture: Analysing the Korean Wave*. Hong Kong, China: Hong Kong University Press, 143–155.

Iwabuchi, K. (1994) "Complicit Exoticism: Japan and Its Other," *Continuum: The Australian Journal of Media & Culture* 8(2): 1–23.

———. (2002) *Recentering Globalization: Popular Culture and Japanese Transnationalism*. Durham, NC: Duke University Press.

——. (2005) "Multinationalizing the Multicultural: The Commodification of 'Ordinary Foreign Residents' in a Japanese TV Talk Show," *Japanese Studies* 25(2): 103–118.
Jaffe, G. (2012, July 24) "Tinted Prejudice in China," *CNN News*. Retrieved from http://www.cnn.com/2012/07/24/world/asia/china-tinted-prejudice/.
Jung, M. (2014, Feb. 3) "Will They Every Get It?," *The Korean Times*. Retrieved from http://www.koreatimes.co.kr/www/news/culture/2015/02/201_150883.html.
Ko, B. (2012) 日本人はなぜ中国人、韓国人とこれほどまで違うのか (*Why Are the Japanese So Different from the Chinese and Koreans?*). Tokyo, Japan: Tokuma Shoten Co. Ltd.
Kuwahara, Y. (2008) "Bob Sapp, Bobby Ologun, Yon-sama, and Jero: The Changing Perception of 'Others' in Contemporary Japan," *The Bulletin of the Center for International Education, Nanzan University* 9, 17–39.
Mori, Y. (2008) "*Winter Sonata* and Cultural Practices of Active Fans in Japan: Considering Middle-Aged Women as Cultural Agents," in C. B. Huat and K. Iwabuchi (eds.), *East Asian Pop Culture: Analysing the Korean Wave*. Hong Kong, China: Hong Kong University Press, 127–141.
Mouer, R. and Sugimoto, Y. (1986) *Images of Japanese Society: A Study in the Structure of Social Reality*. London: Routledge and Kegan Paul.
Oh, C. (2014) "The Politics of the Dancing Body: Racialized and Gendered Femininity in Korean Pop," in Y. Kuwahara (ed.), *The Korean Wave: Korean Popular Culture in Global Context*. New York: Palgrave-Macmillan, 53–81.
Otmazgin, N. K. (2008) "Japanese Popular Culture in East and Southeast Asia: Time for a Regional Paradigm?," *The Asia–Pacific Journal: Japan Focus*. Retrieved from http://www.japanfocus.org/-Nissim_Kadosh-Otmazgin/2660.
Russell, J. (1991, Feb.) "Race and Reflexivity: The Black Other in Contemporary Japanese Mass Culture," *Cultural Anthropology* 6(1): 3–25.
Shiroyama, T. (2014, Dec. 20) 台湾メディアと韓国メディアは犬猿の仲？双方が「感情的な報道控えよう」と呼びかけ―台湾メディア ("Taiwanese Media and Korean Media Are Like Cat and Dog? Both Sides Appeal to Refrain from Emotional Reporting—Taiwanese Media"), *Yahoo! Japan News*. Retrieved from http://headlines.yahoo.co.jp/hl?a=20141220-00000022-xinhua-cn.
Song, M. (2014) "The S(e)oul of Hip-Hop: Locating Space and Identity in Korean Rap," in Y. Kuwahara (ed.), *The Korean Wave: Korean Popular Culture in Global Context*. New York: Palgrave-Macmillan, 133–148.
Suzuki, H. (2015) 邦画の歴史年表と代表的作品 ("History of Japanese Films and Notable Works"), *Pop Culture of the 20th Century*. Retrieved from http://www3.ocn.ne.jp/~zip2000/japanfilm.htm.
Vittachi, N. (2015, Jan. 3) "China's Crime-Free Crime Films," *New York Times*. Retrieved from http://www.nytimes.com/2015/01/04/opinion/sunday/chinas-crime-free-crime-films.html?emc=eta1&_r=1.
Washington, M. (2000) "Sambo: The Black Image in Contemporary Japan," *The Mid-Atlantic Almanack* 9: 23–36.

# Further Reading

Hassid, J. (2008) "Controlling the Chinese Media: An Uncertain Business," *Asian Survey* 48(3): 414–430. (Examination of the governmental control of increasingly liberal Chinese media.)
Iwabuchi, K. (2015) *Resilient Borders and Cultural Diversity: Internationalism, Brand Nationalism and Multiculturalism in Japan*. Lanham, MD: Lexington Books. (Examination of the effect of transnational flow of media products and of people on Japanese millennials.)
Kim, D. K. and Kim M. S. (eds.) (2011) *Hallyu: Influence of Korean Popular Culture in Asia and Beyond*. Seoul, South Korea: Seoul National University Press. (Analysis of the popularity of Korean popular culture in the global context by Korean scholars from diverse perspectives.)
Kowner, R. (2014) *Race and Racism in Modern East Asia*. Leiden, The Netherlands: Brill Academic Publishers. (An analysis of the construction and evolution of the race concept in East Asia and its relationship with the Western concept.)
Pew Research Center. (2014) "Chapter 4: How Asians View Each Other, Global Opposition to U.S. Surveillance and Drones, But Limited Harm to America's Image." Retrieved from http://www.pewglobal.org/2014/07/14/chapter-4-how-asians-view-each-other/. (Results of a survey conducted in Asia which reveal the perceptions of one another among China, Japan, South Korea, and Taiwan.)

# 26

# INDIA

## Insecurities of a Nation on the Rise

*Sidharth Muralidharan*

India is the world's second largest country, with a population of 1.2 billion people (India Census 2011). It also has one of the world's fastest growing economies and, despite its reputation as a third-world nation, findings indicate that improved economic conditions, in terms of increasing levels of individual income, are occurring in both urban and rural areas (Banerjee and Banik 2014). In spite of its progress, India is still plagued with internal issues like discrimination based on skin color, racism against Africans and Indians of the Northeast, and violence against women of Scheduled Castes and Tribes. As this chapter will show, these are not issues that have recently sprung up; they have roots in Indian society's formulation of the caste system centuries ago. British colonialism and, more recently, the advertising industry have been instrumental in propagating racism in India. The objective of this chapter is, first, to describe the twenty-first-century issues that are relevant to the discourse on race and media in India and, second, to further the discussion on how to address the related problems.

### An Obsession with Fair Skin

India's perception of beauty is defined by fair skin, or "whiteness," emanating from a centuries-old social hierarchy created by the Hindu caste system and, later, British colonialism. India historically consisted of two primary races, namely Caucasian Aryans who migrated to India from the north around 1500 BC and the darker-skinned indigenous Dravidians of the south (Shevde 2008; Glenn 2008; Parameswaran and Cardoza 2009). To suppress and exert dominance over the Dravidians, the powerful and more civilized Aryans created the first caste system and divided society into various groups based on color ("varna") and occupation. The upper caste consisted of Brahmins, or priests, who were synonymous with whiteness, purity, and cleanliness; Kshatriyas or warriors were denoted by "red"; Vaishyas or merchants/traders were given the color "yellow"; and the lower caste—Shudras—were associated with black, which symbolized ugliness, dirt, and impurity (Shevde 2008; Arif 2004).

Other writings on the origins of colorism in India described the privileged as having a pale hue since they lived a sheltered life, while those who toiled in the sun had a darker hue (Khan 2009). As centuries passed, Great Britain colonized India and, during its rule,

Western notions of beauty were introduced and white supremacy was enforced. Fair skin was again seen as a symbol of power, dominance, and superiority (Shevde 2008). In India, as in many cultures around the world, the white woman, and especially the tall, thin, blonde, and upper-class white woman, was seen as the epitome of beauty and "is a complex identity born out of differentiations of race, color, and class" (Osuri 2008: 115). The English woman soon became the benchmark of beauty and cultivated a desire among Indian women to emulate their lighter skin tone. In terms of "aspirational" skin tones, there are variations of whiteness, ranging from the white skin color of Northern European Caucasians to the olive skin color of Southern European Caucasians and the North Indian Punjabi community (Parameswaran and Cardoza 2009: 218).

Skin color can play a significant role in India's highly patriarchal matrimony scene. Light skin color is a visible social capital that would help ensure an Indian woman finds a good and accomplished husband. Those with dark-skin, however, face social obstacles where to compensate for the lack of fairness, parents have to pay a high dowry to the groom's family (Grewal 2003). Dowry is the "monetary measure of a woman's value as a person" and the darker the skin, the higher the dowry (Phillips 2004: 269). On the other hand, those with lighter skin have the advantage of negotiating conditions for dowry (Phillips 2004; Varsha and Khandare 2013). Findings from a survey of the popular Indian matrimonial website, shaadi.com, revealed that close to half of the male members wanted brides who were fair (Singh 2011).

In a more comprehensive study of Indian matrimonial websites, men used words such as "beautiful" and "lovely" to describe the preferred qualities of their prospective brides (Jha and Adelman 2009: 65). The authors add that matrimonial websites display the wedding photos of "success stories" in which all the photos were of light-skinned brides; dark-skinned couples were invisible. Research has also indicated that in their profiles Indian women highlight their light skin color far more than men (Pandey 2004), and the need for fair-skinned grooms was non-existent in matrimonial ads (Deshpande 2002). These notions are gradually changing as men have been found to also highlight their physical attractiveness, including light skin color, in matrimonial ads (Ramasubramanian and Jain 2009). This can possibly be attributed to the influence of mass media messages that are propagating the attractiveness of light skin color and toned physiques. Nonetheless, these idealized notions of beauty continue to be considered much more often when evaluating women than men (Jain 2005).

Beauty pageants like "Miss World" and "Miss Universe" have played a tremendous role in propelling Indian models like Aishwarya Rai, Priyanka Chopra, and Sushmita Sen to international stardom. The beauty queens these widely televised events produce have become "symbols of Indian women's new visibility in the public sphere" (Parameswaran 2004: 6). With the popularity of beauty pageants growing, the concept of beauty itself was transformed to "fairer, taller, slimmer, and straighter-haired" (Lal 2003), which is seen as a more acceptable image on a global stage. The beauty queen is seen as a symbol of India's success in the international arena and, furthermore, this success can be attributed to fairer skin color (Osuri 2008).

Winning these titles can also mean lucrative careers in the world's largest film industry, Bollywood, a conduit through which Indian culture is portrayed and a media machine that disseminates the culture of consumption (Osuri 2008). Through its "re-enactment of patriarchal and caste-based identities," Bollywood has a tremendous influence on the psyche of the Indian viewers (Kapur 2009: 221). Models and, later on, stars like Aishwarya Rai are living symbols of Bollywood femininity (Osuri 2008). Even dark-skinned background dancers in Bollywood movies and award functions have been replaced with fair-skinned Indians or Caucasians (Joseph 2000).

A more explicit example of the attraction for fair skin was seen in 2008 when a group of mostly white National Football League cheerleaders from the US were flown in to support the Bangalore Royal Challengers in the Indian Premiere League (IPL) "Twenty20" cricket series (Wax 2008). Cricket organizers were trying to attract a younger male audience, and the novelty of scantily clad cheerleaders at an erstwhile "gentleman's game" quickly became popular in a nation where cricket exists in the same plane as religion. Since then, each team in the league has adopted its own cheerleading squad, with a majority of the cheerleaders from Russia, Ukraine, Belgium, Norway, and South Africa.

India's obsession with fair skin long ago caught the eye of marketers, but it was not until the early 1990s that India liberalized its economy and opened its doors to foreign investors (Banks and Natarajan 1995). Soon after, Indian cosmetic brands like Lakmé and Pond's started to face stiff competition in the form of international companies like Revlon, Avon, and L'Oreal. For marketers, the attraction to India lies in its massive population of 1.2 billion people and their increasing disposable income. According to the India Census (2011), the birthrate of women increased substantially between 2001 and 2011, and the gender ratio has gone up in both rural (where 48.6 percent of the population is female) and urban (48.1 percent) areas. Fairness products aimed at 18–35-year-olds (Shevde 2008) are not limited to middle-class, urban women. According to MART (2012), a leading rural marketing consultancy in India, the combination of the country's rural villages and small towns translates into a $1 trillion market with 1 billion consumers. It is the largest market of "Fast Moving Consumer Goods" and consumer durables, and there are an estimated 10 million operational retail outlets in India, of which 68 percent are in rural areas (Banerjee and Banerjee 2000). For example, the India Tobacco Company's (ITC) *Choupal Saagars* are hypermarkets that sell not only agricultural products to farmers but also consumer products like packaged goods, apparel, appliances, and cosmetics, thus giving consumers in rural India a wide-ranging shopping experience (Himatsingka 2010; Craig and Douglas 2011). Compared to urbanites, rural women are more likely to face color discrimination, and they buy fairness creams to overcome the social stigma of their dark skin. They see skin lightening as an opportunity to not only gain social acceptance but also allow for personal and professional pursuits that would not otherwise be possible (Shevde 2008).

Historically, the Indian perception of upper-class white femininity in the United States was formed through a relationship to valuable things, like fashion, cosmetics, and household goods (Heneghan 2003). More recently, white femininity and its association with success has been commodified by Western marketers and treated as a trait to be desired among Indian women in general (Osuri 2008). Marketers recognize that the image of a white woman in advertisements can be used as a seductive tool to sell products and experiences in markets where darker shades of skin color are more prominent.

Research has shown that dark-skinned models are a rarity in Indian print ads. According to a content analysis of print ads (1997–2002) in *Femina*, India's oldest and largest women's magazine, the majority of the models were light-skinned and models with darker shades of skin tone were nearly invisible (Reddy 2005). Li et al. (2008) found that 82 percent of Indian print ads had Indian models and celebrities, reaffirming the dominance of beauty pageant winners and Bollywood stars in the mass media. However, the skin color of most of the models appeared more Caucasian-looking than Indian.

On critically evaluating Indian ads, Parameswaran and Cardoza (2009) found many brands tend to portray their products as "magnified images of commodities against the backdrop of pale surfaces" (240).

In the branding process, marketers try to associate existing cultural meanings with their products, mainly to distinctly position themselves in the consumer's mind, to break through the clutter in a crowded marketplace, and to promote overt consumption (McCracken 1988). Advertising as a practice survives on symbolism and aids in the transference of meaning, helping consumers perceive "essential similarity" between the cultural world and the product (77). The drawback to this process is the unintended effects; that is, with consistent advertising, the link between fairness and beauty becomes stronger and at the same time perpetuates cultural stereotypes like the pairing of dark skin with inferiority. In the guise of meeting the desires of consumers, corporations are known to manipulate cultural symbols in their advertising to feed their bottom lines. Skin-whitening brands in India especially fuel the cultural beliefs established by the caste system and reinforced by British colonization. Twenty-first-century advertisements for L'Oreal's "White Perfect" feature Bollywood actress Sonam Kapoor as the endorser who suggests that fair skin equates to perfect skin. As Mire (2005) has observed, L'Oreal's ads reinforce white supremacy and tie this notion back to the cultural sphere of the fair-skinned woman as one who is privileged.

With a market share of 57 percent (Singh 2013), one brand that has revolutionized and increased the demand for fair skin products in the Indian market is Hindustan Unilever's "Fair & Lovely." Touted as "the world's first safe and effective skin lightening product" (www.fairandlovely.in), the brand, since 1975, has aggressively promoted fair skin color as a symbol of beauty and success that can enhance one's personal and professional life. Apart from deep underlying cultural beliefs, advertising and Bollywood have transformed fairness creams from a "want" to a "need." To illustrate, many Bollywood celebrities like Juhi Chawla, Hema Malini, Yami Gautam, and cricketers like Virat Kohli and Rohit Sharma are major endorsers of the brand. Even though the Dove brand falls under the Unilever umbrella, its advertising message promotes "natural" beauty and empowerment while Fair & Lovely, in contrast, promotes beauty and success that can be achieved by overcoming flaws like dark skin (Shevde 2008). A close competitor to the Fair & Lovely brand is Emami's "Fair and Handsome," which has capitalized on the men's fairness market since 2005, and Bollywood heartthrob Shah Rukh Khan became its brand endorser in 2007. In the ads, the actor attributes his success to fair skin.

The widespread advertising of fairness creams has not gone unchallenged in India and has led to a public outcry from women's empowerment groups like "Women of Worth," whose mission is to enlighten, encourage, empower, and equip women to value and reach their full potential. Their 2009 campaign called "Dark is Beautiful" (2014) was launched to combat the corroding effects of the fairness stigma as a yardstick of beauty. The awareness campaign also seeks to celebrate diversity and beauty in all skin tones. Internationally renowned actress and director Nandita Das joined the cause and became the face of the campaign, and her presence helped bring a sharp focus to this ongoing debate. Amidst criticism from the All India Democratic Women's Association regarding their ads, the Fair & Lovely Foundation was established in 2003 (Glenn 2008). The foundation's mission is to help women become self-reliant by economically empowering them to achieve their dreams. As per their website, the foundation has given out 1,000 scholarships to applicants in areas like higher education, vocational training, and business start-ups. It cannot be denied that the brand has attempted to instill self-confidence and self-esteem in Indian women, but the disparity created through its ad messages in terms of color prejudice is a cause for concern for future generations. Glenn (2008) iterates that men and women need to be reeducated on the beauty of different shades of skin color and thus have whiteness removed as the benchmark.

The Advertising Standards Council of India (ASCI) (2014) is a self-regulatory voluntary organization that addresses advertisements that are considered false, misleading, indecent, illegal, or that lead to unsafe practices or unfair competition. In August 2014, in response to public feedback and consumer activism regarding the depiction of dark-skinned people as inferior, ASCI released four major guidelines for the advertising of skin-whitening cream: (1) Advertising should not communicate any discrimination as a result of skin color. Specifically, advertising should not directly or implicitly show people with darker skin in a way which is widely seen as unattractive, unhappy, depressed, or concerned; (2) the expression of the model/s in the real and graphical representation should not be negative in a way which is widely seen as unattractive, unhappy, depressed, or concerned; (3) advertising should not associate darker or lighter color skin with any particular socio-economic strata, caste, community, religion, profession, or ethnicity; and (4) advertising should not perpetuate gender-based discrimination because of skin color. These guidelines are commendable and if strictly enforced then advertisers would involuntarily have to change their messaging.

It appears that Indian resistance to skin-lightening advertising has had some impact on the cosmetics industry. According to Nielsen's Moving Annual Total, the $464 million fairness cream market saw a 4.5 percent dip in sales (Singh 2013). Fair & Lovely experienced a dip of 4.2 percent while close competitor Emami's Fair and Handsome experienced a decline of 14 percent.

## Caste and Gendered Violence Against Minorities

As mentioned earlier, the caste system's use of color as an identifier has made life difficult for those in India with dark skin, but when combined with a second factor—gender—the problems deepen considerably. Advertising and television campaigns to counter the problems have not yet had much impact. Rural women in India, especially Scheduled Castes, or "Dalits," and Scheduled Tribes, or "Adivasis," face a combination of racial and gender discrimination in the form of violence by men from upper castes. Scheduled Castes primarily consist of "untouchables"—the 160 million Indians whose births into the caste system have for centuries deemed them less than human (Mayell 2003). Though officially banned by the Indian government in 1950, overt prejudice, discrimination, and violence against the untouchables remain. As Mayell reported for *National Geographic News*:

> India's Untouchables are relegated to the lowest jobs, and live in constant fear of being publicly humiliated, paraded naked, beaten, and raped with impunity by upper-caste Hindus seeking to keep them in their place. Merely walking through an upper-caste neighborhood is a life-threatening offense.
>
> *(2003)*

The classification of Scheduled Tribes refers to the indigenous tribal communities (Sharma 2013). Both Scheduled Castes and Scheduled Tribes suffer from "stigmatized ethnic identity" due to their perceived unworthiness in society, experienced as oppression and exclusion (Berreman 1971: 2).

According to the National Family Health Survey (2007) conducted between 2005 and 2006, rural women in India were more likely to experience physical violence than their urban counterparts. Findings from the comprehensive report also indicate that violence decreases with higher levels of education and wealth. Sexual violence is used as a tactic to assert dominance over lower-caste women, and the "Prevention of Atrocities" Act of 1989, designed to protect the Dalits and Scheduled Tribes from hate crimes, has clearly not been enforced by the local authorities (Sharma 2013). In a 2014 tragedy in which two Dalit girls were raped and hanged in the state of Uttar Pradesh (UP), the first question one of the fathers was asked when reporting his daughter's disappearance to the police was "What is your caste?" (Fontanella-Khan 2014). In 2007 alone, 90 percent of the rape victims from the state of UP were Dalit women, a crisis also seen in other Indian states like Bihar and Haryana (Fontanella-Khan 2014). The major emphasis here is not on gender disparity that is largely prevalent in a patriarchal society like India but to re-emphasize the role played by social hierarchy defined by the caste system. According to Deshpande (2002), a prospective bride in rural India has to first satisfy the requirements of caste, region, and class *before* skin color is even considered. Deshpande believes that exposure to mass media, especially television, can complement education in turning the tides in favor of underprivileged women. TV has now become the most popular medium and Direct-to-Home (DTH) television connections—i.e., the use of personal satellite dishes to receive TV programming—in rural India was more than double the number in urban areas (Nielsen 2010). These signify changing trends, albeit slowly.

Among a few notable awareness campaigns on the issue, the ad agency Taproot partnered with Save Our Sisters to launch the "Abused Goddesses" advertising campaign that garnered a lot of media attention, especially online (Oberoi 2013). The ads had photos of models dressed up as prominent Hindu deities with bruised faces; it instantly went viral. The campaign declares, "Pray that we never see this day. Today, more than 68 percent of women in India are victims of domestic violence. Tomorrow, it seems like no woman shall be spared. Not even the ones we pray to." The campaign was not without its controversy. It received a lot of attention, but Save the Children India did not endorse or approve it, citing that battling domestic violence was not its mission. A disclaimer was provided on its website to clarify its stance on the issue:

> A project of Save the Children India does not endorse the campaign on abused goddesses. Taproot had created the campaign for Save Our Sisters but it was not approved to represent us or use in any form or shape in association with us. The campaign does not represent the work or ideology of the Save Our Sisters movement which is working towards the prevention of trafficking of women from sources areas and the active rehabilitation of rescued victims of trafficking.

The campaign received mixed responses, with some critics accusing the campaign of trivializing Hindu goddesses (Oberoi 2013). Nonetheless, the novel campaign did create some awareness and helped continue the conversation on a critical issue that is downplayed frequently in India.

Not long after the goddess campaign, a second effort to expand the discussion arrived with the launch of a new comic book called "Priya's Shakti," the brainchild of Indian-American filmmaker Ram Devineni (it can be viewed at www.priyashakti.com), designed to combat gender-based violence. The story was inspired by the internationally reported story of Jyoti Singh Pandey, a 23-year-old who was beaten and gang raped by a group of men in a private bus in 2012. She succumbed to her injuries and died 13 days after the rape. The incident garnered national and international protests and resulted in a new law called the Criminal Law (Amendment) Ordinance (and known as the anti-rape bill) passed in 2013. According to the law, jail terms were increased and the death penalty was instituted for a repeat offense of rape, or rape that causes coma. In an interview after the brutal attack, Devineni recalled that a policeman placed the blame on the victim, saying that "no good girl walks alone at night" (Pandey 2014). The statement, according to Devineni, confirms the notion that violence against women is a cultural issue in India. The gruesome incident inspired Devineni and his team to come up with a comic book character, Priya, who is a rape survivor and, with the help of the Goddess Parvati, she fights gender-based crimes. The award-winning comic book targets children and teenagers and, by intertwining Hindu mythology with gender-based violence, the aim is to reach out and educate children at an early age.

The comic book is the first of its kind to use augmented reality; by downloading a free app called Blippar, readers point their mobile devices to certain portraits in the comic book which tell the real-life stories of rape survivors, which have been animated to conceal their true identities (Pundir 2014). As part of the campaign, local artists painted murals on walls replicating the character Priya and the Goddess Parvati at a few locations in Dharavi (Mumbai), one of the largest slums in the world. Being novel and timely in its execution, Priya's Shakti raised the discourse about race and gender in Indian media. It is interesting to note that even though the deceased Pandey was an urbanite in New Delhi, her reincarnation as "Priya" is of a rural girl who is depicted as dark-skinned, wearing traditional Indian clothes, and living in a village, recognizing that rural Indian women are the primary targets of physical and sexual abuse. In the comic book, Priya is described as one who is curious and hardworking with dreams to become a teacher, but as she grows older her father, who is traditional in his ways, instructs her to stay at home and take care of the house. The plotline mirrors the current scenario faced by the Scheduled Castes and Scheduled Tribes in rural villages. Furthermore, this example shows how innovation in new media technology like augmented reality, a tool typically used in advertising campaigns, can also be used to spread awareness of race and gender-based violence.

## Racism and Ethnic Discrimination in India

Newspapers in India and international news organizations regularly report on incidents of racism, much of it related to discrimination against émigrés from Africa. There exists a growing number of Africans from nations like Kenya, Ivory Coast, Ghana, Nigeria, Tanzania, Uganda, and Sudan who come to India to pursue higher education (Soumya 2013). Unfortunately, Indians in general view Africans as suspect; men are stereotyped as troublemakers and drug-traffickers and women as sex-workers. These negative associations have routinely resulted in discrimination against Africans in India, which is widely reported by news organizations. In 2013, a Nigerian national was murdered in the Western state of Goa, which sparked statewide protests by Nigerians and further caused a political rift between the two countries (Soumya 2013). In 2014, three African students were brutally attacked in the nation's capital of New Delhi; such treatment is not uncommon, and is extended to African Americans as well, as reported in *The Hindustan Times* (Vasudeva et al. 2014). One of the men who was beaten told *Al Jazeera*,

"Africans are familiar with Indians due to the huge diaspora in most parts of Africa. It's only now that Africans are coming here and I feel they [Indians] are not prepared for us" (Soumya 2013).

The Indian mass media play a huge role in shaping the public's perception toward Africans. For example, global brands like Coca-Cola's Sprite, Parle Agro's LMN (a lemon drink), and British Petroleum's Castrol engine oil have launched campaigns in India where Africans are portrayed as savages and cannibals (Singh 2010). Singh explains that even though there are many documented instances of discrimination against those from the Indian diaspora abroad, including in media representations (e.g., Ashton Kutcher playing an Indian character "Raj" in a commercial for PopChips), it still doesn't deter Indians from propagating racial stereotypes of other cultures in their home country. Color prejudice is also seen in sports, especially in the country's greatest national pastime, cricket. Event management companies that advertise, interview, and select Indian Premier League cheerleaders primarily focus on skin tone, prompting reasonable allegations about racism. *The Telegraph* reported that for an IPL match in Mohali, British cheerleaders Ellesha Newton and Sherinne Anderson, both of African descent, were prevented from entering the cricket grounds by an organizer of Wizcraft International Entertainment, who explained, "People here don't want to see dark people" (Allen 2008). Decisions such as this continue to propagate discrimination and reiterate the existence of a color divide in India, which can be tied back to the underlying attitudes and behavior against those with dark skin that have been established by the caste system and British colonization.

Another group that has experienced repeated discrimination at the hands of their own countrymen are Indians from the Seven Sister states of the northeast—Arunachal Pradesh, Assam, Manipur, Meghalaya, Mizoram, Nagaland, and Tripura. The more liberal and progressive culture of the northeast has resulted in disturbing stereotypes—men as incompetent and drug-addled and women as prostitutes, as *Al Jazeera* has reported (Das 2014). With communal unrest plaguing the seven states, coupled with the lack of job opportunities and better education, the major Indian metro areas have witnessed an influx of northeasterners (about 15,000 per year) who want to pursue higher education and start a new life but who face frightful prejudice (Bhowmick 2014).

Social media in India has had mixed results in its contributions to the dialogue on race in India. Its power to bring about collective change is undeniable: social media was used to help win Barack Obama the presidential election in 2008, to rally protesters in the 2011 Egyptian revolution, and to voice the opinions of African Americans about the 2014 police shooting in Ferguson, Missouri. At the same time, such a tool can also be used to threaten and invoke fear in minorities. When power struggles between Bengali immigrant Muslims in Assam and the indigenous Bodo tribe led to an insurgency in the northeast, social media platforms like Facebook and Twitter were the tools of choice through which videos and morphed photos of northeasterners attacking Muslims in Assam were disseminated, causing communal violence against the large northeastern community (Magnier 2012). Hate messages were also sent via Short Message Service, warning northeasterners to leave for their respective states before the end of the holy month of Ramadan. The fear of escalation prompted a massive exodus of northeasterners from the South Indian cities of Pune, Bangalore, Chennai, and Hyderabad. The increased train traffic due to the exodus pushed the railway authorities to increase the number of trains to the northeast. With the government stepping in by beefing up security and assuring safety, many of the northeasterners returned after the situation was stabilized, thus gradually ending the exodus. Northeasterners have faced casual racism since their arrival but the exodus marked the emergence of a more acute mindset born from inherent racial biases.

The *Times of India* reported in 2014 that Lulminlal Haokip, 21, and Lepmin Len, 18, who hailed from Manipur, were verbally abused and then physically assaulted by a group of local youths in South Delhi. The assaulters were later taken into custody but the deep scars caused by racism remained. Similar incidents have been reported in major Indian metros like Bangalore and Gurgaon. The turning point came when Nido Taniam, 20, from Arunachal Pradesh was ridiculed for his hair and clothes and soon a brawl ensued (Agarwal 2014). His injuries were so severe that he died, which led to several protests by students in New Delhi to highlight the country's penchant for racism against northeasterners. India is devoid of an anti-racism law and, in response, a committee headed by M. P. Bezbaruah, a member of the Northeast council, was formed with its major goal being the prosecution of assailants "under specific provisions that recognize such crimes as racially motivated" (Malhotra 2014).

Citizens of Nepal, a sovereign country nestled between India and China, are also subject to discrimination in India. About a fifth of Nepal's 28 million residents live and work in India (Prasad 2014). Due to the similarity in the Tibeto-Mongoloid features of the Nepalese with Indians of the northeast, they have been perceived as a single group and have been similarly abused. An ad campaign was created around the negative stereotypes associated with Nepalese men as night watchmen. The Asian Center for Human Rights (ACHR 2014) labeled a recent ad by "Champions League T20 – #T20Nights Are Back!" as racist. In one of the ads, a Nepalese character sings the lines, "Woh Raatein Bhi Kya Raatein Thi, Naach te teh, gaate teh, chilla te teh, purra mohalla ko, haami toh jagate teh" (*What nights were those nights, used to dance, used to sing, used to shout, we are the ones who used to wake up the entire locality*). The words in connection with the actor's nationality clearly implied that Nepalese are stereotyped as night watchmen and, to drive home the point, accompanying radio ads employed a heavy Nepalese accent. Stereotypical simplifications showcase a false perception of diversity, and consistent media portrayals reinforce the minority's outside status in the host culture. Generalizing diverse cultures can create a set of incorrect beliefs about the entire group but, more importantly, "in-group bias" (Brewer 1979) is generated where members of the in-group (mainland India) see themselves superior to out-groups (northeast).

The effects of violence coupled with media stereotyping can slow down the acculturation process and make minorities feel the host culture is indifferent to their values. Even though the Seven Sister states fall under one flag, people of "mainland India" see themselves as physically and culturally different from the northeasterners and vice-versa. Apart from proximity and language barriers, former Nagaland Chief Secretary Alemtemshi Jamir points out that "even if the government enacts an anti-racist law, as long as people don't understand other cultures within its own territory it won't help in solving this issue" (Kharmujai 2014). Kharmujai cites a major flaw in the Indian educational system, in which awareness of the various cultural nuances existing in the northeast is limited, and more comprehensive media coverage of social and current affairs in the region is needed to prevent alienation and promote successful integration between the mainland and the northeast.

## The Future

To truly progress as an advanced country, India has to first empower its people by overcoming social stigmas like colorism and gender disparity, and the country's media system could be central to that effort. Scheduled Castes comprise nearly 17 percent and Scheduled Tribes nearly 9 percent of the total population (India Census 2011). These numbers indicate that their advancement is critical in the country's road to progress. Dark skin color, which is more prevalent in rural India, will have to stop being treated as a handicap, especially for women. Also, race, gender, and violence are inextricably linked in the country, and constructing social boundaries with respect to caste is an impediment as women bear the brunt of discrimination and physical/sexual violence. Research has confirmed that there are long-term economic benefits from investing in women's futures (Marquis et al. 2010), and discrimination based on skin color and social designation can negatively impact their self-esteem and ability to successfully pursue their personal and professional lives. In terms of racist tendencies against the African diaspora and the northeast Indians, further media introspection is needed. As Ayyar and Khandre (2013) point out, it would be prudent for India to borrow the cultural significance of the Sanskrit saying, "Atithi Devo Bhava" (74) [*Guests are God or should be treated like God*], which was seen in the Ministry of Tourism's "Incredible India!" campaign that promoted India as a prime tourist destination to a global audience. In retrospect, the current scenario is a far cry from how India treats not only its guests but also its brethren. Nonetheless, in the light of slowly changing perceptions of beauty and governmental intervention in unison with self-regulation by the mass media, India appears to be on the path of breaking from the shackles of its insecurities and racial biases.

## References

Advertising Standards Council of India. (2014, Aug. 19) "ASCI Releases Advertising Guidelines for the Skin Whitening Products Category." Retrieved from http://www.ascionline.org/images/pdf/press-release-on-asci-sets-up-new-guidelines-for-the-fairness-products-category-2-.pdf.

Agarwal, V. (2014, Feb. 3) "Student's Death Highlights Racial Abuse," *Wall Street Journal*. Retrieved from http://blogs.wsj.com/indiarealtime/2014/02/03/death-of-northeastern-puts-spotlight-on-racial-abuse/.

Allen, N. (2008, May 22) "Indian Premier League: British Cheerleaders 'Banned for Being Black,'" *The Telegraph*. Retrieved from http://www.telegraph.co.uk/news/2007056/Indian-Premier-League-British-cheerleaders-banned-for-being black.html.

Arif, H. (2004) "Woman's Body as a Color Measuring Text: A Signification of Bengali Culture," *Semiotica* 150(1/4): 579–595.

Asian Center for Human Rights. (2014, Dec. 15) "Champions League T-20 Advertisements Promoting Stereotyping and Racial Prejudices Against Nepalese and North Easterners." Retrieved from http://www.achrweb.org/press/2014/IND10-2014.html.

Ayyar, V. and Khandare, L. (2013) "Mapping Color and Caste Discrimination in Indian Society," in R. E. Hall (ed.), *The Melanin Millennium*. The Netherlands: Springer, 71–95.

Banerjee, A. and Banerjee, B. (2000) "Effective Retail Promotion Management: Use of Point of Sales Information Resources," *Vikalpa* 25: 54–55.

Banerjee, A. and Banik, N. (2014) "Is India Shining?," *Review of Development Economics* 18(1): 59–72.

Banks, P. and Natarajan, G. (1995) "India: The New Asian Tiger?," *Business Horizons* 38: 47–50.

Berreman, G. (1971) "Self, Situation and Escape from Stigmatized Ethnic Identity," ERIC Database. Retrieved from http://www.eric.ed.gov/PDFS/ED058344.pdf.

Bhowmick, N. (2014, Feb. 6) "What the Death of Nido Taniam Tells Us about Racism in India," *Time*. Retrieved from http://time.com/4876/nido-taniam-india-racism/.

Brewer, M. B. (1979) "In-group Bias in the Minimal Intergroup Situation: A Cognitive-Motivational Analysis," *Psychological Bulletin* 86(2): 307–324.

Craig, C. S. and Douglas, S. P. (2011) "Empowering Rural Consumers in Emerging Markets," *International Journal of Emerging Markets* 6(4): 382–393.

Dark is Beautiful. (2014) "About the Campaign." Retrieved from http://darkisbeautiful.blogspot.com/p/about-us.html.

Das, B. (2014, Feb. 19) "India's Northeast Speaks Out Against Racism," *Al Jazeera*. Retrieved from http://www.aljazeera.com/indepth/features/2014/02/voices-from-india-northeast-201421811314600858.html.

Deshpande, A. (2002) "Assets versus Autonomy? The Changing Face of the Gender-Caste Overlap in India," *Feminist Economics* 8(2): 19–35.

Fontanella-Khan, A. (2014, June 4) "India's Feudal Rapists," *New York Times*. Retrieved from http://www.nytimes.com/2014/06/05/opinion/indias-feudal-rapists.html?_r=0.

Glenn, E. N. (2008) "Yearning for Lightness: Transnational Circuits in the Marketing and Consumption of Skin Lighteners," *Gender and Society* 22(3): 281–302.

Grewal, I. (2003) "Transnational America: Race, Gender and Citizenship after 9/11," *Social Identities* 9(4): 535–562.

Heneghan, B. T. (2003) *Whitewashing America: Material Culture and Race in the Antebellum Imagination*. Jackson, MS: University Press of Mississippi.

Himatsingka, A. (2010, April 12) "ITC e-Choupal to Quintuple Reach," *The Economic Times*. Retrieved from http://articles.economictimes.indiatimes.com/2010-04-12/news/27612204_1_choupal-itc-plans-agri-reforms.

India Census. (2011, July 15) "Rural Urban Distribution of Population," *Census of India*. Retrieved from http://censusindia.gov.in/2011-prov-results/paper2/data_files/india/Rural_Urban_2011.pdf.

Jain, P. (2005, Nov.) "The Fairer Sex: Constructions of Beauty in Indian Film." Paper presented at the Annual Conference of National Communication Association, Boston, MA.

Jha, S. and Adelman, M. (2009) "Looking for Love in All the White Places: A Study of Skin Color Preferences on Indian Matrimonial and Mate-seeking Websites," *Studies in South Asian Film and Media* 1(1): 65–83.

Kapur, J. (2009) "An 'Arranged Love' Marriage: India's Neoliberal Turn and the Bollywood Wedding Culture Industry," *Communication, Culture, & Critique* 2(2): 221–233.

Khan, A. (2009) "'Caucasian', 'Coolie', 'Black', or 'White'? Color and Race in the Indo-Caribbean Diaspora," in E. Glenn (ed.), *Shades of Difference: Transnational Perspectives on How and Why Skin Color Matters*. Palo Alto, CA: Stanford University Press, 95–113.

Kharmujai, R. (2014, Dec. 3) "Attacks on Northeasterners Due to Lack of Knowledge of Region," *The Assam Tribune*. Retrieved from http://www.assamtribune.com/scripts/detailsnew.asp?id=dec0314/at048.

Lal, P. (2003, Dec. 18) "Bollywood from beyond: Beauty Queens and Fairness Creams," *Pop Matters*. Retrieved from http://www.popmatters.com/columns/lal/031218.shtml.

Li, E. P. H., Min, H. J., Belk, R. W., Kimura, J., and Bahl, S. (2008) "Skin Lightening and Beauty in Four Asian Cultures," *Advances in Consumer Research* 25: 444–449.

Magnier, M. (2012, Aug. 18) "Northeasterners' Exodus in India Underlines Power of Social Media," *Los Angeles Times*. Retrieved from http://articles.latimes.com/2012/aug/18/world/la-fg-india-social-media-20120819.

Malhotra, A. (2014, Oct. 17) "Attacks on Northeasterners Renew Calls for Anti-Racism Law in India," *Wall Street Journal*. Retrieved from http://blogs.wsj.com/indiarealtime/2014/10/17/attacks-on-northeasterners-renew-calls-for-anti-racism-law-in-india/.

Marquis, C., Rangan, V. K., and Ross, C. (2010) "Goldman Sachs: The 10,000 Women Initiative," Harvard Business Case No. 9-509-042. Boston, MA: Harvard Business School Publishing.

MART. (2012) "Rural Growth Story," *MART Knowledge Series*. Retrieved from http://martrural.com/wp-content/themes/themetastic/img/pdf/MART-Rural-Growth-Story-2012.pdf.

Mayell, H. (2003, June 2) "India's 'Untouchables' Face Violence, Discrimination," *National Geographic News*. Retrieved from http://news.nationalgeographic.com/news/2003/06/0602_030602_untouchables.html.

McCracken, G. (1988) *Culture and Consumption*. Bloomington, IN: Indiana University Press.

Mire, A. (2005, July 28) "Pigmentation and Empire: The Emerging Skin-Whitening Industry," *Counterpunch*. Retrieved from http://www.counterpunch.org/mire07282005.html.

National Family Health Survey. (2007) "National Family Health Survey (NFHS-3), 2005–06," *International Institute for Population Sciences (IIPS)*. Retrieved from http://hetv.org/india/nfhs/nfhs3/NFHS-3-Chapter-15-Domestic-Violence.pdf.

Nielsen. (2010) "India's Rural FMCG Market to Grow to $100 billion by 2025," *Nielsen*. Retrieved from http://www.nielsen.com/us/en/insights/news/2010/india-rural-fmcg-market-to-grow-to-100-billion-by-2025.html.

Oberoi, R. K. (2013, Oct. 25) "Critics Slam Art that Depicts Abused Indian Goddesses, Raises Awareness for Domestic Violence," *The Huffington Post*. Retrieved from http://www.huffingtonpost.com/2013/10/25/abused-goddess-campaign_n_4164256.html.

Osuri, G. (2008) "Ash-coloured Whiteness: The Transfiguration of Aishwarya Rai," *South Asian Popular Culture* 6(2): 109–123.

Pandey, G. (2014, Dec. 7) "India's New Comic 'Super Hero': Priya, the Rape Survivor," *BBC News*. Retrieved from http://www.bbc.com/news/world-asia-india-30288173.

Parameswaran, R. and Cardoza, K. (2009) "Melanin on the Margins: Advertising and the Cultural Politics of Fair/Light/White Beauty in India," *Journalism & Communication Monographs* 11(3): 213–274.

Philips, A. (2004) "Gendering Color: Identity, Femininity and Marriage in Kerala," *Anthropologica* 46(2): 253–272.

Prasad, J. (2014, Aug. 2) "A New Template for India-Nepal Ties," *The Hindu*. Retrieved from http://www.thehindu.com/opinion/lead/a-new-template-for-indianepal-ties/article6272963.ece.

Pundir, P. (2014, Sept. 22) "Priya's Shakti Project Tackles Gender-based Violence Through the Story of a Rape Victim," *The Indian Express*. Retrieved from http://indianexpress.com/article/lifestyle/power-of-one-2/.

Ramasubramanian, S. and Jain, P. (2009) "Gender Stereotypes and Normative Heterosexuality in Matrimonial Ads from Globalizing India," *Asian Journal of Communication* 19(3): 253–269.

Reddy, V. (2006) "The Nationalization of the Global Indian Woman: Geographies of Beauty in Femina," *South Asian Popular Culture* 4(l): 61–85.

Sharma, S. (2013) "Hate Crimes in India: An Economic Analysis of Violence and Atrocities against Scheduled Castes and Scheduled Tribes," *The Association of Religion Data Archives*. Retrieved from http://www.thearda.com/asrec/archive/papers/Sharma%20-%20Hate%20crimes%20in%20india.pdf.

Sheehan, K. (2014) *Controversies in Contemporary Advertising*. Thousand Oaks, CA: Sage Publications.

Shevde, N. (2008) "All's Fair in Love and Cream: A Culture Case Study of Fair and Lovely in India," *Advertising & Society Review* 9(2): 1–9.

Singh, A. (2011, May 15) "Fair is Lovely," *The Indian Express*. Retrieved from http://www.newindianexpress.com/magazine/article470182.ece.

Singh, M. (2010, June 21) "Why Do Black African Racial Stereotypes Persist in India?," *Time*. Retrieved from http://content.time.com/time/world/article/0,8599,1997936,00.html.

Singh, R. (2013, Aug. 18) "Fairness Creams' Segment Slows Down: Has the Nation Overcome Its Dark Skin Complex?," *The Economic Times*. Retrieved from http://articles.economictimes.indiatimes.com/2013-08-18/news/41421066_1_fairness-cream-fairness-products-skin-colour.

Soumya, E. (2013, Dec. 2) "Africans Decry 'Discrimination' in India," *Al Jazeera*. Retrieved from http://www.aljazeera.com/indepth/2013/11/africans-decry-discrimination-india-201311139485418912.html.

*Times of India*. (2014, Sept. 15) "2 Manipur Boys Beaten Up in South Delhi," *Times of India*. Retrieved from http://timesofindia.indiatimes.com/city/delhi/2-Manipur-boys-beaten-up-in-south-Delhi/articleshow/42482802.cms.

Vasudeva, R., Joshi, R., Mondal, S., and Kohli, N. (2014, Oct. 12) "Their Indian Horror: Africans Recount Everyday Racism," *The Hindustan Times*. Retrieved from http://www.hindustantimes.com/india-news/their-indian-horror-africans-recount-everyday-racism/article1-1274437.aspx.

Wax, E. (2008, April 19) "Redskins Cheerleaders Shake Up Cricket In Modest India," *The Washington Post*. Retrieved from http://www.washingtonpost.com/wp-dyn/content/article/2008/04/18/AR2008041803577.html.

## Further Reading

Mehta, P. (2013) "Imagining Sikhs: The Ethics of Representation and the Spectacle of Otherness in Bollywood Cinema," *Sikh Formations* 9(1): 73–95. (Studies the Sikh community through a cultural lens and explores how the belittling or exaggerated portrayals in Bollywood cinema mask the community's true identity.)

Parameswaran, R. E. (2005) "Global Beauty Queens in Post-liberalization India," *Peace Review: A Journal of Social Justice* 17(4): 419–426. (An in-depth look at the road traversed by Indian beauty pageant winners and the impact of media narratives weaved around them on the Indian middle and lower class.)

Parameswaran, R. E. and Cardoza, K. (2009) "Immortal Comics, Epidermal Politics," *Journal of Children and Media* 3(1): 19–34. (Examines the symbolic meanings associated with the skin color of historical and religious characters in India's most popular comic book series for children, *Amar Chitra Katha*.)

# 27
# GENDER AND BLACK FEMINIST THEORY

## Examining Difference

*Mia Moody-Ramirez*

Feminist scholarship about the media is often guided by three key themes, including: (1) stereotypes of women in advertising, film, television, and other media; (2) differences among media representations of women of color; and (3) the role of women in the interlocking axes of race, gender, class, and sexuality. The purpose of this chapter is to, first, offer a glimpse of media stereotypes of women of color. Second, it defines terms relevant to the study of feminist theory as they relate to the study of race. Finally, it explores the primary teachings of Black Feminists, which are central to the scholarship about race and gender.

### Stereotypes, Gender, and Race

Lippmann (1922) defines stereotypes as a form of perception that imposes ways of seeing. In other words, "stereotypes are 'mental cookie cutters'—they force a simple pattern upon a complex mass and assign a limited number of characteristics to all members of the group" (Nachbar and Lausé 1992: 236). Stereotypes are particularly important in gender studies because media messages help citizens make sense of the world around them, especially for depictions of traditionally marginalized groups. It is often through media images that people negotiate identities, ideas, and relationships with other people (see, for example, Hall 1998, 2000; Enriques 2001; and Ono 2009). Additionally, stereotyping is a social tool that builds group solidarity and creates an "us versus them" mentality. The dominant group – the cultural elite – uses stereotypes to dehumanize other cultural groups that differ in values, beliefs, or physical characteristics to maintain its own political power and social control (Lassiter 1999).

Feminist and Critical Race Theorists are concerned with stereotypes because dominant ideologies serve to reproduce social relations of domination and subordination (Hammer and Kellner 2009; Moody and Dates 2014). Van Zoonen (1994) explained how stereotypes fulfill the structural needs of a patriarchal and capitalist society by reinforcing gender differences and inequalities. Carter and Steiner (2003) assert that sexist images reproduced by the media make hierarchical and distorted sex-role stereotypes appear normal.

Researchers have consistently found negative, biased news coverage of racial and ethnic minorities. U.S. entertainment media and news coverage of people of color have historically reflected and reinforced racial stereotypes by portraying them as lazier, less intelligent, less moral, and more prone to crime than whites (see, for example, Martindale 1990; Bagdikian 1969; Entman 1990; Chaudhary 1980; Dixon and Linz 2000; Sylvie 1995; Dates and Barlow 1993; Wilson and Gutierrez 2003; Signorielli 2009; Campbell 1995; Campbell et al. 2012). For most racial groups, stereotypes are divided along gender lines, which are explored in the following section.

### *Asian-American Women*

Stereotypes characterizing Asians in movies and TV shows in the US have remained constant over the decades (Spooner 2001). Asian stereotyping began as people form Asian countries migrated to America to help mine gold during the Gold Rush in the middle of the nineteenth century. They worked hard, saved money, opened shops, and eventually competed with Anglos for desirable jobs. In response, early artifacts in popular culture—advertising, newspapers, theater—often depicted members of the ethnic group negatively, as clannish and deceptive. Those messages persisted well into the twentieth century, and the few Asian characters in film and television dramas were often portrayed as villains or owners of laundry shops and restaurants (Harris 1999).

Asian males often played asexual characters and nerds with varying skills in martial arts, ranging from Kung Fu Masters to evil gangsters (Chon-Smith 2006). On the other hand, Asian females were highly sexualized in U.S. movies and television shows, and China doll and geisha stereotypes were extremely exotic and erotic. In stark contrast to that stereotype was the dragon lady, highly skilled in martial arts. In the 1990s and 2000s, Asian women's images improved somewhat as they appeared in a wider range of crucial roles (e.g., Fong 2002; Paek and Shah 2003). However, their stereotypical sexual power and attractiveness to Anglo males has been deeply ingrained in Americans' perceptions and in the U.S. media, and Asian women in film and on TV are typically paired with a white co-star (Tierney 2006; Wang and Cooper 2008).

Also worth noting is that not all Asian stereotypes are negative. While media stereotype other people of color as "problem" minorities, they often cast Asian Americans as the "model" minority. The model minority ideal portrays the group as hard working and dedicated to education. Thus, they achieve success and assimilation. The term "model minority" was first coined by sociologist William Peterson in 1966 in an article, "Success Story: Japanese-American Style" published in the *New York Times Magazine* (Peterson). He suggested that although Asian Americans, as an ethnic minority, were marginalized, they had achieved much more success in the United States than other minority groups.

The "tiger mom" phenomenon added a new dimension to the model minority stereotype and is used to explain why many Asian students excel. On January 8, 2011, the *Wall Street Journal* published an excerpt of, "Why Chinese Mothers Are Superior," written by Yale law professor Amy Chua in her memoir, *Battle Hymn of the Tiger Mother*. In the book, Chua (2011) ridiculed Western-parenting styles as too soft. She held up Chinese parenting as the epitome of successful child-rearing, and the book attracted considerable public attention after the *Wall Street Journal* published the excerpt.

Studies indicate that during the 1990s and 2000s, images of Asian women improved. Asian women during this period appeared in a wider variety of major roles, in affluent settings, and with positive images. In terms of interactions with other people, Asian women are portrayed as somewhat more active and approachable than their male counterparts, which is consistent with previous studies of sexual stereotypes that permeated Asian females with stereotypical sexual power and attractiveness.

### *Native-American Women*

The longest-standing portrayals of Native Americans are also dichotomous. On one hand, the "ignoble savage" is a stereotypically violent Indian (Griffiths 2001). Once conquered, he or she becomes a thief, a drunkard, and a beggar, unwilling to work but willing to accept government handouts. On the other hand, the "noble savage" is the good or redeemable Indian who is close to nature (Griffiths 2001). The male noble savage is often shown hunting buffalo or displaying expert equestrian skill, while the female noble savage combines elements of innocent, natural beauty with forbidden, exotic sexuality (Merskin 1998).

Popular culture portrayals of Native Americans have not redressed historical wrongs (Lobo and Talbot 2001). For instance, from *Seinfeld*, a classic television situation comedy of the 1990s, came the episode in which the hero continually finds himself insulting the Native-American woman he wishes to date, using idioms such as "Indian-giver" to draw laughs (Lobo and Talbot 2001). More recently, Lacroix (2011) examined examples from several popular television shows, concluding that representations have not changed much. Native Americans on shows such as *The Sopranos, Saturday Night Live, Chappelle's Show, Family Guy, Drawn Together*, and *South Park* include depictions of Native Americans that reference age-old racist stereotypes of the ignoble savage while simultaneously working to construct a new trope—"the casino Indian." Lacroix (2011) charted the themes of this stereotype and concluded that while the ignoble savage of the past posed a threat of violence, the contemporary casino Indian image poses economic and political threats. Findings demonstrate Native-American women are still portrayed as exotic and often the prize for a lead character who is usually white or black. Rarely are they in a starring role next to a male counterpart of the same race.

### *Latinas*

Likewise, representations of Hispanics are divided along gender lines. Typically, males are identified by their youthful appearance, aggressive nature, dishonesty, and unkempt appearances. The Latin lover has a hot temper and is sexually aggressive, while the comic or buffoon has secondary status and a lack of intelligence and motivation to succeed (Berg 2002; Mastro and Behm-Morazwitz 2005). Stereotypical behavioral characteristics assigned to Latinas include romantic, sensual, sexual, dependent, powerless, naive, childlike, pampered, and irresponsible (e.g., Mastro and Behm-Morawitz 2005; Berg 2002). According to Berg (2002), Latinas continue to be characterized as maids who are subservient yet hot tempered (Soto 2008). Similarly, the "dark lady" is dichotomously portrayed as both exotic and erotic, and virginal and aristocratic (Berg 2002; Shugart 2007).

In many cases, historical stereotypes extend to modern representations. For instance, the popular TV drama *Desperate Housewives*, which aired from 2004 to 2012, featured Eva Longoria in the role of Gabrielle Solis, a Latina who fits many of the stereotypes outlined above (Merskin 2007). At first glance, Longoria's role appears to be a breakthrough for Latinas. However, a critical reading of the program shows that Gabrielle's role is stereotypical (Shugart 2007). For instance, in one storyline, she portrayed a conniving gold-digger who cheated on her husband with a much younger "pool boy." Latina actress and singer Jennifer Lopez also demonstrated the longevity of negative portrayals of Latinas. Media coverage and movie roles featuring the actress often focused on her curviness rather than her talent, which Guzman (2010) argues might be acceptable in the construction of Lopez as a Latina celebrity, but is not considered acceptable for Anglo celebrities. The researcher concluded that this construction thereby complied with mainstream expectations of Latina beauty, which make it okay for media outlets to focus primarily on sexuality.

## Arab and Muslim Women

When describing the media's treatment of Arabs and Muslim, Akram (2002) explains how media never depict members of this group as "ordinary people, families with social interactions, or outstanding members of communities." Instead, representations of Arabs and Muslims conjure images of "holy war," terrorism, and oppressive patriarchy among the American public (66).

Portrayals of Arab and Muslim women are particularly negative. Historically, media have portrayed women in the Arab and Muslim worlds as either mysteriously exotic or oppressed and backward. Many images of Afghan women focus on the burqa, the traditional head-to-toe cover that shields women from public view (Ferree and Tripp 2006). Eltantawy (2007) examined articles that feed into the dominating yet distorted stereotype of the victimized and oppressed Muslim woman. She concluded that, especially after 9/11, newspapers increased their photos of mostly Afghani women with their faces veiled to the outside world.

## African-American Women

As with other ethnic groups, stereotypes of African Americans tend to differ based on gender (Qasim, Hayat, and Asmat 2012). Historically, stereotypes of African-American women have institutionalized white and male supremacist ideologies that produce "specific images, representations of race, of blackness that support and maintain the oppression, exploitation and overall domination of all Black people" (hooks 1992: 2). Wallace (1979) asserted that the myth of the black superwoman essentially consists of stereotypes deeply rooted in slavery and the idea that although black women are able to do more physical labor than the average woman, "they consistently sacrifice themselves for others, have no emotion, and are really just men" (107). She adds that the matriarchal structure of the black family led by a strong black woman during slavery is often credited for the emasculation of the black man and subsequently the dysfunctional nature of the black family. She writes:

> Less of a woman in that the Black woman is depicted as less 'feminine' and helpless, she is really more of a woman in that she is the embodiment of Mother Earth, the quintessential mother with infinite sexual, life-giving, and nurturing reserves. In other words, she is a superwoman.
>
> *(107)*

These myths of the black superwoman have helped shape the negative perceptions of them as a whole, which carries over to present-day stereotypes found in imagery of black women. Representations of black women are often dichotomous in nature. They include the idea that they are either extremely "dumb" or extremely educated, ambitious or listless, attractive or ugly (Boylorn 2008). The sexually promiscuous black woman, also known as the "oversexed-black-Jezebel," is an extreme opposite of the "mammy," who is nurturing and passive (Moody and Dates 2014).

Sapphire, another opposite to mammy's character, is a wisecracking, emasculating black woman whom media often depict in movies and television shows with her hands on her hips. She lets everyone know she is the boss (Yarborough and Bennett 2000). Scholars argue that Sapphire's character is a control-agent for her counterpart, the corrupt African-American male character, whose lack of integrity and use of trickery provides her with an opportunity to emasculate him with her smart, insulting mouth (Yarborough and Bennett 2000; Collins 2005).

## Feminist Theory

To counteract these negative stereotypes of women, feminist-informed research methods put race, gender, and gender-related issues at the center of analysis and highlight notions of power in various methods (Krolokke and Sorensen 2006). Gender-schema theory proposes that people see the world through the lens of gender and that cultural norms tend to polarize females and males by organizing social life around mutually exclusive gender roles (Bem 1981). Kamler (1999) defined "gender" as fluid, negotiable, and complex, versus "sex," which is biological. Gender also refers to social, cultural, and psychological traits linked to males and females through particular social contexts (Holmes 2007).

Film, print, Web content, and broadcast news reflect ideological positions and help reproduce dominant forms of social power, whether based on race or gender. In her seminal work, *Sexual Politics*, Millett (1969) outlined the twin principles of patriarchy: "Male shall dominate female, elder male shall dominate younger" (20). Media coverage often follows the patriarchal paradigm as outlined by Hartmann (1981), who defines the model as a set of materially based social relations that create a solidarity among men of all races and classes "who are united in their shared relationship of dominance over their women" (14–15).

In media studies, scholars study gender as it relates to power relationships because dominant groups establish and control communication methods (Orbe 1998; Gramsci 1971; Millett 1969). Scholars often apply Gramsci's (1971) idea of hegemony to analyze mass media messages. Hegemony refers to "manufactured consent" rather than a deceitful plan crafted purposefully by those in positions of power to manipulate the system to serve dominant interests (Chomsky and Herman 1988). Hegemonic processes aim to build consensus among the masses that a certain ideology is normal and that any contradictions to it are deviant (Gramsci 1971). Considerable research has confirmed the existence of hegemonic representations through the study of race, physical appearance, and gender stereotypes (see Collins 2005; Ludvig 2006; Zinn and Dill 1994; Hall 1980; hooks 1981; Moraga and Anzaldúa 1981; Carter and Steiner 2003; van Zoonen 1994; Campbell 1995).

### *Feminist Theory Timeline*

Historically, the dates 1890–1940 typically coincide with the first wave of feminism and its educational, suffragist, socialist, and professional agendas. As Scott (2008) observed, "Feminist activism and ideology of the period, as well as reactions against them, made gender a field of contention, sometimes labeled the 'sex wars'" (7). The feminist "first wave" is generally identified with the mobilization of strong feminist movements in the mid-nineteenth and early twentieth centuries in Europe and North America that were concerned with a number of egalitarian and radical issues, which included equal rights for women, educational and legal reform, slavery, and the right to vote (Vavrus 2010). Issues of sexuality and gratification for women and reproductive rights and birth control were highly controversial dimensions of the first wave (Kellner 2002).

"Second-wave" feminists included young women and girls who were part of the massive baby boom generation (1946–64), born during the period of economic prosperity that followed WWII. Many were the first in their families to receive university educations and were greatly influenced by and involved in the civil rights movement. Societal conventions following the war disenchanted others who went back into conventional roles, often as full-time wives and mothers. Betty Friedan, in the 1963 bestseller *The Feminine Mystique*, examined the role of women's magazines, Freudian psychology, and educational institutions in keeping women in a subservient position. Building upon the suffrage movement of the late nineteenth and early twentieth centuries, she described "the problem that has no name" or the widespread unhappiness of women in the 1950s and early 1960s (Friedan 1963). It was during this period that Friedan, who died in 2006, was a prominent leader of the feminist movement. She was a founding member of the National Organization for Women (NOW), the National Abortion Rights Action, and the National Women's Political Caucus (Betty Friedan Biography 2012).

The feminist "third wave," as described by Rebecca Walker and others, began in the early 1990s in response to shortcomings of the "second wave" (Gillis, Gillian, and Munford 2007). During this period, women examined not only gender equality but also the intersections between race, class, and culture. Third-wave feminists also distinguished themselves by focusing on issues of sexuality, challenging female heterosexuality and celebrating sexuality as a means of female empowerment. During this wave, there was an increased understanding of bisexual and trans identities. Third-wave feminism was heavily influenced by academic investigations of queer theory (Munro 2014). Queer theory posits that gender and sexuality are fluid categories and do not easily translate into binary understandings of "male" and "female" (Jakubowski 2014).

Second-wave feminists treated women as homogenous groups without paying attention to the many axes of difference that cleave apart the singular category of "women," so the first two feminist waves limited participation by African-American women. Marbley (2005) noted both the feminist and black movements rendered African-American females and black feminism virtually invisible in mainstream politics and economics. bell hooks' seminal *Ain't I a Woman* (1981) noted the devaluation of black femininity and the invisibility of women of color in the feminist movement. She argued that these actions reinforced racism and classism within the movement. hooks' book drew attention to the need for multiple feminisms; therefore, it was pivotal in the development of the third wave of feminism.

The women's movement was quiet through the early 2000s, which are sometimes characterized as the "ladette" years, a culture marked by young women engaging in the heavy drinking sessions and bad behavior once reserved for men (Macrae 2013). But, as Coleman (2009) observed, new movements surfaced:

> The past fifteen years has witnessed a proliferation of new feminisms: post-feminism, third wave feminism, cyberfeminism, power feminism, even DIY feminism. Depending on what you read, we are either in a postfeminist era or in the third wave of feminism.
>
> (3)

In 2013, the women's movement came back with force (Cochrane 2013). Today, the movement's concerns shift constantly as activists personally encounter pay gaps, rising childcare costs, and pregnancy discrimination (Cochrane 2013). With the magnitude of these pressing issues, feminists fight on several fronts. The campaigns of the 2010s were started by individuals or small groups, who have responded to issues about which they feel strongly (Cochrane 2013).

Many commentators argue that the Web has enabled a shift from "third-wave" to "fourth-wave" feminism (e.g., Munro 2014; Martin and Valenti 2012; Schuster 2013). As Phillips and Cree wrote, "We are currently witnessing a resurgence of interest in feminism across the world, with a claim that we are experiencing a 'fourth wave' in the global North that has its birthplace primarily on the Internet" (2014: 930). The Internet has created a "call-out" culture, in which "sexism or misogyny can be 'called out' and challenged" (Munro 2014, para. 7). This culture is indicative of the continuing influence of the third wave, with its focus on challenging bigotry and misogyny in everyday rhetoric in mass media messages (Munro 2014).

Fourth-wave feminism combines finances, politics, mental health, and stability in an overarching vision of change (Diamond 2009). Sheryl Sandberg, the COO of Facebook, detailed her struggle to achieve equality in a historically male-dominated workplace environment in her 2013 book, *Lean In*. She encourages women to take their places at decision-making tables and to "lean in" to their careers. Sandberg offers strategies for women to pursue career advancement without sacrificing family life. She argues that it is no longer necessary for women to choose between having children *or* careers.

*Lean In*'s reviews were mixed, with critics praising it for its insightful advice on how to balance both career and family and panning it for a seemingly elitist perspective. For instance, hooks (2013) discussed Sandberg's definition of feminism, which she stated, "begins and ends with the notion that it's all about gender equality within the existing social system." hooks continued:

> From this perspective, the structures of imperialist white supremacist capitalist patriarchy need not be challenged. And she makes it seem that privileged white men will eagerly choose to extend the benefits of corporate capitalism to white women who have the courage to "lean in."
>
> *(para. 5)*

hooks adds that Sandberg's construction of simple categories (women and men) was long ago challenged by visionary feminist thinkers, particularly individual black women and women of color.

## The Black Feminist Movement

The long and arduous fight for equal rights for black women began during the slave era (Gines 2011). In 1831, Maria Stewart published a pamphlet critiquing the prevailing assumptions that blacks were "an inferior race" (275) and men were superior to women. She called on black women to unite in support of one another (Gines 2011). The booklet also discussed class oppression and emphasized the exploitation of black women as free labor. During the same period, Sojourner Truth fought for the abolition of slavery and for women's suffrage (Guy-Sheftall 1995). This was the beginning of the fight for equality for black women.

Studies included in the Black Feminist literature have shown that while media and societal structures are unjust to both black and white women, they marginalize black women to a greater extent (e.g., Wallace 1979; Collins 2005; Benedict 1997; hooks 1992; Squires 2007). Alice Walker (1983), Angela Davis (1983), bell hooks (1981), Moraga and Anzaldúa (1981), and many other womanists argued that black women experienced a different and more intense kind of oppression from that of white women.

In *Black Feminist Thought* (1990), Patricia Hill Collins identifies Black Feminists as "women who theorize the experiences and ideas shared by ordinary black women that provide a unique angle of vision on self, community, and society" (22). Black Feminists assert that one cannot conceive of black women's experience of various issues as separable from their experience of racism. That is, women of color do not experience sexism in addition to racism, but sexism in the context of racism. Stereotypes in popular culture—described earlier in this chapter—illustrate key differences (Mathis 2007). hooks (1992) labels this matrix a *politic of domination* and describe how it operates along interlocking axes of race, class, and gender oppression. Black Feminists contend that the liberation of black women entails freedom for all people, since it would require the end of racism, sexism, and class oppression.

### The Concept of Intersectionality

Debates about the adequacy of gender as the central concern of feminist theory led to the useful concept of intersectionality (Crenshaw 2004), which emphasizes the study of intersections between forms or systems of oppression, domination, and discrimination. Beale (1970) identified multiple systems of oppression facing black women along the lines of race, class, gender, and sex in *Double Jeopardy: To Be Black and Female*. Black feminists make the perspectives of black women central by embracing a paradigm of race, class, and gender as interlocking systems of oppression (see Zinn and Dill 1994; Dill 1979; Davis 1983; Collins 1990; hooks 1981; Moraga and Anzaldúa 1981). Davis (2008) points out the complications of the concept:

> Since its inception, the concept of "intersectionality"—the interaction of multiple identities and experiences of exclusion and subordination—has been heralded as one of the most important contributions to feminist scholarship. Despite its popularity, there has been considerable confusion concerning what the concept actually means and how it can or should be applied in feminist inquiry.
>
> *(67)*

Subsequent studies have used intersectionality to examine how whiteness is privileged and to expose how the dominant "gaze" of whiteness shapes and shades societal understandings of black femininity (e.g., Griffin 2014; Collins 1990; hooks 1992; Benedict 1997; hooks 1992; Squires 2007; Schell 2003). Black Feminist Theory and the notion of intersectionality have been applied in a variety of studies of the media, including several described in the next portion of this chapter.

### Applying Feminist Theory

A number of scholars have observed that journalistic coverage of white women who have "gone missing" is far different from the coverage of missing African-American women.

Liebler (2010) cited the examples of two California college students, Kristin Smart and April Gregory, who both disappeared over the same weekend. Kristin, who was white and from an upper-middle-class background, received a great deal of media attention. On the other hand, April, an African-American student at Syracuse University, received very little media coverage. Her university even failed to announce her disappearance. Liebler (2010) writes that one stark difference between the two young women, besides race, was class. While Kristin was a principal's daughter, April worked at a McDonald's. Liebler argues that middle-class missing women have media-savvy parents who can help to shape the media's portrayal of their daughters, resulting in inequitable media treatment across class lines. The author noted that April had two strikes against her—her class and her race.

Similarly, Moody, Dorries, and Blackwell (2009) concluded that national news coverage of missing black women demonstrated numerous inconsistencies in comparison to the coverage of missing white women. For instance, just the number of transcripts found in the research suggested that coverage of missing white women was more prominent and lengthier than missing black women. This skewed coverage of missing, white, young, attractive, middle- to upper-class women became so commonplace in the mid-2000s, PBS Journalist Gwen Ifill referred to the phenomenon as "missing white woman syndrome" at the Unity Convention of Journalists in 2004 (Johnson 2005).

Conservative political commentator Michelle Malkin referred to this trend in June 2005 as "missing pretty girl syndrome" and "damsel in distress syndrome" (Malkin 2005). The assumption, backed by media ratings, is that white viewers may not connect with stories unless they see themselves as possible victims (Kane 2004). Eventually, this oversight led to self-criticism focusing on the disparity in coverage. Journalists admitted wealthy, attractive, white women were much more likely to receive attention and coverage than missing black, older, and unattractive women (Moody, Dorries, and Blackwell 2009).

A second media representation that Black Feminist Theorists have examined is the portrayal of black, female athletes, who have been found to receive less media attention or who are victimized by biased coverage. One study that examined sports magazines such as *Sports Illustrated* and *Women's Sports and Fitness* found that black women were scarce. Maas and Hasbrook (2001) found that when they were depicted, black women were more likely than white women to be depicted in team sports, which they argued are considered "more masculine" than individual sports. Such depictions imply black female athletes do not meet white American standards of beauty and are defeminized. Studies have found that U.S. sports media often give women of color considerably less coverage than they give their white female counterparts (Blinde and McCallister 1999; Maas and Holbrook 2001).

The absence of minority women supports the traditional belief that sports are solely for white, heterosexual, non-disabled women. Such portrayals are of concern because they play a role in how people treat black women. For example, Ruggiero and Lattin (2008) concluded female intercollegiate coaches, like their male counterparts, often believe they can arbitrarily use the power granted to them within the sports organization to perpetuate racial and gender stereotypes.

Rap music is a third topic that has been frequently examined from a Black Feminist perspective. Traditionally, African-American youth mainly used rap music to attract attention to social issues like poverty, police violence, and discrimination (Cheney 2005). However, some studies suggest rap music in the 2000s is more likely to promote violence, drug use, materialism, and degradation of women (Kubrin 2005; Zillmann et al. 1995; Dines and Humez 2002; Rose 1994; Sommers-Flanagan and Davis 1983; Conrad, Dixon, and Zhang 2009).

Based on a textual analysis of rap lyrics, Tyree (2009) concluded black women are the primary focus of misogynistic rap lyrics, and the targets of a sustained historical misogynistic American ideology. The analysis of 24 songs about rappers' mothers and "baby mamas"—the unmarried mothers of their children—revealed that black male rappers saw their mothers as worthy of love, adoration, and respect, while "baby mamas" were sexual conquests portrayed as worthless, unethical gold-diggers and freaks. Tyree argued that the "baby mama" was usually young, single, poor, and urban, unlike the "black queen" who is middle-class and usually has a husband (Tyree 2009). A study by Reid-Brinkley (2007) also revealed a dichotomy between "good" black women media deem the "queens" or "princesses" and "bad" black women, who rappers characterize as whores.

Moody (2011) concluded that while rap songs depicting the "independent woman" present a somewhat positive representation of women, as they focus on "superwomen" skills and not drugs or violence, the songs often contain mixed messages. Both male and female rappers use misogynistic language to describe women; however, they juxtapose images of independence with material wealth and unrealistic ideals of beauty. Male rappers were more likely to include images of beautiful, overachieving women paired with average men while female rappers focus on their own sexual prowess.

To assess the effects of such lyrics, many scholars have explored audience responses to misogynistic lyrics (e.g., Devine 1989; Dunning and Sherman 1997). Cobb and Boettcher (2007) concluded that exposure to misogynistic rap lyrics "primed" sexist attitudes in males and defensive attitudes in females. Likewise, Conrad, Dixon, and Zhang (2007) found that viewing more misogynistic videos predicted greater acceptance of female degradation and less likelihood to believe that the music actually degraded females. Another study concluded only males showed higher levels of sexism towards women when viewing high-sex videos (Kistler and Lee 2009).

## The Future of Gender and Black Feminist Studies

The studies highlighted in this brief review of the literature provide crucial insights regarding the ideas and positions society are likely to embrace about women. They also demonstrate that historical representations of women of color are still strong and have an impact on modern portrayals of the marginalized group. Cultural narratives and stereotypes send viewers, readers, and listeners hidden messages that suggest a story's importance and, ultimately, people's importance within society.

Future media studies must reexamine the way media outlets portray women of color in new media platforms. While censorship is undesirable, scholars must advocate for literacy programs that encourage students to identify and seek positive, accurate messages in mass media. Leaders in the entertainment industry must advocate for positive depictions of women. Reporters must also seek diverse sources and representations that characterize the wide spectrum of women. Furthermore, scholars might encourage public discussions and texts such as this one, which will help keep issues of race, class, and culture on citizens' minds.

Maintaining both the invisibility and the negative representation of women and their ideas has been critical in maintaining social inequalities. Squires (2011) encourages critical communication scholars to identify and promote counter-frames to intervene and counteract stereotypical portrayals in popular culture. She argues that this type of advocacy becomes necessary as old discourses of colorblindness morph into celebrations of a "post-racial" millennium. As Squires (2011) argues, "By diversifying our tactics and approaches to the problem, we can creatively and proactively make some headway and by doing so, set important examples for our students and colleagues in the process" (47).

## References

Akram, S. (2002) "The Aftermath of September 11, 2001: The Targeting of Arabs and Muslims in America," *Arab Studies Quarterly* 24(2 and 3): 61.

Bagdikian, B. (1969) *The Press and Its Crisis of Identity: Mass Media in a Free Society*. Lawrence, KS: University of Kansas Press.

Beale, F. (1970) *Double Jeopardy: To Be Black and Female*. New York: Third World Women's Alliance.

Bem, S. (1981) "Gender Schema Theory: A Cognitive Account of Sex Typing," *Psychological Review* 88(July): 354–364.

Berg, C. (2002) *Latino Images in Film: Stereotypes, Subversion, and Resistance*. Austin, TX: University of Texas Press.

Blinde, E. and McCallister, S. (1999) "Women, Disability and Sport and Physical Activity: The Intersection of Gender and Disability Dynamics," *Research Quarterly for Exercise and Sport* 70: 303–312.

Campbell, C. (1995) *Race, Myth, and the News*. Thousand Oaks, CA: Sage.

Campbell, C., LeDuff, K., Jenkins, C., and Brown, R. (2012) *Race and News: Critical Perspectives*. New York: Routledge.

Carter, C. and Steiner, L. (2003) *Critical Readings: Media and Gender*. Maidenhead, UK: Open University Press.

Chaudhary, A. (1980) "Press Portrayals of Black Officials," *Journalism Quarterly* 57: 636–641.

Cheney, C. (2005) *Brothers Gonna Work It Out: Sexual Politics in the Golden Age of Rap Nationalism*. New York: New York University Press.

Chomsky, N. and Herman, S. (1988) *Manufacturing Consent: The Political Economy of the Mass Media*. New York: Pantheon Books.

Chon-Smith, C. (2006) *Asian American and African American Masculinities: Race, Citizenship, and Culture in Post-Civil Rights*. Dissertation, UC San Diego. Retrieved from http://escholarship.org/uc/item/0c8255gj.

Chua, A. (2011) *Battle Hymn of the Tiger Mother*. New York: Penguin Press.

Cobb, M. and Boettcher, W. (2007) "Ambivalent Sexism and Misogynistic Rap Music: Does Exposure to Eminem Increase Sexism?," *Journal of Applied Social Psychology* 37: 3025–3042.

Coleman, J. (2009) "An Introduction to Feminisms in a Postfeminist Age," *Women's Studies Journal* 23(2): 3–13.

Collins, P. (1990) *Black Feminist Thought: Knowledge, Consciousness, and the Politics of Empowerment*. New York: Routledge.

——. (2005) *Black Sexual Politics: African Americans, Gender, and the New Racism*. New York: Routledge.

Conrad, K., Dixon. T., and Zhang, Y. (2009) "Rap Music Videos and African American Women's Body Image: The Moderating Role of Ethnic Identity," *Journal of Broadcasting and Electronic Media* 53(1): 134–138.

Covert, J. and Dixon, T. (2008) "A Changing View: Representation and Effects of the Portrayal of Women of Color in Mainstream Women's Magazines," *Communication Research* 35(2): 232–256.

Crenshaw, K. (2004) "Intersectionality: The Double Bind of Race and Gender," *Perspectives Magazine* 2.

Dates, J. and Barlow, W. (1993) *Split Image: African-Americans in the Mass Media*. 2nd ed. Washington, D.C.: Howard University Press.

Dates, J. and Pease, E. (1994) "Warping the World: Media's Mangled Images of Race," *The Freedom Forum Media Studies* 8(3): 81–88.

Davis, A. (1983) *Women, Race, and Class*. New York: Vintage.

Davis, K. (2008) "Intersectionality as Buzzword: A Sociology of Science Perspective on What Makes a Feminist Theory Successful," *Feminist Theory* 9: 167–185.

Devine, P. (1989) "Stereotypes and Prejudice: Their Automatic and Controlled Components," *Journal of Personality and Social Psychology* 56: 5–18.

Diamond, D. (2009) "The Fourth Wave of Feminism: Psychoanalytic Perspectives," *Studies In Gender and Sexuality* 10(4): 213–223.

Dill, B. (1979) "The Dialectics of Black Womanhood," *Signs* 4: 543–555.

Dines, G. and Humez, J. (2002) *Gender, Race, and Class in Media: A Text-Reader*. Thousand Oaks, CA: Sage Publications.

Dixon, T. and Linz, D. (2000) "Overrepresentation and Underrepresentation of African Americans and Latinos as Lawbreakers on Television News," *Journal of Communication* 50(2): 131–154.

Dunning, D. and Sherman, D. (1997) "Stereotypes and Tacit Inference," *Journal of Personality and Social Psychology* 73: 459–471.

Eltantawy, N. M. A. (2007) *U.S. Newspaper Representation of Muslims and Arab Women Post 9/11*. Unpublished UMI Thesis. College of Arts and Sciences, Georgia State University.

Enriques, E. (2001) *Feminism and Feminist Criticism: An Overview of Various Feminist Strategies for Reconstructing Knowledge*. Manila, The Philippines: Isis International.

Entman, R. (1990) "Modern Racism and the Images of Blacks in Local Television," *Critical Studies in Mass Communication* 7(4): 332–345.

Ferree, M. and Tripp, A. (2006) *Global Feminism: Transnational Women's Activism, Organizing, and Human Rights*. New York: New York University Press.

Fong, T. (1998) *The Contemporary Asian American Experience: Beyond the Model Minority*. Upper Saddle River, NJ: Prentice Hall.

Friedan, B. (1963) *The Feminine Mystique. The Problem that Has No Name*. New York: W. W. Norton.

Gandy, O. (1998) *Communication and Race: A Structural Perspective*. London: Arnold.

Gillis, S., Gillian, H., and Munford, R. (2007) *Third Wave Feminism: A Critical Exploration*. Basingstoke, UK: Palgrave Macmillan.

Gines, K. (2011) "Black Feminism and Intersectional Analyses: A Defense of Intersectionality," *Philosophy Today* 55: 275–284.

Gramsci, A. (1971) *Selections from the Prison Notebooks*. New York: International Publishers.

Griffin, C. (1996) "Experiencing Power: Dimensions of Gender, 'Race,' and Class," in N. Charles and F. Hughes-Freeland (eds.), *Practicing Feminism: Identity, Difference and Power*. London: Routledge, 180–201.

Griffin, R. (2013) "Gender Violence and the Black Female Body: The Enduring Significance of 'Crazy' Mike Tyson," *Howard Journal of Communications* 24(1): 71–94.

Griffiths, A. (1996) "Science and Spectacle: Native American Representation in Early Cinema," in S. E. Bird (ed.), *Dressing in Feathers: The Construction of the Indian in American Popular Culture*. Boulder, CO: Westview Press, 79–95.

Guy-Sheftall, B. (1995) *Religion and the Pure Principles of Morality, the Sure Foundation on Which We Must Build*. New York: The New Press.

Guzman, M. (2010) *Dangerous Curves: Latina Bodies in the Media*. New York: New York University Press.

Hall, S. (1992) "Race, Culture, and Communications: Looking Backward and Forward at Cultural Studies," *Rethinking Marxism: A Journal of Economics, Culture, and Society* 5(1): 10–18.

———. (1998) "Notes on Deconstructing 'The Popular,'" in J. Storey (ed.), *Cultural Theory and Popular Culture: A Reader*. Upper Saddle River, NJ: Prentice Hall, 443–453.

———. (2000) "Racist Ideologies and the Media," in P. Marris and S. Thornham (eds.), *Media Studies: A Reader*. New York: New York University Press, 271–282.

Hammer, R. and Kellner, D. (2009) *Media/Cultural Studies: Critical Approaches*. New York: Peter Lang.

Hartmann, H. (1981) "The Unhappy Marriage of Marxism and Feminism: Towards a More Progressive Union," in L. Sargent (ed.), *Women and Revolutions: A Discussion of the Unhappy Marriage of Marxism and Feminism*. Boston: South End Press, 1–41.

Holmes, M. (2007) *What is Gender? Sociological Approaches*. Thousand Oaks, CA: Sage Publications.

hooks, b. (1981) *Ain't I a Woman?: Black Women and Feminism*. New York: Routledge.

———. (1992) *Black Looks: Race and Representation*. Boston, MA: South End Press.

———. (2013) "Dig Deep: Beyond Lean In," *The Feminist Wire*, thefeministwire.com.

Jakubowski, K. (2014) "*Too Queer for Your Binary: Everything You Need to Know and More about Non-Binary Identities*." Retrieved from http://everydayfeminism.com/2014/03/too-queer-for-your-binary/.

Kamler, B. (1999) *Constructing Gender and Difference: Critical Research Perspectives in Early Childhood*. Cresskill, NJ: Hampton Press.

Kellner, D. (2002) "Cultural Studies, Multiculturalism and Media Culture," in G. Dines and J. Humez (eds.), *Gender, Race and Class in Media: A Text-Reader*. London: Sage Publications, 9–20.

Kistler, M. and Lee, J. (2009) "Does Exposure to Sexual Hip-Hop Music Videos Influence the Sexual Attitudes of College Students?," *Mass Communication and Society* 13: 1.

Kubrin, C. (2005) "Gangstas, Thugs and Hustlas: Identity and the Code of the Street in Rap Music," *Social Problems* 52(3): 360–378.

Lacroix, C. (2011) "High Stakes Stereotypes: The Emergence of the 'Casino Indian' Trope in Television Depictions of Contemporary Native Americans," *The Howard Journal of Communications* 22(1): 1–23.

Lassiter, J. (1999) "Meta-Anthropology, Normative Culture and the Anthropology of Development." Paper presented at the Annual Meeting of the Northwest Anthropological Conference, Eugene, Oregon.

Liebler, C. (2010) "Me(dia) Culpa: The 'Missing White Woman Syndrome' and Media Self Critique," *Communication, Culture, and Critique* 3(4): 549–565.

Lippmann, W. (1922) *Public Opinion*. New York: Macmillan.

Lobo, S. and Talbot, S. (2001) *Native American Voices: A Reader*. New York: Prentice Hall.

Maas, K. and Holbrook (2001) "Media Promotion of the Paradigm Citizen/Golfer: An Analysis of Golf Magazines' Representations of Disability, Gender, and Age," *Sociology of Sport Journal* 18: 21–36.

Macrae, F. (2013) "Ladettes are Blamed for Rise in Females with Broken Noses," *The Daily Mail*. Retrieved from http://www.dailymail.co.uk/news/article-2477163/Women-behaving-badly-Ladettes-blamed-rise-females-broken-noses.html.

Malkin, M. (2005, June 11) "Missing Pretty Girl Syndrome." Retrieved from http://michellemalkin.com/archives/002712.htm.

Marbley, A. (2005) "African-American Women's Feelings on Alienation from Third-Wave Feminism: A Conversation with My Sisters," *Western Journal Of Black Studies* 29(3): 605–614.

Martin, C. and Valenti, V. (2012) *New Feminist Solutions Volume 8. #FemFuture: Online Feminism*. New York: Barnard Center for Research on Women, Columbia University.

Martindale, C. (1990) "Changes in Newspaper Images of Africans Americans," *Newspaper Research Journal* 11(1): 46–48.

Mastro, D. E. and Behm-Morawitz, E. (2005) "Latino Representation on Primetime Television," *Journalism and Mass Communication Quarterly* 82(1): 110–130.

Mathis, S. (2007) "Can White Be Black?: Cultural Work in the Reality TV Series, *Black. White*." Paper presented at 2007 National Communication Association Conference, Chicago.

Merskin, D. (1998) "Sending Up Signals: A Survey of Native American Media Use and Representation in the Mass Media," *Howard Journal of Communications* 9: 333–345.

——. (2007) "Three Faces of Eva: Perpetuation of the Hot-Latina Stereotype in *Desperate Housewives*," *Howard Journal of Communications* 18(2): 133–151.

Millett, K. (1969) *Sexual Politics*. New York: Doubleday.

Moody, M. (2011) "The Meaning of 'Independent Woman' in Music," *ETC: A Review of General Semantics* 68(2): 187–198.

Moody, M., Dorries, B., and Blackwell, H. (2009) "The Invisible Damsel: Differences in How National Media Outlets Framed the Coverage of Missing Black And White Women in the Mid-2000s." Paper presented at the annual meeting of the International Communication Association, Montreal.

Moody, M. and Dates, J. (2014). *The Obamas and Mass Media: Race, Gender, Religion, and Politics*. New York: Palgrave MacMillan.

Moraga, C. and Anzaldua, G. (1981) *This Bridge Called My Back: Writings by Radical Women of Color*. London: Persephone Press.

Munro, E. (2014) *Feminism: A Fourth Wave?* London: Political Studies Association.

Nachbar, J. and Lausé, K. (1992) *Popular Culture: An Introductory Text*. Bowling Green, OH: Bowling Green State University Press.

Paek, H. and Shah, H. (2003) "Racial Ideology, Model Minorities, and the 'Not-So-Silent Partner': Stereotyping of Asian Americans in U.S. Magazine Advertising," *The Howard Journal of Communication* 14: 225–243.

Peterson, W. (1966, Jan. 9) "Success Story: Japanese-American Style," *New York Times Magazine*: 20–21, 33, 36, 38, 40.

Phillips, R. and Cree, V. (2014) "What does the 'Fourth Wave' Mean for Teaching Feminism in Twenty-First Century Social Work?," *Social Work Education* 33(7): 930–943.

Qasim, K., Hayat, M., and Asmat, U. (2012) "Black Women and Racial Stereotypes: A Black Feminist Reading of Morrison's Novels," *Language in India* 12(5): 211–225.

Reid-Brinkley, S. (2007) "The Essence of Res(ex)pectability: Black Women's Negotiation of Black Femininity in Rap Music and Music Video," *Meridians: Feminism, Race, Transnationalism* 8(1): 236–260.

Robinson, E. (2005, June 10) "(White) Women We Love." *The Washington Post*, p. A23.

Rose, T. (1994) *Black Noise: Rap Music and Black Culture in Contemporary America*. Middletown, CT: Wesleyan University Press.

Ruggiero, T. and Lattin, K. (2008) "Intercollegiate Female Coaches' Use of Verbally Aggressive Communication Toward African American Female Athletes," *Howard Journal of Communications* 19(2): 105–124.

Sandberg, S. (2013) *Lean In: Women Work and the Will to Lead*. New York: Knopf.

Schell, B. (2003) "(Dis)empowering images? Media Representations of Women in Sport. Women's Sports Foundation Web Site," Women's Sports Foundation. Retrieved from http://www.womenssportsfoundation.org/cgibin/iowa/issues/media/article.html?record=881.

Schuster, J. (2013) "Invisible Feminists? Social Media and Young Women's Political Participation," *Political Science* 65(1): 8–24.

Scott, B. (2008) *Gender and Modernism: Critical Concepts in Literary and Cultural Studies*. New York. Routledge.

Shugart, H. (2007) "Crossing Over: Hybridity and Hegemony in the Popular Media," *Communication and Critical/Cultural Studies* 4(2): 115–141.

Signorielli, N. (2009) "Minorities Representation in Prime Time: 2000 to 2008," *Communication Research Reports* 26(4): 323–336.

Sommers-Flanagan, R., Sommers-Flanagan, J., and Davis, B. (1993) "What's Happening on Music Television: A Gender Role Content Analysis," *Sex Roles* 28(11/12): 745–753.

Soto, R. (2008) "'Made to Be the Maid?' An Examination of the Latina as Maid in Mainstream Film and Television," in M. Meyers (ed.), *Women in Popular Culture: Representation and Meaning*. Cresskill, NJ: Hampton Press, 85–100.

Spooner, T. (2001) "Asian Americans and the Internet," *Pew Research Internet Project*. Retrieved from http://www.pewinternet.org/2001/12/12/asian-americans-and-the-internet/.

Squires, C. (2007) *Dispatches from the Color Line: The Press and Multiracial America*. Albany, NY: State University of New York Press.

——. (2011) "Bursting the Bubble: A Case Study of Counter-Framing in the Editorial Pages," *Critical Studies in Media Communication* 28(1): 30–49.

Sylvie, G. (1995) "Black Mayoral Candidates and the Press: Running for Coverage," *Howard Journal of Communications* 6: 89–101.

Tierney, S. (2006) "Themes of Whiteness in *Bulletproof Monk*, *Kill Bill*, and *The Last Samurai*," *Journal of Communication* 56: 607–624.

Tyree, T. (2009) "Lovin' Momma and Hatin' on Baby Mama: A Comparison of Misogynistic and Stereotypical Representations in Songs about Rappers' Mothers and Baby Mamas," *Women and Language* 32(2): 50–58.

van Zoonen, L. (1994) *Feminist Media Studies*. London: Sage Publications.

Vavrus, M. (2010) "Unhitching from the Post (of Postfeminism)," *Journal of Communication Theory* 34(3): 222–227.

Walker, A. (1983) *In Search of Our Mothers' Gardens: Womanist Prose*. New York: Harcourt.

Wallace, M. (1979) *Black Macho and the Myth of the Superwoman*. New York: Verso.

Yarborough, M. and Bennett, Y. (2000) "Mammy Sapphire Jezebel and Their Sisters," *Journal of Gender, Race and Justice* Spring 2002: 626–657, 634–655.

Zillmann, D., Aust, C., Hoffman, K., Love, C., Ordman, V. L., Pope, J., Seigler, P., and Gibson, R. (1995) "Radical Rap: Does It Further Ethnic Division?," *Basic and Applied Social Psychology* 16(1–2): 1–25.

Zinn, M. and Dill, B. (1994) *Women of Color in U.S. Society*. Philadelphia, PA: Temple University Press.

## Further Reading

Crenshaw, K. (2004) "Intersectionality: The Double Bind of Race and Gender," *Perspectives Magazine*: 2. Retrieved from http://www.americanbar.org/content/dam/aba/publishing/perspectives_magazine/women_perspectives_Spring2004CrenshawPSP.authcheckdam.pdf. (Explores how cultural patterns of oppression are bound together and influenced by the intersectional systems of society. Examples of this include race, gender, sexuality, class, and ability.)

May, V. and Cooper, A. (2007) *Visionary Black Feminist: A Critical Introduction*. New York: Routledge. (Explores the theoretical and political contributions of Anna Julia Cooper, a renowned black feminist scholar, educator, and activist.)

Nakamura, L. and Chow-White, P. (2012) *Race after the Internet*. New York: Taylor and Francis. (Examines the persistence of social inequity along racial lines despite the equalizing force of the Internet.)

Walker, A. (1983) *In Search of Our Mothers' Gardens: Womanist Prose*. New York: Harcourt. (In this collection of nonfiction, Alice Walker speaks out as a black woman, writer, mother, and feminist. The topics in the 36 pieces range from personal to political.)

# 28
# RACE AND SEXUALITY
## Whitewashing Representation
### *Robert D. Byrd, Jr.*

University of Mississippi student Sierra Mannie caused a raucous debate among many white gay bloggers and readers in early July 2014 with an opinion piece posted on the *Daily Mississippian* online, later posted on Time.com, titled "Dear White Gays: Stop Stealing Black Female Culture" (Mannie 2014). In the piece, Mannie argues white gay men often appropriate the stereotyped culture of black women by adopting racist dialectical, physical, and affectational characteristics of black women. Mannie contends:

> I need some of you to cut it the hell out. Maybe, for some of you, it's a presumed similar appreciation for Beyoncé and weave that has you thinking that I'm going to be amused by you approaching me in your best "Shanequa from around the way" voice. I don't know. What I do know is that I don't care how well you can quote Madea, who told you that your booty was getting bigger than hers, how cute you think it is to call yourself a strong black woman, who taught you to twerk, how funny you think it is to call yourself Quita or Keisha or for which black male you've been bottoming—you are not a black woman, and you do not get to claim either blackness or womanhood. It is not yours. It is not for you.

Mannie tells readers to check their privilege and be part of the solution rather than continuing the "foolery" of acting the part of a "strong black woman . . . or a ghetto girl." However adept many of Mannie's observations and arguments may have been, several white gay bloggers responded, in many instances with vitriol and condemnation.

One commenter claimed gay, white men are not afforded white privilege and, thus, are not complicit in perpetuating white dominance and oppression over racial and gender minorities. Another blogger, published on *Huffington Post* more than a week after Mannie's commentary first appeared, appropriately notes that Mannie's argument, while correct in the way of racial appropriation, ventures into transphobic territory by privileging cisgender identity (D'Agostino 2014). D'Agostino contends Mannie's piece works to legitimize "gender normative rhetoric that de-legitimizes gay men and trans-women." D'Agostino argues:

> Some men are as authentically feminine as some women. And some feminine men who are white grow up around black people who are feminine, so, yeah, their femininity might seem a little "black" to you. Really not their fault. Really none

of your business. This is to say, your heterodominant feminist fantasy of owning "womanhood" is not the reality of queer people or feminine men. Femininity is theirs *also* and it is not for *you* to allow or deny their gender expression.

However, D'Agostino's argument does not fully adhere to his earlier admission that appropriation of black culture is damaging and the product of white privilege. Instead, D'Agostino provides an escape plan for those white gay men who do not fully adhere to gender norms from their privilege, thus legitimizing white gay racial appropriation and sexism via exclusion from the heterodominant culture. By excluding white gay men from the broader scope of white privilege, he allows a space for them within black womanhood—supporting the argument made by Mannie.

The exclusion of white gay men from white male privilege is not a new concept. For decades, white gay men have operated from the assumption that their sexual minority status excludes them from dominant forms of oppression and privilege; however, previous researchers have pointed to the dangers of viewing sexual minority status as an exclusionary factor in racism and sexism (Johnson 2003; King 2009; Nero 2005; Shugart 2003; Stone and Ward 2011; Ward 1999; Ward 2008; Yep and Elia 2012). In this chapter, I will discuss how white gay men are often given a pass, in the media, from white male privilege. This pass comes not only by way of their sexual minority status but also through the symbolic annihilation of people at the intersections of race, gender, and sexuality. White gay men then stand in as a representation for all queer people despite race and/or gender identity, which works to further privilege white men and subordinate people of color. First, I provide a brief discussion of white male privilege before discussing previous literature on race and sexuality and symbolic annihilation of LGBTQ (Lesbian, Gay, Bisexual, Transgendered, and Queer) people of color. Finally, I provide a contemporary example of the representations of race and sexuality that illustrates these concepts.

## White Gay Male Privilege

Any discussion of white male privilege should include a discussion of the invisible and imbalanced nature of privilege. Carbado (2005) concludes there are two categories of male privilege about which men should develop awareness. First, the invisible advantages that men can count on each day without ever having to work to earn them. The other, he argues, "includes a series of disadvantages that men do not experience precisely because they are men" (195). Men, Carbado maintains, do not have to envision themselves as engendered because "a white heterosexual man lives on the white side of race, the male side of gender, and the straight side of sexual orientation. He is, in this sense, the norm. Mankind. The baseline. He is our reference. We are all defined with him in mind. We are the same as or different from him" (192). However, Carbado argues, not all men experience and enjoy the same advantages to an equal level.

Men at the intersection of race, gender identity, and sexual orientation must contend with other factors that negatively affect their privilege because those men must "simultaneously contend with and respond to negative identity signification. That is, we simultaneously live with and contest our nonnormativity. We are 'different,' and our identities have negative social meanings" (193). Thus, he contends, listing all male privileges is problematic because a universal manhood does not exist, and constructing such a universal would obscure or trivialize those men outside the white, middle-class, heterosexual construction of manhood. Further, he argues that class, race, and sexual orientation impact male identities and may either limit or expand their privilege.

## Race, Sexuality, and Privilege

Despite the limitations of nonnormative gender, racial, and sexual identities, much of the rhetoric of the gay rights movement works to eliminate difference and relies on a narrative of sameness whereby sexuality trumps other identities. Yep and Elia (2012) argue the "new homonormativity" relies on the hegemonic view of racism as a thing of the past, and reduces any instance of oppression or discrimination as a product of homophobia, not a combination of sexuality, race, gender performance, and class. By focusing solely on homophobia, only the concerns of white queers are reflected. They contend, "Queers of color cannot afford to ignore how their 'other' differences interplay with their sexuality" (899) because those differences are salient in day-to-day life.

Stone and Ward (2011) argue that "Blackness" has been used by whites on both sides of the "modern gay rights discourse" to help forward their own causes and arguments (606), especially for white pro-gay rights activists during much of the movement's history. They claim these activists have "relied on Blackness as the dominant metaphor for difference, victimization, and resistance, or as a rhetorical device to achieve specific political ends, such as mobilizing voters, coalition building, or discrediting their opposition" (606). Stone and Ward (2011) also claim the vernacular of the gay rights movement reflects white privilege. For example, they argue, concepts such as "the closet," "coming out," "lifestyle," and "sexual identity" are "rooted in white, middle-class, and American conceptualizations of the relationship between self, sexuality, and community, thereby rendering the same-sex desires and queer subjectivities of people of color unintelligible or invisible within U.S. queer politics" (606–7). In other words, most people of color are eliminated from the discourse of the gay rights movement via privileged language that embodies whiteness.

Teunis (2007) argues the "gay community" in the United States is predominantly a white community regardless of the claims that it is more inclusive. He contends, "It projects whiteness through a projection of an image of normalcy which is inherently a white image" (268). By aligning the movement with a broader normalized society (i.e., white, middle class, and heterosexual), gay rights activists and members of the white gay community are able to gain access to social institutions and spaces not previously available to them because of their sexuality. For example, the movement's push for marriage equality is generally led by white men and women, according to Teunis, "who display little or no concern for critical political issues that face gays and lesbians of color" (269). He argues the issues do not cause the promotion of whiteness inherently. Whiteness, he claims, is given dominance by the way the issues are promoted, which overshadows other issues within the larger LGBTQ community.

## Coopting Blackness

In general, race has been used in the modern gay rights movement as a model for gaining particular rights and privileges that, more than anything, benefit white gay and lesbian members. The discussion of race is subordinated by the discussion of sexuality and gay identity. However, racial issues have often served as a talking point for anti-gay and lesbian rhetoric since the beginning of the modern gay rights movement. Stone and

Ward (2011) claim the anti-gay campaigns resemble white segregationist movements during the 1960s black Civil Rights Movement. Principally white religious conservatives, who traditionally opposed racial justice causes, led the groups. In recent years, they have attempted to build a coalition with blacks by pitting gay rights versus black rights. Stone and Ward (2011) argue that while the gay rights focus has shifted in the 2000s to military service and marriage rights, gay rights activists "have taken up direct analogies between gayness and blackness that have fuelled white racism in the movement, and reinforced the white construction of homosexuality" (608). Further, white anti-gay conservatives, during this same period, framed their cause as a fight to protect children against sexual immorality and/or sexual assault, which "prompted gay activists to work at humanizing LGBT people by drawing parallels to other historically maligned and oppressed groups (Jews, interned Japanese Americans, 'Third World People,' women and working class people)" (608).

In contrast, anti-gay white leaders, according to Stone and Ward, work to demonstrate their solidarity with black voters by dismantling connections or comparisons between the black rights movement and the gay rights movement even though this connection works to obscure queer people of color, enfeeble arguments for affirmative action, and coopt black civil rights as a rhetorical weapon for causes and groups with no interests in furthering black civil rights. They argue that the deployment of race by the religious right and gay and lesbian activists suggests that both are similar in their willingness to cite race in troublesome ways. Gay rights activists, as a result of coopting black civil rights rhetoric, exclude LGBTQ people of color from the gay rights narrative. This marginalization translates to symbolic annihilation in the mass media, a process by which the mass media ignore, exclude, marginalize, or trivialize a group of people via exclusion from its products (Klein and Shiffman 2009). In other words, exclusion from the work of the "gay community" leads to exclusion from media portrayals of the "gay community," and, thus, exclusion from the dominant culture, which, in turn, leads to further marginalization and trivialization.

## Symbolically Annihilating LGBTQ People of Color

Filmmaker Marlon Riggs (1991) wrote in a poem published in the anthology *Brother to Brother: New Writings by Black Gay Men*, which was also used in the production of Riggs' 1989 PBS documentary *Tongues Untied*, about the invisibility of black gay men or men of color in the "gay community" and media aimed at gay men. Riggs conveys his internal struggle regarding the absence of black images in the gay community—an absence that inevitably has an intractable effect on the black gay male psyche. In the poem titled "Tongues untied," he wrote:

> Maybe from time to time
> a brother glanced my way.
> I never noticed.
> I was immersed in vanilla.
> I savored this single flavor,
> one deliberately not my own.
> I avoided the question, why?
> Pretended not to notice

> the absence of black images
> in this new gay life,
> in bookstores
> poster shops
> film festivals,
> my own fantasies.
> Tried not to notice
> the few images of blacks
> that were most popular:
> joke
> fetish
> cartoon caricature
> or disco diva adored
> from a distance.
>
> *(252)*

Riggs' observations are grounded in a nearly complete absence of the black body or body of color from the gay rights movement and gay culture, which in many ways in the 1970s and early 1980s included the images of the sexual revolution and early political movements.

The prevalence of whiteness in the "gay community" has been the topic of discussion for several scholars. Teunis (2007) argues that whiteness in the gay community "is visible, palpable, if for no other reason than that images of men of color are absent" (269). He references a study in which he examines all issues of *Out* magazine from 2002. He claims men of color are only featured in one of two sections. Teunis writes, "First, Latino gay men are represented only as musicians, whose work is reviewed in the appropriate pages. Second, black men model the peak of health in advertisements for HIV treatment drugs" (269–70). He further argues the "gay community" has benefited from symbolically annihilating LGBTQ people of color in several ways. First, he concludes that the portrayal of whiteness has been used to lend to the gay community an air of respectability, and that the portrayal of whiteness lends to the myth of the affluent gay male, which is a created market to attract advertisers to gay and lesbian media outlets (Sender 2001).

Nero (2005) argues that racism and homophobia keep black gay men invisible or marginal in American film and television. He contends that the dual dominant ideological beliefs that African-American males are hyper-masculine and that white masculinity produces same-sex attraction eliminate black gay men from the dominant gay community and movement. Therefore, he argues, black gay men "cannot exist" (235). Black gay men are positioned then as imposters. Nero adds,

> Like the controlling images of black women as mammy, jezebel, and welfare queen, the ubiquitous image of the black gay male as an impostor or a fraud naturalizes and normalizes the exclusion of black gay men from sites of territorial economies where wealth is created.
>
> *(235)*

By casting black gay men as imposters or frauds in television programming, Nero contends, black gay men are then excluded from participation in queer cultures, which "reveals white hostility toward black gay men" (240). This exclusion, he argues, is participation in an "unspoken pact to keep blacks on the bottom," a concept introduced by Bell (1992) in *Faces at the Bottom of the Well*. Bell argues, "Americans achieve a measure of social stability through their unspoken pact to keep blacks on the bottom—an aspect of social functioning that more than any other has retained its viability and its value to general stability from the very beginning of the American experience down to the present day" (152).

## Reifying White Supremacist Patriarchy in *Noah's Arc*

The unspoken pact referenced by Nero could be a possible accounting of perceived homophobia from the African-American community directed toward white gay men. Teunis (2007) maintains the resistance by the white gay community to integrate race into the discussion of sexuality

> makes White gay men blind to the possibility that the perceived homophobia in African American communities is very race specific. If a gay identity is a white identity, which it is in the eyes of many though certainly not all African Americans, then homophobia is also directed towards white gay men, who are perceived to be wealthy, and therefore part of the problem rather than part of the solution of racial inequality.
>
> *(270)*

Riggs' (1989) critique of gay life and media images from the 1970s and 1980s remains accurate in terms of contemporary media representations of people of color. GLADD, a nonprofit organization that monitors the media for LGBTQ representations, reported in its 2015 television programming report, "Where We Are on TV," that only 11 percent of the LGBTQ characters on broadcast television programming were black, 10 percent of the LGBTQ characters on cable were black, and 11 percent of broadcast and cable LGBTQ characters were Latino(a). The percentages of characters of Asian heritage were even smaller at 3 percent for broadcast and 5 percent for cable (Townsend 2015). While many of these percentages have increased in the last several years, the numbers still reflect significant discrepancies from actual population data.

One of the few, if not only, television shows centered around black gay men, *Noah's Arc*, presented a homonormative, depoliticized representation for audiences in the mid-2000s. The show, though groundbreaking in some respects, worked to reify gay, white supremacy through sanitized representations of race, gender, and class—ultimately creating black replicas of white gay respectability (Yep and Elia 2012). While the show's central characters were all black and race is "hypervisible" (899), racism is rendered invisible. In essence, the characters' sexuality is given eminence over race as if to say racism is a thing of the past and homophobia is the most pressing concern for gay men of color.

Furthermore, Yep and Elia (2012) argue that *Noah's Arc* worked to commodify blackness through the ever-present buff black bodies of the characters. The hypersexualized black body is not new to media representations of black bodies (hooks 2003; McBride 2005; Orbe, Warren, and Cornwell 2000; Yep and Elia 2012). The hypersexual black body is comfortable for white audiences to the point of allying with preconceived notions of the primitive black man with "mythically proportioned manhood" (Perez 2005: 185). Further, the show works to reify the gender binary by privileging the masculine and subverting the feminine, and presents monogamy (a dominant, middle-class, white relational norm) as the only "appropriate relational arrangement for gay men" (Yep and Elia 2012: 905).

## Conclusions

In general, media representations of LGBTQ people often work to reify a white supremacist patriarchy that privileges white gay men above all others. LGBTQ people of color are further marginalized via media representations through (1) coopted black civil rights rhetoric that positions sexual identity as equivalent to ethnic and racial identity, (2) colorblind racist assumptions that give sexual identity prominence over race, (3) commodified blackness that emasculates and fetishizes black men, and (4) reinforced gender roles through a reification of the gender binary. The whitewashed queer body is more palatable to a white audience, and by adhering to representations that position people of color in familiar roles, media producers avoid instilling fear in white consumers of their products. Thus, the heteronormative and homonormative constructions of race, gender, sexuality, and class work not to transgress or change existing power structures, but only work to bolster the status quo, leaving LGBTQ people of color pushed further to the margins of society.

What does this mean for LGBTQ people of color? LGBTQ people of color are more likely to live below the poverty line, experience food insecurities, or experience homelessness than their white counterparts (Gates 2014). Unfortunately, another critical point in American history—a time when change was a real possibility—has again (thus far) been squandered by neoliberal assimilationists. By forgoing the initial radical goals of the gay and lesbian movement of the early 1970s, goals of equality through difference, the movement has now instead worked to fortify a model that reifies white supremacy and makes real change more elusive than ever for LGBTQ people of color. Media representations, or lack of representations, of LGBTQ people of color reflect this phenomenon in the LGBTQ rights movement where gay bodies are presented via either white representation or whitewashed representations of color. An authentic representation of the intersection of sexuality and race is rarely ever presented or discussed in a way that challenges the existing power structures. A few bright spots in media exist in the mid-2010s, like the Netflix original program *Orange Is the New Black*, but the bigger story of intersectionality eludes even shows where LGBTQ characters of color appear or news stories that involve newsmakers at the intersection of LGBTQ and racial minority status.

## References

Bell, D. (1992) *Faces at the Bottom of the Well*. New York: Basic Books.
Carbado, D. W. (2005) "Privilege," in E. P. Johnson and M. G. Henderson (eds.), *Black Queer Studies: A Critical Anthology*. Durham, NC: Duke University Press, 190–212.
D'Agostino, A. M. (2014, July 17) "'Bye Sierra': A Slightly Angry Queer Response to the Sierra Mannie Controversy," *Huffington Post Gay Voices*. Retrieved from http://www.huffingtonpost.com/anthony-michael-dagostino/bye-sierra-mannie-a-slightly-ang_b_5588108.html.
Duggan, L. (2003) *The Twilight of Equality? Neoliberalism, Cultural Politics, and the Attack on Democracy*. Boston, MA: Beacon Press.
Gates, G. J. (2014) *Food Insecurity and SNAP (Food Stamps) in LGBT Communities*. Los Angeles, CA: Williams Institute, UCLA School of Law.
hooks, b. (2004) *We Real Cool: Black Men and Masculinity*. New York: Routledge.
Johnson, E. P. (2003) *Appropriating Blackness: Performance and the Politics of Authenticity*. Durham, NC: Duke University Press.
King, S. (2009) "Homonormativity and the Politics of Race: Reading Sheryl Swoopes," *Journal of Lesbian Studies* 13(3): 272–290.
Klein, H. and Shiffman, K. (2009) "Underrepresentation and Symbolic Annihilation of Socially Disenfranchised Groups ("Out Groups") in Animated Cartoons," *Howard Journal of Communication* 20(1): 55–72.

Mannie, S. (2014, July 8) "Dear White Gays," *The DM Online*. Retrieved from http://thedmonline.com/dear-white-gays/.

McBride, D. A. (2005) *Why I Hate Abercrombie and Fitch: Essays on Race and Sexuality*. New York: New York University Press.

Nero, C. I. (2005) "Why Are the Gay Ghettoes White?," in P. E. Johnson and M. G. Henderson (eds.), *Black Queer Studies: A Critical Anthology*. Durham, NC: Duke University Press, 228–245.

Orbe, M. P., Warren, K. T., and Cornwell, N. C. (2000) "Negotiating Societal Stereotypes: Analyzing the Real World Discourse By and about African American Men," *International and Intercultural Communication Annual* 23: 107–134.

Riggs, M. (Producer and Director). (1989) *Tongues Untied* (Documentary film). Available from California Newsreel at http://newsreel.org/video/TONGUES-UNTIED.

Riggs, M. (1991) "Tongues Untied," in E. Hemphill (ed.), *Brother to Brother: New Writings By Black Gay Men*. Boston, MA: Alyson Publications, 200–205.

Sender, K. (2001) "Gay Readers, Consumers, and a Dominant Gay Habitus: 25 Years of the Advocate Magazine," *Journal of Communication* 51: 73–99.

Shugart, H. A. (2003) "Reinventing Privilege: The New (Gay) Man in Contemporary Popular Media," *Critical Studies in Media Communication* 20(1): 67–91.

Stone, A. L. and Ward, J. (2011) "From 'Black People Are Not a Homosexual Act' to 'Gay Is the New Black': Mapping White Uses of Blackness in Modern Gay Rights Campaigns in the United States," *Social Identities* 17(5): 605–624.

Teunis, N. (2007) "Sexual Objectification and the Construction of Whiteness in the Gay Male Community," *Culture, Health and Sexuality* 9(3): 263–275.

Tilsen, J. and Nylund, D. (2010) "Resisting Normativity: Queer Musings on Politics, Identity, and the Performance of Therapy," *The International Journal of Narrative Therapy and Community Work* 3: 67–72.

Townsend, M. (2015) "GLAAD's 'Where We Are on TV' Report Calls for More Diverse, Substantive LGBT Characters," *GLAAD.org*. Retrieved from http://www.glaad.org/blog/glaads-where-we-are-tv-report-calls-more-diverse-substantive-lgbt-characters.

Ward, J. (1999) "Queer Sexism: Rethinking Gay Men and Masculinity," in P. M. Nardi (ed.), *Gay Masculinities*. Thousand Oaks, CA: Sage Publications, 152–175.

——. (2008) "Dude-Sex: White Masculinities and 'Authentic' Heterosexuality among Dudes Who Have Sex with Dudes," *Sexualities* 11(4): 414–434.

Ward, J. and Schneider, B. (2009) "The Reaches of Heteronormativity: An Introduction," *Gender and Society* 23(4): 433–439.

Yep, G. A. and Elia, J. P. (2012) Racialized Masculinities and the New Homonormativity in LOGO'S Noah's Arc," *Journal of Homosexuality* 59(7): 890–911.

## Further Reading

Cooky, C., Wachs, F., Messner, M., and Dworkin, S. L. (2010) "It's Not about the Game: Don Imus, Race, Class, Gender and Sexuality in Contemporary Media," *Sociology of Sport Journal* 27: 139–159. (A critical analysis of mainstream news media's response to Don Imus' on-air comments about the 2007 women's NCAA basketball championship game.)

Gray, H. (1995) *Watching Race: Television and the Struggle for "Blackness."* Minneapolis, MN: University of Minnesota Press. (An examination of television representations of blackness from the beginning of television through the early 1990s.)

Hemphill, E. (ed.) (1991) *Brother to Brother: New Writings by Black Gay Men*. Washington, D.C.: Redbone Press. (Anthology of writings, essays, and poetry, based on the lived experiences of black gay men.)

Holtzman, L. and Sharpe, L. (2014) *Media Messages: What Film, Television, and Popular Music Teach Us about Race, Class, Gender, and Sexual Orientation*. New York: Routledge. (A large-scale examination of television and representations of race, class, gender, and sexuality and the intersections of identities.)

Skidmore, E. (2011) "Constructing the 'Good Transsexual': Christine Jorgensen, Whiteness, and Heteronormativity in the Mid-twentieth-century Press," *Feminist Studies* 2(37): 270–300. (An analysis of the presentation of normative transgender bodies as it relates to the intersection of race and class.)

# INDEX

Aboriginal Australians 17, 189
activism: Asian Americans 239n1; feminist 293–294; gay rights 306, 307; Mexicans 110; salsa music 100; social media 117
Adare, S. 51
Adivasis 280–281
adolescents 113
advertising 4, 7, 148–159; African Americans 199; Asian Americans 232; assimilation 151, 152–153; cultural attitudes model 152; equal presentation model 150–151; ethnic stereotyping 153–156; India 278–279, 280, 281; Native Americans 226, 227–228; political 59; social reality model 151–152; stereotypes 45; women 289
affinity thesis 36
affirmative action 65, 80, 145, 307
African Americans 199–209; advertising 148–150, 151, 152, 153–154; anti-Other subframe 23–25, 28; apparel 140; Black Feminism 295–298; criminal justice 31–32; digital divide 112–113, 119; East Asian popular culture 273–274; ethnic media 167; fear of crime 37; feminism 294; film 45, 89, 93; framing 19, 21; gaming communities 114; gay men 308–309; historical media analysis 44, 45, 46–49; images of violence and criminality 1, 11, 33, 69; interracial marriage 252; journalism 3, 126–137, 141–142; killed by police 11, 17, 31, 69–70, 108, 112, 117, 119–120, 126, 129, 132–134; music 98–99, 103; "new racism" 17; news coverage 213; "one-drop rule" 251; primetime television 78–80; priming 58; public memory analysis 46; public opinion of the police 38, 39; racial myths 14–16; reality television 4, 201–207; social media 117, 119, 121, 283; sports media 173–174, 176, 179–180, 181, 187; television company ownership 22; voting by 121; women 118, 188, 292–293; *see also* Civil Rights Movement
Africans: East Asian views of 273; in India 276, 282–283
agenda-setting 20, 66, 180
aggression 55, 56, 80
Ahn, Ji-Hyun 5, 250–258
AIM *see* American Indian Movement
*Akeelah and the Bee* 232
Akram, S. 292
*Al Jazeera* 282–283
Alaska Natives 222–223, 227
Alba, Jessica 255
Alba, R. 160
alcohol use 223
*Aliens in America* 247
*All-American Muslim* 247
Allen, B. J. 213
*Aloha* (2015) 87, 88, 93–94
Alsultany, Evelyn 5, 16, 241–249
Althusser, Louis 13
Amerasians 251, 256
American Dream 14, 205, 231
American Indian Movement (AIM) 226
American Society of News Editors (ASNE) 127, 128, 135–136, 141, 142
American Spirit cigarettes 228
*America's Next Top Model* 254
Anderson, K. 78
Andrejevic, M. 202, 203
Andrews, D. L. 187
Anguiano, C. 212–213, 218
ANP *see* Associated Negro Press
anti-Other subframe 21, 22, 23–27, 28

# INDEX

anti-racism projects 186
Anzaldúa, Gloria 109, 250, 296
apparel 140
Arabs 5, 16–17, 66, 83, 241–249, 292
Asian Americans 5, 118, 231–240; advertising 155–156; film 89; historical media analysis 44, 50; Internet use 119; journalists 135–136, 141–142; LGBTQ representation on television 309; multiracial 254, 255; "new" 162; news coverage 213; primetime television 82–83; sports media 181; television company ownership 22; women 290–291
Asians 189, 232, 233, 234, 235, 238; *see also* East Asia
ASNE *see* American Society of News Editors
assimilation 206, 310; advertising 151, 152–153; colorblind ideology 254; ethnic media 163; Hawaii 251; "model minority" 290; myth of 15; Native Americans 226
Associated Negro Press (ANP) 48
asylum seekers 260, 261
Atkins, Tyler 119–120
Atlanta Braves 227, 229n4
Attewell, P. 112
audiences: effects studies 77, 84; film 93; framing 20–21; Latin@s 216, 217; Native Americans 83; sports 189, 190–191, 192
Aunt Jemima 149
Australia: Aboriginal identity 17; ethnic media 163, 164, 167; immigrants and sporting loyalty 191; sports media 189
Austria 261, 263, 264
availability heuristic 57
Axelrod, Jim 117
Ayre, Chris 227
Ayyar, V. 285

Back, L. 179
Bacon, Jacqueline 48
Bae Yung-joon 270
Báez, J. 214
Bailey, O. G. 168
Ball-Rokeach, S. J. 161, 166
*Bamboozled* (2000) 92
Banks, A. J. 59
Banks, Tyra 254
Barlow, W. 199–200
Barnet, Claude 48
Barrow, L. 48
Barthes, Roland 13
baseball 49, 181
basketball 174, 176, 179–180
*Basketball Wives* 204
*The Battle of Algiers* (1967) 91
*Battlestar Galactica* 254
Baudry, Jean-Louis 89

Bazin, André 88, 89
Beale, F. 296
beauty 6, 277, 279, 285, 292, 297
Behm-Morawitz, E. 81
Belgium 261, 263
Bell, Derrick 65, 66, 68, 309
Bell, M. A. 59
Bell-Jordan, K. E. 202–203
Belton, Danielle C. 134–135
Beltrán, Mary 251, 253, 254
Benetton 157
Bennett, P. D. 204, 206
Berg, C. 291
Berger, B. K. 234
Beristain, Natalia 110
Berkhofer, R. F. 223
Berman, Chris 176
Bernardi, Daniel 45
Bernstein, A. 192
Bertrand, Michael 97–98
*The Beulah Show* 79
Beur FM 168
Beyoncé 70–71
Bhabha, Homi 89, 250
bias 15, 20, 129, 130, 152
*The Big Bang Theory* 84
Big Chief Sugar 227
bilingualism 217
Billings, A. C. 192
*Billy Jack* 226
*The Birth of a Nation* (1915) 252
Bishop, A. P. 119
Black Feminism 6, 71, 295–298
Black Lives Matter 7, 65, 69, 108, 114–115
Black Nationalist Movement 45
Black Panther Party 71, 90
Black Power Movement 239n1
Black Rock Coalition (BRC) 103
Blacklava 239n3
Blackwell, Chris 101, 102, 104n3, 104n4
Blackwell, H. 297
*Blazing Saddles* (1974) 92
blogs 119, 134–135, 264, 271, 304
blues music 96, 97, 98, 102
Bobo, J. 93
bodies 107, 309, 310
Boettcher, W. 298
Bogle, Donald 45, 93
Bollywood 277–278, 279
Bonilla-Silva, Eduardo 111–112
Born, Georgina 97
boyd, danah 113, 114
Boyle, R. 190
Bradbury, S. 188
Braga, Sonia 154
Brando, Marlon 226

313

# INDEX

brands 227–228, 278–279, 283
*Braxton Family Values* 205–206
BRC *see* Black Rock Coalition
Brewer, P. R. 136
Brock, A. 121
Broussard, Jinx 47
Brown, Michael 11, 17, 31, 69, 117, 120, 129, 139
Brown, Rockell A. 4, 199–209
Browne, D. R. 168
Bruce, T. 192
Bruckman, A. 113
Buchanan, S. 261
Bullock, Penelope 47
Burrowes, C. 48
Bush, George H. W. 153
Byerly, C. 127
Byrd, Robert D. Jr. 6, 304–311

California 215, 232
Callanan, Valerie J. 2, 31–42
Campbell, Christopher P. 1–7, 11–18, 69, 142–143, 177, 181
Campbell, Richard 14
Campbell, S. 199, 201, 203–204
Canada 161–162, 163, 164, 165, 167
Canclini, Néstor García 250
capitalism 45, 207, 232, 238, 289, 295
Carbado, D. W. 305–306
Cardoza, K. 279
Carey, James 45–46
Carpentier, Francesca R. Dillman 2, 55–64
Carrington, B. 187
Carroll, B. 49
Carter, C. 289
Casetti, Francesco 88
Castañeda, M. 212–213, 214, 218
caste 276, 279, 280–281, 283, 285
Castillo, Guadalupe 49
celebrities: Bollywood 279; East Asia 273; priming 59; sports 186, 187
censorship 45
CEOs *see* chief executive officers
Chae, Young Eun 271
Chan, Jachinson 231
Chao, L. M. 139, 140
Charo 154
Chawla, Juhi 279
Cheerios 153
Chen, Gina Masullo 3, 117–125
Chen, Steve 5, 235–238
Chicanos 145, 251; *see also* Latin@s
Chidester, P. 108
chief executive officers (CEOs) 234–235, 238
children 228
Childs, Erica 254–255

China 269–272, 273
Chinese immigrants 50, 156, 162, 166, 231
Chiricos, T. 38
Chiu, Herman B. 50
Chopra, Priyanka 277
Chua, Amy 290
cinema *see* film
civic engagement 117, 122
Civil Rights Movement 31, 32, 65, 71, 148, 307; Asian Americans 231, 239n1; Critical Race Theory 66; ethnic media 165; historical media analysis 45, 46, 48, 49
Clark, Dick 104n2
class: advertising 151; Black Feminism 296; ghettoes 114; Hollywood 251; intersectionality 296; reality television 206; women 289
Cleveland Indians 83, 227
Cliff, Jimmy 102, 104n3
clothing 140
Cobb, M. 298
Cody, Buffalo Bill 224
Coffey, A. J. 141
Colby, D. 202, 203
Cole, Nat King 150
Coleman, J. 294
Coleman, Milton 134
collective memory 46
Collins, Patricia Hill 6, 200, 202, 296
colonialism 90, 243–244, 251, 252, 276–277
colorblindness 110, 111–112, 114, 298–299; Asian Americans 231; colorblind casting 254; journalism 130; multiracial trope 254; priming 60; sexual identity 310; sports media 188
comedies 78–79, 81, 92
commentators 179, 187, 189
commercialization 175
commonsense culture 177, 181
Communication Infrastructure Theory 166
*Community* 247
conflict 202, 262
Conrad, K. 298
content analysis 180, 260, 264, 278
Cooper, C. 48
*COPS* 33, 37
copycat advertising 150–151, 157
corporations 33
Cortese, Anthony J. 4, 148–159
*The Cosby Show* 14, 79, 200, 205, 206
Cosell, Howard 175
Couldry, N. 167
counter-frames 21, 28
counterstereotypes 60
Courtney, Susan 252
Coward, John 50–51
Crazy Horse Malt Liquor 227
Cree, V. 295

314

Crenshaw, Kimberlé Williams 6, 65, 66–67, 68, 71
cricket 278, 283
crime 1, 2, 11, 16, 33; criminal justice 31–32, 35–36, 38–39, 223; Critical Race Theory 66, 69; cultural attitudes 152; fear of 33–34, 35, 36–37, 39; ghettocentric logic 187; immigrants portrayed as criminals 139–140, 141; Latin@s 141, 143; media literacy training 60; Native Americans 223; news media 55, 144, 261; priming 56–57; punishment 33, 35, 38–39; stereotypes 153, 205
Cripps, Thomas 45
*Cristela* 81
Critical Race Theory (CRT) 2, 65–73, 118, 212–213, 218, 289
Cronin, Mary 48–49
Crowe, Cameron 87, 88
CRT *see* Critical Race Theory
Cruz, Ted 153
Cuarón, Alfonso 210
cultivation theory 2, 32–39, 66
cultural attitudes model 152
cultural distance 262
"Cultural Indicators Project" 32–34
cultural maps 174, 177
cultural studies 1, 11, 12, 14
culture, definition of 12
Curtis, E. M. 180
Custer, General George Armstrong 224
cyberfeminism 107
Czech Republic 259

D'Agostino, A. M. 304–305
*The Daily Show* 17
Dalits 280–281
*Dances with Wolves* (1990) 227
Daniels, J. 110, 111
*The Danny Thomas Show* 244
Das, Nandita 279
Dash, Julie 92
Dates, J. L. 199–200
*Daughter of the Dragon* 156
Davies, David 49, 131
Davis, Angela 6, 296
Davis, F. J. 251
Day of the Dead 145
decoding 12–13
Deggans, E. 130, 131, 132–133
Del Rio, Delores 154
Delgado, R. 66, 68–69
Delonas, Sean 24–25
DeLoria, Vine Jr. 228
democracy 243, 272
Democrats 68
Derrida, Jacques 103
Desantis, A. 48

desegregation 49
DeSensi, J. 180
Deshpande, A. 281
*Desperate Housewives* 291
*Despicable Me 2* (2013) 19, 25–27
Devine, P. G. 57–58
Devineni, Ram 281–282
diasporic media 161, 162
diegesis 91
Diesel, Vin 254
difference, myth of 15
digital divide 112–114, 117, 119, 122
digital technology 4; film 89, 93; Latin@s 216–217; *see also* Internet
discourses: colorblind 231; hegemonic 189–190; identity 109; nationalist 191; political 263–264; sports 186, 187, 190, 192
discrimination 1, 149, 163–164; African Americans 199; Arabs and Muslims 242, 243, 245, 247; Black Feminism 296; colorblindness 188; cultural attitudes 152; East Asia 269, 270, 273; Europe 6; film 87–88; homophobia 306; India 276, 278, 280, 282–284, 285; Latin@s 82, 212; news media 15; sports 176, 186; white racial frame 21, 28; *see also* racism
diversity: journalism 128, 130–132, 134–135, 141–142, 214; multiculturalism 60; public broadcasting 261; sports 186
Dixon, T. L. 56–57, 141, 144, 214, 298
Dolan, K. 129–130
Dolezal, Rachel 87, 88
dominant ideology 12, 21, 199, 200, 203, 206–207
Domke, D. 47
Dorries, B. 297
Douglass, Frederick 47
Dowler, K. 37
dowries 277
"Dragon Lady" stereotype 156
drama 37, 38
Dreher, T. 167
drugs 32
Duany, Jorge 99, 100
DuBois, W. E. B. 47
Dubrofsky, R. E. 202, 203, 206
Duncan, M. C. 189
Dyer, Richard 89

East Asia 6, 256, 269–275
Eastern Europe 259, 260
Ebo, B. 118
education 212
EEO *see* Equal Employment Opportunity
effects studies 77, 82, 84
El Gringo 168
El Rey Network 218

Elam, Michelle 255
Elantawy, N. M. A. 292
elections 67–68, 121–122, 167
Elia, J. P. 306, 309
*Elle* 157
Elling, A. 190, 191
Emami 279, 280
empowerment 2, 43, 117
Engelhardt, T. 91
Enlightenment 89, 130
entertainment 7; Latin@s 214–216; priming 55; *see also* film; television
Entman, R. M. 80, 180
Equal Employment Opportunity (EEO) 127, 163
equal presentation model 150–151
Eschholz, S. 37–38
Eskimos 45
ESPN 175
*Esprit* 157
essentialism 96, 103, 162, 252
ethnic media 4, 160–172; *see also* minority media
ethnic minorities 259–265
ethnicity/race distinction 186, 259–260
Eurocentrism 3, 89, 93
Europe 6, 259–268; advertising 157; ethnic media 164–165, 168; sports media 4, 185–195; white racial frame 22
Everett, A. 110
exposure 80, 82, 84

Facebook 117, 120, 121, 283, 295; *see also* social media
Fair and Lovely 279–280
*The Fast and the Furious* (2001) 254
*Father Hood* 205
fatherhood 205
*Fatima* (1897) 243
FCC *see* Federal Communication Commission
Feagin, Joe R. 1–2, 19–30
Federal Communication Commission (FCC) 127, 163
Fehr, Oded 242
femininity 204, 277, 278, 304–305
feminism 289, 293–295; Black 6, 71, 295–298; cyberfeminism 107
Ferguson, Missouri 11, 17, 31, 69, 117, 119–120, 129, 138, 283
Ferry, Danny 23
festivals 143, 144–145
Figueroa-Caballero, Andrea 2–3, 77–86
film 3, 87–95, 118, 149; African Americans 199; anti-Other subframe 25–27; Arabs and Muslims 242, 243–244, 245, 246; Asian Americans 156, 290; blues music 97; Bollywood 277–278; historical media analysis 45; Japan 272; Latin@s 154–155, 215, 216; mixed race people 251–253, 254; Native Americans 224–225, 227; women 289
Fiorina, Carly 234–235
Fisher, Max 272
Fiske, J. 12–13, 14
Fitzgerald, M. 51
*500 Nations* 227
Flamiano, Dolores 50
*Flavor of Love* 203–204
Florini, S. 121
Fojas, Camilla 251, 253
Folkerts, Jean 44
football (American) 173, 174, 176, 180, 181, 187
football (soccer) 185–186, 188, 189, 190, 191, 192
Ford, Christopher 272
Ford, John 225
formats 35–36
*Forrest Gump* (1994) 90
Foucault, Michel 90, 109
Fox 70
framing 1–2, 19–30, 66, 129, 180–181, 214
France 166, 168, 185, 260, 263
Francis, D. 224
Fraser, N. 109
Freed, Alan 104n2
Freeman, Alan 66
Friedan, Betty 294
Friedhofer, Hugo 91
Fuhlhage, M. 49
Fusion.net 217–218

Gabbidon, S. L. 39
gaming 111, 113, 114, 217
Gandy, O. 163
gangsta rap 99, 104
Garcia-Castañon, M. 121
Garner, Eric 69, 108, 138, 139
Garvey, Marcus 47
Gautam, Yami 279
gay men 6, 304–310
Geertz, Clifford 13
gender 6, 289–303; CEOs 234–235; ethnic minorities in Europe 261; feminist theory 293–295; Hollywood 251; India 280, 281–282, 285; intersectionality 296; Latin@s 154–155, 212; LGBTQ people of color 310; queer theory 294; reality television 206; sports media 188–189, 191; *see also* femininity; masculinity; women
genocide 21, 224
genres: film 92; music 96, 97; television 79
*The George Lopez Show* 81
Georgiou, M. 161, 163, 165
Gerbner, George 2, 32–34, 35–36, 37, 39

Germany 164–165, 166, 260, 261–262, 263, 264
Gertz, M. 38
ghettocentric logic 187
ghettoes 113–114, 119
Giacobbi, P. 180
Giannino, S. S. 199, 201, 203–204
*Gimme a Break* 79
Girls' Generation 273–274
Giroux, H. A. 107–108
Gitlin, T. 19, 20, 167
Givenchy 157
*Glee* 254
Glenn, E. N. 280
globalization 4, 160, 256
Goff, Victoria 49
Goffman, E. 19
Gold, Riva 135
Goldman, A. Y. 202, 204, 205–206
golf 174, 181
Gomez, Jeff 218
*Gone with the Wind* 149
González, Juan 44, 211
González de Bustamante, Celeste 4–5, 210–221
*Good Times* 79
Google 235, 237, 238
Gramsci, Antonio 13, 293
Gray, Freddie 69, 129
Gray, Herman 14, 16, 200, 206, 246
Gray, Kishonna L. 3, 107–116
Great Britain: colonialism in India 276–277; ethnic media 163, 165, 166; ethnic minorities in Europe 261; immigrants 260, 262; political discourse 263; sports media 174, 190
Greece 185
Green, M. K. 225, 227, 228
Green, Nancy 149
Gregory, April 297
Greising, Dave 236
*Grey's Anatomy* 254
Gross, Bella 48
Gross, L. 34
Grossman, R. 48
Guerrero, Ed 92
*Guess Who's Coming to Dinner* (1967) 90, 252, 253
Guo, Jeff 70
Gutiérrez, Felix 49, 139, 140
Guzman, M. 292

hailing 13
Hall, Stuart 34, 118, 120; cultural maps 174, 181; hegemonic discourses 189; hybridity 250; levels of analysis 12–13; representation 1, 11–12, 14, 17
*Hallelujah* (1929) 154
Halse, Rolf 17

Hardy, A. 202, 203, 206
Harindranath, R. 168
Harper, P. B. 199
Harris, Eric 69
Hartley, J. 12–13, 14
Hartmann, D. 176, 177, 293
Harwood, J. 78
hashtags 3, 108, 120–121, 122
hate crimes 247, 281
Hawaii 142, 143, 144, 251
Hayek, Salma 154
Hayes, D. 134–135
Hayes, Tom 101
Haynes, R. 190
Hayworth, Rita 154
hegemonic identities 107–109
hegemony 13, 293; Western 274; white 28, 176, 177
Heider, Don 142, 143–144
Heitner, Deborah 45
Hermes, J. 191
Hesmondhalgh, David 97
Heuterman, Thomas 50
Higginbotham, A. Leon 69
Higgin, T. 111
Higgins, G. E. 39
Himmelstein, H. 14
hip-hop 99, 140, 273
Hispanics: fear of crime 37; historical media analysis 49; images of violence and criminality 1; journalism 135–136, 144, 145; use of the term 219n1; *see also* Latin@s
historical media analysis 2, 43–54
Hoffman, D. L. 112–113
Hogan, Lawrence 48
Hollifield, C. A. 127
Hollywood 87, 97; Arabs and Muslims 242, 243; Japan 272; Latin@s 154–155, 210, 213, 215, 216; mixed race people 251–253, 254, 255; Native Americans 225; *see also* film
*Homeland* 246
homonormativity 306, 310
homophobia 306, 308, 309
hooks, bell 6, 226–227, 292, 294, 295, 296
Hopson, M. 202
Horton, Willie 153
Hughes, M. 34
hulu.com 162
human rights 152
Hume, Janice 46
Humphrey, R. 152
Hungary 185, 259
Hurley, Chad 235–237
Hurt, Byron 98–99
Husband, C. 167
Hutton, F. 47

hybridity 250
Hylton, K. 178, 187, 188, 191–192
hypermasculinity 26–27, 55

identity: advertising 151; Arabs and Muslims 242; black 121; ethnic 59; Foucault on 109; gay men 305, 309; hegemonic 107–109; identity politics 89–90; journalists 129, 130; Latin@s 213; mixed race people 251, 252; multiple identities 162, 165; music and 96; sexual 310; sports influence on 175
ideology 90, 93; coding of media messages 13; colorblind 111–112, 114, 254; dominant 12, 21, 199, 200, 203, 206–207; film 3, 91; hegemony 293; priming 59; racist 44, 148; ruling-class 201; sports 185
Ifekwunigwe, Jayne 253
Ifill, Gwen 297
images: advertising 148; Asian-American women 290; counter-frames 28; criminality 1, 11; film 90; Native Americans 223, 227–228; white racial frame 23, 24, 28; *see also* representation
*Imitation of Life* (1934) 149, 252
immigrants: Asian 156; cast as deviant and dangerous 1; ethnic media 4, 160, 161, 163–164, 166; Europe 6, 185, 259, 260, 261, 262, 263; historical media analysis 43, 50; Latin@s 139–140, 144, 210, 211, 214, 219n2, 219n3; Puerto Ricans 99–100; sports media 191
Iñárritu, Alejandro González 210
incarceration 31
incomes 112–113
India 6, 276–288
Indians 83–84
indigenous people 161
inequalities 145, 178; advertising 151–152; colorblind ideology 112; gender 289, 298; Internet 109, 112–114, 115, 119; social media 122
inferential racism 118, 120
information processing 20, 57
Instagram 117, 121
institutional process analysis 32–33
institutional racism 32, 186, 247
integration: advertising 152; ethnic media 163, 164, 166; European 265
Internet 3, 93–94, 107–116, 118–119; Asian Americans 5, 234–238; control 110–112; counter-frames 28; development of the 233–234; digital divide 112–114, 119, 122; feminism 295; hegemonic identities 107–109; Latin@s 216, 217–218; marginality 109–110; online video services 162; white racist framing 24; *see also* social media; YouTube

interpellation 13
interracial marriage 153, 251, 252, 254–255
intersectionality 6, 294; Black Feminism 296; Critical Race Theory 71; LGBTQ people of color 310; sports media 191
invisibility 2, 15, 118; Arab women 244; Latin@s 213, 215; women 298
Iorio, S. H. 132
Iran hostage crisis 245
Irish Americans 89
Islam 241, 245; *see also* Muslims
Island Records 101
Israel 192, 244
Italian Americans 89
Italy 261, 263
Iwabuchi, Koichi 270, 273

Jackson, M. 223
Jaffe, G. 273
Jamaica 101
James, LeBron 181
Jamir, Alemtemshi 284
*Jane the Virgin* 81, 215
Jansen, S. C. 189
Japan 157, 256, 269–271, 272–274
Japanese Americans 50
Jeep Cherokee 155
*The Jeffersons* 79
Jenkins, Cheryl D. 3, 126–137
Jewish Americans 89
"Jezebel" stereotype 23, 153–154, 201, 203, 204, 293
Jhally, S. 16
Jobs, Steve 238
Johnson, Charles S. 47
Johnson, Linton Kwesi 102
Jones, R. L. 190
Joo, Sung-Hee 232
Jordan, William 48
Joseph, Ralina 253–254, 255
journalism 1, 7; African Americans 3, 126–137; ethnic minorities in Europe 262, 264–265; framing 20; historical media analysis 44, 45–46, 47, 51; Latin@s 3–4, 138–147, 214, 218; minority journalists 127–129, 131–132, 134–136, 141–142, 144; myth-making capacity of 14; Native Americans 225–226; racial myths 15–16; *see also* news media; newspapers
Juffer, J. 181
*Julia* 79, 200

Kalinak, K. 91
Kamler, B. 293
Kansas City Chiefs 227
Kapoor, Sonam 279

# INDEX

Karim, Jawed 5, 235–237
Karim, K. H. 161, 167
Katz, V. 161
Kawai, Y. 232
Kellner, D. 177
Kerner Commission 127
Khan, Shah Rukh 279
Khandare, L. 285
Kharmujai, R. 284
Kilpatrick, J. 51
Kim Dae-jung 270
Kimbro, C. W. 127
King, Martin Luther 46
King, Rodney 142
King-O'Riain, R. C. 256
Kirk, Andrew 50
Kitch, Carolyn 46
Klibanoff, Hank 49
Klopotek, B. 229n2
Knoppers, A. 190, 191
Ko, Mika 256
Kohli, Virat 279
Kolko, B. E. 111
Kopkind, Andrew 102–103
Kornweibel, T. 48
K-pop 271, 273
Ku Klux Klan (KKK) 45, 65, 114
Kumar, Anil 242
Kuwahara, Yasue 6, 269–275
Kvasny, L. 113

Lacroix, C. 291
Lal, P. 277
Lamb, Chris 49
language: ethnic media 161–162; Latin@s 26, 212, 216, 217; linguistic profiling 114
Larson, Stephanie 144
*Last of the Mohicans* (1992) 227
Latin@s 4–5, 118, 149, 210–221; advertising 150–151, 154–155; anti-Other subframe 25–27, 28; demographics 211–212; digital divide 113; ethnic media 167; film 89; gaming 114; historical media analysis 44; identity 109; images of violence and criminality 33; journalism 3–4, 135–136, 138–147, 214; LGBTQ representation on television 308, 309; primetime television 80–82; public opinion of the police 38; salsa music 99–100; social media 119; sports media 189; television company ownership 22; use of the term 219n1; voting by 121; women 154–155, 291–292; *see also* Hispanics; Mexican Americans
LatinoLens 218
Lattin, K. 297
*Law and Order* 37, 246
Lawrence, S. 187, 191–192

LeDuff, Kim M. 2, 65–73
Lee, K. 232
Lee, Robert E. 15
Lee, Spike 92
Leeroy Jenkins character 111
Leggett, S. 189
Lehrman, S. 126
Leslie, M. 45
Lewis, J. 16
LGBTQ people 6, 304–310
Liebler, C. 297
Lin, Jeremy 181
Linden, Paul 3, 96–106
linguistic minorities 160, 161–162
linguistic profiling 114
Lippmann, W. 289
*Little Mosque on the Prairie* 247
Littlefeather, Shasheen 226
Livingstone, S. 34
Long, J. 178
Longoria, Eva 291
Lopez, Jennifer 154, 255, 291–292
L'Oreal 278, 279
Los Angeles 140, 142, 167–168, 212, 215, 222, 273
*Love & Hip Hop* 204, 205
*Loving v. Virginia* (1967) 251, 252–253
Lucas, George 92
*Luis* 81
"Luscious Latina" stereotype 154–155
Lynn, Marvin 67

MacMillin, K. 142
Maddox, K. B. 56–57
magazines: advertising 150, 157; black female athletes 297; India 278; Native Americans 224
Magnuson, Karen 136
Mahtani, Minelle 255
mainstream media, definition of 160–161
mainstreaming 34, 35
Malini, Hema 279
Malkin, Michael 297
Mamdani, Mahmood 16
"mammy" stereotype 23, 79, 118, 148, 149, 200, 201, 293
Mandela, Nelson 176
Mangun, Kimberly 48
Mannie, Sierra 304, 305
Maoris 17
Marbley, A. 294
Marchi, R. M. 144–145
marginality 15, 109–110, 118
marginalization 114, 118, 131, 167, 264, 307, 310
marketing 278–279; *see also* advertising
Marley, Bob 3, 101, 102

marriage: India 277; interracial 153, 251, 252, 254–255
Martin, Trayvon 69, 120–121, 126, 129, 132–134, 139, 140
Martin Luther King, Jr. Day 15–16, 145
*Mary Mary* 205–206
masculinity: Black 204; East Asian popular culture 274; gay men 308; hegemonic 234; hypermasculinity 26–27, 55; Native Americans 224, 227; sports 187
*M.A.S.H.* 244
master/slave relationship 110–111
Mastro, Dana 2–3, 77–86
*The Matrix* 254
Matsaganis, M. 160–161
Mayell, H. 280
Maynard, Dori J. 129
McAlister, Melani 245
McCarthy, D. 190
McChesney, R. W. 175
McCombs, M. E. 180
McCormick, E. 180, 187
McDonald's 151
McGwire, Mark 181
McKinney, Nina Mae 154
media concentration 33
media formats 35–36
media literacy 112; critical 148; training 60
media mapping 165
Mehra, B. 119
memory: priming 55, 56, 57, 60; public 46
Merkel, C. 119
Merskin, Debra 5, 222–230
message systems analysis 32–33
*mestizaje* 250, 251
metaphors 92, 99, 140, 262
Metro 168
Mexican Americans 49, 110, 138–139, 140, 144; *see also* Latin@s
Mexicans 44, 49, 109–110, 210, 219n2
Mignon, P. 188
Miller, Count Prince 101
Millett, K. 293
*The Mindy Project* 84
Minh-Ha, Trinh T. 92
minority media 43–44, 45–46, 47–49, 51, 132–133, 136; *see also* ethnic media
Minow, Newton 77
minstrelsy 200, 201, 203, 204, 205, 207
Miranda, Carmen 154
Mire, A. 279
miscegenation 251, 252–253
misogyny 16, 295; Arabs and Muslims 243, 245; *Flavor of Love* 204; rap music 58, 99, 298
mixed race people 5, 26, 250–258
Mizuno, Takeya 50

mobile technology 113, 119, 216–217, 218, 282
mode of address 92
"model minority" stereotype 82, 231–233, 234, 237, 238, 290
models 150, 157, 277
*Modern Family* 81, 254
Moffatt, Tracy 92
Mok, T. A. 82–83
monkey imagery 24
Moody, M. 132, 297, 298
Moody-Ramirez, Mia 6, 289–303
Moraga, C. 296
Moreno, Rita 154
Morris, James McGrath 47
movies *see* film
MSNBC 70
Muhammad, Nisa 133
mulatto 251–252, 253
Müller, F. 188
Müller, Phillip 6, 259–268
multiculturalism 16, 60, 90, 253; advertising 157; African-American media representations 200–201, 204–205, 206, 207; Canada 164; colorblind ideology 254; ethnic media 164, 168; Europe 185
multilingualism 162
multiraciality 250, 251, 254, 255
*The Mummy* 242
Muralidharan, Sidharth 6, 276–288
Murillo, Jesus 110
Murphree, Vanessa 2, 43–54
Murrell, A. J. 180
music 3, 58, 59, 96–106; Black Feminist critique of rap music 297–298; East Asia 272, 273, 274; in film 91; K-pop 271
Muslims 5, 16–17, 66, 68, 241–249; Europe 260, 262; France 166; India 283; primetime television 83; sports media 189; women 292
MySpace 113
myths 13, 14, 15

NAACP *see* National Association for the Advancement of Colored People
Naber, Nadine 241–242
Nacos Brigitte 245
Naficy, H. 161
NAHJ *see* National Association of Hispanic Journalists
Nakamura, L. 110, 111
NALIP *see* National Association of Latino Independent Producers
Naomi, Jane 50
narratives 67–68
National Association for the Advancement of Colored People (NAACP) 45, 87

National Association of Hispanic Journalists (NAHJ) 213, 214
National Association of Latino Independent Producers (NALIP) 218
National Basketball Association (NBA) 176, 179, 181
National Football League (NFL) 173–174, 181
nationalism 191
Native Americans 5, 17, 222–230; advertising 155; film 45, 88, 89, 93; genocide 21; historical media analysis 43, 44, 49, 50–51; journalists 135–136; news media 15; primetime television 83; use of the term 229n2; women 291
*Naturally Native* (1998) 227
NBA *see* National Basketball Association
NBC 87
Neal, Mark A. 99
Neale, Steve 90
Nee, V. 160
negativity 6, 55, 56, 80, 261–262
Negus, Keith 96, 99, 100, 103
Nelson, Angela M. S. 199, 200–201, 203, 204–205, 206, 207
neoliberalism 163–164, 310
Nepal 284
Nerad, J. 252
Nero, C. I. 308–309
Netflix 92
Netherlands 185, 189, 191, 261, 262, 264
"new racism" 17, 112
New York 38, 222
New Zealand 17, 192
news media: African Americans 3, 126–137, 199; Arabs and Muslims 245; Asian Americans 234, 238; black women 296–297; Critical Race Theory 69, 70; ethnic media 166; ethnic minorities in Europe 261–263, 264–265; fear of crime 36; framing 20; Latin@s 3–4, 138–147, 213–214, 217–218; LGBTQ people of color 310; minority media 44; narratives 68; Native Americans 225–226; priming 55, 56–57; public opinion of the police 37–38; racial myths 15–16; representation 14, 141–143; violent crime 32; *see also* journalism
newspapers: black press 47–49, 132–134; ethnic minorities in Europe 262; fear of crime 36; historical media analysis 43, 44, 47–51; lack of diversity 135; Latin@s 214; minority journalists 128; Native Americans 224, 225–226; South Korea 271; *see also* journalism
NFL *see* National Football League
Nichols, Marisa 242
*Nihonjinron* 269–270
Nilsen, S. 254

9/11 terrorist attacks 66, 241, 242, 260, 262, 292; *see also* Muslims
*Nip/Tuck* 254
Nishikawa, K. A. 131, 144
Nishime, Leilani 254
Nixon, Richard 32
*Noah's Arc* 309
Norander, S. 234–235
Nordin, K. 48
norms 131, 148, 149, 177, 251
*Northern Exposure* 83, 227
Norway 259
*Not Without My Daughter* (1991) 246
Novak, T. P. 112–113

Obama, Barack 19, 32, 65, 68, 114; post-racial society 1, 255; priming 60; racial myths 16; social media 121, 283; white racist framing 23, 24–25
Obeidellah, Dean 68
Oliveira, M. D. 120
"one-drop rule" 251
Ono, Kent A. 5, 231–240
oppression: Black Feminism 296; gay men 305; homophobia 306; India 280; internalized 222; music 102–103; white racial frame 21, 22, 26, 28
*Orange is the New Black* 310
Orbe, M. P. 202, 213
Orientalism 243, 245
Ortega, Frank J. 1–2, 19–30
*The Ortegas* 81
Orwell, George 152
Osajima, K. 231
Osuri, G. 277
Other/Otherness: Arabs and Muslims 243; film 90, 91, 93; Latin@s 212; Native Americans 227; sports media 191; white racial frame 21

Padilla, Felix 100
Paek, H. J. 232
Pakistanis 83–84, 242, 260
Palestinians 245
Pandey, Jyoti Singh 281–282
Papacharissi, Z. 120
Parameswaran, R. 277, 279
*Parenthood* 254
Park, D. J. 234
Parker, D. 253
Parker, Laurence 67
*Parks and Recreation* 84
Pasco shooting (2015) 138–139
Pastorius, Francis Daniel 223
patriarchy 16, 26–27, 293, 295; Arabs and Muslims 245, 292; India 277, 281; miscegenation narrative 252; stereotypes 289; white supremacist 310

# INDEX

Payne, Ethel 47
Pears Soap 150
Pease, E. 177
Penn, Garland 47
Penn, Sean 210
Perry, B. 222
Peterson, William 231, 290
Pham, Vincent N. 5, 231–240
Phillips, R. 295
Phua, J. 232
*Pinky* (1949) 252
Plana, Tony 242
*Pocahontas* 83, 225
Poindexter, P. M. 142
Poitier, Sidney 90
police: cultivation theory 33–34, 35, 37–38, 39; killing of black people by 11, 17, 31, 69–70, 108, 112, 117, 119–120, 126, 129, 132–134; Pasco shooting 138–139
policy: criminal justice 32; ethnic media 163–165, 167, 168; Europe 259, 263; USA PATRIOT Act 247
politics: ethnic minorities in Europe 263–264; European integration 265; presidential elections 67–68; priming and political ideology 59; racial 32; social media 121–122
Pontecorvo, Gillo 91
popular culture: African Americans 199; Barthes on 13; East Asia 269, 270–271, 272–274; mixed race people 255; Native Americans 226; white hegemony 28; whiteness 108, 115; women 298
postcolonialism 90, 250
post-racial society 1, 15, 254, 255, 298–299
poststructuralism 92
Potrac, P. 190
poverty 223
Powell, Tracy 133
power: advertising 149; Critical Race Theory 65, 68–70, 118; discourse and 109; gender 293; Internet 107–108; of the media 178
Pozner, Jennifer 201, 203, 206
*The Practice* 246
*Predator* (1987) 92
predator image 153
prejudice: Europe 6, 264, 265; everyday 186; ideology 90; India 283; priming 57–58; sports media 177; *see also* discrimination; racism
presidential elections 67–68
Presley, Elvis 3, 97–98
Pride, Armistead S. 47
priming 2, 20, 55–64, 232
producers 213, 216, 218
protests 69, 71
public broadcasting 261
public memory 46

public opinion: European 259; fear of crime 36–37; police 37–38, 39; punishment 38–39
public relations 44–45
Puerto Ricans 99, 144, 219n2
punishment 35, 38–39, 69

qualitative research 178–179
quantitative research 180, 260
queer theory 294
Quinn, Francesco 242

racialization 188, 189, 191, 212, 241–242
racism 1, 7, 148; advertising 152; American Dream 14; Arabs and Muslims 16, 241–242, 247; Black Feminism 296; black gay men 308, 309; colorblind ideology 111–112; Critical Race Theory 65–66, 68–70, 118; critique of 17; cultural attitudes 152; East Asia 272–273; "enlightened" 188, 205; environmental 143, 145; feminist theory 294; film 92; framing 21, 23, 24–25, 27, 28; gay rights movement 307; hegemonic 207; historical media analysis 2, 43, 44; homonormativity 306; immigrants 140; India 276, 282–284, 285; inferential 118, 120; institutional 32, 186, 247; internalized 207; Internet 114; journalism 129; master/slave relationship 110–111; mixed race people 251; Netherlands 185; "new" 17, 112; normalization of 188; politics 68; reality television 202, 203, 205; reception studies 93; sports 185–186; symbolic 32, 60, 157; systemic 21–22, 23, 114, 203; "traditional" 15; transmission of racist ideology 44; *see also* discrimination; prejudice
radio 165, 166; African Americans 199; historical media analysis 44, 45; Latin@s 216
Raheja, M. 51
Rai, Aishwarya 277
Raiford, L. 46
Rainville, R. E. 180, 187
Ramirez, Margaret 100
Rana, Junaid 242
rap music 58, 59, 98–99, 104, 273, 297–298
rape 26, 281–282
Rashad, Amad 179, 180, 181
Rastafarianism 102–103
Ratzlaff, A. 132
Reagan, Ronald 232
*The Real Housewives of Atlanta* 204
*The Real World* 202, 203
realism 68–70, 88, 92
reality television: African-Americans in 4, 201–207; crime-based 33, 36, 37–38
reception studies 93
*Reel Injuns* (2009) 226
Reeves, Keanu 254, 255

refugees 260, 262
reggae 96–97, 101–103, 104
Reid-Brinkley, S. 298
Reilly, H. J. 225
Reis, Raul 3–4, 138–147
Renaissance 89
representation 1, 2–3, 11–12, 14, 17; African Americans 4, 199–207; Arabs and Muslims 5, 243–247; Asian Americans 5, 233; ethnic minorities in Europe 261; film 87–88; Latin@s 4–5, 212–213; LGBTQ people of color 309, 310; mixed race people 5, 250; Native Americans 5, 223, 226, 227, 228; news media 141–143; sports media 186; *see also* images
Republicans 68, 145
resonance 34
Retis, Jessica 4–5, 210–221
Rhodes, Jane 43–44
Rice, Tamir 69
*The Ridiculous Six* (2015) 88, 92
Riess, S. A. 175
Riggins, R. H. 163
Riggs, Marlon 92, 307–308, 309
Rigoni, I. 166
Rios, Herminio 49
Rivers, Doc 179, 180, 181
*Road Rules* 202, 203
Roberts, Gene 49
Roberts, Jeff John 133, 135
Robin, Corey 69
Robinson, Cedric 45
Robinson, Jackie 49
Rock, Chris 17
rock music 101, 102–103, 104
rock 'n' roll 98, 103, 272
Rodriguez, Gina 215
Rodriguez, Robert 218
role models 59
Romano, R. 46
*Romeo Must Die* (2000) 254
Ronaldo, Cristiano 191–192
Roosevelt, Franklin D. 48
Root, Maria 253
Rosenberger, Jared S. 2, 31–42
Ross, F. 48
Rowe, D. 191
Rowe, Mike 97, 104n1
Ruggiero, T. 297
*Run's House* 205
Russell, John 272–273

Sabo, D. 189
Said, Edward 90, 245
Saliba, Therese 244
salsa 96, 99–100, 104
*San Andreas* (2015) 215

Sandberg, Sheryl 295
Santa Ana, O. 139–140, 213, 214
"sapphire" stereotype 200, 201, 203, 204, 293
Sautman, Barry 273
Savage, Barbara Dianne 45
Save the Children 281
Schaller, M. 178
Scheduled Castes/Tribes 280–281, 282, 285
Schemer, Christian 6, 259–268
Schudson, Michael 139
Schuman, H. 152
science fiction 92
Scott, B. 293
Scott, William Alexander 48
*The Searchers* (1956) 91
secondary assimilation 152–153
*Seinfeld* 291
Seiter, E. 177
self-alienation 166
self-Orientalism 270, 272
semiology 103
Semmerling, Tim Jon 243
Sen, Sushmita 277
Serrano, Nestor 242
sexism 207, 289, 295; Black Feminism 296; gay men 305; rap music 298
sexual violence 281–282, 285
sexuality 6, 191, 304–311; African Americans 202, 203, 206, 293; Asian-American women 291; feminist theory 294; Hollywood 251; Latinas 81, 154, 156, 219n4, 292; queer theory 294; reality television 206; women 289
Shah, H. 232
Shaheen, Jack G. 242, 243, 244, 245
*Shahs of Sunset* 247
Shankar, S. 232
Sharma, Rohit 279
Shaw, D. L. 180
Sheerin, M. 142
*The Sheik* (1921) 243
Sherman, Richard 23, 173–174, 176–177, 178, 181
Shim, D. 232
Shively, JoEllen 93
Shohat, Ella 90, 91, 246
*The Siege* (1998) 246
signification 1, 13, 17
Signorielli, N. 78–79
*The Silent Enemy* (1930) 224
Silk, M. L. 187
Sim, Gerald 3, 87–95
Simmons, Kimora Lee 254
Singh, M. 283
Sink, Alexander 2–3, 77–86
Sinocentrism 271–272
Sipocz, Daniel 4, 173–184

skin color 276–280, 285
slavery 21, 23, 152, 251, 252, 292, 295
*Sleeper Cell* 242, 246
Sloan, David 44
Smalls, Millie 101
Smart, Kristin 297
smartphones 113, 119, 217
Smith, Debra C. 205
Smith, Douglas 45
Smith, S. 203, 207
Smits, Jimmy 59
*Smoke Signals* (1998) 227
Snapchat 117
Snoop Dogg 205
Snorgrass, J. 48
social change 43
social constructionism 96
social control 32
social justice 228
social media 3, 113, 117–125; Black Lives Matter 7; counter-frames 28; East Asia 271; ethnic minorities in Europe 264; framing 24; India 283; Latin@s 210; Michael Brown shooting 11, 17; sports media 192; *see also* Facebook; Twitter; YouTube
social reality model 151–152
Solomos, J. 179
Song, M. 253
Sosa, Sammy 181
South Korea 17, 256, 269–271, 272, 273, 274
Soviet Republics, former 260
Spaaij, Ramon 191
Spain 261, 264
Spanish language 26, 216, 217
spectators 93
Spence, L. 91
Spickard, Paul 253
sports: anti-black subframe 23–24; Beyoncé's Super Bowl performance 70–71; black female athletes 297; Europe 4, 185–195; historical media analysis 49; India 278, 283; United States 4, 173–184, 187, 297
Squires, C. R. 251–252, 255, 298–299
St. Cyr, Lillian 224
*Stagecoach* 225
Stahl, John 252
Stam, Robert 90, 91, 246
Stangor, C. 178
*Star Wars* 92
Stefancic, J. 66, 68–69
Steiner, L. 289
stereotypes 2, 7, 32, 129, 149, 254, 289–290; advertising 148, 152, 153–156, 158; African Americans 23, 199, 200–205, 207, 292–293; Arabs and Muslims 16–17, 245–247, 292; Asian Americans 231–233, 237, 239n3;

290–291; definition of 289; East Asia 274; ethnic minorities in Europe 264; everyday 186; film 89–90, 92, 118; historical media analysis 45, 50; India 279, 283, 284; journalism 131; Latin@s 139–141, 144–145, 212, 214, 219n4, 291–292; media literacy training 60; mixed race people 251, 252, 254; Native Americans 5, 50–51, 222–228, 291; news media 15, 68; priming 56, 57–58, 59, 60–61; reality television 4, 201, 202–203, 204, 205, 207; sports media 4, 173–174, 176–182, 188–191; television 77, 79–82, 84; video games 111; white racial frame 21, 28; women 290–293, 297, 298
Sterling, Donald 23
Stern, B. B. 232
Stewart, A. 192
Stewart, Jacqueline 93
Stewart, Maria 295
stigmatization 262, 264, 280
Stone, A. L. 306–307
Stone, Emma 87
Stormfront 114
storytelling 67–68
Streitmatter, Roger 47
subjectivity 89, 250
substitution thesis 35–36, 37, 39
Suggs, Henry 48
suicide 223
Sundance Film Festival 227
Super Bowl 70–71, 153, 181
Surace, S. J. 140
Sweden 168, 259
Switzerland 261, 262, 263, 264
symbolic racism 32, 60, 157
systemic racism 21–22, 23, 114, 203

Tahmahkera, D. 51
Taiwan 271, 273
Tamir, I. 192
Tate, D. 189
Taylor, C. R. 232
Taylor, Rebecca Stiles 48
technologies of the self 109
technology: Asian Americans 232, 233; film 89; Latin@s 216–217; *see also* Internet
Teel, Leonard Ray 48
Teeter, Dwight 44
Telemundo 217
television 2–3, 77–86; advertising 154; African Americans 14–16, 78–80, 199–200, 201–207; Arabs and Muslims 16–17, 83, 242, 244, 246–247; Asian Americans 82–83, 155, 290; Critical Race Theory 66; cultivation theory 2, 32–39; decoding 12–13; East Asia 270–271, 272, 273, 274; ethnic media 161–162, 163,

# INDEX

167; ethnic minorities in Europe 261–262; historical media analysis 44, 45, 50; India 281; Indians and Pakistanis 83–84; Latin@s 80–82, 215, 216, 217; LGBTQ representation 308, 309; meanings of 12; mixed race people 254–255; Native Americans 83, 223, 227, 291; news media 141–142; priming 55; reality television 4, 33, 36, 37–38, 201–207; sports media 175; white ownership 22; women 289
Temoignage 168
terrorism 5, 16, 241, 242, 243, 292; Arabs and Muslims 244, 245, 246, 247; Critical Race Theory 66; Europe 262, 263
Teunis, N. 306, 308, 309
texts 178; decoding 12–13
Thailand 256
*That 70s Show* 81
theGrio 133
*The Thief of Baghdad* (1924) 156, 243
Thornton, B. 48
*Three Kings* (1999) 246
*The Today Show* 87
Torres, Joseph 44
Torres-Reyna, Oscar 245
Trainor, Sean 71
translation 104
transphobia 304
tribes 222
Tripp, Bernell 47
Trump, Donald 140, 153
Truth, Sojourner 295
Tuchman, G. 19, 213
Turner, Frederick Jackson 93
Turner, R. H. 140
Turner, S. E. 254
Turner, Ted 227, 229n4
*Tushka* (1998) 227
TVQX 273–274
*24* 17, 242, 246
*Twilight* franchise 227
Twitter 108, 117, 119–121, 192, 210, 283; *see also* social media
Tyree, T. 202, 207, 298

*Ugly Betty* 81, 215
U.N. Declaration of Human Rights 163
Unilever 279
United States 1; advertising 148–149, 152, 153–157; Arabs and Muslims 5, 16–17, 241–242, 243, 244, 245, 247; Critical Race Theory 65–66, 67–72; ethnic media 162, 163, 164, 165, 167; gay rights movement 306; historical media analysis 43, 46–51; immigration 164; mainstream media 160–161; military presence in East Asia 256; mixed race people 250–255; music 97–99, 103; racial mythology 15; sports media 4, 173–184, 187, 297; stereotypes 289–290; television 77–84; white racial frame 21, 22; *see also* African Americans; Asian Americans; Latin@s; Native Americans
Univision 217
Unnever, J. D. 39
Urman, Jennie Snyder 215
U.S. Commission on Civil Rights 77, 78
USA PATRIOT Act 247

Valentino, N. A. 59
values: American 152; ethnic media 165; framing 129; journalists 130; middle American 14
van Sterkenburg, Jacco 4, 185–195
van Zoonen, L. 289
*The Vanishing Family: Crisis in Black America* 14
Vargas, L. 213, 214
Velez, Lupe 154
Vercellotti, T. 136
video games 55, 111, 113, 114, 217
Vine 117
violence: African-American media representations 202, 203; Arabs and Muslims 243, 244; cultivation theory 33–34, 37; India 276, 281–282, 284, 285; Native Americans 222–223; news media 32, 261; rap music 58, 99, 104, 297; *see also* crime
Virginia 45
visual culture 254
Vittachi, N. 271
Vosloo, Arnold 242
voting 121–122, 167

Waits, Tom 96, 103
Walker, Alice 6, 296
Walker, Rebecca 294
Wallace, M. 292
Wal-Mart 157
Wang, Wayne 92
Ward, J. 306–307
Warschauer, M. 113
Washburn, Patrick 48
Washington, Fredi 252
Washington, Michael 272–273
*The Washington Post* 152–153
Washington Redskins 83, 155, 227
Watson, Carmen Ashurst 99
Watts, Stuart 101
Wayne, John 225
Welch, K. 38
Welch, Raquel 154
Wells, Ida B. 47
Wenner, L. A. 175, 176–177
Weston, M. A. 226
Whannel, G. 174

*What's Happening* 79
White Citizens Councils 45
white people: actors 87–88; advertising 148, 149–150, 152; audiences 190–191; Critical Race Theory 118; cultural attitudes 152; digital divide 113; fear of crime 37; journalists 128, 129–130; news media 142–143; priming 56–57, 58, 59; public opinion of the police 38, 39; punitiveness 38–39; reality television 201; sports 176, 179–180, 187–188, 189–190, 191–192; views on Latin@s 82
white privilege 22, 88, 108; colorblind ideology 111–112; Critical Race Theory 67; film 3; gay men 6, 304, 305–306, 310; sports media 177
white racial frame 19, 21–28
white supremacy 93, 114, 207, 254; anti-Other subframe 25, 26; LGBTQ representation 309, 310; L'Oreal adverts 279
whiteness: discourses of 109; East Asia 256, 274; film 88, 89; gay community 306, 308; India 6, 276–277; Internet 3, 107–108, 111, 115; intersectionality 296; reality television 201–202; sports media 191–192
*Whoopi* 247
Wiegman, R. 89
Wilkins, Karin Gwinn 243
Williams, C. L. 141, 144, 214
Williams, R. M. Jr. 152
Williams, Richard 101
Wilson, Clint C. 47, 127, 139, 140
Winfrey, Oprah 60
Wolseley, Roland 47
women: advertising 150, 151; African Americans 201, 202, 204, 205–206, 292–293; Arabs and Muslims 243, 244, 292; Asian Americans 156, 232, 290–291; CEOs 234–235; cyberfeminism 107; ethnic minorities in Europe 261; fear of crime 37; feminist theory 293–295; *Flavor of Love* 204; India 6, 277, 278, 279–280, 281–282, 285; journalists 47, 128; Latinas 81, 154–155, 219n4, 291–292; Native Americans 224, 225, 291; "new racism" 17; sports media 188–189; stereotypes 153–154, 290–293
Wong, Anna Mae 156
Wong, Russell 254
Woo, Deborah 231
Woods, Tiger 180–181, 254, 255
World of Warcraft 111
World War II 48, 50, 244, 256, 269
Wounded Knee protest (1973) 226
Wynn, C. A. 113

Xbox Live 113, 114
xenophobia 263–264

Yardi, S. 113
Yasso, Tara 66
"yellow peril" 232
Yep, G. A. 309
Young, P. B. 47
*The Young Lions* (1958) 91
Youngdeer, James 224
YouTube 192, 218; Asian Americans 5, 233, 235–238, 239n2; Latin@s 216; Mexican activism 110; stereotypes on 118
Yu, Sherry S. 4, 160–172
Yúdice, G. 211

Zack, Naomi 253
Zambrano-Montes, Antonio 138–139
Zhang, Y. 298
Zimmerman, George 120, 126, 132–133
Zinkhan, G. 45
Ziploc 149